GALE
DIRECTORY OF
PUBLICATIONS AND
BROADCAST MEDIA
Update

137th Edition

GALE DIRECTORY OF PUBLICATIONS AND BROADCAST MEDIA

Update

An Interedition Service Providing New Listings
and Updates to Listings in the Main Volumes
See Introduction for Details

Alan Hedblad, Editor

GALE®

THOMSON

GALE

Detroit • New York • San Diego • San Francisco • Cleveland • New Haven, Conn. • Waterville, Maine • London • Munich

THOMSON
™
GALE

Gale Directory of Publications and Broadcast Media, 137th Edition Supplement

Project Editor
Alan Hedblad

Editorial
Jeff Sumner

Editorial Support Services
Edward J. David

Imaging and Multimedia
Cynthia Baldwin

Composition and Electronic Capture
Evi Seoud

Manufacturing
NeKita McKee

ISBN 0-7876-6202-X (Update)
ISBN 0-7876-6196-1 (Complete set w/Update)
ISSN 1048-7972

Printed in the United States of America
10 9 8 7 6 5 4 3 2 1

Contents

Introduction

This *Update* to the *Gale Directory of Publications and Broadcast Media* (*GDPBM*) presents the latest industry information, including:

- Nearly 1,800 new entries
- Additional E-mail and URL information

Preparation, Content, and Arrangement

Published midway between editions of *GDPBM*, this *Update* is sent free to all subscribers. Information presented is obtained from questionnaire responses, brochures, catalogs, faxes, and phone calls.

Entries for newly established or newly identified media outlets are listed. All entries contain full text as in the main volume.

More detail regarding the scope and coverage of *GDPBM* listings is contained in the Sample Entries following this introduction.

Available in Electronic Formats

Licensing. *Gale Directory of Publications and Broadcast Media* is available for licensing. The complete database is provided in a fielded format and is deliverable on such media as disk or CD-ROM. For more information, contact Gale's Business Development Group at 1-800-877-GALE, or visit us on our web site at www.galegroup.com/bizdev.

Online. *Gale Directory of Publications and Broadcast Media* (along with *Directories in Print* and *Newsletters in Print*) is accessible as File 469: *Gale Database of Publications and Broadcast Media* through the Dialog Corporation's DIALOG service. *GDPBM* is also accessible as PUBBRD through LexisNexis. For more information, contact The Dialog Corporation, 11000 Regency Parkway, Ste. 400, Cary, NC 27511; phone: (919) 462-8600; toll-free: 800-3-DIALOG; or LexisNexis, P.O. Box 933, Dayton, OH 45401-0933; phone (937) 865-6800; toll-free: 800-227-4908.

The *Directory* is also available through InfoTrac as part of *Gale's Ready Reference Shelf*. For more information, call 800-877-GALE.

Acknowledgments

The editors are grateful to the many media professionals who generously responded to our requests for information, provided additional data by telephone or fax, and helped in the shaping of this *Update* with their comments and suggestions throughout the year. Special thanks also go to Hilary White for her contributions.

Comments and Suggestions Welcome

If you have questions, concerns, or comments about *Gale Directory of Publications and Broadcast Media (GDPBM)* or other Gale products, please contact **Alan Hedblad,** Managing Editor, Business Product.

Matters pertaining to specific listings in *GDPBM,* as well as suggestions for new listings, should be directed to **Jeff Sumner,** Editor.

Please write or call:

Gale Directory of Publications and Broadcast Media
Gale Group
27500 Drake Rd.
Farmington Hills, MI 48331-3535

Phone: (248) 699-4253
Toll-free: 800-347-GALE
Fax: (248) 699-8070
Email: BusinessProducts@gale.com

Sample Entries

The samples that follow are fabricated entries in which each numbered section designates information that might appear in a listing. The numbered items are explained in the descriptive paragraphs following each sample.

SAMPLE PUBLICATION LISTING

① **222** ② **American Computer Review**
③ Black Cat Publishing Company, Inc.
④ 199 E. 49th St.   ⑤ Phone: (518)555-9966
  PO Box 724866   ⑥ Fax: (518)555-1028
  Salem, NY 10528-5555   ⑦ Free: 800-555-0212
⑧ **Publication E-mail:** acr@bcpci.com
⑨ **Publisher E-mail:** bcpci@bcpci.com
⑩ Magazine for users of Super Software Plus products. ⑪ **Subtitle:** The Programmer's Friend. ⑫ **Founded:** June 1979.
⑬ **Freq:** Monthly (combined issue July/Aug.). ⑭ **Print Method:** Offset. ⑮ **Trim Size:** 8/12 x 11. ⑯ **Cols./Page:** 3.
⑰ **Col. Width:** 24 nonpareils. ⑱ **Col. Depth:** 294 agate lines. ⑲ **Key Personnel:** Dan Carne, Editor, phone (518)555-1010, fax (518)555-0710, dcarne@jdpci.com; Ryan Boyce, Publisher; Lingl Mungo Jr., Advertising Mgr. ⑳ **ISSN:** 5555-6226.
㉑ **Subscription Rates:** $25; $30 Canada; $2.50 single issue. ㉒ **Remarks:** Color advertising not accepted.
㉓ **Online:** Lexis-Nexis **URL:** http://www.acrmagazine.com. ㉔ **Alternate Format(s):** Braille; CD-ROM; Microform.
㉕ **Variant Name(s):** Formerly: Computer Software Review (Dec. 13, 1986). ㉖ **Feature Editors:** Kit Mungo, *Consumer Affairs, Editorials,* phone (518)555-2306, fax (518)555-2307, km@jdpci.com. ㉗ **Additional Contact Information: Advertising:** 123 Main St., New York, NY 10016, (201)555-0417, fax: (201)555-6812.
㉘ **Ad Rates:** BW: $850   ㉙ **Circulation:** 25,000
         PCI: $.75

---

① **Symbol/Entry Number.** Each publication entry number is preceded by a symbol (a magazine or newspaper) representing the publishing industry. Entries are numbered sequentially. Entry numbers, rather than page numbers, are used in the index to refer to listings.

② **Publication Title.** Publication names are listed *as they appear on the masthead or title page*, as provided by respondents.

③ **Publishing Company.** The name of the commercial publishing organization, association, or academic institution, as provided by respondents.

④ **Address.** Full mailing address information is provided wherever possible. This may include: street address; post office box; city; state or province; and ZIP or postal code. ZIP plus-four numbers are provided when known.

⑤ **Phone.** Phone numbers listed in this section are usually the respondent's switchboard number.

⑥ **Fax.** Facsimile numbers are listed when provided.

⑦ **Free.** Toll-free numbers are listed when provided.

⑧ **Publication E-mail.** Electronic mail addresses for the publication are included as provided by the listee.

⑨ **Publisher E-mail:** Electronic mail addresses for the publishing company are included as provided by the listee.

⑩ **Description.** Includes the type of publication (i.e., newspaper, magazine) as well as a brief statement of purpose, intended audience, or other relevant remarks.

⑪ **Subtitle.** Included as provided by the listee.

⑫ **Founded.** Date the periodical was first published.

⑬ **Frequency.** Indicates how often the publication is issued--daily, weekly, monthly, quarterly, etc. Explanatory remarks sometimes accompany this information (e.g., for weekly titles, the day of issuance; for collegiate titles, whether publication is limited to the academic year; whether certain issues are combined.)

⑭ **Print Method.** Though offset is most common, other methods are listed as provided.

⑮ **Trim Size.** Presented in inches unless otherwise noted.

⑯ **Number of Columns Per Page.** Usually one figure, but some publications list two or more, indicating a variation in style.

⑰ **Column Width.** Column sizes are given exactly as supplied, whether measure in inches, picas (6 picas to an inch), nonpareils (each 6 points, 72 points to an inch), or agate lines (14 to an inch).

⑱ **Column Depth.** Column sizes are given exactly as supplied, whether measure in inches, picas (6 picas to an inch), nonpareils (each 6 points, 72 points to an inch), or agate lines (14 to an inch).

⑲ **Key Personnel.** Presents the names and titles of contacts at each publication. May include phone, fax, and e-mail addresses if different than those for the publication and company.

⑳ **International Standard Serial Number (ISSN).** Included when provided. Occasionally, United States Publications Serial (USPS) numbers are reported rather than ISSNs.

㉑ **Subscription Rates.** Unless otherwise stated, prices shown in this section are the individual annual subscription rate. Other rates are listed when known, including multiyear rates, prices outside the United States, discount rates, library/institution rates, and single copy prices.

㉒ **Remarks.** Information listed in this section further explains the Ad Rates (see ㉘ below).

㉓ **Online.** If a publication is accessible online via computer, that information is listed here. If the publication is available online but the details of the URL (universal resource locator) or vendor are not known, the notation '**Available Online**' will be listed.

㉔ **Alternate Format(s).** Lists additional mediums in which a publication may be available (other than online), including CD-ROM and microform.

㉕ **Variant Name(s).** Lists former or variant names of the publication, including the year the change took place, when known.

㉖ **Feature Editors.** Lists the names and beats of any feature editors employed by the publication.

㉗ **Additional Contact Information.** Includes mailing, advertising, news, and subscription addresses and phone numbers when different from the editorial/publisher address and phone numbers.

㉘ **Ad Rates.** Respondents may provide non-contract (open) rates in any of six categories:

> GLR = general line rate
> BW = one-time black & white page rate
> 4C = one-time four-color page rate
> SAU = standard advertising unit rate
> CNU = Canadian newspaper advertising unit rate
> PCI = per column inch rate

Occasionally, explanatory information about other types of advertising appears in the Remarks section of the entry (see ㉒ above.)

㉙ **Circulation.** Figures represent various circulation numbers; the figures are accompanied by a symbol (except for sworn and estimated figures). Following are explanations of the eight circulation classifications used by *GDPBM*, the corresponding symbols, if any, are listed at the bottom of each right hand page. All circulation figures *except* publisher's reports and estimated figures appear in boldface type.

These audit bureaus are independent, nonprofit organizations (with the exception of VAC, which is for-profit) that verify circulation rates. Interested users may contact the association for more information.

ABC: Audit Bureau of Circulations, 900 N. Meacham Rd., Schaumburg, IL 60173; (847)605-0909
CAC: Certified Audit of Circulations, Inc., 155 Willowbrook Blvd., 4th Fl., Wayne, NJ 07470-7036; (973)785-3000
CCAB: Canadian Circulations Audit Board, 90 Eglinton Ave. E, Ste. 980, Toronto, ON Canada M4P 2Y3; (416)487-2418
VAC: Verified Audit Circulation, 517 Jacoby St., Ste. A, San Rafael, CA 94901; (800)775-3332
Post Office Statement: These figures were verified from a U.S. Post Office form.
Publisher's Statement: These figures were accompanied by the signature of the editor, publisher, or other officer.
Sworn Statement: These figures, which appear in **boldface** without a symbol, were accompanied by the notarized signature of the editor, publisher, or other officer of the publication.
Estimated Figures: These figures, which are shown in lightface without a symbol, are the unverified report of the listee.

The footer on every odd-numbered page contains a key to circulation and entry type symbols, as well as advertising abbreviations.

SAMPLE BROADCAST LISTING

① **111** ② **WDOG-AM - 1530**
③ 34 N South St.   ④ Phone: (518)678-9288
 PO Box 09876   ⑤ Fax: (518)412-3456
 Sahko, NY 10789-0198   ⑥ Free: 800-724-5678
⑦ **E-mail:** wdog@wdog.com
⑧ **Format:** Classical. ⑨ **Simulcasts:** WDOG-FM. ⑩ **Network(s):** Westwood One Radio; ABC. ⑪ **Owner:** Sheltie Communications, Inc., at above address. ⑫ **Founded:** 1990. ⑬ **Variant Name(s):** Formerly: WCHA-AM (1992). ⑭ **Operating Hours:** Continuous; 85% local, 15% network. ⑮ **ADI:** Elmira, NY. ⑯ **Key Personnel:** Michael Vainio, General Mgr., phone (518)556-1020, fax (518)556-1010, mvainio@wdog.com; Josh Butland, Program Dir. ⑰ **Cities Served:** Salem, NY. ⑱ **Postal Areas Served:** 10528; 10529. ⑲ **Local Programs:** Who's Beethoven? Richard Jim, Contact, (518)556-1031, fax (518)556-1032. ⑳ **Wattage:** 3000. ㉑ **Ad Rates:** Underwriting available. $20-25 for 30 seconds; $50-55 for 60 seconds. Combined advertising rates available with WPAN-FM. ㉒ **Additional Contact Information:** Mailing address: PO Box 661, Elmira, NY, 10529.
㉓ **URL:** http://www.wdog.com.

---

① **Entry Number.** Each broadcast or cable entry is preceded by a symbol (a microphone) representing the broadcasting industry. Entries are numbered sequentially. Entry numbers (rather than page numbers) are used in the index to refer to listings.

② **Call Letters and Frequency/Channel** or **Cable Company Name**.

③ **Address.** Location and studio addresses appear as supplied by the respondent. If provided, alternate addresses are listed in the Additional Contact Information section of the entries (see ㉒ below).

④ **Phone.** Telephone numbers are listed as provided.

⑤ **Fax.** Facsimile numbers are listed when provided.

⑥ **Free.** Toll-free numbers are listed when provided.

⑦ **E-mail.** Electronic mail addresses are included as provided by the listee.

⑧ **Format.** For television station entries, this subheading indicates whether the station is commercial or public. Radio station entries contain industry-defined (and, in some cases, station-defined) formats as indicated by the listee.

⑨ **Simulcasts.** Lists stations that provide simulcasting.

⑩ **Network(s).** Notes national and regional networks with which a station is affiliated. The term 'independent' is used if indicated by the listee.

⑪ **Owner.** Lists the name of an individual or company, supplemented by the address and telephone number, when provided by the listee. If the address is the same as that of the station or company, the notation 'at above address' is used, referring to the station or cable company address.

⑫ **Founded.** In most cases, the year the station/company began operating, regardless of changes in call letters/names and ownership.

⑬ **Variant Name(s).** For radio and television stations, former call letters and the years in which they were changes are presented as provided by the listee. Former cable company names and the years in which they were changed are also noted when available.

⑭ **Operating Hours.** Lists on-air hours and often includes percentages of network and local programming.

⑮ **ADI (Area of Dominant Influence).** The Area of Dominant Influence is a standard market region defined by the Arbitron Ratings Company for U.S. television stations. Some respondents also list radio stations as having ADIs.

⑯ **Key Personnel.** Presents the names and titles of contacts at each station or cable company.

⑰ **Cities Served.** This heading is primarily found in cable system entries and provides information on channels and the number of subscribers.

⑱ **Postal Areas Served.** This heading is primarily found in cable system entries and provides information on the postal (zip) codes served by the system.

⑲ **Local Programs.** Lists names, air times, and contact personnel of locally-produced television and radio shows.

⑳ **Wattage.** Applicable to radio stations, the wattage may differ for day and night in the case of AM stations. Occasionally a station's ERP (effective radiated power) is given in addition to, or instead of, actual licensed wattage.

㉑ **Ad Rates.** Includes rates for 10, 15, 30, and 60 seconds as provided by respondents. Some stations price advertisement spots "per unit" regardless of length; these units vary.

㉒ **Additional Contact Information.** Includes mailing, advertising, news, and studio addresses and phone numbers when different from the station, owner, or company address and phone numbers.

㉓ **URL.** If a radio station or cable company is accessible online via computer, that information is listed here. If the station or company is available online but the details of the URL (universal resource locator) or vendor are not known, the notation '**Available Online**' will be listed.

Entry information appearing in the Sample Entries portion of this directory has been fabricated. The entries named here do not, to the best of our knowledge, exist.

Index Notes

Following the main body of the *Update* is the Master Name and Keyword Index. Citations in this index are listed alphabetically regardless of media type.

Publication citations include the following:

- ◆ titles
- ◆ important keywords within titles
- ◆ former titles
- ◆ foreign language titles
- ◆ alternate titles

Broadcast media citations include the following:

- ◆ station call letters
- ◆ cable company names
- ◆ former station call letters
- ◆ former cable company names

Indexing is word-by-word rather than letter-by-letter. For example, "New York" is listed before "News". Current listings in the Index include geographic information and entry number.

INDEXING SAMPLE

① Administration in Mental Health ② (New York, NY) 575

① Allied Cable Systems ② (Lancaster, NH) 476

③ Mental Health; Administration in (New York, NY) ④575

⑤ Metro Tattler (Chicago, IL) *Ceased*

⑥ Administration in Mental and Physical Health 575*

⑦ WMDC-TV (Detroit, MI) *Unable to Locate*

---

① The full name (i.e. publication title, station call letters, or cable company name) of each entry is cited as it appears in the main body.

② Citations include in parentheses the city and state (or province and country for Canadian entries) in which the entry is located.

③ Publications are also indexed by subject keywords and other important words within titles.

④ References are to entry numbers rather than page numbers.

⑤ Notices of cessations are included.

⑥ Former names and call letters are indicated by an * and do not include a geographic designation.

⑦ Notices are included in cases where the editors have not been able to verify the location or continued existence of a publication, broadcast station, or cable company.

Abbreviations, Symbols, and Codes

Miscellaneous Abbreviations

& .... And
4C .... One-Time Four Color Page Rate

ABC .... Audit Bureau of Circulations
Acad. .... Academy
Act. .... Acting
Adm. .... Administrative, Administration
Admin. .... Administrator
AFB .... Air Force Base
AM .... Amplitude Modulation
Amer. .... American
APO .... Army Post Office
Apt. .... Apartment
Assn. .... Association
Assoc. .... Associate
Asst. .... Assistant
Ave. .... Avenue

Bldg. .... Building
Blvd. .... Boulevard
boul. .... boulevard
BPA .... Business Publications Audit of Circulations
BTA .... Best Time Available
BW .... One-time Black & White Page Rate

C .... Central
CAC .... Certified Audit of Circulations
CCAB .... Canadian Circulations Audit Board
CEO .... Chief Executive Officer
Chm. .... Chairman
Chwm. .... Chairwoman
CNU .... Canadian Newspaper Advertising Unit Rate
c/o .... Care of
Col. .... Column
Coll. .... College
Comm. .... Committee
Co. .... Company
COO ....Chief Operating Officer
Coord. .... Coordinator
Corp. .... Corporation
Coun. .... Council
CP .... case postale
Ct. .... Court

Dept. .... Department
Dir. .... Director
Div. .... Division
Dr. .... Doctor, Drive

E .... East
EC .... East Central

ENE .... East Northeast
ERP .... Effective Radiated Power
ESE .... East Southeast
Eve. .... Evening
Exec. .... Executive
Expy. .... Expressway

Fed. .... Federation
Fl. .... Floor
FM .... Frequency Modulation
FPO .... Fleet Post Office
Fri. .... Friday
Fwy. .... Freeway

Gen. .... General
GLR ....General Line Rate

Hd. .... Head
Hwy. .... Highway

Inc. .... Incorporated
Info. .... Information
Inst. .... Institute
Intl. .... International
ISSN .... International Standard Serial Number

Jr. ....Junior

Libn. .... Librarian
Ln. ....Lane
Ltd. .... Limited

Mgr. .... Manager
mi. ....miles
Mktg. .... Marketing
Mng. .... Managing
Mon. .... Monday
Morn. .... Morning

N. .... North
NAS .... Naval Air Station
Natl. .... National
NC .... North Central
NE .... Northeast
NNE .... North Northeast
NNW .... North Northwest
No. .... Number
NW .... Northwest

Orgn. .... Organization

PCI	Per Column Inch Rate
Pkwy.	Parkway
Pl.	Place
PO	Post Office
Pres.	President
Prof.	Professor
Rd.	Road
RFD	Rural Free Delivery
Rm.	Room
ROS	Run of Schedule
RR	Rural Route
Rte.	Route
S.	South
Sat.	Saturday
SAU	Standard Advertising Unit Rate
SC	South Central
SE	Southeast
Sec.	Secretary
Soc.	Society
Sq.	Square
Sr.	Senior
SSE	South Southeast
SSW	South Southwest
St.	Saint, Street
Sta.	Station

Ste.	Sainte, Suite
Sun.	Sunday
Supt.	Superintendent
SW	Southwest
Terr.	Terrace
Thurs.	Thursday
Tpke.	Turnpike
Treas.	Treasurer
Tues.	Tuesday
Univ.	University
USPS	United States Publications Serial
VAC	Verified Audit Circulation
VP	Vice President
W.	West
WC	West Central
Wed.	Wednesday
WNW	West Northwest
WSW	West Southwest
x/month	Times per Month
x/week	Times per Week
x/year	Times per Year

U.S. State and Territory Postal Codes

AK	Alaska
AL	Alabama
AR	Arkansas
AZ	Arizona
CA	California
CO	Colorado
CT	Connecticut
DC	District of Columbia
DE	Delaware
FL	Florida
GA	Georgia
HI	Hawaii
IA	Iowa
ID	Idaho
IL	Illinois
IN	Indiana
KS	Kansas
KY	Kentucky
LA	Louisiana
MA	Massachusetts
MD	Maryland
ME	Maine
MI	Michigan
MN	Minnesota
MO	Missouri
MS	Mississippi

MT	Montana
NC	North Carolina
ND	North Dakota
NE	Nebraska
NH	New Hampshire
NJ	New Jersey
NM	New Mexico
NV	Nevada
NY	New York
OH	Ohio
OK	Oklahoma
OR	Oregon
PA	Pennsylvania
PR	Puerto Rico
RI	Rhode Island
SC	South Carolina
SD	South Dakota
TN	Tennessee
TX	Texas
UT	Utah
VA	Virginia
VT	Vermont
WA	Washington
WI	Wisconsin
WV	West Virginia
WY	Wyoming

Canadian Province and Territory Postal Codes

AB .... Alberta

BC .... British Columbia

MB .... Manitoba

NB .... New Brunswick

NF .... Newfoundland

NS .... Nova Scotia

NT .... Northwest Territories

ON .... Ontario

PE .... Prince Edward Island

QC .... Quebec

SK .... Saskatchewan

YT .... Yukon Territory

UNITED STATES

ALABAMA

FORT PAYNE

1 Dekalb Advertiser
PO Box 680559
Fort Payne, AL 35968-1606   Phone: (256)845-6156

Community newspaper. **Freq:** Weekly. **Cols./Page:** 6. **Key Personnel:** Jerry E. Whittle, Publisher. **Subscription Rates:** $12 individuals; $24 out of area. **Remarks:** Accepts advertising.
Ad Rates: 4C: $130   **Circ:** Paid ⊕**6,172**
                  PCI: $9.10   Non-paid ⊕**60**

ARIZONA

FORT HUACHUCA

2 Commander
Intelligence Center and Fort Huachuca
ATZS-FDR-CB   Phone: (520)538-0979
Fort Huachuca, AZ 85613-6000   Fax: (520)538-1007
Publisher E-mail: mipb@hua.army.mil

Military professional journal. **Subtitle:** Military Intelligence Professional Bulletin. **Founded:** 1974. **Freq:** Quarterly. **Print Method:** Offset. **Trim Size:** 8 1/2 x 11. **Cols./Page:** 3. **Col. Width:** 2 1/16 inches. **Col. Depth:** 9 inches. **Key Personnel:** Michael Ley, Managing Editor, michael.ley@hua.army.mil. **ISSN:** 0026-4028. **Subscription Rates:** $19 individuals; $26.60 Other Countries; $3.50 single issue; $5 single issue Other Countries. **Remarks:** Advertising not accepted. **URL:** http://www.huachuca-usaic.army.mil/mip-bhome/welcome.htm. **Formerly:** Military Intelligence Professional Bulletin.
                  Circ: Paid ‡**2,300**
                  Controlled ‡**5,000**

ARKANSAS

FAYETTEVILLE

3 KREB-AM - 1190
1780 W. Holly St.   Phone: (479)582-3776
Fayetteville, AR 72703-1307   Fax: (479)571-0995

Format: Eclectic; News; Talk. **Networks:** ABC. **Founded:** 1954. **Formerly:** KAMO-AM (1902). **Operating Hours:** Continuous. **Key Personnel:** Dave Clark, Program Dir.; Stephen Butler, President. **Wattage:** 1000. **Ad Rates:** $8 for 30 seconds; $10 for 60 seconds.

FORT SMITH

4 KWHN-AM - 1650
423 Garrison Ave.   Phone: (479)782-8888
Fort Smith, AR 72901-1931   Fax: (479)785-5946
E-mail: info@kwhn.com

Format: News; Talk; Sports. **Networks:** ABC. **Founded:** 2000. **Operating Hours:** Continuous; 25% network, 75% other. **ADI:** Fort Smith, AR. **Key Personnel:** Paul Swint, General Mgr., phone (479)782-8888, fax (479)782-1947, paulswint@clearchannel.com; Gary Elmore, Program Dir., phone

(479)782-8888, fax (479)782-0366, garyelmore@clearchannel.com. **Wattage:** 10,000. **Ad Rates:** $10-25 for 30 seconds; $15-60 for 60 seconds. KMAG-FM, KZBB-FM, KKBD-FM, KYHN-AM.

5 KZBB-FM - 97.9
423 Garrison Ave.   Phone: (479)782-8888
Fort Smith, AR 72901-1931   Fax: (479)785-5946
E-mail: b98@kzbb.com

Format: Contemporary Hit Radio (CHR). **Owner:** Clear Channel Communications, Inc., at above address. **Founded:** 1947. **ADI:** Fort Smith, AR. **Key Personnel:** Paul Swint, General Mgr., phone (479)782-8888, fax (479)782-1947, paulswint@clearchannel.com; Lee Matthews, Program Dir., phone (479)782-8888, fax (479)782-0366, leematthews@clearchannel.com. **Wattage:** 100,000. **Ad Rates:** $15-36 per unit. KMAG-FM, KKBD-FM, KWHN-AM, KYHN-AM.

CALIFORNIA

BERKELEY

6 California Law Review
Joe Christensen, Inc.
School of Law
592 Simon Hall, Boalt Hall   Phone: (510)642-7562
Berkeley, CA 94720   Fax: (510)642-3476

Legal journal. **Founded:** 1912. **Freq:** 6/year (during the academic year). **Print Method:** Offset. **Trim Size:** 5 1/2 x 8. **Cols./Page:** 1. **Col. Width:** 57 nonpareils. **Col. Depth:** 105 agate lines. **Key Personnel:** Kira Abrams, Publications Coordinator, kabrams@law.berkeley.edu. **ISSN:** 0008-1221. **Subscription Rates:** $45 individuals; $20 out of country surface postage; $11 single issue; $50 institutions; $15 single issue special issues. **Remarks:** Advertising not accepted. **URL:** http://www.ucpress.edu/journals/.
                  Circ: ‡**1,500**

EMERYVILLE

7 Remix
Primedia Business
6400 Hollis St., Ste. 12   Phone: (510)653-3307
Emeryville, CA 94608   Fax: (510)653-5142
                  Free: (800)541-7706

Consumer magazine covering underground music performance and DJ performance. **Freq:** Monthly. **Key Personnel:** Chris Gill, Editor, remixeditorial@primediabusiness.com; Kylee Swenson, Assoc. Editor, remixeditorial@primediabusiness.com; Erin Hutton, Copy Editor, erhutton@primediabusiness.com; Paul Lehrman, Web Editor, mixonline@gis.net; Alex Butkus, Art Dir., abutkus@primediabusiness.com; John Pledger, Publisher, jpledger@primediabusiness.com; Joanne Zola, Advertising Dir., jzola@primediabusiness.com; Josh Egelston, West Coast Sales Rep., jegelston@primediabusiness.com; Angela Muller Rehm, Marketing Mgr., arehm@primediabusiness.com; Robin Boyce-Trubitt, Classifieds/Marketplace Adv. Dir., rboyce@primediabusiness.com. **ISSN:** 1532-1327. **Subscription Rates:** $30 individuals; $35 out of country. **Remarks:** Accepts advertising. **URL:** http://www.remixmag.com.
                  Circ: (Not Reported)

Ad Rates: GLR = general line rate; BW = one-time black & white page rate; 4C = one-time four color page rate; SAU = standard advertising unit rate; CNU = Canadian newspaper advertising unit rate; PCI = per column inch rate.
Circulation: ★ = ABC; △ = BPA; ♦ = CAC; • = CCAB; ▢ = VAC; ⊕ = PO Statement; ‡ = Publisher's Report; Boldface figures = sworn; Light figures = estimated.
Entry type: ▢ = Print; 🎙 = Broadcast.

1

FOLSOM

📖 **8 Converge**
e.Republic, Inc.
100 Blue Ravine Rd.   Phone: (916)932-1300
Folsom, CA 95630   Fax: (916)932-1470

Magazine covering education and technology. **Freq:** Bimonthly. **Key Personnel:** Marina Leight, Publisher, mleight@convergemag.com; Bernard Percy, Editor-in-Chief, bpercy@convergemag.com; Olga Amador, Managing Editor/Web Mgr., oamador@convergemag.com; Miriam Jones, Assoc. Editor, mjones@convergemag.com; Christy Harvey, Art Dir., charvey@erepublic.com; Kristin Sims, Promotion Mgr./Marketing Asst., ksims@convergemag.com; Erin Leight, Circ. Dir., eleight@convergemag.com; Shelley Ballard, Advertising Exec., sballard@convergemag.com; Sherese Graves, Founding Publisher. **Remarks:** Accepts advertising. **URL:** http://www.convergemag.com.
Circ: (Not Reported)

FRESNO

🎤 **9 KFSR-FM - 90.7**
California State University Fresno
5201 N. Maple Ave
Mail Stop No. 119   Phone: (559)278-2598
Fresno, CA 93740   Fax: (559)278-6985
E-mail: kfsrfresno@hotmail.com

Format: Eclectic; Adult Album Alternative; Jazz; Blues; Hip Hop; Reggae; Soft Rock. **Networks:** Independent. **Owner:** California State University, Fresno, at above address. **Founded:** 1982. **Operating Hours:** Continuous. **ADI:** Fresno-Visalia (Hanford), CA. **Key Personnel:** Andrew Bunnell, Program Dir., phone (559)278-4500; Jason Anaforian, News Dir.; Patricia Chavez, Sports Dir., phone (559)278-2598; Mathew Boam, Public Affairs and Traffic Dir., phone (559)278-6981; Jason Tarver, Promotions Dir., phone (559)278-6982; Joe Moore, Station Mgr., phone (559)278-2598. **Local Programs:** *Hip Hop* 9:00 a.m. - 12:00 a.m. Fri.-Sun., Jason Tarver, Urban Music Dir., (209)278-6981; *Jazz* 6:00 a.m. - 12:00 p.m. Monday-Friday, Joe Moore, Station Mgr., (209)278-4500; *Progressive* 12:00 p.m. - 6:00 p.m. Monday-Friday, Manny Carr, Music Dir., (559)278-4500. **Wattage:** 2600. **Ad Rates:** $5-20 per unit. **URL:** http://www.csufresno.edu/kfsr/.

HUNTINGTON BEACH

📖 **10 Home Business**
United Marketing and Research Company, Inc.
8855 Atlanta Ave., Ste. 368   Phone: (714)968-0331
Huntington Beach, CA 92646   Fax: (714)962-7722
Publication E-mail: henderson@ix.netcom.com

Magazine covering the home-based business market, including sales and marketing, business start-ups, business operations, raising money, productivity, and related issues. **Founded:** Jan. 1994. **Freq:** Bimonthly. **Print Method:** Web. **Trim Size:** 8 3/8 x 10 7/8. **Cols./Page:** 3. **Key Personnel:** Stacy Henderson, Pub./CEO, henderson@ix.netcom.com; Richard Henderson, Pub./CFO; Sandy Larson, Managing Editor; Stacy Ann Henderson, Editor-in-Chief; David Rifkin, Nat'l. Sales Dir.; Marilyn Ellis, Office Mgr.; Mark Manusz, Circulation Mgr.; Dan Howard, Advertising Sales. **ISSN:** 1092-4779. **Subscription Rates:** $15 individuals; $3.99 single issue; $5.99 single issue Canada. **Remarks:** Accepts advertising. **URL:** http://www.homebusinessmag.com.
Ad Rates: BW: $2,375   **Circ:** (Not Reported)
              4C: $2,850
              PCI: $165

📖 **11 New Era Magazine**
22152 Jonesport Ln.   Phone: (714)962-1351
Huntington Beach, CA 92646   Fax: (714)962-1354
                                       Free: (888)565-8236

Publication E-mail: 4newera@gte.net

Magazine for laundry and dry cleaning managers, owners, and operators. **Subtitle:** Laundry and Cleaning Lines. **Founded:** 1959. **Freq:** Monthly. **Print Method:** Offset. **Trim Size:** 8 3/8 x 11 7/8. **Cols./Page:** 3. **Col. Width:** 28 nonpareils. **Col. Depth:** 140 agate lines. **Key Personnel:** Judith E. Frye,

Publisher. **ISSN:** 1068-7076. **Subscription Rates:** $30 individuals; $5 single issue. **Remarks:** Accepts advertising.
Ad Rates: BW: $3,175   **Circ:** Controlled ‡18,211
              4C: $4,525

LOS ANGELES

📖 **12 Variety**
Reed Business Information
5700 Wilshire Blvd., Ste. 120   Phone: (323)857-6600
Los Angeles, CA 90036   Fax: (323)965-2475

Newspaper (tabloid) reporting on theatre, television, radio, music, records, and movies. **Subtitle:** The International Entertainment Weekly. **Founded:** 1905. **Freq:** Weekly (Mon.). **Print Method:** Heatset. **Trim Size:** 10 3/4 x 14 1/2. **Cols./Page:** 5. **Col. Width:** 11 picas. **Col. Depth:** 196 agate lines. **Key Personnel:** Peter Bart, Editor; Charles Koones, Publisher. **ISSN:** 0042-2738. **Subscription Rates:** $129. **Remarks:** Accepts advertising.
Ad Rates: BW: $3,200   **Circ:** Mon. 34,293
              4C: $5,000
              PCI: $75

🎤 **13 KIRN-AM - 670**
1645 N. Vine St.   Phone: (323)466-4726
Los Angeles, CA 90028   Fax: (323)461-4772

Format: Ethnic; Full Service. **Founded:** 1983. **Formerly:** KVCA-AM. **Operating Hours:** Continuous. **Key Personnel:** John Paley, General Mgr., phone (323)769-2222, jpaley@679amkirn.com. **Wattage:** 5000. **Ad Rates:** $20-124 for 30 seconds; $25-155 for 60 seconds. **URL:** http://www.670amkirn.com.

RIVERSIDE

📖 **14 Healthy Cooking**
Sunwest Publishing
3769 Tibbetts St., Ste. A   Phone: (909)682-3026
Riverside, CA 92506-2606   Fax: (909)682-0246
Publication E-mail: iemail@pacbell.net

Consumer magazine covering cooking and recipes. **Freq:** Bimonthly. **Subscription Rates:** $39.95 individuals; $44.95 two years. **Remarks:** Accepts advertising. **URL:** http://www.inlandempiremagazine.com/hcinthisissue.html.
Circ: (Not Reported)

📖 **15 Pasta Magazine**
Sunwest Publishing
3769 Tibbetts St., Ste. A   Phone: (909)682-3026
Riverside, CA 92506-2606   Fax: (909)682-0246
Publication E-mail: iemail@pacbell.net

Consumer magazine covering Italian cooking and lifestyle. **Subtitle:** The Journal of Fine Culture and Italian Cuisine. **Freq:** Bimonthly. **Subscription Rates:** $44.95 individuals; $54.95 two years. **Remarks:** Accepts advertising. **URL:** http://www.inlandempiremagazine.com/pastafall01.html.
Circ: (Not Reported)

📖 **16 Southern California Brides**
Sunwest Publishing
3769 Tibbetts St., Ste. A   Phone: (909)682-3026
Riverside, CA 92506-2606   Fax: (909)682-0246
Publication E-mail: iemail@pacbell.net

Consumer magazine covering brides in Southern California. **URL:** http://www.inlandempiremagazine.com/brides.html.

📖 **17 Southern California Golf**
Sunwest Publishing
3769 Tibbetts St., Ste. A   Phone: (909)682-3026
Riverside, CA 92506-2606   Fax: (909)682-0246

Consumer magazine covering golf in Southern California. **Freq:** Annual. **URL:** http://www.inlandempiremagazine.com/socalgolflead01.html.

SANTA ANA

📖 **18 Union Hidpana**
Union Hispana
611 W. Civic Center Dr.   Phone: (714)541-6007
Santa Ana, CA 92701   Fax: (714)541-1603
Publication E-mail: uhnews@hotmail.com

Bilingual, Latino community newspaper. **Freq:** Weekly. **Print Method:** Offset. **Cols./Page:** 5. **Col. Width:** 11 picas. **Key Personnel:** Juan Garcia, Editor; Luis H. Arrhola, Publisher. **Remarks:** Accepts advertising.
Ad Rates: GLR: $18.45   **Circ:** Non-paid 35,000
          BW: $1,365
          4C: $1,765

SANTA CLARA

📖 **19 Hume Studies**
Philosophy Documentation Center
c/o Elizabeth S. Radcliffe, Editor, Hume
   Studies
Department of Philosophy
Santa Clara University
500 El Camino Real
Santa Clara, CA 95053-0310
Publication E-mail: order@pdcnet.org
Publisher E-mail: order@pdcnet.org

Scholarly journal covering work on the thought of David Hume. **Freq:** Semiannual. **Key Personnel:** Elizabeth Radcliffe, Editor; Kenneth Winkler, Editor. **ISSN:** 0319-7336. **Subscription Rates:** $40 institutions; $20 single issue institutions; $17.50 single issue individuals. **URL:** http://www.pdcnet.org/hume.html.

SPRINGVILLE

📖 **20 The Tule Times**
PO Box 692
Springville, CA 93265   Phone: (559)539-3166
                           Fax: (559)539-2942
Publisher E-mail: trtval@sosinet.net

Community newspaper. **Subtitle:** Serving the Tule River Foothill and Mountain Communities. **Founded:** Aug. 1979. **Freq:** Weekly. **Print Method:** Offset. **Trim Size:** 10 x 11 3/4. **Cols./Page:** 5. **Col. Width:** 1 7/8 inches. **Col. Depth:** 11 3/4 inches. **Key Personnel:** Valeri Barnes, Editor and Publisher; Chelsea McDonald, Asst. Editor. **Subscription Rates:** $22; $25 out of county; $20 senior citizen. **Remarks:** Color advertising accepted; rates available upon request. **Formerly:** Tule River Times (1902).
Ad Rates: BW: $308.75   **Circ:** Paid ‡2,200
          PCI: $8.60   Free ‡100

VAN NUYS

📖 **21 Dayspa**
Creative Age Publications, Inc.
7628 Densmore Ave.   Phone: (818)782-7328
Van Nuys, CA 91406-2042   Fax: (818)782-7450
                           Free: (800)442-5667

Professional magazine covering issues for salon/spa owners. **Freq:** Monthly. **Trim Size:** 8 x 10 3/4. **Cols./Page:** 3. **Key Personnel:** Linda W. Lewis, Exec. Editor, llewis@creativeage.com. **ISSN:** 1089-3199. **Subscription Rates:** $24 individuals; $5 single issue. **Remarks:** Accepts advertising.
Ad Rates: BW: $2,911   **Circ:** Controlled 32,564
          4C: $4,005

WALNUT CREEK

📖 **22 The Institutional Real Estate Letter**
Institutional Real Estate, Inc.
1475 N. Broadway, Ste. 300   Phone: (925)933-4040
Walnut Creek, CA 94596   Fax: (925)934-4099
Publication E-mail: n.gordon@irei.com
Publisher E-mail: circulation@irei.com

Monthly publication covering the pension, foundation, and endowment investment market. Provides information on investment patterns, trends, and strategies. **Subtitle:** The Information Source for Tax-Exempt Real Estate Investors. **Founded:** 1989. **Freq:** Monthly. **Print Method:** Sheet fed offset press. **Trim Size:** 8 1/2 x 11. **Cols./Page:** 3. **Key Personnel:** Geoffrey Dohrmann, Publisher and CEO, g.dohrmann@irei.com; Nyia Dohrmann, Pres. and COO, n.dohrmann@irei.com; Nancy Gordon, Editor, n.gordon@irei.com; Sandy Terranova, Marketing Dir., s.terranova@irei.com; Amanda Baak, Advertising Coordinator, a.baak@irei.com. **ISSN:** 1044-1662. **Subscription Rates:** $1,995 individuals; $185 single issue. **Remarks:** Accepts advertising.
Ad Rates: BW: $3,595   **Circ:** Paid 500
          4C: $4,095   Non-paid 1,000

📖 **23 REITStreet Magazine**
Institutional Real Estate, Inc.
1475 N. Broadway, Ste. 300   Phone: (925)933-4040
Walnut Creek, CA 94596   Fax: (925)934-4099
Publication E-mail: m.lester@irei.com
Publisher E-mail: circulation@irei.com

Professional magazine covering the real estate investment trust (REIT) industry for individual investors and REIT executives. **Subtitle:** The Stock Investor's Roadmap to Real Estate. **Founded:** Jan. 2001. **Freq:** Quarterly. **Print Method:** Sheetfed offset. **Trim Size:** 8'' x 11. **Cols./Page:** 2. **Key Personnel:** Geoffrey Dohrmann, Pub./CEO, g.dohrmann@irei.com; Nyia Dohrmann, Pres./COO, n.dohrmann@irei.com; Michael Lester, Editor, l.clodfelter@irei.com; Sandy Terranova, Mktg. Dir., s.terranova@irei.com; Amanda Baak, Adv. Coord., a.baak@irei.com. **ISSN:** 1090-0551. **Subscription Rates:** Free. **Remarks:** Accepts advertising.
Ad Rates: 4C: $4,095   **Circ:** Non-paid 4,000

COLORADO

BOULDER

📖 **24 Natural Foods Merchandiser**
New Hope Natural Media
1401 Pearl St., Ste. 200   Phone: (303)939-8440
Boulder, CO 80302   Fax: (303)447-1164
                           Free: (800)933-8440
Publication E-mail: nfm@newhope.com

Natural foods industry trade magazine. **Founded:** Feb. 1979. **Freq:** Monthly. **Print Method:** Offset. **Trim Size:** 10 3/4 x 14 3/4. **Cols./Page:** 4. **Col. Width:** 27 nonpareils. **Col. Depth:** 140 agate lines. **Key Personnel:** Karen Raterman, Vice President, kraterman@newhope.com; Kim Paulsen, Publisher; Marty Traynor-Spencer, Editor; Lauren Piscopo, Managing Editor; Ian Davis, Art Dir. **ISSN:** 0164-338X. **Subscription Rates:** $95 U.S.; $110 Canada; $125 other countries surface mail; $195 other countries air mail. **Remarks:** Accepts advertising. **URL:** http://www.newhope.com.
Ad Rates: BW: $4,045   **Circ:** Paid △15,003
          4C: $4,760

COLORADO SPRINGS

📖 **25 Colorado Springs Independent**
121 E. Pikes Peak Ave., Ste. 455
Colorado Springs, CO 80903

Community newspaper. **Freq:** Weekly. **Print Method:** Web. **Trim Size:** 10 x 12''. **Cols./Page:** 6. **Key Personnel:** John Weiss, Publisher, jw@csindy.com. **Subscription Rates:** Free. **URL:** http://www.csindy.com.
                           Circ: Combined 36,300

DENVER

📖 **26 Plastics Auxiliaries & Machinery**
Canon Communications LLC
55 Madison St., Ste. 770   Phone: (303)321-2322
Denver, CO 80206   Fax: (303)321-3552
Publication E-mail: editorial@immnet.com

Trade magazine for the plastics processing industry. **Freq:** Monthly. **Trim**

Ad Rates: GLR = general line rate; BW = one-time black & white page rate; 4C = one-time four color page rate; SAU = standard advertising unit rate; CNU = Canadian newspaper advertising unit rate; PCI = per column inch rate.
Circulation: ★ = ABC; △ = BPA; ♦ = CAC; ● = CCAB; ❑ = VAC; ⊕ = PO Statement; ‡ = Publisher's Report; Boldface figures = sworn; Light figures = estimated.
Entry type: 📖 = Print; 🎙 = Broadcast.

3

Size: 11 x 16. Cols./Page: 5. Key Personnel: Merle Snyder, Editor, msnyder@immnet.com; Kevin O'Grady, Publisher, phone (310)445-3705, kogrady@immnet.com; Jackie Dalzell, Assoc. Publisher, phone (440)239-4984, fax (440)239-4595, jdalzell@immnet.com. Remarks: Accepts advertising. URL: http://www.plasticsaux.mach.com. Former name: Plastics Auxiliaries.

Ad Rates: BW: $5,175   Circ: Controlled 30,000
           4C: $6,825

STEAMBOAT SPRINGS

📖 **27 Rocky Mountain Golf Magazine**
Mac Media, Inc.
PO Box 774328   Phone: (970)879-5250
Steamboat Springs, CO 80477-4328   Fax: (970)879-4650
                                Free: (800)686-6247

Consumer magazine covering golf in the Rocky Mountain region. Founded: 2000. Freq: Annual. Print Method: Web offset. Trim Size: 8 3/8 x 10 7/8. Key Personnel: Don Berger, Editor, phone (970)949-9170, fax (970)949-9176, bergerd@vail.net; Joel Schulman, Production Mgr., phone (970)879-5250, fax (970)879-4652, jschulm@mtnmags.com; Sandy Jacobs, Office Mgr., phone (970)879-5250, fax (970)879-4652, sjacobs@mtnmags.com. Subscription Rates: $5 individuals. Remarks: Accepts advertising. Former name: Vail Valley Golf.

Ad Rates: 4C: $4,137   Circ: Combined ‡60,000

📖 **28 Vail International Dance Festival**
Mac Media, Inc.
PO Box 774328   Phone: (970)879-5250
Steamboat Springs, CO 80477-4328   Fax: (970)879-4650
                                Free: (800)686-6247

Official publication for the Vail International Dance Festival. Founded: 1999. Freq: Annual. Print Method: Web offset. Trim Size: 8 3/8 x 10 7/8. Key Personnel: Don Berger, Editor, phone (970)949-9170, fax (970)949-9176, bergerd@vail.net; Joel Schulman, Production Mgr., phone (970)879-5250, fax (970)879-4652, jschulm@mtnmags.com; Sandy Jacobs, Office Mgr., phone (970)879-5250, fax (970)879-4652, sjacobs@tnmags.com. Subscription Rates: Free. Remarks: Accepts advertising.

Ad Rates: 4C: $2,300   Circ: Non-paid ‡10,000

CONNECTICUT

DANBURY

📖 **29 Junior Scholastic**
Scholastic Library Publishing
90 Sherman Tpke.
Danbury, CT 06816   Fax: (203)797-3657
                                Free: (800)621-1115
Publication E-mail: jr@scholastic.com
Publisher E-mail: custserv@scholastic.com

Social studies magazine. Founded: Sept. 18, 1937. Freq: 18/year (issued Sept. thru May). Print Method: Offset. Cols./Page: 3. Col. Width: 27 nonpareils. Col. Depth: 140 agate lines. Key Personnel: Lee Baier, Editor; David Goody, Publisher; William Kelchner, Advertising Mgr. ISSN: 0022-6688. Subscription Rates: $8.25 individuals; $1.25 single issue. Remarks: Accepts advertising.

Ad Rates: BW: $8,260   Circ: Paid 591,038
           4C: $12,080

TORRINGTON

📖 **30 The Dolphin**
Journal Register Inc.
190 Water St.
PO Box 58   Phone: (860)489-3121
Torrington, CT 06790   Fax: (860)489-6790
                                Free: (800)489-1450
Publication E-mail: dolphin@ctcentral.com

Military newspaper. Freq: Weekly. Key Personnel: Sheryl Walsh, Editor; Chris Lough, Editorial Asst. Remarks: Accepts advertising. URL: http://www.dolphin-news.com.

                                Circ: (Not Reported)

WILLIMANTIC

📖 **31 Campus Lantern**
Eastern Connecticut State College
110 Student Ctr.
83 Windham St.   Phone: (860)465-4445
Willimantic, CT 06226-2308   Fax: (860)465-4685
Publication E-mail: lantern.adv@stu.easternct.edu

College campus-oriented newspaper (tabloid). Founded: 1949. Freq: Weekly (Wed.). Print Method: Offset. Cols./Page: 5. Col. Width: 1 7/10 inches. Col. Depth: 11 1/2 inches. Key Personnel: Jordan Zukley, Editor-in-Chief, lantern@stu.easternct.edu; Jen Fernandez, Managing Editor. Subscription Rates: Free; $9 by mail. Remarks: Accepts advertising.

Ad Rates: BW: $408   Circ: Controlled 2,900
           PCI: $7.10

DELAWARE

DOVER

📖 **32 Delaware State News**
Independent Newspapers, Inc.
PO Box 737   Phone: (302)674-3600
Dover, DE 19903   Fax: (302)741-8261
                                Free: (800)282-8586
Publication E-mail: dsnnews@newszap.com

Community newspaper. Subtitle: the downstate daily. Founded: 1953. Freq: Mon.-Sun. Print Method: Offset. Trim Size: 13 1/2 x 22 1/2. Cols./Page: 6. Col. Width: 11 picas. Col. Depth: 21 1/2 inches. Key Personnel: Andrew West, Editor, phone (302)741-8204, awest@newszap.com; Tonda Parks, Advertising Mgr., phone (302)741-8205, fax (302)741-8261, Tonda_Park@aol.com. USPS: 152-160. Subscription Rates: $145.60 individuals. Remarks: Accepts advertising. Monday-Friday: GLR: $2.36; BW: $2,832.84; 4C: $3,072.84; PCI: $21.96; Sunday: GLR: $2.84; BW: $3,405.60; 4C: $3,693.60; PCI: $26.40. URL: http://www.newszap.com. Merged with: The Daily Whale (June 1997).

                             Circ: Mon.-Sat. 17,693
                                  Sun. 25,316

DISTRICT OF COLUMBIA

WASHINGTON

📖 **33 Kerem**
3035 Porter St. NW
Washington, DC 20008   Phone: (202)364-3006

Religious, literary journal on Jewish themes. Subtitle: Creative Explorations in Judaism. Founded: 1992. Freq: Irregular. Trim Size: 6 x 9. Key Personnel: Gilah Langner, Editor, phone (202)364-3006, langner@erols.com; Sara R. Horowitz, Editor, srh@yorku.ca. ISSN: 1068-6975. Subscription Rates: $8.50 individuals; $15 2 issues. Remarks: Advertising accepted; rates available upon request. URL: http://www.kerem.org.

                                Circ: (Not Reported)

📖 **34 Nation's Cities Weekly**
National League of Cities
1301 Pennsylvania Ave. NW, Ste 550   Phone: (202)626-3000
Washington, DC 20004-1763   Fax: (202)626-3043
Publication E-mail: weekly@nlc.org
Publisher E-mail: inet@nlc.org

Tabloid newspaper covering municipal government and urban affairs. Founded: 1978. Freq: Weekly. Print Method: Offset. Trim Size: 11 3/8 x 14 1/2. Cols./Page: 5. Col. Width: 27 nonpareils. Col. Depth: 189 agate lines. Key Personnel: Michael Reinemer, Editor, phone (202)626-3123, reinemer@nlc.org; Cinty Hogan, Managing Editor, phone (202)626-3048, hogan@nlc.org. ISSN: 0164-5935. Subscription Rates: $96 individuals; $149 two years; $192 For 3 years. Remarks: Accepts advertising. Online: UMI.

Ad Rates: GLR: $12   Circ: ‡32,500
           BW: $3,890
           4C: $4,390

FLORIDA

BAREFOOT BAY

📖 **35 The Barefoot Tattler**
937 Barefoot Blvd., Ste. B
PO Box 779-176
Barefoot Bay, FL 32976
Phone: (772)664-9381
Fax: (772)664-6236
Publisher E-mail: melba@barefoot-tattler.com

Community newspaper for a predominantly senior audience. **Founded:** Sept. 1978. **Freq:** Monthly. **Print Method:** Offset. **Trim Size:** 11 x 16. **Cols./Page:** 4. **Col. Width:** 14 picas. **Col. Depth:** 16 inches. **Key Personnel:** Melba Lochmandy, Publisher, melba@barefoot-tattler.com; John Lochmandy, Editor, editor@barefoot-tattler.com; Ray Olinger, Sales Mgr. **Subscription Rates:** Free. **Remarks:** Accepts advertising. **URL:** http://www.barefoot-tattler.com. **Feature Editors:** Wally Beery, *Garden/Home*; Joan Doton, *Features*; Lynn Mickley, *Features*; Bob Pearsall, *Features*; Bob Smith, *Features*.

Ad Rates:	GLR: $11	Circ: Combined ⊕**6,850**
	BW: $704	
	4C: $880	
	PCI: $11	

BONITA SPRINGS

📖 **36 Cultic Studies Review**
American Family Foundation
PO Box 2265
Bonita Springs, FL 34133
Phone: (239)514-3081
Publisher E-mail: aff@affculting.serve.com

Online journal covering cults and related groups. **Freq:** Triennial. **Subscription Rates:** $25 individuals online only; $45 individuals print & online eds.; $55 Canada and Mexico print & online eds.; $65 elsewhere print & online eds. **URL:** http://www.csj.org. **Formed by the merger of:** Cultic Studies Journal; The Cult Observer.

FORT LAUDERDALE

📖 **37 Waterfront News**
Ziegler Publishing Co., Inc.
1515 SW 1 Ave.
Fort Lauderdale, FL 33315
Phone: (954)524-9450
Fax: (954)524-9464
Free: (800)226-9464
Publication E-mail: publisher@waterfront-news.com

Community newspaper. **Subtitle:** South Florida's Nautical Newspaper. **Founded:** Mar. 1984. **Freq:** Monthly. **Print Method:** Offset. **Trim Size:** 11 x 17. **Cols./Page:** 3. **Col. Width:** 3 1/3 inches. **Col. Depth:** 16 inches. **Key Personnel:** John Ziegler, Publisher, publisher@waterfront-news.com; Jennifer Heit, Editor, editor@waterfront-news.com; David Lewis, Web Site Coord., web@waterfront-news.com. **ISSN:** 8756-0038. **Subscription Rates:** $12 by mail. **Remarks:** Accepts advertising. **Available Online. URL:** http://waterfront-news.com.

Ad Rates:	GLR: $5	Circ: Paid ‡750
	BW: $1,200	Free ‡36,000
	4C: $1,500	
	PCI: $30	

FT. PIERCE

📖 **38 International Journal of Applied Philosophy**
Philosophy Documentation Center
c/o Elliot D. Cohen, Editor
Indian River Community College
3209 Virginia Ave.
Ft. Pierce, FL 34981-5596
Publication E-mail: order@pdcnet.org
Publisher E-mail: order@pdcnet.org

Scholarly journal covering philosophy in the areas of education, business, law, government, health care, psychology, science, and the environment. **Freq:** Semiannual. **Key Personnel:** Elliot D. Cohen, Editor, ecohen@ircc.cc.fl.us.

ISSN: 0739-098X. **Subscription Rates:** $40 institutions; $22 individuals; $20 single issue institutions; $11 single issue individuals. **URL:** http://www.pdcnet.org/ijap.html.

ORLANDO

📖 **39 Hinge Music Magazine**
The Performing Artist
5005 City St., No. 1326
Orlando, FL 32839
Phone: (407)852-7078
Publication E-mail: hingemusicmag@aol.com

Consumer magazine covering music. **Subtitle:** Opening Doors to Florida's Music Mecca. **Founded:** Aug. 2001. **Freq:** Monthly. **Trim Size:** 8'' x 10. **Key Personnel:** Jennifer Bair, Publisher. **Subscription Rates:** Free; $18 by mail. **Remarks:** Accepts advertising.

| Ad Rates: | 4C: $600 | Circ: Non-paid 15,000 |

SARASOTA

📖 **40 Intermarket Review**
International Institute for Economic Research
1539 S Orange Ave.
Sarasota, FL 34239
Phone: (941)364-5850
Fax: (941)364-9463
Free: (800)221-7514
Publication E-mail: info@pring.com
Publisher E-mail: info@pring.com

Professional journal covering financial markets worldwide for investment brokers and others. **Freq:** Monthly. **Key Personnel:** Lisa H. Pring, Managing Editor, lpring@home.com. **ISSN:** 1096-1747. **Subscription Rates:** $315 U.S. **URL:** http://www.pring.com.

TALLAHASSEE

📖 **41 The Florida Bar Journal**
The Florida Bar
650 Apalachee Pkwy.
Tallahassee, FL 32399-2300
Phone: (850)561-5600
Fax: (850)561-3859
Publication E-mail: journal@flabar.org

Legal journal. **Founded:** Aug. 1927. **Freq:** Monthly. **Print Method:** Offset. **Trim Size:** 8 1/8 x 10 7/8. **Cols./Page:** 3. **Col. Width:** 13.5 picas. **Col. Depth:** 58 picas. **Key Personnel:** Cheryle Dodd, Editor, phone (850)561-5680, cdodd@flabar.org; John F. Harkness, Jr., Publisher; Cassandra Conrad, Advertising Mgr., phone (850)561-5601, dixon@flabar.org. **ISSN:** 0015-3915. **Subscription Rates:** $50 individuals; $5 single issue. **Remarks:** Accepts advertising. **Online:** Westlaw. **URL:** http://www.flabar.org. **Alt. Formats:** Microform.

| Ad Rates: | BW: $2,040 | Circ: ‡63,762 |
| | 4C: $2,685 | |

📖 **42 Psychomusicology**
Florida State University
Music and Arts Publications
1211 Brandt Dr.
Tallahassee, FL 32308-5210
Fax: (850)644-6100

Scholarly journal covering research in music. **Founded:** 1981. **Freq:** Semiannual. **Print Method:** Offset. **Trim Size:** 6 x 9. **Cols./Page:** 1. **Col. Width:** 4 inches. **Col. Depth:** 7 inches. **Key Personnel:** Jack Taylor, Managing Editor, taylor@cmr.fsu.edu. **ISSN:** 0275-3987. **Subscription Rates:** $27 individuals; $33 other countries; $16 single issue U.S.; $19 single issue other countries. **Remarks:** Advertising not accepted. **URL:** http://otto.cmr.fsu.edu/psychomus.

Circ: (Not Reported)

GEORGIA

ATHENS

📖 43 College and Research Libraries
Association of College and Research Libraries
50 E. Huron St.
Chicago, IL 60611

Phone: (312)280-2513
Fax: (312)280-2520
Free: (800)545-2433

Publisher E-mail: acrl@ala.org

Journal for ACRL members. **Founded:** Dec. 1939. **Freq:** Bimonthly. **Print Method:** Offset. **Trim Size:** 6 1/8 x 9 1/4. **Cols./Page:** 2. **Col. Width:** 29 nonpareils. **Col. Depth:** 105 agate lines. **Key Personnel:** William G. Potter, Editor, phone (706)542-0621, fax (706)542-4144, wpotter@arches.uga.edu; Stuart Foster, Advertising Mgr., phone (203)347-3764. **ISSN:** 0010-0870. **Subscription Rates:** $60 nonmembers. **Remarks:** Accepts advertising.
Ad Rates: BW: $935   **Circ:** ‡12,000
           4C: $1,710

DOUGLAS

🎙 44 WDMG-FM - 99.5
620 E. Ward St.
Douglas, GA 31533-3915

Phone: (912)389-0995
Fax: (912)383-8552

E-mail: wdmg@amfm.com

Format: News; Talk; Sports; Classic Rock. **Networks:** USA Radio; Gannett News. **Operating Hours:** Continuous. **ADI:** Savannah, GA. **Key Personnel:** Bob Ganzak, President, phone (229)386-9898; John Higgs, Station Mgr./News Dir., johnovidhiggs@hotmail.com. **Wattage:** 100,000. **Ad Rates:** $8-22 for 30 seconds; $12-30 for 60 seconds. Combined advertising rates available with WDMG-AM.

GLENVILLE

📖 45 Glenville Sentinel
Glennville Sentinel
PO Box 218
Glennville, GA 30427-0218

Phone: (912)654-2515
Fax: (912)654-2527

Publication E-mail: sentinel@pineland.net

Community newspaper. **Founded:** 1925. **Freq:** Weekly. **Cols./Page:** 6. **Col. Width:** 2 inches. **Col. Depth:** 21 inches. **Key Personnel:** Pam Waters, Editor and Publisher; Sarah Reed, Asst. Editor. **ISSN:** 2199-0000. **Subscription Rates:** $17.12 individuals; $21.40 out of state. **Remarks:** Accepts advertising. **URL:** http://www.glennvillesentinel.net. **Alt. Formats:** CD-ROM.
Ad Rates: PCI: $5   **Circ:** Paid ⊕4,300

PERRY

🎙 46 WCOP-FM - 99.9
1006 1st St.
Perry, GA 31069-3592

Phone: (478)218-7756
Fax: (478)988-7977
Free: (800)705-8770

E-mail: mail@wcopradio.com

Format: Religious. **Networks:** USA Radio. **Founded:** June 1995. **Formerly:** WAVC-AM; WCOP-FM. **Operating Hours:** Continuous. **Key Personnel:** Bill Bruton, Station Mgr., billbruton@aol.com; Bill Best, Sales Mgr.; Nelda Bruton, Office Mgr. **Wattage:** 6000. **Ad Rates:** $5.50-8.00 for 30 seconds; $8.46-11.00 for 60 seconds. **URL:** http://www.wcopradio.com.

ILLINOIS

CHAMPAIGN

📖 47 Ethnomusicology
University of Illinois Press
1325 S. Oak St.
Champaign, IL 61820-6903

Phone: (217)333-0950
Fax: (217)244-8082
Free: (800)545-4703

Publisher E-mail: uipress@uillinois.edu

Journal covering ethnomusicology for musicians, musicologists, folklorists, popular culture scholars, and cultural anthropologists. **Freq:** Triennial. **Key Personnel:** Bruno Nettl, Editor, b-nettl@uiuc.edu; Clydette Wantland, Advertising, phone (217)244-6496, fax (217)244-8082, cwant-lan@uillinois.edu. **ISSN:** 0014-1836. **Subscription Rates:** $75 institutions; $85 institutions out of country; $60 individuals; $70 individuals out of country; $18.50 single issue. **Remarks:** Accepts advertising. **URL:** http://www.press.uillinois.edu/journals/ethno.html.
Ad Rates: BW: $350   **Circ:** (Not Reported)

📖 48 Northwestern University Law Review
University of Illinois Press
1325 S. Oak St.
Champaign, IL 61820-6903

Phone: (217)333-0950
Fax: (217)244-8082
Free: (800)545-4703

Publisher E-mail: uipress@uillinois.edu

Law journal. **Founded:** 1892. **Freq:** Quarterly. **Print Method:** Offset. **Key Personnel:** Barbara Hunt, Contact, phone (312)503-2035, fax (312)503-5950, b-hunt2@law.northwestern.edu. **ISSN:** 0029-3571. **Subscription Rates:** $40 institutions U.S.; $45 institutions, other countries; $40 individuals U.S.; $45 individuals other countries; $9 single issue U.S.; $10 single issue other countries. **Remarks:** Advertising not accepted.
                               Circ: ‡1,500

📖 49 Perspectives on Work
University of Illinois Press
1325 S. Oak St.
Champaign, IL 61820-6903

Phone: (217)333-0950
Fax: (217)244-8082
Free: (800)545-4703

Publisher E-mail: uipress@uillinois.edu

Journal covering industrial relations and human resources. Official publication of the Industrial Relations Research Association. **Freq:** Semiannual. **Key Personnel:** Charles J. Whalen, Editor; Clydette Wantland, Advertising, phone (217)244-6496, fax (217)244-8082, cwantlan@uillinois.edu. **ISSN:** 1534-2976. **Subscription Rates:** $170 institutions; $185 institutions out of country; $85 individuals; $100 individuals out of country; $28 institutions journal only, without IRRA membership. **Remarks:** Accepts advertising. **URL:** http://www.press.uillinois.edu/journals/pow.html.
Ad Rates: BW: $500   **Circ:** (Not Reported)

📖 50 State Politics & Policy Quarterly
University of Illinois Press
1325 S. Oak St.
Champaign, IL 61820-6903

Phone: (217)333-0950
Fax: (217)244-8082
Free: (800)545-4703

Publisher E-mail: uipress@uillinois.edu

Official journal of the State Politics and Policy section of the American Political Science Association covering studies that develop general hypotheses of the political behavior and policymaking and test those hypotheses using methodological advantages of the states. **Freq:** Quarterly. **Key Personnel:** Christopher Z. Mooney, Editor; Clydette Wantland, Advertising, phone (217)244-6496, fax (217)244-8082, cwantlan@uillinois.edu. **ISSN:** 1532-4400. **Subscription Rates:** $95 institutions; $135 institutions out of country; $40 individuals; $80 individuals out of country; $48 single issue institutions; $12 single issue individuals. **Remarks:** Accepts advertising. **URL:** http://www.press.uillinois.edu/journals/sppq.html.
Ad Rates: BW: $225   **Circ:** (Not Reported)

CHICAGO

📖 51 Archives of Physical Medicine and Rehabilitation
Elsevier Science
330 N. Wabash Ave., Ste. 2510
Chicago, IL 60611-3604

Phone: (312)464-9550
Fax: (312)464-9554

Publication E-mail: archivesmail@aapmr.org
Publisher E-mail: markmrvica@mrvica.com

Journal concerning physical medicine and rehabilitation. **Freq:** Monthly. **Key Personnel:** Kenneth M. Jaffe, MD, Editor-in-Chief; Rebecca Craik, PhD, Congress Editor; Jeffrey R. Basford, MD, Academy Editor. **ISSN:** 0003-9993. **Subscription Rates:** $207 individuals U.S.; $296 institutions U.S.; $90 students and residents, U.S.; $262 individuals other countries; $355 institutions other countries; $131 students and residents, other countries; $30 single issue. **Remarks:** Advertising accepted; rates available upon request. **Online:** MEDLINE. **URL:** http://www.archives-pmr.org.
                            Circ: 11,500

📖 **52 City & Community**
Blackwell Publishers
University of Illinois at Chicago
1007 W. Harrison St.
Chicago, IL 60607-7140
Publisher E-mail: subscrip@blackwellpub.com

Official journal of the Community and Urban Sociology Section covering research and theory about communities and metropolitan areas. **Freq:** Quarterly. **Key Personnel:** Anthony Orum, Editor. **ISSN:** 1535-6841. **Subscription Rates:** $237 institutions print & premium online; $214 institutions print & standard online; $195 institutions premium online only; $63 nonmembers; $25 students. **Remarks:** Accepts advertising. **Available Online.** **URL:** http://www.asanet.org/.
Ad Rates: BW: $100   **Circ:** (Not Reported)

📖 **53 The Cremationist of North America**
Cremation Association of North America
401 N Michigan Ave.   Phone: (312)644-6610
Chicago, IL 60611   Fax: (312)321-4098
Publisher E-mail: cana@sba.com

Trade magazine on cremation. **Founded:** July 1965. **Freq:** Quarterly. **Print Method:** Offset. **Trim Size:** 8 1/2 x 11. **Cols./Page:** 3. **Col. Width:** 26 nonpareils. **Col. Depth:** 140 agate lines. **Key Personnel:** Barbara Nelson, Administrative Dir., phone (312)673-4705, barb_nelson@sba.com; Cathryn McClelland, Art Director. **Subscription Rates:** $24 individuals; $36 two years; $5 single issue. **Remarks:** Accepts advertising. **URL:** http://www.cremationassociation.org.
Ad Rates: GLR: $513   **Circ:** ‡1,600
             BW: $513
             4C: $1,348
             PCI: $79

📖 **54 Equipment Solutions**
Talcott Communications Corp.
20 N. Wacker Dr., Ste. 1865   Phone: (312)849-2220
Chicago, IL 60606   Fax: (312)849-2174
                                                                 Free: (800)229-1967
Publication E-mail: equipmentsolutions@talcott.com
Publisher E-mail: giftwarenews@talcott.com

Trade magazine covering the foodservice business, equipment, serving operators, equipment dealers, trends, and related issues for foodservice operators. **Founded:** Feb. 1998. **Freq:** Bimonthly. **Print Method:** Web press. **Trim Size:** 10 5/8 x 14 3/8. **Cols./Page:** 4. **Col. Width:** 2 3/8 inches. **Col. Depth:** 13 3/4 inches. **Key Personnel:** Don Knapp, Publisher; Rita Negrete, Consulting Editor; James J. Hodl, Technical Editor. **Subscription Rates:** Free to qualified subscribers; $26.60 individuals; $35 two years; $34.60 Canada. **Remarks:** Accepts advertising. **URL:** http://www.equipsolu.com.
Ad Rates: BW: $4,995   **Circ:** Paid ‡1,265
             4C: $5,895   Non-paid ‡29,054

📖 **55 Flora Magazine**
Cenflo, Inc.
205 W Wacker Dr., Ste. 1040   Phone: (312)739-5000
Chicago, IL 60606-3508   Fax: (312)739-0739
                                                                 Free: (800)732-4581
Publisher E-mail: kbcenflo@aol.com

Magazine for volume buyers of floral products. **Founded:** 1982. **Freq:** Bimonthly. **Print Method:** Web offset. **Trim Size:** 8 1/2 x 11. **Cols./Page:** 3. **Col. Width:** 1 7/8 inches. **Col. Depth:** 10 inches. **Key Personnel:** Erin Hallstom, Editor, kbcenflo@aol.com; Eric Benjamin, Publisher. **Subscription Rates:** $20. **Remarks:** Accepts advertising. **URL:** http://www.cenflo.com/floramag.
Ad Rates: BW: $1,840   **Circ:** ‡17,100
             4C: $2,755
             PCI: $37

📖 **56 Law and History Review**
University of Illinois Press
c/o Christopher Tomlins
American Bar Foundation
750 N. Lake Shore Dr.   Phone: (312)988-6553
Chicago, IL 60611   Fax: (312)988-6579
Publisher E-mail: uipress@uillinois.edu

Journal covering legal history in the U.S., England, Europe and ancient legal history. **Freq:** Triennial. **Key Personnel:** Christopher Tomlins, Editor, clt@abfn.org; Clydette Wantland, Advertising, phone (217)244-6496, fax (217)244-8082, cwantlan@uillinois.edu. **ISSN:** 0738-2480. **Subscription Rates:** $85 institutions; $95 institutions out of country; $50 individuals; $60 individuals out of country; $28 single issue. **Remarks:** Accepts advertising. **URL:** http://www.press.uillinois.edu/journals/lhr.html.
Ad Rates: BW: $315   **Circ:** (Not Reported)

📖 **57 Midwest Engineer**
Western Society of Engineers
28 E Jackson Blvd.   Phone: (312)913-1730
Chicago, IL 60604   Fax: (312)913-1731
Publisher E-mail: wse@wsechicago.org

Subtitle: News Magazine of the Western Society of Engineers. **Founded:** 1890. **Freq:** 6/year. **Print Method:** Offset. **Trim Size:** 8 3/4 x 10 7/8. **Cols./Page:** 3 and 2. **Col. Width:** 32 and 42 nonpareils. **Col. Depth:** 135 agate lines. **Key Personnel:** Kristy Galgan. **ISSN:** 0026-3370. **Subscription Rates:** $15 individuals. **URL:** http://www.wsechicago.org.
Ad Rates: GLR: $.50   **Circ:** ‡1,000
             BW: $645

📖 **58 The Owl of Minerva**
Philosophy Documentation Center
c/o Ardis B. Collins, Editor
Department of Philosophy
Loyola University
6525 North Sheridan Rd.
Chicago, IL 60626
Publication E-mail: order@pdcnet.org
Publisher E-mail: order@pdcnet.org

Journal of the Hegel Society of America covering issues pertaining to Hegel and a Hegleian approach to philosophical issues. **Freq:** Semiannual. **Key Personnel:** Ardis B. Collins, Editor, acollin@luc.edu. **ISSN:** 0030-7580. **Subscription Rates:** $25 institutions; $20 individuals; $10 students/retirees; $12.50 single issue institutions; $10 single issue individuals. **URL:** http://www.pdcnet.org/owl.html.

📖 **59 Roctober**
Roctober Magazine
1507 E. 53rd St., No. 617
Chicago, IL 60615
Publication E-mail: editor@roctober.com

Consumer magazine covering rock and other types of music, pop culture, and comics. **Freq:** Triennial. **Key Personnel:** Jake Austen, Editor-in-Chief; Benjamin Edmonds, Online Editor; John Battles, Asst. Contrib. Editor; James Porter, Asst. Contrib. Editor; Jacqueline Stewart, Asst. Contrib. Editor; Ken Burke, Asst. Contrib. Editor. **Subscription Rates:** $10 individuals; $15 Canada and Mexico; $20 elsewhere. **Remarks:** Accepts advertising. **URL:** http://www.roctober.com.
                                                                 Circ: (Not Reported)

HAZEL CREST

📖 **60 Muslim Journal**
Muslim Journal Enterprises, Inc.
929 W 171st. St.
Hazel Crest, IL 60429-1901   Phone: (708)647-9600
                                                                 Fax: (708)647-0754
                                                                 Free: (800)837-8402
Publication E-mail: muslimjrnl@aol.com

International Islamic newspaper. **Founded:** 1975. **Freq:** Weekly (Fri.). **Print Method:** Offset. **Cols./Page:** 5. **Col. Width:** 22 nonpareils. **Col. Depth:** 208 agate lines. **Key Personnel:** Ayesha K. Mustafaa, Editor/Contact, aveshak-

Ad Rates: GLR = general line rate; BW = one-time black & white page rate; 4C = one-time four color page rate; SAU = standard advertising unit rate;
CNU = Canadian newspaper advertising unit rate; PCI = per column inch rate.
Circulation: ★ = ABC; △ = BPA; ♦ = CAC; • = CCAB; ❑ = VAC; ⊕ = PO Statement; ‡ = Publisher's Report; Boldface figures = sworn; Light figures = estimated.
Entry type: ❑ = Print; ⚍ = Broadcast.

7

mustafaa@msn.com; Monte I Fateen, Circulation Mgr.; NGina Muhammad-Ali, Advertising Dir., nginamuhammad@hotmail.com. **ISSN:** 0883-816X. **Subscription Rates:** $49 individuals; $79 two years. **URL:** http://www.muslimjournal.com. **Alt. Formats:** Microfiche.

Ad Rates:	BW: $910	Circ: ‡16,000
	4C: $1,092	
	SAU: $14	
	PCI: $14	

NAPERVILLE

📖 61 Batavia Sun
Sun Publications
1500 W. Ogden Ave.
PO Box 269   Phone: (630)355-0063
Naperville, IL 60566-0269   Fax: (630)416-5163
Publisher E-mail: thesun@scni.com

Community newspaper. **Founded:** Oct. 26, 2000. **Freq:** Weekly. **Key Personnel:** Gina Allen, Editor; Greg Melis, General Mgr.; Laurie K. Kagann, News Libn., phone (630)416-5202. **URL:** http://www.suburbanchicagonews.com.
Circ: Combined 280,876

📖 62 Downers Grove Sun
Sun Publications
1500 W. Ogden Ave.
PO Box 269   Phone: (630)355-0063
Naperville, IL 60566-0269   Fax: (630)416-5163
Publisher E-mail: thesun@scni.com

General newspaper. **Founded:** Apr. 19, 2001. **Freq:** Weekly (Thurs.). **Key Personnel:** Gina Allen, Editor; Greg Melis, General Mgr.; Laurie K. Kagann, News Libn. **URL:** http://www.suburbanchicagonews.com.

📖 63 The Fox Valley Villages/60504 Sun
Sun Publications
1500 W. Ogden Ave.
PO Box 269   Phone: (630)355-0063
Naperville, IL 60566-0269   Fax: (630)416-5163
Publisher E-mail: thesun@scni.com

Community newspaper. **Founded:** Aug. 16, 1984. **Freq:** Weekly (Thurs.). **Print Method:** Offset. **Cols./Page:** 5. **Col. Width:** 24 nonpareils. **Col. Depth:** 224 agate lines. **Key Personnel:** Gina Allen, Editor; Gerg Melis, General Mgr.; Laurie K. Kagann, News Libn., phone (630)416-5202. **Subscription Rates:** $10 individuals; $11.50 out of area. **Remarks:** Accepts advertising. **URL:** http://www.suburbanchicagonews.com.

Ad Rates:	GLR: $.21	Circ: Combined 280,786
	BW: $235.20	
	4C: $685.20	
	PCI: $2.94	

📖 64 Geneva Sun
Sun Publications
1500 W. Ogden Ave.
PO Box 269   Phone: (630)355-0063
Naperville, IL 60566-0269   Fax: (630)416-5163
Publisher E-mail: thesun@scni.com

Community newspaper. **Freq:** Weekly. **Key Personnel:** Gina Allen, Editor; Greg Melis, General Mgr.; Laurie K. Kagann, News Libn., phone (630)416-5202. **URL:** http://www.suburbanchicagonews.com.
Circ: Combined 280,786

📖 65 Glen Ellyn Sun
Sun Publications
1500 W. Ogden Ave.
PO Box 269   Phone: (630)355-0063
Naperville, IL 60566-0269   Fax: (630)416-5163
Publisher E-mail: thesun@scni.com

General newspaper. **Founded:** Apr. 20, 2001. **Freq:** Weekly (Fri.). **Key Personnel:** Gina Allen, Editor; Greg Milis, General Mgr.; Laurie K. Kagann, News Libn. **URL:** http://www.suburbanchicagonews.com.

📖 66 Homer/Lockport/Lemont Sun
Sun Publications
1500 W. Ogden Ave.
PO Box 269   Phone: (630)355-0063
Naperville, IL 60566-0269   Fax: (630)416-5163
Publisher E-mail: thesun@scni.com

Community newspaper. **Freq:** Weekly. **Key Personnel:** Gina Allen, Editor; Greg Melis, General Mgr.; Laurie K. Kagann, News Libn., phone (630)416-5202. **URL:** http://www.suburbanchicagonews.com.
Circ: Combined 280,786

📖 67 Lincoln-Way Sun
Sun Publications
1500 W. Ogden Ave.
PO Box 269   Phone: (630)355-0063
Naperville, IL 60566-0269   Fax: (630)416-5163
Publisher E-mail: thesun@scni.com

Community newspaper. **Freq:** Weekly. **Key Personnel:** Gina Allen, Editor; Greg Melis, General Mgr.; Laurie K. Kagann, News Libn., phone (630)416-5202. **URL:** http://www.suburbanchicagonews.com.
Circ: Combined 280,786

📖 68 The Lisle Sun
Sun Publications
1500 W. Ogden Ave.
PO Box 269   Phone: (630)355-0063
Naperville, IL 60566-0269   Fax: (630)416-5163
Publisher E-mail: thesun@scni.com

Community newspaper. **Founded:** 1938. **Freq:** Weekly (Fri.). **Print Method:** Offset. **Cols./Page:** 5. **Col. Width:** 24 nonpareils. **Col. Depth:** 224 agate lines. **Key Personnel:** Gina Allen, Editor; Greg Melis, General Mgr.; Laurie K. Kagann, News Libn., phone (630)416-5202. **USPS:** 314-800. **Subscription Rates:** $10.50 individuals; $16.35 out of county. **Remarks:** Accepts advertising. **URL:** http://www.suburbanchicagonews.com.

Ad Rates:	GLR: $.33	Circ: Combined 280,786
	BW: $526	
	4C: $871	
	PCI: $4.70	

📖 69 The Naperville Sun
Sun Publications
1500 W. Ogden Ave.
PO Box 269   Phone: (630)355-0063
Naperville, IL 60566-0269   Fax: (630)416-5163
Publisher E-mail: thesun@scni.com

Community newspaper. **Founded:** July 1935. **Freq:** 3/week. **Print Method:** Offset. Uses mats. **Cols./Page:** 5. **Col. Width:** 2 1/16 inches. **Col. Depth:** 224 agate lines. **Key Personnel:** Gina Allen, Editor; Greg Melis, General Mgr.; Laurie K. Kagann, News Libn., phone (630)416-5202. **Subscription Rates:** $40 individuals; $75 out of area. **Remarks:** Accepts advertising. **URL:** http://www.suburbanchicagonews.com.

Ad Rates:	BW: $698.75	Circ: Sun. 20,828
	4C: $948.75	Wed. 21,234
	PCI: $10.75	Fri. 21,234

📖 70 Plainfield Sun
Sun Publications
1500 W. Ogden Ave.
PO Box 269   Phone: (630)355-0063
Naperville, IL 60566-0269   Fax: (630)416-5163
Publisher E-mail: thesun@scni.com

Community newspaper. **Freq:** Wed. through Fri. **Key Personnel:** Gina Allen, Editor; Greg Melis, General Mgr.; Laurie K. Kagann, News Libn., phone (630)416-5202. **URL:** http://www.suburbanchicagonews.com.
Circ: Combined 280,786

📖 71 St. Charles Sun
Sun Publications
1500 W. Ogden Ave.
PO Box 269   Phone: (630)355-0063
Naperville, IL 60566-0269   Fax: (630)416-5163
Publisher E-mail: thesun@scni.com

Community newspaper. **Founded:** Oct. 25, 2000. **Freq:** Weekly. **Key**

Personnel: Gina Allen, Editor; Greg Melis, General Mgr.; Laurie K. Kagann, News Libn., phone (630)416-5202. **URL:** http://www.suburbanchicagonews.com.

Circ: Combined 280,786

📖 **72 Wheaton Sun**
Sun Publications
1500 W. Ogden Ave.
PO Box 269   Phone: (630)355-0063
Naperville, IL 60566-0269   Fax: (630)416-5163
Publisher E-mail: thesun@scni.com

General newspaper. **Founded:** 1910. **Freq:** Weekly. **Cols./Page:** 6. **Col. Width:** 24 nonpareils. **Col. Depth:** 301 agate lines. **Key Personnel:** Gina Allen, Editor; Greg Melis, General Mgr.; Laurie K. Kagann, News Libn., phone (630)416-6202. **Subscription Rates:** $78 individuals. **Remarks:** Accepts advertising. **URL:** http://www.suburbanchicagonews.com. **Formerly:** The Daily Journal (1992).
Ad Rates: BW: $1,549.13   **Circ:** Combined 280,786
              4C: $1,729.13
              PCI: $12.15

NORTHFIELD

📖 **73 McKnight's Long-Term Care News**
One Northfield Plz., Ste. 521   Phone: (847)784-8706
Northfield, IL 60093   Fax: (847)784-9346
Publication E-mail: ltcnews@medec.com
Publisher E-mail: ltcnews@mltcn.com

Professional magazine. **Founded:** 1980. **Freq:** Monthly 16 per year. **Print Method:** Offset. **Trim Size:** 10 7/8 x 14. **Cols./Page:** 4. **Col. Width:** 28 nonpareils. **Col. Depth:** 140 agate lines. **Key Personnel:** John O'Connor, Publisher; Bob Santini, National Sales Mgr. **ISSN:** 1084-3314. **Subscription Rates:** Free to qualified subscribers in U.S.; $5 single issue; $9 single issue back issue; $54.95 Canada; $59.95 foreign. **Remarks:** Accepts advertising. **Formerly:** Today's Nursing Home.
Ad Rates: BW: $4,695   **Circ:** Paid ‡850
              4C: $5,955   Controlled ‡50,025
              PCI: $120

OAK PARK

📖 **74 Femme Fatales**
Cinefantastique
Box 270   Phone: (708)366-5566
Oak Park, IL 60303   Fax: (708)366-1441
Publisher E-mail: cinefan@earthlink.net

Consumer magazine covering women in science fiction, horror and fantasy movies. **Freq:** Monthly. **Trim Size:** 8'' x 11. **Key Personnel:** Latonja Stephenson, Customer Svc. **Subscription Rates:** $48 individuals; $55 Canada; $62 elsewhere; $89 two years; $103 two years Canada; $116 two years elsewhere. **Remarks:** Accepts advertising.
Ad Rates: BW: $900   **Circ:** (Not Reported)
              4C: $1,700

ST. CHARLES

📖 **75 Food & Drug Packaging**
Stagnito Communications
Packaging Group
210 S 5th St.   Phone: (630)377-0100
St. Charles, IL 60174   Fax: (630)377-1678
                                                     Free: (800)346-6229

Trade magazine for packaging professionals in food and pharmaceutical industries. **Founded:** Jan. 1, 1959. **Freq:** Monthly. **Print Method:** Web offset. **Trim Size:** 11 x 15 3/4. **Cols./Page:** 3. **Key Personnel:** Lisa Pierce, Editor-in-Chief, phone (630)377-0100 x24, fax (630)377-1082, lpierce@stagnito.com. **ISSN:** 1085-2077. **Subscription Rates:** $65 individuals; $75 Canada; $140 other countries; $10 single issue. **Remarks:** Accepts

advertising. **URL:** http://www.fdp.com. **Former name:** The New Food & Drug Packaging.
Ad Rates: BW: $6,080   **Circ:** Combined 70,000
              4C: $7,950
              PCI: $100

SPRINGFIELD

📖 **76 Journal of the Abraham Lincoln Association**
University of Illinois Press
Illinois State Historical Library
One Old State Capital Plaza   Phone: (217)782-2118
Springfield, IL 62701-1507   Fax: (217)785-7937
Publisher E-mail: uipress@uillinois.edu

Scholarly journal covering Abraham Lincoln. **Freq:** Semiannual. **Key Personnel:** Thomas Schwartz, Editor, tschwart@hpa084r1.state.il.us; Clydette Wantland, Advertising, phone (217)244-6496, fax (217)244-8082, cwantland@uillinois.edu. **ISSN:** 0898-4212. **Subscription Rates:** $25 institutions; $30 institutions out of country; $25 individuals; $30 individuals out of country; $14 single issue; $19 single issue out of country. **Remarks:** Accepts advertising. **URL:** http://www.press.uillinois.edu/journals/jala.html.
Ad Rates: BW: $225   **Circ:** (Not Reported)

INDIANA

BERNE

📖 **77 Crazy for Cross Stitch**
House of White Birches
306 E. Parr Rd.   Phone: (219)589-4000
Berne, IN 46711   Fax: (219)589-8093
Publication E-mail: customer_service@whitebirches.com
Publisher E-mail: customer_service@whitebirches.com

Consumer magazine covering cross stitch techniques, products, information, and designs for every skill level. **Freq:** Bimonthly. **Print Method:** Offset. **Trim Size:** 8 x 10 3/4. **Key Personnel:** Vicki Blizzard, Editor, phone (877)282-4724, fax (707)667-7558; John Boggs, Adv. Sales Dir., phone (877)282-4724, fax (707)667-7558, john_boggs@drgnetwork.com; Cindy Elzey, Display Sales; Patsy Franz, Display Sales, patsy_franz@drgnetwork.com; Tamara Hanes, Display Sales; Jeremiah Abbott, Ad Materials; Karen Ousley, Traffic. **Subscription Rates:** $19.97 individuals; $3.99 single issue. **Remarks:** Accepts advertising. **URL:** http://www.whitebirches.com.
Ad Rates: BW: $1,439.9   **Circ:** Combined 60,000
              4C: $1,694

📖 **78 Crochet!**
House of White Birches
306 E. Parr Rd.   Phone: (219)589-4000
Berne, IN 46711   Fax: (219)589-8093
Publication E-mail: customer_service@whitebirches.com
Publisher E-mail: customer_service@whitebirches.com

Consumer magazine covering crochet techniques, stitches, fiber options and other facts about crochet. **Founded:** Mar. 2002. **Freq:** Bimonthly. **Print Method:** Offset. **Trim Size:** 8 x 10 3/4. **Key Personnel:** John Boggs, Adv. Sales Dir., phone (877)282-4724, fax (707)667-7558, john_boggs@drgnetwork.com; Cindy Elzey, Display Sales; Patsy Franz, Display Sales, patsy_franz@drgnetwork.com; Tamara Hanes, Display Sales; Jeremiah Abbott, Ad Materials; Karen Ousley, Traffic. **Subscription Rates:** $19.97 individuals; $4.95 single issue. **Remarks:** Accepts advertising. **URL:** http://www.whitebirches.com.
Ad Rates: 4C: $2,625   **Circ:** Combined 56,000

📖 **79 Sewing Savvy**
House of White Birches
306 E. Parr Rd.   Phone: (219)589-4000
Berne, IN 46711   Fax: (219)589-8093
Publication E-mail: customer_service@whitebirches.com
Publisher E-mail: customer_service@whitebirches.com

Consumer magazine covering home decor sewing techniques, patterns and

Ad Rates: GLR = general line rate; BW = one-time black & white page rate; 4C = one-time four color page rate; SAU = standard advertising unit rate; CNU = Canadian newspaper advertising unit rate; PCI = per column inch rate.
Circulation: ★ = ABC; △ = BPA; ♦ = CAC; • = CCAB; ❑ = VAC; ⊕ = PO Statement; ‡ = Publisher's Report; Boldface figures = sworn; Light figures = estimated.
Entry type: 📖 = Print; 🎙 = Broadcast.

9

product information for home sewers. **Founded:** 2000. **Freq:** Bimonthly. **Print Method:** Offset. **Trim Size:** 8 x 10 3/4. **Key Personnel:** Meta J. Hoge, Editor, sewingmeta@earthlink.net; John Boggs, Adv. Sales Dir., phone (877)282-4724, fax (707)667-7558, john_boggs@drgnetwork.com; Cindy Elzey, Display Sales; Patsy Franz, Display Sales, patsy_franz@drgnetwork.com; Tamara Hanes, Display Sales; Jeremiah Abbott, Ad Materials; Karen Ousley, Traffic. **Subscription Rates:** $19.97 individuals; $3.95 single issue. **Remarks:** Accepts advertising. **URL:** http://www.whitebirches.com.

Ad Rates: BW: $1,092.25　　　　　　**Circ:** Paid 57,000
4C: $1,285

IOWA

CEDAR FALLS

📖 **80 Implement & Tractor**
Agra USA
PO Box 7　　　　　　　　　　　Phone: (319)277-3599
Cedar Falls, IA 50613　　　　　　Fax: (319)277-3783
　　　　　　　　　　　　　　　Free: (800)959-3276

Publisher E-mail: informa@cfu.net

Magazine on farm and industrial machinery, trends and technology. **Founded:** 1886. **Freq:** Bimonthly and annual. **Print Method:** Web. **Trim Size:** 8 1/8 x 10 7/8. **Cols./Page:** 3. **Col. Width:** 2 1/8 inches. **Col. Depth:** 10 inches. **Key Personnel:** Bob Van Voorhis, Editor, rvanvooris@cfu.net; Mary Shepherd, Publisher, mshepherd@cfu.net; Jack Cooney, Advertising Sales; Paul Hurst, Advertising Sales. **ISSN:** 0019-2953. **Subscription Rates:** $33 U.S. and Canada; $90 other countries; $60 two years. **Remarks:** Accepts advertising.
Ad Rates: BW: $1,890　　　　　**Circ:** Paid ‡4,500
4C: $2,690　　　　　　　　　　Non-paid ‡3,500

DES MOINES

📖 **81 Successful Farming**
Meredith Corp.
1716 Locust St.
Des Moines, IA 50309-3023　　　Fax: (515)284-3563
　　　　　　　　　　　　　　Free: (800)678-2659

Agricultural magazine. **Subtitle:** For Families That Make Farming and Ranching Their Business. **Founded:** 1902. **Freq:** Monthly two issues Feb./Mar./Dec., no issue Jun. or Jul. **Print Method:** Offset. **Trim Size:** 8 x 10 1/2. **Cols./Page:** 3. **Col. Width:** 2.5 picas. **Col. Depth:** 140 agate lines. **Key Personnel:** Loren Kruse, Editor-in-Chief, phone (515)284-2897, fax (515)284-3127, lkruse@mdp.com; Tom Davis, Publisher, tdavis@mdp.com. **ISSN:** 0039-4432. **Subscription Rates:** $15.95 U.S.; $27 other countries. **Remarks:** Accepts advertising. **URL:** http://www.agriculture.com.
Ad Rates: BW: $39,910　　　　　**Circ:** Paid ‡442,000
4C: $57,090

IOWA CITY

📖 **82 Special Recreation Digest**
John A. Nesbitt
701 Oaknoll Dr.
Iowa City, IA 52246-5168　　　　Phone: (319)466-3192
Publisher E-mail: john-nesbitt@uiowa.edu

Magazine offering information on recreation needs of people with disabilities. **Subtitle:** Special Recreation for disABLED. **Founded:** 1980. **Freq:** Quarterly. **Print Method:** offset. **Trim Size:** 8 1/2 x 11. **Key Personnel:** John A. Nesbitt, Ed. D., Editor. **Subscription Rates:** $39.95 individuals. **Remarks:** Advertising not accepted.
　　　　　　　　　　　　　　　　Circ: (Not Reported)

KANSAS

LEAVENWORTH

📖 **83 Leavenworth Times**
PO Box 144
Leavenworth, KS 66048

General newspaper. **Founded:** Mar. 7, 1857. **Freq:** Daily (eve.), Sunday (morn.). **Print Method:** Offset. **Trim Size:** 12.5 X 22.75 IN. **Cols./Page:** 6. **Col. Width:** 24 nonpareils. **Col. Depth:** 294 agate lines. **Key Personnel:**

Tom Throne III, Publisher; Ron Piche', Editor; Lautz Trapania, Advertising Mgr. **USPS:** 308-180. **Subscription Rates:** $10.55 individuals a month. **Remarks:** Accepts advertising.
Ad Rates: GLR: $2.11　　　　　　**Circ:** Mon.-Fri. 6,592
BW: $1297.80　　　　　　　　　　Sun. 7,294
4C: $1437.80

KENTUCKY

PIPPA PASSES

🎙 **84 WWJD-FM - 91.7**
100 Purpose Rd.　　　　　　　　Phone: (606)368-6015
Pippa Passes, KY 41844　　　　　Fax: (606)368-2125
　　　　　　　　　　　　　　　Free: (888)280-4252

Format: Contemporary Christian. **Networks:** Independent. **Founded:** 1985. **Formerly:** WOAL-FM. **Operating Hours:** Continuous. **Key Personnel:** Jamie Hughes, General Mgr. **Local Programs:** *Morning Message* 8a.m.-9.a.m. Mon. Wed. Fri., Sonya Slone. **Wattage:** 7300.

RUSSELLVILLE

📖 **85 Bluegrass Music News**
Kentucky Music Educators Association
1007 Granville Ln.　　　　　　　Phone: (270)726-6427
Russellville, KY 42276　　　　　Fax: (270)726-2291

Magazine for school music educators who teach kindergarten through university-level. **Founded:** Apr. 1, 1950. **Freq:** Quarterly (Oct., Dec., Mar., May). **Print Method:** Offset. **Trim Size:** 8 1/2 x 11. **Cols./Page:** 3. **Col. Width:** 28 nonpareils. **Col. Depth:** 140 agate lines. **Key Personnel:** Hazel O. Carver, Editor, hcarv@logantele.com. **ISSN:** 0006-5129. **Subscription Rates:** $15 individuals; $18 Canada; $20 other countries.
Ad Rates: BW: $325　　　　　　　**Circ:** ‡2,100
4C: $499

MARYLAND

BALTIMORE

📖 **86 Crisis**
4805 Mount Hope Dr.
Baltimore, MD 21215-3206

Consumer magazine covering issues for African Americans. **Freq:** Bimonthly. **Print Method:** Web offset. **Key Personnel:** Victoria Valentine, Editor, vvalentine@naacpnet.org; India Artis, Business Mgr., phone (410)486-9216, fax (410)318-6712, lartis@naacpnet.org. **ISSN:** 0011-1422. **Subscription Rates:** $12 individuals. **Remarks:** Accepts advertising.
Ad Rates: BW: $6,600　　　　　　**Circ:** (Not Reported)
4C: $9,320
PCI: $200

📖 **87 Journal of the History of Philosophy**
Johns Hopkins University Press
2715 N. Charles St.　　　　　　　Phone: (410)516-6900
Baltimore, MD 21218-4363　　　　Fax: (410)516-6968
　　　　　　　　　　　　　　　Free: (800)548-1784

Publisher E-mail: jlorder@jhupress.jhu.edu

History journal of Western philosophy (English, French, German, and Italian). **Founded:** Oct. 1963. **Freq:** Quarterly. **Print Method:** Offset. **Trim Size:** 6 1/4 x 10. **Cols./Page:** 1. **Col. Width:** 30 picas. **Col. Depth:** 45.5 picas. **Key Personnel:** Gerald Press, Editor. **ISSN:** 0022-5053. **Subscription Rates:** $26 individuals; $76 institutions; $98.80 institutions print and online. **Remarks:** Accepts advertising. **URL:** http://www.press.jhu.edu/press/journals/hph.htm.
Ad Rates: BW: $200　　　　　　　　**Circ:** 1,600

📖 **88 Modernism/Modernity**
Johns Hopkins University Press
2715 N. Charles St.　　　　　　　Phone: (410)516-6900
Baltimore, MD 21218-4363　　　　Fax: (410)516-6968
　　　　　　　　　　　　　　　Free: (800)548-1784

Publisher E-mail: jlorder@jhupress.jhu.edu

Scholarly journal covering modernist studies, including art, music, architecture, literary theory, history and related areas. **Founded:** 1995. **Freq:**

Quarterly. **Trim Size:** 5.5 x 8. **Key Personnel:** Robert von Hallberg, Editor; Lawrence Rainey, Editor; Tamara Barnes, Advertising Mgr., phone (410)516-6984, trichter@mail.press.jhu.edu; Cassandra Laity, Editor. **ISSN:** 1071-6068. **Subscription Rates:** $36 individuals print version; $99 institutions print version; $84.10 institutions online; $128.70 institutions online and print; $11 single issue individuals; $30 single issue institutions. **Remarks:** Accepts advertising. **URL:** http://www.press.jhu.edu/journals.
Ad Rates: BW: $225 **Circ:** Combined 637

📖 **89 Molecular Medicine**
Johns Hopkins University Press
2715 N. Charles St.
Baltimore, MD 21218-4363
Phone: (410)516-6900
Fax: (410)516-6968
Free: (800)548-1784

Publication E-mail: jlorder@jhunix.hcf.jhu.edu
Publisher E-mail: jlorder@jhupress.jhu.edu

Journal covering research in molecular sciences for research scientists, molecular biologists, pharmaceutical scientists, clinical doctors, geneticists, and related professionals. **Freq:** Monthly. **Key Personnel:** David Weatherall, Editor-in-Chief; Yvonne Cole, Ph.D., Managing Editor. **ISSN:** 1076-1551. **Subscription Rates:** $160 individuals print ed.; $196 individuals out of country; $575 institutions print ed.; $517.50 institutions elec. ed. only; $747.50 institutions print & elec. eds. **Remarks:** Accepts advertising. **Online:** Project Muse. **URL:** http://muse.jhu.edu/journals/mm/.
Ad Rates: BW: $450 **Circ:** Combined 500

📖 **90 Philosophy, Psychiatry & Psychology**
Johns Hopkins University Press
2715 N. Charles St.
Baltimore, MD 21218-4363
Phone: (410)516-6900
Fax: (410)516-6968
Free: (800)548-1784

Publisher E-mail: jlorder@jhupress.jhu.edu

Scholarly journal covering overlap between philosophy, psychiatry, and psychology. **Freq:** Quarterly. **Key Personnel:** K.W.M. Fulford, Editor; John Z. Sadler, M.D., Editor; Tamara Barnes, Advertising Mgr., phone (410)516-6984, fax (410)516-3866, trichter@mail.press.jhu.edu. **ISSN:** 1071-6076. **Subscription Rates:** $85 individuals print version; $158 institutions print version; $142.30 institutions online; $205.40 institutions online and print; $25.50 single issue individuals; $47.50 single issue institutions. **Remarks:** Accepts advertising. **URL:** http://www.press.jhu.edu/journals/ppp/htm.
Ad Rates: BW: $200 **Circ:** Paid 592

📖 **91 Portal**
Johns Hopkins University Press
2715 N. Charles St.
Baltimore, MD 21218-4363
Phone: (410)516-6900
Fax: (410)516-6968
Free: (800)548-1784

Publisher E-mail: jlorder@jhupress.jhu.edu

Scholarly journal covering academic information services for academic librarians. **Subtitle:** Libraries and the Academy. **Freq:** Quarterly. **Key Personnel:** Charles Lowry, Exec. Editor, clowry@deans.umd.edu; Susan Martin, Exec. Editor, martinsk@gusun.georgetown.edu; Gloriana St. Clair, Managing Editor, gstclair@andrew.cmu.edu; Martha Bright Anandakrishnan, Copy Editor; Cindy Stell Carroll, Editorial Asst.; Don Bosseau, Column Editor, bosseau@miami.edu; Nicholas Burckel, Column Editor, burcklen@vmsb.cad.mu.edu; Neal Kaske, Column Editor, nk20@umail.umd.edu. **ISSN:** 1531-2542. **Subscription Rates:** $154 institutions; $48 individuals; $200.20 institutions print and online; $46.50 single issue institutions; $14.50 single issue individuals; $160 institutions Canada & Mexico; $54 individuals Canada & Mexico; $166 elsewhere institutions; $60 elsewhere individuals. **Remarks:** Accepts advertising. **Online:** Project Muse. **URL:** http://www.press.jhu.edu/press/journals/pla.htm.
Ad Rates: BW: $450 **Circ:** Combined 1,500

📖 **92 Theory & Event**
Johns Hopkins University Press
2715 N. Charles St.
Baltimore, MD 21218-4363
Phone: (410)516-6900
Fax: (410)516-6968
Free: (800)548-1784

Publication E-mail: theory@amherst.edu
Publisher E-mail: jlorder@jhupress.jhu.edu

Scholarly journal covering political theory in the humanities and social sciences. **Freq:** Quarterly. **Key Personnel:** Thomas Dumm, Editor, tldumm@amherst.edu; William Chaloupka, Editor; Kathy Ferguson, Review Editor; William Connolly, Advising Editor; Brenda Bright, Managing Editor. **ISSN:** 1092-311X. **Subscription Rates:** $25 individuals; $61 institutions. **Remarks:** Advertising not accepted. **Online:** Project Muse. **URL:** http://muse.jhu.edu/journals/tae/.
Circ: (Not Reported)

LINTHICUM HEIGHTS

📖 **93 Information Systems Research (ISR)**
The Institute for Operations Research and the Management Sciences
901 Elkridge Landing Rd., Ste. 400
Linthicum Heights, MD 21090-2909
Phone: (410)850-0300
Fax: (410)684-2963
Free: (800)446-3676

Publisher E-mail: informs@informs.org

Journal covering information systems in organizations, institutions, the economy and society worldwide. **Freq:** Quarterly. **Key Personnel:** Chris F. Kemerer, Editor, phone (412)648-1572, fax (412)624-2983, ckemerer@katz.pitt.edu; Sirkka Jarvenpaa, Sr. Editor; Salvatore T. March, Sr. Editor; Tridas Mukhopadhyay, Sr. Editor; Geoff Walsham, Sr. Editor; Robert W. Zmud, Sr. Editor; Ronald T. Cenfetelli, Managing Editor; Molly O'Donnell, Production Ed.; Christine Bullen, Dir. of Mktg. & Circ. **ISSN:** 1047-7047. **Subscription Rates:** $198 institutions; $56 members; $28 student/retired members; $112 nonmembers. **URL:** http://www.informs.org.

📖 **94 INFORMS Journal on Computing**
The Institute for Operations Research and the Management Sciences
901 Elkridge Landing Rd., Ste. 400
Linthicum Heights, MD 21090-2909
Phone: (410)850-0300
Fax: (410)684-2963
Free: (800)446-3676

Publisher E-mail: informs@informs.org

Professional journal covering computing. **Freq:** Quarterly. **Key Personnel:** Dr. W. David Kelton, Editor-in-Chief. **ISSN:** 0899-1499. **Subscription Rates:** $56 members print ed.; $40 members online ed.; $73 members print & online eds.; $28 student/retired member, print; $20 student/retired member, online; $36 student/retired member, print & online eds.; $112 nonmembers print; $80 nonmembers online; $146 nonmembers print & online eds. **URL:** http://joc.pubs.informs.org/.

📖 **95 M&SOM (Manufacturing & Service Operations Management)**
The Institute for Operations Research and the Management Sciences
901 Elkridge Landing Rd., Ste. 400
Linthicum Heights, MD 21090-2909
Phone: (410)850-0300
Fax: (410)684-2963
Free: (800)446-3676

Publication E-mail: msom@mgmt.purdue.edu
Publisher E-mail: informs@informs.org

Journal covering manufacturing and service operations management. **Freq:** Quarterly. **Key Personnel:** Leroy B. Schwarz, Editor-in-Chief, lee@mgmt.purdue.edu; Aleda Roth, Deputy Editor; Lisa R. Ratliff, Managing Editor, phone (765)494-4420, fax (765)496-1778; Molly O'Donnell, Production Ed., phone (410)691-7820, fax (410)691-6095, molly.odonnell@informs.org. **ISSN:** 1523-4614. **Subscription Rates:** $226 institutions; $56 members; $28 retired/student members; $112 nonmembers. **URL:** http://www.mgmt.purdue.edu/centers/msom/.

📖 **96 OR/MS Today**
The Institute for Operations Research and the Management Sciences
901 Elkridge Landing Rd., Ste. 400
Linthicum Heights, MD 21090-2909
Phone: (410)850-0300
Fax: (410)684-2963
Free: (800)446-3676

Publisher E-mail: informs@informs.org

Professional magazine covering operations research and management sciences. **Freq:** Bimonthly. **Key Personnel:** John Llewellyn, President; Peter R. Horner, Editor; Tracy Jean Benn, Managing Editor; James J. Swain, Assoc. Editor; Ramesh Sharda, Computer Science Editor; Susan Palocsay, Software Review Editor; Sharon Baker, Advertising Mgr. **ISSN:** 1085-1038. **Subscription Rates:** Free to qualified subscribers; $34 nonmembers; $50 out of country; $54 institutions; $70 institutions out of country. **Remarks:** Accepts advertising. **URL:** http://www.orms-today.com.

Circ: (Not Reported)

SILVER SPRING

📖 97 NADmag
National Association of the Deaf
814 Thayer Ave.   Phone: (301)587-1788
Silver Spring, MD 20910-4500   Fax: (301)587-1791
Publication E-mail: editor@nad.org
Publisher E-mail: nadinfo@nad.org

Magazine for deaf and hard of hearing people, and their parents and educators. **Founded:** 2001. **Freq:** 6/year. **Trim Size:** 8 1/2 x 11. **Subscription Rates:** Free to members; $30 institutions. **Remarks:** Accepts advertising. **Formerly:** The NAD Broadcaster.

Ad Rates: BW: $1,000   **Circ:** 7,000
           4C: $1,200

MASSACHUSETTS

BOSTON

📖 98 The Bulletin of Symbolic Logic
Association for Symbolic Logic
c/o Akihiro Kanamori
Department of Mathematics
Boston University
Boston, MA 02215
Publisher E-mail: asl@vassar.edu

Journal covering all aspects of logic, including mathematical or philosophical logic; logic in computer science or linguistics; history and philosophy of logic; and application of logic to other fields. **Founded:** 1995. **Key Personnel:** Andreas R. Blass, Managing Editor, ablass@umich.edu; John P. Burgess, Editor, jburgess@pucc.princeton.edu; Matt Foreman, Editor, mforeman@math.uci.edu; Phokion G. Kolaitis, Editor, kolaitis@cs.ucsc.edu; Manuel Lerman, Editor, mlerman@math.uconn.edu; Dugald Macpherson, Editor, pmthdm@amsta.leeds.ac.uk. **Subscription Rates:** $425 nonmembers. **URL:** http://www.aslonline.org/journals-bulletin.html. **Alt. Formats:** Microfiche; Microfilm.

📖 99 Newbury Street and Back Bay Guide
Jacaranda Publishing, Inc.
143 Newbury St., 6th Fl.   Phone: (617)424-9005
Boston, MA 02116   Fax: (617)424-8944
Publisher E-mail: info@jacaranda-media.com

Travel and tourist newspaper. **Founded:** 1991. **Freq:** Biweekly. **Print Method:** Web offset. **Key Personnel:** Sarie Booy, Publisher, sarie@jacaranda-media.com; Eileen Lee, Managing Editor; Phyllis Sterbakov, Sales Dir. **Subscription Rates:** $35 individuals. **Remarks:** Accepts advertising. **URL:** http://backbayguide.com. **Feature Editors:** Julie Hatfield, *Fashion*; Lynda Saltz, *Art*.

Ad Rates: BW: $885   **Circ:** Combined 10,000

CAMBRIDGE

📖 100 American Police Beat
4 Brattle St., Ste. 308
Cambridge, MA 02138-3714   Fax: (617)354-6515
                    Free: (800)234-0056
Publication E-mail: info@apbweb.com

Professional magazine covering law enforcement. **Founded:** 1994. **Freq:** 10/year. **Print Method:** Heatset. **Trim Size:** 10 3/4 x 13 3/4. **Cols./Page:** 5. **Col. Depth:** 12 inches. **Key Personnel:** Cynthia Brown, Publisher, cynthia@apbweb.com; George Chateauneuf, Mktg. Dir., phone (800)579-4911, george@apbweb.com. **Subscription Rates:** Free to qualified subscribers; $16.95 individuals; $3 single issue. **Remarks:** Accepts advertising. **URL:** http://www.apbweb.com.

Ad Rates: BW: $3,655   **Circ:** Paid ★11,500
          4C: $4,305   Non-paid ★45,500

📖 101 International Organization
The MIT Press
WCFIA/Harvard University
1033 Massachusetts Ave.
Cambridge, MA 02138
Publication E-mail: io@ucsd.edu
Publisher E-mail: journals-info@mit.edu; mitpress-order-inq@mit.edu

Journal on international politics and economics including political economy, foreign policy, history, and comparative politics. **Founded:** 1947. **Freq:** Quarterly. **Print Method:** Offset. **Trim Size:** 6 x 9 1/4. **Cols./Page:** 1. **Col. Width:** 54 nonpareils. **Col. Depth:** 105 agate lines. **Key Personnel:** Lisa L. Martin, Editor-in-Chief; Rebecca L. Webb, Managing Editor. **ISSN:** 0020-8183. **Subscription Rates:** $43 individuals; $140 institutions; $14 single issue. **Remarks:** Accepts advertising. **Online:** OCLC; EBSCO; SWETSNET; Blackwell; Dawson's.

Ad Rates: BW: $350   **Circ:** ‡3,000

CONCORD

📖 102 Bank Accounting & Finance
Aspen Publishers
129 Everett St.   Phone: (978)369-6285
Concord, MA 01742   Fax: (978)371-2961
Publisher E-mail: nacas@cfw.com

Journal for bank financial and accounting officers. **Founded:** 1987. **Freq:** 6/year. **Trim Size:** 8 1/2 x 11. **Key Personnel:** Claire Green, Editor, clairegreene@clairegreene.cnchost.com; Shawn Hood, Marketing Mgr., phone (212)597-0213, hood@aspenpubl.com. **Remarks:** Advertising accepted; rates available upon request. **URL:** http://www.aspenpublishers.com.

Circ: Paid 1,000

FLORENCE

📖 103 Verse
Verse Press
221 Pine St., Studio 2A3
Florence, MA 01062
Publisher E-mail: sales@versepress.org

Consumer magazine covering poetry worldwide. **Key Personnel:** Brian Henry, Founder/Editor; Andrew Zawacki, Editor; Matthew Zapruder, Founder. **Subscription Rates:** $18 individuals. **URL:** http://www.versepress.org.

WORCESTER

📖 104 Idealistic Studies
Philosophy Documentation Center
c/o Prof. Gary Overvold, Editor
Department of Philosophy
Clark University
950 Main St.
Worcester, MA 01610-1407   Phone: (508)793-7416
Publication E-mail: order@pdcnet.org
Publisher E-mail: order@pdcnet.org

Scholarly journal covering the tradition and legacy of philosophical Idealism. **Subtitle:** An Interdisciplinary Journal of Philosophy. **Founded:** 1971. **Freq:** Triennial. **Key Personnel:** Gary Overvold, Editor, govervold@clarku.edu. **ISSN:** 0046-8541. **Subscription Rates:** $48 institutions; $30 individuals; $18 single issue institutions; $10 single issue individuals. **URL:** http://www.pdcnet.org/is.html.

MICHIGAN

ANN ARBOR

📖 105 FOUND
FOUND Magazine
3455 Charing Cross Rd.
Ann Arbor, MI 48108-1911
Publication E-mail: info@foundmagazine.com

Consumer magazine covering found items. **Freq:** Triennial. **Subscription Rates:** $21.21 individuals; $5 single issue. **Remarks:** Accepts advertising. **URL:** http://www.foundmagazine.com.

Circ: (Not Reported)

BIG RAPIDS

106 Ferris State Torch
Ferris State University
805 Campus Dr.
Rankin Center
Box 15
Big Rapids, MI 49307

Phone: (231)591-2609
Fax: (231)591-3617

Collegiate newspaper. **Founded:** 1931. **Freq:** Weekly. **Print Method:** Offset. **Trim Size:** 9 3/4 x 15. **Cols./Page:** 5. **Col. Width:** 23 nonpareils. **Col. Depth:** 196 agate lines. **Key Personnel:** Laura Anger, Advertising Mgr., Laura_Anger@ferris.edu; Chris Miller, Editor-in-Chief, phone (231)591-5978; Dennis Ruzicka, Faculty Advisor, phone (231)591-3609. **Subscription Rates:** Free; $45 by mail. **Remarks:** Accepts advertising. **URL:** http://www.ferris.edu/torch.
Ad Rates: PCI: $6.75

Circ: Free ‡6,000

KENTWOOD

107 WJNZ-AM - 1680
3777 44th St. SE
Kentwood, MI 49512-3945
E-mail: jamz@wjnz.com

Phone: (616)656-0586
Fax: (616)656-9326

Format: Urban Contemporary. **Networks:** American Urban Radio. **Owner:** Goodrich Radio Marketing, Inc., at above address. **Formerly:** WKWM-AM. **Operating Hours:** Continuous. **ADI:** Grand Rapids-Kalamazoo-Battle Creek, MI. **Key Personnel:** Mike St. Cyr, General Mgr., mstcyr@mjnz.com. **Wattage:** 10,000. **Ad Rates:** $15-40 for 60 seconds.

ROYAL OAK

108 Big City Blues Magazine
PO Box 1805
Royal Oak, MI 48068
Publication E-mail: blues@bigcitybluesmag.com

Phone: (248)582-1544
Fax: (248)582-8242

Consumer magazine covering blues music. **Freq:** Bimonthly. **Remarks:** Accepts advertising. **URL:** http://www.bigcitybluesmag.com.

Circ: (Not Reported)

WESTLAND

109 theIndian
theINDIAN Group
PO Box 858030
Westland, MI 48185
Publication E-mail: theindianguru@yahoo.com

Phone: (734)447-0028

Publication for the East Indian American community worldwide. **Freq:** Monthly. **Key Personnel:** A. Gupta, Pub./CEO; A. Garg, Editor-in-Chief; S. Chaudhry, Art Prod.; A. Rahim Salaam, Circ.; A. K. Abdoulli, Production; A. J. Chaudhry, Distribution.

MINNESOTA

BROOKLYN CENTER

110 Brooklyn Center Sun-Post
Minnesota Sun Publications
10917 Valley View Rd.
Eden Prairie, MN 55344-3730
Publication E-mail: brooklyncentersunpost@mnsunpub.com

Phone: (952)392-6835
Fax: (952)941-3588

Community newspaper. **Founded:** 1955. **Freq:** Weekly (Wed.). **Print Method:** Offset. **Cols./Page:** 4. **Col. Width:** 2 1/2 inches. **Col. Depth:** 15 inches. **Key Personnel:** Doug Dance, Publisher, phone (612)896-4787, ddane@mnsunpub.com; Pamela Austin, Editor, phone (612)897-5486; Tom Losey, Marketing Dir. **Subscription Rates:** $15. **URL:** http://www.mnsunpub.com.

Circ: Paid ◆736
Non-paid ◆5,831

BURNSVILLE

111 Burnsville/Savage Sun Current
Minnesota Sun Publications
10917 Valley View Rd.
Eden Prairie, MN 55344-3730
Publication E-mail: burnsvillesuncurrent@mnsunpub.com

Phone: (952)392-6835
Fax: (952)941-3588

Community newspaper (tabloid). **Founded:** 1984. **Freq:** Weekly (Wed.). **Print Method:** Offset. **Cols./Page:** 4. **Col. Width:** 2 1/2 inches. **Col. Depth:** 15 inches. **Key Personnel:** Doug Dane, Publisher, phone (612)896-4787; Pamela Austib, Advertising Dir., phone (612)897-5486. **URL:** http://www.mnsun.com.

Circ: Paid ◆298
Non-paid ◆19,161

EAGAN

112 Eagan Sun Current
Minnesota Sun Publications
10917 Valley View Rd.
Eden Prairie, MN 55344-3730
Publication E-mail: eagansuncurrent@mnsunpub.com

Phone: (952)392-6835
Fax: (952)941-3588

Community newspaper (tabloid). **Freq:** Weekly (Wed.). **Print Method:** Offset. **Cols./Page:** 4. **Col. Width:** 2 1/2 inches. **Col. Depth:** 15 inches. **Key Personnel:** Doug Dane, Publisher, phone (612)896-4787; Pamela Austin, Advertising Dir., phone (612)897-5486. **URL:** http://www.mnsun.

Circ: Paid ◆166
Non-paid ◆16,808

EDEN PRAIRIE

113 Bloomington Sun Current
Minnesota Sun Publications
10917 Valley View Rd.
Eden Prairie, MN 55344-3730

Phone: (952)392-6835
Fax: (952)941-3588

Community newspaper (tabloid). **Founded:** 1984. **Freq:** Weekly (Wed.). **Print Method:** Offset. **Cols./Page:** 4. **Col. Width:** 2 1/2 inches. **Col. Depth:** 15 inches. **Key Personnel:** John Gannet Hawley, Publisher; Robert Stjern, Advertising Mgr.

Circ: Paid ◆2,384
Non-paid ◆24,968

Brooklyn Center Sun-Post - See Brooklyn Center

114 Brooklyn Park Sun-Post
Minnesota Sun Publications
10917 Valley View Rd.
Eden Prairie, MN 55344-3730

Phone: (952)392-6835
Fax: (952)941-3588

Community newspaper (tabloid). **Founded:** 1962. **Freq:** Weekly (Wed.). **Print Method:** Offset. **Cols./Page:** 4. **Col. Width:** 2.5 inches. **Col. Depth:** 15 inches. **Remarks:** Accepts advertising.

Circ: Paid ◆513
Non-paid ◆19,170

Burnsville/Savage Sun Current - See Burnsville

Eagan Sun Current - See Eagan

115 Eden Prairie Sun Current
Minnesota Sun Publications
10917 Valley View Rd.
Eden Prairie, MN 55344-3730

Phone: (952)392-6835
Fax: (952)941-3588

Community newspaper (tabloid). **Founded:** 1984. **Freq:** Weekly (Wed.). **Print Method:** Offset. **Cols./Page:** 5. **Col. Width:** 1 15/16 inches. **Col. Depth:** 16 inches. **Key Personnel:** Don Thurlow, Publisher; Ed Shur, Editor; Paul Johnson, Advertising Dir.; Bonnie Laux, Sales Mgr. **Subscription**

Ad Rates: GLR = general line rate; BW = one-time black & white page rate; 4C = one-time four color page rate; SAU = standard advertising unit rate; CNU = Canadian newspaper advertising unit rate; PCI = per column inch rate.
Circulation: ★ = ABC; △ = BPA; ◆ = CAC; ● = CCAB; ❑ = VAC; ⊕ = PO Statement; ‡ = Publisher's Report; Boldface figures = sworn; Light figures = estimated.
Entry type: ▥ = Print; ♪ = Broadcast.

13

Rates: $20 Biannual voluntary subscription. **Remarks:** Accepts advertising. **Formerly:** Sun Prarie Sailor.

Ad Rates:	GLR: $14	Circ: Free ◆12,361
	BW: $1,120	Paid ◆379
	PCI: $11.90	

Edina Sun Current - See Edina

Hopkins/East Minnetonka Sailor-Sun - See Hopkins

New Hope/Golden Valley Sun-Post - See New Hope

Richfield Sun Current - See Richfield

South St. Paul/Inver Grove Heights Sun Current - See South St. Paul

EDINA

116 Edina Sun Current
Minnesota Sun Publications
10917 Valley View Rd.
Eden Prairie, MN 55344-3730

Phone: (952)392-6835
Fax: (952)941-3588

Community newspaper (tabloid). **Founded:** 1984. **Freq:** Weekly (Wed.). **Print Method:** Offset. **Cols./Page:** 4. **Col. Width:** 2 1/2 inches. **Col. Depth:** 15 inches. **Key Personnel:** John Gannet Hawley, Publisher; Robert Stjern, Advertising Mgr.

Circ: Paid ◆1,337
Non-paid ◆13,860

HOPKINS

117 Hopkins/East Minnetonka Sailor-Sun
Minnesota Sun Publications
10917 Valley View Rd.
Eden Prairie, MN 55344-3730

Phone: (952)392-6835
Fax: (952)941-3588

Community newspaper (tabloid). **Freq:** Weekly (Wed.). **Print Method:** Offset. **Cols./Page:** 5. **Col. Width:** 1 15/16 inches. **Col. Depth:** 16 inches. **Key Personnel:** Frank Chilinski, Publisher, phone (612)392-6851, fax (612)392-6868, frank@citilink.com; Kevin True, Advertising Dir., phone (612)392-6807, ktrue@mnsunpub.com. **Remarks:** Accepts advertising.

Ad Rates:	GLR: $24.94	Circ: Paid ◆234
	BW: $830	Non-paid 4,657
	4C: $1,473	
	PCI: $21	

LAKEVILLE

118 FATE Magazine
Fate Magazine
PO Box 460
Lakeville, MN 55044
Publication E-mail: fate@fatemag.com

Paranormal magazine focusing on UFOs, hauntings, psychic phenomena, mystery animals, ancient mysteries, and personal mystical experiences. **Subtitle:** True Reports of the Strange and Unknown. **Founded:** 1948. **Freq:** Monthly. **Print Method:** Web offset. **Trim Size:** 8 1/8 x 10 3/4. **Cols./Page:** 3. **Col. Width:** 13 picas. **Col. Depth:** 9 1/2 inches. **Key Personnel:** Phyllis Galde, President, phone (952)431-2050, fax (951)891-6091, phyllisg@fatemag.com. **ISSN:** 0014-8776. **Subscription Rates:** $29.95; $5 single issue. **URL:** http://www.fatemag.com. **Alt. Formats:** Microform, MSI.

Ad Rates:	BW: $1,865	Circ: Paid 30,000
	4C: $2,265	Free 350
	PCI: $140	

MINNEAPOLIS

119 Cultural Critique
University of Minnesota Press
Dept. of Cultural Studies & Comparative
  Literature
9 Pleasant St. SE
350 Folwell Hall
University of Minnesota
Minneapolis, MN 55455
Publication E-mail: jlorder@jhunix.hcf.jhu.edu

Publisher E-mail: ump@tc.umn.edu

Scholarly journal covering issues in culture, theory and politics. **Founded:** 1985. **Freq:** Triennial. **Trim Size:** 6 x 9. **Key Personnel:** John Mowitt, Editor, culcrit@umn.edu; Jochen Schulte-Sasse, Editor; Keya Ganguly, Editor; Margie Weinstein, Asst. Editor; Tom Roach, Asst. Editor. **ISSN:** 0882-4371. **Subscription Rates:** $30 individuals; $78 institutions; $35 other countries; $83 institutions, other countries; $12 single issue individuals; $30 single issue institutions. **Remarks:** Accepts advertising. **Online:** Project Muse. **URL:** http://muse.jhu.edu/journals/cul/.

Ad Rates: BW: $200   Circ: (Not Reported)

120 Far Eastern Affairs
East View Publications
3020 Harbor Ln. N
Minneapolis, MN 55447

Phone: (763)550-0961
Fax: (763)559-2931
Free: (800)477-1005

Publisher E-mail: eastview@eastview.com

Journal covering developments in China, Japan, and the Asia-Pacific region. **Freq:** Quarterly. **ISSN:** 0206-149X. **Subscription Rates:** $39 individuals; $69 out of country; $210 institutions; $39 individuals online ed.; $95 institutions online ed. **Remarks:** Accepts advertising. **URL:** http://www.eastview.com/evjournals.asp.

Circ: (Not Reported)

NEW HOPE

121 New Hope/Golden Valley Sun-Post
Minnesota Sun Publications
10917 Valley View Rd.
Eden Prairie, MN 55344-3730

Phone: (952)392-6835
Fax: (952)941-3588

Publication E-mail: goldenvalleysunpost@mnsunpub.com

Community newspaper (tabloid). **Founded:** 1963. **Freq:** Weekly (Wed.). **Print Method:** Offset. **Key Personnel:** Doug Dane, Publisher, phone (612)896-4787; Pamela Austin, Advertising Mgr., phone (612)897-5486.

Circ: Paid ◆1,106
Non-paid ◆10,092

NORTHFIELD

122 German Studies Review
Carleton College
300 N College St.
Northfield, MN 55057

Phone: (507)646-4158
Fax: (507)646-4146

Scholarly journal covering research in German history, literature, politics, and related fields. **Founded:** Feb. 1978. **Freq:** Quarterly. **Key Personnel:** Prof. Diethelm Prowe, Editor, dprowe@carleton.edu; Judith Ricker, Book Review Editor, phone (479)575-2951, fax (479)575-6795, jricker@comp.uark.edu. **Subscription Rates:** $40 individuals; $45 Canada; $50 elsewhere; $15 single issue. **Remarks:** Accepts advertising.

Ad Rates: BW: $125   Circ: Combined 2,050

RICHFIELD

123 Richfield Sun Current
Minnesota Sun Publications
10917 Valley View Rd.
Eden Prairie, MN 55344-3730

Phone: (952)392-6835
Fax: (952)941-3588

Publication E-mail: richfieldsuncurrent@mnsunpub.com

Community newspaper (tabloid). **Freq:** Weekly (Wed.). **Print Method:** Offset. **Cols./Page:** 4. **Col. Width:** 2 1/2 inches. **Col. Depth:** 15 inches. **Key Personnel:** Doug Dance, Publisher, phone (612)896-4787; Pamela Austin, Advertising Dir., phone (612)897-5486. **Remarks:** Advertising accepted; rates available upon request. **Available Online.** **URL:** http://www.mnsun.pub.com.

Circ: Paid ◆1,113
Non-paid ◆8,611

SOUTH ST. PAUL

124 South St. Paul/Inver Grove Heights Sun Current
Minnesota Sun Publications
10917 Valley View Rd.
Eden Prairie, MN 55344-3730

Phone: (952)392-6835
Fax: (952)941-3588

Publication E-mail: southstpaulsuncurrent@mnsunpub.com

Community newspaper (tabloid). **Founded:** 1984. **Freq:** Weekly (Wed.). **Print Method:** Offset. **Cols./Page:** 4. **Col. Width:** 2 1/2 inches. **Col. Depth:** 15 inches. **Key Personnel:** Doug Dane, Publisher, phone (612)896-4787; Pamela Austin, Advertising Mgr., phone (612)897-5486. **URL:** http://www.mnsun.

Circ: Paid ◆224
Non-paid ◆**14,362**

MISSISSIPPI

BELMONT

📖 **125 Belmont-Tishomingo Journal**
The Belmont and Tishomongo Journal, Inc.
PO Box 70   Phone: (662)454-7196
Belmont, MS 38827   Fax: (662)454-7196

Community newspaper. **Founded:** 1970. **Freq:** Weekly (Wed.). **Print Method:** Web press. **Cols./Page:** 6. **Col. Width:** 1 7/8 inches. **Col. Depth:** 21 1/2 inches. **Key Personnel:** Catherine Mitchell, Editor; M.W. Mitchell, Publisher. **Subscription Rates:** $16 individuals; $24 out of area. **Remarks:** Advertising not accepted for liquors, tobacco, gambling.
Ad Rates: PCI: $5   **Circ:** ‡2,100

HATTIESBURG

📖 **126 Hattiesburg American**
Gannett Co., Inc.
825 N. Main St.
PO Box 1111   Phone: (601)582-4321
Hattiesburg, MS 39401   Fax: (601)583-8244

General newspaper. **Freq:** Daily (eve.), Sat. and Sun. (morn.). **Print Method:** Offset. **Trim Size:** 13 3/4 x 22 3/4. **Cols./Page:** 6. **Col. Width:** 1.833 inches. **Col. Depth:** 21 1/2 inches. **Key Personnel:** Marilyn Mitchell, Editor, phone (601)584-3125, fax (601)584-3130, mmitchel@hattiesb.gannett.com; David Petty, Publisher, phone (601)584-3000, fax (601)583-9914, dpetty@hattiesb.gannett.com; Brent Powers, Advertising Dir., phone (601)584-3089, fax (601)584-3075, bpowers@hattiesb.gannett.com. **Subscription Rates:** $144; $225 out of area. **Remarks:** Accepts advertising. **URL:** http://www.hattiesburgamerican.com.
Ad Rates: GLR: $1.62   **Circ:** Mon.-Sat. 22,741
BW: $3,128.25   Sun. 26,958
4C: $3,698.25
SAU: $22.72
PCI: $24.25

MONTANA

MISSOULA

📖 **127 Montana Kaimin**
University of Montana
U of M Journalism 206
Missoula, MT 59812   Phone: (406)243-4310

Collegiate newspaper. **Founded:** 1898. **Freq:** Tues.-Fri. (morn.). **Print Method:** Offset. **Trim Size:** 9 1/2 x 12 1/2. **Cols./Page:** 5. **Col. Width:** 19 nonpareils. **Col. Depth:** 175 agate lines. **Subscription Rates:** $75 individuals. **URL:** http://www.kaimin.org.
Ad Rates: GLR: $1   **Circ:** Free 6,000
BW: $552.75
SAU: $13.13

NEW HAMPSHIRE

CONWAY

📖 **128 Northern Light**
PO Box 2230   Phone: (603)447-3824
Conway, NH 03818   Fax: (603)447-3825

Newspaper. **Subtitle:** Northern Light. **Founded:** 1980. **Freq:** Weekly (Sat.).

Print Method: Offset. **Trim Size:** 11 3/4 x 13 1/2. **Cols./Page:** 5. **Col. Width:** 2 1/4 inches. **Col. Depth:** 13 inches. **Key Personnel:** Gaye Berry-Hodgdon, Editor. **USPS:** 145-. **Remarks:** Accepts advertising.
Ad Rates: GLR: $.35   **Circ:** Non-paid 34,759
BW: $581.75
4C: $681.75
SAU: $8.95
PCI: $8.60

PETERBOROUGH

📖 **129 Consulting**
Kennedy Information, Inc.
One Pheonix Mill Ln., 5th Fl.   Phone: (603)924-1006
Peterborough, NH 03458   Fax: (603)924-4034
                                                  Free: (800)531-0007
Publisher E-mail: bookstore@kennedyinfo.com

Professional magazine covering management consulting. **Freq:** Monthly. **Key Personnel:** Jack Sweeney, Editor-in-Chief, phone (212)557-7883, jsweeney@kennedyinfo.com; Mina Landriscina, Managing Editor, phone (212)557-7882, mlandriscina@kennedyinfo.com; Brian Cuthbert, Editorial Asst., bcuthbert@kennedyinfo.com. **Subscription Rates:** $99 individuals; $129 out of country. **Remarks:** Accepts advertising. **URL:** http://www.consultingcentral.com.

Circ: (Not Reported)

📖 **130 Shareholder Value**
Kennedy Information, Inc.
One Pheonix Mill Ln., 5th Fl.   Phone: (603)924-1006
Peterborough, NH 03458   Fax: (603)924-4034
                                                  Free: (800)531-0007
Publisher E-mail: bookstore@kennedyinfo.com

Professional magazine covering managing expectations and the creation of shareholder value for executives. **Freq:** Bimonthly. **Key Personnel:** William F. Mahoney, Exec. Editor. **Subscription Rates:** $99 individuals; $129 out of country. **Remarks:** Accepts advertising. **URL:** http://www.kennedyinfor.com/ir/svm/svm.html.

Circ: (Not Reported)

WARNER

📖 **131 Warner's New Paper**
PO Box 92   Phone: (603)456-1423
Warner, NH 03278   Fax: (603)456-3087
Publication E-mail: thepaper98@hotmail.com

Community newspaper. **Founded:** Mar. 1, 1998. **Freq:** Monthly. **Key Personnel:** Richard Senor, Editor. **Subscription Rates:** $15. **Remarks:** Accepts advertising. **URL:** http://www.geocities.com/Athens/Styx/9323. **Alt. Formats:** CD-ROM.
Ad Rates: BW: $95   **Circ:** 1,000

NEW JERSEY

BERNARDSVILLE

📖 **132 The Bernardsville News**
Recorder Publishing Co., Inc.
17-19 Morristown Rd.
Bernardsville, NJ 07924-2312
Publication E-mail: bernardsvillenews@recordernewspapers.com
Publisher E-mail: editor@recordernewspapers.com

Community newspaper. **Founded:** 1897. **Freq:** Weekly (Thurs.). **Print Method:** Offset. **Cols./Page:** 6. **Col. Width:** 26 nonpareils. **Col. Depth:** 300 agate lines. **Key Personnel:** Charles Zavalick, Editor; Cortlandt Parker, Publisher; Allison Spinella, Advertising Mgr., phone (908)766-3900. **Subscription Rates:** $30 individuals. **Remarks:** Combined advertising rates available with other Recorder publications.
Ad Rates: GLR: $1.03   **Circ:** Combined 8,880

Ad Rates: GLR = general line rate; BW = one-time black & white page rate; 4C = one-time four color page rate; SAU = standard advertising unit rate; CNU = Canadian newspaper advertising unit rate; PCI = per column inch rate.
Circulation: ★ = ABC; △ = BPA; ◆ = CAC; ● = CCAB; ❑ = VAC; ⊕ = PO Statement; ‡ = Publisher's Report; Boldface figures = sworn; Light figures = estimated.
Entry type: 📖 = Print; 🎤 = Broadcast.

15

📖 **133 New England Wine Gazette**
Recorder Publishing Company Inc.
17-19 Morristown Rd.
PO Box 687   Phone: (908)766-3900
Bernardsville, NJ 07924   Fax: (908)766-6365

Newspaper covering wine and the wine industry in New England. **Founded:** 1988. **Freq:** Quarterly. **Print Method:** Photo offset. **Key Personnel:** David Nelson, Circ. Exec. **Subscription Rates:** Free.

         Circ: Non-paid ◆**18,418**

CHESTER

📖 **134 Mount Olive Chronicle**
Recorder Publishing Co., Inc.
PO Box 600
Chester, NJ 07930-0600   Phone: (908)879-4100
Publication E-mail: mountolivechronicle@recordernewspapers.com
Publisher E-mail: editor@recordernewspapers.com

Community newspaper. **Founded:** Sept. 1979. **Freq:** Weekly (Thurs.). **Print Method:** Offset. **Cols./Page:** 6. **Col. Width:** 26 nonpareils. **Col. Depth:** 300 agate lines. **Key Personnel:** Phil Garber, Editor; Cortlandt Parker, Publisher; Allison Spinella, Advertising Mgr., phone (908)766-3900. **Subscription Rates:** $16. **Remarks:** Combined advertising rates available with other Recorder newspapers.

         Circ: Combined 2,683

📖 **135 Observer-Tribune**
Recorder Publishing Co., Inc.
PO Box 600   Phone: (908)879-4100
Chester, NJ 07930-0600   Fax: (908)647-5952
Publication E-mail: observertribune@recordernewspapers.com
Publisher E-mail: editor@recordernewspapers.com

Local newspaper. **Founded:** 1936. **Freq:** Weekly (Thurs.). **Print Method:** Offset. **Cols./Page:** 6. **Col. Width:** 12.2 picas. **Col. Depth:** 21 inches. **Key Personnel:** Phil Garber, Editor; Cortlandt Parker, Sr., Publisher; Allison Spinella, Advertising Mgr. **Subscription Rates:** $20. **Remarks:** Accepts advertising.
Ad Rates: SAU: $21.25   **Circ:** Combined 7,115
          PCI: $15

Roxbury Register - See Roxbury Township

ELIZABETH

📖 **136 Mensaje**
Latin American News and Books Corp.
PO Box 2109   Phone: (908)355-8835
Elizabeth, NJ 07207-2109   Fax: (908)527-9160

Community newspaper (Spanish). **Subtitle:** Un Periodico Veraz Y Combativo. **Founded:** Oct. 10, 1980. **Freq:** Daily. **Cols./Page:** 5. **Col. Depth:** 15 inches. **Key Personnel:** Jose Tenreiro, Editor. **Subscription Rates:** $.35 single issue. **Formerly:** Mensaje Newsleder.
Ad Rates: BW: $1260   **Circ:** Paid 52,000
          4C: $1610
          PCI: $18

HOBOKEN

📖 **137 BB Gun Magazine**
PO Box 5074
Hoboken, NJ 07030
Publication E-mail: bbgunmagazine@aol.com

Consumer magazine covering music and underground culture. **Key Personnel:** Bob Bert, Editor; Linda Wolfe, Editor. **Subscription Rates:** $7 single issue; $10 single issue out of country. **Remarks:** Accepts advertising. **URL:** http://www.bbgun.org.

         Circ: (Not Reported)

RED BANK

📖 **138 Business Facilities**
Group C Communications, Inc.
PO Box 2060   Phone: (732)919-1716
Red Bank, NJ 07701   Fax: (732)919-7532
          Free: (800)524-0337

Professional magazine focusing on corporate expansion, commercial/industrial real estate, and economic development. **Subtitle:** The Source For Corporate Site Selectors. **Founded:** 1967. **Freq:** Monthly. **Print Method:** Offset. **Trim Size:** 8 x 10 3/4. **Cols./Page:** 3. **Col. Width:** 27 nonpareils. **Col. Depth:** 140 agate lines. **Key Personnel:** David Goldstein, Publisher, phone (732)842-7433, fax (732)758-6634, dgoldstein@groupc.com; Donna Clapp, Editor, phone (732)842-7433, fax (732)758-6634, dclapp@groupc.com. **ISSN:** 0746-0023. **Subscription Rates:** $36.75. **Remarks:** Accepts advertising. **URL:** http://www.facilitycity.com.
Ad Rates: BW: $5,849   **Circ:** Free 43,500
          4C: $7,349

📖 **139 Today's Facility Manager**
Group C Communications, Inc.
PO Box 2060   Phone: (732)919-1716
Red Bank, NJ 07701   Fax: (732)919-7532
          Free: (800)524-0337

Tabloid for facility design and management. **Subtitle:** The Facility Decision Maker's Source for Products and Services. **Founded:** Sept. 1988. **Freq:** Monthly. **Print Method:** Web offset. **Trim Size:** 10 7/8 x 13 3/4. **Cols./Page:** 4. **Col. Width:** 2 1/2 inches. **Col. Depth:** 13 inches. **Key Personnel:** Heidi Schwartz, Editor, phone (732)842-7433, schwartz@groupc.com; Susan Coene, Publisher, phone (732)842-7433, fax (730)842-1684, scoene@groupc.com. **USPS:** 003-776. **Subscription Rates:** $31.50 individuals. **Remarks:** Accepts advertising. **Online:** compuserve. **URL:** http://www.facilitycity.com. **Formerly:** Business Interiors; Corporate Design; Realty.
Ad Rates: BW: $5,321   **Circ:** Controlled ❑**50,000**
          4C: $6,681

ROXBURY TOWNSHIP

📖 **140 Roxbury Register**
Recorder Publishing Co., Inc.
PO Box 600
Chester, NJ 07930-0600
Publication E-mail: roxburyregister@recordernewspapers.com
Publisher E-mail: editor@recordernewspapers.com

Community newspaper. **Founded:** 1988. **Freq:** Weekly (Thurs.). **Print Method:** Offset. **Cols./Page:** 6. **Col. Width:** 2 1/4 inches. **Col. Depth:** 22 inches. **Key Personnel:** Elizabeth K. Parker, Editor and Publisher, phone (908)645-1187, eparker@recordernewspapers.com; Philip J. Nardone, Managing Editor; Cortlandt Parker, Publisher; Allison Spinella, Advertising Mgr.; Mike Condon, Editor, phone (908)879-4100. **Subscription Rates:** $18. **Remarks:** Accepts advertising. **URL:** http://www.roxburyregister.com.
Ad Rates: PCI: $15.95   **Circ:** Combined 2,356

SECAUCUS

📖 **141 Business Travel Planner - European Edition**
Northstar Travel Media
500 Plaza Dr.   Phone: (201)902-2000
Secaucus, NJ 07094-3626   Fax: (201)902-1888

Directory containing information on travel to and through Europe, including country basics, city destination data, hotel/motel listings, airport diagrams, city and country maps, and reservation directories. **Founded:** June 1978. **Freq:** Quarterly. **Print Method:** Offset. **Trim Size:** 8 x 10 1/2. **Cols./Page:** 2. **Key Personnel:** Marie Mason, Publisher, phone (201)802-7734, mmason@cahners.com. **ISSN:** 0894-1718. **Subscription Rates:** $149 individuals. **Remarks:** Accepts advertising. **Formerly:** OAG Business Travel Planner.
Ad Rates: BW: $3,940   **Circ:** (Not Reported)
          4C: $5,250

📖 **142 Business Travel Planner - North American Edition**
Northstar Travel Media
500 Plaza Dr.   Phone: (201)902-2000
Secaucus, NJ 07094-3626   Fax: (201)902-1888

Magazine covering business and leisure travel. **Founded:** 1959. **Freq:**
Quarterly. **Print Method:** Offset. **Trim Size:** 8 x 10 1/2. **Key Personnel:**
Carlo DeCarlo, Managing Editor, phone (201)902-7918, cdecar-
lo@ntmllc.com; Linda Hadley, Marketing Mgr., phone (201)902-1576,
lhadley@ntmllc.com. **ISSN:** 0894-1726. **Subscription Rates:** $149 individu-
als. **Remarks:** Accepts advertising. **Formerly:** OAG Travel Planner Hotel &
Motel Redbook (North American Edition); OAG Business Travel Planner,
North American Edition; OAG Business Travel Planner.
Ad Rates: BW: $8,720   **Circ:** (Not Reported)
               4C: $8,880

📖 **143 Business Travel Planner - Pacific/Asia Edition**
Northstar Travel Media
500 Plaza Dr.   Phone: (201)902-2000
Secaucus, NJ 07094-3626   Fax: (201)902-1888

Directory containing information on travel to and through the Pacific Rim,
including country basics, hotel/motel listings, airport diagrams, city and
country maps, and reservation directories. **Founded:** 1985. **Freq:** Quarterly.
Print Method: Offset. **Trim Size:** 8 x 10 1/2. **Cols./Page:** 2. **Col. Width:** 40
nonpareils. **Col. Depth:** 140 agate lines. **Key Personnel:** Carlo DeCarlo,
Managing Editor, phone (201)902-7918, cdecarlo@ntmllc.com; Linda Hadley, Marketing Mgr., phone (201)902-1576, lhadley@ntmllc.com. **ISSN:**
0894-1734. **Subscription Rates:** $149 individuals. **Remarks:** Accepts
advertising. **Formerly**: OAG Business Travel Planner; OAG Business Travel
Planner.
Ad Rates: BW: $3,940   **Circ:** (Not Reported)
               4C: $5,250

THOROFARE

📖 **144 Journal of Nursing Education**
SLACK Inc.
6900 Grove Rd.   Phone: (856)848-1000
Thorofare, NJ 08086-9447   Fax: (856)848-6091
                                                Free: (800)257-8290

Publication E-mail: jne@slackinc.com

Professional journal covering research and teaching in nursing education.
Founded: 1962. **Freq:** Monthly. **Trim Size:** 8 1/8 x 10 7/8. **Key Personnel:**
Christine A. Tanner, Ph.D., Editor; Karen Stanwood, Managing Editor,
kstanwood@slackinc.com; Richard N. Roash, VP/Group Publisher; John C.
Carter, VP, Publishing Operations; Lester J. Robeson, Circulation Dir. **ISSN:**
0148-4834. **Subscription Rates:** $79 individuals; $19 single issue; $109
institutions; $109 institutions, Canada plus 7% tax; $39.50 nursing students w/
qualifying letter. **Remarks:** Accepts advertising.
Ad Rates: BW: $900   **Circ:** Paid 4,000
               4C: $1,335

📖 **145 Journal of Psychosocial Nursing and Mental Health
    Services**
SLACK Inc.
6900 Grove Rd.   Phone: (856)848-1000
Thorofare, NJ 08086-9447   Fax: (856)848-6091
                                                Free: (800)257-8290

Publication E-mail: jpn@slackinc.com

Journal presenting original, peer-reviewed articles on psychiatric/mental
health nursing. **Founded:** 1963. **Freq:** Monthly. **Print Method:** Web press.
Trim Size: 8 1/8 x 10 7/8. **Cols./Page:** 3. **Col. Width:** 13 picas. **Col. Depth:**
58 agate lines. **Key Personnel:** Shirley A. Smoyak, R.N., Ph.D; Richard
Roash, Publisher, fax (856)848-6091, rroash@slackinc.com; Karen Stanwood,
Managing Editor, kstanwood@slackinc.com; Meredith Roash, Advertising
Mgr., mroash@slackinc.com. **ISSN:** 0279-3695. **Subscription Rates:** $49;
$74 institutions; $19 single issue. **Remarks:** Accepts advertising. **Formerly:**
Journal of Psychiatric Nursing (July 1, 1981).
Ad Rates: BW: $2,290   **Circ:** ‡6,000
               4C: $3,685

TRENTON

📖 **146 New Jersey Reporter**
Public Policy Center of New Jersey
36 W Lafayette St.   Phone: (609)392-2003
Trenton, NJ 08608-2011   Fax: (609)392-1770
Publication E-mail: njreporter@aol.com
Publisher E-mail: publicpolicynj@aol.com

Subtitle: A Journal of Public Issues. **Founded:** 1970. **Freq:** 10/year. **Print
Method:** Offset. **Trim Size:** 8 1/2 x 11. **Cols./Page:** 3. **Col. Width:** 13 1/2
picas. **Col. Depth:** 140 agate lines. **Key Personnel:** Lauren Otis, Managing
Editor, lotis@castle.com. **ISSN:** 0195-3192. **Subscription Rates:** $50 indi-
viduals; $4.95 single issue. **Remarks:** Accepts advertising. **URL:** http://
www.njreporter.org.

                                                Circ: Paid ‡1,200
                                                Controlled ‡500

WILLINGBORO

📖 **147 The Post**
Burlington Times, Inc.
4284 Rte. 130   Phone: (609)871-8000
Willingboro, NJ 08046   Fax: (609)877-2706

Military newspaper. **Founded:** 1925. **Freq:** Weekly (Fri.). **Print Method:**
Photo offset. **Key Personnel:** Stanley M. Ellis, Publisher; Frank E. Leon,
Circ. Exec. **Subscription Rates:** Free. **Remarks:** Accepts advertising.
                                                Circ: Non-paid ♦9,196

NEW MEXICO

ALBUQUERQUE

📖 **148 American Literary Realism**
University of Illinois Press
Department of English
Humanities 217
University of New Mexico   Phone: (505)277-3015
Albuquerque, NM 87131-1106   Fax: (505)277-5573
Publisher E-mail: uipress@uillinois.edu

Journal covering American literature from the late nineteenth and early
twentieth centuries. **Freq:** Triennial. **Key Personnel:** Gary Scharnhorst,
Editor, gscharn@unm.edu; Andrew Flood, Managing & Book Editor,
flood@unm.edu; Clydette Wantland, Advertising, phone (217)244-6496, fax
(217)244-8082, cwantlan@uillinois.edu. **ISSN:** 0002-9823. **Subscription
Rates:** $40 institutions; $50 institutions out of country; $35 individuals; $45
individuals out of country; $12 single issue; $15 single issue out of country.
URL: http://www.press.uillinois.edu/journals/alr.html.

NEW YORK

BINGHAMTON

📖 **149 Medical Reference Services Quarterly**
The Haworth Press Inc.
10 Alice St.   Phone: (607)722-5857
Binghamton, NY 13904-1580   Fax: (607)722-6362
                                                Free: (800)429-6784
Publisher E-mail: getinfo@haworthpressinc.com

Journal for medical and health sciences librarians. **Founded:** 1982. **Freq:**
Quarterly. **Trim Size:** 6 x 8 3/8. **Cols./Page:** 1. **Col. Width:** 4 3/8 inches.
Col. Depth: 7 1/8 inches. **Key Personnel:** M. Sandra Wood, Editor, phone
(717)531-8630, fax (717)531-8635, mswood@psghs.edu; Bill Cohen, Publisher; Kellie N. Kaneshiro, Editor. **ISSN:** 0276-3869. **Subscription Rates:**
$60 individuals USA; $250 institutions/libraries/agencies USA; $81 individu-
als Canada; $337.50 institutions/libraries/agencies Canada; $87 individuals
elsewhere; $362.50 institutions/libraries/agencies elsewhere. **Remarks:** Ac-
cepts advertising. **URL:** http://www.haworthpress.com. **Alt. Formats:** Microform.
Ad Rates: BW: $315   **Circ:** 1,295
               4C: $550

BROOKLYN

📖 **150 Wax Poetics**
Wax Poetics, LLC
655 Fulton St., No. 181
Brooklyn, NY 11217-1112   Phone: (718)826-0616

Consumer magazine covering hip hop music, culture and record collecting.
Freq: Quarterly. **Subscription Rates:** $32 individuals; $40 Canada; $65
elsewhere. **Remarks:** Accepts advertising. **URL:** http://waxpoetics.com/html/
home.php.
                                           Circ: (Not Reported)

LOWVILLE

📖 **151 Lewis County Historical Society Journal**
Lewis County Historical Society
7552 S. State St.
Box 446
Lowville, NY 13367   Phone: (315)376-8957
Publisher E-mail: histsoc@northnet.org

Journal covering local history. **Founded:** Dec. 1966. **Freq:** Annual. **Key
Personnel:** Lisa Becker, Museum Dir. **Subscription Rates:** $5 single issue
plus S&H. **Remarks:** Advertising not accepted.
                                           Circ: (Not Reported)

MELVILLE

📖 **152 Oncology**
PRR, Inc.
A Division of SCP Communications, Inc.
48 South Service Rd.   Phone: (631)777-3800
Melville, NY 11747-2335   Fax: (631)777-8700
Publication E-mail: info@prrnet.com

Journal featuring articles for practicing oncologists, with reviews by peers in
relevant specialties published concurrently. **Founded:** Mar. 1987. **Freq:**
Monthly. **Print Method:** Offset. **Trim Size:** 7 3/4 x 10 3/4. **Cols./Page:** 3.
Key Personnel: Cara H. Glynn, Sr. Editorial Dir.; Joseph Schuldner,
Publisher, phone (973)726-5293, joe.schuldner@scp.com; Kelly McNulty,
National Accounts Mgr., kelly.mcnulty@scp.com. **ISSN:** 0890-9091. **Sub-
scription Rates:** $112 U.S.; $118 Canada; $96 students/nurses; $135 out of
country; $18 single issue. **Remarks:** Accepts advertising. **URL:**
www.cancernetwork.com.
Ad Rates: BW: $3,335   **Circ:** Controlled △30,016
               4C: $4,910   Paid △1,875

NEW YORK

📖 **153 Abdominal Imaging**
Springer-Verlag New York Inc.
175 5th Ave.   Phone: (212)460-1500
New York, NY 10010   Fax: (212)473-6272
                                           Free: (800)777-4643
Publisher E-mail: journals@springer-ny.com

Medical journal providing information on diagnostic imaging of the alimenta-
ry tract to radiologists, internists, and surgeons. **Founded:** 1973. **Freq:**
Bimonthly. **Print Method:** Offset. **Trim Size:** 8 1/4 x 11. **Cols./Page:** 2. **Col.
Width:** 38 nonpareils. **Col. Depth:** 128 agate lines. **Key Personnel:** Morton
Meyers, Editor, phone (212)460-1571; Rob Albano, Marketing Mgr. Medicine, ralbano@springer-ny.com; Jay Feinman, Advertising Sales, phone
(212)460-1682, fax (212)533-0108. **ISSN:** 0942-8925. **Subscription Rates:**
$131 individuals; $309 institutions. **Remarks:** Accepts advertising. **URL:**
http://www.springer-ny.com. **Alt. Formats:** Microform. **Formerly:** Gastroin-
testinal Radiology.
Ad Rates: BW: $655   **Circ:** Combined 1,350
               4C: $1,375

📖 **154 Algorithmica**
Springer-Verlag New York Inc.
175 5th Ave.   Phone: (212)460-1500
New York, NY 10010   Fax: (212)473-6272
                                           Free: (800)777-4643
Publisher E-mail: journals@springer-ny.com

Publication containing original papers on the development and application of
algorithms. **Subtitle:** An International Journal in Computer Science. **Found-**

ed: 1986. **Freq:** Monthly. **Trim Size:** 6 1/2 x 9 1/2. **Key Personnel:** Dr. C.K.
Wong, Editor; Robert Vrooman, Advertising Mgr., phone (212)460-1700, fax
(212)533-5617. **ISSN:** 0178-4617. **Subscription Rates:** $116 individuals;
$264 institutions. **Remarks:** Accepts advertising.
Ad Rates: BW: $575   **Circ:** Combined 750
               4C: $1,295

📖 **155 Applied Mathematics and Optimization**
Springer-Verlag New York Inc.
175 5th Ave.   Phone: (212)460-1500
New York, NY 10010   Fax: (212)473-6272
                                           Free: (800)777-4643
Publisher E-mail: journals@springer-ny.com

Mathematics journal. **Founded:** 1974. **Freq:** Bimonthly. **Print Method:**
Offset. **Trim Size:** 6 1/2 x 9 1/2. **Cols./Page:** 1. **Col. Width:** 57 nonpareils.
Col. Depth: 107 agate lines. **Key Personnel:** G. Kallianpur, Editor; Robert
Vrooman, Advertising Mgr., phone (212)460-1700, fax (212)533-5617. **ISSN:**
0095-4616. **Subscription Rates:** $329 individuals. **Remarks:** Accepts
advertising.
Ad Rates: BW: $500   **Circ:** Combined 700
               4C: $1,100

📖 **156 Calcified Tissue International**
Springer-Verlag New York Inc.
175 5th Ave.   Phone: (212)460-1500
New York, NY 10010   Fax: (212)473-6272
                                           Free: (800)777-4643
Publisher E-mail: journals@springer-ny.com

Journal dealing with the structure and function of bone and other mineralized
systems in living organisms. **Founded:** 1967. **Freq:** Monthly. **Print Method:**
Offset. **Trim Size:** 8 1/4 x 11. **Cols./Page:** 2. **Col. Width:** 38 nonpareils. **Col.
Depth:** 128 agate lines. **Key Personnel:** Louis Avioli, M.D., Editor; Jay
Feinmen, Advertising Mgr., phone (212)460-1682, fax (212)533-0108; Rob
Albano, Marketing Mgr. Medicine, ralbano@springer-ny.com. **ISSN:** 0171-
967X. **Subscription Rates:** $162 individuals; $750 institutions. **Remarks:**
Accepts advertising. **URL:** http://www.springer-ny.com. **Alt. Formats:**
Microform.
Ad Rates: BW: $640   **Circ:** 1,650
               4C: $1,390

📖 **157 Cardiovascular and Interventional Radiology**
Springer-Verlag New York Inc.
175 5th Ave.   Phone: (212)460-1500
New York, NY 10010   Fax: (212)473-6272
                                           Free: (800)777-4643
Publisher E-mail: journals@springer-ny.com

Journal providing medical and radiology news. **Founded:** 1977. **Freq:**
Bimonthly Plus one supplement. **Print Method:** Offset. **Trim Size:** 8 1/4 x
11. **Cols./Page:** 2. **Col. Width:** 37 nonpareils. **Col. Depth:** 140 agate lines.
Key Personnel: Jay Feinman, Advertising Mgr., phone (212)460-1682, fax
(212)533-0108; Rob Albano, Marketing Mgr. Medicine, ralbano@springer-
ny.com. **ISSN:** 0174-1551. **Subscription Rates:** $147 individuals; $287
institutions. **Remarks:** Accepts advertising. **URL:** http://www.springer-
ny.com. **Alt. Formats:** Microform.
Ad Rates: BW: $1,660   **Circ:** Combined 2,800
               4C: $2,535

📖 **158 Chance**
Springer-Verlag New York Inc.
175 5th Ave.   Phone: (212)460-1500
New York, NY 10010   Fax: (212)473-6272
                                           Free: (800)777-4643
Publisher E-mail: journals@springer-ny.com

Magazine about new approaches to statistics, including reviews of statistical
computer programs and other statistical methodology. **Subtitle:** New Direc-
tions for Statistics and Computing. **Founded:** Jan. 1988. **Freq:** Quarterly.
Print Method: Web offset. **Trim Size:** 8 1/4 x 11. **Key Personnel:** Patrick
Ferencz, Editor; Brian Skepton, Advertising Mgr., phone (212)460-1575, fax
(212)533-0108. **ISSN:** 0933-2480. **Subscription Rates:** $35. **Remarks:**
Accepts advertising.
Ad Rates: BW: $750   **Circ:** Combined 5,000
               4C: $1,470   Paid 4,000

159 Constructive Approximation
Springer-Verlag New York Inc.
175 5th Ave.   Phone: (212)460-1500
New York, NY 10010   Fax: (212)473-6272
                                                  Free: (800)777-4643
Publisher E-mail: journals@springer-ny.com

Mathematics journal. **Freq:** Quarterly. **Key Personnel:** Thomas Heitzman, Editor; Ronald LeVore, Advertising Mgr. **ISSN:** 0176-4276. **Subscription Rates:** $149.
Ad Rates: BW: $400   **Circ:** Combined 550
              4C: $920

160 Current Microbiology
Springer-Verlag New York Inc.
175 5th Ave.   Phone: (212)460-1500
New York, NY 10010   Fax: (212)473-6272
                                                  Free: (800)777-4643
Publisher E-mail: journals@springer-ny.com

Microbiology journal. **Subtitle:** An International journal. **Founded:** 1978. **Freq:** Monthly. **Print Method:** Offset. **Trim Size:** 8 1/4 x 11. **Cols./Page:** 2. **Col. Width:** 36 nonpareils. **Col. Depth:** 130 agate lines. **Key Personnel:** Albert Balows, Editor; Bob Vrooman, Advertising Mgr., phone (212)4601700. **ISSN:** 0343-8651. **Subscription Rates:** $455 institutions. **Remarks:** Accepts advertising. **URL:** http://link.springer-ny.com.
Ad Rates: BW: $500   **Circ:** Combined 700
              4C: $1,220

161 Discrete and Computational Geometry
Springer-Verlag New York Inc.
175 5th Ave.   Phone: (212)460-1500
New York, NY 10010   Fax: (212)473-6272
                                                  Free: (800)777-4643
Publisher E-mail: journals@springer-ny.com

Mathematics and computer science journal. **Founded:** 1986. **Freq:** 8/year. **Trim Size:** 6 1/2 x 9 1/2. **Key Personnel:** Robert Vrooman, Advertising Mgr.; Richard Pollack, Editor. **ISSN:** 0179-5376. **Subscription Rates:** $229 individuals.
Ad Rates: BW: $575   **Circ:** Combined 675
              4C: $1,295

162 Dysphagia
Springer-Verlag New York Inc.
175 5th Ave.   Phone: (212)460-1500
New York, NY 10010   Fax: (212)473-6272
                                                  Free: (800)777-4643
Publisher E-mail: journals@springer-ny.com

Journal concerning the disorders of swallowing. **Subtitle:** An International Multidisciplinary Journal Devoted to Swallowing and Its Disorders. **Founded:** 1986. **Freq:** Quarterly. **Print Method:** Offset. **Trim Size:** 8 1/4 x 11. **Key Personnel:** Brian Skepton, Advertising Mgr., phone (212)460-1575, fax (212)533-0108; Rob Albano, Marketing Mgr. Medicine, ralbano@springer-ny.com. **ISSN:** 0179-051X. **Subscription Rates:** $124 individuals; $246 institutions. **Remarks:** Accepts advertising. **URL:** http://www.springer-ny.com. **Alt. Formats:** Microform.
Ad Rates: BW: $710   **Circ:** Combined 2,200
              4C: $1,485

163 Fence
Fence Books
14 Fifth Ave., Ste. 1A
New York, NY 10011
Publisher E-mail: editor@fencebooks.com

Literary magazine featuring poems and fiction. **Freq:** Semiannual. **Key Personnel:** Rebecca Wolff, Editor; Brett Fletcher Lauer, Assoc. Editor; Caroline Crumpacker, Poetry Editor; Matthew Rohrer, Poetry Editor; Max Winter, Poetry Editor; Ben Marcus, Fiction Editor; Frances Richard, Nonfiction Editor; Chris Gage, Production Mgr. **Subscription Rates:** $14 individuals; $26 two years; $200 lifetime subscription; $8 single issue. **URL:** http://www.fencemag.com.

164 Foreign Affairs
Council on Foreign Relations Press
58 E 68th St.   Phone: (212)434-9525
New York, NY 10021   Fax: (212)861-2759
Publication E-mail: foraff@email.cfr.org

Magazine on international relations, trade, and economics. **Founded:** 1922. **Freq:** 6/year. **Print Method:** Offset. **Trim Size:** 7 x 10. **Cols./Page:** 1. **Col. Width:** 28 picas. **Col. Depth:** 49 picas. **Key Personnel:** James F. Hoge, Jr., Editor; David Kellogg, Publisher; David Hilmer, Advertising Dir. **ISSN:** 0015-7120. **Subscription Rates:** $44 individuals; $7.95 single issue. **Online:** LEXIS-NEXIS.
Ad Rates: BW: $7,300   **Circ:** Paid 109,206
              4C: $10,250

165 International Railway Journal
Simmons-Boardman Publishing Corp.
345 Hudson St.   Phone: (212)620-7200
New York, NY 10014   Fax: (212)633-1165
                                                  Free: (800)895-4389
Publisher E-mail: bdemarco@sbpub.com

Magazine focusing on international railways and rail transit. Summaries in French, German and Spanish. **Subtitle:** Rapid Transit Review. **Founded:** 1960. **Freq:** Monthly. **Print Method:** Offset. **Trim Size:** 8 1/4 x 11 3/8. **Cols./Page:** 3. **Col. Width:** 26 nonpareils. **Col. Depth:** 140 agate lines. **Key Personnel:** Robert P. DeMarco, Publisher, Bdemarco@sbpub.com; David Briginshaw, Editor-in-Chief, dbrigenshaw@railjournal.com. **ISSN:** 0744-5326. **Subscription Rates:** $95. **Remarks:** Accepts advertising.
Ad Rates: BW: $2,310   **Circ:** Combined 10,314
              4C: $3,500
              PCI: $80

166 Journal of Membrane Biology
Springer-Verlag New York Inc.
175 5th Ave.   Phone: (212)460-1500
New York, NY 10010   Fax: (212)473-6272
                                                  Free: (800)777-4643
Publisher E-mail: journals@springer-ny.com

Journal containing articles examining the nature, structure, function, and genesis of biological membranes, and the physics and chemistry of artificial membranes relevant to biomembranes. **Subtitle:** An International Journal for Studies on the Structure, Function, and Genesis of Biomembranes. **Founded:** 1969. **Freq:** 18/year. **Print Method:** Offset. **Trim Size:** 8 1/4 x 11. **Cols./Page:** 2. **Col. Width:** 57 nonpareils. **Col. Depth:** 107 agate lines. **Key Personnel:** W.R. Loewenstein, Editor; Bob Vrooman, Advertising Mgr., phone (212)460-1700, fax (212)533-0108. **ISSN:** 0022-2631. **Subscription Rates:** $1399 institutions. **Remarks:** Accepts advertising. **URL:** http://link.springer-ny.com.
Ad Rates: BW: $750   **Circ:** Paid 900
              4C: $1,295

167 Journal of Molecular Evolution
Springer-Verlag New York Inc.
175 5th Ave.   Phone: (212)460-1500
New York, NY 10010   Fax: (212)473-6272
                                                  Free: (800)777-4643
Publisher E-mail: journals@springer-ny.com

Journal containing articles about the various fields of molecular evolution. **Subtitle:** The Journal of the International Society of Molecular Evolution. **Founded:** 1971. **Freq:** Monthly. **Print Method:** Sheetfed offset. **Trim Size:** 8 1/4 x 11. **Cols./Page:** 2. **Key Personnel:** Robert Vrooman, Advertising Mgr., phone (212)460-1700, fax (212)533-0108; Emile Zuckerkandl, Editor-in-Chief. **ISSN:** 0022-2844. **Subscription Rates:** $999 institutions /Industry. **Remarks:** Accepts advertising. **URL:** http://link.springer-ny.com.
Ad Rates: BW: $565   **Circ:** Combined 1,075
              4C: $1,285

168 Journal of Nonlinear Science
Springer-Verlag New York Inc.
175 5th Ave.
New York, NY 10010

Phone: (212)460-1500
Fax: (212)473-6272
Free: (800)777-4643

Publisher E-mail: journals@springer-ny.com

Science journal. **Freq:** Quarterly. **Key Personnel:** Robert Vrooman, Advertising Mgr. **ISSN:** 0938-8974. **Subscription Rates:** $98 individuals; $299 institutions. **Remarks:** Accepts advertising.

Ad Rates:	BW: $400	Circ: Combined 450
	4C: $1,120	

169 Journal of Plant Growth Regulation
Springer-Verlag New York Inc.
175 5th Ave.
New York, NY 10010

Phone: (212)460-1500
Fax: (212)473-6272
Free: (800)777-4643

Publisher E-mail: journals@springer-ny.com

Science journal. **Subtitle:** Published in cooperation with the Plant Growth Regulator Society of America and the International Plant Growth Substances Association. **Founded:** 1982. **Freq:** Quarterly. **Trim Size:** 8 1/4 x 11. **Key Personnel:** Robert Vrooman, Advertising Mgr., phone (212)460-1700, fax (212)533-0108. **ISSN:** 0721-7595. **Subscription Rates:** $226 institutions. **Remarks:** Accepts advertising. **URL:** http://link.springer-ny.com.

Ad Rates:	BW: $395	Circ: Combined 825
	4C: $1,195	

170 Kidney
Springer-Verlag New York Inc.
175 5th Ave.
New York, NY 10010

Phone: (212)460-1500
Fax: (212)473-6272
Free: (800)777-4643

Publisher E-mail: journals@springer-ny.com

Journal containing article summaries on nephrology literature. **Subtitle:** A Current Survey of World Literature. **Founded:** 1992. **Freq:** Bimonthly. **Key Personnel:** Jay Feinman, Advertising Rep., phone (212)460-1682; Rob Albano, Mktg. Mgr. of Medicine, phone (212)460-1571, ralbano@springerny.com. **ISSN:** 0940-7936. **Subscription Rates:** $99 individuals; $155 institutions. **Remarks:** Accepts advertising. **Alt. Formats:** Microform.

Ad Rates:	BW: $825	Circ: Combined 850
	4C: $1,625	

171 Lung
Springer-Verlag New York Inc.
175 5th Ave.
New York, NY 10010

Phone: (212)460-1500
Fax: (212)473-6272
Free: (800)777-4643

Publisher E-mail: journals@springer-ny.com

Journal featuring articles, reviews, editorials, case reports, and technical notes on aspects of clinical and basic research dealing with lungs, airways, and breathing. **Founded:** 1903. **Freq:** Bimonthly. **Print Method:** Offset. **Trim Size:** 6 1/2 x 9 1/2. **Key Personnel:** Jay Feinman, Advertising Rep., phone (212)460-1682, fax (212)533-0108; Rob Albano, Mktg. Mgr. of Medicine, phone (212)460-1571, ralbano@springer-ny.com. **ISSN:** 0341-2040. **Subscription Rates:** $122 individuals; $299 institutions. **Remarks:** Accepts advertising. **Available Online. URL:** http://www.springer-ny.com. **Alt. Formats:** Microform.

Ad Rates:	BW: $525	Circ: Combined 725
	4C: $1,125	

172 Mammalian Genome
Springer-Verlag New York Inc.
175 5th Ave.
New York, NY 10010

Phone: (212)460-1500
Fax: (212)473-6272
Free: (800)777-4643

Publisher E-mail: journals@springer-ny.com

Genetics journal. **Subtitle:** Official Journal of the International Mammalian Genome Society. **Founded:** 1990. **Freq:** Monthly. **Print Method:** Offset. **Trim Size:** 8 1/4 x 11. **Cols./Page:** 2. **Key Personnel:** Lee M. Silver, Editor; Joseph H. Nadeau, Editor; Bob Vrooman, Advertising Manager. **ISSN:** 0938-8990. **Subscription Rates:** $199; $499 institutions. **URL:** http://link.springer-ny.com.

Ad Rates:	BW: $685	Circ: Combined 1,050
	4C: $1,405	

173 The Mathematical Intelligencer
Springer-Verlag New York Inc.
175 5th Ave.
New York, NY 10010

Phone: (212)460-1500
Fax: (212)473-6272
Free: (800)777-4643

Publisher E-mail: journals@springer-ny.com

Mathematics journal. **Founded:** 1978. **Freq:** Quarterly. **Trim Size:** 8 1/4 x 11. **Key Personnel:** Brian Skepton, Advertising Mgr., phone (212)460-1575, fax (212)533-0108. **ISSN:** 0343-6993. **Subscription Rates:** $39.

Ad Rates:	BW: $825	Circ: Combined 5,000
	4C: $1,600	

174 Microbial Ecology
Springer-Verlag New York Inc.
175 5th Ave.
New York, NY 10010

Phone: (212)460-1500
Fax: (212)473-6272
Free: (800)777-4643

Publisher E-mail: journals@springer-ny.com

Journal containing articles in all areas of ecology involving microorganisms. **Subtitle:** An International Journal. **Founded:** 1974. **Freq:** Bimonthly. **Print Method:** Offset. **Trim Size:** 8 1/4 x 11. **Cols./Page:** 1. **Col. Width:** 54 nonpareils. **Col. Depth:** 105 agate lines. **Key Personnel:** S.K. Frederick, Editor-in-Chief; Robert Vrooman, Advertising Mgr., phone (212)460-1700, fax (212)533-0108. **ISSN:** 0095-3628. **Subscription Rates:** $140 individuals; $399 institutions Industry. **Remarks:** Accepts advertising. **URL:** http://link.springer-ny.com.

Ad Rates:	BW: $485	Circ: Combined 1,500
	4C: $1,085	

175 Open City
Open City, Inc.
225 Lafayette St., Ste. 1114
New York, NY 10012
Publication E-mail: editors@opencity.org
Publisher E-mail: editors@opencity.org

Phone: (212)625-9048
Fax: (212)625-2030

Consumer literary magazine covering fiction, poetry, and essay. **Founded:** 1990. **Freq:** Triennial. **Key Personnel:** Thomas Beller, Editor; Daniel Pinchbeck, Editor; Joanna Yas, Managing Editor; Nick Stone, Art Dir.; Robert Bingham, Founding Pub.; Stephen Macgillivray, Webmaster. **Subscription Rates:** $30 individuals; $55 two years; $10 single issue. **URL:** http://www.opencity.org.

176 Pain Digest
Springer-Verlag New York Inc.
175 5th Ave.
New York, NY 10010

Phone: (212)460-1500
Fax: (212)473-6272
Free: (800)777-4643

Publisher E-mail: journals@springer-ny.com

Journal featuring abstracts on pain literature. **Founded:** 1991. **Freq:** Bimonthly. **Key Personnel:** Vicki Finiello, Assoc. Ed.; Rob Albano, Mktg. Mgr., Medicine, phone (212)460-1571, ralbano@springer-ny.com; Jay Feinman, Advertising Mgr., phone (212)460-1682. **ISSN:** 0938-9016. **Subscription Rates:** $119 individuals; $219 institutions. **Remarks:** Accepts advertising. **Alt. Formats:** Microform.

Ad Rates:	BW: $660	Circ: Combined 1,000
	4C: $1,380	

177 Pediatric Cardiology
Springer-Verlag New York Inc.
175 5th Ave.
New York, NY 10010

Phone: (212)460-1500
Fax: (212)473-6272
Free: (800)777-4643

Publisher E-mail: journals@springer-ny.com

Journal devoted to the diagnosis and management of heart disease in young people. **Founded:** 1979. **Freq:** Bimonthly. **Print Method:** Offset. **Cols./Page:** 2. **Col. Width:** 40 nonpareils. **Col. Depth:** 138 agate lines. **Key Personnel:** Rob Albano, Mktg. Mgr., Medicine, phone (212)460-1571, ralbano@springer-ny.com; Jay Feinman, Advertising Representative, phone (212)460-1682. **ISSN:** 0172-0643. **Subscription Rates:** $99 individuals; $242 institutions. **Remarks:** Accepts advertising. **Available Online. URL:** http://www.springer-ny.com. **Alt. Formats:** Microform.

Ad Rates:	BW: $645	Circ: Combined 1,375
	4C: $1,395	

☐ **178 Radical History Review**
Duke University Press
Tamiment Library
New York University
70 Washington Sq. S., 10th Fl.
New York, NY 10012   Phone: (212)998-2632
Publication E-mail: rhr@igc.org

Journal focusing on historical scholarship from a political perspective. **Freq:** 3/year. **Trim Size:** 4 7/8 x 7 3/4. **ISSN:** 0163-6545. **Subscription Rates:** $90 institutions; $81 institutions electronic only; $35 individuals; $22 students. **Remarks:** Accepts advertising. **Available Online.**
Ad Rates: BW: $440   **Circ:** Paid 1,200

☐ **179 Railway Age**
Simmons-Boardman Publishing Corp.
345 Hudson St.   Phone: (212)620-7200
New York, NY 10014   Fax: (212)633-1165
                                           Free: (800)895-4389
Publication E-mail: railwayage@aol.com
Publisher E-mail: bdemarco@sbpub.com

Magazine focusing on railroad and rail transit. **Founded:** 1856. **Freq:** Monthly. **Print Method:** Offset. **Trim Size:** 8 x 10 7/8. **Cols./Page:** 3. **Col. Width:** 26 nonpareils. **Col. Depth:** 140 agate lines. **Key Personnel:** William Vantuono, Editor; Robert P. DeMarco, Publisher. **ISSN:** 0033-8826. **Subscription Rates:** $55 individuals. **Remarks:** Accepts advertising.
Ad Rates: GLR: $4,080   **Circ:** Paid 998
        BW: $4,800   Non-paid 23,730
        4C: $6,735

☐ **180 Semigroup Forum**
Springer-Verlag New York Inc.
175 5th Ave.   Phone: (212)460-1500
New York, NY 10010   Fax: (212)473-6272
                                           Free: (800)777-4643
Publisher E-mail: journals@springer-ny.com

Journal containing survey and research articles, announcements of new results, research problems, short notes, and abstracts and bibliographic items of completed works on semigroup theory. **Founded:** 1970. **Freq:** Bimonthly (Jan.,Mar.,May,July,Sept.,Nov.). **Print Method:** Offset. **Trim Size:** 6 1/2 x 9 1/2. **Cols./Page:** 1. **Col. Width:** 54 nonpareils. **Col. Depth:** 124 agate lines. **Key Personnel:** Robert Vrooman, Advertising Mgr. **ISSN:** 0037-1912. **Subscription Rates:** $130; $249 Industry. **Remarks:** Accepts advertising.
Ad Rates: BW: $400   **Circ:** Combined 550
        4C: $920

☐ **181 Skyscraper**
Skyscraper Magazine
PO Box 1595
New York, NY 10276

Consumer magazine covering music. **Key Personnel:** Peter Bottomley, Advertising. **Remarks:** Accepts advertising. **URL:** http://www.skyscrapermagazine.com.
                                          Circ: (Not Reported)

☐ **182 Soviet Metal Technology**
Primary Sources
PO Box 472, Cooper Sta.
New York, NY 10276-0472   Phone: (212)254-8748
Publication E-mail: primsrc@aol.com
Publisher E-mail: Primsrc@aol.com

Publication covering selected papers from four Russian periodicals: *Koks I Khimiya (Coke and Chemistry), Stal' (Steel), Tsvetnye Metally (Non-Ferrous Metals),* and *Zavodskaya Laboratoriya (Factory Laboratory)..* **Freq:** Quarterly. **ISSN:** 1958-1959. **Subscription Rates:** $223 individuals; $190 universities.

☐ **183 World Journal of Surgery**
Springer-Verlag New York Inc.
175 5th Ave.   Phone: (212)460-1500
New York, NY 10010   Fax: (212)473-6272
                                           Free: (800)777-4643
Publisher E-mail: journals@springer-ny.com

Medical journal covering surgical developments. **Founded:** 1977. **Freq:** Monthly. **Print Method:** Offset. **Trim Size:** 8 1/4 x 11. **Cols./Page:** 2. **Col. Width:** 38 nonpareils. **Col. Depth:** 128 agate lines. **Key Personnel:** Ronald K. Tompkins, Editor; Brian Skepton, Advertising Mgr., phone (212)460-1575, fax (212)533-0108; Rob Albano, Mktg. Mgr., Medicine, phone (212)460-1571, ralbano@springer-ny.com. **ISSN:** 0364-2313. **Subscription Rates:** $166 individuals; $340 institutions. **Remarks:** Accepts advertising. **Available Online. URL:** http://www.springer-ny.com. **Alt. Formats:** Microform.
Ad Rates: BW: $950   **Circ:** Combined 5,000
        4C: $1,695

ROCHESTER

☐ **184 Catholic Courier**
Rochester Catholic Press Association
PO Box 24379   Phone: (585)529-9530
Rochester, NY 14624-0379   Free: (800)600-3628
Publication E-mail: newsroom@catholiccarrier.com
Publisher E-mail: info@catholiccourier.com

Catholic and non-political newspaper. **Founded:** 1889. **Freq:** Weekly (Thurs.) except last Thurs. in Dec. **Print Method:** Offset. **Trim Size:** 11 1/4 x 12 1/2. **Cols./Page:** 4. **Col. Width:** 13 1/2 picas. **Col. Depth:** 11.625 inches. **Key Personnel:** Most Rev. Matthew H. Clark, Publisher; Karen M. Franz, General Mgr./Editor; Jennifer Ficcaglia, Asst. Editor; Donna Stubbings, Circulation Mgr., dstubbings@catholiccourier.com; Kim Parks, Graphics Manager, kparks@catholiccourier.com. **USPS:** 135-580. **Subscription Rates:** $20. **Remarks:** Accepts advertising. **URL:** http://www.catholiccourier.com. **Alt. Formats:** Microform. **Formerly:** Courier-Journal; Catholic Courier-Journal.
Ad Rates: BW: $1,698   **Circ:** Paid ⊕43,471
        4C: $2,098
        PCI: $46

NORTH CAROLINA

BOONE

☐ **185 Appalachian Journal**
Appalachian State University
Belk Library
PO Box 32026   Phone: (828)262-4072
Boone, NC 28608   Fax: (828)262-2553

Scholarly journal covering regional Appalachian history, politics, literature and culture. **Subtitle:** A Regional Studies Review. **Founded:** 1972. **Freq:** Quarterly. **Print Method:** Offset. **Trim Size:** 10 1/2 x 7. **Key Personnel:** Sandra L. Ballard, ballardsl@appstate.edu. **ISSN:** 0090-3779. **Subscription Rates:** $18 individuals; $6 single issue. **Remarks:** Advertising not accepted.
                                          Circ: Paid 500

CHAPEL HILL

☐ **186 Beethoven Forum**
University of Illinois Press
University of North Carolina at Chapel Hill
Department of Music
Hill Hall, CB3320
Chapel Hill, NC 27599-3320
Publisher E-mail: uipress@uillinois.edu

Scholarly journal covering the work of Beethoven. **Freq:** Semiannual. **Key Personnel:** Mark Evan Bonds, Editor-in-Chief, mbonds@nc.rr.com; Clydette Wantland, Advertising, phone (217)244-6496, fax (217)244-8082, cwantlan@uillinois.edu. **ISSN:** 1059-5031. **Subscription Rates:** $65 institutions; $75 institutions out of country; $35 individuals; $45 individuals out of

Ad Rates: GLR = general line rate; BW = one-time black & white page rate; 4C = one-time four color page rate; SAU = standard advertising unit rate; CNU = Canadian newspaper advertising unit rate; PCI = per column inch rate.
Circulation: ★ = ABC; △ = BPA; ♦ = CAC; ● = CCAB; ☐ = VAC; ⊕ = PO Statement; ‡ = Publisher's Report; Boldface figures = sworn; Light figures = estimated.
Entry type: ☐ = Print; ♨ = Broadcast.

21

country; $35 single issue. **Remarks:** Accepts advertising. **URL:** http://www.press.uillinois.edu/journals/bf.html.
Ad Rates: BW: $225   **Circ:** (Not Reported)

📖 **187 The Carolina Quarterly**
University of North Carolina at Chapel Hill
Greenlaw Hall, CB 3520   Phone: (919)962-0244
Chapel Hill, NC 27599-3520   Fax: (919)962-3520
Publication E-mail: cquarter@unc.edu

Literary journal covering fiction, poetry, essays, nonfiction, artwork and reviews. **Founded:** 1948. **Freq:** Triennial. **Trim Size:** 6 x 9. **ISSN:** 0008-6797. **Subscription Rates:** $12 individuals; $5 single issue; $15 other countries; $15 institutions; $18 other countries institutions. **Remarks:** Accepts advertising. **URL:** http://www.unc.edu/student/orgs/cquarter. **Alt. Formats:** Microform.
Ad Rates: BW: $80   **Circ:** Combined 900

📖 **188 Village Advocate**
The Village Publishing Corp.
505 W. Franklin St.   Phone: (919)932-2000
Chapel Hill, NC 27516   Fax: (919)932-2027

Shopper. **Founded:** 1969. **Freq:** Semiweekly (Wed. and Sun.). **Print Method:** Offset. **Cols./Page:** 4. **Col. Width:** 27 nonpareils. **Col. Depth:** 197 agate lines. **Key Personnel:** Douglas F. Rogers, Publisher. **Subscription Rates:** Free. **Remarks:** Advertising accepted; rates available upon request.
                 Circ: Wed. ◆**17,848**
                      Sun. ◆**17,735**

GREENSBORO

📖 **189 The Shuttle Sheet**
Pace Communications, Inc.
1301 Carolina St.   Phone: (336)378-6065
Greensboro, NC 27401-1001   Fax: (336)274-2679

In-flight magazine covering events and news relevant to Boston, Washington, DC, and New York. **Print Method:** Web offset. **Trim Size:** 8 x 10 7/8. **Cols./Page:** 3. **Subscription Rates:** Free. **Remarks:** Accepts advertising. **URL:** http://www.shuttlesheet.com.
Ad Rates: 4C: $8,415   **Circ:** (Not Reported)

OHIO

BOWLING GREEN

📖 **190 Inquiry**
Philosophy Documentation Center
Dan Fasko, Editor
550 Education Bldg.
Bowling Green University
Bowling Green, OH 43403-0151
Publication E-mail: order@pdcnet.org
Publisher E-mail: order@pdcnet.org

Scholarly journal covering critical thinking in post-secondary educational contexts. **Subtitle:** Critical Thinking Across the Disciplines. **Freq:** Quarterly. **Key Personnel:** Dan Fasko, Editor, dfasko@bgnet.bgsu.edu. **ISSN:** 1093-1082. **Subscription Rates:** $70 institutions; $30 individuals; $17 single issue institutions; $8 single issue individuals. **URL:** http://www.pdcnet.org/inq.html.

CHILLICOTHE

📖 **191 County Line Advertiser**
Add Inc.—Ohio Group
147 W. Water St.   Phone: (740)773-5010
Chillicothe, OH 45601   Fax: (740)773-5021

Shopping guide. **Founded:** 1999. **Freq:** Weekly (Sun.). **Print Method:** Photo offset. **Key Personnel:** Mike Ricken, Publisher; Skip Heinlein, Circ. Exec. **Subscription Rates:** Free. **Remarks:** Accepts advertising.
             Circ: Non-paid ◆**3,881**

CLEVELAND

📖 **192 The Montrose Sun**
Sun Newspapers
5510 Cloverleaf Pkwy.   Phone: (216)986-2600
Cleveland, OH 44125-4887   Fax: (216)986-2380
                     Free: (800)362-8008

Publication E-mail: sun@sunnews.com
Publisher E-mail: sun@sunnews.com

Community newspaper. **Founded:** 2000. **Freq:** Weekly (Thurs.). **Trim Size:** 11 5/8 x 21 1/4. **Cols./Page:** 6. **Col. Width:** 1 5/6 inches. **Col. Depth:** 21 1/4 inches. **Key Personnel:** John M. Urbancich, Pres./General Mgr.; Tom Kessler, Editor; Dwight Schulz, Operations Mgr.; W. Peter Deverall, VP Sales/Mktg.; Tim Schmidt, Operations Dir./Circ. Dir.; Linda Kinsey, Exec. Editor. **USPS:** 369-490. **Subscription Rates:** $33.80 by mail. **Remarks:** Accepts advertising. **URL:** http://www.sunnews.com. **Feature Editors:** Barbara Collier, *Food*; Sharyn Hinman, *Features*; Dennis Seeds, *Features*; Stan Urankar, *Entertainment*.
Ad Rates: BW: $2,486.25   **Circ:** Combined ‡22,741
            PCI: $19.50

📖 **193 The Sun**
Sun Newspapers
5510 Cloverleaf Pkwy.   Phone: (216)986-2600
Cleveland, OH 44125-4887   Fax: (216)986-2380
                     Free: (800)362-8008

Publication E-mail: sun@sunnews.com
Publisher E-mail: sun@sunnews.com

Community newspaper. **Founded:** 1990. **Freq:** Weekly (Thurs.). **Trim Size:** 11 5/8 x 21 1/4. **Cols./Page:** 6. **Col. Width:** 1 5/6 inches. **Col. Depth:** 21 1/4 inches. **Key Personnel:** John M. Urbancich, Pres./General Mgr.; Kevin Burns, Editor; Dwight Schulz, Operations Mgr.; W. Peter Deverall, VP Sales/Mktg.; Tim Schmidt, Operations Dir./Circ. Dir.; Linda Kinsey, Exec. Editor. **USPS:** 012-731. **Subscription Rates:** $33.80 by mail. **Remarks:** Accepts advertising. **URL:** http://www.sunnews.com. **Feature Editors:** Barbara Collier, *Food*; Sharyn Hinman, *Features*; Dennis Seeds, *Features*; Stan Urankar, *Entertainment*.
Ad Rates: BW: $1,402.50   **Circ:** Combined ★**3,409**
            PCI: $11

📖 **194 West Akron Sun**
Sun Newspapers
5510 Cloverleaf Pkwy.   Phone: (216)986-2600
Cleveland, OH 44125-4887   Fax: (216)986-2380
                     Free: (800)362-8008

Publication E-mail: sun@sunnews.com
Publisher E-mail: sun@sunnews.com

Community newspaper. **Founded:** 2001. **Freq:** Weekly (Thurs.). **Trim Size:** 11 5/8 x 21 1/4. **Cols./Page:** 6. **Col. Width:** 1 5/6 inches. **Col. Depth:** 21 1/4 inches. **Key Personnel:** John M. Urbancich, Pres./General Mgr.; Tom Kessler, Editor; Dwight Schulz, Operations Mgr.; W. Peter Deverall, VP Sales/Mktg.; Tim Schmidt, Operations Dir./Circ. Dir.; Linda Kinsey, Exec. Editor. **Subscription Rates:** $33.80 by mail. **Remarks:** Accepts advertising. **URL:** http://www.sunnews.com. **Feature Editors:** Barbara Collier, *Food*; Sharyn Hinman, *Features*; Dennis Seeds, *Features*; Stan Urankar, *Entertainment*.
Ad Rates: BW: $2,486.25   **Circ:** Combined ‡22,741
            PCI: $19.50

NEW PHILADELPHIA

📖 **195 The National Hobby News**
NHN Publishing
PO Box 612
New Philadelphia, OH 44663-0612   Phone: (330)339-6338
Publication E-mail: ru1219@webtv.net
Publisher E-mail: ru1219@webtv.net

Newspaper covering antiques and collecting for hobbyists and small businesses. **Founded:** Oct. 1980. **Freq:** Triennial. **Key Personnel:** Woody Russell, Editor and Publisher; Marsha Mariatt, Managing Editor; Kay Conner, Prod. Asst. & Review Editor; Jill L. Martinelli, Circulation. **Subscription Rates:** $5 two years. **Remarks:** Accepts advertising.
Ad Rates: PCI: $10   **Circ:** (Not Reported)

WESTERVILLE

📖 **196 Ceramic Source**
The American Ceramic Society
735 Ceramic Pl.   Phone: (614)794-4700
Westerville, OH 43081   Fax: (614)794-6109
Publication E-mail: customersrvc@acers.org
Publisher E-mail: customersrvc@acers.org

Trade magazine covering materials and equipment used to manufacture ceramic products or buyers and sellers. **Freq:** Annual. **Print Method:** Offset. **Trim Size:** 8 1/8 x 10 7/8. **Cols./Page:** 3. **Col. Width:** 27 nonpareils. **Col. Depth:** 140 agate lines. **Key Personnel:** Patricia A. Janeway, Editor, phone (614)794-5826, pjaneway@acers.org; Peter Scott, Advertising Mgr., phone (614)794-5844, pscott@acers.org. **Subscription Rates:** Free to qualified subscribers; $25 nonmembers. **Remarks:** Accepts advertising. **URL:** http://www.ceramicsource.org.

Ad Rates: BW: $3,925   **Circ:** Paid 14,500
                 4C: $5,325   Non-paid 6,000

OKLAHOMA

CHICKASHA

🎙 **197 KWCO-FM - 105.5**
PO Box 1268   Phone: (405)224-1560
Chickasha, OK 73023-1268   Fax: (405)224-2890
E-mail: kwco@aol.com

Format: Classic Rock. **Simulcasts:** KWCO-AM. **Founded:** 1968. **Formerly:** KXXK-FM. **Operating Hours:** Continuous. **Key Personnel:** Bruce McGrew, General Mgr.; Jennifer McGrew, Business Mgr.; Bruce McGrew, General Sales Mgr. **Wattage:** 6000. **Ad Rates:** $10-16 for 30 seconds; $12-20 for 60 seconds.

GRANDFIELD

📖 **198 Big Pasture News**
PO Box 608
Grandfield, OK 73546-0608

Community newspaper. **Founded:** 1907. **Freq:** Weekly. **Print Method:** Offset. **Cols./Page:** 5. **Col. Width:** 28 nonpareils. **Col. Depth:** 294 agate lines. **Key Personnel:** Kent Kinzer, Publisher, phone (580)479-5757, fax (580)479-5232. **USPS:** 005-588. **Subscription Rates:** $15 individuals.

Ad Rates: GLR: $2.50   **Circ:** Paid ‡520

OREGON

PORTLAND

📖 **199 Today's OEA**
Oregon Education Association
6900 SW Atlanta St.   Phone: (503)684-3300
Portland, OR 97223-2513   Fax: (503)684-8063

Membership magazine covering educational issues statewide and in the U.S. **Freq:** Bimonthly September through June. **Key Personnel:** Amber Cole, Editor; Kris Kain, President; Joann Waller, Exec. Dir.; Janine Leggett, Communications Specialist, janine.leggett@oregoned.org. **ISSN:** 0030-4689. **Subscription Rates:** Free to qualified subscribers; $10 nonmembers. **Remarks:** Accepts advertising.

Circ: (Not Reported)

PENNSYLVANIA

ALLENTOWN

📖 **200 The Morning Call**
101 N. 6th St., No. 1260   Phone: (610)820-6500
Allentown, PA 18101-1403   Fax: (610)820-6617

General newspaper. **Founded:** 1888. **Freq:** Mon.-Sun. (morn.). **Print**

Method: Letterpress. **Cols./Page:** 6. **Col. Width:** 25 nonpareils. **Col. Depth:** 300 agate lines. **Key Personnel:** Lawrence Hymans, Editor; Gary K. Shorts, Publisher; Robert Richelderfer, Advertising Mgr. **Remarks:** Accepts advertising. **Online:** Dialog (The Dialog Corporation). **Feature Editors:** Joel Bieler, *Photo*, phone (215)820-6537; Van Cavett, *Editorials*, phone (215)820-6728; Paul F. Reinhard, *Sports*, phone (215)820-6515; Charles Jaffe, *Financial/Business*, phone (215)820-6694; Jame Kelly, *Family*, phone (215)820-6117; James Kelly, *Lifestyle*, phone (215)820-6741; Randy Kraft, *Travel*, phone (215)820-6557; Sylvia Lawler, *TV*, phone (215)820-6733; Linda Luther, *Sunday*, phone (215)820-6656; Polly Rayner, *Fashion, Society, Women's*, phone (215)820-6515; Al Roberts, *City, News, Political, Real Estate, Rural Development*, phone (215)820-6566; Rosa Salter, *Science*, phone (215)820-6750; Diane Stoneback, *Food, Garden/Home*, phone (215)820-6526; David Venditta, *Religion*, phone (215)820-6566; Paul Willistein, *Book, Drama, Features, Movie, Music*, phone (215)820-6546; Ann Wlazelek, *Medical*, phone (215)820-6745.

Ad Rates: PCI: $32.45   **Circ:** Mon.-Sat. 127,175
                                               Sun. 170,744

EDINBORO

🎙 **201 WXTA-FM - 97.9**
471 Robison Rd.   Phone: (814)868-5355
Erie, PA 16509-5425   Fax: (814)868-1876

Format: Country. **Owner:** Regent Broadcasting of Erie, Inc., at above address. **Founded:** 1988. **Operating Hours:** Continuous. **ADI:** Erie, PA. **Key Personnel:** Gary Spurgeon, General Mgr., GSpurgeon@Regentcomm.com; Donna Palowitz, Sales Dir., fax (814)864-4837, DPalowitz@Regentcomm.com; Ed Benks, Sales Mgr., fax (814)868-4837, EBenks@Regenterie.com; Marcia Diehl, Business Mgr., fax (814)864-5816, MDiehl@Regentcomm.com; Fred Horton, Program Dir., Unclefred@Regenterie.com. **Wattage:** 10,000. **Ad Rates:** $25-60 per unit.

ERIE

🎙 **WXTA-FM** - See Edinboro

HANOVER

📖 **202 Sun Marketplace**
The Evening Sun
135 Baltimore St.   Phone: (717)637-3736
Hanover, PA 17331   Fax: (717)637-7730

Community newspaper. **Founded:** 1997. **Freq:** Weekly (Wed.). **Print Method:** Photo offset. **Key Personnel:** Norman C. Bollack, Circ. Exec. **Subscription Rates:** Free.

Circ: Non-paid ♦28,489

LANSDALE

📖 **203 The Reporter**
Journal Register Co.
307 Derstine Ave.   Phone: (215)855-8440
Lansdale, PA 19446-3532   Fax: (215)855-3432
                                             Free: (800)220-8440

General newspaper. **Founded:** 1870. **Freq:** Daily (eve.) and Sat. (morn.). **Print Method:** Offset. **Cols./Page:** 6. **Col. Width:** 1.833 inches. **Col. Depth:** 301 agate lines. **Key Personnel:** Phil Freedman, Editor, phone (215)364-8820, fax (215)855-3432, pfreedman@thereporteronline.com; Al Frattura, Publisher, phone (215)361-8801, fax (215)361-2142, afrattura@journalregister.com; Craig Schwartz, Advertising Dir., phone (215)361-8855, fax (215)855-6147, cschwartz@thereporteronline.com. **Subscription Rates:** $117. **Remarks:** Accepts advertising.

Ad Rates: GLR: $2.50   **Circ:** 18,602
                 BW: $3,208.23
                 4C: $3,678.23
                 SAU: $24.87

Ad Rates: GLR = general line rate; BW = one-time black & white page rate; 4C = one-time four color page rate; SAU = standard advertising unit rate; CNU = Canadian newspaper advertising unit rate; PCI = per column inch rate.
Circulation: ★ = ABC; △ = BPA; ♦ = CAC; ● = CCAB; ❏ = VAC; ⊕ = PO Statement; ‡ = Publisher's Report; Boldface figures = sworn; Light figures = estimated.
Entry type: 📖 = Print; 🎙 = Broadcast.

MOUNT JOY

📖 **204 Where & When Pennsylvania's Travel Guide**
Enge Printing and Publishing Company
1425 W. Main St.
PO Box 500
Mount Joy, PA 17552

Phone: (717)492-2536
Fax: (717)653-6165
Free: (800)800-1833

Guide to travel, events, and activities across Pennsylvania. **Subtitle:** Pennsylvania's Travel Guide. **Founded:** 1966. **Freq:** Quarterly. **Print Method:** Web. **Trim Size:** 5 3/8 x 8 1/4 INS. **Cols./Page:** 2. **Col. Width:** 32 nonpareils. **Col. Depth:** 114 agate lines. **Key Personnel:** Marty P. Wilcox, Publications Mgr., phone (800)326-9584, fax (814)238-3415, mimi@barashgroup.com. **USPS:** 494-950. **Remarks:** Accepts advertising. **URL:** http://www.whereandwhen.com. **Formerly:** Where & When Magazine.
Ad Rates: BW: $2,375   **Circ:** Combined ‡100,000
           4C: $2,875

PENN STATE UNIVERSITY

Pennsylvania History - See State College

PHILADELPHIA

📖 **205 Journal of Musicological Research**
Taylor & Francis
325 Chestnut St., Ste. 800
Philadelphia, PA 19106

Phone: (215)625-8900
Fax: (215)625-2940
Free: (800)354-1420

Publisher E-mail: customerservice@taylorandfrancis.com

Publication covering music. **Freq:** Quarterly. **Trim Size:** 6 x 9. **Key Personnel:** Jill Millard, Contact, Jill.Millard@taylorandfrancis.com; Craig Pacelli, Contact, Craig.Pacelli@taylorandfrancis.com. **ISSN:** 0141-1896. **Online:** Gale Group. **Formerly:** Music & Man.

📖 **206 L I T: Literature Interpretation Theory**
Taylor & Francis
325 Chestnut St., Ste. 800
Philadelphia, PA 19106

Phone: (215)625-8900
Fax: (215)625-2940
Free: (800)354-1420

Publisher E-mail: customerservice@taylorandfrancis.com

Publication covering literature and writing. **Freq:** Quarterly. **Trim Size:** 6 x 9. **Key Personnel:** Jill Millard, Contact, Jill.Millard@taylorandfrancis.com; Craig Pacelli, Contact, Craig.Pacelli@taylorandfrancis.com. **ISSN:** 1043-6928. **Subscription Rates:** $89 individuals; $315 institutions; $479 corporate. **Online:** Gale Group.

📖 **207 Molecular Cancer Research**
American Association for Cancer Research, Inc.
150 S. Independence Mall West, Ste. 826
Philadelphia, PA 19106-3483

Phone: (215)440-9300
Fax: (215)440-9354

Publication E-mail: pubs@aacr.org
Publisher E-mail: aacr@aacr.org

Journal of the American Association for Cancer Research covering molecular biology. **Founded:** 1990. **Freq:** Monthly. **Print Method:** Web press. **Trim Size:** 8 3/8 x 10 7/8. **Key Personnel:** Joseph R. Nevins, Ph.D., Editor-in-Chief, phone (919)681-9749, fax (919)684-2790; Robert Eisenman, Editor; Eric R. Fearon, Editor. **ISSN:** 1541-7786. **Subscription Rates:** $50 members; $140 nonmembers; $180 nonmembers out of country. **Remarks:** Accepts advertising. **URL:** http://mcr.aacrjournals.org. **Formerly:** Cell Growth & Differentiation (Nov. 1902).
Ad Rates: BW: $805   **Circ:** Paid 2,400
           4C: $855

📖 **208 World Futures**
Taylor & Francis
325 Chestnut St., Ste. 800
Philadelphia, PA 19106

Phone: (215)625-8900
Fax: (215)625-2940
Free: (800)354-1420

Publisher E-mail: customerservice@taylorandfrancis.com

Publication covering philosophy and religion. **Freq:** Monthly. **Print Method:** Sheetfed. **Trim Size:** 6 x 9. **Key Personnel:** Jill Millard, Contact, Jill.Millard@taylorandfrancis.com; Craig Pacelli, Contact, Craig.Pacelli@taylorandfrancis.com. **ISSN:** 0260-4027. **Subscription Rates:** $177 individuals; $546 institutions; $847 corporate. **Online:** Gale Group.

PITTSBURGH

📖 **209 Public Affairs Quarterly**
University of Illinois Press
University of Pittsburgh
Department of Philosophy
1012 Cathedral of Learning
Pittsburgh, PA 15260

Phone: (412)624-5950
Fax: (412)383-7506

Publisher E-mail: uipress@uillinois.edu

Scholarly journal covering social and political philosophy. **Freq:** Quarterly. **Key Personnel:** Sam Wheeler, Editor; Nicholas Rescher, Exec. Editor, rescher@pitt.edu; Clydette Wantland, Advertising, phone (217)244-6496, fax (217)244-8082, cwantlan@uillinois.edu. **ISSN:** 0887-0373. **Subscription Rates:** $220 institutions; $55 individuals; $75 single issue institutions; $30 single issue individuals. **URL:** http://www.press.uillinois.edu/journals/paq.html.

STATE COLLEGE

📖 **210 Pennsylvania History**
Pennsylvania Historical Association
108 Weaver Bldg.
Penn State University, PA 16802

Phone: (814)238-4053
Fax: (814)863-7840

Publication E-mail: wap1@psuvm.psu.edu
Publisher E-mail: jbf2@psu.edu

Journal on all aspects of Pennsylvania and the middle Atlantic region's history. **Subtitle:** A Journal of Mid-Atlantic Studies. **Founded:** Jan. 1934. **Freq:** Quarterly. **Print Method:** Offset. **Trim Size:** 6 x 9. **Cols./Page:** 1. **Key Personnel:** William Pencak, Editor, wap1@psu.edu; John B. Frantz, Manager, jbfz@psu.edu. **ISSN:** 0031-4528. **Subscription Rates:** $30 individuals per year; $35 institutions per year; $15 students per year. **Remarks:** Accepts advertising.
Ad Rates: BW: $150   **Circ:** ‡1,000

UNIVERSITY PARK

📖 **211 American Philosophical Quarterly**
University of Illinois Press
Pennsylvania State University
Department of Philosophy
240 Sparks Bldg.
University Park, PA 16802-5201

Publisher E-mail: uipress@uillinois.edu

Scholarly journal covering philosophy. **Founded:** 1964. **Freq:** Quarterly. **Key Personnel:** Dale Jacquette, Editor, dlj4@psu.edu. **ISSN:** 0003-0481. **Subscription Rates:** $220 institutions; $55 individuals; $75 single issue institutions; $30 single issue individuals. **URL:** http://www.press.uillinois.edu/journals/apq.html.

VILLANOVA

📖 **212 Epoche**
Philosophy Documentation Center
Walter Brogan, Editor Epoche
Deparment of Philosophy
800 Lancaster Ave.
Villanova University
Villanova, PA 19085-1699

Phone: (610)519-4712
Fax: (610)519-4639

Publication E-mail: order@pdcnet.org
Publisher E-mail: order@pdcnet.org

Scholarly journal covering the history of philosophy. **Subtitle:** A Journal for the History of Philosophy. **Founded:** 1994. **Freq:** Semiannual. **Key Personnel:** Walter Brogan, Editor, walter.brogan@villanova.edu. **ISSN:** 1085-1968. **Subscription Rates:** $80 institutions; $35 individuals; $20 students/retirees; $18 single issue. **URL:** http://www.pdcnet.org/epoche.html.

WILKES BARRE

🎤 **213 WCLH-FM - 90.7**
84 W. South St.
Wilkes Barre, PA 18766

Phone: (570)408-5907
Fax: (570)408-5908
Free: (800)WILKES-U

E-mail: wclh@wclh.net

Format: Alternative/New Music/Progressive; Heavy Metal. **Networks:** AP.

Owner: Wilkes University, PO Box 111, Wilkes Barre, PA 18766, **Free:** (800)WILKES-U. **Founded:** 1972. **Operating Hours:** Continuous; 100% local. **ADI:** Wilkes Barre-Scranton, PA. **Key Personnel:** Dr. Mark Stine, Faculty Adviser, phone (570)408-4169, stine@wilkes.edu; Cory Rosenberger, Station Mgr., phone (570)408-5907, manager@wclh.net; Justin D'Angelo, Music Dir., phone (570)408-2908, music@wclh.net; Leroy Mrozowski, Asst. Music Dir., phone (570)408-2908, metal@wclh.net; Tim Millard, Production Dir., phone (570)408-5907, production@wclh.net; Amanda Darbenzio, Public Relations/Underwriting Dir., phone (570)408-5907, underwriting@wclh.net; Edin Greaney, Sports Dir., phone (570)408-5907, sports@wclh.net; Leroy Mrozowski, Web Master, phone (570)408-2908, webmaster@wclh.net. **Wattage:** 175. **Ad Rates:** Noncommercial; underwriting available. **URL:** http://www.wclh.net; http://www.wclh.org.

RHODE ISLAND

BRISTOL

📖 214 Shopping News South

East Bay Newspapers
1 Bradford St.
PO Box 90   Phone: (401)253-6000
Bristol, RI 02809   Fax: (401)253-6055

Shopping guide. **Freq:** Weekly (Wed.). **Print Method:** Photo offset. **Trim Size:** 11 x 17. **Cols./Page:** 6. **Col. Width:** 1 5/8 inches. **Col. Depth:** 1 inches. **Key Personnel:** R.S. Bosworth, Jr., Publisher. **Subscription Rates:** Free locally.
Ad Rates: PCI: $2.50   **Circ:** Non-paid ♦**7,290**

CRANSTON

📖 215 Cranston Herald

Beacon Communications of Rhode Island
789 Park Ave.   Phone: (401)732-3100
Cranston, RI 02910   Fax: (401)732-3110

Community newspaper. **Founded:** 1923. **Freq:** Weekly (Thurs.). **Print Method:** Offset. **Cols./Page:** 6. **Col. Width:** 12 1/2 picas. **Col. Depth:** 21 1/2 inches. **Key Personnel:** Suda Prohaska, Editor; John Howell, Publisher; Richard Fleischer, Advertising Mgr. **Subscription Rates:** $18. **Remarks:** Accepts advertising.
Ad Rates: BW: $806.25   **Circ:** Paid ♦**2,651**
                4C: $1,074   Non-paid ♦**80**
                PCI: $6.25

PROVIDENCE

📖 216 Bedroom

RTP Publications
301 Friendship St.   Phone: (401)351-0787
Providence, RI 02903-4507   Fax: (401)351-0788
Publisher E-mail: jtatulli@rtppub.com

Trade journal covering construction and benefits of mattresses and sleep surfaces, including innerspring, flotation, foam, visco-elastic foam, latex, adjustable beds, and sleep accessories. **Founded:** 1995. **Freq:** Quarterly. **Print Method:** Web offset. **Trim Size:** 8 3/8 x 10 7/8. **Cols./Page:** 3. **Col. Width:** 2 3/8 inches. **Col. Depth:** 7 inches. **Key Personnel:** Dale T. Read, Publisher/Editor-in-Chief, daler@ertp.com; Jeffrey Flynn, Art Dir., jeflynn@ertp.com; Ann Pearson, Asst. Editor, apearson@ertp.com; Carol Giusti, Production, cgiusti@ertp.com. **ISSN:** 1534-1984. **Subscription Rates:** $16.95 individuals; $39.95 out of country; $5 single issue; $10.95 single issue out of country. **Remarks:** Accepts advertising. **URL:** http://www.specialtybed.com.
Ad Rates: BW: $2,067   **Circ:** Controlled 21,700
                4C: $3,689

WAKEFIELD

📖 217 South County Independent

South County Newspapers, Inc.
202 Church St.   Phone: (401)789-6000
Wakefield, RI 02879-2912   Fax: (401)792-9176
Publisher E-mail: business@scindependent.com

Community newspaper. **Founded:** 1997. **Freq:** Weekly (Thurs.). **Print Method:** Photo offset. **Key Personnel:** Fredrick J. Wilson III, Publisher; Mary Jane Mann, Adv. Exec.; Jerald L. Devine, Circ. Exec.
                                   Circ: Combined ♦**4,741**

SOUTH CAROLINA

BAMBERG

📖 218 Advertizer-Herald

Kilgus Publishing Co.
PO Box 929   Phone: (803)245-5204
Bamberg, SC 29003-0929   Fax: (803)245-3900

Community newspaper. **Founded:** 1967. **Freq:** Weekly (Thurs.). **Print Method:** Offset. **Trim Size:** 13 x 20.5. **Cols./Page:** 6. **Col. Width:** 2 inches. **Col. Depth:** 20.5 inches. **Key Personnel:** Cindy K. Nichols, General Mgr., phone (803)245-5204. **ISSN:** 1535-9131. **Subscription Rates:** $20 individuals. **Remarks:** Accepts advertising. **Formerly:** The Bamberg Herald; The Advertizer.
Ad Rates: BW: $664.20   **Circ:** Paid ⊕**2,504**
                4C: $814.20   Non-paid ⊕**496**
                PCI: $5.40

📖 219 North Trade Journal

Kilgus Publishing Co.
PO Box 929   Phone: (803)245-5204
Bamberg, SC 29003-0929   Fax: (803)245-3900

Community newspaper. **Founded:** 1957. **Freq:** Weekly (Thurs.). **Print Method:** Offset. **Trim Size:** 13 x 20 1/2. **Cols./Page:** 6. **Col. Width:** 2 inches. **Col. Depth:** 20 1/2 inches. **Key Personnel:** Cindy K. Nichols, General Mgr. **USPS:** 303-830. **Subscription Rates:** $17.50 individuals. **Remarks:** Accepts advertising.
Ad Rates: BW: $571.95   **Circ:** Paid ⊕**905**
                4C: $721.95   Non-paid ⊕**395**
                PCI: $4.65

ORANGEBURG

📖 220 Psychology and Education

PO Box 7487, SCSU   Phone: (803)836-7133
Orangeburg, SC 29117   Fax: (803)536-8492

Professional journal covering behavioral sciences and education. **Subtitle:** An Interdisciplinary Journal. **Founded:** 1964. **Freq:** Quarterly. **Trim Size:** 8 1/2 x 5 3/4 in. **Key Personnel:** Dr. Joseph P. Cangemi, Editor, phone (270)842-3436, fax (270)842-0436; Dr. Casimir J. Kowalski, Managing Editor, phone (803)536-2133, fax (803)536-8492. **Subscription Rates:** $24 individuals; $8.50 single issue. **Remarks:** Accepts advertising. **Alt. Formats:** Microform. **Formerly:** Psychology—A Journal of Human Behavior.
Ad Rates: BW: $75   **Circ:** (Not Reported)

SOUTH DAKOTA

DOLAND

📖 221 Conde News

Doland Times Record
PO Box 387   Phone: (605)897-6636
Doland, SD 57436-0387   Fax: (605)897-6636
Publication E-mail: eastarea@nvc.net

Community newspaper. **Freq:** Weekly. **Cols./Page:** 6. **Col. Width:** 13 inches. **Col. Depth:** 21'' inches. **Key Personnel:** Alina Becker, Editor and Publisher;

Tina Sanderson, Asst. Editor. **Subscription Rates:** $25 individuals; $30 out of state. **Remarks:** Accepts advertising.
Ad Rates: PCI: $13   **Circ:** Paid 570

222 Doland Times Record
PO Box 387   Phone: (605)897-6636
Doland, SD 57436-0387   Fax: (605)897-6636
Publication E-mail: eastarea@nvc.net

Community newspaper. **Freq:** Weekly. **Cols./Page:** 6. **Col. Width:** 13 inches. **Col. Depth:** 21'' inches. **Key Personnel:** Alina Becker, Editor and Publisher; Tina Sanderson, Asst. Editor. **Subscription Rates:** $25 individuals; $30 out of state. **Remarks:** Accepts advertising.
Ad Rates: PCI: $13   **Circ:** Paid 570

TENNESSEE

NASHVILLE

223 X-Ray News
Adventures in Publishing
4721 Trousdale Dr., Ste. 120
Nashville, TN 37220   Phone: (615)333-9600
                                              Fax: (615)333-0171
Publisher E-mail: aip@res-xraynews.com

Continuing education publication for X-Ray technician certification. **Freq:** Quarterly. **Subscription Rates:** $95 individuals; $180 two years. **URL:** http://www.res.-xraynews.com/xrn.html.

TEXAS

AUSTIN

224 The American Journal of Criminal Law
The University of Texas School of Law Publications Inc.
727 E Dean Keeton St.   Phone: (512)232-1149
Austin, TX 78705   Fax: (512)471-6988
Publication E-mail: ajcl@mail.law.utexas.edu
Publisher E-mail: publications@mail.law.utexas.edu

Professional journal covering areas of interest to legal scholars and practitioners worldwide, especially in the area of criminal law. **Founded:** 1972. **Freq:** Quarterly. **Print Method:** Web offset. **Trim Size:** 6 3/4 x 10. **ISSN:** 0092-2315. **Subscription Rates:** $30 individuals; $35 other countries. **Remarks:** Accepts advertising. **URL:** http://www.ajcl.org.
                                              Circ: Combined 600

225 Texas Forum on Civil Liberties and Civil Rights
The University of Texas School of Law Publications Inc.
727 E Dean Keeton St.   Phone: (512)232-1149
Austin, TX 78705   Fax: (512)471-6988
Publication E-mail: tfclcr@mail.law.utexas.edu
Publisher E-mail: publications@mail.law.utexas.edu

Scholarly journal covering civil rights and liberties. **Founded:** 1992. **Freq:** Biennial. **Print Method:** Web offset. **Trim Size:** 6 3/4 x 10. **ISSN:** 1085-942X. **Subscription Rates:** $25 individuals; $28 other countries. **Remarks:** Accepts advertising. **Online:** Lexis; Westlaw. **URL:** http://www.tfclcr.org.
Ad Rates: BW: $250   **Circ:** Combined 400

226 Texas Intellectual Property Law Journal
The University of Texas School of Law Publications Inc.
727 E Dean Keeton St.   Phone: (512)232-1149
Austin, TX 78705   Fax: (512)471-6988
Publication E-mail: tiplj@mail.law.utexas.edu
Publisher E-mail: publications@mail.law.utexas.edu

Professional journal covering developments in the areas of patent, copyright, trademark, unfair competition, and trade secret law. **Founded:** 1993. **Freq:** 3 per year. **Print Method:** Web offset. **Trim Size:** 6 3/4 x 10. **Key Personnel:** Paul Goldman, Contact. **ISSN:** 1068-1000. **Subscription Rates:** $25 individuals; $28 other countries. **Remarks:** Accepts advertising. **URL:** http://www.tiplj.org.
Ad Rates: BW: $250   **Circ:** Combined 1,800

227 Texas International Law Journal
The University of Texas School of Law Publications Inc.
727 E Dean Keeton St.   Phone: (512)232-1149
Austin, TX 78705   Fax: (512)471-6988
Publication E-mail: tilj@mail.law.utexas.edu
Publisher E-mail: publications@mail.law.utexas.edu

Professional journal covering international law. **Founded:** 1964. **Freq:** Triennial. **Print Method:** Offset. **Trim Size:** 6 3/4 x 10. **Key Personnel:** Paul Goldman, Publications Mgr. **ISSN:** 0163-7479. **Subscription Rates:** $30 individuals; $35 other countries. **Remarks:** Accepts advertising. **Online:** LEXIS-NEXIS; Westlaw. **URL:** http://www.texasinternationallawjournal.org.
Ad Rates: BW: $250   **Circ:** Paid 600

228 Texas Journal of Women and the Law
The University of Texas School of Law Publications Inc.
727 E Dean Keeton St.   Phone: (512)232-1149
Austin, TX 78705   Fax: (512)471-6988
Publication E-mail: tjwl@mail.law.utexas.edu
Publisher E-mail: publications@mail.law.utexas.edu

Professional journal addressing legal issues that concern women for legal scholars and practitioners. **Founded:** 1990. **Freq:** Semiannual. **Print Method:** Web offset. **Trim Size:** 6 3/4 x 10. **ISSN:** 1058-5427. **Subscription Rates:** $25 individuals; $28 other countries. **Remarks:** Accepts advertising. **URL:** http://www.tjwl.org; http://lexis/nexis.westlaw.
                                              Circ: Combined 450

229 Texas Law Review
The University of Texas School of Law Publications Inc.
727 E Dean Keeton St.   Phone: (512)232-1149
Austin, TX 78705   Fax: (512)471-6988
Publication E-mail: tlr@www.utexas.edu
Publisher E-mail: publications@mail.law.utexas.edu

Journal for the legal profession and legal academics. **Founded:** 1922. **Freq:** 7/year (Nov., Dec., Feb., Mar., Apr., May, Jun.). **Print Method:** Web offset. **Trim Size:** 6 3/4 x 10. **Cols./Page:** 1. **Col. Width:** 60 nonpareils. **Col. Depth:** 98 agate lines. **Key Personnel:** Paul Goldman, Contact. **ISSN:** 0040-4411. **Subscription Rates:** $44 individuals; $50 out of country. **Online:** West Group. **URL:** http://www.texaslawreview.org. **Alt. Formats:** Microform.
Ad Rates: BW: $200   **Circ:** ‡1,800

DALLAS

230 Cowboys & Indians
USFR Media Group
8214 Westchester Dr., Ste. 800   Phone: (214)750-8222
Dallas, TX 75225   Fax: (214)750-4522
                                              Free: (800)982-5370
Publication E-mail: queries@cowboysindians.com

Western lifestyle magazine for general consumers. **Subtitle:** The Premier Magazine of the West. **Founded:** 1992. **Freq:** 8/year. **Key Personnel:** Eric O'Keefe, Editor, eokeefe@cowboysindians.com. **Subscription Rates:** $34 individuals; $5 single issue. **Remarks:** Accepts advertising. **URL:** http://www.cowboysindians.com.
Ad Rates: 4C: $6,465   **Circ:** Paid 101,225

HOUSTON

231 Clear Lake Citizen & Exchange News
Houston Community Newspapers
17511 El Camino   Phone: (281)488-1108
Houston, TX 77058-3049   Fax: (281)286-0750

Community newspaper. **Founded:** 1967. **Freq:** Weekly. **Print Method:** Offset. **Cols./Page:** 6. **Col. Width:** 2 1/8 inches. **Col. Depth:** 21 1/2 inches. **Key Personnel:** Sharon Rickel, Publisher, srickel@hcnonline.com; Mary Alys Cherry, Editor, mcherry@hcnonline.com. **Subscription Rates:** Free. **Remarks:** Accepts advertising.
Ad Rates: PCI: $19.38   **Circ:** 26,700

232 Pipeline News
Oildom Publishing Company of Texas Inc.
PO Box 941669   Phone: (281)558-6930
Houston, TX 77079   Fax: (281)558-7029

Supplement to *Underground Construction* magazine, covering pipeline construction and large civil pipeline projects worldwide. **Freq:** Monthly. **Trim Size:** 8 1/4 x 10 7/8. **Key Personnel:** Oliver C. Klinger III, Pres./Pub., oklinger@oildompublishing.com; Traci Read, Editor, traci@oildompublishing.com; Sheila Coats, Asst. Editor/Circ. Mgr., scoats@oildompublishing.com; Robert Carpenter, Editorial Dir., rcarpenter@oildompublishing.com; Laura Apatini, Art Dir., lapatini@oildompublishing.com. **Subscription Rates:** $85 individuals; $95 Canada; $110 elsewhere; $160 two years; $180 two years Canada; $210 two years elsewhere. **Remarks:** Combined advertising rates available with Underground Construction and Pipeline & Gas Journal. **URL:** http://www.oildompublishing.com/pln/plnewsabout.html.

| Ad Rates: | BW: $800 | Circ: (Not Reported) |
| | 4C: $1,825 | |

📖 **233 Power & Gas Marketing**
Oildom Publishing Company of Texas Inc.
PO Box 941669   Phone: (281)558-6930
Houston, TX 77079   Fax: (281)558-7029

Professional magazine covering power and gas marketing. **Subtitle:** Information and Technology for the Energy Manager. **Freq:** Bimonthly. **Print Method:** Offset. **Trim Size:** 8'' x 10 7/8. **Key Personnel:** Oliver C. Klinger III, Publisher, oklinter@oildompublishing.com; Jamie Craddock, Dir., Marketing/Sr. Editor, craddockent@hotmail.com; Jeff Share, Editor, jshare@oildompublishing.com; Rita Tubb, Managing Editor, rita@oildompublishing.com; Linda Rader, Exec. Consulting Editor, natgas101@worldnet.att.net; Sheri W. Biscardi, Art Dir., biscardi@oildompublishing.com. **Remarks:** Accepts advertising. **URL:** http://www.powerandgasmarketingonline.com.

| Ad Rates: | BW: $4,255 | Circ: Combined **20,000** |
| | 4C: $5,680 | |

📖 **234 Rehabilitation Technology**
Oildom Publishing Company of Texas Inc.
PO Box 941669   Phone: (281)558-6930
Houston, TX 77079   Fax: (281)558-7029
Publication E-mail: ginfo@undergroundinfo.com

Professional magazine covering solutions, technology and equipment available to utilities, municipalities, engineers and contractors design, repair and rehabilitate the underground piping infrastructure. Special supplement to *Underground Construction.* **Freq:** Monthly. **Key Personnel:** Oliver C. Klinger, Pres./Pub., oklinger@undergroundinfo.com; Robert Carpenter, Editor, rcarpen@undergroundinfo.com; Rita Tubb, Managing Editor, rita@undergroundinfo.com; Jeff Griffin, Sr. Editor, upfront@fullnet.net; Traci Read, Assoc. Editor, tread@undergroundinfo.com; Elizabeth Bailey, Art Dir., ebailey@undergroundinfo.com; Sheila Coats, Admin. Mgr., scoats@undergroundinfo.com. **Remarks:** Accepts advertising. **URL:** http://www.oildompublishing.com.

                                       Circ: Combined 32,000

KINGWOOD

📖 **235 Kingwood Observer**
1129 Kingwood Dr.   Phone: (281)359-2799
Kingwood, TX 77339-3033   Fax: (281)359-0017

Community newspaper. **Subtitle:** Kingwood's Local Newspaper. **Founded:** Nov. 1977. **Freq:** Weekly. **Key Personnel:** Cynthia Calvert, Editor, ccalvert@hcnonline.com. **Subscription Rates:** Free. **Remarks:** Accepts advertising. **URL:** http://www.thekingwoodobserver.com.

                                       Circ: Non-paid ❏**25,000**

MARBLE FALLS

📖 **236 101 Fun Things to Do**
Victory Publishing
PO Box 10   Phone: (830)693-7152
Marble Falls, TX 78654   Fax: (830)693-3085

Consumer magazine covering local travel and recreation for residents and visitors. **Founded:** 2000. **Freq:** Triennial. **Print Method:** Web. **Trim Size:** 8 1/4 x 10 3/4. **Cols./Page:** 2. **Col. Width:** 3'' inches. **Col. Depth:** 9'' inches. **Key Personnel:** Dana Lee Alvey, Publisher; Paulette Turner, Operations Mgr., paulette@thepicayune.com; Lindsay Bickerton, Advertising Dir., lind-

say@thepicayune.com; Chris Crews, Editor. **Subscription Rates:** Free. **Remarks:** Accepts advertising.

| Ad Rates: | 4C: $726 | Circ: Non-paid 20,000 |

📖 **237 The Picayune**
Victory Publishing
PO Box 10   Phone: (830)693-7152
Marble Falls, TX 78654   Fax: (830)693-3085

Community newspaper. **Founded:** Apr. 1992. **Freq:** Weekly. **Print Method:** Offset. **Cols./Page:** 6. **Col. Width:** 1 7/8 inches. **Col. Depth:** 21 inches. **Key Personnel:** Dana Lee Alvey, Publisher; Paulette Turner, Operations Mgr., paulette@thepicayune.com; Lindsay Bickerton, Advertising Dir., lindsay@thepicayune.com; Chris Crews, Editor. **Subscription Rates:** Free; $15 by mail. **Remarks:** Accepts advertising.

| Ad Rates: | BW: $1,396 | Circ: Controlled 22,250 |
| | PCI: $11.78 | |

📖 **238 River Cities Tribune**
Victory Publishing
PO Box 10   Phone: (830)693-7152
Marble Falls, TX 78654   Fax: (830)693-3085

Community newspaper. **Freq:** Weekly. **Print Method:** Offset. **Cols./Page:** 6. **Col. Width:** 1 7/8 inches. **Col. Depth:** 21 inches. **Key Personnel:** Dana Lee Alvey, Publisher; Paulette Turner, Operations Mgr., paulette@thepicayune.com; Lindsay Bickerton, Advertising Dir., lindsay@thepicayune.com; Chris Crews, Editor. **Subscription Rates:** $26 individuals; $40 out of state. **Remarks:** Accepts advertising.

                                       Circ: Combined ⊕**4,650**

MCKINNEY

📖 **239 American Cueist Magazine**
5100 Eldorado Pkwy., Ste. 102
PMB 728
McKinney, TX 75070
Publication E-mail: editor@theamericancueist.com

Consumer magazine for pool players. **Founded:** Jan. 1, 1987. **Freq:** Monthly. **Print Method:** Offset. **Trim Size:** 10 3/4 X 8 1/4. **Key Personnel:** Jeff Swan, Editor and Publisher, phone (214)544-1899, fax (972)542-8721, jeff@theamericancueist.com. **Subscription Rates:** $17.95 individuals. **Remarks:** Accepts advertising. **URL:** http://www.theamericancueist.com.

| Ad Rates: | BW: $600 | Circ: Paid 1,000 |
| | 4C: $1,200 | Non-paid 100 |

PEARLAND

📖 **240 Friendswood Journal**
Houston Community Newspapers
PO Box 1830   Phone: (281)485-2785
Pearland, TX 77588   Fax: (281)485-4464

Community newspaper. **Founded:** 1971. **Freq:** Weekly (Wed.). **Print Method:** Offset. **Cols./Page:** 6. **Col. Width:** 12 picas. **Col. Depth:** 21 1/2 inches. **Key Personnel:** Jennifer Hookstra, Editor, jhookstra@hcnonline.com; Sharon Rickel, Publisher, srickel@hcnonline.com. **USPS:** 936-820. **Subscription Rates:** $26 individuals. **URL:** http://www.friendswoodjournal.com.

Ad Rates:	GLR: $10.80	Circ: 3,200
	BW: $619.20	
	4C: $1,046.91	
	SAU: $4.80	

📖 **241 Pearland Journal**
Houston Community Newspapers
PO Box 1830   Phone: (281)485-2785
Pearland, TX 77588   Fax: (281)485-4464

Community newspaper. **Founded:** 1975. **Freq:** Weekly (Wed.). **Print Method:** Offset. **Cols./Page:** 6. **Col. Width:** 12 picas. **Col. Depth:** 21 1/2 inches. **Key Personnel:** Jennifer Hookstra, Editor, jhookstra@hcnonline.com; Sharon Rickel, Publisher, srickel@hcnonline.com. **USPS:** 314-150. **Subscrip-**

Ad Rates: GLR = general line rate; BW = one-time black & white page rate; 4C = one-time four color page rate; SAU = standard advertising unit rate; CNU = Canadian newspaper advertising unit rate; PCI = per column inch rate.
Circulation: ★ = ABC; △ = BPA; ◆ = CAC; • = CCAB; ❏ = VAC; ⊕ = PO Statement; ‡ = Publisher's Report; Boldface figures = sworn; Light figures = estimated.
Entry type: 📖 = Print; 🎤 = Broadcast.

27

tion Rates: $26 individuals. URL: http://www.pearlandjournal.com. **Former-ly**: The Journal (1989).
Ad Rates: PCI: $6.17   **Circ:** ‡3500

VICTORIA

📖 **242 Symploke**
University of Nebraska Press
c/o Jeffrey R. Di Leo, Editor
University of Houston-Victoria
3007 N. Ben Wilson   Phone: (361)570-4201
Victoria, TX 77901   Fax: (361)570-4207
Publication E-mail: jlorder@jhunix.hcf.jhu.edu
Publisher E-mail: pressmail@unl.edu

Scholarly journal covering comparative literature and theory. **Subtitle:** A journal for the intermingling of literary, cultural and theoretical scholarship. **Founded:** 1993. **Freq:** Semiannual. **Trim Size:** 6 x 9. **Key Personnel:** Jeffrey R. Di Leo, Editor-in-Chief, editor@symploke.org. **ISSN:** 1069-0697. **Subscription Rates:** $30 institutions and libraries; $15 individuals; $32.50 institutions and libraries; out of country; $17.50 individuals out of country. **Remarks:** Advertising accepted; rates available upon request. **Online:** Project Muse. **URL:** http://muse.jhu.edu/journals/sym/.
                                              Circ: (Not Reported)

UTAH

SALT LAKE CITY

📖 **243 Journal of Pain and Palliative Care Pharmacotherapy**
The Haworth Press Inc.
College of Pharmacy
Univ. of Utah
305 2000 E. Rm. 258   Phone: (801)581-5986
Salt Lake City, UT 84112-5820   Fax: (801)585-6160
Publisher E-mail: getinfo@haworthpressinc.com

Journal covering pain and symptom control. **Subtitle:** Advances in Acute, Chronic & End-of-Life Symptom Control. **Founded:** 1993. **Freq:** Quarterly. **Trim Size:** 6 x 8 3/8. **Cols./Page:** 1. **Col. Width:** 4 3/8 inches. **Col. Depth:** 7 1/8 inches. **Key Personnel:** Arthur Lipman, Editor, fax (801)585-6160, alipman@pharm.utah.edu; Bill Cohen, Publisher. **ISSN:** 1536-0288. **Sub-scription Rates:** $34 individuals 30% more for Canada; 40% more for other countries; $45 institutions 30% more for Canada; 40% more for other countries; $125 libraries 30% more for Canada; 40% more for other countries. **Remarks:** Advertising not accepted. **URL:** http://www.haworthpress.com. **Alt. Formats:** Microform. **Absorbed:** The Hospice Journal. **Formerly**: Journal of Pharmaceutical Care in Pain and Symptom Control (Jan. 1902); Journal of Pharmacotherapy (1993).
                                              Circ: Paid 3,000

📖 **244 Western Humanities Review**
University of Utah
English Dept.
255 S. Central Campus Dr., Rm. 3500   Phone: (801)581-6070
Salt Lake City, UT 84112-0494   Fax: (801)585-5167
Publication E-mail: whr@mail.hum.utah.edu

Journal of literature, culture, and history. **Founded:** Jan. 1947. **Freq:** Semiannual. **Print Method:** Offset. **Trim Size:** 6 x 9. **Cols./Page:** 1. **Col. Width:** 58 nonpareils. **Col. Depth:** 107 agate lines. **Key Personnel:** Barry Weller, Editor, phone (801)581-6168, barry.weller@m.cc.utah.edu; Paul Ketzle, Managing Editor. **ISSN:** 0043-3845. **Subscription Rates:** $16 U.S. and Canada; $20 institutions U.S. & Canada; $26 other countries; $10 single issue. **Remarks:** Advertising not accepted. **URL:** http://www.hum.utah.edu/whr.
                                              Circ: ‡1,033

VIRGINIA

ALEXANDRIA

📖 **245 American Brewer**
PO Box 20268   Phone: (703)567-1962
Alexandria, VA 22320-1268   Free: (800)474-7291
Publisher E-mail: jimd@brewingnews.com

Magazine covering micro brewing among small to medium sized brewers in the United States. **Subtitle:** The Buisiness of Beer. **Founded:** 1986. **Freq:** 4/year. **Print Method:** Offset. **Trim Size:** 8 1/2 x 11. **Cols./Page:** 3. **Col. Width:** 2 1/4 inches. **Col. Depth:** 9 1/2 inches. **Key Personnel:** Jim Dorsch, Publisher; Bill Metzger, Publisher, bill@brewingnews.com; Greg Kitscok, Editor, greg@brewingnews.com; Jamie Magee, Publisher. **ISSN:** 0887-7418. **Subscription Rates:** $50 individuals; $100 out of country; $10 single issue. **Remarks:** Accepts advertising. **URL:** http://www.americanbrewer.com. **For-merly**: American Brewer (Oct. 9, 1900).
Ad Rates: BW: $1,250   **Circ:** Combined 3,000
                 4C: $1,875

📖 **246 Journal of Counseling and Development**
American Counseling Association
5999 Stevenson Ave.   Phone: (703)823-9800
Alexandria, VA 22304   Fax: (703)823-0252
                                            Free: (800)422-2648
Publisher E-mail: www@counseling.org

Journal for counseling and human development professionals concerning research, empirical data on current issues, and emerging counseling trends. **Freq:** Quarterly. **Print Method:** Offset. **Trim Size:** 8 1/2 x 11. **Key Personnel:** Kathy McGuire, Advertising Dir., phone (317)873-1800, fax (317)873-1899, kmaguire@counseling.org. **ISSN:** 0748-9633. **Subscription Rates:** $40 individuals; $175 institutions. **URL:** http://www.counseling.org.
                                              Circ: Paid 59,000

📖 **247 The Prosecutor**
National District Attorneys Association
99 Canal Center Plaza, Ste. 510   Phone: (703)549-9222
Alexandria, VA 22314   Fax: (703)836-3195

Professional magazine covering law for prosecuting attorneys. **Freq:** Bi-monthly. **Available Online.** **URL:** http://www.ndaa-apri.org.

CHARLOTTESVILLE

📖 **248 Augustinian Studies**
Philosophy Documentation Center
PO Box 7147   Phone: (434)220-3300
Charlottesville, VA 22906-7147   Fax: (434)220-3301
                                            Free: (800)444-2419
Publication E-mail: order@pdcnet.org
Publisher E-mail: order@pdcnet.org

Scholarly journal covering the life, teachings and influence of Augustine of Hippo. **Freq:** Semiannual. **Key Personnel:** Allan D. Fitzgerald, Editor. **ISSN:** 0094-5323. **Subscription Rates:** $40 institutions; $30 individuals; $20 single issue institutions; $15 single issue individuals. **URL:** http://www.pdcnet.org/august.html.

📖 **249 HYLE**
Philosophy Documentation Center
PO Box 7147   Phone: (434)220-3300
Charlottesville, VA 22906-7147   Fax: (434)220-3301
                                            Free: (800)444-2419
Publication E-mail: order@pdcnet.org
Publisher E-mail: order@pdcnet.org

Scholarly journal covering the philosophical aspects of chemistry worldwide. **Subtitle:** An International Journal for the Philosophy of Chemistry. **Freq:** Annual. **Key Personnel:** Joachim Schummer, Editor, editor@hyle.org. **ISSN:** 1433-5158. **Subscription Rates:** $35 institutions; $22 individuals. **URL:** http://www.pdcnet.org/hyle.html.

📖 **250 Philosophy Now**
Philosophy Documentation Center
PO Box 7147   Phone: (434)220-3300
Charlottesville, VA 22906-7147   Fax: (434)220-3301
                                            Free: (800)444-2419
Publication E-mail: order@pdcnet.org
Publisher E-mail: order@pdcnet.org

Magazine covering philosophy for specialists and the general public. **Founded:** 1991. **Freq:** Bimonthly. **Key Personnel:** Richard Lewis, Editor. **ISSN:** 0961-5970. **Subscription Rates:** $49 institutions; $28 individuals; $9 single issue institutions; $7 single issue individuals. **URL:** http://www.pdcnet.org/pn.html.

📖 251 Questions
Philosophy Documentation Center
PO Box 7147   Phone: (434)220-3300
Charlottesville, VA 22906-7147   Fax: (434)220-3301
                                                Free: (800)444-2419

Publication E-mail: order@pdcnet.org
Publisher E-mail: order@pdcnet.org

Journal covering philosophical questions and answers of young students and their teachers. **Subtitle:** Philosophy for Young People. **Freq:** Annual. **Key Personnel:** Jana Mohr Lone, Editor-in-Chief. **ISSN:** 1541-4760. **Subscription Rates:** $25 individuals; $50 schools. **URL:** http://www.pdcnet.org/questions.html.

DILLWYN

📖 252 EGA Needle Arts Magazine
Embroiderers Guild of America, Inc.
Route 1, Box 4510   Phone: (804)983-3021
Dillwyn, VA 23936   Fax: (804)983-1074
Publication E-mail: egahq@aol.com
Publisher E-mail: EGAHQ@aol.com

Technical, trade magazine for needleworkers. **Freq:** Quarterly. **Print Method:** Web offset. **Trim Size:** 8 1/8 x 10 7/8. **Cols./Page:** 3. **Col. Width:** 13 picas. **Col. Depth:** 9'' inches. **Key Personnel:** Susanna Lawson, Managing Editor, chrysolis@hovac.com; Carol S. Lawson, Art Dir., lawson@aba.org. **Remarks:** Accepts advertising.

                                                Circ: Paid 30,000

WASHINGTON

FERNDALE

📖 253 The North American Technocrat
Technocracy, Inc.
2475 Harksell Rd.   Phone: (360)366-1012
Ferndale, WA 98248   Fax: (360)366-1409
Publication E-mail: tech-mag@juno.com
Publisher E-mail: chqlll@aol.com

Magazine promoting technocracy, a science dedicated to illuminating social phenomena in a technical, scientific context. **Founded:** 1939. **Freq:** Quarterly. **Trim Size:** 8 1/4 x 11. **Key Personnel:** George Wright, Editor; Grace Sheldon, Ed. Asst. **ISSN:** 1540-2797. **Subscription Rates:** $6 U.S., Canada, and Mexico; $8 other countries. **Remarks:** Advertising not accepted. **Formerly:** The Northwest Technocrat (Aug. 1, 1902).

                                                Circ: 1,500

OAK HARBOR

📖 254 Crosswind
Sound Publishing, Inc.
800 SE
Oak Harbor, WA 98277

Community and naval base newspaper. **Founded:** 1965. **Freq:** Weekly (Fri.). **Print Method:** Offset. **Trim Size:** 11 x 17. **Cols./Page:** 5. **Col. Width:** 12 1/2 picas. **Col. Depth:** 16 1/2 inches. **Key Personnel:** Gregg McConnell, Publisher; Marcia Smith, Advertising Dir. **Remarks:** Accepts advertising.
Ad Rates: GLR: $3   **Circ:** Non-paid ♦7,041
            BW: $948.75
            4C: $1398.75
            SAU: $11.50

PORT ORCHARD

📖 255 The Port Orchard Independent
Sound Publishing, Inc.
2950 SE Mile Hill Dr.   Phone: (360)876-4414
Port Orchard, WA 98366   Fax: (360)876-4458

Community newspaper. **Founded:** 1890. **Freq:** Weekly Wed. and Sat. **Print Method:** Offset. **Trim Size:** 10 1/4 x 15. **Cols./Page:** 6. **Col. Width:** 1 9/16

inches. **Col. Depth:** 15 inches. **Key Personnel:** Dan Ivanis, Editor; Michael Shepard, Publisher; Rich Peterson, Advertising Mgr.; Pat Jenkins, Editor. **Subscription Rates:** $26 individuals; $40 out of area; $78 out of state. **Remarks:** Accepts advertising. **URL:** http:// www.portorchardindependent.com. **Formerly:** Port Orchard Advantage.
Ad Rates: GLR: $13   **Circ:** Paid ♦1,332
            BW: $1,170   Non-paid ♦14,364
            4C: $1,620
            SAU: $12.65
            PCI: $13

PULLMAN

📖 256 The Western Journal of Black Studies
Washington State University Press
70C Cleveland Hall   Phone: (509)335-8681
Pullman, WA 99164   Fax: (509)335-6959
Publication E-mail: wjbs@wsu.edu
Publisher E-mail: wsupress@wsu.edu

Black studies. **Founded:** 1977. **Freq:** Quarterly. **Print Method:** Offset. **Trim Size:** 8 x 10. **Cols./Page:** 2. **Col. Width:** 36 nonpareils. **Col. Depth:** 113 agate lines. **Key Personnel:** E. Lincoln James, Editor, phone (509)335-3911; Cicely Clinkenbeard, Ed. Asst. **ISSN:** 0197-4327. **Subscription Rates:** $30 individuals hard copy; $20 individuals online; $45 individuals hard copy and online; $90 institutions (online not available to institutions); $55 two years individuals, hard copy; $35 two years individuals, online; $85 two years individuals, hard copy and online; $170 two years institutions; $12 single issue. **Remarks:** Accepts advertising.
Ad Rates: BW: $300   **Circ:** Paid ‡400
                                                Non-paid ‡30

SEATTLE

📖 257 Capitol Hill Times
Pacific Publishing Co.
4000 Aurora Ave. N, Ste. 100   Phone: (206)461-3333
Seattle, WA 98103-7853   Fax: (206)461-1316

Community newspaper. **Founded:** 1926. **Freq:** Weekly (Wed.). **Print Method:** Offset. **Cols./Page:** 5. **Col. Width:** 12 picas. **Col. Depth:** 16 inches. **Key Personnel:** Brenda L. French, Publisher, phone (206)461-1303; Doug Schwartz, Editor, editor@capitalhilltimes.com; Jim Christenson, Circulation Mgr., phone (206)461-1337. **Subscription Rates:** $28 individuals. **Remarks:** Combined advertising rates available with other Flaherty Newspapers.
Ad Rates: BW: $1,760   **Circ:** Paid 15,000
            4C: $2,135
            SAU: $25

📖 258 Seattle University Spectator
Seattle University
900 Broadway   Phone: (206)296-6470
Seattle, WA 98122-4460   Fax: (206)296-6477
Publication E-mail: spectator@seattleu.edu

Collegiate newspaper. **Founded:** 1933. **Freq:** Weekly (Thurs.). **Print Method:** Offset. **Cols./Page:** 5. **Col. Width:** 23 nonpareils. **Col. Depth:** 210 agate lines. **Key Personnel:** Steven Ford, Editor; Katie Ching, Managing Editor, phone (206)296-6471; Brandy Gevers, Business Mgr., phone (206)296-6474; Romie Ponce, Advertising Mgr. **Subscription Rates:** $20. **Remarks:** Accepts advertising. **URL:** http://www.seattleu.edu/student/spec/.
Ad Rates: GLR: $2.00   **Circ:** 4,200
            BW: $600
            4C: $910
            SAU: $8.25
            PCI: $8

📖 259 Seattle's Child (Snohomish County Edition)
Northwest Parent Publishing
123 NW 36th St., Ste. 215   Phone: (206)441-0191
Seattle, WA 98107-4959   Fax: (206)441-4919
Publication E-mail: scnwpp@aol.com

Consumer magazine for parents of children under 12 years old. **Founded:** Apr. 1979. **Freq:** Monthly. **Print Method:** Offset. **Trim Size:** 10 3 1/6 x 13

Ad Rates: GLR = general line rate; BW = one-time black & white page rate; 4C = one-time four color page rate; SAU = standard advertising unit rate; CNU = Canadian newspaper advertising unit rate; PCI = per column inch rate.
Circulation: ★ = ABC; △ = BPA; ♦ = CAC; • = CCAB; 📖 = VAC; ⊕ = PO Statement; ‡ = Publisher's Report; Boldface figures = sworn; Light figures = estimated.
Entry type: 📖 = Print; 🕮 = Broadcast.

29

1/2. **Cols./Page:** 4. **Col. Width:** 2 1/4 inches. **Key Personnel:** Karen Matthee, Editor, kmatthee@unitedad.com. **Subscription Rates:** $15 individuals. **Remarks:** Accepts advertising.

Ad Rates: BW: $2,100   **Circ:** Combined 8,850
            4C: $2,600
            PCI: $25

📖 **260 Working Money**
Technical Analysis Inc.
4757 California Ave. SW   Phone: (206)938-0570
Seattle, WA 98116-4499   Fax: (206)938-1307
                           Free: (800)832-4642

Publication E-mail: mail@traders.com
Publisher E-mail: circ@traders.com

Consumer magazine covering investment strategies, mutual funds, money management, and financial planning. **Key Personnel:** Jayanthi Gopalakrishnan, Editor; Jack K. Hutson, Publisher. **Subscription Rates:** $14.99 individuals; $3.99 single issue. **Remarks:** Accepts advertising. **URL:** http://www.working-money.com.

Ad Rates: BW: $7,447   **Circ:** Paid 165,000
            4C: $8,936

SILVERDALE

📖 **261 Central Kitsap Reporter**
Sound Publishing, Inc.
9989 Silverdale Way, Ste. 109   Phone: (360)308-9161
Silverdale, WA 98383   Fax: (360)308-9363

Community newspaper, twice weekly. **Founded:** 1984. **Freq:** Semiweekly (Wed. and Sat.). **Print Method:** Web, Offset. **Trim Size:** 101/4 x 15. **Cols./Page:** 6. **Col. Width:** 1 9/16 inches. **Col. Depth:** 15 inches. **Key Personnel:** Michael Dillon, Publisher, phone (360)308-9161, fax (360)308-9363; Vince Dice, Editor, vdice@centralkitsapreporter.com. **Subscription Rates:** $26 individuals; $120.00 out of state. **Formerly:** Central Kitsap Style.

Ad Rates: GLR: $1.36   **Circ:** Paid ♦443
            BW: $1,350   Non-paid ♦16,999
            4C: $1,800
            SAU: $16.38
            PCI: $15

📖 **262 N.W. Navigator**
Sound Publishing Inc.
9989 Silverdate Way, Ste. 109   Phone: (360)308-9161
Silverdale, WA 98383   Fax: (360)308-9363

Military newspaper. **Founded:** 2000. **Freq:** Weekly (Fri.). **Print Method:** Photo offset. **Key Personnel:** Jim Long, Publisher. **Subscription Rates:** Free; $39 by mail. **Remarks:** Accepts advertising.
                         Circ: Combined ♦6,696

WENATCHEE

📖 **263 El Mundo**
El Mundo Communications Inc.
PO Box 2231   Phone: (509)663-5737
Wenatchee, WA 98007   Fax: (509)663-6957
Publication E-mail: elmundo1@nwi.net

Spanish language community newspaper. **Founded:** Mar. 1989. **Freq:** Weekly. **Print Method:** Offset. **Trim Size:** 12'' x 21''. **Cols./Page:** 6. **Col. Width:** 1 5/6 inches. **Col. Depth:** 20 1/4 inches. **Key Personnel:** Jim Tiffany, Managing Editor; Carlos Rossetti, Sales Mgr., phone (425)609-9480, fax (425)603-0282. **ISSN:** 1526-9698. **Subscription Rates:** Free; $36 by mail. **Remarks:** Accepts advertising. **URL:** http://www.elmundocom.net.

Ad Rates: BW: $2,126.25   **Circ:** Paid ❏235
            4C: $2,276.25   Non-paid ❏14,643
            PCI: $17.50

WEST VIRGINIA

CIRCEVILLE

📖 **264 Combat**
PO Box 3
Circleville, WV 26804
Publication E-mail: majordomo@combatmagazine.ws

Electronic consumer magazine covering wartime literature, poetry and essay. **Founded:** Jan. 2003. **Freq:** Quarterly. **URL:** http://www.combatmagazine.ws/.

HAMLIN

📖 **265 Lincoln Times**
The Lincoln Journal, Inc.
328 Walnut St.   Phone: (304)824-5101
PO Box 308   Fax: (304)824-5210
Hamlin, WV 25523   Free: (800)319-4204
Publication E-mail: lincolnjnl@aol.com
Publisher E-mail: LincolnJnl@aol.com

Shopping guide. **Founded:** Jan. 1982. **Freq:** Weekly (Fri.). **Print Method:** Offset. **Cols./Page:** 6. **Col. Depth:** 21 inches. **Key Personnel:** Thomas A. Robinson, Publisher; Fred Pace, Editor. **Subscription Rates:** Free. **Remarks:** Accepts advertising. **URL:** http://www.lincolnjournal.com.

Ad Rates: 4C: $240   **Circ:** Non-paid ⊕12,400
            PCI: $9.65

WISCONSIN

APPLETON

📖 **266 Milk & Liquid Food Transporter**
Glen Street Publications, Inc.
W4652 Glen St.   Phone: (920)749-4880
Appleton, WI 54913-9563   Fax: (920)749-4877
Publication E-mail: mlft@glenstreet.com

Magazine covering transportation and processing of bulk milk and liquid foods. **Founded:** 1960. **Freq:** Monthly. **Print Method:** Sheet fed, saddle stitched. **Trim Size:** 8 3/8 x 10 7/8. **Cols./Page:** 3. **Col. Width:** 2 9/16 inches. **Key Personnel:** Jane Plout, Publisher, Advertising/Business Mgr., jplout@glenstreet.com; Laurie Arendt, Editor. **Subscription Rates:** Free to qualified subscribers; $12 individuals; $21 two years. **Remarks:** Accepts advertising.

Ad Rates: GLR: $7   **Circ:** Controlled 4,772
            BW: $800
            4C: $1,350
            PCI: $36

MADISON

📖 **267 American Orthoptic Journal**
University of Wisconsin Press
1930 Monroe St., 3rd Fl.   Phone: (608)263-0668
Madison, WI 53711   Fax: (608)263-1173
Publisher E-mail: journals@uwpress.wisc.edu

Professional medical journal covering amblyopia, strabismus, and pediatric opthalmology. **Founded:** 1950. **Freq:** Annual. **Print Method:** 7 x 10. **Key Personnel:** Dr. Thomas France, Editor; Adrienne Omen, Advertising Mgr., phone (608)263-0534. **ISSN:** 0065-955X. **Subscription Rates:** $32 individuals; $94 institutions. **Remarks:** Accepts advertising. **URL:** http://www.wisc.edu/wisconsinpress/journals. **Alt. Formats:** Mailing labels.

Ad Rates: BW: $450   **Circ:** Paid 1,500
            4C: $1,000

📖 **268 L'Anello Che Non Tiene**
University of Wisconsin
Department of French and Italian
618 Vanhise Hall
Madison, WI 53706

Journal covering Italian literature. **Subtitle:** Journal of Modern Italian Literature. **Founded:** 1998. **Freq:** Semiannual. **Key Personnel:** Ernesto Livorni, Editor, phone (608)262-4068, fax (608)265-3892, elivorni@wisc.edu. **ISSN:** 0099-5273. **Subscription Rates:** $15 individuals. **Remarks:** Accepts advertising.

Ad Rates: BW: $100   **Circ:** (Not Reported)

📖 **269 Arctic Anthropology**
University of Wisconsin Press
1930 Monroe St., 3rd Fl.   Phone: (608)263-0668
Madison, WI 53711   Fax: (608)263-1173
Publisher E-mail: journals@uwpress.wisc.edu

Professional journal covering the study of Arctic regions worldwide. **Freq:** Semiannual. **Trim Size:** 8 x 11. **Key Personnel:** Susan Kaplan, Editor; Adrienne Omen, Advertising Mgr., phone (608)263-0534. **ISSN:** 0065-955X. **Subscription Rates:** $48 individuals; $150 institutions. **Remarks:** Accepts advertising. **URL:** http://www.wisc.edu/wisconsinpress/journals. **Alt. Formats:** Mailing labels.
Ad Rates: BW: $330   **Circ:** Paid 700

📖 **270   Journal of Human Resources**
University of Wisconsin Press
1930 Monroe St., 3rd Fl.   Phone: (608)263-0668
Madison, WI 53711   Fax: (608)263-1173
Publisher E-mail: journals@uwpress.wisc.edu

Examines labor, health, education, welfare and retirement issues, focusing on policy implications. **Founded:** 1966. **Freq:** Quarterly. **Trim Size:** 6 1/8 x 9 1/4. **Cols./Page:** 1. **Key Personnel:** Jonathan Skinner, Editor; Jan Levine Thal, Managing Editor; Adrienne Omen, Advertising Mgr., phone (608)263-0534. **ISSN:** 0022-166X. **Subscription Rates:** $60 individuals; $150 institutions. **Remarks:** Accepts advertising. **URL:** http://www.wisc.edu/wisconsinpress/journals. **Alt. Formats:** Mailing labels.
Ad Rates: BW: $350   **Circ:** Controlled 2,200

📖 **271   Landscape Journal**
University of Wisconsin Press
1930 Monroe St., 3rd Fl.   Phone: (608)263-0668
Madison, WI 53711   Fax: (608)263-1173
Publisher E-mail: journals@uwpress.wisc.edu

Scholarly journal covering research, investigation, and technical information on landscape architecture. **Freq:** Semiannual. **Trim Size:** 8 x 11. **Key Personnel:** Kenneth Helphand, Editor; Adrienne Omen, Advertising Mgr., phone (608)224-3884. **ISSN:** 0277-2426. **Subscription Rates:** $42 individuals; $135 institutions. **Remarks:** Accepts advertising. **URL:** http://www.wisc.edu/wisconsinpress/journals.
Ad Rates: BW: $330   **Circ:** Paid 1,000

📖 **272   Madison Review**
University of Wisconsin at Madison
Department of English
Helen C. White Hall
600 N. Park St.   Phone: (608)263-0566
Madison, WI 53706   Fax: (608)563-3709
Publication E-mail: madreview@mail.studentorg.wisc.edu

Fiction and poetry journal. **Freq:** Semiannual. **Subscription Rates:** $8 individuals; $20 two years. **Remarks:** Advertising not accepted. **URL:** http://mendota.english.wisc.edu/~MadRev.
Ad Rates: BW: $50   **Circ:** (Not Reported)

MILWAUKEE

📖 **273   Philosophy & Theology**
Marquette University Press
PO Box 3141   Phone: (414)288-1564
Milwaukee, WI 53201-3141   Fax: (414)288-7813
                                                  Free: (800)247-6553
Publication E-mail: andrew.tallon@marquette.edu

Scholarly journal covering philosophy and theology. **Subtitle:** Marquette University Journal. **Founded:** 1986. **Freq:** Semiannual. **Trim Size:** 5 1/2 x 8 1/2. **Key Personnel:** Philip Rossi, Editor, phone (414)288-3738, fax (414)288-5548; Robert Masson, Assoc. Editor, phone (414)288-6952, fax (414)288-5548, robert.masson@marquette.edu; Pamela Swope, Fulfillment, phone (434)220-3300, order@pdcnet.org. **ISSN:** 0890-2461. **Subscription Rates:** $35 individuals print; $20 individuals diskette; $43 out of country print; $28 out of country diskette; $20 single issue print, U.S.; $20 single issue print, other countries. **Remarks:** Advertising not accepted. **URL:** http://www.nlx.com. **Alt. Formats:** CD-ROM; Diskette.
                                                  Circ: Paid 500

Ad Rates: GLR = general line rate; BW = one-time black & white page rate; 4C = one-time four color page rate; SAU = standard advertising unit rate; CNU = Canadian newspaper advertising unit rate; PCI = per column inch rate.
Circulation: ★ = ABC; △ = BPA; ♦ = CAC; • = CCAB; ❑ = VAC; ⊕ = PO Statement; ‡ = Publisher's Report; Boldface figures = sworn; Light figures = estimated.
Entry type: 📖 = Print; 🕮 = Broadcast.

31

CANADA

ALBERTA

CALGARY

📖 **274 Journal of Advanced Transportation**
Institute for Transportation Inc.
4625 Varsity Dr. NW, No. 305, Ste. 68   Phone: (403)286-7676
Calgary, AB, Canada T3A 0Z9   Fax: (403)286-9638
Publisher E-mail: wirasing@advanced-transport.com

Journal covering transportation technology and engineering. **Founded:** 1967.
Freq: Triennial. **Trim Size:** 6 x 9. **Cols./Page:** 1. **Col. Width:** 5 inches. **Col.
Depth:** 8 inches. **Key Personnel:** Dr. S. C. Wirasinghe, Editor-in-Chief,
phone (403)220-7180, fax (403)284-3697, wirasing@advanced-transport.com.
ISSN: 0197-6729. **Subscription Rates:** $125 individuals; $135 other
countries airmail; $45 single issue. **Remarks:** Advertising not accepted.
URL: http://www.advanced-transport.com.

Circ: Combined 355

EDMONTON

📖 **275 LawNow**
Legal Studies Program
Faculty of Extension
Univ. of Alberta
11019-90 Ave.   Phone: (403)492-1751
Edmonton, AB, Canada T6G 1A6   Fax: (403)492-6180
Publisher E-mail: lawnow@ualberta.ca

Magazine covering the law, the legal process and their relationship to life in
Canada. **Founded:** 1976. **Freq:** Bimonthly. **Available Online. URL:** http://
www.extension.ualberta.ca/lawnow/. **Former name:** Resource News (1988).

BRITISH COLUMBIA

BURNABY

📖 **276 GardenWise Magazine**
Canada Wide Magazines & Communications Ltd.
4180 Lougheed Hwy., 4th Fl.   Phone: (604)299-7311
Burnaby, BC, Canada V5C 6A7   Fax: (604)299-9188
                                               Free: (800)663-0518
Publication E-mail: mag@britishcolumbiagardner.com
Publisher E-mail: cwm@canadawide.com

Consumer magazine covering gardening in British Columbia. **Freq:** 6/year.
Key Personnel: Samantha Legge-Stollery, slegge@canadawide.com. **Subscription Rates:** $21.35 individuals; $40.61 two years; $29.95 U.S.; $34.95
elsewhere. **Remarks:** Accepts advertising. **URL:** http://
www.britishcolumbiagardner.com/. **Former name:** Coastal Grower Magazine; British Columbia Gardener.

Circ: (Not Reported)

VANCOUVER

📖 **277 Canadian Traveller**
OP Travel & Tourism Marketing, Inc.
104-1260 Hornby St.   Phone: (604)699-9990
Vancouver, BC, Canada V6Z 1W2   Fax: (604)699-9993
Publication E-mail: info@canadiantraveller.net

Destination sales resource for travel professionals. **Founded:** 1983. **Freq:**
Monthly. **Print Method:** Web offset. **Trim Size:** 8 1/8 x 10 7/8. **Cols./Page:**
3. **Col. Width:** 2.292 inches. **Col. Depth:** 10 inches. **Key Personnel:** Rex
Armstead, Editor and Publisher, rexarmstead@canadiantraveller.net; Janice
Strong, Assoc. Ed., janicestrong@canadiantraveller.net; Stephen Fountaine,
Assoc. Publisher, phone (250)861-9006, fax (250)861-4811; Leo Antonelli,
Assoc. Ed., phone (416)481-8037, fax (416)481-3074, leonantonel-
li@canadiantraveller.net; Nicole Verni, Eastern Regional Sales Mgr., phone
(416)907-7524, fax (416)907-7525, nicoleverni@canadiantraveller.net. **ISSN:**
1207-1463. **Subscription Rates:** $36; $54 U.S.; $72 other countries.
Remarks: Accepts advertising. **Formerly:** MLD Canadian Traveller.
Ad Rates: BW: $2,850   **Circ:** Combined ‡14,954
              4C: $3,600

📖 **278 Cottage**
OP Publishing Ltd.
1080 Howe St., Ste. 900   Phone: (604)606-4644
Vancouver, BC, Canada V6Z 2T1   Fax: (604)687-1925
Publication E-mail: info@cottagemagazine.com
Publisher E-mail: oppublishing@oppublishing.com

Consumer magazine for rural and recreational property owners in Western
Canada. **Subtitle:** Country Living in Western Canada. **Freq:** Bimonthly.
Subscription Rates: $20.33 individuals. **Remarks:** Accepts advertising.
URL: http://www.cottagemagazine.com.

Circ: (Not Reported)

📖 **279 History of Philosophy Quarterly**
University of Illinois Press
University of British Columbia
Department of Philosophy
1866 Main Mall, E-370
Vancouver, BC, Canada V6T 1Z1
Publisher E-mail: uipress@uillinois.edu

Scholarly journal covering the history of philosophy. **Freq:** Quarterly. **Key
Personnel:** Catherine Wilson, Editor, catherine.wilson@ubc.ca; Clydette
Wantland, Advertising, phone (217)244-6496, fax (217)244-8082, cwant-
lan@uillinois.edu. **ISSN:** 0740-0675. **Subscription Rates:** $220 institutions;
$55 individuals; $75 single issue institutions; $30 single issue individuals.
URL: http://www.press.uillinois.edu/journals/hpq.html.

📖 **280 The Outdoor Edge**
OP Publishing Ltd.
1080 Howe St., Ste. 900   Phone: (604)606-4644
Vancouver, BC, Canada V6Z 2T1   Fax: (604)687-1925
Publisher E-mail: oppublishing@oppublishing.com

Magazine for hunters and anglers in Western Canada. **Founded:** 1991. **Freq:**
6/year.

Circ: Paid 48,915

Ad Rates: GLR = general line rate; BW = one-time black & white page rate; 4C = one-time four color page rate; SAU = standard advertising unit rate;
CNU = Canadian newspaper advertising unit rate; PCI = per column inch rate.
Circulation: ★ = ABC; △ = BPA; ◆ = CAC; ● = CCAB; ❑ = VAC; ⊕ = PO Statement; ‡ = Publisher's Report; Boldface figures = sworn; Light figures = estimated.
Entry type: 📖 = Print; 🎙 = Broadcast.

MANITOBA

WINNIPEG

📖 **281 Ars Combinatoria**
Charles Babbage Research Centre
PO Box 272, St. Norbert Postal Sta.
Winnipeg, MB, Canada R3V 1L6   Phone: (204)772-2612

Mathematical journal. **Subtitle:** A Canadian Journal of Combinatorics. **Freq:** Quarterly. **Key Personnel:** Scott Vanstone, Editor-in-Chief; Jeff Allston, Managing Editor. **Subscription Rates:** $212 individuals. **URL:** http://bkocay.cs.umanitoba.ca/artscomb/artscomb.html.

📖 **282 Bar & Beverage Business Magazine**
Mercury Publications Ltd.
1839 Inkster Blvd.   Phone: (204)954-2085
Winnipeg, MB, Canada R2X 1R3   Fax: (204)954-2057
     Free: (800)337-6372
Publisher E-mail: mp@mercury.mb.ca; ads@mercury.mb.ca

Trade magazine for managers, owners and staff of nightclubs, bars, cabarets, and hotel/restaurant lounges in Canada. **Freq:** Bimonthly. **Subscription Rates:** $46 Canada; $66 elsewhere; $70 two years Canada; $93 two years elsewhere. **Remarks:** Accepts advertising. **URL:** http://www.mercury.mb.ca/bbmain.html.
Ad Rates: BW: $2,830   **Circ:** Combined 16,077
     4C: $3,810

📖 **283 C Store Canada**
Mercury Publications Ltd.
1839 Inkster Blvd.   Phone: (204)954-2085
Winnipeg, MB, Canada R2X 1R3   Fax: (204)954-2057
     Free: (800)337-6372
Publisher E-mail: mp@mercury.mb.ca; ads@mercury.mb.ca

Trade magazine for managers, owners and staff of convenience stores in Canada. **Freq:** Quarterly. **Subscription Rates:** $40 Canada; $60 elsewhere; $57 two years Canada; $85.50 two years elsewhere. **Remarks:** Accepts advertising. **URL:** http://www.mercury.mb.ca/.
     Circ: (Not Reported)

📖 **284 The Manitoba Museum Annual Report**
Manitoba Museum of Man and Nature
190 Rupert Ave.   Phone: (204)956-2830
Winnipeg, MB, Canada R3B 0N2   Fax: (204)942-3679
     Free: (888)231-9739
Publisher E-mail: info@manitobamuseum.mb.ca

Annual report. **Freq:** Annual. **Print Method:** Offset. **Key Personnel:** Karen Pankiw, Editor, phone (204)988-0614. **Subscription Rates:** Free to qualified subscribers. **Remarks:** Advertising not accepted. **Available Online. Formerly:** Manitoba Museum of Man and Nature Annual Report.
     Circ: Non-paid 2,700

📖 **285 Western Hotelier**
Mercury Publications Ltd.
1839 Inkster Blvd.   Phone: (204)954-2085
Winnipeg, MB, Canada R2X 1R3   Fax: (204)954-2057
     Free: (800)337-6372
Publisher E-mail: mp@mercury.mb.ca; ads@mercury.mb.ca

Trade magazine covering hotel management in Western Canada and U.S. western border states. **Freq:** Quarterly. **Subscription Rates:** $32 Canada; $42.50 elsewhere; $42 two years Canada; $66 two years elsewhere. **Remarks:** Accepts advertising. **URL:** http://www.mercury.mb.ca/.
Ad Rates: BW: $1,679   **Circ:** Combined 4,342

NEW BRUNSWICK

FREDERICTON

📖 **286 ellipse**
471 Smythe, No. 27009   Phone: (506)451-0408
Fredericton, NB, Canada E3B 3E3   Fax: (506)455-9980

Journal covering Canadian poetry in French and English. **Subtitle:** textes en traduction/literary translation. **Founded:** 1968. **Freq:** Semiannual. **Key**

Personnel: Jo-Anne Elder, Editor, phone (506)455-0413, elder@nb.sympatico.ca. **ISSN:** 0046-1830. **Subscription Rates:** $12 individuals; $14 institutions; $7 single issue. **Remarks:** Advertising not accepted.
     Circ: Combined 560

ONTARIO

BELLEVILLE

📖 **287 The Canadian Fly Fisher**
389 Bridge St. W., RR2   Phone: (613)966-8017
Belleville, ON, Canada K8N 4Z2   Fax: (613)966-5002
     Free: (888)805-5608
Publication E-mail: canflyfish@canflyfish.com

Consumer magazine covering fishing in Canada. **Freq:** Quarterly. **Key Personnel:** Chris Marshall, Editor and Publisher; Mark Anthony Krupa, Photo Editor. **Subscription Rates:** $21.95 U.S. and Canada; $40 elsewhere; $41 U.S. and Canada two years; $72 elsewhere two years. **Remarks:** Accepts advertising. **URL:** http://www.canflyfish.com.
Ad Rates: BW: $1,233   **Circ:** (Not Reported)
     4C: $1,530

MARKHAM

📖 **288 Canadian Home and Country**
Avid Media Inc.
210-340 Ferrier St.   Phone: (905)475-8440
Markham, ON, Canada L3R 2Z5   Fax: (905)475-9246
Publisher E-mail: general@avidmediainc.com

Consumer magazine covering traditional homes in Canada. **Founded:** 1983. **Freq:** 7/year. **Print Method:** Web offset. **Key Personnel:** Eron McLaughlin, Editor, mclaughlin@centuryborne.com; Jacqueline Howe, Publisher, howe@avidmediainc.com; Carina Cassidy, Vice President, cassidy@avidmediainc.com. **ISSN:** 0838-9330. **Subscription Rates:** $22.95 individuals; $4.25 single issue. **Remarks:** Accepts advertising. **URL:** www.centuryhome.com. **Formerly:** Century Home.
Ad Rates: 4C: $4,625   **Circ:** Paid ‡68,000

OAKVILLE

📖 **289 Tourist**
Metroland Printing, Publishing and Distributing
467 Speers Rd.   Phone: (905)815-0017
Oakville, ON, Canada L6K 3S4   Fax: (905)337-5571
     Free: (800)265-3673

Publication covering travel and tourism for Canadians. **Subtitle:** Canada's Newsmagazine for Travellers. **Freq:** Monthly. **Key Personnel:** Ian Oliver, Publisher; Neil Oliver, Assoc. Publisher; Cathryn Oliver, General Mgr.; Val Saunders, Bus. Dev. & Advertising Sales; Don Wall, Editor; Teri Casas, Office Mgr.; Brad Marple, Nat'l. Sales Dir.; Janet Humphreys, Production Mgr. **ISSN:** 0827-6854. **Remarks:** Accepts advertising.
     Circ: (Not Reported)

OTTAWA

📖 **290 Canadian Pharmaceutical Journal**
Canadian Pharmacists Association
1785 Alta Vista Dr.   Phone: (613)523-7877
Ottawa, ON, Canada K1G 3Y6   Fax: (613)523-0445
     Free: (800)917-9489
Publisher E-mail: cpha@pharmacists.ca

Pharmacy journal. **Subtitle:** The Voice of Canadian Pharmacy. **Founded:** 1868. **Freq:** Monthly (Dec./Jan. and July/Aug. combined). **Print Method:** Offset. **Trim Size:** 8 1/8 x 10 7/8. **Cols./Page:** 3. **Col. Width:** 26 nonpareils. **Col. Depth:** 115 agate lines. **Key Personnel:** Blair Jarvis, Editor; Leesa D. Bruce, Publisher. **ISSN:** 0828-6914. **Subscription Rates:** $70. **Remarks:** Advertising accepted; rates available upon request. **URL:** http://www.pharmacists.ca.
     Circ: Non-paid 8,298
     Paid 9,600

📖 **291 Compendium of Pharmaceuticals and Specialties**
Canadian Pharmacists Association
1785 Alta Vista Dr. Phone: (613)523-7877
Ottawa, ON, Canada K1G 3Y6 Fax: (613)523-0445
  Free: (800)917-9489
Publisher E-mail: cpha@pharmacists.ca

Medical periodical covering all Canadian prescription drugs. **Freq:** Annual. **ISSN:** 0069-7966. **Subscription Rates:** $150 Canada Standard; $154 Canada French; $209 Canada On CD ROM. **Alt. Formats:** CD-ROM.

TORONTO

📖 **292 Canadian Transportation & Logistics**
Business Information Group
1450 Don Mills Rd. Phone: (416)445-6641
Toronto, ON, Canada M3B 2X7 Fax: (416)442-2213
  Free: (800)668-2374

Professional trade magazine covering transportation and integrated logistics management, for professionals who manage product flow from manufacturer to point-of-sale. Focuses on reporting, analysis, and interpretation of Canadian logistics trends and issues. **Founded:** 1898. **Freq:** Monthly. **Print Method:** Offset. **Trim Size:** 8 1/8 x 10 7/8. **Cols./Page:** 3. **Col. Width:** 26 nonpareils. **Col. Depth:** 140 agate lines. **Key Personnel:** Kevin Sharp, Publisher, phone (416)442-2075, fax (416)442-2069, ksharp@ctl.ca; Nick Krukowski, Acct. Mgr., phone (416)442-2050, fax (416)2069, nkrukowski@ctl.ca; Lou Smyrlis, Editor, phone (416)442-2099, fax (416)442-2214, lsmyrlis@businessinformationgroup.ca; John Desroche, Market Production Mgr., phone (416)510-6756, jdesroche@businessinformationgroup.ca. **Subscription Rates:** Free to qualified subscribers; $51.95 Canada; $65.95 U.S.; $82.85 two years; $5.89 single issue, Canada. **Remarks:** Accepts advertising. **URL:** http:/ /www.ctl.ca. **Formerly:** Canadian Transportation (1992); Canadian Transportation Logistics; Canadian Transportation and Distribution Management; Canadian Transportation Logistics/Including Canadian Warehousing Logistics.
Ad Rates: BW: $3,700 **Circ:** Combined ‡18,382
  4C: $4,915
  PCI: $125

📖 **293 Journal of Orthomolecular Medicine**
Canadian Schizophrenia Foundation
16 Florence Ave. Phone: (416)733-2117
Toronto, ON, Canada M2N 1E9 Fax: (416)733-2352
Publisher E-mail: centre@orthomed.org

Professional medical journal. **Subtitle:** Journal of Orthomolecular Medicine; Nutrition & Mental Health. **Founded:** 1969. **Freq:** Quarterly. **Key Personnel:** Steven Carter, Managing Editor. **Subscription Rates:** $55 individuals. **Remarks:** Accepts advertising. **URL:** http://www.orthomed.org.
  Circ: (Not Reported)

📖 **294 Klublife**
Klublife Publishing Inc.
275 King St. E. Phone: (416)861-9884
Toronto, ON, Canada M5A 1K2 Fax: (416)861-1557
Publication E-mail: feedback@klublife.com

Consumer magazine covering music and urban lifestyle in Canada. **Freq:** Monthly. **Key Personnel:** Nicola Gregory, Publisher/Editor-in-Chief; Emerson Segura, Assoc. Publisher; Jason Thomas, Marketing Dir.; Susan Oh, Managing Editor. **ISSN:** 1490-2907. **Remarks:** Accepts advertising. **URL:** http://www.klublife.com.
  Circ: Combined 40,000

📖 **295 The Northern Miner**
Business Information Group
1450 Don Mills Rd. Phone: (416)445-6641
Toronto, ON, Canada M3B 2X7 Fax: (416)442-2213
  Free: (800)668-2374

Trade newspaper for the mining industry. **Freq:** Weekly. **Key Personnel:** James Cohyte, Editor, phone (416)510-6747, tmm@northernminer.com; Brian

Warriner, Sales Rep., phone (416)442-2172, bwarriner@northernminer.com. **Remarks:** Accepts advertising. **URL:** http://www.northernminer.com.
  Circ: (Not Reported)

📖 **296 PrintAction**
Youngblood Publishing Ltd.
4580 Dufferin St., Ste. 404 Phone: (416)665-7333
Toronto, ON, Canada M3H 5Y2 Fax: (416)665-7226
  Free: (800)363-3261
Publication E-mail: info@printaction.com

Printing trade newspaper (tabloid). **Subtitle:** Canada's Monthly Graphic Arts Journal. **Founded:** 1971. **Freq:** Monthly. **Print Method:** Sheetfed offset. **Trim Size:** 10 3/8 x 13 1/2. **Key Personnel:** Jon Robinson, Editor, jon@printaction.com; Sara Young, President, sara@printaction.com; John Galbraith, Publisher, johng@printaction.com. **Subscription Rates:** $28.95 Canada; $34.35 U.S. (U.S. dollars); $55 elsewhere (U.S. dollars). **Remarks:** Advertising accepted; rates available upon request. **URL:** http://www.printaction.com.
  Circ: Combined 10,287

📖 **297 Renaissance and Reformation/Renaissance et Reforme**
Centre for Reformation and Renaissance Studies
Victoria University at the University of Toronto
71 Queen's Park Crescent Phone: (416)585-4485
Toronto, ON, Canada M5K 1S7 Fax: (416)585-4430
Publisher E-mail: crrs.publications@utoronto.ca

Scholarly journal covering history and literature in early modern Europe. **Founded:** 1965. **Freq:** Quarterly. **Cols./Page:** 1. **Key Personnel:** Richard Hillman, Contact, phone ( )33 02 47701700, fax ( )33 02 47701700, rhillman@wanadoo.fr. **ISSN:** 0034-429X. **Subscription Rates:** $37 individuals;' $49 institutions; $10 single issue. **Remarks:** Accepts advertising.
Ad Rates: BW: $50 **Circ:** Combined 700

📖 **298 RINSE**
RINSE Magazine
599B Yonge St., No. 346
Toronto, ON, Canada M4Y 1Z4
Publication E-mail: info@rinsemag.com

Consumer magazine covering music and alternative culture. **Freq:** Bimonthly. **Key Personnel:** John Tan, Publisher; Ziaud Baksh, Sales Dir.; Richard Yuzon, Editor-in-Chief; Alex Shoukas, Creative Dir.; Christie Burton, Project Mgr.; Victor Chen, Music Dir.; Jocelyn Dickey, New Dir.; Laura Pitts, Fashion Dir.; Nico Oved, Copy Editor; Yvonne Gaynor, Photo Editor. **Remarks:** Accepts advertising. **URL:** http://rinsemag.com.
  Circ: (Not Reported)

📖 **299 Satellite 1-416**
PO Box 176, Sta. E
Toronto, ON, Canada M6H 4E2 Phone: (416)530-4232
  Fax: (416)530-0069
Publication E-mail: satellite1-416@logers.com

Czechoslovakian newspaper. **Founded:** Apr. 17, 1991. **Freq:** Biweekly. **Cols./Page:** 4. **Col. Width:** 2 1/4 inches. **Col. Depth:** 12 inches. **Key Personnel:** Ales Brezina, phone (416)530-4222. **Subscription Rates:** $34 Canada; $34 U.S. **Remarks:** Accepts advertising. **URL:** http://www.satellite1-416.com.
Ad Rates: GLR: $1.50 **Circ:** Combined 1,500
  BW: $400
  4C: $60
  PCI: $22

WATERLOO

📖 **300 Kinema**
University of Waterloo
Department of Fine Arts and Film Studies
Waterloo, ON, Canada N2L 3G1 Phone: (519)885-1211
  Fax: (519)746-4982
Publication E-mail: kinema@watarts.uwaterloo.ca

Scholarly journal covering film and audiovisual media. **Subtitle:** A Journal for Film and Audiovisual Media. **Founded:** 1993. **Freq:** Semiannual. **Trim**

Ad Rates: GLR = general line rate; BW = one-time black & white page rate; 4C = one-time four color page rate; SAU = standard advertising unit rate; CNU = Canadian newspaper advertising unit rate; PCI = per column inch rate.
Circulation: ★ = ABC; △ = BPA; ♦ = CAC; • = CCAB; ❑ = VAC; ⊕ = PO Statement; ‡ = Publisher's Report; Boldface figures = sworn; Light figures = estimated.
Entry type: 📖 = Print; 🎙 = Broadcast.

35

Size: 5.5 X 8.5 in. **Key Personnel:** Jan Uhde, Editor, juhde@watarts.uwaterloo.ca. **ISSN:** 1192-6252. **Subscription Rates:** $13 U.S. and Canada single issue; $22 U.S. and Canada; $34 institutions U.S. and Canada; $15 single issue other countries; $25 individuals other countries; $44 institutions other countries. **Remarks:** Accepts advertising. **URL:** http://arts.uwaterloo.ca/FINE/juhde/kinemahp.html.

Ad Rates: BW: $95   **Circ:** (Not Reported)

QUEBEC

BEAUPORT

301 Beauport Express
3333, rue du Carrefour, Ste. 212   Phone: (418)663-6131
Beauport, QC, Canada G1C 5R9   Fax: (418)663-3469
Publication E-mail: beauport.express@globetrotter.net

Community newspaper. **Founded:** 1983. **Freq:** Weekly (Sat.). **Trim Size:** 10 x 16 1/2. **Cols./Page:** 10. **Col. Depth:** 165 agate lines. **Key Personnel:** Yuan Rancourt, Editor. **ISSN:** 0383-7572. **Subscription Rates:** $85 taxes. **Remarks:** Accepts advertising. **URL:** http://www.hebdosquebecor.com. **Absorbed:** L'Exclusif (1990).

Ad Rates: GLR: $0.96   **Circ:** 38,287
               BW: $1,237.50
               4C: $1,608
               PCI: $14.40

DORVAL

302 Silk & Satin
1604, Boul. St-Regis
Dorval, QC, Canada H9P 1H6   Free: (888)500-4747

Consumer magazine covering lingerie and fashion. **Freq:** Quarterly. **Key Personnel:** Karine Wascher, Managing Editor. **Subscription Rates:** $2.50 single issue. **Remarks:** Accepts advertising.

                                            Circ: (Not Reported)

MONTREAL

303 Montreal Serai
PO Box 72
Succursale NDG
Montreal, QC, Canada H4A 3P4

Consumer arts magazine covering fiction, non-fiction, poetry and reviews of film, music, art, exhibitions, theater and dance. **Founded:** 1986. **Key Personnel:** Rana Bose, Editor, editor@montrealserai.com; Robert J. Lewis, Arts & Music Editor, robert55@videotron.ca. **Remarks:** Accepts advertising. **URL:** http://www.montrealserai.com.

                                            Circ: (Not Reported)

INTERNATIONAL

ARGENTINA

BUENOS AIRES

📖 **304 Cotal**
Confederation of Latin American Tourism Organizations
Confederacion de Organizaciones Turisticas
Viamonte 640, Piso 8   Ph: 54 11 4322 4003
1053 Buenos Aires, Argentina   Fax: 54 11 4393 5696
Publisher E-mail: cotal@tournet.com.ar

Spanish language publication covering travel. **Freq:** Bimonthly. **Key Personnel:** Maria T. Compos, Secretaria General. **Subscription Rates:** Free.
Circ: 5,000

📖 **305 Integration and Trade**
Institute for the Integration of Latin America and the Caribbean
Instituto para la Integracion de America Latina y el Caribe
Esmeralda 130, piso 17   Ph: 54 1143201850
1035 Buenos Aires, Argentina   Fax: 54 1143201865
Publisher E-mail: int/inl@iadb.org

Publication covering trade issues in English and Spanish. **Founded:** 1996. **Freq:** 2/year. **Key Personnel:** Mariela Marchisio, Contact, phone 54 1143201874, marielam@iadb.org. **ISSN:** 1027-5703. **Subscription Rates:** US$30 Argentina; US$35 Bolivia, Brazil, Chile, Paraguay, and Uruguay; US$45 rest of the Americas; US$50 other countries. **Remarks:** Advertising not accepted. **URL:** http://www.iadb.org/intal.
Circ: (Not Reported)

📖 **306 Journal of Argentine Dermatology**
Argentinian Association of Dermatology
Asociacion Argentina de Dermatologia
Mexico 1720   Ph: 54 13812737
1100 Buenos Aires, Argentina   Fax: 54 13812737
Publisher E-mail: aaderm@hotbot.com

English and Spanish language publication covering dermatology. **Subtitle:** Revista Argentina de Dermatologia. **Founded:** 1907. **Freq:** 4/year. **Print Method:** Offset. **Trim Size:** 18 x 26 cm. **ISSN:** 0325-2787. **Subscription Rates:** US$150. **Remarks:** Advertising accepted; rates available upon request.
Circ: (Not Reported)

AUSTRALIA

ARMIDALE

📖 **307 Australasian Victorian Studies Journal**
Australasian Victorian Studies Association
School of English, Communication and
   Theatre
University of New England
Armidale, NSW 2351, Australia
Publication E-mail: avsj@metz.une.edu.au

Journal covering Australasian Victorian studies, including archaeology, architecture, art, economics, history, sociology and related areas. **Founded:** 1995. **Freq:** Annual. **Key Personnel:** Dr. Cathy Waters, Editor, cwaters@metz.une.edu.au; Dr. Elizabeth Hale, Editor, ehale@metz.une.edu.au;

Dr. Jennifer McDonell, Editor, jmcdonel@metz.une.edu.au; Dr. Robert Dingley, Editor, rdingley@metz.une.edu.au. **ISSN:** 1327-8746. **Subscription Rates:** $A 40 single issue individuals; $A 50 single issue institutions. **Remarks:** Advertising accepted; rates available upon request. **URL:** http://www.une.edu.au/arts/AVSJ.
Circ: 150

BALMAIN

📖 **308 Jacket**
c/o Australian Literary Management
2-A Booth St.
Balmain, NSW 2041, Australia

Online publication covering poetry and prose. **Freq:** 3-4/year. **Key Personnel:** John Tranter, Editor. **ISSN:** 1440-4737. **Subscription Rates:** Free. **URL:** http://jacketmagazine.com/.

BRISBANE

📖 **309 CALL-EJ Online**
School of Languages & Linguistics
Nathan Campus
Griffith University
Brisbane, QLD 4111, Australia   Ph: 61 738756766

Online publication covering computers and language education. **Key Personnel:** Prof. Kazunori Nozawa, Editor, nozawa@ec.ritsumei.ac.jp; Dr. Mike Levy, Editor, michael.levy@mailbox.gu.edu.au. **ISSN:** 1442-438X. **Subscription Rates:** Free. **Remarks:** Advertising not accepted. **URL:** http://www.clec.ritsumei.ac.jp/english/callejonline/. **Formed by the merger of:** CALL EJ; ON-CALL.
Circ: (Not Reported)

CANBERRA

📖 **310 Royal Australian Navy News**
R8-LG-039 12
Dept. of Defence   Ph: 61 2 6266 7605
Canberra, ACT 2600, Australia   Fax: 61 2 6265 6690
Publication E-mail: navynews@defencenews.gov.au

Official newspaper of the Royal Australian Navy. **Founded:** 1958. **Freq:** Biweekly. **Print Method:** Offset. **Trim Size:** 380 x 262 mm. **Cols./Page:** 7. **Col. Width:** 36 millimeters. **Col. Depth:** 380 millimeters. **Key Personnel:** R. Horan, Editor, phone 61 1 6266 7707, rod.horan@defencenews.gov.au; G. Davis, Sub Editor, phone 61 2 9359 2494, fax 61 2 9359 2499; G. Howard, Advertising Mgr., geoff.howard@defencenews.gov.au. **Remarks:** Accepts advertising. **URL:** http://www.navy.gov.au.
Circ: Non-paid 22,000

CASTLEMAINE

📖 **311 Acoustics Australia**
Australian Acoustical Society
PO Box 903   Ph: 61 354706381
Castlemaine, VIC 3450, Australia   Fax: 61 354706381
Publisher E-mail: watkinsd@castlemaine.net

Publication covering acoustics. **Founded:** 1972. **Freq:** 3/year. **Print Method:**

Offset. **Trim Size:** A4. **Key Personnel:** Marion Burgess, Contact, phone 61 262688241, fax 61 262688276, acoust-aust@adfa.edu.au. **ISSN:** 0814-6039. **Subscription Rates:** $A 57.20 Australia; $A 64 other countries. **Remarks:** Accepts advertising. **URL:** http://www.acoustics.asn.au.

Ad Rates: BW: $A 605   **Circ:** Paid ‡600
           4C: $A 1,045

COMO

▥ 312 Australian Journal of Educational Technology
c/o Dr. Roger Atkinson, Production Editor
Unit 5, 202 Coode St.
Como, WA 6152, Australia   Ph: 61 893671133
Publication E-mail: ajet-editor@cleo.murdoch.edu.au

Journal covering educational technology, instructional design, educational applications of computer technolgies, educational telecommunications and related areas. **Founded:** 1985. **Freq:** 3/year. **Print Method:** Offset. **Trim Size:** A5. **Key Personnel:** Roger Atkinson, Production Editor, rjatkinson@bigpond.com. **ISSN:** 0814-673X. **Subscription Rates:** $A 30 individuals Australia, New Zealand, Singapore, Malaysia; $A 30 individuals Indonesia, Papua New Guinea, Asia/Pacific zone; $A 40 elsewhere. **Remarks:** Advertising not accepted. **URL:** http://www.ascilite.com.au/ajet/.
                          Circ: Paid 700

DEAKIN

▥ 313 Nutrition & Dietetics
Dietitians Association of Australia
1/8 Phipps Close   Ph: 61 262829555
Deakin, ACT 2600, Australia   Fax: 61 262829888
Publication E-mail: journal@daa.asn.au

Scientific journal covering food, nutrition and dietetics. **Freq:** Quarterly. **Key Personnel:** Dr. Margaret Allman-Farinelli, Editor; Margaret Ruhfus, Managing Editor; Julie Bernsons, Subscriptions, nationaloffice@daa.asn.au. **ISSN:** 1446-6368. **Subscription Rates:** $A 77 individuals; $A 90 out of country surface mail; $A 110 out of country airmail. **Remarks:** Accepts advertising. **URL:** http://www.ajnd.org.au/. **Formerly:** Australian Journal of Nutrition and Dietetics.
                      Circ: (Not Reported)

MELBOURNE

▥ 314 Law in Context
The Federation Press
La Trobe University   Ph: 61 2 9552 2200
Melbourne, VIC 3083, Australia   Fax: 61 2 9552 1681

Law periodical. **Founded:** 1983. **Freq:** Semiannual. **Key Personnel:** Olive Mendelsohn, phone 61 3 9479 1297, fax 61 3 9479 1607, o.mendelsohn@latrobe.edu.au. **ISSN:** 0811-5796. **Subscription Rates:** $A 40 individuals Australia; $A 60 elsewhere; $A 50 institutions Australia; $A 75 institutions, other countries; $A 25 single issue. **Online:** Gale Group.

▥ 315 Sophia
Ashgate Publishing Ltd.
Philosophy Dept., PO Box 4230
The University of Melbourne   Ph: 61 383444778
Melbourne, VIC 3052, Australia   Fax: 61 383444280
Publisher E-mail: info@gowerpub.com

Journal covering the philosophy of religion, metaphysical theology and ethics worldwide. **Founded:** 1962. **Freq:** Semiannual. **Key Personnel:** Purushottama Bilimoria, Editor-in-Chief; Patrick Hutchings, Assoc. Editor; Nicky Staszkiewicz, Subscriptions, phone 44 1252 351804, fax 44 1252 351839, nstaszkiewicz@ashgatepub.co.uk. **ISSN:** 0038-1527. **Subscription Rates:** $A 30 individuals; $A 60 institutions. **URL:** http://www.ashgate.com.

REDCLIFFE NORTH

▥ 316 Peace and Freedom
Women's International League for Peace and Freedom - Australia
PO Box 2064
Redcliffe North, QLD 4020, Australia
Publisher E-mail: wilpf@macbbs.com.au

Publication covering peace. **Founded:** 1960. **Freq:** Quarterly. **Print Method:** Offset.
                          Circ: 500

ST. LUCIA

▥ 317 Australian Literary Studies
University of Queensland Press
PO Box 6042   Ph: 61 733652452
St. Lucia, QLD 4067, Australia   Fax: 61 733651988

Publication covering literature and writing. **Freq:** Semiannual. **Trim Size:** 175 x 250 mm. **Key Personnel:** Rosemary Chay, Contact, rosichay@uqp.uq.edu.au. **ISSN:** 0004-9697. **Subscription Rates:** $A 43.80 individuals; $A 55 other countries; $A 90 institutions, other countries. **Remarks:** Advertising not accepted. **Online:** Gale Group.
                          Circ: 750

▥ 318 Australian Women's Book Review
Hecate Press
PO Box 6099
St. Lucia, QLD 4067, Australia   Ph: 61 733652799

Academic journal focusing on books and literature of interest to women. **Founded:** 2000. **ISSN:** 1033-9434.

▥ 319 Hecate
Hecate Press
PO Box 6099
St. Lucia, QLD 4067, Australia   Ph: 61 733652799

Academic journal focusing on women's issues and gender studies. **Subtitle:** A Womens' Interdiciplinary Journal. **Founded:** 1975. **Freq:** Semiannual. **Key Personnel:** Carole Ferrier. **ISSN:** 0311-4198. **Subscription Rates:** $A 35 individuals. **Remarks:** Accepts advertising. **Online:** Gale Group.

Ad Rates: BW: $A 300   **Circ:** 1,800

▥ 320 Journal of Australian Studies
University of Queensland Press
PO Box 6042   Ph: 61 733652452
St. Lucia, QLD 4067, Australia   Fax: 61 733651988

Cultural studies publication focusing on Australia. **Freq:** Semiannual. **Trim Size:** 175 x 250 mm. **Key Personnel:** Rosemary Chay, Contact, rosichay@uqp.uq.edu.au. **ISSN:** 1444-3058. **Subscription Rates:** $A 72 individuals; $A 103 other countries; $A 22 single issue. **Remarks:** Advertising not accepted. **Online:** Gale Group.
                          Circ: 1,000

▥ 321 University of Queensland Law Journal
University of Queensland Press
PO Box 6042   Ph: 61 733652452
St. Lucia, QLD 4067, Australia   Fax: 61 733651988

Law periodical. **Freq:** Annual. **Trim Size:** 175 x 250 mm. **Key Personnel:** Rosemary Chay, Contact, rosichay@uqp.uq.edu.au. **ISSN:** 0083-4041. **Subscription Rates:** $A 46 individuals; $A 63.50 other countries. **Remarks:** Advertising not accepted. **Online:** Gale Group.
                    Circ: (Not Reported)

SOUTH MELBOURNE

▥ 322 Journal of Pharmacy Practice and Research
Society of Hospital Pharmacists of Australia
Ste. 3, 27-33 Raglan St.   Ph: 61 396906733
South Melbourne, VIC 3205, Australia Fax: 61 396967634
Publication E-mail: jppr@shpa.org.au
Publisher E-mail: shpa@shpa.org.au

Journal covering hospital pharmacy. **Founded:** Jan. 1966. **Freq:** Quarterly. **Trim Size:** 297 x 210 mm. **Key Personnel:** John Low, Editor-in-Chief; Rosie McKew, Managing Editor; Reg Arulappu, Advertising Mgr., phone 61 393372095, martya@ozemail.com.au. **ISSN:** 1445-937X. **Subscription Rates:** $A 100 individuals; $A 125 out of country. **URL:** http://www.shpa.org.au/austra.htm. **Formerly:** The Australian Journal of Hospital Pharmacy.

Ad Rates: BW: $A 2,090   **Circ:** (Not Reported)
           4C: $A 1,830
           PCI: $A 28

STRAWBERRY HILLS

📖 **323 The Medical Journal of Australia**
Australasian Medical Publishing Company Ltd.
Locked Bag 3030   Ph: 61 295626666
Strawberry Hills, NSW 2012, Australia   Fax: 61 295626600
Publication E-mail: mja@ampco.com.au
Publisher E-mail: ampco@ampco.com.au

Health publication. **Founded:** 1914. **Freq:** Biweekly. **ISSN:** 0025-729X.
Subscription Rates: $A 284.90 individuals; $A 396 other countries; $A 539
other countries airmail; $A 55 students. **Remarks:** Advertising accepted; rates
available upon request. **Online:** Gale Group.

Circ: 27,459

AUSTRIA

ST. POLTEN

📖 **324 St. Polten Konkret**
Rathausplatz 1   Ph: 43 27423332800
A-3100 St. Polten, Austria   Fax: 43 27423332809
Publisher E-mail: oeffarb@st-poelten.gv.at

Consumer magazine covering local lifestyle. **Subtitle:** Amtsblatt der Landesh-
auptstadt St. Polten. **Founded:** 1974. **Freq:** Monthly. **Print Method:** Offset.
Key Personnel: Dr. Siegfried Nasko, sinasko@st-poelten.gv.at; Mag. Matt-
hias Stadler, phone 43 27423332812, mastadler@st-poelten.gv.at; Johannes
Reichl, Feature Editor, Culture, phone 43 27423332803, joreichl@st-poel-
ten.gv.at; Heinz Steinbrecher, Feature Editor, Economy & City, phone 43
27423332804, hesteinbrecher@st-poelten.gv.at; Doris Schmidt, Feature Editor, Health & Society, phone 43 27423332806, doschmidt@st-poelten.gv.at;
Judith Goritschnig, Feature Editor, School & Education, phone 43
27423332806, jugoritschnig@st-poelten.gv.at. **Remarks:** Accepts advertising. **URL:** http://www.st-poelten.gv.at.
Ad Rates: BW: €1,620   **Circ:** Non-paid ⊕28,000
                BW: €2,142   Non-paid ⊕65,000
                4C: €1,800
                4C: €2,380

BAHRAIN

MANAMA

📖 **325 Bahrain This Month**
Red House Marketing
PO Box 20461   Ph: 973 789600
Manama, Bahrain   Fax: 973 785745
Publisher E-mail: redhouse@batelco.com.bh

Magazine covering local leisure and entertainment in Bahrain. **Founded:**
Sept. 1997. **Freq:** Monthly. **Trim Size:** 270 X 206 mm. **Key Personnel:**
George F. Middleton, Publishing & Mng. Dir.,
george@bahrainthismonth.com; Roy Kietzman, Editor,
roy@bahrainthismonth.com; Lini Madhavan, Production Editor,
lini@bahrainthismonth.com; Samson Vaz, Media Coord., sam-
son@bahrainthismonth.com; Leena Roshni Dias, Editorial Asst., rosh-
ni@bahrainthismonth.com; Cherryl Chisholm, Advertising Sales, cher-
ryl@bahrainthismonth.com; Bambi Manalese, Advertising Sales, bam-
bi@bahrainthismonth.com; M. Reghunath, Circ. & Subscriptions, re-
ghu@bahrainthismonth.com; Abdul Rahman, Distribution. **Subscription
Rates:** BD 15 individuals. **URL:** http://www.bahrainthismonth.com/.
Ad Rates: BW: US$1,715   **Circ:** Combined 10,000
                4C: US$2,185

BARBADOS

ST. MICHAEL

📖 **326 Caribbean Law Review**
Caribbean Law Publishing Co. Ltd.
University of the West Indies
Faculty of Law
Cave Hill Campus   Ph: (246)417-4217
St. Michael, Barbados   Fax: (246)424-1788
Publication E-mail: tmayers@uwichiu.edu.bb
Publisher E-mail: cariblaw@colis.com

Law periodical. **Founded:** 1991. **Freq:** Semiannual. **ISSN:** 1018-3671.
Subscription Rates: US$55; US$30 single issue. **Online:** Gale Group.

BELGIUM

GENVAL

📖 **327 Colmed**
Sciences Today
rue de Rixensart 18/17   Ph: 32 26532158
B-1332 Genval, Belgium   Fax: 32 26532158

Magazine covering arts, history, and general culture. **Freq:** Bimonthly. **Key
Personnel:** Dr. J. Andris, Editor-in-Chief, phone 32 2 653 0781, fax 32 2 652
0184, ja@diffu-sciences.com. **Subscription Rates:** 795 BFr individuals.
Remarks: Accepts advertising.
Ad Rates: 4C: 2,500 BFr   **Circ:** Combined 15,000

📖 **328 Folia Ugentia**
Sciences Today
rue de Rixensart 18/17   Ph: 32 26532158
B-1332 Genval, Belgium   Fax: 32 26532158

Professional magazine covering medical emergencies for general practition-
ers. **Freq:** Bimonthly. **Print Method:** Offset. **Key Personnel:** Dr. J. Andris,
Editor-in-Chief, phone 32 2 653 0781, fax 32 2 652 0184, ja@diffu-
sciences.com. **Subscription Rates:** Free to qualified subscribers. **Remarks:**
Accepts advertising.
Ad Rates: 4C: 2,500 BFr   **Circ:** Non-paid ⊕15,000

OOSTENDE

📖 **329 Motorhome ABC**
Uitgeverij de Groeve
Postbus 728   Ph: 32 59702814
B-8400 Oostende, Belgium   Fax: 32 59702834

Consumer magazine covering recreational vehicles in French and Dutch.
Founded: 2001. **Freq:** Annual. **Print Method:** Offset litho. **Cols./Page:** 4.
Col. Width: 45 millimeters. **Col. Depth:** 273 millimeters. **Key Personnel:**
Jan De Groeve, Editor; Albrecht De Groeve, Editor. **Subscription Rates:**
€4.95 single issue. **Remarks:** Accepts advertising.
Ad Rates: BW: €1,750   **Circ:** Paid ‡29,750
                4C: €2,500

OOSTERZELE-BAL

📖 **330 European Journal of Hospital Pharmacy**
European Association of Hospital Pharmacists
Association Europeene des Pharmaciens des Hopitaux
Walzegem, 6   Ph: 32 93603789
B-9860 Oosterzele-Bal, Belgium   Fax: 32 93613010
Publisher E-mail: lukcism@pandora.be

European journal covering pharmacy. **Freq:** Periodic. **Key Personnel:** Luc P.
Haesebeyt, Prof. Secretary. **ISSN:** 0939-9437. **Subscription Rates:** 48 BFr.
Remarks: Advertising accepted; rates available upon request.

Circ: (Not Reported)

RUMBEKE

📖 **331 CORE Magazine**
Uitgeverij New Idea
Gebr. Van Raemdonckstraat 5   Ph: 32 51207909
B-8800 Rumbeke, Belgium   Fax: 32 51202966

Consumer magazine covering "fun fashion" and the active lifestyle. **Subtitle:** Fun Fashion & Active Life. **Freq:** Semiannual. **Print Method:** Offset. **Trim Size:** A4. **Cols./Page:** 3. **Key Personnel:** Guy Hochepied, Director, guy@newidea.be; A. Santens, Editor; Antoinette Hoorne, Editor, antoinette.hoorne@skynet.be; V. Symoens, Editor. **Subscription Rates:** Free in fashion shops and sportswear stores. **Alt. Formats:** CD-ROM.
Ad Rates: BW: €1,450   **Circ:** 30,000
               4C: €1,735

WILRIJK

📖 **332 Anatomia, Histologia, Embryologia**
World Association of Veterinary Anatomists
Department of Veterinary Science
Anatomy and Embryology of Domestic
   Animals
Gebouw U
Universiteitsplein 1   Ph: 32 38202434
B-2810 Wilrijk, Belgium   Fax: 32 38202433
Publisher E-mail: andre.weyns@ua.ac.be

Professional publication covering veterinary medicine. **Subtitle:** Journal of the World Association of Veterinary Anatomists. **Freq:** Quarterly.

BRAZIL

CAMPINA GRANDE

📖 **333 SBA: Controle e Automacao**
Brazilian Society for Automation
Sociedade Brasileira de Automatica
DEE/UFPB
CP 10.105
58109-970 Campina Grande, Pernambuco,   Ph: 55 19 37883767
   Brazil   Fax: 55 19 32891395
Publication E-mail: revista_sba@fee.umicamp.br
Publisher E-mail: sba@dee.ufpb.br

English, Portuguese and Spanish language publication covering automation. **Founded:** 1989. **Freq:** Quarterly. **Key Personnel:** Joao B.R. Do Val, Editor-in-Chief. **ISSN:** 0103-1759. **Remarks:** Advertising not accepted. **URL:** http://www.fee.unicamp.br/revista_sba.
                                               Circ: 800

RIO DE JANEIRO

📖 **334 Ciencia Hoje**
Brazilian Association for the Advancement of Science
Sociedade Brasileira para o Progresso da Ciencia
Av. Venceslau Bras
71 Fundos
Casa 27   Ph: 55 2122954846
22290-140 Rio de Janeiro, RJ, Brazil   Fax: 55 2125415342
Publisher E-mail: chojered@sbpcnet.org.br

Portuguese language publication covering science. **Founded:** July 1982. **Freq:** Monthly. **Trim Size:** 21 x 28 cm. **Key Personnel:** Alicia Ivanissevich, Contact, alicia@sbpcnet.org.br. **ISSN:** 0101-8515. **Subscription Rates:** US$100 individuals; US$10 single issue. **Remarks:** Accepts advertising. **URL:** http://www.ciencia.org.br.
                                               Circ: Paid 13,000

📖 **335 Ciencia Hoje das Criancas**
Brazilian Association for the Advancement of Science
Sociedade Brasileira para o Progresso da Ciencia
Av. Venceslau Bras
71 Fundos
Casa 27   Ph: 55 2122954846
22290-140 Rio de Janeiro, RJ, Brazil   Fax: 55 2125415342
Publication E-mail: chcred@cbpf.br
Publisher E-mail: chojered@sbpcnet.org.br

Portuguese language science magazine for children. **Founded:** Dec. 1986. **Freq:** Monthly. **Trim Size:** 21 x 28 cm. **Key Personnel:** Bianca Encarnagao, Contact. **ISSN:** 0103-2054. **Subscription Rates:** US$73 individuals; US$7 single issue. **Remarks:** Advertising accepted; rates available upon request.
                                               Circ: Paid 194,000

SAO PAULO

📖 **336 RTI—Redes, Telecom and Instalacoes**
Aranda Editora Ltda
Alameda Olga, 315   Ph: 55 1138245300
01155-900 Sao Paulo, SP, Brazil   Fax: 55 1136669585
Publication E-mail: inforti@arandanet.com.br
Publisher E-mail: info@arandanet.com.br

Technical magazine covering for the telecom, datacom, and building systems markets in Brazil. **Freq:** Monthly. **Key Personnel:** Jose Rubens Alves de Souza, Editor-in-Chief; Sandra Mogami, Editor; Edgard Laureano da Cunha, Jr., Director; Ronaldo Amorim Barbosa, Production Mgr.; Clayton Delfino, Circulation; Silvio Paulo da Silva, Advertising Dir.; Elcio S. Cavalcanti, Advertising Mgr.; Patricia Rudek, Sales Rep.; Alexandre Rodrigues, Sales Rep. **Subscription Rates:** Free to qualified subscribers. **URL:** http://www.arandanet.com.br/rti/.
Ad Rates: BW: US$1,930   **Circ:** Non-paid 12,000
               4C: US$2,881

PEOPLE'S REPUBLIC OF CHINA

BEIJING

📖 **337 Acta Agronomica Sinica**
Crop Science Society of China
12 Zhonggguancun South Rd.   Ph: 86 10689186816
Beijing 100081, People's Republic of China   Fax: 86 1062174865
Publication E-mail: xbzw@chinajournal.net.cn
Publisher E-mail: yguo@public.bta.net.cn

Chinese and English language publication covering agricultural development. **Founded:** 1950. **Freq:** Bimonthly. **Key Personnel:** Zhuang Qiaosheng, Editor-in-Chief, phone 86 01068919111, fax 86 01068919111. **ISSN:** 0496-3490. **Subscription Rates:** 26 Yu. **Formerly:** Journal of Agricultural Research (1952); Academic Journal of Agriculture (1961).
Ad Rates: BW: US$200   **Circ:** 12,000
               4C: US$500

📖 **338 Acta Geographica Sinica**
Bldg. 917, Datun Rd.   Ph: 86 1064889295
Beijing 100101, People's Republic of China   Fax: 86 1064889598
Publication E-mail: acta@igsnrr.ac.cn
Publisher E-mail: gsc@igsnrr.ac.cn

Chinese language publication covering geography. **Founded:** 1934. **Freq:** Bimonthly. **Trim Size:** 188 x 260 mm. **Key Personnel:** Yao Lufeng, Contact. **ISSN:** 0375-5444. **Subscription Rates:** 26 Yu. **Remarks:** Accepts advertising. **URL:** http://www.igsnrr.ac.cn/geo/index.jsp. **Alt. Formats:** CD-ROM.
Ad Rates: BW: US$550   **Circ:** 1,700
               4C: US$750

📖 **339 Auto China**
China Daily
15 Huixindongjie
Chaoyang District   Ph: 86 1064924488
Beijing 100029, People's Republic of China   Fax: 86 1064918377
Publication E-mail: autochina@chinadaily.com.cn
Publisher E-mail: office@chinadaily.com.cn

Periodical covering Chinese automotive industry. **Freq:** Biweekly. **Subscription Rates:** US$598. **URL:** http://bdu.chinadaily.com.cn/autochina-2.shtml.

📖 **340 Beijing Review**
Beijing Review Publishing Co.
24 Baiwanzhuang Rd.
Beijing 100037, People's Republic of China   Ph: 86 108315599
Publication E-mail: bjreviewdd@fm365.com

Periodical covering political, economic, and social developments in China today. **Subtitle:** A Magazine of Chinese News and Views. **Founded:** 1958. **Freq:** Weekly. **Key Personnel:** Lii Haibo, Editor-in-Chief. **ISSN:** 1000-9140.

Subscription Rates: US$64. **Remarks:** Advertising accepted; rates available upon request. **URL:** http://www.bjreview.com.cn.

Circ: Paid 100,000

341 Beijing This Month
Asia Systems Media Corp.
Asian Games Garden
Building No. 2-6A
No. 12 Xiaoying Lu
Chao Yang District
Beijing 100101, People's Republic of China   Ph: 86 1084634451
Publication E-mail: consultants@cbw.com

General interest periodical. **Freq:** Monthly. **Key Personnel:** Li Mingxia, Deputy Editor-in-Chief. **URL:** http://www.cbw.com/btm.

342 Business Beijing
Asia Systems Media Corp.
Asian Games Garden
Building No. 2-6A
No. 12 Xiaoying Lu
Chao Yang District
Beijing 100101, People's Republic of China   Ph: 86 1084634451
Publication E-mail: consultants@cbw.com

Chinese business magazine. **Freq:** Monthly. **URL:** http://cbw.com/busbj.

343 China Aero Information
Aviation Industry Press
14 Xiaoguan Dongli
Xiaoguan Dongli
Anwai
Beijing 100029, People's Republic of China   Ph: 86 1064918417

Periodical covering the Chinese aviation industry. **Freq:** Monthly. **Key Personnel:** Zhang Yong, Editor. **ISSN:** 1003-6008. **Subscription Rates:** US$100. **Remarks:** Advertising accepted; rates available upon request. **Available Online.**

Circ: (Not Reported)

344 China and Africa
Ministry of Culture Foreign Language Bureau
23 Baiwanzhuang Lu
Fuwai
Beijing 100037, People's Republic of China   Ph: 86 108315599

Journal dealing with political ties between China and Africa. **Freq:** Monthly. **Key Personnel:** Zhang Lifang, Editor.

345 China Auto
China Automotive Technology and Research Center
45 Zengguang Rd.
Haidian
Beijing 100037, People's Republic of China   Ph: 86 108424477

Publication providing comprehensive analysis of the automotive industry in China. **Founded:** 1991. **Freq:** Bimonthly. **Key Personnel:** Zhu Dezhao, Editor. **ISSN:** 1002-0918. **Subscription Rates:** US$150. **Remarks:** Advertising accepted; rates available upon request.

Circ: (Not Reported)

346 China Books
China International Book Trading Corp.
PO Box 339C
Beijing 100037, People's Republic of China   Ph: 86 1068413849
Publication E-mail: cibtc@mail.cibtc.com.cn

Journal dealing with publishing and book trade. **Founded:** 1981. **Freq:** Quarterly.

347 China Business
China Business (Press) Hong Kong
No. 23 Building
Guanying Yuan Xiqu
Xicheng District
Beijing 100035, People's Republic of China   Ph: 86 1066160951
Publication E-mail: xinli@chinabusiness-press.com

English-language business magazine approved-by-the-Ministry-of Foreign Trade and Economic Cooperation, the People's Republic of China. **Founded:** 1993. **URL:** http://www.chinabusiness-press.com.

348 China Chemical Week
No. 2 Beixiaojie
Liupukang
Xicheng District   Ph: 86 1082032247
Beijing 100011, People's Republic of China   Fax: 86 1082030116
Publication E-mail: arzuo@vip.sina.com

Newspaper covering the Chinese chemical industry. **Founded:** 1994. **Freq:** Weekly. **Key Personnel:** Zu Yinxue. **Subscription Rates:** US$50. **Remarks:** Advertising accepted; rates available upon request. **URL:** http://www.chemweek.com.cn.

Circ: Paid 100,000

349 China Computer Reseller World
IDG China
Rm. 616
COFCO Plaza
Jianguomennei Dajie
Beijing 100005, People's Republic of China   Ph: 86 1065260959
Publication E-mail: dumin@idg.com.cn

Journal dealing with computers. **Key Personnel:** Weisheng Wang, Editor. **Available Online.**
Ad Rates: 4C: 20,000 Yu   **Circ:** (Not Reported)

350 China Environment News
Circulation Dept
15 A, Xiaoxinglong Jie
Beijing 100062, People's Republic of China   Ph: 86 1067122478
Publication E-mail: cnenv@public3.bta.net.cn

Newspaper featuring information about Chinese policies, technologies and research for environmental protection in industry and agriculture. **Founded:** 1989. **Freq:** Monthly. **Key Personnel:** Zhenglong Xu, Editor. **Subscription Rates:** US$24.

Circ: Paid 20,000

351 China Pictorial
China Pictorial Publishing House
33 Chegongzhuang West Rd.
Haidian District
Beijing 100044, People's Republic of China   Ph: 86 1068412390

Magazine featuring China's magnificent scenery, the life of its people, and its works of art. **Founded:** 1950. **Freq:** Monthly. **ISSN:** 0009-4420. **Subscription Rates:** US$24.60.

Circ: Paid 500,000

352 China Screen
China Film Import & Export Corp.
25 Xinjiekouwai Dajie
Beijing 100088, People's Republic of China

Periodical covering new Chinese films. Features articles on actors, actresses, directors, and films. **Founded:** 1980. **Freq:** Quarterly. **Subscription Rates:** US$12.

353 China Sports
People's Sports Publishing House
8 Tiyuguan Lu
Chongwen-qu
Beijing 100061, People's Republic of China   Ph: 86 1067112086

Periodical covering athletic events, sports training, traditional Chinese sports and martial arts. **Founded:** 1957. **Freq:** Monthly. **ISSN:** 0577-8948. **Subscription Rates:** US$36.70. **Remarks:** Advertising accepted; rates available upon request.
Circ: 50,000

354 China & the World
Beijing Review Publishing Co.
24 Baiwanzhuang Rd.
Beijing 100037, People's Republic of China   Ph: 86 108315599

Publication dealing with political science. **Subtitle:** Beijing Review Foreign Affairs Series. **Founded:** 1982. **Key Personnel:** Zhou Guo, Editor.

355 China's Foreign Trade
China Chamber of International Commerce (CCOIC)
1 Fuxingmenwai St
Beijing 100860, People's Republic of China   Ph: 86 1068513344

Periodical containing articles on Chinese economic development and specialty products, as well as information on Chinese imports and exports, and related policies and regulations. **Founded:** 1956. **Freq:** Monthly. **Key Personnel:** Xinyi Li, Editor. **ISSN:** 0009-4498. **Subscription Rates:** US$99.40. **Remarks:** Advertising accepted; rates available upon request.
Circ: Paid 70,000

356 Chinese Medical Journal
Chinese Medical Association
ATTN: Wang De
42 Dongsi Xidajie
Beijing 100710, People's Republic of China   Ph: 86 1065271226
Publication E-mail: order@cmj.org

Journal related to medicine. **Freq:** Monthly. **Key Personnel:** De Wang, Scientific Editor, editor@cmj.org. **ISSN:** 0366-6999. **Subscription Rates:** US$240. **URL:** http://www.cmj.org/YW.htm. **Alt. Formats:** CD-ROM.

357 Journal of Aeronautical Materials
Chinese Society of Aeronautics and Astronautics
PO Box 81   Ph: 86 1062458063
Beijing 100095, People's Republic of China   Fax: 86 1062456212
Publisher E-mail: hkclxb@biam.ac.cn

Chinese journal covering aerospace. **Subtitle:** Hangkong Cailao Xuebao. **Founded:** 1989. **Freq:** Quarterly. **Print Method:** Offset. **Trim Size:** 210 x 296 mm. **Key Personnel:** Yan Minggao, Contact, phone 86 1062458029, fax 86 1062456212, minggao.yan@biam.ac.cn. **ISSN:** 1005-5053. **Subscription Rates:** 20 Yu individuals; 5 Yu single issue. **Remarks:** Advertising not accepted. **Online:** Ei (Compendex). **URL:** http://mail.periodicals.net.cn; http://www.cnki.net. **Alt. Formats:** CD-ROM.
Circ: (Not Reported)

358 Journal of Aerospace Power
Chinese Society of Aeronautics and Astronautics
37 Xueyuan Rd.
Beijing 100083, People's Republic of China   Ph: 86 1082317410
Publisher E-mail: hkclxb@biam.ac.cn

Chinese language journal covering aerospace. **Founded:** 1986. **Freq:** Bimonthly. **Trim Size:** 162 x 255 mm. **Key Personnel:** Cao Chuanjun, Contact, phone 86 1082313794, JAP@ns.ngl.buaa.edu.cn. **ISSN:** 1000-8055. **Subscription Rates:** US$120 individuals U.S.; US$20 single issue U.S. **Remarks:** Accepts advertising. **Available Online. Formerly:** Wu Yi Huang.
Circ: Paid 3,000

359 Journal of the China University of Geosciences
China University of Geosciences
29 Xueyuan Lu
Beijing 100083, People's Republic of China   Ph: 86 2787481794
Publication E-mail: xbb@dns.cug.edu.cn

Journal related to earth science. **Founded:** 1957. **Freq:** Bimonthly. **Key Personnel:** Pengda Zhao, Editor, xbb@dns.cug.edu.cn. **Available Online.**

360 Journal of Geographical Sciences
Bldg. 917, Datun Rd.   Ph: 86 1064870663
Beijing 100101, People's Republic of China   Fax: 86 1064889598
Publication E-mail: jgs@igsnrr.ac.cn
Publisher E-mail: gsc@igsnrr.ac.cn

Professional journal covering geographical science. **Founded:** 1990. **Freq:** Quarterly. **Trim Size:** 188 x 260 mm. **Key Personnel:** Zhao Xin, Contact, phone 86 1064889293. **ISSN:** 1009-637X. **Subscription Rates:** US$120 individuals; US$30 single issue. **Remarks:** Accepts advertising. **URL:** http://www.igsnrr.ac.cn/geo/index.jsp.
Ad Rates: BW: 550 Yu   **Circ:** Paid ‡700
4C: 750 Yu

361 Motor China
China North Vehicle Research
Building 8
Cuiwei Nanli
Wanshou Rd.
Haidian District
Beijing 100036, People's Republic of China   Ph: 86 1068217240

Periodical offering Chinese mechanics and automotive technicians with the latest information about automotive technology impacting the Chinese market. **Founded:** 1996. **Freq:** Monthly. **Key Personnel:** Li Qiang, Managing Editor, lq@motorchina.com. **Remarks:** Advertising accepted; rates available upon request. **URL:** http://www.motorchina.com/2002.11/main_eng.htm.
Circ: (Not Reported)

362 People's Daily
People's Daily Online
Jintaixi Rd. No. 2
Chaoyang District
Beijing 100733, People's Republic of China   Ph: 86 1065368361
Publication E-mail: info@peopledaily.com.cn

General online newspaper. **Founded:** 1948. **Freq:** Daily. **Remarks:** Advertising accepted; rates available upon request. **URL:** http://english.peopledaily.com.cn/home.shtml.
Circ: 3,000,000

HENAN

363 China's Refractories
Jinxiang Wang
No. 43 Xiyuan Lu
Jianxi-qu Luoyang
Henan 471039, People's Republic of China   Ph: 86 3794913501
Publication E-mail: nhcl@public2.lyptt.ha.cn.

Publishes important news and statistical data on the Chinese refractories market as well as technical and academic discussions. **Founded:** 1992. **Freq:** Quarterly. **Key Personnel:** Liu Jiehua, Editor-in-Chief, jiehua@public2.lyptt.ha.cn. **ISSN:** 1004-4493. **Subscription Rates:** US$76. **Remarks:** Advertising accepted; rates available upon request. **URL:** http://www.china-refract.org/cr/default.htm.
Circ: (Not Reported)

HONG KONG

364 Action Asia
19/F, Winsome House
73 Wyndham St., Central
Hong Kong, People's Republic of China   Ph: 852 21652800

Magazine of environment, health and tourism. **Freq:** Monthly. **Subscription Rates:** HK$250. **Remarks:** Advertising accepted; rates available upon request. **URL:** http://www.actionasia.com/.
Circ: (Not Reported)

365 Arts of Asia
Arts of Asia Publications Ltd.
1309 Kowloon Centre
29-39 Ashley Rd.
Kowloon
Hong Kong, People's Republic of China   Ph: 852 23762228
Publication E-mail: info@artsofasianet.com

Magazine of Asian arts. **Founded:** 1970. **Freq:** Bimonthly. **ISSN:** 0004-4083. **URL:** http://www.artsofasianet.com.

📖 **366 Artslink**
Hong Kong Arts Centre
2 Harbour Rd., Wanchai
Hong Kong, People's Republic of China   Ph: 852 25820200
Publication E-mail: hkac@hkac.org.hk

Periodical featuring all programs and activities presented by the Hong Kong Arts Center. **Freq:** Monthly. **Key Personnel:** Joanne Chiu, Editor, jchao@hkac.org.hk. **URL:** http://www.hkac.org.hk.

Circ: 40,000

📖 **367 Asia Asset Management**
PO Box 33743
Sheung Wan Post Office
Hong Kong SAR
Hong Kong, People's Republic of China   Fax: 852 25489544
Publication E-mail: enquiries@asiaasset.com

Periodical focusing on the institutional fund management industry. **Founded:** 1996. **Freq:** 11/year. **Key Personnel:** Tan Lee Hock, Editor, editor@asiaasset.com. **ISSN:** 1029-5305. **Subscription Rates:** US$1,200. **Remarks:** Advertising accepted; rates available upon request. **URL:** http://www.asiaasset.com/eng/aboutus.shtml.

Circ: (Not Reported)

📖 **368 Asia Labour Monitor**
Asia Monitor Resource Center
444 Nathan Rd., 8-B
Kowloon
Hong Kong, People's Republic of China
Publication E-mail: admin@amrc.org.hk

Publication focusing on Asian labour concerns. **Founded:** 1983. **Freq:** Bimonthly. **ISSN:** 0258-0268. **URL:** http://www.amrc.org.hk.

📖 **369 Asia Law and Practice**
Euromoney Publications (Jersey) Ltd.
5/F Printing House
6 Duddell St., Central
Hong Kong, People's Republic of China   Ph: 852 25233399
Publication E-mail: info@euromoneyasia.com

Law magazine. **Freq:** Monthly. **Key Personnel:** Alison Shaw, Editorial Dir., ashaw@alphk.com. **Remarks:** Advertising accepted; rates available upon request. **URL:** http://www.asialaw.com/.

Circ: (Not Reported)

📖 **370 Asia Money**
Asiamoney
Rm. 203-206, 2/F Printing House
6 Duddell St.
Central
Hong Kong, People's Republic of China   Ph: 852 29128050

Publication providing information on Asian finance, banking, investment and treasury. **Freq:** Monthly. **Key Personnel:** Chris Wright, Editor, chris.wright@asiamoney.com. **Remarks:** Advertising accepted; rates available upon request. **URL:** http://www.asiamoney.com.

Circ: (Not Reported)

📖 **371 Asia Textile & Apparel Journal**
Adsale Publishing Co.
4/F Stanhope House
734 King's Rd.
North Point
Hong Kong, People's Republic of China   Ph: 852 28118897
Publication E-mail: cta.ata@adsale.com.hk

Trade magazine on the textile and apparel industry. **Freq:** Bimonthly. **Remarks:** Advertising accepted; rates available upon request. **URL:** http://www.2456.com/eng/epub/content.asp?epubiid=4&pg=1.

Circ: Controlled 15,432

📖 **372 Asian Affairs**
PO Box 10086
15/F Supreme Commercial Bldg.
368 King's Rd., North Point
Hong Kong, People's Republic of China   Ph: 852 29802824
Publication E-mail: editor@asian-affairs.com

Publication focusing on business, economics, politics and review. **Founded:** 1997. **Freq:** Quarterly. **ISSN:** 1029-1903. **Subscription Rates:** US$100. **URL:** http://www.asian-affairs.com/Frame/hongkong.html.

📖 **373 Asian Financial Law Briefing**
Pacific Business Press Ltd.
Ste. 2701
27/F, 8 Wing Hing St.
Causeway Bay
Hong Kong, People's Republic of China   Ph: 852 25420505
                                               Fax: 852 25750004
Publication E-mail: sales@pbpress.com
Publisher E-mail: sales@pbpress.com

Asia's leading business and legal forum. **Freq:** Monthly. **Key Personnel:** Arun Sudhaman, Managing Editor, sudhaman@pbpress.com. **Subscription Rates:** HK$1,550.

📖 **374 Asian IP**
Pacific Business Press Ltd.
Ste. 2701
27/F, 8 Wing Hing St.
Causeway Bay
Hong Kong, People's Republic of China   Ph: 852 25420505
                                               Fax: 852 25750004
Publication E-mail: sales@pbpress.com
Publisher E-mail: sales@pbpress.com

Publication focusing on the growing world of intellectual property from a uniquely Asian perspective. **Freq:** Monthly. **Key Personnel:** Arun Sudhaman, Managing Editor, sudhaman@pbpress.com. **Subscription Rates:** HK$2,995.

📖 **375 The Asset**
Asset Publishing & Research Limited
15th Fl., Trust Tower
68 Johnston Rd.
Wanchai
Hong Kong, People's Republic of China   Ph: 852 25736078
Publication E-mail: info@assetglobal.com

Finance magazine. **Founded:** 1999. **Freq:** Monthly. **Key Personnel:** Daniel Yu, Editor-in-Chief. **Subscription Rates:** US$280. **Remarks:** Advertising accepted; rates available upon request. **URL:** http://www.theassetonline.com/.

Circ: (Not Reported)

📖 **376 Building Journal Hong Kong**
China Trend Building Press Ltd.
Rm. 901, C C Wu Bldg.
302 Hennessy Rd.
Wanchai
Hong Kong, People's Republic of China   Ph: 852 28026299

Journal covering building and construction. **Freq:** Monthly. **Subscription Rates:** HK$500. **URL:** http://www.building.com.hk/bjhk/bjindex.html.
Ad Rates: BW: HK$6,500   **Circ:** (Not Reported)
                  4C: HK$9,500

📖 **377 Canada Hong Kong Business**
The Canadian Chamber of Commerce in Hong Kong
Ste. 1003 Kinwick Center
32 Hollywood Rd., Central
Hong Kong, People's Republic of China   Ph: 852 21108700

Publication of the Canadian Chamber of Commerce in Hong Kong. **Freq:** Bimonthly. **URL:** http://www.cancham.org/html/advertising_chkb.htm.

☐ 378 CFO Asia
CFO Publishing Corporation
18 Harbour Rd.
Wanchai
Hong Kong, People's Republic of China   Ph: 852 25853888
Publication E-mail: heathermartino@economist.com

Magazine for Asia's leading corporate financial executives. **Founded:** 1998. **Freq:** Monthly. **Key Personnel:** Tom Leander, Editor-in-Chief, tomleander@economist.com. **ISSN:** 1560-3539. **Remarks:** Advertising accepted; rates available upon request. **URL:** http://www.cfoasia.com/index.html.
Circ: (Not Reported)

☐ 379 Computer Today Monthly
Modern Electronic & Computing Publishing Co. Ltd.
15-17 Shing Yip St.
9/F, Rm. 1, Kwun Tong
Kowloon
Hong Kong, People's Republic of China   Ph: 852 23428299
Publication E-mail: computertoday@electronictechnology.com

Comprehensive magazine specially designed for computer's end user. **Founded:** 1988. **Freq:** Monthly. **URL:** http://www.electronictechnology.com.

☐ 380 Coutoure
Communication Management Ltd.
1811 Hong Kong Plaza
188 Connaught Rd. W.
Hong Kong   Ph: 852 25477117
Hong Kong, People's Republic of China   Fax: 852 28582671
Publication E-mail: cmail@cmlink.com

Magazine on apparel & fashion. **Key Personnel:** Lina Ross, Editor. **Remarks:** Advertising accepted; rates available upon request. **URL:** http://www.hkcouture.com/index2.html.
Circ: (Not Reported)

☐ 381 Hinge
Hinge Marketing Ltd.
2/F West, Sincere Insurance Bldg.
6 Hennessy Rd.
Wanchai
Hong Kong, People's Republic of China   Ph: 852 25202468
Publication E-mail: hinge@hingenet.com

Architecture and design magazine. **Founded:** 1993. **Freq:** Monthly. **URL:** http://www.hingenet.com.
Ad Rates: 4C: HK$9,600   **Circ:** (Not Reported)

☐ 382 Home Journal
Communication Management Ltd.
1811 Hong Kong Plaza
188 Connaught Rd. W.
Hong Kong   Ph: 852 25477117
Hong Kong, People's Republic of China   Fax: 852 28582671
Publication E-mail: home@cmlink.com

Magazine on interior design. **Founded:** 1980. **Freq:** Monthly. **URL:** http://www.hkhomejournal.com.

☐ 383 Hong Kong Apparel
Hong Kong Trade Development Council
38th Fl., Office Tower, Convention Plaza
1 Harbour Rd.
Wanchai
Hong Kong, People's Republic of China   Ph: 852 25844333

Publication providing information on high-quality ready-to-wear and designer fashions and accessories. **Founded:** 1969. **Freq:** Semiannual. **Subscription Rates:** HK$240 two years. **URL:** http://www.tdctrade.com/prodmag/apparel/apparel.htm.
Ad Rates: 4C: HK$11,500   **Circ:** (Not Reported)

☐ 384 Hong Kong for the Business Visitor
Hong Kong Trade Development Council
38th Fl., Office Tower, Convention Plaza
1 Harbour Rd.
Wanchai
Hong Kong, People's Republic of China   Ph: 852 25844333
Publication E-mail: hktdc@tdc.org.hk

Journal of travel, tourism, business and economics. **Founded:** 1997. **Freq:** Annual. **ISSN:** 1028-1606. **Remarks:** Advertising accepted; rates available upon request. **URL:** http://www.tdc.org.hk.
Circ: 40,000

☐ 385 Hong Kong Dermatology and Venereology Bulletin
Medcom Limited
Rm. 1310, Olympia Plaza
255 King's Rd., North Point
Hong Kong, People's Republic of China   Ph: 852 25783833

Magazine of dermatology. **Freq:** Monthly. **URL:** http://www.medicine.org.hk/hksdv/bulletin.htm.

☐ 386 Hong Kong Design Services
Hong Kong Trade Development Council
38th Fl., Office Tower, Convention Plaza
1 Harbour Rd.
Wanchai
Hong Kong, People's Republic of China   Ph: 852 25844333
Publication E-mail: hktdc@tdc.org.hk

Journal of interior design and decoration. **Founded:** 1997. **Freq:** Annual. **ISSN:** 1026-6704. **URL:** http://www.tdc.org.hk.

☐ 387 Hong Kong Electronic Components & Parts
Hong Kong Trade Development Council
38th Fl., Office Tower, Convention Plaza
1 Harbour Rd.
Wanchai
Hong Kong, People's Republic of China   Ph: 852 25844333

Guide for electronic components and parts manufacturers, traders and agents in Hong Kong. **Founded:** 1996. **Freq:** Quarterly. **Subscription Rates:** HK$250. **URL:** http://www.tdctrade.com/prodmag/elecom/elecom.htm.
Ad Rates: 4C: HK$12,000   **Circ:** (Not Reported)

☐ 388 Hong Kong Electronics
Hong Kong Trade Development Council
38th Fl., Office Tower, Convention Plaza
1 Harbour Rd.
Wanchai
Hong Kong, People's Republic of China   Ph: 852 25844333

Publication focusing on innovative electronic products. **Founded:** 1985. **Freq:** Bimonthly. **ISSN:** 1021-8866. **Subscription Rates:** HK$480. **URL:** http://www.tdctrade.com/prodmag/electron/electron.htm.
Ad Rates: 4C: HK$12,000   **Circ:** Paid 50,000

☐ 389 Hong Kong Enterprise
Hong Kong Trade Development Council
38th Fl., Office Tower, Convention Plaza
1 Harbour Rd.
Wanchai
Hong Kong, People's Republic of China   Ph: 852 25844333
Publication E-mail: hktdc@tdc.org.hk

Journal of gifts, toys and clothing trade. **Founded:** 1967. **Freq:** Monthly. **ISSN:** 1021-5611. **Subscription Rates:** HK$1,620. **URL:** http://www.tdctrade.com/prodmag/enterpri/enterpri.htm.
Ad Rates: 4C: HK$16,800   **Circ:** Paid 150,000

☐ 390 Hong Kong Fabrics & Accessories
Hong Kong Trade Development Council
38th Fl., Office Tower, Convention Plaza
1 Harbour Rd.
Wanchai
Hong Kong, People's Republic of China   Ph: 852 25844333

Fabrics and accessories magazine. **Founded:** 1995. **Freq:** Semiannual.

Subscription Rates: HK$240 two years. **URL:** http://www.tdctrade.com/prodmag/fabrics/fabrics.htm.
Ad Rates: 4C: HK$11,500   **Circ:** (Not Reported)

📖 **391 Hong Kong Fashion Flash**
Hong Kong Trade Development Council
Fashion Dept.
38th Fl., Office Tower, Convention Plaza
1 Harbour Rd.
Wanchai
Hong Kong, People's Republic of China   Ph: 852 25844333

Fashion design magazine. **Freq:** Semiannual. **Key Personnel:** Patrick Lam, Editor-in-Chief. **ISSN:** 1563-2644. **Subscription Rates:** HK$40; HK$50 other countries.

📖 **392 Hong Kong Footwear**
Hong Kong Trade Development Council
38th Fl., Office Tower, Convention Plaza
1 Harbour Rd.
Wanchai
Hong Kong, People's Republic of China   Ph: 852 25844333

Publication focusing on the footwear industry. **Founded:** 1997. **Freq:** Semiannual. **Subscription Rates:** HK$240 two years. **URL:** http://www.tdctrade.com/prodmag/footwear/footwear.htm.
Ad Rates: 4C: HK$11,500   **Circ:** (Not Reported)

📖 **393 Hong Kong Gifts, Premiums & Stationery**
Hong Kong Trade Development Council
38th Fl., Office Tower, Convention Plaza
1 Harbour Rd.
Wanchai
Hong Kong, People's Republic of China   Ph: 852 25844333

Publication focusing on innovative gifts and creative premiums. **Founded:** 1986. **Freq:** Quarterly. **Subscription Rates:** HK$290. **URL:** http://www.tdctrade.com/prodmag/gifts/gifts.htm.
Ad Rates: 4C: HK$13,000   **Circ:** (Not Reported)

📖 **394 Hong Kong Household**
Hong Kong Trade Development Council
38th Fl., Office Tower, Convention Plaza
1 Harbour Rd.
Wanchai
Hong Kong, People's Republic of China   Ph: 852 25844333

Publication providing information on all sorts of household and hardware products. **Founded:** 1983. **Freq:** Semiannual. **Subscription Rates:** HK$300 two years. **URL:** http://www.tdctrade.com/prodmag/house/house.htm.
Ad Rates: 4C: HK$11,500   **Circ:** (Not Reported)

📖 **395 Hong Kong Industrialist**
Federation of Hong Kong Industries
4-F, Hankow Centre
5-15 Hankow Rd.
Tsim Sha Tsui
Kowloon
Hong Kong, People's Republic of China   Ph: 852 27323188
Publication E-mail: fhki@fhki.org.hk

Journal covering business and economics. **Founded:** 1962. **Freq:** Monthly. **Subscription Rates:** HK$400. **Remarks:** Advertising accepted; rates available upon request. **URL:** http://www.fhki.org.hk.
                                                Circ: Paid 35,000

📖 **396 Hong Kong Jewellery Collection**
Hong Kong Trade Development Council
38th Fl., Office Tower, Convention Plaza
1 Harbour Rd.
Wanchai
Hong Kong, People's Republic of China   Ph: 852 25844333

Magazine on jewellery collection. **Founded:** 1985. **Freq:** Semiannual.

Subscription Rates: HK$240 two years. **URL:** http://www.tdctrade.com/prodmag/jewell/jewell.htm.
Ad Rates: 4C: HK$11,500   **Circ:** (Not Reported)

📖 **397 Hong Kong Jewelry Express Magazine**
Hong Kong Jewelry Manufacturers Association
Unit G, 2/F, Phase 2, Kaiser Estate
51 Man Yue St.
Hunghom
Kowloon   Ph: 852 27663002
Hong Kong, People's Republic of China   Fax: 852 23623647
Publication E-mail: hkjma@jewelry.org.hk
Publisher E-mail: hkjma@jewelry.org.hk

Publication of the Hong Kong Jewelry Manufacturers' Association. **Founded:** 1997. **Freq:** Quarterly. **ISSN:** 1682-7333. **Subscription Rates:** HK$200. **URL:** http://www.jewelry.org.hk/.

📖 **398 Hong Kong Journal of Applied Linguistics**
The University of Hong Kong
The English Centre
Pokfulam Rd.
Hong Kong, People's Republic of China   Ph: 852 28592004
Publication E-mail: hkjal@hkucc.hku.hk

Publication catering to those who use English as a second or foreign language and have Chinese as their first language. **Founded:** 1996. **Freq:** Semiannual. **Key Personnel:** Vivien Berry, Editor, fax 85225473409, vberry@hkucc.hku.hk. **ISSN:** 1028-4435. **URL:** http://ec.hku.hk/hkjal/default.htm.

📖 **399 Hong Kong Journal of Mental Health**
Mental Health Association of Hong Kong
Jockey Club Building, 2
Kung Lok Rd.
Kwun Tong
Kowloon
Hong Kong, People's Republic of China   Ph: 852 25280196
Publication E-mail: mhahkho@mhahk.org.hk

Mental health journal. **Founded:** 1968. **Freq:** Semiannual. **ISSN:** 1560-9294. **URL:** http://www.mhahk.org.hk.

📖 **400 The Hong Kong Journal of Orthopaedic Surgery**
Pamela Youde Nethersole Eastern Hospital
Dept. of Orthopaedics and Traumatology
3 Lok Man Rd.
Chai Wan
Hong Kong, People's Republic of China

Journal that aims to serve as the communication channel for ideas and knowledge exchange in the field of orthopedic surgery among surgeons and the paramedical personnel. **Founded:** 1997. **Freq:** Semiannual. **Key Personnel:** Wu Wing-Cheung, Editor-in-Chief, wuwc@ha.org.hk. **ISSN:** 1028-2637. **Subscription Rates:** US$30. **URL:** http://www.hkjos.org/.

📖 **401 Hong Kong Journal of Paediatrics**
Medcom Limited
Dept. of Paediatrics
University of Hong Kong
Queen Mary Hospital
Pokfulam Rd.
Hong Kong, People's Republic of China

Official publication of the Hong Kong College of Pediatricians and Hong Kong Paediatric Society. **Founded:** 1984. **ISSN:** 1013-9923. **URL:** http://www.medicine.org.hk/hkcpaed/journal/home.htm.

Ad Rates: GLR = general line rate; BW = one-time black & white page rate; 4C = one-time four color page rate; SAU = standard advertising unit rate; CNU = Canadian newspaper advertising unit rate; PCI = per column inch rate.
Circulation: ★ = ABC; △ = BPA; ◆ = CAC; ● = CCAB; ❑ = VAC; ⊕ = PO Statement; ‡ = Publisher's Report; Boldface figures = sworn; Light figures = estimated.
Entry type: 📖 = Print; 🎙 = Broadcast.

45

402 The Hong Kong Journal of Psychiatry
The Hong Kong College of Psychiatrists
Rm. 906, Hong Kong Academy of
  Medicine Jockey Club Bldg.
99 Wong Chuk Hang Rd.
Aberdeen
Hong Kong, People's Republic of China   Ph: 852 28718777
Publication E-mail: admin@hkjpsych.com

Official journal of Hong Kong College of Psychiatrists. Aims to promote Chinese psychiatric research and practice. **Founded:** 1994. **Freq:** Annual. **ISSN:** 1026-2121. **URL:** http://www.hkjpsych.com/.

403 The Hong Kong Journal of Social Work
Hong Kong Social Workers Association Limited
Rm. 703, Duke of Windsor Social Service
  Bldg.
15 Hennessy Rd.
Wanchai
Hong Kong, People's Republic of China   Ph: 852 25281802
Publication E-mail: hkswa@hkswa.org.hk

Publication committed to the improvement of practice, extension of knowledge and promotion of communications in the broad field of social work. **Freq:** Semiannual. **Key Personnel:** Lai-chong Joyce Ma, Chief Editor. **ISSN:** 0219-2462. **Subscription Rates:** US$70 institutions and libraries. **URL:** http://www.worldscinet.com/hkjsw/hkjsw.shtml.

**404 The Hong Kong Journal of Sports Medicine and Sports
  Science**
Dr. Stephen Hui Research Centre for Physical Recreation and Wellness
Hong Kong Baptist University
c/o Dept. of Physical Education
Kowloon Tong
Kowloon
Hong Kong, People's Republic of China

Publishes articles in the field of sports medicine and sports science. **Freq:** Bimonthly. **Key Personnel:** Frank Fu, Chief Editor.

405 Hong Kong Law Reports & Digest
Sweet & Maxwell Asia
20/F Sunning Plaza
10 Hysan Ave.
Causeway Bay
Hong Kong, People's Republic of China   Ph: 852 28632600

Journal of law. **Founded:** 1997. **Freq:** Monthly. **ISSN:** 1029-7324.

406 Hong Kong Lawyer
The Law Society of Hong Kong
12/F, Hennessy Centre
500 Hennessy Rd.
Causeway Bay
Hong Kong, People's Republic of China   Fax: 852 2976 0840
Publication E-mail: june.tsui@butterworths-hk.com

Official journal of the Law Society of Hong Kong. **Freq:** Monthly. **Key Personnel:** Steven K. Lee, Gen. Editor, steven.lee@butterworths-hk.com. **ISSN:** 1025-9554. **URL:** http://www.hk-lawyer.com.

407 Hong Kong Leather Goods & Bags
Hong Kong Trade Development Council
38th Fl., Office Tower, Convention Plaza
1 Harbour Rd.
Wanchai
Hong Kong, People's Republic of China   Ph: 852 25844333

Publication providing information on leather goods and bags. **Founded:** 1993. **Freq:** Quarterly. **Subscription Rates:** HK$290. **URL:** http://www.tdctrade.com/prodmag/leather/leather.htm.
Ad Rates: 4C: HK$12,000   **Circ:** (Not Reported)

408 The Hong Kong Medical Diary
Medcom Limited
Rm. 1310, Olympia Plaza
255 King's Rd., North Point
Hong Kong, People's Republic of China   Ph: 852 25783833
Publication E-mail: fmshk@medcom.com.hk

Official publication of the Federation of Medical Societies of Hong Kong. **Freq:** Monthly. **Key Personnel:** Kwok Tin-fook, Editor-in-Chief. **URL:** http://medicine.org.hk/fmshk/hkmd.htm.
   Circ: 8,000

409 Hong Kong Medical Journal
10th Fl.
99 Wong Chuk Hang Rd.
Aberdeen
Hong Kong, People's Republic of China   Ph: 852 28718822
Publication E-mail: hkmj@hkam.org.hk

Publication of the Hong Kong Academy of Medicine (HKAM) and the Hong Kong Medical Association (HKMA). **Founded:** 1995. **Freq:** Bimonthly. **Key Personnel:** Y.L. Yu, Editor. **ISSN:** 1024-2708. **Subscription Rates:** HK$600. **URL:** http://www.hkmj.org.hk/hkmj.
Ad Rates: BW: **Circ:** Paid 7,100
         HK$10,000
         4C: HK$13,500

410 The Hong Kong Nursing Journal
Medcom Limited
College of Nursing, Hong Kong
12th Fl., Hyde Centre, 221 Gloucester Rd.
Wanchai
Hong Kong, People's Republic of China

Journal committed to the improvement of the standard of clinical practice, extension of nursing knowledge and promotion of communication in the nursing profession. **URL:** http://www.fmshk.com.hk/conhk/hknj/home.htm.

411 Hong Kong Optical
Hong Kong Trade Development Council
38th Fl., Office Tower, Convention Plaza
1 Harbour Rd.
Wanchai
Hong Kong, People's Republic of China   Ph: 852 25844333

Publication focusing on opticals and eyewears. **Founded:** 1992. **Freq:** Annual. **Subscription Rates:** HK$120 two years. **URL:** http://www.tdctrade.com/prodmag/optical/optical.htm.
Ad Rates: 4C: HK$10,000   **Circ:** (Not Reported)

412 Hong Kong Packaging
Hong Kong Trade Development Council
38th Fl., Office Tower, Convention Plaza
1 Harbour Rd.
Wanchai
Hong Kong, People's Republic of China   Ph: 852 25844333

Publication providing information on a comprehensive range of packaging materials, machinery and services for safe transport and appropriate presentation of any product. **Founded:** 1996. **Freq:** Semiannual. **Subscription Rates:** HK$240 two years. **URL:** http://www.tdctrade.com/prodmag/package/package.htm.
Ad Rates: 4C: HK$11,500   **Circ:** (Not Reported)

413 Hong Kong Physiotherapy Journal
Hong Kong Physiotherapy Association Ltd.
PO Box 10139
General Post Office
Hong Kong, People's Republic of China

Physiotherapy journal. **Founded:** 1978. **Freq:** 3/month. **Key Personnel:** Gladys Cheing, Editor-in-Chief, rsgladys@polyu.edu.hk. **ISSN:** 1013-7025. **URL:** http://www.hongkongpa.com.hk/publication/journal.htm.

414 The Hong Kong Practitioner
Medcom Limited
The Hong Kong College of Family
  Physicians
7th Fl., HKAM Jockey Club Bldg.
99 Wong Chuk Hang Rd.   Ph: 852 25286618
Hong Kong, People's Republic of China   Fax: 852 28660616

Journal for the medical practitioners of Hong Kong. **Freq:** Monthly. **Key Personnel:** D.V.K. Chao, Editor. **ISSN:** 1027-3948. **URL:** http://www.hkcfp.org.hk/journal.htm.

☐ **415 Hong Kong Printing**
Hong Kong Trade Development Council
38th Fl., Office Tower, Convention Plaza
1 Harbour Rd.
Wanchai
Hong Kong, People's Republic of China   Ph: 852 25844333
Publication E-mail: hktdc@tdc.org.hk

Journal covering printing. **Founded:** 1997. **Freq:** Semiannual. **ISSN:** 1027-6327. **URL:** http://www.tdc.org.hk.

☐ **416 Hong Kong Productivity News**
Hong Kong Productivity Council
HKPC Bldg, 78 Tat Chee Av
Kowloon
Hong Kong, People's Republic of China   Ph: 852 27885678

Journal covering business and economics. **Founded:** 1967. **Freq:** Monthly. **Remarks:** Advertising accepted; rates available upon request.
                                                  Circ: 7,000

☐ **417 The Hong Kong Racing Journal**
The Hong Kong Racing Journal Limited
Ste. 801-802, Lansing House
41-47 Queen's Rd., Central
Hong Kong, People's Republic of China
Publication E-mail: raceinfo@horseracing.com.hk

Publication providing racing application and custom services. **Founded:** 1995. **URL:** http://www.horseracing.com.hk/~journal.

☐ **418 Hong Kong Toys**
Hong Kong Trade Development Council
38th Fl., Office Tower, Convention Plaza
1 Harbour Rd.
Wanchai
Hong Kong, People's Republic of China   Ph: 852 25844333

Periodical covering innovative electronic games, traditional plush toys, and educational toys. **Founded:** 1969. **Freq:** Semiannual. **Subscription Rates:** HK$540. **URL:** http://www.tdctrade.com/prodmag/toys/toys.htm.
Ad Rates: 4C: HK$17,800   **Circ:** (Not Reported)

☐ **419 Hong Kong Trade Services**
Hong Kong Trade Development Council
38th Fl., Office Tower, Convention Plaza
1 Harbour Rd.
Wanchai
Hong Kong, People's Republic of China   Ph: 852 25844333

Publication providing detailed, practical information to help small and medium enterprises take full advantage of the wide scope of trade services available through Hong Kong. **Founded:** 2001. **Freq:** Biennial. **URL:** http://www.tdctrade.com/prodmag/trade/trade.htm.
Ad Rates: 4C: HK$16,800   **Circ:** 55,000

☐ **420 Hong Kong Watches and Clocks**
Hong Kong Trade Development Council
38th Fl., Office Tower, Convention Plaza
1 Harbour Rd.
Wanchai
Hong Kong, People's Republic of China   Ph: 852 25844333

Periodical aimed at providing access to elegant yet stylish, classic yet ornate, sophisticated yet competitively-priced timepieces produced by Hong Kong. **Founded:** 1985. **Freq:** Quarterly. **Subscription Rates:** HK$250. **URL:** http://www.tdctrade.com/prodmag/watch/watch.htm.
Ad Rates: 4C: HK$12,000   **Circ:** (Not Reported)

☐ **421 Hongkong Tatler**
Communication Management Ltd.
1811 Hong Kong Plaza
188 Connaught Rd. W.
Hong Kong   Ph: 852 25477117
Hong Kong, People's Republic of China   Fax: 852 28582671
Publication E-mail: circulation@cmlink.com

Lifestyle magazine. **Freq:** Monthly. **Print Method:** Offset. **Subscription Rates:** HK$315. **URL:** http://www.hktatler.com/main.html.
Ad Rates: BW: **Circ:** (Not Reported)
                HK$26,970
                4C: HK$47,570

☐ **422 In-House Briefing Asia Pacific**
Pacific Business Press Ltd.
Ste. 2701
27/F, 8 Wing Hing St.
Causeway Bay   Ph: 852 25420505
Hong Kong, People's Republic of China   Fax: 852 25750004
Publication E-mail: sales@pbpress.com
Publisher E-mail: sales@pbpress.com

Addresses the issues and concerns confronting in-house lawyers in the Asia-Pacific region. **Freq:** Monthly. **Key Personnel:** Arun Sudhaman, Managing Editor, sudhaman@pbpress.com. **Subscription Rates:** HK$1,550.

☐ **423 International Journal of Computer Processing of Oriental Languages**
World Scientific Publishing (HK) Co. Ltd.
Kowloon Central Post Office
PO Box 72482
Hong Kong, People's Republic of China   Ph: 852 27718791
Publication E-mail: wsped@pacific.net.hk

Periodical covering all aspects related to the computer processing of Oriental languages. **Founded:** 1993. **Freq:** Quarterly. **Key Personnel:** S.K. Chang, Editor-in-Chief, changsk@branden.edu. **ISSN:** 0219-4279. **Subscription Rates:** US$180 institutions and libraries. **URL:** http://www.worldscinet.com/ijcpol/ijcpol.shtml.

☐ **424 International Journal of Image and Graphics**
World Scientific Publishing (HK) Co. Ltd.
Dept. of Computing
Hong Kong Polytechnic University
Kowloon   Ph: 852 27667271
Hong Kong, People's Republic of China   Fax: 852 27740842
Publication E-mail: wsped@pacific.net.hk

Publication covering efficient and effective image and graphics technologies and systems. **Freq:** Quarterly. **Key Personnel:** David Zhang, Editor-in-Chief, csdzhang@comp.polyu.edu.hk. **ISSN:** 0219-4678. **Subscription Rates:** US$240 institutions and libraries. **URL:** http://www.worldscinet.com/ijig/mkt/editorial.shtml.

☐ **425 Journal of the Hong Kong College of Cardiology**
Medcom Limited
Rm. 1310, Olympia Plaza
255 King's Rd., North Point
Hong Kong, People's Republic of China   Ph: 852 25783833
Publication E-mail: mcl@medcom.com.hk

Official publication of the Hong Kong College of Cardiology. **Founded:** 1993. **Freq:** Quarterly. **ISSN:** 1027-7811. **URL:** http://www.medicine.org.hk/hkcc/journal/home.htm.

☐ **426 The Journal of the Hong Kong Geriatrics Society**
Medcom Limited
The Hong Kong Geriatrics Society
Rm. 3-031, Lai King Bldg., Princess
   Margaret Hospital
10 Lai Kong St., Kwai Chung
Kowloon   Ph: 852 27498228
Hong Kong, People's Republic of China   Fax: 852 27440249
Publication E-mail: ccmlum@cuhk.edu.hk

Ad Rates: GLR = general line rate; BW = one-time black & white page rate; 4C = one-time four color page rate; SAU = standard advertising unit rate; CNU = Canadian newspaper advertising unit rate; PCI = per column inch rate.
Circulation: ★ = ABC; △ = BPA; ♦ = CAC; ● = CCAB; ☐ = VAC; ⊕ = PO Statement; ‡ = Publisher's Report; Boldface figures = sworn; Light figures = estimated.
Entry type: ☐ = Print; ♨ = Broadcast.

Official journal of the Hong Kong Geriatrics Society. Publishes articles on geriatric medicine. **Freq:** Semiannual. **Key Personnel:** Christopher Chor-ming Lum, Editor-in-Chief. **URL:** http://www.fmshk.com.hk/hkgs/journal.htm.

Circ: 1,800

427 Journal of Modern Literature in Chinese
Lingnan College
Centre for Literature and Translation
Tuen Mun
Hong Kong, People's Republic of China   Ph: 852 26168056

Journal providing a forum for discussing issues related to any aspect of modern or contemporary literature in Chinese. **Freq:** Semiannual. **Key Personnel:** Leo Tak-hung Chan, Editor, chanleo@ln.edu.hk. **URL:** http://www.ln.edu.hk/clt/info/jmlc.htm.

428 Journal of Physical Education & Recreation
Dr. Stephen Hui Research Centre for Physical Recreation and Wellness
Hong Kong Baptist University
c/o Dept. of Physical Education
Kowloon Tong
Kowloon
Hong Kong, People's Republic of China

Periodical covering research or reviews in physical education, recreation, sports and fitness. **Key Personnel:** Lobo H. Louie, Editor.

429 Malaysia Tatler
Communication Management Ltd.
1811 Hong Kong Plaza
188 Connaught Rd. W.
Hong Kong   Ph: 852 25477117
Hong Kong, People's Republic of China   Fax: 852 28582671
Publication E-mail: mtatler@cmlink.com

Consumer publication. **Founded:** 1989. **Freq:** Monthly. **ISSN:** 1394-7354. **Subscription Rates:** US$26. **Remarks:** Advertising accepted; rates available upon request. **URL:** http://www.malaysiatatler.com.

Circ: Paid 16,400

430 Mode Hong Kong
Communication Management Ltd.
1811 Hong Kong Plaza
188 Connaught Rd. W.
Hong Kong   Ph: 852 25477117
Hong Kong, People's Republic of China   Fax: 852 28582671

Magazine covering apparel and fashion. **Key Personnel:** Lina Ross, Editor.

431 Nikkei Electronics Asia
Nikkei Business Publications Asia Ltd.
23rd Fl.
111 Leighton Rd.
Causeway Bay
Hong Kong, People's Republic of China   Ph: 852 25758301
Publication E-mail: neacir@nikkeibp.com.hk

Magazine for engineers and managers. **Freq:** Monthly. **Remarks:** Advertising accepted; rates available upon request. **URL:** http://www.nikkeibp.asiabiztech.com/index.shtml.

Circ: (Not Reported)

432 Orient Aviation
Wilson Press Ltd.
Ste. 3D Tung Shan Villa
2, Tung Shan Terrace, Happy Valley
Hong Kong, People's Republic of China   Ph: 852 28933676
Publication E-mail: orientav@netvigator.com

Periodical covering Asia-Pacific's commercial aviation scene. **Founded:** 1993. **Freq:** 10/year. **ISSN:** 1027-6572. **Subscription Rates:** US$90. **URL:** http://www.orienaviation.com.
Ad Rates: BW: US$3,890   **Circ:** Paid 10,700
                  4C: US$5,185

433 Orientations
Orientations Magazine Ltd.
17th Fl., 200 Lockhart Rd.
Hong Kong, People's Republic of China   Ph: 852 25111368
Publication E-mail: omag@netvigator.com

Publication providing information on the many and varied aspects of the arts of East Asia, the Indian Subcontinent and Southeast Asia. **Freq:** 10/year. **Key Personnel:** Carl Horwell, Managing Editor. **Subscription Rates:** HK$680. **Remarks:** Advertising accepted; rates available upon request.

Circ: (Not Reported)

434 PC World Hong Kong
IDG Communications (HK) Ltd.
Ste. 601, K. Wah Centre
191 Java Rd.
North Point   Ph: 852 28613238
Hong Kong, People's Republic of China   Fax: 852 28610953
Publication E-mail: infohk@idg.com.hk
Publisher E-mail: infohk@idg.com.hk

Computers magazine. **Key Personnel:** Winston Raj, Editor, w.raj@idg.com.hk. **Remarks:** Advertising accepted; rates available upon request. **URL:** http://www.pcworld.com.

Circ: (Not Reported)

435 Profile
Communications and Public Affairs Office
The Hong Kong Polytechnic University
Hung Hom
Kowloon
Hong Kong, People's Republic of China   Ph: 852 27665100

Published by the Communications and Public Affairs Office for staff and friends of The Hong Kong Polytechnic University. **Key Personnel:** David Poon, Editor. **URL:** http://www.polyu.edu.hk/cpa/profile/01feb/index.html.

436 Review of Modern Literature in Chinese
Lingnan College
Centre for Literature and Translation
Tuen Mun
Hong Kong, People's Republic of China   Ph: 852 26168056
Publication E-mail: chengcw@ln.edu.hk

Periodical aimed at providing a review of modern Chinese literature. **Freq:** Semiannual. **Key Personnel:** Laurence Wong, Chief Editor. **URL:** http://www.ln.edu.hk/clt/info/rmlc_e.htm.

437 The Standard
Sing Tao Holdings (Ltd)
3/F Sing Tao Bldg.
1 Wang Kong Rd.
Kowloon Bay   Ph: 852 27982798
Hong Kong, People's Republic of China   Fax: 852 27953009
Publication E-mail: editor@thestandard.com.hk

Newspaper covering Hong Kong, China & world business news. **Subscription Rates:** HK$1,872. **Remarks:** Advertising accepted; rates available upon request. **URL:** http://www.thestandard.com.hk.

Circ: (Not Reported)

438 Telecom Asia
Advanstar Asia Ltd.
26/F Pacific Plaza
410 Des Voeux Rd. West
Hong Kong, People's Republic of China   Ph: 852 25592772
Publication E-mail: customer_service@telecomasia.net

Magazine of telecommunications. **Founded:** 1990. **Freq:** Monthly. **Key Personnel:** Robert Clark, Group Editor, rclark@telecomasia.net. **ISSN:** 1681-181X. **Subscription Rates:** HK$480. **URL:** http://www.telecomasia.net.

439 Time Asia
TIME Magazine
30/F Oxford House, Taikoo Pl.
979 King's Rd.
Quarry Bay
Hong Kong, People's Republic of China   Ph: 852 31283333
Publication E-mail: ivy_choi@timeinc.com

Magazine for decision makers who value reliable, timely and authoritative news coverage. **Freq:** Weekly. **URL:** http://www.time.com/time/asia/.

Ad Rates: BW:
US$36,790
4C: US$52,550

Circ: 306,081

JINAN

📖 **440 Openings**
484 Wei Yi Rd.
Jinan 250001, Shandong, People's Republic
of China
Publication E-mail: info@chinatoday.com

Ph: 86 5316915823

Magazine providing up-to-date information on cultural, economic and scientific matters in Shandong Province, China. **Key Personnel:** Zhu Lei, Chief Managing Editor. **URL:** http://www.chinatoday.com/med/sd/a.htm.

SHANGHAI

📖 **441 Shanghai Today**
Today Publications Ltd.
10/F Peng Xin Apartment
811 Tian Yao Qiao Rd.
Shanghai 200030, People's Republic of
China
Publication E-mail: peiling@online.sh.cn

Ph: 86 2164825237

General Interest magazine. **Freq:** Bimonthly. **Remarks:** Accepts advertising. **URL:** http://www.todaypublications.com.

Ad Rates: BW: US$4,900
4C: US$7,000

Circ: (Not Reported)

SHENYANG

📖 **442 Zhongguo Yike Daxue Xuebao**
Chinese University of Medical Sciences
6 Sanhao Jie 1 Duan
Heping-qu
Shenyang 393501, Liaoning, People's
Republic of China

Journal pertaining to medical science. **Founded:** 1982. **Freq:** Bimonthly. **ISSN:** 0258-4646.

CZECH REPUBLIC

PRAGUE

📖 **443 Papir a Celuloza (Paper & Pulp)**
SPPaC—The Czech Pulp and Paper Association
K Hrusovu 4
102 23 Prague 10, Czech Republic
Publisher E-mail: sppac@sppac.cz

Ph: 420 271081131
Fax: 420 271081136

Trade journal for the paper and pulp industry. **Subtitle:** Journal of the Czech Pulp & Paper Industry. **Founded:** 1946. **Freq:** Monthly. **Print Method:** Offset. **Trim Size:** 215 x 310 mm. **Key Personnel:** Milos Lesikar, Editor-in-Chief, phone 420 271081125, fax 420 271081136; Ivana Drahosova, Editor, phone 420 271081136, fax 420 271081135. **ISSN:** 0031-1421. **Subscription Rates:** US$57 individuals; US$6 single issue. **Remarks:** Accepts advertising. **Former name:** Svaz prumyslu papiru a celulozy/SPPaC.

Circ: Paid ‡2,000

DENMARK

CHARLOTTENLUND

📖 **444 Copenhagen This Week**
Politikens Lokalaviser Grafisk A/S
Ordrupvej 101, 3rd Fl.
DK-2920 Charlottenlund, Denmark
Publication E-mail: ctw@ctw.dk

Ph: 45 33132230
Fax: 45 33328674

Consumer magazine covering local tourism. **Founded:** 1972. **Freq:** Monthly. **Key Personnel:** Charlotte Breum, Contact, cb@polagrafisk.dk. **Subscription Rates:** 217 DKr individuals; 256 DKr individuals Scandinavia; 364 DKr individuals Europe; 532 DKr elsewhere. **Remarks:** Advertising accepted; rates available upon request. **URL:** http://www.ctw.dk/.

Circ: (Not Reported)

FREDERIKSBERG

📖 **445 Hotel, Restaurant & Turisme**
Association of the Hotel, Restaurant, and Tourism Industry in Denmark
Hotel-, Restaurant- and Turisterhvervets Arbejdsgiverforening
Vodroffsvej 32
DK-1900 Frederiksberg C, Denmark
Publication E-mail: hrt@horesta.dk
Publisher E-mail: horesta@horesta.dk

Ph: 45 35248080
Fax: 45 35248088

Publication covering hospitality industries, in Danish. **Founded:** 1882. **Freq:** Monthly. **Trim Size:** A4. **ISSN:** 1395-3028. **Subscription Rates:** 450 DKr in Denmark; 700 DKr overseas. **Remarks:** Accepts advertising.

Ad Rates: BW: 10,400
DKr
4C: 16,100
DKr

Circ: 19,400

📖 **446 Tool and Tillage**
International Secretariat for Research on the History of Agrarian and
Food Technology
Royal Veterinary and Agricultural University
Bulowsoej 17
DK-1870 Frederiksberg, Denmark
Publisher E-mail: gle@kvl.dk

Ph: 45 35283746
Fax: 45 35283746

Publication covering the history of the tools of cultivation and agricultural processes. **Subtitle:** A Journal on the History of the Implements of Cultivation and Other Agricultural Processes. **Founded:** 1968. **Freq:** Annual. **Key Personnel:** G. Lerche, Contact, gle@kvl.dk; G. Lerche, Contact, gle@kvl.dk. **ISSN:** 0563-8887. **Remarks:** Advertising not accepted.

Circ: (Not Reported)

RINGSTEN

📖 **447 Ulvehunden**
Irsk Ulvehunde Klub
Sigerstedvej 66
DK-4100 Ringsten, Denmark

Ph: 45 57 616232
Fax: 45 57 616221

Danish language publication covering dogs. **Founded:** 1986. **Freq:** Quarterly. **Print Method:** Offset. **Remarks:** Advertising accepted; rates available upon request.

Circ: (Not Reported)

ECUADOR

QUITO

📖 **448 Correo Poblacional y de Gerencia en Salud**
Population and Responsible Parenthood Studies Center
Centro de Estudios de Poblacion y Desarrollo Social
Casilla 1701-2327
Toribio Montes 423 y Daniel Hidalgo
Quito, Ecuador
Publisher E-mail: cepar@cepar.org.ec

Ph: 593 2526018
Fax: 593 2233851

Spanish language publication covering population. **Freq:** Trimestral. **Key Personnel:** Nelson Oviedo, Contact. **ISSN:** 1390-08XX. **Remarks:** Advertising accepted; rates available upon request. **URL:** http://www.cepar.org.ec. **Former name:** Endemain.

Circ: (Not Reported)

ESTONIA

TALLINN

📖 **449 Arhitektuuriajakiri MAJA**
Kirjastus Maja Ou
Paldiski Maantee 26a   Ph: 372 6613754
EE-10149 Tallinn, Estonia   Fax: 372 6613754
Publication E-mail: maja@arhitektuur.ee

Magazine reviewing architecture. **Founded:** 1994. **Freq:** Quarterly. **Key Personnel:** Triin Ojari, Editor-in-Chief, phone 372 5059120, triin@arhitektuur.ee. **ISSN:** 1023-0742. **Subscription Rates:** US$50. **Remarks:** Accepts advertising. **URL:** http://maja.arhitektuur.ee.
Ad Rates: BW: €1,025   **Circ:** (Not Reported)
          4C: €1,025

FINLAND

A-LEHDET

📖 **450 AKK-Motorsport**
A-lehdet Oy
Hitsaajankatu 10/2   Ph: 358 975961
FIN-00081 A-lehdet, Finland   Fax: 358 97596373

Magazine covering Finish motor sports for members of the Finnish Motor Sports Association and interested others. **Freq:** Bimonthly. **Trim Size:** 280 x 400 mm. **Cols./Page:** 5. **Key Personnel:** Terhi Heloaho, Editor-in-Chief, phone 3589 7258 2200, terhi.heloaho@akkry.fi; Pekka Virtanen, Managing Editor, phone 3589 759 6303, pekka.virtanen@a-lehdet.fi; Timo Puumalainen, Sales Mgr., phone 3589 759 6371, timo.puumalainen@a-lehdet.fi; Liisa Tarvainen, Advertising Sec., phone 3589 759 6378, liisa.tarvainen@a-lehdet.fi. **Remarks:** Accepts advertising.
Ad Rates: BW: FM 1,680   **Circ:** Combined 32,000

📖 **451 Apu**
A-lehdet Oy
Hitsaajankatu 10/2   Ph: 358 975961
FIN-00081 A-lehdet, Finland   Fax: 358 97596373

Consumer magazine covering food, home, travel, fashion, pets and other issues for families. **Founded:** 1933. **Freq:** Weekly. **Print Method:** Engraved rotogravure. **Trim Size:** 216 x 265 mm. **Cols./Page:** 4. **Key Personnel:** Matti Saari, Editor-in-Chief, phone 3589 759 6307, matti.saari@a-lehdet.fi; Anne Lyytikainen-Palmroth, Editor-in-Chief, phone 3589 759 6357, anne.lyytikainen-palmrith@a-lehdet.fi; Tuuli Toivainen, Sales Mgr., phone 3589 759 6556, tuuli.toivainen@a-lehdet.fi; Jatta Waarala, Advertising Sec., phone 3589 759 6374, jatta.waarala@a-lehdet.fi. **Remarks:** Accepts advertising.
Ad Rates: 4C: FM 7,600   **Circ:** Combined 256,709

📖 **452 Avotakka**
A-lehdet Oy
Hitsaajankatu 10/2   Ph: 358 975961
FIN-00081 A-lehdet, Finland   Fax: 358 97596373

Consumer magazine covering interior decoration in Finland. **Founded:** 1967. **Freq:** Monthly. **Trim Size:** 230 x 273 mm. **Cols./Page:** 4. **Key Personnel:** Soili Ukkola, Editor-in-Chief, phone 3589 759 6286, soili.ukkola@a-lehdet.fi; Salme Kantonen, Sales Mgr., phone 3589 759 6552, salme.kantonen@a-lehdet.fi; Riikka Mayranen, Advertising Sec., phone 3589 759 6380, riikka.mayranen@a-lehdet.fi. **Remarks:** Accepts advertising.
Ad Rates: 4C: FM 5,500   **Circ:** Paid 102,594

📖 **453 Demi**
A-lehdet Oy
Hitsaajankatu 10/2   Ph: 358 975961
FIN-00081 A-lehdet, Finland   Fax: 358 97596373

Consumer magazine covering issues for girls aged 12 to 19 years. **Founded:** 1998. **Freq:** Monthly. **Trim Size:** 230 x 273 mm. **Cols./Page:** 4. **Key Personnel:** Oona Tyomi, Editor-in-Chief, phone 3589 759 6339, oona.tuomi@a-lehdet.fi; Johanna Mikkonen, Sales Mgr., phone 3589 759 6271, johanna.mikkonen@a-lehdet.fi; Jutta Kuusela, Advertising Sec., phone 3589 759 6563, jutta.kuusela@a-lehdet.fi. **Remarks:** Accepts advertising. **URL:** http://www.demi.fi.
Ad Rates: 4C: FM 2,860   **Circ:** Paid 43,127

📖 **454 Eeva**
A-lehdet Oy
Hitsaajankatu 10/2   Ph: 358 975961
FIN-00081 A-lehdet, Finland   Fax: 358 97596373

Consumer magazine covering general issues for women. **Founded:** 1934. **Freq:** Monthly. **Print Method:** Offset. **Trim Size:** 230 x 273 mm. **Cols./Page:** 4. **Key Personnel:** Liisa Jappinen, Editor-in-Chief, phone 3589 759 6635, liisa.jappinen@a-lehdet.fi; Riitta Sihvonen, Sales Mgr., phone 3589 759 6277, riitta.sihvonen@a-lehdet.fi; Jutta Kuusela, Advertising Sec., phone 3589 759 6563, jutta.kuusela@a-lehdet.fi. **Remarks:** Accepts advertising.
Ad Rates: 4C: FM 5,285   **Circ:** Paid 102,505

📖 **455 F1 Racing**
A-lehdet Oy
Hitsaajankatu 10/2   Ph: 358 975961
FIN-00081 A-lehdet, Finland   Fax: 358 97596373

Consumer magazine covering Forumla 1 racing. **Founded:** 1994. **Freq:** Monthly. **Print Method:** Offset. **Trim Size:** 221 x 297 mm. **Cols./Page:** 4. **Key Personnel:** Lauri Larmela, Editor-in-Chief, phone 3589 759 6298, lauri.larmela@a-lehdet.fi; Timo Puumalainen, Sales Mgr., phone 3589 759 6371, timo.puumalainen@a-lehdet.fi; Liisa Tarvainen, Advertising Sec., phone 3589 759 6378, liisa.tarvainen@a-lehdet.fi. **Remarks:** Accepts advertising.
Ad Rates: 4C: FM 2,860   **Circ:** Paid 18,709

📖 **456 Futari**
A-lehdet Oy
Hitsaajankatu 10/2   Ph: 358 975961
FIN-00081 A-lehdet, Finland   Fax: 358 97596373

Consumer magazine covering football (soccer) in Finland. **Founded:** 1982. **Freq:** 10/year. **Print Method:** Offset. **Trim Size:** 230 x 280 mm. **Cols./Page:** 4. **Key Personnel:** Juha Kuosa, Editor-in-Chief; Suomen Palloliitto, Editor-in-Chief; Jouko Vuorela, Managing Editor, phone 3589 759 6593; Jorma Riipinen, Sales Mgr., phone 3589 759 6557, jorma.riipinen@a-lehdet.fi; Jatta Waarala, Advertising Sec., phone 3589 759 6374, jatta.waarala@a-lehdet.fi. **Remarks:** Accepts advertising.
Ad Rates: 4C: FM 2,110   **Circ:** Paid 75,478

📖 **457 Hippo**
A-lehdet Oy
Hitsaajankatu 10/2   Ph: 358 975961
FIN-00081 A-lehdet, Finland   Fax: 358 97596373

Finnish and Swedish language children's magazine for ages 5 to 12 years. **Founded:** 1980. **Freq:** Quarterly. **Print Method:** Offset. **Trim Size:** 210 x 297 mm. **Cols./Page:** 4. **Key Personnel:** Katri Korpikallio, Editor-in-Chief; Jorma Riipinen, Sales Mgr., phone 3589 759 6557, jorma.riipinen@a-lehdet.fi; Jatta Waarala, Advertising Sec., phone 3589 759 6374, jatta.waarala@a-lehdet.fi. **Remarks:** Accepts advertising.
Ad Rates: 4C: FM 2,500   **Circ:** Combined 199,536

📖 **458 Hirsilehti**
A-lehdet Oy
Hitsaajankatu 10/2   Ph: 358 975961
FIN-00081 A-lehdet, Finland   Fax: 358 97596373

Consumer magazine covering log housing and summer cottages in Finland. **Founded:** 1977. **Freq:** Semiannual. **Print Method:** Offset. **Trim Size:** 225 x 297 mm. **Cols./Page:** 4. **Key Personnel:** Eero Saarelainen, Editor-in-Chief; Ilkka Palomaki, Sales Mgr., phone 3589 759 6270, ilkka.palomaki@a-lehdet.fi; Riikka Mayranen, Advertising Sec., phone 3589 759 6380, riikka.mayranen@a-lehdet.fi. **Remarks:** Accepts advertising.
Ad Rates: 4C: FM 2,800   **Circ:** Combined 40,000

📖 **459 Hyva Ateria**
A-lehdet Oy
Hitsaajankatu 10/2   Ph: 358 975961
FIN-00081 A-lehdet, Finland   Fax: 358 97596373

Trade magazine for restaurants and institutional kitchens. **Founded:** 1986. **Freq:** 9/year. **Print Method:** Offset. **Trim Size:** 230 x 273 mm. **Cols./Page:** 4. **Key Personnel:** Marita Joutjarvi, Editor-in-Chief, phone 3589 759 6261, marita.joutjarvi@a-lehdet.fi; Ari Ylonen, Sales Mgr., phone 3589 759 6379, ari.ylonen@a-lehdet.fi; Liisa Tarvainen, Advertising Sec., phone 3589 759 6378, liisa.tarvainen@a-lehdet.fi. **Remarks:** Accepts advertising.
Ad Rates: 4C: FM 3,170   **Circ:** Paid 16,000

📖 **460 Katso**
A-lehdet Oy
Hitsaajankatu 10/2   Ph: 358 975961
FIN-00081 A-lehdet, Finland   Fax: 358 97596373

Consumer magazine covering television, movies, games, technology and entertainment. **Founded:** 1960. **Freq:** Weekly. **Print Method:** Offset. **Trim Size:** 230 x 302 mm. **Cols./Page:** 4. **Key Personnel:** Markku Veijalainen, Editor-in-Chief, phone 3589 759 6368, markku.veijalainen@a-lehdet.fi; Jarkko Jokinen, Sales Mgr., phone 3589 759 6554, jarkko.jokinen@a-lehdet.fi; Jatta Waarala, Advertising Sec., phone 3589 759 6374, jatta.waarala@a-lehdet.fi. **Remarks:** Accepts advertising. **URL:** http://www.katso.fi.
Ad Rates: 4C: FM 2,860   **Circ:** Paid 72,540

📖 **461 Kauneus Jaterveys**
A-lehdet Oy
Hitsaajankatu 10/2   Ph: 358 975961
FIN-00081 A-lehdet, Finland   Fax: 358 97596373

Consumer magazine covering health and fitness for women. **Founded:** 1956. **Freq:** Monthly. **Print Method:** Offset. **Trim Size:** 230 x 273 mm. **Cols./Page:** 4. **Key Personnel:** Irmeli Castren, Editor-in-Chief, phone 3589 759 6585, irmeli.castren@a-lehdet.fi; Elise Lammi, Sales Mgr., phone 3589 759 6264, elise.lammi@a-lehdet.fi; Jutta Kuusela, Advertising Sec., phone 3589 759 6563, jutta.kuusela@a-lehdet.fi. **Remarks:** Accepts advertising.
Ad Rates: 4C: FM 5,500   **Circ:** Paid 76,708

📖 **462 Kultaraha**
A-lehdet Oy
Hitsaajankatu 10/2   Ph: 358 975961
FIN-00081 A-lehdet, Finland   Fax: 358 97596373

Consumer magazine covering banking, economics and investing. **Founded:** 1939. **Freq:** 5/year. **Print Method:** Offset. **Trim Size:** 230 x 297 mm. **Cols./Page:** 4. **Key Personnel:** Stina Suominen, Editor-in-Chief; Jorma Riipinen, Sales Mgr., phone 3589 759 6557, jorma.riipinen@a-lehdet.fi; Jatta Waarala, Advertising Sec., phone 3589 759 6374, jatta.waarala@a-lehdet.fi. **Remarks:** Accepts advertising.
Ad Rates: 4C: FM 6,400   **Circ:** Combined 739,191

📖 **463 Madame**
A-lehdet Oy
Hitsaajankatu 10/2   Ph: 358 975961
FIN-00081 A-lehdet, Finland   Fax: 358 97596373

Consumer magazine covering issues for mature women. **Founded:** 1996. **Freq:** 5/year. **Print Method:** Offset. **Trim Size:** 230 x 273 mm. **Cols./Page:** 4. **Key Personnel:** Irmeli Castren, Editor-in-Chief, phone 3589 759 6585, irmeli.castren@a-lehdet.fi; Elise Lammi, Sales Mgr., phone 3589 759 6264, elise.lammi@a-lehdet.fi; Jutta Kuusela, Advertising Sec., phone 3589 759 6563, jutta.kuusela@a-lehdet.fi. **Remarks:** Accepts advertising.
Ad Rates: 4C: FM 4,210   **Circ:** Paid 43,555

📖 **464 Meidan Mokki**
A-lehdet Oy
Hitsaajankatu 10/2   Ph: 358 975961
FIN-00081 A-lehdet, Finland   Fax: 358 97596373

Consumer magazine covering travel and leisure in Finland. **Founded:** 1997. **Freq:** Bimonthly. **Print Method:** Offset. **Trim Size:** 230 x 273 mm. **Cols./Page:** 4. **Key Personnel:** Paivi Anttila, Editor-in-Chief, phone 3589 759 6292, paivi.anttila@a-lehdet.fi; Ilkka Palomaki, Sales Mgr., phone 3589 759 6270, ilkka.palomaki@a-lehdet.fi; Riikka Mayranen, Advertising Sec., phone 3589 759 6380, riikka.mayranen@a-lehdet.fi. **Remarks:** Accepts advertising.
Ad Rates: 4C: FM 3,900   **Circ:** Paid 49,070

📖 **465 Meidan Talo**
A-lehdet Oy
Hitsaajankatu 10/2   Ph: 358 975961
FIN-00081 A-lehdet, Finland   Fax: 358 97596373

Consumer magazine covering home and garden. **Founded:** 1959. **Freq:** 10/year. **Print Method:** Offset. **Trim Size:** 230 x 273 mm. **Cols./Page:** 4. **Key Personnel:** Timo Paasky, Editor-in-Chief, phone 3589 759 6533, timo.paasky@a-lehdet.fi; Ilkka Palomaki, Sales Mgr., phone 3589 759 6270, ilkka.palomaki@a-lehdet.fi; Riikka Mayranen, Advertising Sec., phone 3589 759 6380, riikka.mayranen@a-lehdet.fi. **Remarks:** Accepts advertising.
Ad Rates: 4C: FM 4,400   **Circ:** Paid 71,948

📖 **466 Soundi**
A-lehdet Oy
Hitsaajankatu 10/2   Ph: 358 975961
FIN-00081 A-lehdet, Finland   Fax: 358 97596373

Consumer magazine covering rock music in Finland and worldwide. **Founded:** 1975. **Freq:** Monthly. **Print Method:** Offset. **Trim Size:** 225 x 297 mm. **Cols./Page:** 4. **Key Personnel:** Timo Kanerva, Editor-in-Chief, phone 3583 3125 3112, timo.kanerva@sound.fi; Veikko Virtanen, Sales Mgr., phone 3589 5627 7110, veikko.virtanen@a-lehdet.fi; Liisa Tarvainen, Advertising Sec., phone 3589 759 6378, liisa.tarvainen@a-lehdet.fi. **Remarks:** Accepts advertising. **URL:** http://www.sound.fi.
Ad Rates: 4C: FM 1,792   **Circ:** Paid 25,000

📖 **467 Tuulilasi**
A-lehdet Oy
Hitsaajankatu 10/2   Ph: 358 975961
FIN-00081 A-lehdet, Finland   Fax: 358 97596373

Consumer magazine covering automobiles. **Founded:** 1963. **Freq:** Monthly. **Print Method:** Offset. **Trim Size:** 217 x 280 mm. **Cols./Page:** 4. **Key Personnel:** Lauri Larmela, Editor-in-Chief, phone 3589 759 6298, lauri.larmela@a-lehdet.fi; Timo Puumalainen, Sales Mgr., phone 3589 759 6371, timo.puumalainen@a-lehdet.fi; Liisa Tarvainen, Advertising Sec., phone 3589 759 6378, liisa.tarvainen@a-lehdet.fi. **Remarks:** Accepts advertising. **URL:** http://www.tuulilasi.fi.
Ad Rates: 4C: FM 5,870   **Circ:** Paid 86,454

📖 **468 Viherpiha**
A-lehdet Oy
Hitsaajankatu 10/2   Ph: 358 975961
FIN-00081 A-lehdet, Finland   Fax: 358 97596373

Consumer magazine covering gardening. **Founded:** 1994. **Freq:** Bimonthly. **Print Method:** Offset. **Trim Size:** 230 x 273 mm. **Cols./Page:** 4. **Key Personnel:** Kiti Andrejew, Editor-in-Chief, phone 3589 759 6209, kiti.andrejew@a-lehdet.fi; Salme Kantonen, Sales Mgr., phone 3589 759 6552, salme.kantonen@a-lehdet.fi; Riikka Mayranen, Advertising Sec., phone 3589 759 6380, riikka.mayranen@a-lehdet.fi. **Remarks:** Accepts advertising.
Ad Rates: 4C: FM 4,500   **Circ:** Paid 105,424

📖 **469 Voi Hyvin**
A-lehdet Oy
Hitsaajankatu 10/2   Ph: 358 975961
FIN-00081 A-lehdet, Finland   Fax: 358 97596373

Consumer magazine covering alternative health. **Founded:** 1986. **Freq:** Bimonthly. **Print Method:** Offset. **Trim Size:** 230 x 273 mm. **Cols./Page:** 4. **Key Personnel:** Arja Sihvola, Editor-in-Chief, phone 3589 759 6207, arja.sihvola@a-lehdet.fi; Riitta Sihvonen, Sales Mgr., phone 3589 759 6277, riitta.sihvonen@a-lehdet.fi; Riikka Mayranen, Advertising Sec., phone 3589 759 6380, riikka.mayranen@a-lehdet.fi. **Remarks:** Accepts advertising.
Ad Rates: 4C: FM 3,400   **Circ:** Paid 64,905

HELSINKI

📖 **470 Aikuiskasvatus**
KVS Foundation
Museokatu 18 A 2
FIN-00100 Helsinki, Finland

Scientific journal covering adult education. **Founded:** 1981. **Freq:** Quarterly. **Print Method:** Offset. **Cols./Page:** 3. **Col. Width:** 420 centimeters. **Col. Depth:** 215 centimeters. **Key Personnel:** Anja Heikkinen, Editor-in-Chief, phone 35814 2601670, anja.heikkinen@edu.jyu.fi; Anneli Kajanto, Editor, phone 3589 5491 8833, fax 3589 5491 8811, anneli.kajanto@kvs.fi. **ISSN:** 0358-6197. **Subscription Rates:** €25 individuals; €7 single issue. **Remarks:** Accepts advertising. **URL:** http://www.kvs.fi.
Ad Rates: GLR: €53   **Circ:** Paid 2,000
            BW: €269   Non-paid 200

Ad Rates: GLR = general line rate; BW = one-time black & white page rate; 4C = one-time four color page rate; SAU = standard advertising unit rate; CNU = Canadian newspaper advertising unit rate; PCI = per column inch rate.
Circulation: ★ = ABC; △ = BPA; ♦ = CAC; ♦ = CCAB; ❏ = VAC; ⊕ = PO Statement; ‡ = Publisher's Report; Boldface figures = sworn; Light figures = estimated.
Entry type: 📖 = Print; 🎙 = Broadcast.

51

471 Arttu!
University of Art and Design Helsinki UIAH
Communications & Publications
Hameentie 135 C   Ph: 358 975630221
FIN-00560 Helsinki, Finland   Fax: 358 975630385
Publication E-mail: info@uiah.fi
Publisher E-mail: info@uiah.fi

Magazine covering design, designers, audiovisual communications, art education and research. **Freq:** Bimonthly. **Trim Size:** 240 x 340 mm. **Key Personnel:** Prof. Yrjo Sotamaa, Editor-in-Chief, yrjo.sotamaa@uiah.fi; Outi Raatikainen, Managing Editor; Paula Haikarainen, Editor. **Subscription Rates:** €23 individuals Finland; €43 elsewhere. **Remarks:** Accepts advertising. **URL:** http://www.uiah.fi.
Ad Rates: BW: €1,667   **Circ:** (Not Reported)
            4C: €2,250

472 Human Rights Report
Finnish League for Human Rights
Unioninkatu 45 B 41   Ph: 358 941552500
FIN-00170 Helsinki, Finland   Fax: 358 941552520
Publisher E-mail: info@ihmisoikeusliitto.fi

Finnish language publication covering human rights. **Subtitle:** Ihmisoikeusraportti. **Freq:** Quarterly. **Key Personnel:** Kristina Kouros, Contact, phone 358 941552550, kristina.kouros@ihmisoikeusliitto.fi. **ISSN:** 1237-0355. **Subscription Rates:** €25. **Remarks:** Advertising accepted; rates available upon request.
                         Circ: 2,000

473 Kuljetusyrittaja
SKAL Kustannus Oy
PL 38   Ph: 358 9478999
FIN-00401 Helsinki, Finland   Fax: 358 95878520
Publisher E-mail: skal@skal.fi

Trade magazine covering legislation, transport economy, product news and related issue of interest to the Finnish Trucking Association and its members. **Founded:** 1993. **Freq:** 10/year. **Print Method:** Heat offset. **Trim Size:** 210 x 297 mm. **Cols./Page:** 4. **Col. Width:** 40 millimeters. **Col. Depth:** 270 millimeters. **Key Personnel:** Jouko Santala, Editor-in-Chief, jouko.santala@skal.fi. **Remarks:** Accepts advertising. **URL:** http://www.skal.fi. **Former name:** Ammattiautoilija.
Ad Rates: BW: €1,660   **Circ:** Controlled 9,446
            4C: €2,500

474 Latu ja Polku
Suomen Latu ry—Central Association for Recreational Sports and
   Outdoor Activities
Fabianinkatu 7   Ph: 358 941591100
FIN-00130 Helsinki, Finland   Fax: 358 9663376
Publisher E-mail: info@suomenlatu.fi

Consumer magazine covering outdoor activities and recreational sport. **Founded:** 1940. **Freq:** 8/year. **Print Method:** Offset. **Trim Size:** 210 x 295 mm. **Key Personnel:** Tuomo Jantunen, Editor-in-Chief, phone 358 941591125, tuomo.jantunen@suomenlatu.fi; Marianne Mertanen, Sub-Editor, phone 358 941591127, helena.collin@suomenlatu.fi. **ISSN:** 0356-2395. **Remarks:** Accepts advertising. **URL:** http://www.suomenlatu.fi.
                       Circ: (Not Reported)

475 Lifelong Learning in Europe
KVS Foundation
Museokatu 18 A 2
FIN-00100 Helsinki, Finland

Journal covering education and lifelong learning in Europe. **Founded:** 1996. **Freq:** Quarterly. **Print Method:** Offset. **Cols./Page:** 4. **Col. Width:** 400 centimeters. **Col. Depth:** 240 centimeters. **Key Personnel:** Kauko Hamalainen, Editor-in-Chief, phone 358405012513, kauko.hamalainen@minedu.fi; Eeva Siirala, Editor, phone 3589 54918855, eeva.siirala@kvs.fi. **ISSN:** 1239-6826. **Subscription Rates:** US$58 individuals; €7 single issue. **Remarks:** Accepts advertising. **URL:** http://www.kvs.fi.
Ad Rates: GLR: FM 53   **Circ:** Paid 400
                                 Non-paid 1,000

476 Nuorten Tasavalta
Youth League of the Coalition Party
Kokoomuksen Nuorten Liitto
Pohjoinen Rautatiekatu 21 B   Ph: 358 969381
FIN-00100 Helsinki, Finland   Fax: 358 96943702
Publisher E-mail: annakaisa@kokoomusnuoret.fi

Political youth publication. **Freq:** 4/year. **Key Personnel:** Henrikki Halme, phone 358 96938263, henrikki@kokoomusnuoret.fi. **ISSN:** 0783-1668. **Subscription Rates:** €25. **Remarks:** Advertising accepted; rates available upon request.
                       Circ: 23,000

477 ptah
The Alvar Aalto Academy
The Alvar Aalto Museum
Tiilimaki 20
FIN-00330 Helsinki, Finland   Ph: 358 942433311
Publication E-mail: ptah@alvaraalto.fi

Publication covering the theory of architecture, design, and art in English. **Freq:** Semiannual (May and Oct.). **Trim Size:** 200 x 270 mm. **Key Personnel:** Esa Laaksonen, Editor-in-Chief, phone 35809 4243 3310, esa.laaksonen@alvaraalto.fi; Merja Vainio, Asst. Editor, phone 35809 4243 3311; Jarmo Valtonen, Advertising, phone 35809 8734 373, fax 35809 8733 756, jarmo.valtonen@mediabookers.fi. **ISSN:** 1239-3401. **Subscription Rates:** €16.80 individuals Finland; €25 elsewhere; €10 single issue. **Remarks:** Accepts advertising. **URL:** http://www.jkl.fi/aalto/academy/ptah/main.htm.
                       Circ: (Not Reported)

478 SAHKO & TELE
Association of Electrical Engineers
Sahkoinsinooriliitto
Merikasarminkatu 7   Ph: 358 96689850
FIN-00160 Helsinki, Finland   Fax: 358 9657562
Publisher E-mail: sil@sil.fi

English, Finnish and Swedish language publication covering engineering. **Subtitle:** A Professional Magazine of Electrical and Electronic Technics and Science. **Founded:** Jan. 1, 1928. **Freq:** 8/year. **Print Method:** Offset. **Trim Size:** A4. **Key Personnel:** Heikki Silvan, Editor-in-Chief, heikki.silvan@sil.fi; Timo Vehmas, Editor; Arto Huttunen, Editor; Tarja Ahokas, Editor; Jaana Lindholm, Editorial Sec. **ISSN:** 0789-676X. **Remarks:** Accepts advertising. **URL:** http://www.sil.fi. **Formerly:** Voima Ja Valo; Sahko-Electricity In Finland.
                       Circ: 10,000

JYVASKYLA

479 International Peat Journal
International Peat Society
Vapaudenkatu 12   Ph: 358 143385440
FIN-40520 Jyvaskyla, Finland   Fax: 358 143385410
Publisher E-mail: ips@peatsociety.fi

Scientific journal covering fertilizer. **Freq:** Annual. **ISSN:** 0782-7784. **Subscription Rates:** €19 single issue nonmembers; €9 single issue members. **Remarks:** Advertising not accepted.
                       Circ: (Not Reported)

480 Peatlands International
International Peat Society
Vapaudenkatu 12   Ph: 358 143385440
FIN-40520 Jyvaskyla, Finland   Fax: 358 143385410
Publisher E-mail: ips@peatsociety.fi

Magazine of the International Peat Society covering fertilizer. **Freq:** 2/year. **ISSN:** 1455-8491. **Subscription Rates:** Free IPS members; €46 nonmembers. **Remarks:** Advertising not accepted.
                       Circ: (Not Reported)

FRANCE

BREZOLLES

481 Chorus
Les Editions du Verbe
BP 28
F-28270 Brezolles, France   Ph: 33 0237436660
        Fax: 33 0237436271
Publication E-mail: chorus@club-internet.fr

Consumer magazine covering chanson music. **Subtitle:** Les Cahiers de la Chanson. **Founded:** Sept. 21, 1992. **Freq:** Quarterly. **Trim Size:** 190 x 270 mm. **Key Personnel:** Fred Hidalgo, Editor-in-Chief; Mauricette Hidalgo, Publication Dir. **ISSN:** 1241-7076. **Subscription Rates:** €13 single issue; €47 individuals France; €89 two years France. **Remarks:** Accepts advertising. **URL:** http://www.chorus-chanson.fr.
Ad Rates: BW: €3,000   **Circ:** (Not Reported)

CLICHY

482 Autocar Infos
SEJT
21 rue Martissot   Ph: 33 161279737
F-92110 Clichy, France   Fax: 33 1612 79730

Professional magazine covering transportation. **Subtitle:** The Coach and Bus Transport Magazine. **Founded:** 1993. **Freq:** Bimonthly. **Print Method:** Offset. **Cols./Page:** 3. **Key Personnel:** Patrice de Saulieu, Director, phone 33 141279737, fax 33 141279730, p.saulieu@routiers.com; Francois Gilbert, Editor-in-Chief, phone 33 141279737, fax 33 141279730, f.gilbert@routiers.com; Francois Deneuter, Advertising, phone 33 141279732, fax 33 141279730, fdeneuter@sejt.com. **ISSN:** 1261-357X. **Subscription Rates:** 3.66 Fr single issue; 18.30 Fr individuals. **Remarks:** Accepts advertising.
Ad Rates: BW: 2,897 Fr   **Circ:** Paid 23,000
        4C: 3,781 Fr

483 Forum Chantiers
SEJT
21 rue Martissot   Ph: 33 161279737
F-92110 Clichy, France   Fax: 33 1612 79730

Professional magazine covering construction and public works. **Subtitle:** The Public Works Magazine. **Founded:** 1990. **Freq:** Monthly 8 per year. **Print Method:** Offset. **Cols./Page:** 3. **Key Personnel:** Patrice de Saulieu, Director, phone 33 141279737, fax 33 141279730, psalieu@routiers.com; Alain Favre, Editor-in-Chief, phone 33 141279737, fax 33 141279730, afavre@routiers.com; Francois Deneuter, Advertising, phone 33 141279732, fax 33 141279730, fdeneuter@sejt.com. **Subscription Rates:** 3.05 Fr single issue; 32.10 Fr individuals. **Remarks:** Accepts advertising.
Ad Rates: BW: 2,440 Fr   **Circ:** Paid 15,000
        4C: 4,344 Fr

484 Guide des Relais Routiers
SEJT
21 rue Martissot   Ph: 33 161279737
F-92110 Clichy, France   Fax: 33 1612 79730

Professional magazine covering restaurants. **Founded:** 1934. **Freq:** Annual. **Key Personnel:** Patrice de Saulieu, Director, phone 33 141279737, fax 33 141279730; Thierry de Saulieu, Editor-in-Chief, phone 33 141279737, fax 33 141279730; Francois Deneuter, Advertising, phone 33 141279732, fax 33 141279730, fdeneuter@sejt.com. **Remarks:** Accepts advertising.
Ad Rates: BW: 2,705 Fr   **Circ:** Paid 50,000
        4C: 3,201 Fr

485 Les Routiers
SEJT
21 rue Martissot   Ph: 33 161279737
F-92110 Clichy, France   Fax: 33 1612 79730

Professional magazine covering regulation, vehicle test, technical innovations and other issues for truck drivers. **Subtitle:** The Road and Truck Drivers Monthly Magazine. **Founded:** 1934. **Freq:** Monthly. **Cols./Page:** 3. **Key** **Personnel:** Patrice de Saulieu, Director, phone 33 141279737, fax 33 141279730; Thierry de Saulieu, Editor-in-Chief, phone 33 141279737, fax 33 141279730; Francois Deneuter, Advertising, phone 33 141279732, fax 33 141279730, fdeneuter@sejt.com. **Remarks:** Accepts advertising.
Ad Rates: BW: 3,329 Fr   **Circ:** Paid 45,000
        4C: 4,369 Fr

486 Stations-Service Acutalites
SEJT
21 rue Martissot   Ph: 33 161279737
F-92110 Clichy, France   Fax: 33 1612 79730

Professional magazine covering the management and development of gas stations. **Subtitle:** The Magazine for Petrol Station Professionals. **Freq:** Bimonthly. **Cols./Page:** 3. **Key Personnel:** Patrice de Saulieu, Director, phone 33 141279737, fax 33 141279730; Laurent de Saulieu, Editor-in-Chief, phone 33 141279737, fax 33 141279730; Francois Deneuter, Advertising, phone 33 141279732, fax 33 141279730, fdeneuter@sejt.com. **Remarks:** Accepts advertising.
Ad Rates: BW: 1,760 Fr   **Circ:** Paid 9,500
        4C: 3,361 Fr

487 Transport Service
SEJT
21 rue Martissot   Ph: 33 161279737
F-92110 Clichy, France   Fax: 33 1612 79730

Professional magazine covering management, financial, material, and other issues for the transportation industry. **Founded:** 1997. **Freq:** Bimonthly. **Cols./Page:** 3. **Key Personnel:** Patrice de Saulieu, Director, phone 33 141279737, fax 33 141279730; David Reibenberg, Editor-in-Chief, phone 33 141279737, fax 33 141279730; Francois Deneuter, Advertising, phone 33 141279732, fax 33 141279730, fdeneuter@sejt.com. **Remarks:** Accepts advertising.
Ad Rates: BW: 3,937 Fr   **Circ:** Paid 30,000
        4C: 4,802 Fr

CRETEIL

488 Journal of Intensive Care Medicine
Springer-Verlag GmbH & Co. KG
Reanimation Medicale - Hopital Henri
  Mondor
Rue Marechal de Tassigny   Ph: 33 149812545
F-94010 Creteil, France   Fax: 33 142079943
Publication E-mail: journal.icm@hmn.ap.hop-paris.fr

Publication covering intensive care medicine. **Freq:** Monthly. **Key Personnel:** Dr. Laurent Brochard, Editor-in-Chief, phone 33 149812386, fax 33 142079943. **Subscription Rates:** Included in membership. **Remarks:** Advertising accepted; rates available upon request. **URL:** http://link.springer.de.
        Circ: (Not Reported)

FONTAINEBLEAU

489 Auto Retro
BP 410
F-77309 Fontainebleau Cedex, France Ph: 33 160396969
        Fax: 33 160396900
Publication E-mail: autoretro@elvea.fr

Consumer magazine popular automobiles and auto sport events. **Founded:** 1992. **Freq:** Monthly. **Key Personnel:** A. Georges, Publication Dir.; Xavier Audio, Editor-in-Chief. **Subscription Rates:** €58 individuals; €4.10 single issue. **Remarks:** Accepts advertising.
        Circ: (Not Reported)

490 La Vie de l'Auto
BP 410
F-77309 Fontainebleau Cedex, France Ph: 33 160396969
        Fax: 33 160396900
Publication E-mail: lva@elvea.fr

Consumer magazine covering classic cars, including events, auctions, and sales. **Founded:** 1976. **Freq:** Weekly. **Key Personnel:** A. Georges, Publica-

tion Dir.; S. Cordey, Editorial Dir.; B. Leroux, Editor-in-Chief. **Subscription Rates:** €96 individuals; €2.60 single issue. **Remarks:** Accepts advertising.
Circ: (Not Reported)

GERMANY

BERLIN

📖 **491 ballet-tanz**
Friedrich Berlin Publishing Group
Reinhardstr. 29   Ph: 49 3025449521
D-10117 Berlin, Germany   Fax: 49 3025449524
Publication E-mail: redaktion@ballet-tanz.de

Magazine covering dance and ballet in Europe. **Founded:** 1994. **Freq:** Monthly (double issue Aug./Sep. and a yearbook). **Trim Size:** 240 x 300 mm. **Key Personnel:** Dr. Michael Merschmeier, Managing Dir.; Heike Drisch, Advertising Mgr.; Marina Dafova, Layout; Sofie Goblirsch, Sec.; Hartmut Regitz, Editor; Arnd Wesemann, Editor. **Subscription Rates:** €90 individuals; €8 single issue. **Remarks:** Accepts advertising. **URL:** http://www.ballet-tanz.de/.
Ad Rates: BW: €1,800   **Circ:** 12,000
     4C: €2,500

📖 **492 Utopie Kreativ**
Neue Zeitungsuerwaltung GmbH
Franz-Mehring-Platz 1   Ph: 49 3029781156
D-10243 Berlin, Germany   Fax: 49 3025781181
Publisher E-mail: FEVAC@t-online.de

German language publication covering political and socio-theoretical affairs and problems. **Subtitle:** Diskussion sozialistischer Alternativen. **Founded:** Sept. 1990. **Freq:** Monthly. **ISSN:** 0863-4890. **Subscription Rates:** €57; €75 overseas. **Remarks:** Accepts advertising. **URL:** http://utopiekreativ.de.
Circ: 1,000

BONN

📖 **493 Adult Education and Development**
Institute of the International Cooperation of the German Adult
   Education Association
Deutscher Volkshochschul-Verband
Obere Wilhelm-Strasse 32   Ph: 49 228975690
D-53225 Bonn, Germany   Fax: 49 2289750930
Publisher E-mail: buero@dvv.vhs.de

English, French and Spanish language publication covering adult education. **Freq:** Semiannual. **ISSN:** 0342-7633. **Subscription Rates:** Free. **Remarks:** Advertising not accepted.
Circ: 21,000

📖 **494 Quantitative Structure-Activity Relationships**
Wiley-VCH Verlag GmbH
c/o Michael Wiese
Rheinische-Friedrich-Wilhelms-University
Institute of Pharmacy, Dept. of
   Pharmaceutical Chemistry
An der Immenburg 4   Ph: 49 228735212
D-53121 Bonn, Germany   Fax: 49 228735212
Publication E-mail: subinfo@wiley.com
Publisher E-mail: subservice@wiley-vch.de

Scientific journal covering molecular modelling, computer graphics and other computer-assisted methods in the design and development of biologically active compounds as applied to medicinal, agricultural and environmental chemistry. For medicinal chemists, organic chemists, biochemists, toxicologists, pharmacologists, and drug designers. **Key Personnel:** Michael Wiese, Editor, m.wiese@uni-bonn.de; Ferenc Darvas, Editor, phone 361214 2306, fax 361214 2310, df@cdk-cgx.hu. **ISSN:** 0931-8771. **Available Online.** **URL:** http://www.interscience.wiley.com.

📖 **495 Report Psychologie**
Deutscher Psychologen Verlag GmbH
Ober Lindweg 2   Ph: 49 2289873170
D-53129 Bonn, Germany   Fax: 49 228641023
Publisher E-mail: dpv@bdp-verband.de

Professional journal covering psychology. **Founded:** 1974. **Freq:** 10/year.

Print Method: Offset. **Cols./Page:** 4. **Col. Width:** 47 millimeters. **Col. Depth:** 259 millimeters. **Key Personnel:** Petra Walkenbach, Editor/Managing Dir., phone 49 228987310, fax 49 228641023; Hans Werner Drewe, News Editor; Chris Schaffmann, Editor-in-Chief. **ISSN:** 0344-9602. **Subscription Rates:** €54 individuals; €72 other countries; €6 single issue.
Ad Rates: BW: DM 1,130   **Circ:** Combined 18,500

HANNOVER

📖 **496 Sonderhefte**
International Gottfried Wilhelm Leibniz Society
Gottfried-Wilhelm-Leibniz-Gesellschaft
Niedersaechsische Landesbibliothek
Waterloostrasse 8   Ph: 49 5111267331
D-30169 Hannover, Germany   Fax: 49 5111267202
Publisher E-mail: leibnizgesellschaft@mail.mlb-hannover.de

Journal covering the history of philosophy and science in English, French and German. **Founded:** 1969. **ISSN:** 0341-0765. **Remarks:** Advertising not accepted.
Circ: (Not Reported)

📖 **497 Studia Leibnitiana Supplementa**
International Gottfried Wilhelm Leibniz Society
Gottfried-Wilhelm-Leibniz-Gesellschaft
Niedersaechsische Landesbibliothek
Waterloostrasse 8   Ph: 49 5111267331
D-30169 Hannover, Germany   Fax: 49 5111267202
Publisher E-mail: leibnizgesellschaft@mail.mlb-hannover.de

Journal covering the history of philosophy and science in English, French and German. **Founded:** 1968. **ISSN:** 0303-5980. **Remarks:** Advertising not accepted.
Circ: (Not Reported)

HERTEN

📖 **498 Flash Opel Scene International**
proMedia GmbH & Co. Verlag KG
Mi Hoffmann und Partner KG
Hertener Mark 7   Ph: 49 2366808104
D-45699 Herten, Germany   Fax: 49 2366808149
Publisher E-mail: j.christ@vest-netz.de

Consumer magazine covering Opel automobiles worldwide. **Founded:** 1991. **Freq:** Monthly. **Print Method:** Offset. **Trim Size:** 210 x 285 mm. **Cols./Page:** 3. **Col. Width:** 55 millimeters. **Key Personnel:** Ansgar Wilkendorf, Editor-in-Chief, a.wilkendorf@vest-netz.de; Andreas Loleit, Managing Editor, a.loleit@vest-netz.de. **ISSN:** 1438-2075. **Subscription Rates:** €3.50 single issue. **Remarks:** Accepts advertising.
Circ: (Not Reported)

📖 **499 VW Scene International**
TV Trend Verlag GmbH
Mi Hoffman und Partner KG
Hertener Mark 7   Ph: 49 2366808100
D-45699 Herten, Germany   Fax: 49 2366808149
Publication E-mail: b.lauf@vest-netz.de

Consumer magazine covering Volkswagen automobiles worldwide. **Founded:** 1989. **Freq:** Monthly. **Print Method:** Offset. **Trim Size:** 210 x 285 mm. **Cols./Page:** 3. **Col. Width:** 55 millimeters. **Key Personnel:** Thomas Ebeling, Editor-in-Chief, t.ebeling@vest-netz.de; Andreas Loleit, Managing Editor, a.loleit@vest-netz.de. **ISSN:** 0942-3257. **Subscription Rates:** DM 3.50 single issue. **Remarks:** Accepts advertising.
Circ: (Not Reported)

MUNICH

📖 **500 Die Pirsch**
Deutscher Landwirtschaftsverlag GmbH
Lothstr. 29   Ph: 49 8912705362
D-80797 Munich, Germany   Fax: 49 8912705542
Publication E-mail: pirschredaktion@dlv.de

Consumer magazine covering hunting. **Founded:** 1948. **Freq:** 2/month. **Print Method:** Offset. **Trim Size:** 210 x 297 mm. **Cols./Page:** 4. **Col. Width:** 45 millimeters. **Col. Depth:** 270 millimeters. **Key Personnel:** Jost Doerenkamp,

Editor. **ISSN:** 1437-4420. **Subscription Rates:** €91 individuals; €4.70 single issue. **Remarks:** Accepts advertising. **URL:** http://www.pirsch.de.

| Ad Rates: | BW: €2,700 | Circ: Combined 48,244 |
| | 4C: €5,098 | |

501 Fraunhofer (English)
Fraunhofer-Gesellschaft zur Forderung der Angewandten Forschung
Leonrodstrasse 54   Ph: 49 89120501
D-80636 Munich, Germany   Fax: 49 891205317
Publication E-mail: presse@zv.fhg.de
Publisher E-mail: info@zv.fhg.de

English language magazine covering research, technology, and innovation. **Freq:** Semiannual. **ISSN:** 1615-7028. **Subscription Rates:** Free to qualified subscribers. **URL:** http://www.fraunhofer.de/english/press/.

502 Official Journal of the European Patent Office
European Patent Office
Europaisches Patentamt
D-80298 Munich, Germany   Ph: 49 8923995225
    Fax: 49 8923995219
Publication E-mail: iwendl@epo.org

Journal covering the European patent office in English, French and German. **Subtitle:** Amtsblatt/Official Journal/Journal officiel. **Founded:** 1978. **Freq:** Monthly. **ISSN:** 0170-9291. **Subscription Rates:** €101 Europe, includes postage; €147 other countries includes postage; €12 single issue plus postage. **Remarks:** Accepts advertising. **URL:** http://www.european-patent-office.org.

| Ad Rates: | BW: €1,227 | Circ: Paid ‡2,200 |
| | | Non-paid ‡2,100 |

503 Schweinzucht und Schweinemast
Umbrella Association of German Pig Production
Postfach 7847   Ph: 49 251510120
D-48042 Munich, Germany   Fax: 49 2515101254
Publisher E-mail: susredaktion@ev-h.de

German language publication covering livestock. **Freq:** 6/year. **ISSN:** 0944-307X. **Subscription Rates:** €36 in Germany; €42 outside Germany. **Remarks:** Advertising accepted; rates available upon request.

    Circ: 15,000

NUREMBERG

504 Alpin
Olympia-Verlag GmbH
Badstr. 4-6   Ph: 49 89 89 31600
D-90402 Nuremberg, Germany   Fax: 49 89 89 316019
Publication E-mail: alpin@bergwelt.de
Publisher E-mail: anteigen@olympia-verlag.de

Consumer magazine covering mountaineering, climbing, and tourism. **Subtitle:** Das Bergwelt Magazin. **Founded:** Oct. 1963. **Freq:** Monthly. **Print Method:** Offset. **Key Personnel:** Bene Benedikt, Editor-in-Chief, b.benedikt@bergwelt.de. **ISSN:** 0177-3542. **Subscription Rates:** DM 44.80 individuals; DM 56.40 out of country; DM 4.60 single issue. **Remarks:** Accepts advertising. **Former name:** Alpinismus.

Ad Rates:	GLR: €3.40	Circ: Combined 30,016
	BW: €2,246	
	4C: €3,853	
	PCI: €3.50	

WIESBADEN

505 Management International Review
Gabler Verlag GmbH
Abraham-Lincoln-Str. 46   Ph: 49 61178780
D-65189 Wiesbaden, Germany   Fax: 49 6117878400

International business publication. **Founded:** Jan. 1, 1960. **Freq:** Quarterly. **ISSN:** 0938-8249. **Subscription Rates:** US$108 individuals; US$212 institu-

tions; US$51 single issue. **Remarks:** Accepts advertising. **Online:** Gale Group.

| Ad Rates: | BW: US$897 | Circ: Paid ‡1,200 |
| | 4C: US$2,029 | |

HUNGARY

BUDAPEST

506 The Gazette of Patents and Trademarks
Hungarian Design Council
Magyar Formatervezesi Tanacs
PO Box 552   Ph: 36 4745586
H-1370 Budapest 5, Hungary   Fax: 36 4745571
Publication E-mail: hirlapelofizetes@posta.hu
Publisher E-mail: varhelyi@hpo.hu

Official publication of the Hungarian Patent Office covering patent, utility model, trade mark, geographic indication and industrial property protection. **Freq:** Monthly. **Subscription Rates:** 14,400 Ft individuals; 1,200 Ft single issue. **URL:** http://www.hpo.hu/english/eszkv.html.

507 Nutrition, Allergy, Diet - Taplalkozas, anyagcsere, dieta
Hungarian Society of Nutrition
Magyar Taplalkozastudomanyi Tarsasag
Szentkiralyi u.14   Ph: 36 486 4820
H-1088 Budapest, Hungary   Fax: 36 486 2761
Publisher E-mail: drbarnam@hotmail.com

Hungarian language publication covering nutrition. **Founded:** 1995. **Freq:** Bimonthly. **ISSN:** 1419-1520. **Subscription Rates:** 1,800 Ft. **Remarks:** Advertising accepted; rates available upon request.

    Circ: (Not Reported)

508 Review of Industrial Property Protection and Copyright
Hungarian Design Council
Magyar Formatervezesi Tanacs
PO Box 552   Ph: 36 4745586
H-1370 Budapest 5, Hungary   Fax: 36 4745571
Publication E-mail: hirlapelofizetes@posta.hu
Publisher E-mail: varhelyi@hpo.hu

Publication covering industrial property protection and copyright. **Freq:** Bimonthly. **URL:** http://www.hpo.hu/english/eszkv.html.

ICELAND

REYKJAVIK

509 Handbok Baenda
Baendasamtok Islands
Baendahoellini vid Hagatorg
Postholf 7080   Ph: 354 15630300
IS-107 Reykjavik, Iceland   Fax: 354 15623058
Publication E-mail: me@bondi.is
Publisher E-mail: bi@bondi.is

Trade publication covering farming. **Founded:** 1951. **Freq:** Annual. **ISSN:** 0251-1940.

    Circ: 1,400

INDIA

ALIGARH

510 Asian Journal of Microbiology, Biotechnology and Environmental Sciences
Global Science Publications
23, Maharashi Dayanad Nagar
Surendra Nagar
Aligarh 202 001, Uttar Pradesh, India   Ph: 91 571404271

Publication covering biology, environmental science, biotechnology, and microbiology. **Founded:** 1999. **Freq:** Quarterly. **Print Method:** Offset. **Key**

Ad Rates: GLR = general line rate; BW = one-time black & white page rate; 4C = one-time four color page rate; SAU = standard advertising unit rate; CNU = Canadian newspaper advertising unit rate; PCI = per column inch rate.
Circulation: ★ = ABC; △ = BPA; ♦ = CAC; • = CCAB; ❏ = VAC; ⊕ = PO Statement; ‡ = Publisher's Report; Boldface figures = sworn; Light figures = estimated.
Entry type: ▢ = Print; ▮ = Broadcast.

55

Personnel: R. K. Trivedy, Editor, phone 91 2164 20369, fax 91 2164 20369. **ISSN:** 0972-3005. **Remarks:** Accepts advertising.

| Ad Rates: | BW: US$100 | Circ: Combined 1,000 |
| | 4C: US$200 | |

511 Indian Journal of Politics
Aligarh Muslim University
Dept. of Political Science
Aligarh 202 002, Uttar Pradesh, India
Ph: 91 0571701720
Fax: 91 0571701617

Publication on political science. **Founded:** 1967. **Freq:** Quarterly. **Key Personnel:** T. A. Nizami, Editor, phone 91 0571703183, fax 91 0571700673, mohsin@ndf.vsnl.net.in. **ISSN:** 0303-9951. **Subscription Rates:** Rs 150; US$40 other countries. **Remarks:** Advertising not accepted. **Alt. Formats:** Large-print.

Circ: 1,000

CALCUTTA

512 Economic Studies
Economic Studies & Journals Publishing Co
2 Private Rd.
Dum Dum
Calcutta 700 074, W. Bengal, India
Ph: 91 0335512288
Fax: 91 0335513635

Periodical focusing on business and economics. **Founded:** 1960. **Freq:** Biweekly. **Print Method:** Web offset. **Cols./Page:** 2. **Key Personnel:** Gautam Mukherjee, Editor. **ISSN:** 0013-0362. **Subscription Rates:** Rs 180; US$80 airmail; US$60 seamail; €70 airmail; €90 airmail. **Remarks:** Accepts advertising.

Ad Rates: BW: Rs 200 Circ: Paid 27,307

513 Indian Journal of Theoretical Physics
Institute of Theoretical Physics
Bignan Kutir
Calcutta 700 004, W. Bengal, India

Scientific journal focusing on physics. **Founded:** 1953. **Freq:** Quarterly. **ISSN:** 0019-5693. **Subscription Rates:** Rs 1200; US$70 other countries; Rs 200 Indian universities, colleges, institutions; Rs 1500 back volumes; US$100 other countries back volumes.

514 The Journal of the Anthropological Survey of India
Anthropological Survey of India
27 Jawaharlal Nehru Marg
Calcutta 700 016, W. Bengal, India
Publication E-mail: anthro@Cal12.vsnl.net.in

Periodical focusing on anthropology. **Founded:** Jan. 1952. **Freq:** Quarterly. **Print Method:** Offset. **Key Personnel:** Shri Deepak Tyagi, Editor/Dir., phone 91 0332497696, fax 91 0332497099. **ISSN:** 0970-3411. **Subscription Rates:** Rs 340; US$106 other countries. **Remarks:** Advertising not accepted. **URL:** http://www.anthsi.com. **Formerly:** Human Science.

Circ: Paid 1,100

515 Journal of the Asiatic Society
Asiatic Society, Calcutta
1 Park St.
Calcutta 700 016, W. Bengal, India
Publisher E-mail: astibcal@cal.vsnl.net.in
Ph: 91 0332290779
Fax: 91 0332172355

Journal covering Oriental studies. **Founded:** 1832. **Freq:** Annual. **ISSN:** 0368-3308. **Subscription Rates:** Rs 200.

516 Journal of Optics
Optical Society of India
c/o Dept. of Applied Physics
University of Calcutta
92 Acharya Prafulla Chandra Rd.
Calcutta 700 009, W. Bengal, India
Ph: 91 333508386
Publisher E-mail: osi@cucc.ernet.in; osi_india@rediffmail.com

Science magazine focusing on optics in India. **Founded:** 1972. **Freq:** Quarterly. **Key Personnel:** L.N. Haera, Gen. Secretary, osi@cubmb.earnet.in. **ISSN:** 0970-0374. **Subscription Rates:** Rs 2,500; US$250 other countries. **Remarks:** Accepts advertising.

Circ: Paid 600

517 Udbodhan
Ramakrishna Math
1 Udbodhan Lane
Calcutta 700 003, W. Bengal, India
Ph: 91 0335542248
Publication E-mail: udbodhan@vsnl.com
Publisher E-mail: udbodhan@vsnl.net

Periodical covering religion and theology. **Founded:** 1899. **Freq:** Monthly. **Trim Size:** 185 x 240 cm. **Key Personnel:** Swami Sarvaganandaji Maharaj, Editor, phone 91 0335542403. **ISSN:** 0971-4316. **Subscription Rates:** Rs 75; Rs 10 single issue. **Remarks:** Accepts advertising. **URL:** http://www.udbodhan.org.

| Ad Rates: | GLR: Rs 125 | Circ: Paid 55,000 |
| | BW: Rs 5,000 | Non-paid 1,000 |

CALICUT

518 Rheedea
Indian Association for Angiosperm Taxonomy
c/o University of Calicut
Department of Botany
Calicut 673 675, Kerala, India

Science magazine focusing on angiosperm taxonomy. **Founded:** 1991. **Freq:** Semiannual. **Print Method:** Offset. **Key Personnel:** K. N. Manilal, Editor. **ISSN:** 0971-2313. **Subscription Rates:** Rs 300 individuals; Rs 400 institutions.

Circ: Paid 500

CHENNAI

519 Review of Development and Change
Madras Institute of Development Studies
79, Second Main Rd.
Gandhi Nagar
Adyar
Chennai 600 020, Tamil Nadu, India
Ph: 91 0444412589
Fax: 91 0444910872
Publication E-mail: pub@mids.tn.nic.in
Publisher E-mail: office@mids.tn.nic.in

General magazine on social sciences. **Founded:** 1996. **Freq:** Semiannual. **Trim Size:** A4. **Key Personnel:** C. T. Kurien, Editor, phone 91 0442350305, fax 91 044412589, ssmids@ren.nic.in; Manabi Majundar, Editor; K. Nagaraj, Editor. **Subscription Rates:** Rs 100 individuals; Rs 150 institutions. **Remarks:** Advertising not accepted.

Circ: Paid 300

520 Theosophist
The Theosophical Publishing House
The Theosophical Society
Adyar
Chennai 600 020, Tamil Nadu, India
Ph: 91 444466613
Fax: 91 444901399
Publication E-mail: theosophist@eth.net
Publisher E-mail: tphindia@vsnl.com; theosophy@netkracker.com

Publication on theosophy, philosophy and religion. **Founded:** 1879. **Freq:** Monthly. **Print Method:** Offset. **Trim Size:** 18 x 24 cm. **Key Personnel:** Radha Burnier, Editor, phone 91 444912808, fax 91 444902706, para_vidya@vsnl.com; T.A. Echikwa, Publications Officer. **ISSN:** 0972-1851. **Subscription Rates:** Rs 40; US$18 other countries. **Remarks:** Accepts advertising.

Circ: Paid 3,000

DHARAMSALA

521 Tibet Journal
Library of Tibetan Works & Archives
Gangchen Kyishong
Dharamsala 176 215, Himachal Pradesh, India
Ph: 91 0189222467
Fax: 91 0189223723
Publisher E-mail: ltwa@vsnl.com

Tibetan history and culture publication. **Subtitle:** A Publication of Tibetan Studies. **Founded:** 1975. **Freq:** Quarterly. **Print Method:** Offset. **Trim Size:** 9 x 6.4. **Key Personnel:** Sonam Tsering, Editor. **ISSN:** 0970-5368. **Subscription Rates:** Rs 260; US$30 other countries. **Remarks:** Accepts advertising. **Online:** EBSCO. **Alt. Formats:** CD-ROM; Diskette.

Circ: Paid 1,000

ERNAKULAM

📖 **522 The Cashew**
P.P. Balasubramanian
Directorate of Cashewnut & Cocoa
  Development
Government of India
Kera Bhavan, Cochin   Ph: 91 0484373239
Ernakulam 682 011, Kerala, India   Fax: 91 0484373239
Publisher E-mail: cashco@vsnl.com

Bulletin on the cashew industry. **Founded:** 1967. **Freq:** Quarterly. **Print
Method:** Offset. **Key Personnel:** Venkatesh N. Hubballi, Editor, phone 91
0484351751, cashco@vsnl.com. **ISSN:** 0970-2423. **Subscription Rates:** Rs
600.
Ad Rates: BW: Rs 300   **Circ:** Paid 250
                4C: Rs 350

HYDERABAD

📖 **523 Indian Journal of American Studies**
Indo-American Centre for International Studies
Osmania University Campus   Ph: 91 0407098608
Hyderabad 500 007, Andhra Pradesh, India   Fax: 91 0407097114
Publisher E-mail: amerlib@hd2.vsnl.net.in; info@iacis-india.org

Publication on American history, literary criticism and collections. **Freq:**
Semiannual. **ISSN:** 0019-5030. **Subscription Rates:** Rs 100; US$10 other
countries.
                                             Circ: 1,000

JAIPUR

📖 **524 Diamond World**
International Journal House
A-95 Journal House
Janta Colony   Ph: 91 0141614398
Jaipur 302 004, Rajasthan, India   Fax: 91 0141602973
Publication E-mail: gemjournal@satyam.net.in
Publisher E-mail: diaworld@sancharnet.in

Periodical covering jewelry. Contains illustrations. **Founded:** 1973. **Freq:**
Biweekly. **Print Method:** Offset. **Trim Size:** 22.8 x 17.75 cm. **Key
Personnel:** Alok Kala, Editor. **ISSN:** 0970-7727. **Subscription Rates:** Rs
375; US$65 other countries airmail. **Remarks:** Accepts advertising.
Ad Rates: BW: US$1,000   **Circ:** 8,000
                4C: US$1,500

📖 **525 Gem & Jewellery Yearbook**
International Journal House
A-95 Journal House
Janta Colony   Ph: 91 0141614398
Jaipur 302 004, Rajasthan, India   Fax: 91 0141602973
Publication E-mail: gemjournal@satyam.net.in
Publisher E-mail: diaworld@sancharnet.in

Publication on antique jewelleries and collectibles. **Founded:** 1974. **Freq:**
Annual. **Print Method:** Offset. **Trim Size:** 17.5 x 11.5 cm. **Key Personnel:**
Alok Kala, Editor. **Subscription Rates:** Rs 750; US$50 other countries
airmail. **Remarks:** Accepts advertising.
Ad Rates: BW: US$500   **Circ:** Paid 4,500
                4C: US$1,000

📖 **526 Journal of Gem Industry**
Gem & Jewellery Information Centre
A-95 Journal House
Janta Colony   Ph: 91 0141614398
Jaipur 302 004, Rajasthan, India   Fax: 91 0141602973
Publication E-mail: gemjournal@satyam.net.in
Publisher E-mail: diaworld@sancharnet.in

Periodical covering the jewelry and gem industry. **Founded:** 1963. **Freq:**
Bimonthly. **Print Method:** Offset. **Trim Size:** 22.8 x 17.75 cm. **Key

Personnel: Alok Kala, Editor. **ISSN:** 0022-1244. **Subscription Rates:** Rs
525; US$60 other countries airmail. **Remarks:** Accepts advertising.
Ad Rates: BW: US$1,100   **Circ:** 8,750
                4C: US$1,600

JAMMU

📖 **527 Kashmir Times**
Kashmir Times Publications
Residency Road
Jammu Tawi   Ph: 91 0191543676
Jammu 180 001, Jammu and Kashmir, India   Fax: 91 0191542028
Publisher E-mail: vbhasin@sancharnet.in

General newspaper of Kashmir. **Founded:** 1955. **Freq:** Daily. **Print Method:**
Offset. **Trim Size:** 53 x 41 cm. **Key Personnel:** Prabodh Jamwal, Editor-in-
Chief, phone 91 0191543676, fax 91 0191542028, prabodh@sancharnet.in.
Subscription Rates: Rs 2 single issue. **Remarks:** Accepts advertising. **URL:**
http://www.kashmirtimes.com.
Ad Rates: GLR: Rs 300   **Circ:** Paid 160,000
                BW: Rs
                127,200
                4C: Rs
                254,400
                PCI: Rs 3,001

KARAD

📖 **528 Ecology, Environment and Conservation**
Enviro Media
2nd Fl.
Rohan Heights
PO Box 90   Ph: 91 216420369
Karad 415 110, Maharashtra, India   Fax: 91 216420369
Publisher E-mail: rktem@pn3.vsnl.net.in

Periodical covering biology, environmental science, and law. **Founded:** 1995.
Freq: Quarterly. **Key Personnel:** R. K. Trivedy, Editor. **ISSN:** 0971-765X.
Remarks: Accepts advertising.
Ad Rates: BW: US$100   **Circ:** 1,500
                4C: US$200

📖 **529 Journal of Industrial Pollution Control**
Enviro Media
2nd Fl.
Rohan Heights
PO Box 90   Ph: 91 216420369
Karad 415 110, Maharashtra, India   Fax: 91 216420369
Publisher E-mail: rktem@pn3.vsnl.net.in

Journal focusing on Indian industrial pollution and control. **Founded:** 1985.
Freq: Semiannual. **Print Method:** Offset. **Trim Size:** A8. **Key Personnel:** R.
K. Trivedy, Editor, phone 91 0216444369. **ISSN:** 0970-2083. **Subscription
Rates:** Rs 150 individuals; Rs 250 institutions. **Remarks:** Accepts advertis-
ing.
Ad Rates: BW: US$50   **Circ:** Paid 2,000
                4C: US$100

📖 **530 Pollution Research**
Enviro Media
2nd Fl.
Rohan Heights
PO Box 90   Ph: 91 216420369
Karad 415 110, Maharashtra, India   Fax: 91 216420369
Publisher E-mail: rktem@pn3.vsnl.net.in

Scientific magazine focusing on environmental sciences and pollution.
Founded: 1982. **Freq:** Quarterly. **Print Method:** Offset. **Trim Size:** A4. **Key
Personnel:** R. K. Trivedy, Editor. **ISSN:** 0257-8050. **Subscription Rates:**
US$90 individuals; US$300 institutions. **Remarks:** Accepts advertising.
Ad Rates: BW: US$100   **Circ:** Paid 2,000
                4C: US$200

Ad Rates: GLR = general line rate; BW = one-time black & white page rate; 4C = one-time four color page rate; SAU = standard advertising unit rate;
CNU = Canadian newspaper advertising unit rate; PCI = per column inch rate.
Circulation: ★ = ABC; △ = BPA; ♦ = CAC; ♦ = CCAB; ❑ = VAC; ⊕ = PO Statement; ‡ = Publisher's Report; Boldface figures = sworn; Light figures = estimated.
Entry type: 📖 = Print; 🎙 = Broadcast.

57

KOCHI

531 Caustic
Travancore-Cochin Chemicals Ltd.
Udyogamandal P.O.   Ph: 91 484545425
Kochi 683 501, Kerala, India   Fax: 91 484545420
Publisher E-mail: tccudl@vsnl.com

Illustrated scientific journal on chemistry. **Freq:** Quarterly. **Key Personnel:** N.I. Paulose, DGM, Contact, phone 91 484546049, fax 91 484546049, salestcc@vsnl.net. **ISSN:** 0008-8579. **URL:** http://www.tcckerala.com.
Circ: Free 1,200

LUCKNOW

532 Indian Veterinary Medical Journal
Institute of Veterinary Biologicals
Badshahbagh
Lucknow 226 007, Uttar Pradesh, India

Medical journal focusing on veterinary science. **Founded:** 1977. **Freq:** Quarterly. **Print Method:** Offset. **Key Personnel:** J. N. S. Yadava, Editor-in-Chief, phone 91 0522371621. **ISSN:** 0250-5266. **Subscription Rates:** US$80 other countries. **Remarks:** Accepts advertising.
Circ: Combined 1,500

533 Journal of Medicinal and Aromatic Plant Science
Central Institute of Medicinal and Aromatic Plants
Post Office CIMAP
CIMAP   Ph: 91 0522359623
Lucknow 226 015, Uttar Pradesh, India Fax: 91 0522342666
Publisher E-mail: cimap@cimap.res.in

Periodical on various areas of medicinal and aromatic plants, gum, dyes, and pharmaceuticals. Presents original findings and information on market prices, export, import, new patents, new books, and current references. **Founded:** 1979. **Freq:** 4/year. **Print Method:** Offset. **Trim Size:** A4. **Key Personnel:** SPS Khanuja, Chief Editor, phone 91 0522359623, director@cimap.res.in; Ashok Sharma, Editor, phone 91 0522357133, ashoksharma@cimap.res.in. **ISSN:** 0253-7125. **Subscription Rates:** Rs 2000; US$150 other countries. **Remarks:** Accepts advertising. **Formerly:** Current Research on Medicinal and Aromatic Plants.
Circ: Paid 250

MARIKUNNU

534 Journal of Spices and Aromatic Crops
Indian Society for Spices
c/o Indian Institute of Spices Research
PO Box 1701
Calicut   Ph: 91 0495730906
Marikunnu 673 012, Kerala, India   Fax: 91 0495730294
Publication E-mail: josac@iisr.org
Publisher E-mail: iss@iisr.org

Scientific journal focusing on research on spices and aromatic crops. **Founded:** 1992. **Freq:** Semiannual. **Key Personnel:** Santhosh J. Eapen, Editor, sjeapen@iissr.org. **ISSN:** 0971-3328. **Subscription Rates:** Rs 300; US$50 other countries. **Remarks:** Advertising not accepted. **URL:** http://www.iisr.org/iss/josac.
Circ: Paid 400

MUMBAI

535 Blind Welfare
National Association for the Blind, India
NAB Louis Braille Memorial Research
  Centre
R.M. Alpaiwalla Complex
124-127, Cotton Depot, Cotton Green   Ph: 91 0223726748
Mumbai, Maharashtra, India   Fax: 91 0223726748
Publisher E-mail: nabin@bom3.vsnl.net.in

Journal for the visually impaired. **Founded:** June 1959. **Freq:** 3/year. **Key Personnel:** Hema Upendra, Editor, phone 91 0223726748, fax 91 0223726748; Dr. Rajendra T. Vyas, Editorial Consultant, phone 91 0224948581, fax 91 0224932539; Wg. Cdr. C.M. Jaywant, Exec. Dir., phone 91 0224935370. **ISSN:** 0006-4823. **Subscription Rates:** Rs 90 print edition; US$25 other countries print edition; Rs 20 Braille edition; US$10 other

countries Braille edition; US$20 U.S. Braille edition. **Remarks:** Accepts advertising. **Available Online. Alt. Formats:** Braille; CD-ROM.
Ad Rates: BW: Rs 1,500   **Circ:** Paid 500

536 Economic Survey of Maharashtra
Directorate of Economics and Statistics
Government of Maharashtra
Administrative Bldg., 8th Fl.
Govt. Colony, Bandra (East)   Ph: 91 0228309801
Mumbai 400 051, Maharashtra, India   Fax: 91 0228309800

Publication containing reviews of various economic and social developments of state. Includes statistical tables. **Founded:** 1962. **Freq:** Annual. **Trim Size:** A4. **Key Personnel:** Shri B.M. Nagrale, Editor. **ISSN:** 0076-2539. **Subscription Rates:** Free. **Remarks:** Advertising not accepted.
Circ: (Not Reported)

537 Indica
Heras Institute of Indian History and Culture
St. Xavier's College, Mahapalika Marg.
Mumbai 400 001, Maharashtra, India   Ph: 91 222620665
Publisher E-mail: herasinstitute@hotmail.com

Periodical focusing on ancient, medieval, and modern Indian history, Indian art and literature, Indian religions and cultures. **Subtitle:** The Journal of the Heras Institute of Indian History and Culture. **Founded:** 1964. **Freq:** Semiannual (March and Sept.). **Print Method:** Offset. **Trim Size:** 16.5 x 24 cm. **Key Personnel:** Dr. Aubrey Mascarenhas, Editor, phone 91 0222620665, aubreyam@hotpop.com. **ISSN:** 0019-686X. **Subscription Rates:** Rs 200 individuals; Rs 300 institutions. **Remarks:** Advertising not accepted.
Circ: Paid 500

538 Journal of Postgraduate Medicine
Seth G.S. Medical College and K.E.M. Hospital
Office of Publications
Mumbai 400 012, Maharashtra, India   Ph: 91 0224132118

Medical journal on postgraduate medicine featuring charts and illustrations. **Founded:** 1955. **Freq:** Quarterly. **Print Method:** Offset. **Trim Size:** 8.5 X 11 inches. **Key Personnel:** K. Radhakrisna Murthy, Editor. **ISSN:** 0022-3859. **Subscription Rates:** Rs 400 individuals; Rs 800 institutions; Rs 150 single issue; US$50 individuals; US$100 institutions. **Remarks:** Accepts advertising. **URL:** http://www.jpgmonline.com. **Alt. Formats:** CD-ROM.
Ad Rates: BW: Rs 5,000   **Circ:** 2,000
                 4C: Rs 10,000

539 Maharashtra Quarterly Bulletin of Economics & Statistics
Directorate of Economics and Statistics
Government of Maharashtra
Administrative Bldg., 8th Fl.
Govt. Colony, Bandra (East)   Ph: 91 0228309801
Mumbai 400 051, Maharashtra, India   Fax: 91 0228309800

Bulletin of economics and statistics. **Founded:** 1960. **Freq:** Quarterly. **Trim Size:** A4. **Key Personnel:** Shri A.G. Wagh, Director, phone 91 0228309807. **ISSN:** 0025-0481. **Subscription Rates:** Rs 200. **Remarks:** Advertising not accepted.
Circ: (Not Reported)

540 Paintindia
Colour Publications Pvt. Ltd.
126-A Dhurwadi
A.V. Nagwekar Marg
Prabhadevi   Ph: 91 224306319
Mumbai 400 025, Maharashtra, India   Fax: 91 2204300601
Publisher E-mail: colorpub@vsnl.com

Technical magazine on Techno commercial journal for coatings, inks and allie and industries. **Founded:** 1951. **Freq:** Monthly. **Print Method:** Offset. **Trim Size:** 21.5 x 27.5 cm. **Key Personnel:** R. V. Raghavan, Editor, phone 91 0224309318, colorpub@vsnl.com; S. Radhaknshnan, Group Editor. **ISSN:** 0030-9540. **Subscription Rates:** Rs 400; US$150 other countries. **Remarks:** Accepts advertising. **Absorbed:** Finish.
Ad Rates: BW: US$600   **Circ:** Paid 9,439
                 4C: US$1200

541 Screen
Indian Express Newspapers (Bombay) Pvt. Ltd.
3/50 Lalbaug Industrial Estate
Dr. Ambedkar Mong, Lalbaug   Ph: 91 0222022627
Mumbai 400 012, Maharashtra, India   Fax: 91 0222022139
Publication E-mail: scrdept-bmy@expressindia.com

English publication on films. **Founded:** 1951. **Freq:** Weekly. **Key Personnel:** Bhawana Somaaya, Editor, phone 91 022 4717677, fax 91 022 4717641, iemumbai@express.indexp.co.in. **ISSN:** 0036-9551. **Subscription Rates:** Rs 10 single issue. **Remarks:** Accepts advertising. **URL:** http://www.expressindia.com/screen.

Circ: Paid 28,700

542 Statistical Abstract of Maharashtra State
Directorate of Economics and Statistics
Government of Maharashtra
Administrative Bldg., 8th Fl.
Govt. Colony, Bandra (East)   Ph: 91 0228309801
Mumbai 400 051, Maharashtra, India   Fax: 91 0228309800

Publication featuring statistics pertaining to various socioeconomic aspects of Maharashtra State. **Founded:** 1951. **Freq:** Annual. **Trim Size:** A4. **Key Personnel:** Shri A.G. Wagh, Director, phone 91 0228309807. **ISSN:** 0081-4709. **Subscription Rates:** Rs 300. **Remarks:** Advertising not accepted.

Circ: (Not Reported)

543 Yoga and Total Health
The Yoga Institute
Santa Cruz East
Mumbai 400 055, Maharashtra, India   Ph: 91 0226110506
Publisher E-mail: yogainstitute@rediffmail.com

Publication on yoga and health. **Founded:** 1933. **Freq:** Monthly. **Key Personnel:** Jayadeva Yogendra, Editor, phone 91 0226122185, yoga@vsnl.net. **ISSN:** 0970-1737. **Subscription Rates:** Rs 150 India; US$25 other countries airmail. **Remarks:** Accepts advertising. **Formerly:** The Journal of the Institute.

Circ: Paid 2,000

NEW DELHI

544 Afro-Asian Journal of Rural Development
Afro-Asian Rural Reconstruction Organization
2 State Guest Houses Complex
Chana Kyapuri   Ph: 91 114100475
New Delhi 100 021, Delhi, India   Fax: 91 116115937
Publisher E-mail: aardohq@nde.vsnl.net.in

English language publication covering agriculture and rural development issues in AFro-Asian countries. **Founded:** Aug. 1966. **Freq:** Semiannual. **Print Method:** Offset. **Key Personnel:** Dr. Bahar Munip, Editor, aardohq@nde.vsnl.net.in. **ISSN:** 0972-3021. **Subscription Rates:** US$15 individuals airmail; US$10 individuals surface mail. **Remarks:** Advertising not accepted.

Circ: Combined 400

545 Biology Today
MTG Learning Media (P) Ltd.
406, Taj Apt.
New Delhi 110 029, Delhi, India   Ph: 91 011 619 1601
      Fax: 91 011 619 1599
Publication E-mail: math2000@vsnl.com

Biology publication covering study material for exams in India. **Freq:** Monthly. **Subscription Rates:** Rs 200 individuals; Rs 375 two years. **URL:** http://www.pcmbtoday.com/mtgpp/biology/.

546 Chemistry Today
MTG Learning Media (P) Ltd.
406, Taj Apt.
New Delhi 110 029, Delhi, India   Ph: 91 011 619 1601
      Fax: 91 011 619 1599
Publication E-mail: math2000@vsnl.com

Chemistry publication featuring study material for IIT-JEE exams in India.

Freq: Monthly. **Subscription Rates:** Rs 200 individuals; Rs 375 two years. **URL:** http://www.pcmbtoday.com/mtgpp/chem/.

547 Communicator (New Delhi)
Indian Institute of Mass Communication
JNU New Campus   Ph: 91 116160940
New Delhi 110 067, Delhi, India   Fax: 91 116107462

Scientific journal covering communication. **Founded:** 1965. **Freq:** Quarterly. **Key Personnel:** K.M. Shrivastava, Editor, phone 91 116166550. **Subscription Rates:** Rs 80 individuals India; US$30 other countries.

548 Ethnobotany
Deep Publications
B-1/118, Paschim Vihar   Ph: 91 0115259514
New Delhi 110 063, Delhi, India   Fax: 91 0116519849

Periodical focusing on botany, pharmacology, alternative medicine, and the ethnobotany of various areas, including ethno-medicine, ethnochemistry, ethnopharmocology, ethnotaxonomy, and ethnopharamacognosy. **Founded:** 1989. **Freq:** Semiannual. **Print Method:** Offset. **Key Personnel:** S.K. Jain, Editor. **ISSN:** 0971-1252. **Subscription Rates:** Rs 400; US$60 other countries. **Remarks:** Accepts advertising.
Ad Rates: BW: US$60   Circ: Paid 575
      4C: US$150

549 In-between
University of Delhi
RLA College
English Dept.
New Delhi 110 021, Delhi, India   Ph: 91 0112715435
      Fax: 91 0112714607
Publication E-mail: inbetween@indiatimes.com
Publisher E-mail: inbetween@rediff.com

Academic journal featuring literary criticism. **Subtitle:** Essays & Studies in Literary Criticism. **Founded:** 1992. **Freq:** Semiannual. **Trim Size:** 5.5 x 8.5. **Key Personnel:** G.R. Taneja, Editor, grtaneja47@hotmail.com. **ISSN:** 0971-9474. **Subscription Rates:** Rs 300; US$28 other countries. **Remarks:** Accepts advertising.
Ad Rates: BW: US$100   Circ: Paid 600
      4C: US$400

550 Indian Dairyman
Indian Dairy Association
I D A House
Sector IV
R.K. Puram   Ph: 91 0116179781
New Delhi 110 022, Delhi, India   Fax: 91 0116174719
Publisher E-mail: ida@nde.vsnl.net.in

Scientific journal focusing on dairying and animal husbandry. **Founded:** 1949. **Freq:** Monthly. **Print Method:** Offset. **Trim Size:** 28 x 21.5 cm. **Key Personnel:** A. Banerjee, Pres./Chairman, Editorial Board. **ISSN:** 0019-4603. **Subscription Rates:** Rs 1,200 individuals; US$120 other countries plus postage; Rs 150 single issue. **Remarks:** Accepts advertising. **Available Online. Alt. Formats:** CD-ROM.
Ad Rates: BW: Rs 3,000   Circ: Paid 2,000
      4C: Rs 6,000

551 Indian Journal of Dairy Science
Indian Dairy Association
I D A House
Sector IV
R.K. Puram   Ph: 91 0116179781
New Delhi 110 022, Delhi, India   Fax: 91 0116174719
Publisher E-mail: ida@nde.vsnl.net.in

Publication on the field of dairy science. **Founded:** 1948. **Freq:** Bimonthly. **Print Method:** Offset. **Trim Size:** 28 x 21.5 cm. **Key Personnel:** A. Banerjee, President, phone 91 0116170781, fax 91 0116174719. **ISSN:** 0019-5146. **Subscription Rates:** Rs 400 individuals; Rs 75 single issue; US$60 other countries. **Remarks:** Accepts advertising. **URL:** http://www.indiandairyassociation.com/link2.htm.
Ad Rates: BW: Rs 1,500   Circ: (Not Reported)

📖 **552 Journal of the International Medical Sciences Academy**
P.D. Gulati
Intl. Medical Sciences Academy Natl.
  Medical Library Bldg.
2nd Fl.
Ansari Nagar
Ring Rd.   Ph: 91 0116964660
New Delhi 110 029, Delhi, India   Fax: 91 0116964660
Publisher E-mail: imsahq@ndl.vsnl.net.in

Journal covering medical science issues. **Founded:** 1987. **Freq:** Quarterly. **Trim Size:** 8 x 10.5. **Key Personnel:** Dr. P.D. Gulati, Editor. **ISSN:** 0971-071X. **Subscription Rates:** Rs 500; US$200 other countries. **Remarks:** Accepts advertising.
Ad Rates: BW: Rs 6,000   **Circ:** Paid 1,200
             4C: Rs 15,000

📖 **553 Physics For You**
MTG Learning Media (P) Ltd.
406, Taj Apt.   Ph: 91 011 619 1601
New Delhi 110 029, Delhi, India   Fax: 91 011 619 1599
Publication E-mail: math2000@vsnl.com

Physics publication featuring study material for exams in India. **Freq:** Monthly. **Subscription Rates:** Rs 200 individuals; Rs 375 two years. **URL:** http://www.pcmbtoday.com/mtgpp/physics/.

📖 **554 Phytotaxonomy**
Deep Publications
B-1/118, Paschim Vihar   Ph: 91 0115259514
New Delhi 110 063, Delhi, India   Fax: 91 0116519849

Journal covering taxonomy of all plant groups. **Founded:** 2001. **Freq:** Annual. **Print Method:** Offset. **Trim Size:** 7 x 9. **Key Personnel:** S. K. Jain, Editor; Dr. D.K. Upreti, Managing Editor. **ISSN:** 0972-4206. **Subscription Rates:** Rs 400 individuals; US$60 out of country. **Remarks:** Accepts advertising.
Ad Rates: BW: US$60   **Circ:** Paid 200
             4C: US$150

📖 **555 Taxation**
174 Jorbagh
New Delhi 110 003, Delhi, India
Publication E-mail: taxation@nda.vsnl.net.in

Finance, economics and taxation journal reporting judgments on direct taxes passed by the Supreme Court of India, all high courts of India, and all benches of income tax appellate tribrunals. Also covers circulars and notifications issued by the Indian Ministry of Finance. **Founded:** 1948. **Freq:** Biweekly. **Print Method:** Offset. **Key Personnel:** B. B. Bhargava, Editor, phone 91 011 461 9558, fax 91 011 335 5584. **Subscription Rates:** Rs 26,901. **Remarks:** Advertising not accepted.
                                              Circ: Paid 6,000

PONDICHERRY

📖 **556 PILC Journal of Dravidic Studies**
Pondicherry Institute of Linguistics and Culture
c/o Director
No. 55, Chinna Subbaraya Pillai St.
Pondicherry 605 001, Pondicherry, India   Ph: 91 041337117
Publication E-mail: pilc@md3.vsnl.net.in

Journal covering cultural and linguistics studies. **Founded:** 1991. **Freq:** Semiannual. **Print Method:** Offset. **Trim Size:** 16.5 x 23.5 cm. **ISSN:** 0971-0957. **Subscription Rates:** Rs 150 individuals; Rs 300 institutions; US$50 other countries. **Remarks:** Advertising not accepted.
                                              Circ: Paid 150

ITALY

COMO

📖 **557 Hobby Zoo**
Vimax Srl
via Rezzonico 23   Ph: 39 031301059
I-22100 Como, Italy   Fax: 39 031301418
Publisher E-mail: vimax@tin.it

Trade magazine covering pet supplies worldwide. **Founded:** 1983. **Freq:** Monthly. **Print Method:** Offset. **Trim Size:** 195 x 265 mm. **Key Personnel:** Adolfo Somigliana, Editor, a.somigliana@zoomark.it. **Subscription Rates:** Free. **Remarks:** Accepts advertising.
                                              Circ: Non-paid 14,000

MILAN

📖 **558 Agro Food**
Teknoscienze srl
Via Aurelio Saffi 23   Ph: 39 024818011
I-20123 Milan, Italy   Fax: 39 024818070
Publication E-mail: subscription@teknoscienze.com
Publisher E-mail: info@teknoscienze.com

Publication covering agricultural technology. **Founded:** 1990. **Trim Size:** 210 x 297 mm. **Key Personnel:** Michaela Carmagnola, Editor, mickycar@tin.it. **Subscription Rates:** €67.30 individuals Italy; €109.60 two years Italy; €189 elsewhere; €311.10 elsewhere two years; €50 institutions Italy; €100 institutions two years; €150 institutions elsewhere; €230 institutions elsewhere; two years. **Remarks:** Accepts advertising. **URL:** http://www.teknoscienze.com/co/co.htm.
                                              Circ: Combined 7,000

📖 **559 Airone**
Editoriale Giorgio Mondadori SpA
Cso Magenta 55
I-20123 Milan, MI, Italy   Ph: 39 02 433131
Publication E-mail: airone@edgm.it

Magazine covering subjects from astrophysics discoveries, animal life, the human mind, and other topics of various interest in nature and science. **Founded:** 1981. **Freq:** Monthly. **Print Method:** Rotary offset. **Cols./Page:** 3. **Key Personnel:** Eliana Ferioli, Director, phone 39 02 43313375, fax 39 02 43313574. **Remarks:** Advertising accepted; rates available upon request.
                                              Circ: (Not Reported)

📖 **560 CDA**
Editoriale Elsevier SpA
via Vittoria Colonna 4   Ph: 39 024859181
I-20149 Milan, Italy   Fax: 39 02485918220
Publisher E-mail: info@elsevier.it

Trade magazine covering heating and cooling. **Freq:** Monthly. **Key Personnel:** Renato Lazzarin, Scientific Dir.; Franco Adami, Editorial Dir. **Remarks:** Accepts advertising.
                                              Circ: (Not Reported)

📖 **561 Chimica Oggi (Chemistry Today)**
Teknoscienze srl
Via Aurelio Saffi 23   Ph: 39 024818011
I-20123 Milan, Italy   Fax: 39 024818070
Publication E-mail: subscription@teknoscienze.com
Publisher E-mail: info@teknoscienze.com

Publication covering chemicals and pharmaceuticals. **Founded:** 1983. **Trim Size:** 210 x 297 mm. **Key Personnel:** Michaela Carmagnola, Editor, mickycar@tin.it. **Subscription Rates:** €95.70 individuals Italy; €155.30 two years Italy; €283 elsewhere; €458 elsewhere two years; €50 institutions Italy; €100 institutions two years; €150 institutions elsewhere; €230 institutions elsewhere; two years. **Remarks:** Accepts advertising. **URL:** http://www.teknoscienze.com/co/co.htm.
                                              Circ: Combined 8,000

📖 **562 Famiglia Cristiana**
Periodici San Paolo
via Giotto 36   Ph: 39 248071
I-20145 Milan, Italy   Fax: 39 248078247
Publication E-mail: famigliacristiana@stpauls.it

Christian family magazine. **Subtitle:** Weekly Magazine of Current News, Information and Culture. **Founded:** 1931. **Freq:** Weekly. **Key Personnel:** Don Antonio Sciortino, Editor-in-Chief, diresionefc@stpauls.it; M. Fulvio Donadei, Advertising Mgr., fax 39 48072360, fulvio.donadei@stpauls.it. **Remarks:** Accepts advertising. **URL:** http://www.famigliacristiana.it.
                                              Circ: 966,671

Ⓠ 563 Jesus
Periodici San Paolo
via Giotto 36
I-20145 Milan, Italy
Ph: 39 248071
Fax: 39 248078247
Publication E-mail: jesus@stpauls.it

Consumer magazine covering religion. **Founded:** 1978. **Freq:** Monthly. **Trim Size:** 21 x 28 cm. **Key Personnel:** Don Vincenzo Marras, Editor-in-Chief, fax 39 048072486, vincenzo.marras@stpaul.it; M. Fulvio Donadei, Advertising Mgr., fulvio.donadei@stpaul.it. **Subscription Rates:** €37.20; €3.10 single issue. **Remarks:** Accepts advertising. **URL:** http://www.sanpaolo.org/jesus.
Circ: 68,173

MODUGNO

Ⓠ 564 La Gazzetta dell'Economia
Tipografia Sedit Servizi Editoriali Srl
Via Orchidee, 1
I-70026 Modugno, BA, Italy
Ph: 39 805857439
Fax: 39 805857427
Publication E-mail: gazeco@tin.it
Publisher E-mail: administrazione@edit.net

Newspaper covering entrepreneurship. **Subtitle:** Settimanale di Informazione Economica di Puglia e Basilicata. **Founded:** May 11, 1996. **Freq:** Weekly. **Print Method:** Offset. **Cols./Page:** 4. **Key Personnel:** Michele Christallo, Editor. **Subscription Rates:** €41.20 individuals; €1.03 single issue. **Remarks:** Accepts advertising.
Circ: (Not Reported)

PONTE LAMBRO

Ⓠ 565 SAGGI-Child Development and Disabilities
Ghedimedia
Associazionela la Nostra Famiglia
Via don Luigi Monza 1
I-22037 Ponte Lambro, Italy
Publication E-mail: redazione.saggi@bp.lnf.it

Italian and English language publication covering child disabilities. **Founded:** 2000. **Freq:** Quarterly. **Key Personnel:** Ada Moretti, Contact, phone 39 031877111, fax 39 031877559, amoretti@bp.lnf.it. **Subscription Rates:** €42 individuals; €15.50 single issue. **Alt. Formats:** CD-ROM.

ROME

Ⓠ 566 Il Fiasco
DeAgostini Professionale SpA
Viale Mazzini 25
I-00195 Rome, Italy
Ph: 39 63217538
Fax: 39 63217808

Professional magazine covering tax law for consultants offices, entrepreneurs, executives and tax law experts. **Founded:** 1977. **Freq:** Weekly. **Key Personnel:** Dr. Pasquale Marino, Editorial Dir., mc9423@mclink.it. **ISSN:** 1124-9307. **Remarks:** Accepts advertising.
Circ: (Not Reported)

Ⓠ 567 L'Industria Italiana del Cemento
Pubblicemento srl
Piazza G. Marconi, 25
I-00144 Rome, Italy
Ph: 39 654210237
Fax: 39 5915408
Publication E-mail: iic@aitecweb.com

Trade magazine covering the construction industry. **Founded:** 1930. **Freq:** Monthly. **Print Method:** Offset. **Cols./Page:** 3. **Col. Width:** 66 millimeters. **Col. Depth:** 229 millimeters. **Key Personnel:** Domenico Burattini, Managing Editor. **ISSN:** 0019-7637. **Subscription Rates:** €88 individuals; €9 single issue. **Remarks:** Accepts advertising.
Circ: Controlled 12,000

VERNASCA

Ⓠ 568 Flortecnica Data e Fiori
ACE/International
via Mocomero 26
I-29010 Vernasca, PC, Italy
Ph: 39 9910719
Fax: 39 9910719
Publication E-mail: flortec@flortec.it

Professional magazine for garden centers and florists. **Founded:** 1979. **Freq:** Quarterly. **Print Method:** Offset litho. **Trim Size:** 210 x 280 mm. **Cols./Page:** 3. **Col. Width:** 5.7 centimeters. **Col. Depth:** 25.7 centimeters. **Key Personnel:** Arturo Croci, Publisher. **ISSN:** 1122-7966. **Subscription Rates:** Free to qualified subscribers. **Remarks:** Accepts advertising. **URL:** http://www.flortec.it. **Formerly:** Data e Fiori.
Circ: Controlled 54,000

JAPAN

AICHI

Ⓠ 569 Chubu Weekly
April Communications
Matsui Bldg. 1-F
1-2-26 Higashi-Sakura
Higashi-ku
Nagoya-shi
Aichi 461-0005, Japan
Ph: 81 529710906
Publication E-mail: cwmail@april.co.jp

General newspaper. **Founded:** 1995. **Freq:** Weekly. **Key Personnel:** John E. Gibson, Editor. **Subscription Rates:** US$35 single issue. **Remarks:** Advertising accepted; rates available upon request. **URL:** http://www.eal.or.jp/CW.
Circ: Paid 5,000

Ⓠ 570 Daily News Nagoya
April Communications
Matsui Bldg. 1-F
1-2-26 Higashi-Sakura
Higashi-ku
Nagoya-shi
Aichi 461-0005, Japan
Ph: 81 529710906

General online newspaper. **Freq:** Daily. **URL:** http://www.eal.or.jp/DNN/.

Ⓠ 571 Environmental Medicine
Nagoya University
Research Institute of Environmental Medicine
Furo-cho Chikusa-ku
Nagoya-shi
Aichi 464-0814, Japan
Ph: 81 527893873

Journal of environmental medicine. **Founded:** 1951. **Freq:** Semiannual. **Key Personnel:** Hideki Yamamura, Editor. **ISSN:** 0287-0517.
Circ: Free 400

Ⓠ 572 Journal of College of International Studies
Chubu University College of International Studies
Kasugai
Aichi, Japan

Journal covering economics. **Founded:** 1985. **Freq:** Annual. **ISSN:** 0910-8882.

Ⓠ 573 Journal of Plasma and Fusion Research
Japan Society of Plasma Science and Nuclear Fusion Research
20-29 Nishiki 2-chome
Naka-ku
Nagoya-shi
Aichi 460-0003, Japan

Journal of nuclear physics. **Founded:** 1958. **Freq:** Monthly. **ISSN:** 0918-7928. **Subscription Rates:** 1,300¥ single issue.

📖 **574 Nanzan Review of American Studies**
Nanzan University
18 Yamazato-cho
Showa-ku
Nagoya-shi
Aichi 466-0824, Japan   Ph: 81 528323111

History journal. **Founded:** 1979. **Freq:** Annual. **Key Personnel:** Charles B. Wordell, Editor, wordell@ic.nanzan-u.ac.jp. **ISSN:** 0288-3872.

📖 **575 Primates**
Japan Monkey Center
26 Inuyama-Kanrin
Inuyama-shi
Aichi 484-0000, Japan   Ph: 81 568612327

Journal of zoology. **Founded:** 1957. **Freq:** Quarterly. **Key Personnel:** Yukimaru Sugiyama, Editor. **ISSN:** 0032-8332. **Subscription Rates:** 15,000¥. **Remarks:** Advertising accepted; rates available upon request.
                 Circ: Paid 800

📖 **576 Regional Development Dialogue**
United Nations Centre for Regional Development
1-47-1 Nagono
Nakamura-ku
Nagoya-shi
Aichi 450-0001, Japan   Ph: 81 525619377

Journal covering economics. **Subtitle:** An International Journal Focusing on Third Wo. **Founded:** 1980. **Freq:** Semiannual. **Key Personnel:** Hideki Kaji, Editor. **ISSN:** 0250-6505. **Subscription Rates:** US$40. **Remarks:** Advertising accepted; rates available upon request.
                 Circ: Paid 1,000

📖 **577 Regional Development Studies**
United Nations Centre for Regional Development
1-47-1 Nagono
Nakamura-ku
Nagoya-shi
Aichi 450-0001, Japan   Ph: 81 525619377

Journal covering economics. **Founded:** 1995. **Freq:** Annual. **ISSN:** 1020-3060. **Subscription Rates:** US$20.
                 Circ: Paid 500

AKITA

📖 **578 Akita Journal of Medicine**
Akita University
School of Medicine
1-1-1 Hondo
Akita 010-8543, Japan

Medical science journal. **Founded:** 1974. **Freq:** Semiannual. **Key Personnel:** Toshihiro Sugiyama, Editor. **ISSN:** 0386-6106. **Subscription Rates:** 20,000¥. **Remarks:** Advertising accepted; rates available upon request.
                 Circ: Paid 800

AMAGASAKI

📖 **579 Daruma Magazine**
Takeguchi Momoko
Mukonoso Higashi 1-12-5
Amagasaki 661-0032, Japan   Ph: 81 664365874
Publication E-mail: momoko@gao.ne.jp

Magazine covering the arts. **Founded:** 1994. **Freq:** Quarterly. **Subscription Rates:** 4,000¥. **URL:** http://www.darumamagazine.com/.

AOMORI

📖 **580 Hirosaki Medical Journal**
Hirosaki University
School of Medicine
5 Zaifu-cho
Hirosaki-shi
Aomori 036-8216, Japan

Medical science journal. **Founded:** 1950. **Freq:** Quarterly. **ISSN:** 0439-1721.
                 Circ: 400

📖 **581 Journal of Aomori Society of Obstetricians and Gynecologists**
Aomoriken Rinsho Sanfujinka Ikai
Hirosaki Daigaku Igakubu Sanfujinka Kyoshitsu
5 Zaifu-cho
Hirosaki-shi
Aomori 036-8216, Japan

Medical science journal. **Founded:** 1986. **Freq:** Semiannual. **ISSN:** 0913-8307.

📖 **582 Medical Journal of Aomori Prefectural Central Hospital**
Aomori Prefectural Central Hospital
2-24 Nagashima 1-chome
Aomori 030-0861, Japan

Medical science journal. **Founded:** 1956. **Freq:** Quarterly. **ISSN:** 0387-0138.

CHIBA

📖 **583 Class NK Magazine**
Nippon Kaiji Kyokai
1-8-5, Ohnodai
Midori-ku
Chiba 267-0056, Japan   Ph: 81 432945451
Publication E-mail: isd@classnk.or.jp

Earth sciences journal. **Founded:** 1973. **Freq:** Annual. **Key Personnel:** Masahiro Murakami, Editor. **ISSN:** 1341-0091. **URL:** http://www.classnk.or.jp/.

📖 **584 Journal of Acarological Society of Japan**
Acarological Society of Japan
c/o Faculty of Horticulture
Chiba University
Matsudo
Chiba, Japan   Ph: 81 776613111
Publication E-mail: yhyano@fmsrsa.fukui-med.ac.jp

Journal of entomology. **Founded:** 1974. **Freq:** Semiannual. **Key Personnel:** Naoki Mori, Managing Editor, mokurin@kais.kyoto-u.ac.jp. **ISSN:** 0918-1067. **Subscription Rates:** 5,000¥. **Remarks:** Advertising accepted; rates available upon request. **URL:** http://www.affrc.go.jp:8001/acari.
                 Circ: Paid 350

📖 **585 Journal of Radiation Research**
Japan Radiation Research Society
c/o National Institute of Radiological Sciences
4-9-1 Anagawa
Inage-ku
Chiba 263-8555, Japan
Publication E-mail: jrr@fml.nirs.go.jp

Publishes original articles in the field of radiation research, including studies in radiation physics, chemistry, biology, radioecology and medicine. **Founded:** 1960. **Freq:** Quarterly. **Key Personnel:** K. Ando, Editor-in-Chief. **ISSN:** 0449-3060. **Subscription Rates:** 8,000¥. **Remarks:** Advertising accepted; rates available upon request. **URL:** http://wwwsoc.nii.ac.jp/jrr/JRReditorial.html.
                 Circ: Paid 1,500

📖 586　Journal of Tokyo Dental College Society
Tokyo Dental College Society
Tokyo Dental College
2-2 Masago 1-chome
Chiba 260, Japan

Journal of dentistry. **Founded:** 1895. **Freq:** Monthly. **Key Personnel:** Tetsuya Kanatake, Editor. **ISSN:** 0037-3710. **Subscription Rates:** 5,000¥. **Remarks:** Advertising accepted; rates available upon request.
Circ: Paid 4,600

📖 587　Journal of Yamashina Institute for Ornithology
Yamashina Institute for Ornithology
115 Aza-Tsutsumine-Konoyama
Abiko-shi
Chiba 270-1100, Japan　　　　Ph: 81 471821101

Journal of ornithology. **Founded:** 1952. **Freq:** Semiannual. **Key Personnel:** Nariko Oka, Editor. **Subscription Rates:** 10,000¥.
Circ: Paid 700

📖 588　Medical Journal of Asahi General Hospital
Asahi General Hospital
I 1326
Asahi-shi
Chiba, Japan

Medical science journal. **Founded:** 1979. **Freq:** Semiannual. **ISSN:** 0285-9017.

📖 589　Research Notes and Memoranda of Applied Geometry for Prevenient Natural Philosophy
Post-RAAG Library
1570 Yotsukaido
Yotsukaido-shi
Chiba, Japan

Mathematics journal. **Founded:** 1973. **Freq:** Monthly. **Key Personnel:** Kazuo Kondo, Editor. **Subscription Rates:** 4,000¥.

FUKUI

📖 590　Journal of Chemical Software
Chemical Software Society of Japan
Dept. of Chemistry & Biology Engineering
Fukui National College of Technology
Geshi-cho, Sabae
Fukui 916-0064, Japan　　　　Ph: 81 778621111
Publication E-mail: tadayosi@fukui-nct.ac.jp

Journal covering chemistry. **Founded:** 1992. **Freq:** Quarterly. **Key Personnel:** Haruo Hosoya, Editor. **ISSN:** 0918-0761. **URL:** http://cssjweb.chem.eng.himeji-tech.ac.jp/Welcome.html.

FUKUOKA

📖 591　Acta Dipterologica
Soshi Gakkai
c/o Biosystematics Laboratory
Graduate School of Social & Cultural Studies
Kyushu University
Ropponmatsu, Chuo-ku
Fukuoka 810-0044, Japan　　　　Ph: 81 927264637

Journal of entomology. **Founded:** 1966. **Key Personnel:** H. Shima, Editor. **ISSN:** 0917-4710.

📖 592　Agricultural Journal of Kyushu University
Kyushu University Faculty of Agriculture
6-10-1 Hakozaki
Higashi-ku
Fukuoka 812-0053, Japan

Journal covering agriculture. **Founded:** 1923. **Freq:** Quarterly. **ISSN:** 0023-6152. **URL:** http://www.agr.kyushu-u.ac.jp/english/.

📖 593　Biotronics
Kyushu University
Biotron Institute
Kyushu University 12
Fukuoka 812-8581, Japan　　　　Ph: 81 926423060

Journal covering biology. **Subtitle:** Environment Control and Environmental Biology. **Founded:** 1972. **Freq:** Annual. **Key Personnel:** Nobuyuki Yamasaki, Editor. **ISSN:** 0289-0011.
Circ: Free 1,000

📖 594　Fukuoka Now
Fukuoka NOW Ltd.
3F Best Kego Bldg.
2-12-27 Kego
Chuo-ku
Fukuoka, Japan
Publication E-mail: info@fukuoka-now.com

General interest online magazine. **Freq:** Monthly. **Key Personnel:** Kanako Yamaguchi, Managing Editor. **URL:** http://www.fukuoka-now.com/index.php.

📖 595　The Gaijin Gleaner
2084-22 Ooaza Masue
Nijou-Machi
Itoshima-gun
Fukuoka, Japan　　　　Ph: 81 923292041
Publication E-mail: gleaner@gol.com

General interest magazine. **Founded:** 1994. **Freq:** Monthly. **Key Personnel:** Nikolas May, Editor. **Subscription Rates:** 1,800¥. **Remarks:** Advertising accepted; rates available upon request. **URL:** http://kyushu.com/gleaner/index.shtml.
Circ: Paid 1,600

📖 596　Japanese Journal of Clinical and Experimental Medicine
Daido Gakkan Shuppan-bu
Kyushu University Medical School
3576 Hakozaki
Higashi-ku
Fukuoka 812-0053, Japan

Periodical covering clinical and experimental medicine. **Founded:** 1924. **Freq:** Monthly. **ISSN:** 0021-4965. **Subscription Rates:** 11,760¥.

📖 597　Journal of University of Occupational and Environmental Health
University of Occupational and Environmental Health Japan
1-1 Iseigaoka
Yahatanishi-ku
Kitakyushu-shi
Fukuoka 807-0804, Japan

Occupational health journal. **Founded:** 1979. **Freq:** Quarterly. **Key Personnel:** Toshiji Koboyashi, Editor. **ISSN:** 0387-821X. **Subscription Rates:** US$48.

📖 598　Kurume Medical Journal
Kurume University School of Medicine
67 Asahi-Machi
Kurume-shi
Fukuoka 830-0011, Japan　　　　Ph: 81 942353311

Medical science journal. **Founded:** 1954. **Freq:** Quarterly. **Key Personnel:**

Takashi Akasu, Editor. **ISSN:** 0023-5679. **Remarks:** Advertising accepted; rates available upon request.

Circ: Paid 550

📖 599 Kyushu American Literature
Kyushu University
College of General Education
4-2-1 Ropponmatsu
Chuo-ku
Fukuoka 810-0044, Japan   Ph: 81 927714161

Journal of literature. **Founded:** 1960. **Freq:** Annual. **Key Personnel:** Adio Shinmura, Editor. **ISSN:** 0454-8132. **Remarks:** Advertising accepted; rates available upon request.

Circ: 450

📖 600 Nippon Tungsten Review
Nippon Tungsten Co. Ltd.
NT Bldg.
2-8 Minoshima 1-chome
Hakata-ku
Fukuoka 812-0017, Japan   Ph: 81 942817710

Journal covering chemistry. **Founded:** 1968. **Freq:** Annual. **Key Personnel:** T. Koumura, Editor. **ISSN:** 0388-0664.

📖 601 Research Reports on Information Science and Electrical Engineering
Kyushu University Graduate School of Information Science and
   Electrical Engineering
Graduate School of Information Science and
   Electrical Engine
Fukuoka, Japan   Ph: 81 926423244
Publication E-mail: isee-rep(a)isee.kyushu-u.ac.jp

Journal of electrical engineering. **Founded:** 1996. **Freq:** Semiannual. **Key Personnel:** Kazuo Ushijima, Editor. **ISSN:** 1342-3819. **URL:** http://www.isee.kyushu-u.ac.jp/rep-isee/index-e.html.

Circ: 1,000

FUKUSHIMA

📖 602 Fukushima Journal of Medical Science
Fukushima Society of Medical Science
Medical College Library
1 Hikarigaoka
Fukushima 960-1247, Japan

Medical science journal. **Founded:** 1954. **Freq:** Semiannual. **Key Personnel:** Teizo Fujita, Editor. **ISSN:** 0016-2590.

Circ: 1,600

📖 603 New Cicada
New Cicada Press
40-11 Kubo
Date-gun
Hobara-machi
Fukushima 960-0602, Japan

Journal of literature. **Subtitle:** Haiku and Short Poetry Magazine. **Founded:** 1984. **Key Personnel:** Tadao Okazaki, Editor. **ISSN:** 0911-6567. **Subscription Rates:** 800¥ single issue.

GIFU

📖 604 Gifu Journal of Maternal Health
Gifu Society of Maternal Health
Dept. of Obstetrics and Gynecology
Gifu University School of Medicine
40 Tsukasa-Machi
Gifu 500-8076, Japan   Ph: 81 582659006

Medical science journal. **Founded:** 1989. **Freq:** 3/year. **Key Personnel:** Yoshitaka Yamada, Editor. **ISSN:** 0915-7557. **Subscription Rates:** 1,000¥. **Remarks:** Advertising accepted; rates available upon request.

Circ: (Not Reported)

📖 605 Japanese Journal of Protozoology
Japan Society of Protozoology
Gifu Daigaku Igakubu Seikagaku Kyoshitsu
40 Tsukasa-Machi
Gifu 500-8076, Japan

Publishes original research on protozoa, and covering all aspects of protozoa. **Founded:** 1968. **Freq:** Annual. **Key Personnel:** Toshinobu Suzaki, Editor-in-Chief, phone 81 788035722, suzaki@kobe-u.ac.jp. **ISSN:** 0388-3752.

HIGASHI-HIROSHIMA CITY

📖 606 Chromosome Science
Society of Chromosome Research
c/o Laboratory of Plant Chromosome and
   Gene Stock
Faculty of Science
Hiroshima University
1-4-3 Kagamiyama
Higashi-Hiroshima City 739-8526, Japan   Ph: 81 824247490

Journal covering biology. **Founded:** 1997. **Freq:** Quarterly. **Key Personnel:** Michihiro Yoshida, Editor. **ISSN:** 1344-1051. **Subscription Rates:** 8,500¥. **Remarks:** Advertising accepted; rates available upon request.

Circ: Paid 400

📖 607 Journal of Faculty of Applied Biological Science of Hiroshima University
Hiroshima University Faculty of Applied Biological Science
4-4, Kagamiyama 1 chome
Higashi-Hiroshima City 739-8528, Japan

Journal covering agriculture. **Founded:** 1955. **Freq:** Semiannual. **ISSN:** 0387-7647.

Circ: Free 1,000

HIROSHIMA

📖 608 Fish Pathology
Japanese Society of Fish Pathology
c/o Fac of Applied Biological Sciences
Hiroshima University
1-4-4 Kagamiyama
Higashihiroshima-shi
Hiroshima 739-0046, Japan   Ph: 81 824247947

Journal of zoology. **Founded:** 1966. **Freq:** Quarterly. **Key Personnel:** K. Ogawa, Editor. **ISSN:** 0388-788X. **Subscription Rates:** 6,000¥. **Remarks:** Advertising accepted; rates available upon request.

Circ: Paid 1,000

📖 609 Hiroshima Journal of Mathematics Education
Hiroshima University
Dept. of Mathematics Education
1-1-2 Kagamiyama
Higashihiroshima-shi
Hiroshima 739-8524, Japan

Publication devoted to the publication of research papers in the field of mathematics education. **Founded:** 1993. **Freq:** Annual. **Key Personnel:** Yoshio Okada, Editor-in-Chief. **ISSN:** 0919-1720. **URL:** http://home.hiroshima-u.ac.jp/matedu/journal/journal.html.

📖 610 Hiroshima Mathematical Journal
Hiroshima University
Faculty of Science
Dept. of Mathematics
Kagamiyama
Higashihiroshima-shi
Hiroshima 739-0046, Japan

Publishes original papers in pure and applied mathematics. **Founded:** 1971. **Freq:** 3/year. **Key Personnel:** Hideyasu Sumihiro, Managing Editor. **ISSN:** 0018-2079. **URL:** http://www.math.sci.hiroshima-u.ac.jp/hmj/.

Circ: 400

611 Journal of Hiroshima City Medical Association
Hiroshimashi Ishikai
1-1 Kanonhon-Machi 1-chome
Nishi-ku
Hiroshima 733-0033, Japan

Medical science journal. **Freq:** Monthly.

612 Journal of Hiroshima University Dental Society
Hiroshima University Dental Society
Daigaku
2-3 Kasumi 1-chome
Minami-ku
Hiroshima 734-0037, Japan

Journal of dentistry. **Founded:** 1969. **Freq:** Semiannual. **Key Personnel:** Nobuo Nagasaka, Editor. **ISSN:** 0046-7472. **Subscription Rates:** US$12. **Remarks:** Advertising accepted; rates available upon request.
Circ: (Not Reported)

613 Medical Journal of Hiroshima Prefectural Hospital
Hiroshima Kenritsu Byoin
5-54 Ujina-Kanda 1-chome
Minami-ku
Hiroshima 734-0004, Japan

Medical science journal. **Founded:** 1969. **Freq:** Annual. **ISSN:** 0387-6454.

614 Medical Journal of Hiroshima University
Hiroshima University School of Medicine
1-2-3 Kasumi
Minami-ku
Hiroshima 734-0037, Japan

Medical science journal. **Founded:** 1951. **Freq:** Quarterly. **Key Personnel:** Yoshiyasu Matsuo, Editor. **ISSN:** 0018-2087. **Subscription Rates:** US$20.
Circ: Paid 600

HOKKAIDO

615 Hokkaido Journal of Medical Science
Hokkaido Medical Society
Hokkaido Daigaku Igakubu
Nishi 7-chome
Kita 15-jo Kita-ku
Sapporo-shi
Hokkaido, Japan
Ph: 81 117065007

Medical science journal. **Founded:** 1923. **Freq:** Bimonthly. **Key Personnel:** Masuo Hosokawa, Editor. **ISSN:** 0367-6102. **Subscription Rates:** 3,000¥. **Remarks:** Advertising accepted; rates available upon request.
Circ: Paid 1,200

616 Illustrated Flora of Hokkaido
Hokkaido University
Faculty of Agriculture
Botanic Garden
Nishi-8-chome
Kita 3-jo
Chuo-ku
Sapporo-shi
Hokkaido 060-0003, Japan

Journal covering botany. **Founded:** 1991. **Key Personnel:** Hideki Takahashi, Editor. **ISSN:** 0917-043X.

617 Xene
Xene Inc
Danke Odori Bldg
6F, 4-27, Odori Nishi 11-chome
Chuo-ku
Sapporo-shi
Hokkaido 060-0042, Japan
Ph: 81 112720757
Publication E-mail: info@xene.net

General interest magazine. **Freq:** Bimonthly. **Key Personnel:** Carey Paterson, Editor. **Subscription Rates:** 1,800¥. **Remarks:** Advertising accepted; rates available upon request. **URL:** http://www.xene.net/english/index.htm.
Circ: (Not Reported)

HYOGO

618 Fujitsu Ten Technical Journal
Fujitsu Ten Ltd.
2-28 Goshodori 1-chome
Hyogo-ku
Kobe-shi
Hyogo 652-0885, Japan

Journal of electrical engineering. **Founded:** 1988. **Freq:** Annual. **ISSN:** 0914-6458. **URL:** http://www.fujitsu-ten.co.jp/english/outline/index1.htm.

619 Funkcialaj Ekvacioj, Serio Internacia
Mathematical Society of Japan
Division of Functional Equations
c/o Kobe Daigaku Rigakubu
Sugaku Kyoshitsu
Rokko-Dai-cho
Nada-ku Kobe-shi
Hyogo 657-0013, Japan

Mathematics journal. **Founded:** 1949. **Freq:** Quarterly. **ISSN:** 0532-8721. **Subscription Rates:** US$210.

620 International Journal of Kobe University Law Review
Kobe University Law Review Association
Faculty of Law Kobe University
Rokko-Dai-cho
Nada-ku
Kobe-shi
Hyogo 657-0013, Japan
Ph: 81 788811212

Periodical covering legal issues in an international scope. **Founded:** 1961. **Freq:** Annual. **Key Personnel:** Noriho Urabe, Editor. **ISSN:** 0075-6423.
Circ: 460

621 Journal of Faculty of Nutriiton of Kobe Gakuin University
Kobe Gakuin Daigaku Eiyogakubu
518 Ikawadanichoarise
Nishi-ku
Kobe-shi
Hyogo 651-2113, Japan

Journal of nutrition. **Founded:** 1969. **Freq:** Annual. **ISSN:** 0911-565X.

622 Journal of Himeji Red Cross Hospital
Himeji Sekijui Byoin
30-1 Tatsuno-Machi 5-chome
Himeji-shi
Hyogo 670-0032, Japan

Medical science journal. **Founded:** 1977. **Freq:** Annual. **ISSN:** 0914-8019.

623 Journal of Hyogo University of Teacher Education Series 3
Hyogo University of Teacher Education
942-1 Shimo-Kume
Yashiro-cho
Kato-gun
Hyogo 673-1415, Japan

Journal covering biology. **Founded:** 1983. **Freq:** Annual. **ISSN:** 0911-6230.

624 Journal of Institute of International Sociology
Institute of International Sociology
Kake International Center for Academic Exchange
c/o Bureau of Sociological Research
Hyogo Kyoiku University
Kato-gun
Yashiro-cho
Hyogo 673-14, Japan

Sociology journal. **Founded:** 1993. **Freq:** Annual. **ISSN:** 0919-3413.

625 Kobe Journal of Mathematics
Kobe University Association for Mathematical Science
2-1 Tsurukabu-To 1-chome
Nada-ku 4
Kobe-shi
Hyogo 657-0011, Japan   Ph: 81 788811212

Mathematics journal. **Founded:** 1984. **Freq:** Semiannual. **Key Personnel:**
Yasutaka Nakanishi, Editor. **ISSN:** 0289-9051.

626 Kobe Journal of Medical Sciences
Kobe University
School of Medicine
7-5-1 Kusunoki-cho 7-chome
Chuo-ku
Kobe-shi
Hyogo 650-0017, Japan   Ph: 81 783825443
Publication E-mail: journal@med.kobe-u.ac.jp

Medical science journal. **Founded:** 1951. **Freq:** Bimonthly. **Key Personnel:**
Takayoshi Kuno, Editor-in-Chief. **ISSN:** 0023-2513. **Subscription Rates:**
6,000¥. **URL:** http://www.med.kobe-u.ac.jp/journal/.
                                              Circ: Paid 650

627 Kobe University Economic Review
Kobe University Graduate School of Economics
Rokkodai
Nada-ku
Kobe-shi
Hyogo 567-8501, Japan   Ph: 81 788031212

Journal covering economics. **Founded:** 1955. **Freq:** Annual. **Key Personnel:**
Kazuhiro Ohtani, Editor. **ISSN:** 0454-1111. **URL:** http://www.econ.kobe-
u.ac.jp/english/.
                                              Circ: 650

IBARAKI

628 Hydrology
Japanese Association of Hydrological Science
Tsukuba Daigaku Chikyu Kagakukei
1-1 Tenno-Dai 1-chome
Tsukuba-shi
Ibaraki 305-0006, Japan

Earth sciences journal. **Founded:** 1967. **Freq:** Quarterly. **ISSN:** 0914-3009.
Subscription Rates: 8,000¥.

629 Japanese Journal of Animal Psychology
Japanese Society for Animal Psychology
c/o University of Tsukuba
Institute of Psychology
1-1-1 Tenno-Dai
Tsukuba-shi
Ibaraki 305-0006, Japan   Ph: 81 298534720

Journal of zoology. **Founded:** 1947. **Freq:** Semiannual. **Key Personnel:**
Hiroshige Okaichi, Editor. **ISSN:** 0916-8419. **Subscription Rates:** 1,700¥
single issue. **Remarks:** Advertising accepted; rates available upon request.
                                              Circ: Controlled 500

630 Japanese Journal of Behavior Therapy
Japanese Association of Behavior Therapy
c/o Masahiko Sugiyama Sec-Gen
Institute of Special Education
University of Tsukuba
1-1-1 Tenno-Dai, Tsukuba-shi
Ibaraki 305-0006, Japan   Ph: 81 298536719

Periodical covering experimental and clinical research in behavior therapy.
Founded: 1974. **Freq:** Semiannual. **Key Personnel:** Yuji Sakano, Editor.
ISSN: 0910-6529. **Subscription Rates:** 3,260¥. **Remarks:** Advertising
accepted; rates available upon request.
                                              Circ: Paid 1,200

631 Japanese Journal of Nematology
Japanese Nematological Society
National Agriculture Research Center
Kannondai
Tsukuba-shi
Ibaraki 305-0856, Japan   Ph: 81 298388840

Journal of zoology. **Founded:** 1972. **Freq:** Semiannual. **ISSN:** 0919-6765.
Subscription Rates: US$35.

632 Japanese Poultry Science
Japan Poultry Science Association
c/o National Institute of Animal Industry
PO Box 5
Ibaraki 305-0901, Japan   Ph: 81 298388777
Publication E-mail: jpsa@affrc.go.jp

Journal of poultry science. **Founded:** 1964. **Freq:** Bimonthly. **Key Person-
nel:** Kiyoshi Shimada, Editor-in-Chief. **ISSN:** 0029-0254. **Subscription
Rates:** 9,000¥. **Remarks:** Advertising accepted; rates available upon request.
URL: http://kakin.ac.affrc.go.jp/index-e.htm.
                                              Circ: Paid 1,300

633 Journal of Clinical Biochemical and Nutrition
Institute of Applied Biochemistry
1-1-1 Tennodai
Tsukuba
Ibaraki 305-8572, Japan   Ph: 81 298534936
Publication E-mail: abc@agbi.tsukuba.ac.jp

Journal covering biochemistry. **Founded:** 1986. **Freq:** Bimonthly. **ISSN:**
0912-0009. **URL:** http://www.agbi.tsukuba.ac.jp/~abc/.

634 Journal of Environmental Chemistry
Japan Society for Environmental Chemistry
Kokuritsu Kankyo Kenkyujo Kaggaku
  Kankyobu
16-2 Onogawa
Tsukuba-shi
Ibaraki 305-0053, Japan

Journal covering chemistry. **Founded:** 1991. **Freq:** Quarterly. **ISSN:** 0917-
2408. **Subscription Rates:** 4,000¥ single issue.

635 Journal of Geodetic Society of Japan
Geodetic Society of Japan
c/o Kokudo Chiri-in — Geographical
  Survey Institute
1 Kita-Sato
Tsukuba-shi
Ibaraki 305-0811, Japan

Journal of geography. **Founded:** 1954. **Freq:** Quarterly. **Key Personnel:**
Yoshitero Kono, Editor. **ISSN:** 0038-0830. **Subscription Rates:** 8,000¥.
                                              Circ: Paid 775

636 Journal of Sericultural Science of Japan
Japanese Society of Sericultural Science
National Institute of Sericultural and
  Entomological Science
1-2 Owashi
Tsukuba-shi
Ibaraki 305-0851, Japan   Ph: 81 0298386056

Journal covering agriculture and sericulture. **Founded:** 1930. **Freq:** Bimonthly. **Key Personnel:** Toshihiko Iizuka, Editor. **ISSN:** 0037-2455. **Subscription Rates:** 7,500¥. **Remarks:** Advertising accepted; rates available upon request.

Circ: Paid 1,300

📖 **637 Mathematical Journal of Ibaraki University**
Ibaraki University
Dept. of Mathematical Science
1-1 Bunkyo 2-chome
Mito-shi
Ibaraki 310-0056, Japan

Mathematics journal. **Founded:** 1968. **Freq:** Annual. **Key Personnel:** Toshio Horiuchi, Editor.

Circ: 350

📖 **638 Papers in Meteorology and Geophysics**
Japan Meteorological Agency Meteorological Research Institute
Office of Planning
1-1 Nagamine
Tsukuba-shi
Ibaraki 305-0052, Japan

Journal of meteorology. **Founded:** 1950. **Freq:** Quarterly. **Key Personnel:** Kenji Okada, Editor. **ISSN:** 0031-126X. **Subscription Rates:** 6,180¥.

📖 **639 Pedologist**
Japanese Society of Pedology
c/o National Institute of Agro-Environmental
   Sciences
3-1-1 Kannondai
Tsukuba-shi
Ibaraki 305-0856, Japan   Ph: 81 298388275

Journal covering agriculture. **Founded:** 1957. **Freq:** Semiannual. **Key Personnel:** Nobufumi Miyauchi, Editor. **ISSN:** 0031-4064. **Subscription Rates:** 5,000¥. **Remarks:** Advertising accepted; rates available upon request.

Circ: Controlled 700

📖 **640 Sago Communication**
Tsukuba Sago Fund
Institute of Applied Biochemistry
791-27 Inaoka
Tsukuba-shi
Ibaraki 305-0071, Japan   Ph: 81 298536631

Journal covering botany. **Founded:** 1990. **Freq:** 3/year. **Key Personnel:** Shigeru Hisajima, Editor, hisajima@sakura.cc.tsukuba.ac.jp. **ISSN:** 0917-6470.

Circ: Free 650

📖 **641 Tsukuba Journal of Mathematics**
University of Tsukuba
Institute of Mathematics
1-1 Tenno-Dai 1-chome
Tsukuba-shi
Ibaraki 305-0006, Japan   Ph: 81 298534384

Mathematics journal. **Founded:** 1977. **Freq:** Semiannual. **Key Personnel:** K. Kajitani, Editor. **ISSN:** 0387-4982. **Subscription Rates:** 36,000¥.

📖 **642 University of Tsukuba Institute of Geoscience Science Reports Section A: Geographical Sciences**
University of Tsukuba Institute of Geoscience
1-1 Tenno-Dai 1-chome
Tsukuba-shi
Ibaraki 305-0006, Japan

Journal of geography. **Founded:** 1980. **Freq:** Annual. **ISSN:** 0388-6174.

ISHIKAWA

📖 **643 Journal of Juzen Medical Society**
Kanazawa University
School of Medicine
Juzen Medical Society
13-1 Takara-Machi
Kanazawa-shi
Ishikawa 920-0934, Japan

Medical science journal. **Founded:** 1896. **Freq:** Bimonthly. **ISSN:** 0022-7226. **Subscription Rates:** 3,000¥. **Remarks:** Advertising accepted; rates available upon request.

Circ: (Not Reported)

📖 **644 Medical Journal of Ishikawa Prefectural Central Hospital**
Ishikawa Kenritsu Chuo Byoin
Nu 153 Minami-Shinbo-Machi
Kanazawa-shi
Ishikawa 920-0064, Japan

Medical science journal. **Founded:** 1978. **Freq:** Annual. **ISSN:** 0287-1777.

IWATE

📖 **645 Medical Journal of Iwate Prefectural Miyako Hospital**
Iwate Kenritsu Miyako Byoin
1-6 Sakae-cho
Miyako-shi
Iwate 027-0076, Japan

Medical science journal. **Founded:** 1990. **Freq:** Annual. **ISSN:** 0917-1177.

KAGOSHIMA

📖 **646 South Pacific Study**
Kagoshima University Research Center for the Pacific Islands
1-21-24 Korimo-To
Kagoshima 890-8580, Japan   Ph: 81 992857394
Publication E-mail: tatoken@kuas.kagoshima-u.ac.jp

Science journal. **Founded:** 1980. **Freq:** Semiannual. **Key Personnel:** Junzo Tsukahara, Editor. **ISSN:** 0916-0752. **URL:** http://cpi.kagoshima-u.ac.jp/.

Circ: Controlled 700

KANAGAWA

📖 **647 Aikido Journal**
KK Aiki News
14-17-103 Matsugae-cho
Sagamihara-shi
Kanagawa 228-0813, Japan   Ph: 81 427482423
Publication E-mail: ajmag@earthlink.net

Sports magazine. **Founded:** 1974. **Freq:** Bimonthly. **Key Personnel:** Stanley Pranin, Editor. **ISSN:** 1340-5624. **Subscription Rates:** US$35. **Remarks:** Advertising accepted; rates available upon request. **URL:** http://www.aikidojournal.com/new/.

Circ: Paid 12,000

📖 **648 Biological Sciences in Space**
Japanese Society for Biological Sciences in Space
Uchu Kagaku Kenkyujo
1-1 Yoshinodai 3-chome
Sagamihara-shi
Kanagawa 229-0022, Japan   Ph: 81 427598230

Journal covering biology. **Founded:** 1987. **Freq:** Quarterly. **Key Personnel:** Kenichi Ijiri, Editor. **ISSN:** 0914-9201. **Subscription Rates:** 4,000¥.

Circ: Paid 500

649 Industrial Health
National Institute of Industrial Health
6-21-1 Nagao
Tama-ku
Kawasaki-city
Kanagawa 214-8585, Japan   Ph: 81 448656111

Occupational health journal. **Founded:** 1963. **Freq:** Quarterly. **Key Personnel:** Haruhiko Sakurai, Editor. **ISSN:** 0019-8366. **URL:** http://www.niih.go.jp.
Circ: 1,100

650 Journal of Fujita Technical Research Institute
Fujita Corporation
Technical Research Institute
2025-1 Ono Atsugi-shi
Kanagawa 243-0125, Japan

Online journal of civil engineering. **Founded:** 2000. **Freq:** Semiannual. **ISSN:** 0389-5068.

651 Journal of Japan Salivary Gland Society
Nihon Daekisen Gakkai
1604 Shimo-Sakunobe
Takatsu-ku
Kawasaki-shi
Kanagawa 213-0033, Japan

Journal covering biology. **Founded:** 1959. **Freq:** Annual. **ISSN:** 0916-1104.

652 Journal of Science of Labour
Institute for Science of Labour
2-8-14 Sugao
Miyamae-ku
Kawasaki-shi
Kanagawa 216-0015, Japan

Occupational health journal. **Founded:** 1924. **Freq:** Monthly. **Key Personnel:** Kazutaka Kogi, Editor. **ISSN:** 0022-443X. **Subscription Rates:** 8,800¥. **Remarks:** Advertising accepted; rates available upon request.
Circ: Paid 2,500

653 Mammalian Mutagenicity Study Group Communications
Environmental Mutagen Society of Japan
Mammalian Mutagenicity Study Group
Shokuhin Yakuhin Anzen Senta Hadano
  Kenkyujo
729-5 Ochiai
Hadano-shi
Kanagawa 257-0025, Japan

Journal of zoology. **Founded:** 1988. **Freq:** Annual. **Key Personnel:** Makoto Hayashi, Editor. **ISSN:** 0918-5976. **Subscription Rates:** 2,000¥. **Remarks:** Advertising accepted; rates available upon request.
Circ: (Not Reported)

654 Neuro-Ophthalmology Japan
Japanese Neuro-Ophthalmology Society
Kitasato University School of Allied Health
  Sciences
15-1 Kitaza-To 1-chome
Sagamihara-shi
Kanagawa 228-0829, Japan   Ph: 81 427789416

Medical science journal. **Founded:** 1984. **Freq:** Quarterly. **Key Personnel:** Satoshi Ishikawa, Editor. **ISSN:** 0289-7024. **Subscription Rates:** 4,000¥ single issue. **Remarks:** Advertising accepted; rates available upon request.
Circ: Paid 1,500

655 Physico-Chemical Biology
Society of Electrophoresis
Azabu Daigaku Juigakubu Kachiku
Eiseigaku Kyoshitsu
17-71 Fuchinobe 1-chome
Sagamihara-shi
Kanagawa 229-0006, Japan

Journal covering biological chemistry. **Founded:** 1951. **Freq:** Bimonthly. **Key Personnel:** Toshitsugu Oda, Editor. **ISSN:** 0031-9082. **Subscription**

Rates: 1,200¥ single issue. **Remarks:** Advertising accepted; rates available upon request.
Circ: Paid 1,600

656 Tensor
Tensor Society
Kawaguchi Surikenkyujo - Kawaguchi
Institute of Mathematical Sciences
7-15 Matsugaoka 2-chome
Chigasaki-shi
Kanagawa 253-0025, Japan

Mathematics journal. **Founded:** 1938. **Freq:** 3/year. **Key Personnel:** Tomoaki Kawaguchi, Editor. **ISSN:** 0040-3504. **Subscription Rates:** US$750.
Circ: Controlled 600

657 Wheat Information Service
Kihara Foundation
641-12 Maioka-cho
Totsuka-ku
Yokohama-shi
Kanagawa 244-0813, Japan   Ph: 81 458253487

Periodical covering the genetics and breeding of wheat (triticum). **Founded:** 1950. **Freq:** Semiannual. **Key Personnel:** Kozo Nishikawa, Editor. **ISSN:** 0510-3517. **Subscription Rates:** 2,000¥. **Remarks:** Advertising accepted; rates available upon request.
Circ: Paid 750

KANAZAWA

658 Journal of Phytogeography and Taxonomy
Society for the Study of Phytogeography and Taxonomy
c/o Mr. Tatemi Shimizu
Kanazawa
Daigaku Rigakubu, 1-1 Marunochi
Ishikawa-ken
Kanazawa 920-0937, Japan

Journal covering botany. **Founded:** 1952. **Freq:** Semiannual. **ISSN:** 0388-6212.

KOBE

659 Journal of Germfree Life and Gnotobiology
Japanese Association of Germfree Life and Gnotobiology
c/o Ms. Kazuko Adachi
Kobe Gakuin Daigaku Eiyogakubu
Arise, Ikawadanicho, Nishi-ku
Hyogo-ken
Kobe, Japan

Journal covering biology. **Founded:** 1971. **Freq:** Semiannual. **ISSN:** 0910-0903.

660 Sea and Sky
Marine Meteorological Society
Kobe Kaiyo Kishodai
14-1 Nakayamatedori 7-chome
Chuo-ku
Hyogo-ken
Kobe 650-0004, Japan   Ph: 81 783410044

Journal of meteorology. **Founded:** 1921. **Freq:** Quarterly. **Key Personnel:** Yoshio Yokota, Editor. **ISSN:** 0503-1567. **Subscription Rates:** 75,000¥.
Circ: Paid 500

KOCHI

661 Gondwana Research
Internationl Association for Godwana Research
Professor of Geology
Dept. of Natural Environmental Science
Faculty of Science, Kochi University
Akebono-cho 2-5-1
Kochi 780-8520, Japan

Earth sciences journal. **Founded:** 1997. **Freq:** Quarterly. **Key Personnel:** M.

Santosh, Editor-in-Chief, msantosh_gr@yahoo.com. **ISSN:** 1342-937X. **URL:** http://gondwanaresearch.com/.

KUMAMOTO

📖 **662 Kumamoto Journal of Mathematics**
Kumamoto University
Faculty of Science
Dept. of Mathematics
39-1 Kurokami 2-chome
Kumamoto 860-0862, Japan   Ph: 81 963423331

Mathematics journal. **Freq:** Annual. **Key Personnel:** Mitsuhiko Kohno, Editor. **ISSN:** 0914-675X.

📖 **663 Kumamoto Medical Journal**
Kumamoto University School of Medicine
2-1 Honjo 2-chome
Kumamoto 860-0811, Japan   Ph: 81 963442111

Medical science journal. **Founded:** 1951. **Freq:** Quarterly. **Key Personnel:** Yasuharu Nishimura, Editor. **ISSN:** 0023-5326.
    Circ: Free 440

📖 **664 Publications of Amakusa Marine Biological Laboratory**
Kyushu University Amakusa Marine Biological Laboratory
2231 Tomioka
Amakusa-gun
Reihoku Cho
Kumamoto 863-2507, Japan   Ph: 81 969350003

Journal covering biology. **Founded:** 1966. **Freq:** Annual. **ISSN:** 0065-6682.
    Circ: 450

KYOTO

📖 **665 Acta Histochemica et Cytochemica**
Japan Society of Histochemistry and Cytochemistry
c/o Nakanishi Printing Co.
Shimotachiuri-Ogawa
Kamikyo-ku
Kyoto, Japan   Ph: 81 754153661

Journal covering biology. **Founded:** 1960. **Freq:** Bimonthly. **Key Personnel:** Tsukasa Ashihara, Editor. **ISSN:** 0044-5991. **Subscription Rates:** 12,000¥. **Remarks:** Advertising accepted; rates available upon request.
    Circ: Paid 1,800

📖 **666 Acta Phytotaxonomica et Geobotanica**
Phytogeographical Society
c/o Faculty of Integrated Human Studies
Kyoto University
Sakyo-ku
Kyoto, Japan

Journal covering biology. **Founded:** 1932. **Freq:** 2/year. **Key Personnel:** Hiroshi Tobe, Editor. **ISSN:** 0001-6799. **Subscription Rates:** 8,000¥.
    Circ: Paid 750

📖 **667 Cell Structure and Function**
Japan Society for Cell Biology
Shimodachuri Ogawa Higashi
Kamigyo-ku
Kyoto 602-8048, Japan   Ph: 81 754153661

Journal covering biology. **Founded:** 1975. **Freq:** Bimonthly. **Key Personnel:** N. Hirokawa, Editor. **ISSN:** 0386-7196. **Subscription Rates:** US$136.
    Circ: Paid 1,600

📖 **668 Congenital Anomalies**
Japanese Teratology Society
Dept. of Anatomy and Developmental
  Biology
Faculty of Medicine
Kyoto University
Kyoto 606-8501, Japan   Ph: 81 757534670

Medical science journal. **Founded:** 1961. **Freq:** Quarterly. **Key Personnel:** Mineo Yasuda, Editor. **ISSN:** 0914-3505. **Subscription Rates:** 8,000¥. **Remarks:** Advertising accepted; rates available upon request.
    Circ: Paid 1,700

📖 **669 Doshisha American Studies**
Doshisha University Center for American Studies
Kyoto 602-8580, Japan

History journal. **Founded:** 1963. **Freq:** Annual. **Key Personnel:** Kenji Yoshida, Editor. **ISSN:** 0420-0918. **Subscription Rates:** 1,000¥.
    Circ: Paid 750

📖 **670 Doshisha Literature**
Doshisha University English Literary Society
Karasuma Imadegawa
Kamikyo-ku
Kyoto, Japan   Ph: 81 752513371

Journal of linguistics. **Founded:** 1927. **Freq:** Annual. **Key Personnel:** Teruhiro Ishiguro, Editor. **ISSN:** 0046-063X. **Subscription Rates:** 1,000¥. **Remarks:** Advertising accepted; rates available upon request.
    Circ: Paid 2,000

📖 **671 International Journal of Hematology**
Japanese Society of Hematology
Kinki Chihou Hatsumei Center
14 Kawaramachi Yoshida
Sakyo-ku
Kyoto 606-8305, Japan   Ph: 81 757518982
Publication E-mail: ijh-ind@umin.ac.jp

Publishes articles in fields of clinical and experimental hematology. **Founded:** 1938. **Freq:** 8/year. **Key Personnel:** Takashi Uchiyama, Editor-in-Chief. **ISSN:** 0925-5710. **Subscription Rates:** 125¥. **Remarks:** Advertising accepted; rates available upon request. **URL:** http://www.jshem.or.jp/english/.
    Circ: Paid 5,000

📖 **672 Japanese Circulation Journal**
Japanese Circulation Society
Kinki Invention Center
14 Yoshidakawara-cho
Sakyo-ku
Kyoto 606-8305, Japan   Ph: 81 757518643

Medical science journal. **Founded:** 1935. **Freq:** Monthly. **Key Personnel:** Masunori Matsuzaki, Editor-in-Chief. **ISSN:** 0047-1828. **Subscription Rates:** 20,000¥. **Remarks:** Advertising accepted; rates available upon request. **URL:** http://www.j-circ.or.jp/english/publications/index.htm.
    Circ: Paid 19,000

📖 **673 Japanese Journal of Herpetology**
Herpetological Society of Japan
Dept. of Zoology
Faculty of Science
Kyoto University
Kitashirakawa-Oiwakecho Sakyo-ku
Kyoto 606-8502, Japan

Journal of zoology. **Founded:** 1964. **Freq:** Semiannual. **ISSN:** 0285-3191. **URL:** http://www.herplit.com/contents/JJH.html.

674 Japanese Journal of Medical Imaging and Information Sciences
Japan Society of Medical Imaging and Information Sciences
Kogei Sen i Daigaku
Kogeigakubu Denki Kogakka
Matsugasaki-Goshokaido-cho
Sakyo-ku
Kyoto 606-0962, Japan

Medical science journal. **Freq:** 3/year. **ISSN:** 0910-1543.

675 The Japanese Journal of Pharmacology
Japanese Pharmacological Society
Kantohya Bldg.
Gokomachi-Ebisugawa
Nakagyo-ku
Kyoto 604-0982, Japan　　　　　　　　　Ph: 81 752524641
Publication E-mail: journal@pharmacol.or.jp

Pharmacy journal. **Founded:** 1951. **Freq:** Quarterly. **Key Personnel:** Masamichi Satoh, Editor. **ISSN:** 0021-5198. **Subscription Rates:** 20,000¥; US$250 other countries. **URL:** http://wwwsoc.nii.ac.jp/tjps/kyoto/jjp/.
　　　　　　　　　　　　　　　　　　Circ: Paid 2,400

676 Japanese Religions
National Christian Council of Japan
Center for the Study of Japanese Religions
Karasuma-Shimotachiuri
Kamikyo-ku
Kyoto, Japan　　　　　　　　　　　　Ph: 81 754321945

Journal covering religion. **Founded:** 1959. **Freq:** Semiannual. **Key Personnel:** Martin Repp, Editor. **ISSN:** 0448-8954. **Subscription Rates:** 3,600¥.
　　　　　　　　　　　　　　　　　　Circ: Paid 500

677 Journal of Applied Medicine
Society of Applied Medicine
108 Shimo-Gamomiyazaki-cho
Sakyo-ku
Kyoto 606-0802, Japan

Medical science journal. **Founded:** 1960. **Freq:** Quarterly.

678 Journal of Japanese Association for Chest Surgery
Nihon Kokyuki Geka Gakkai
Kyoto Daigaku Kyobu Shikkan Kenkyujo
　Kyobu Geka
53, Shogoin Kawaracho
Sakyo-ku
Kyoto, Japan

Medical science journal. **Founded:** 1987. **Freq:** Bimonthly. **Key Personnel:** Hiromi Wada, Editor. **Remarks:** Advertising accepted; rates available upon request.
　　　　　　　　　　　　　　　　　　Circ: (Not Reported)

679 Journal of Kyoto Entomological Society
Kyoto Entomological Society
Furitsu Daigaku Konchugaku Kenkyushitsu
1-5 Shimo-Gamohangi-cho
Sakyo-ku
Kyoto 606-0823, Japan

Journal covering biology. **Founded:** 1974. **Freq:** Annual. **ISSN:** 0389-2751.

680 Journal of Kyoto Prefectural University of Medicine
Kyoto Prefectural University of Medicine
Kyoto Foundations for the Promotion of Medical Science
Hirokoji
Kawara-machi
Kamigyo-ku
Kyoto 602-8566, Japan　　　　　　　　Ph: 81 752125466

Medical science journal. **Founded:** 1927. **Freq:** Monthly. **Key Personnel:** Jiro Imanishi, Editor. **ISSN:** 0023-6012. **Subscription Rates:** 7,200¥. **Remarks:** Advertising accepted; rates available upon request. **URL:** http://www.kpu-m.ac.jp/index_e.html.
　　　　　　　　　　　　　　　　　　Circ: Paid 1,400

681 Kyoto Journal
Heian Bunka Center
35 Minamigosho-machi
Okazaki
Sakyo-ku
Kyoto, Japan　　　　　　　　　　　　Ph: 81 757611433
Publication E-mail: kyotojournal@gol.com

Journal of oriental studies. **Subtitle:** An International Quarterly on Culture and Jap. **Founded:** 1987. **Freq:** Quarterly. **Key Personnel:** John Einarsen, Editor. **ISSN:** 0913-5200. **Subscription Rates:** US$35. **Remarks:** Advertising accepted; rates available upon request. **URL:** http://www.kampo.co.jp/kyoto-journal.
　　　　　　　　　　　　　　　　　　Circ: Paid 3,000

682 The Kyoto Shimbun News
The Kyoto Shimbun Newspaper Co., Ltd.
Karasuma Ebisugawa-agaru
Nakagyo-ku
Kyoto, Japan　　　　　　　　　　　　Ph: 81 752415277
Publication E-mail: kpdesk@mb.kyoto-np.co.jp

General newspaper. **Freq:** Daily. **URL:** http://www.kyoto-np.co.jp/kp/english/index.html.

683 Kyoto University Research Activities in Civil Engineering and Related Fields
Kyoto University School of Civil Engineering
Yoshidahon-Machi
Sakyo-ku
Kyoto 606-8317, Japan　　　　　　　　Ph: 81 757535088

Journal covering civil engineering. **Founded:** 1963. **Freq:** Triennial. **ISSN:** 0075-7365.

684 Material Science Study
Bussei Kenkyu Kankokai
c/o Yukawa Hall
Kyoto University
Kyoto 606-8502, Japan　　　　　　　　Ph: 81 757537051

Physics journal. **Founded:** 1963. **Freq:** Monthly. **Key Personnel:** Ken Sekimoto, Editor. **ISSN:** 0525-2997. **Subscription Rates:** 19,200¥.
　　　　　　　　　　　　　　　　　　Circ: Paid 400

685 Physiology and Ecology Japan
Physiology and Ecology Japan Editorial Office
Kyoto Daigaku Rigakubu Dobutsugaku
　Kyoshitsu
Kitashirakawa
Sakyo-ku
Kyoto, Japan

Journal of physiology. **Founded:** 1947. **Freq:** Semiannual. **Key Personnel:** Hiroya Kawanabe, Editor. **ISSN:** 0370-9612. **Subscription Rates:** US$30.
　　　　　　　　　　　　　　　　　　Circ: Paid 700

686 Progress of Theoretical Physics
Yukawa Institute for Theoretical Physics
c/o Yukawa Hall
Kyoto University
Kyoto 606-8502, Japan　　　　　　　　Ph: 81 757223540
Publication E-mail: ptp@yukawa.kyoto-u.ac.jp

Physics journal. **Founded:** 1946. **Freq:** Monthly. **Key Personnel:** Humitaka Sato, Editor. **ISSN:** 0033-068X. **Subscription Rates:** 75,000¥. **URL:** http://www2.yukawa.kyoto-u.ac.jp/~ptpwww/.

687 Progress of Theoretical Physics - Supplement
Yukawa Institute for Theoretical Physics
c/o Yukawa Hall
Kyoto University
Kyoto 606-8502, Japan　　　　　　　　Ph: 81 757223540
Publication E-mail: ptp@yukawa.kyoto-u.ac.jp

Physics journal. **Founded:** 1955. **Freq:** Quarterly. **Key Personnel:** Humitaka Sato, Editor. **ISSN:** 0375-9687. **Subscription Rates:** 16,800¥ members; 57,000¥ nonmembers. **URL:** http://www2.yukawa.kyoto-u.ac.jp/~ptpwww/supple-info.html.

📖 **688 Psychologia**
Psychologia Society
Dept. of Cognitive Psychology in Education
Graduate School of Education
Kyoto University
Kyoto 606-8501, Japan   Ph: 81 757533051
Publication E-mail: psysoc@www.educ.kyoto-u.ac.jp

Publishes symposia, general surveys, reviews, brief reports, notes and discussions, as well as representative original works in very broad fields of psychology. **Founded:** 1957. **Freq:** Quarterly. **Key Personnel:** Masuo Koyasu, Editor. **ISSN:** 0033-2852. **Subscription Rates:** 8,000¥; 11,000¥ institutions. **Remarks:** Advertising accepted; rates available upon request. **URL:** http://www.educ.kyoto-u.ac.jp/cogpsy/psychologia.
Circ: Paid 900

📖 **689 Science and Engineering Review of Doshisha University**
Doshisha Daigaku Rikogaku Kenkyujo
Kyo-tanabe
Kyoto 610-0321, Japan

Journal of engineering. **Founded:** 1960. **Freq:** Quarterly. **Key Personnel:** M. Miki, Editor. **ISSN:** 0036-8172. **Subscription Rates:** 1,200¥.
Circ: Paid 4,340

📖 **690 Study of Elementary Particles**
Research Group on the Theory of Particle and Nuclear Physics
c/o Yukawa Hall
Kyoto University
Kyoto 606-8502, Japan   Ph: 81 757223540

Journal of nuclear physics. **Founded:** 1948. **Freq:** Monthly. **Key Personnel:** Masafumi Fukuma, Editor. **ISSN:** 0371-1838. **Subscription Rates:** 9,600¥.
Circ: Paid 500

MATSUDO CITY

📖 **691 Soil Microorganisms**
Japanese Society of Soil Microbiology
648 Matsundo
Matsudo City 271-8510, Japan   Ph: 81 473088823

Journal of microbiology. **Founded:** 1960. **Freq:** Semiannual. **Key Personnel:** Masanori Saito, Editor. **ISSN:** 0912-2184. **Subscription Rates:** 3,500¥.

MATSUMOTO

📖 **692 Journal of Sedimentological Society of Japan**
Sedimentological Society of Japan
c/o Dept. of Environmental Sciences
Faculty of Science
Shinshu University
Asahi 3-1-1
Matsumoto 390-8621, Japan   Ph: 81 263372479

Journal of geology. **Founded:** 1969. **Freq:** Semiannual. **Key Personnel:** Osam Takano, Editor. **ISSN:** 1342-310X. **Subscription Rates:** 3,000¥ single issue.

MIE

📖 **693 Journal of the Faculty of Fisheries Prefectural University Mie**
Mie University
Faculty of Fisheries
2-80 Edobashi
Tsu-shi
Mie 514-0001, Japan

Journal of fisheries. **Founded:** 1950. **Freq:** Annual.

MINAMIMINOWA

📖 **694 New Entomologist**
Entomological Society of Shinshu
Shinshu Daigaku Nogakubu Oyo
Konchugaku Kyoshitsu
8304 Kamiina-gun
Nagano-ken
Minamiminowa 399-4511, Japan

Journal of entomology. **Founded:** 1951. **Freq:** Semiannual. **Key Personnel:** Nagao Koyama, Editor. **ISSN:** 0028-4955. **Subscription Rates:** 3,000¥.

MITO

📖 **695 Entomological Science**
Entomological Society of Japan
c/o Dept. of Zoology
National Science Museum (Natl. Hist.)
Faculty of Science
Ibaraki University
Mito 310-8512, Japan   Ph: 81 292288377

Journal of entomology. **Founded:** 1998. **Freq:** Quarterly. **Key Personnel:** Soichi Yamane, Editor. **ISSN:** 1343-8786. **URL:** http://wwwsoc.nii.ac.jp/entsocj/e/e-3.htm.

MIYAGI

📖 **696 Ecological Review**
Tohoku Daigaku Hakkodasan Shokubutsu Jikkenjo
c/o Botanical Garden
Tohoku University
Kawauch
Miyagi 980-0862, Japan   Ph: 81 222176765

Journal covering biology. **Founded:** 1935. **Freq:** Annual. **Key Personnel:** Tadaki Hirose, Editor. **ISSN:** 0371-0548.

📖 **697 Research and Practice in Forensic Medicine**
Tohoku University
School of Medicine
Dept. of Forensic Medicine
Sendai-shi
Miyagi, Japan   Ph: 81 227178110

Journal of forensic medicine. **Founded:** 1954. **Freq:** Annual. **Key Personnel:** Kaoru Sagisaka, Editor. **ISSN:** 0289-0755. **Subscription Rates:** 4,000¥.
Circ: Paid 1,000

📖 **698 Tohoku Geophysical Journal**
Tohoku University
Faculty of Science
Geophysical Institute
Aoba
Aramaki
Sendai-shi
Miyagi 980, Japan

Journal of geophysics. **Founded:** 1949. **Key Personnel:** Yoshiaki Toba, Editor. **ISSN:** 0040-8794.
Circ: 700

📖 **699 Tohoku Journal of Agricultural Research**
Tohoku University
Faculty of Agriculture
1-1 Tsutsumi-dori Amamiya-cho
Sendai-shi
Miyagi 981, Japan

Journal covering agriculture. **Founded:** 1950. **Freq:** Quarterly. **ISSN:** 0040-8719.
Circ: 1,000

⚫ **700 Tohoku Journal of Experimental Medicine**
Tohoku University Medical Press
2-1 Seiryo-cho
Aoba-ku
Sendai-shi
Miyagi 980-8575, Japan   Ph: 81 227178184

Journal of experimental medicine. **Founded:** 1920. **Freq:** Monthly. **Key Personnel:** Hiroshi Satoh, Editor. **ISSN:** 0040-8727. **Subscription Rates:** US$410.

Circ: Paid 800

⚫ **701 Tohoku Mathematical Journal**
Tohoku University
Mathematical Institute
Aramaki aza Aoba
Aoba-ku
Sendai-shi
Miyagi 980-8578, Japan

Mathematics journal. **Founded:** 1911. **Freq:** Quarterly. **Key Personnel:** Yasuo Morita, Editor. **ISSN:** 0040-8735. **Subscription Rates:** US$208.

Circ: Paid 1,000

⚫ **702 Tohoku Psychologica Folia**
Tohoku University
Faculty of Arts and Letters
Dept. of Psychology
Kawauchi
Aoba-ku
Sendai-shi
Miyagi 980-0862, Japan   Ph: 81 222176048

Journal of psychology. **Founded:** 1933. **Freq:** Annual. **Key Personnel:** Hideshi Ohashi, Editor. **ISSN:** 0040-8743.

Circ: 525

MIYAZAKI

⚫ **703 Journal of Japan Glaucoma Society**
Nihon Ryokunaisho
Miyazaki Ika Daigaku Gankagaku Kyoshitsu
5200 Kihara
Miyazaki-gun
Kiyotake-cho
Miyazaki 889-1601, Japan

Medical science journal. **Founded:** 1990. **Freq:** Annual. **ISSN:** 0917-4338.

NAGANO CITY

⚫ **704 The Shinano Mainichi Shimbun**
The Shinano Mainichi Shimbun Inc.
Minami-agatamachi 657
Nagano City, Japan
Publication E-mail: center@shinmai.co.jp

General newspaper. **Founded:** 1873. **Freq:** Daily. **Remarks:** Advertising accepted; rates available upon request. **URL:** http://www.shinmai.co.jp/shinmai/shim1e.html.

Circ: 47,5000

NAGASAKI

⚫ **705 Acta Medica Nagasakiensia**
Nagasaki University
School of Medicine
12-4 Sakamo-To
Nagasaki-shi
Nagasaki 852-8102, Japan   Ph: 81 958497353

Medical science journal. **Founded:** 1939. **Freq:** Irregular. **Key Personnel:** Kuniaki Hayashi, Editor. **ISSN:** 0001-6055.

Circ: 350

⚫ **706 Japanese Journal of Tropical Medicine and Hygiene**
Japanese Society of Tropical Medicine
c/o Institute of Tropical Medicine
12-4 Sakamo-To
Nagasaki 852-8523, Japan

Medical science journal. **Founded:** 1959. **Freq:** Quarterly. **Key Personnel:** Masahiro Takagi, Editor. **ISSN:** 0304-2146. **Subscription Rates:** 7,000¥.

Circ: Paid 700

⚫ **707 Tropical Medicine**
Nagasaki University
Institute of Tropical Medicine
1-12-4 Sakamoto
Nagasaki 852-8523, Japan   Ph: 81 958497822

Medical science journal. **Founded:** 1959. **Freq:** Quarterly. **Key Personnel:** Yoshiki Aoki, Editor, aoki@net.nagakaki-u.ac.jp. **ISSN:** 0041-3267.

Circ: 450

NAGOYA

⚫ **708 Journal of Plasma and Fusion Research**
The Japan Society of Plasma Science and Nuclear Fusion Research
2-20-20-2 F, Nishiki
Naka-ku
Nagoya 460-0003, Japan   Ph: 81 522314535
Publication E-mail: jspf@nifs.ac.jp

Journal of nuclear physics. **Founded:** 1958. **Freq:** Monthly. **ISSN:** 0918-7928. **Subscription Rates:** 1,300¥ single issue. **URL:** http://jspf.nifs.ac.jp/index-e.html.

⚫ **709 Nagoya Mathematical Journal**
Nagoya University
Graduate School of Mathematics
Chikusa-ku
Nagoya 464-8602, Japan

Mathematics journal. **Founded:** 1950. **Freq:** Quarterly. **Key Personnel:** Yoshiyuki Kitaoka, Editor. **ISSN:** 0027-7630. **Subscription Rates:** 22,000¥. **Remarks:** Advertising accepted; rates available upon request. **URL:** http://www.math.nagoya-u.ac.jp/nagoyamath-e.html.

Circ: Controlled 1,150

NARA

⚫ **710 Biology of Inland Waters**
Nara Scientific Research Society of Inland Water Biology
c/o Nara Joshi Daigaku Rigakubu
Seibutsugaku Kyoshitsu
Kita-Uoyanishi-Machi
Nara 630-8263, Japan   Ph: 81 742203424

Journal covering biology. **Founded:** 1980. **Freq:** Annual. **Key Personnel:** Makoto Nagoshi, Editor. **ISSN:** 0286-8172. **Subscription Rates:** 4,000¥.

Circ: Paid 300

⚫ **711 Journal of Tezukayama College Food Sciences**
Tezukayama Association for Food Sciences
Tezukayama Tanki Daigaku
1-3, Gakuen Minami 3-chome
Nara-shi
Nara 631, Japan   Ph: 81 742414755

Journal of food science. **Founded:** 1979. **Freq:** Annual. **Key Personnel:** Takeshi Mineshita, Editor.

NIIGATA

712 Acta Medica et Biologica
Niigata University
School of Medicine
Ichiban-cho
Asahimachi-dori
Niigata, Japan

Medical science journal. **Founded:** 1953. **Freq:** Irregular. **ISSN:** 0567-7734. **Subscription Rates:** 10,000¥.

Circ: Paid 100

713 Archives of Histology and Cytology
Japan Society of Histological Documentation
c/o Dept. of Anatomy, University School of
    Medicine
Asahima-cho
Niigata 951-8122, Japan

Journal covering biology. **Founded:** 1950. **Freq:** 5/year. **Key Personnel:** Tsuneo Fujita, Editor. **ISSN:** 0914-9465. **Subscription Rates:** US$250. **Remarks:** Advertising accepted; rates available upon request.

Circ: Controlled 700

714 Nihonkai Mathematical Journal
Niigata University
Sado Marine Biological Station
2-8050 Igarashi
Niigata, Japan

Publishes original contributions to all disciplines in mathematics. **Founded:** 1964. **Freq:** Semiannual. **Key Personnel:** Nobuhiro Innami, Editor-in-Chief. **URL:** http://mathweb.sc.niigata-u.ac.jp/nmj.html.

OKAYAMA

715 Acta Medica Okayama
Okayama University
School of Medicine
2-5-1 Shikata-cho
Okayama-shi
Okayama 700-0914, Japan   Ph: 81 862357057

Medical science journal. **Founded:** 1928. **Freq:** Bimonthly. **Key Personnel:** Tadaatsu Akagi, Editor. **ISSN:** 0386-300X. **Remarks:** Advertising accepted; rates available upon request.

Circ: Controlled 600

716 Journal of Brain Science
Japan Neurosciences Research Association
c/o Japan Brain Science Society Business
    Office
Dept. of Neurochemistry Institute for
    Neurobiology
University Medical School
2-5-1 Shikata-Cho
Okayama 700-0914, Japan

Journal covering biology. **Founded:** 1975. **Freq:** Bimonthly. **Key Personnel:** Koichi Ishikawa, Editor. **ISSN:** 1341-5301. **Subscription Rates:** 10,000¥. **Remarks:** Advertising accepted; rates available upon request.

Circ: Paid 800

717 Journal of Japanese Society of Autologous Blood Transfusion
Nihon Jikoketsu Yuketsu Kenkyukai
Kawasaki Ika Daigaku Masuika
577 Matsushima
Kurashiki-shi
Okayama 701-0114, Japan   Ph: 81 86462111

Medical science journal. **Founded:** 1987. **Freq:** Semiannual. **Key Personnel:** Takeshi Fuji, Editor. **ISSN:** 0915-0188. **Subscription Rates:** 5,000¥.

718 Kawasaki Medical Journal
Kawasaki Medical Society
577 Matsushima
Kurashiki-shi
Okayama 701-0114, Japan

Medical science journal. **Founded:** 1975. **Freq:** Quarterly. **Key Personnel:** Yoshihito Yawata, Editor. **ISSN:** 0385-0234. **Subscription Rates:** 20,000¥.

Circ: Paid 800

719 Mathematical Journal of Okayama University
Okayama University
Faculty of Science
Dept. of Mathematics
3-1-1 Tsushima-Naka
Okayama 700-8530, Japan

Mathematics journal. **Founded:** 1952. **Freq:** Semiannual. **Key Personnel:** Yasuyuki Hirano, Editor, yhirano@math.okayama-u.ac.jp. **ISSN:** 0030-1566. **URL:** http://www.math.okayama-u.ac.jp/mjou/index.html.

OKINAWA

720 Island Studies in Okinawa
University of Ryukyus
College of Science, Dept. of Biology
Iriomote Cat Research Laboratory
1 Senbaru
Nakagami-gun
Nishihara-cho
Okinawa 903-0129, Japan   Ph: 81 988958541

Earth sciences journal. **Founded:** 1983. **Freq:** Annual. **Key Personnel:** Masako Izawa, Editor. **ISSN:** 0289-7857.

OKINAWA CITY

721 Japan Update
K K Japan Update
1-36-10 Chuo
Okinawa City 904-0004, Japan   Ph: 81 988961925

General weekly newspaper. **Founded:** 1986. **Freq:** Weekly. **Key Personnel:** Kari Valtaoja, Contact, kari@japanupdate.com. **ISSN:** 0912-3474. **URL:** http://japanupdate.com/.
Ad Rates: BW: 7,000¥   **Circ:** (Not Reported)
              4C: 14,000¥

OSAKA

722 Acta Arachnologica
Arachnological Society of Japan
Biological Laboratory
Otemon-Gakuin University
2-1-15 Nishiai
Ibaraki-shi
Osaka 567-0008, Japan

Journal on biology. **Founded:** 1936. **Freq:** Semiannual. **ISSN:** 0001-5202. **Subscription Rates:** 7,000¥. **Remarks:** Advertising accepted; rates available upon request.

Circ: Paid 600

723 Acta Medica Kinki University
Kinki University Medical Association
377 Ono-Higashi
Osakasayama-shi
Osaka 589-0014, Japan   Ph: 81 723660221

Medical science journal. **Founded:** 1976. **Key Personnel:** Takanori Tomura, Editor. **ISSN:** 0386-6092. **Subscription Rates:** 4,000¥.

Circ: Paid 1,300

724 Hitachi Zosen News
Hitachi Zosen Corporation
3-22 Sakurajima 1-chome
Konohana-ku
Osaka 554-0031, Japan

Journal covering economics. **Founded:** 1976. **Freq:** Semiannual. **Key Personnel:** T. Nishijima, Editor. **ISSN:** 0439-2795.
Circ: Free 2,800

725 Hypertension Research - Clinical and Experimental
Japanese Society of Hypertension Center for Academic Societies Osaka
Senri Life Science Center Bldg., 14th Fl.
4-2 Shinsenri-Higashi-Machi
Toyonaka-shi
Osaka 565-0082, Japan   Ph: 81 68732301

Medical science journal. **Founded:** 1978. **Freq:** Quarterly. **Key Personnel:** Osamu Iimura, Editor, o-edit@bcasj.or.jp. **ISSN:** 0916-9636. **Subscription Rates:** US$120. **Remarks:** Advertising accepted; rates available upon request.
Circ: (Not Reported)

726 Japanese Journal of Environment, Entomology and Zoology
Japanese Society of Environmental Entomology and Zoology
12-19 Nishi-Hon-Machi 1-chome
Nishi-ku
Osaka 550-0005, Japan

Journal of entomology. **Founded:** 1989. **Freq:** Quarterly. **ISSN:** 0915-4698.

727 Journal of Bioscience and Bioengineering
The Society for Fermentation and Bioengineering Japa
Business Office c/o Faculty of Engineering
Osaka University
2-1 Yamada-Oka
Suita-shi
Osaka 565-0871, Japan   Ph: 81 68775111

Publication devoted to the advancement and dissemination of knowledge concerning fermentation technology, biochemical engineering, food technology and microbiology. **Founded:** 1923. **Freq:** Monthly. **Key Personnel:** Yoshikatsu Murooka, Editor-in-Chief. **ISSN:** 1389-1723. **Subscription Rates:** US$1,278 all countries except Japan and Europe; €1,143 Europe. **URL:** http://www.elsevier.com/locate/jfermbio.

728 Journal of the Faculty of Science and Technology of Kinki University
Kinki University
Faculty of Science and Technology
4-1 Kowakae 3-chome
Higashiosaka-shi
Osaka 577-0818, Japan

Journal of science and technology. **Founded:** 1966. **Freq:** Annual. **ISSN:** 0386-4928.

729 Journal of Geosciences
Osaka City University
Dept. of Geosciences
Faculty of Science
3-3-138 Sugimoto
Sumiyoshi-ku
Osaka 558-8585, Japan   Ph: 81 666052504

Earth sciences journal. **Founded:** 1954. **Freq:** Annual. **ISSN:** 0449-2560.
Circ: 1,000

730 Journal of Kansai Medical University Journal
Kansai Medical University
1 Fumizono-cho
Moriguchi-shi
Osaka 570-0074, Japan

Medical science journal. **Founded:** 1948. **Freq:** Quarterly. **Subscription Rates:** 1,000¥. **Remarks:** Advertising accepted; rates available upon request.
Circ: (Not Reported)

731 Journal of Kansai Society of Naval Architects
Kansai Society of Naval Architects
c/o Graduate School of Engineering, Osaka University
2-1 Yamada-oka
Suita
Osaka 565-0871, Japan   Ph: 81 68797593
Publication E-mail: office@ksnaj.or.jp

Journal of transportation. **Founded:** 1912. **Freq:** Semiannual. **ISSN:** 0389-9101. **Subscription Rates:** 5,000¥. **URL:** http://www.ksnaj.or.jp/english/.

732 Journal of Microwave Surgery
Medical Review Co., Ltd.
7-3 Hirano-Machi 1-chome
Chuo-ku
Osaka 541-0046, Japan   Ph: 81 62231556

Medical science journal. **Founded:** 1988. **Freq:** Annual. **Key Personnel:** Hatsuoka Jabuse, Editor. **ISSN:** 0917-7728. **Subscription Rates:** 3,000¥.

733 Journal of Osaka Dental University
Osaka Odontological Society
8-1 Kuzuha-Hanazono-cho
Hirakata-shi
Osaka 573-1121, Japan

Journal of dentistry. **Founded:** 1967. **Freq:** Semiannual. **Key Personnel:** Tatsuo Kawamoto, Editor. **ISSN:** 0475-2058.

734 Journal of Pesticide Science
Pesticide Science Society of Japan
Research Institute for Advanced Science and Technology
Osaka Prefecture University
1-2 Gakuen-cho
Sakai
Osaka 599-8570, Japan   Ph: 81 722526776
Publication E-mail: jsps@riast.osakafu-u.ac.jp

Publishes original scientific papers in English or Japanese which deal with pesticides in a broad sense. **Founded:** 1992. **Freq:** Quarterly. **Key Personnel:** Keiichiro Nishimura, Editor. **ISSN:** 0916-9962. **Subscription Rates:** US$40. **URL:** http://wwwsoc.nii.ac.jp/pssj2/index-e.html.
Circ: Paid 2,000

735 Journal of Textile Engineering
Textile Machinery Society of Japan
1-8-4 Utsubo Honmachi
Nishi-ku
Osaka 550-0004, Japan   Ph: 81 664434691
Publication E-mail: JDH04707@nifty.ne.jp

Journal of textile engineering. **Freq:** Quarterly. **ISSN:** 1346-8235. **URL:** http://wwwsoc.nii.ac.jp/tmsj/english/index.html.

736 Kansai Scene
P & K Inc.
Dai 3 Silver Bldg. 2F
Nishi-Nakajima 2-15-13
Yodogawa-ku
Osaka 532-0011, Japan   Ph: 81 663013054

General interest magazine on Kansai. **Freq:** Monthly. **Remarks:** Advertising accepted; rates available upon request. **URL:** http://www.kansaiscene.com.
Circ: (Not Reported)

737 Mathematica Japonica
Japanese Association of Mathematical Sciences
Shin Sakai-Higashi Bldg.
2-1-18 Minami Hanadaguchi
Sakai
Osaka 590-0075, Japan   Ph: 81 722221850
Publication E-mail: pbls@jams.or.jp

Publishes original papers in mathematical sciences submitted from all over the world. **Founded:** 1948. **Freq:** Bimonthly. **Key Personnel:** Tadashige

Ishihara, Managing Editor, edtr@jams.or.jp. **ISSN:** 0025-5513. **Subscription Rates:** US$360. **URL:** http://www.jams.or.jp/mj/mj.html.

Circ: Paid 950

738 Orthopaedic Ceramic Implants
Seikei Geka Seramikku Inpuranto Kenkyukai
Kokuritsu Osaka Minami Byoin Seikei Geka
677-2 Kido-cho
Kawachinagano-shi
Osaka 586-0001, Japan

Journal of orthopedics. **Founded:** 1981. **Freq:** Annual. **ISSN:** 0289-2855.

739 Osaka Journal of Mathematics
Osaka University
Graduate School of Science
Dept. of Mathematics
1-1 Machikaneyama-cho
Toyonaka-shi
Osaka 560-0043, Japan

Publication devoted entirely to the publication of original works in mathematics and related fields. **Founded:** 1964. **Freq:** Quarterly. **Key Personnel:** Masayoshi Miyanishi, Editor. **ISSN:** 0030-6126. **Subscription Rates:** US$346. **URL:** http://www.math.sci.osaka-u.ac.jp/ojm.

740 Peptide Information
Protein Research Foundation Peptide Institute
4-1-2 Ina
Mino-shi
Osaka 562-0015, Japan   Ph: 81 727294124
Publication E-mail: query@prf.or.jp

Journal covering biology. **Founded:** 1975. **Freq:** Biweekly. **ISSN:** 0385-8847. **Subscription Rates:** US$450. **URL:** http://www.prf.or.jp/en/pi.htm.

741 Questions and Answers in General Topology
Symposium of General Topology
Uzumasa Higashiga-oka
13-2 Neyagawa-shi
Osaka 572-0000, Japan

Publication devoted primarily to rapid publication of questions and answers that arise from research in general topology and related areas. **Founded:** 1983. **Freq:** Semiannual. **Key Personnel:** Juniti Nagata, Managing Editor. **ISSN:** 0918-4732. **Subscription Rates:** 6,000¥.

Circ: Paid 200

742 Rare Earths
Rare Earth Society of Japan
Osaka Daigaku Kogakubu Oyo Kagakka
2-1 Yamada-oka
Suita-shi
Osaka 565-0871, Japan   Ph: 81 68797352

Journal of metallurgy. **Founded:** 1982. **Freq:** Semiannual. **Key Personnel:** Gin Ya Adachi, Editor. **ISSN:** 0910-2205.

743 Review of Economics and Business
Kansai University Press
3-3-35 Yamate-cho
Suita-shi
Osaka 564-0073, Japan

Journal covering economics. **Founded:** 1972. **Freq:** Semiannual. **Key Personnel:** Shigeru Shoji, Editor. **ISSN:** 0302-6574.

Circ: 600

744 Review of Laser Engineering
Laser Society of Japan
2-6 Yamada-Oka
Suita-shi
Osaka 565-0871, Japan

Physics journal. **Founded:** 1973. **Freq:** Monthly. **ISSN:** 0387-0200. **Subscription Rates:** 1,500¥ single issue.

745 Science and Industry
Osaka Society of Industrial Research
Osaka-shiritsu Kogyo Kenkyujo
6-50 Morinomiya 1-chome
Joto-ku
Osaka 536-0025, Japan

Science journal. **Founded:** 1926. **Freq:** Monthly. **ISSN:** 0368-5918.

746 Setsunan University Review of Humanities and Social Sciences
Setsunan Daigaku
17-8 Ikedanaka-Machi
Neyagawa-shi
Osaka 572-0074, Japan

Humanities journal. **Founded:** 1994. **Freq:** Annual. **ISSN:** 1341-9315.

747 Spinal Surgery
Japanese Society of Spinal Surgery
Shiritsu Daigaku Igakubu No Shinkei
  Gekagaku Kyoshitsu
5-7 Asahi-Machi 1-chome
Abeno-ku
Osaka 545-0051, Japan   Ph: 81 66452157

Medical science journal. **Founded:** 1987. **Freq:** Annual. **Key Personnel:** Hiroshi Abe, Editor. **ISSN:** 0914-6024. **Subscription Rates:** 3,000¥.

748 Trends in Glycoscience and Glycotechnology
Gakushin Company Ltd.
1-1-8 Tarumi-cho
Suita-shi
Osaka 564-0062, Japan   Ph: 81 663300956

Journal of organic chemistry. **Founded:** 1989. **Freq:** Bimonthly. **Key Personnel:** Tatsuya Yamagata, Editor. **ISSN:** 0915-7352. **Subscription Rates:** 5,000¥. **Remarks:** Advertising accepted; rates available upon request.
Circ: (Not Reported)

749 Viva Origino
Society for the Study of the Origin and Evolution of Life
Osaka Furitsu Daigaku Sogo Kagakubu
Seimei Kagaku Koza
Mozu-Ume-Machi
Sakai-shi
Osaka 591-8032, Japan

Journal covering biology. **Founded:** 1971. **Freq:** 3/year. **ISSN:** 0910-4003. **Subscription Rates:** 4,000¥.

SAITAMA

750 Infrared and Raman Spectroscopy
Raman and Infrared Analysis Committee
c/o Saitama University
Faculty of Science
Dept. of Chemistry
Urawa
Saitama 338-8570, Japan

Journal covering physical chemistry. **Founded:** 1978. **Freq:** Bimonthly. **Key Personnel:** Mitsuo Tasumi, Editor. **Subscription Rates:** 5,000¥. **Remarks:** Advertising accepted; rates available upon request.
Circ: Paid 200

751 Journal of National Defense Medical College
Defense Agency
National Defense Medical College
3-2 Namiki
Tokorozawa-shi
Saitama 359-0042, Japan

Medical science journal. **Founded:** 1976. **Freq:** Quarterly. **Key Personnel:** Akira Ishibashi, Editor. **ISSN:** 0385-1796.

752 Saitama Mathematical Journal
Saitama University
Faculty of Science
Dept. of Mathematics
Urawa-shi
Saitama 338-8570, Japan
Publication E-mail: smjeditor@rimath.saitama-u.ac.jp

Publishes original papers in pure and applied mathematics. **Founded:** 1952. **Freq:** Annual. **Key Personnel:** Madoka Ebihara, Editor, smjeditor@rimath.saitama-u.ac.jp. **ISSN:** 0289-0739. **URL:** http://www.rimath.saitama-u.ac.jp/research/authinst.html.
Circ: 500

SAPPORO

753 Clinical Pediatric Endocrinology
Japanese Society for Pediatric Endocrinology
Dept. of Pediatrics
Hokkaido University School of Medicine
N-15, W-7
Kita-ku
Sapporo 060-8638, Japan

Journal of pediatric endocrinology. **Founded:** 1989. **Freq:** Semiannual. **Key Personnel:** Kenji Fujieda, Editor, ken-fuji@medlhokudai.ac.jp. **ISSN:** 0918-5739. **Subscription Rates:** 2,000¥. **Remarks:** Advertising accepted; rates available upon request.
Circ: (Not Reported)

754 Economic Journal of Hokkaido University
Hokkaido University Faculty of Economics
North 9, West 7
Kita-ku
Sapporo 060-0809, Japan Ph: 81 117064112

Journal covering economics. **Founded:** 1969. **Freq:** Annual. **ISSN:** 0916-4650. **Available Online.**
Circ: Controlled 560

755 Geophysics Journal of Hokkaido University
Hokkaido University Faculty of Science
Nishi-8-chome
Kita-10-jo
Kita-ku
Sapporo 060-8589, Japan

Earth sciences journal. **Founded:** 1957. **Freq:** Annual. **Key Personnel:** Yasunori Nishida, Editor. **ISSN:** 0441-067X.
Circ: 400

756 Hokkaido Journal of Primary Care
Hokkaido Puraimari Kea Kenkyukai Kaiho
Hokkaido Ishikai
Nishi 6-chome
Odori
Chuo-ku
Sapporo, Japan

Medical science journal. **Founded:** 1985. **Freq:** Annual.

757 Hokkaido Mathematical Journal
Hokkaido University
Faculty of Science
Dept. of Mathematics
Nishi-8-chome
Kita-10-jo
Kita-ku
Sapporo 060-0810, Japan
Publication E-mail: journal@math.sci.hokudai.ac.jp

Publishes significant research articles in all areas of mathematics. **Founded:** 1972. **Freq:** 3/year. **Key Personnel:** Asao Arai, Managing Editor, phone 81 117062634, fax 81 117063419. **ISSN:** 0385-4035. **Subscription Rates:** US$388. **URL:** http://www.math.hokudai.ac.jp/hmj/.
Circ: Paid 720

758 Japanese Journal of Veterinary Research
Hokkaido University Faculty of Veterinary Medicine
Nishi-9-chome
Kita-18-jo
Sapporo, Japan Ph: 81 117065215

Journal of veterinary science. **Founded:** 1954. **Freq:** Quarterly. **Key Personnel:** Misao Onuma, Editor. **ISSN:** 0047-1917.
Circ: 650

759 Journal of Northern Occupational Health
Association of Northern Occupational Health
c/o Dept. of Hygiene and Preventive
    Medicine
Hokkaido University School of Medicine
Kita-15 nishi-7
Kita-ku
Sapporo, Japan Ph: 81 117065066

Occupational health journal. **Founded:** 1939. **Freq:** Biennial. **Key Personnel:** Naoki Sugawara, Editor. **ISSN:** 0911-3363.

760 Language and Culture
Hokkaido University Institute of Language and Culture Studies
Nishi-8-chome
Kita 17
Kita-ku
Sapporo 060-0817, Japan Ph: 81 117065129
Publication E-mail: kobayakw@ilcs.hokudai.ac.jp

Journal of linguistics. **Founded:** 1982. **Freq:** Semiannual. **ISSN:** 0286-3855. **URL:** http://www.hokudai.ac.jp/lang/index-e.html.
Circ: Controlled 400

761 Sapporo Medical Journal
Sapporo Medical University
Nishi-17-chome
Minami-1-jo
Chuo-ku
Sapporo 060-8556, Japan Ph: 81 116112111

Medical science journal. **Founded:** 1950. **Freq:** Bimonthly. **ISSN:** 0036-472X.
Circ: 500

762 Tumor Research: Experimental and Clinical
Sapporo Medical University
Nishi-17-chome
Minami-1-jo
Chuo-ku
Sapporo 060-8556, Japan Ph: 81 116112111

Journal of oncology. **Founded:** 1966. **Freq:** Semiannual. **Key Personnel:** Yohichi Mochizuki, Editor. **ISSN:** 0041-4093.
Circ: 550

SENDAI

📖 **763 Japanese Journal of Crop Science**
Crop Science Society of Japan
c/o Graduate School of Agriculture
Tohoku University
1-1 Tsutsumidori Amemiya-cho
Aoba
Sendai, Japan   Ph: 81 227178638

Journal covering agriculture. **Founded:** 1927. **Freq:** Quarterly. **Key Personnel:** Toshiro Kuroda, Editor. **Subscription Rates:** 6,000¥.
                                        Circ: Paid 2,000

📖 **764 Journal of Japanese Paediatric Orthopaedic Association**
Japanese Paediatric Orthopaedic Association
Dept. of Orthopaedic Surgery
Tohoku University School of Medicine
1-1 Seiryou-machi
Sendai 980-8575, Japan   Ph: 81 227177245
Publication E-mail: kokubun@mail.cc.tohoku.ac.jp

Medical science journal. **Founded:** 1991. **Freq:** Semiannual. **ISSN:** 0917-6950. **Subscription Rates:** 4,500¥ single issue.

📖 **765 Journal of Mineralogy, Petrology and Economic Geology**
Japanese Association of Mineralogists Petrologists and Economic
  Geologists
c/o Graduate School of Science
Tohoku University
Sendai 980-8578, Japan   Ph: 81 222243852

Earth sciences journal. **Founded:** 1929. **Freq:** Monthly. **Key Personnel:** Hirokazu Fujimaki, Editor. **ISSN:** 0914-9783. **Subscription Rates:** 14,000¥. **Remarks:** Advertising accepted; rates available upon request. **URL:** http://wwwsoc.nii.ac.jp/jampeg/journals.htm.
                                        Circ: Paid 1,300

📖 **766 Pharmacometrics**
Japanese Society of Pharmacometrics
PO Box 180
Sendai 980-8691, Japan   Ph: 81 222673810

Pharmacy journal. **Founded:** 1967. **Freq:** Monthly. **Key Personnel:** Hikaru Ozawa, Editor. **ISSN:** 0300-8533. **Subscription Rates:** 10,000¥. **Remarks:** Advertising accepted; rates available upon request.
                                        Circ: Paid 1,200

📖 **767 Solvent Extraction Research and Development, Japan**
Japan Association of Solvent Extraction
c/o Professor Kenichi Akiba
Institute for Advanced Materials Processing,
  Tohoku Universi
2-1-1 Katahira, Aoba-ku
Miyagi-ken
Sendai 980-0812, Japan   Ph: 81 222175141

Journal of organic chemistry. **Founded:** 1994. **Freq:** Annual. **Key Personnel:** Kenichi Akiba, Editor, akiba@iamp.tohoku.ac.jp. **ISSN:** 1341-7215. **Subscription Rates:** 5,000¥.
                                        Circ: Paid 200

SHIGA

📖 **768 Japanese Journal of Rheumatism and Joint Surgery**
Nihon Ryumachi Kansetsu Geka Gakkai
Shiga Ika Daigaku Seikei Gekagaku
  Kyoshitsu
Seta Tsukiwacho
Otsu-shi
Shiga, Japan

Medical science journal. **Founded:** 1982. **Freq:** Quarterly. **ISSN:** 0287-3214.

SHIMANE

📖 **769 Shimane Journal of Medical Science**
Shimane Medical University
89-1 Enya-cho
Izumo-shi
Shimane 693-0021, Japan

Medical science journal. **Founded:** 1977. **Freq:** Annual. **Key Personnel:** Yuzuru Kato, Editor. **ISSN:** 0386-5959.

SHIZUOKA

📖 **770 Genes & Genetic Systems**
Genetics Society of Japan
c/o National Institute of Genetics
1111 Yata
Mishima-shi
Shizuoka 411-0801, Japan   Ph: 81 668798317

Journal of genetics. **Founded:** 1921. **Freq:** Bimonthly. **Key Personnel:** Hideo Shinagawa, Editor, phone 81 668798317, fax 81 668798320, shinagaw@biken.osaka-u.ac.jp. **ISSN:** 1341-7568. **Subscription Rates:** US$130. **Remarks:** Advertising accepted; rates available upon request.
                                        Circ: Paid 2,000

📖 **771 Japanese Journal of Obstetrical, Gynecological and Neonatal Hematology**
Japanese Society of Obstetrical Gynecological and Neonatal Hematology
Hamamatsu University School of Medicine
Dept. of Obstetrics and Gynecology
3600 Handa-cho
Hamamatsu-shi
Shizuoka 431-3124, Japan   Ph: 81 534352309

Medical science journal. **Founded:** 1977. **Freq:** Quarterly. **Key Personnel:** Terao Toshihiko, Editor. **ISSN:** 0916-8796. **Subscription Rates:** 8,000¥.
                                        Circ: Paid 1,500

📖 **772 Journal of Faculty of Marine Science and Technology of Tokai University**
Tokai University
Faculty of Marine Science and Technology
20-1 Ori-Do 3-chome
Shimizu-shi
Shizuoka 424-0902, Japan

Journal of oceanography. **Founded:** 1966. **Freq:** Semiannual. **ISSN:** 0375-3271.

📖 **773 Journal of Marine Science Museum of Tokai University**
Tokai Daigaku Kaiyo Kagaku Hakubutsukan
2389 Miho
Shimizu-shi
Shizuoka 424-0901, Japan

Journal of oceanography. **Founded:** 1971. **Freq:** Bimonthly. **ISSN:** 0386-4197. **Subscription Rates:** 800¥.

TANASHI

📖 **774 Plant Production Science**
Crop Science Society of Japan
c/o Faculty of Agriculture
University of Tokyo
Midori-cho
Tanashi 188-0002, Japan   Ph: 81 424631611
Publication E-mail: asahito@hongo.ecc.u-tokyo.ac.jp

Publishes original research reports on field crops and resource plants, their production and related subjects, covering a wide range of sciences; physiology, biotechnology, morphology, ecology, cropping system, production technology and post harvest. **Founded:** 1998. **Freq:** Quarterly. **Key Personnel:** Makie Kokubun, Editor. **ISSN:** 1343-943X. **Subscription Rates:**

6,000¥. **Remarks:** Advertising accepted; rates available upon request. **URL:** http://wwwsoc.nii.ac.jp/cssj/pps.

Circ: (Not Reported)

TOCHIGI

775 Dokkyo Journal of Medical Sciences
Dokkyo University School of Medicine
Dokkyo Medical Society
Mibu
Tochigi, Japan
Ph: 81 282861111

Medical science journal. **Founded:** 1974. **Freq:** Quarterly. **Key Personnel:** Susumu Wakai, Editor. **ISSN:** 0385-5023. **Subscription Rates:** 5,000¥. **Remarks:** Advertising accepted; rates available upon request.
Circ: Paid 1,300

776 Grassland Science
Japanese Society of Grassland Science
c/o National Grassland Research Institute
768 Senbonmatsu
Nasu-gun
Nishinasuno-machi
Tochigi 329-2747, Japan
Ph: 81 287360111

Publishes original contributions in the field of grassland science and technology. **Founded:** 1955. **Freq:** Bimonthly. **Key Personnel:** Hirsohi Kobayashi, Editor. **ISSN:** 0447-5933. **Subscription Rates:** 8,000¥. **Remarks:** Advertising accepted; rates available upon request.
Circ: Paid 1,400

TOKUSHIMA

777 Journal of Mathematics
University of Tokushima
Faculty of Integrated Arts and Sciences
1-1 Minamijosanjima-cho
Tokushima 770-8503, Japan
Ph: 81 886567103
Publication E-mail: ohbuchi@ias.tokushima-u.ac.jp

Mathematics journal. **Founded:** 1967. **Freq:** Annual. **ISSN:** 0075-4293. **URL:** http://www-math.ias.tokushima-u.ac.jp/journal/.

778 Journal of Medical Investigation
Tokushima University
School of Medicine
18-15 Kuramoto-cho 3-chome
Tokushima 770-0042, Japan
Ph: 81 886337104

Journal of experimental medicine. **Founded:** 1954. **Freq:** Semiannual. **Key Personnel:** Saburo Sone, Editor. **ISSN:** 1343-1420.

779 Social Science Research of University of Tokushima
University of Tokushima
Faculty of Integrated Arts and Sciences
1-1 Minamijosanjima-cho
Tokushima 770-8503, Japan
Ph: 81 886567103

Social science journal. **Founded:** 1988. **Freq:** Annual.

TOKYO

780 A & U
A & U Publishing Co. Ltd.
30-8 Yushima 2-chome
Bunkyo-ku
Tokyo 113-0034, Japan
Ph: 81 338162935
Publication E-mail: aandu@nisiq.net

Journal on architecture. **Subtitle:** Architecture and Urbanism. **Founded:** 1971. **Freq:** Monthly. **Key Personnel:** Nobuyuki Yoshida, Editor. **ISSN:** 0389-9160. **Subscription Rates:** 30,000¥. **Remarks:** Advertising accepted; rates available upon request.
Circ: Paid 25,000

781 ACCJ Journal
American Chamber of Commerce in Japan
Masonic 39 Mori Bldg., 10F
2-4-5 Azabudai Minato-ku
Tokyo 106-0041, Japan
Ph: 81 334335381
Fax: 81 334338454
Publisher E-mail: info@accj.or.jp

Magazine of the American Chamber of Commerce in Japan (ACCJ), the most influential foreign business organization in Japan. **Freq:** Monthly. **Key Personnel:** Peter Kenny, Editor-in-Chief, phone 81 354787941, fax 81 354787942, peterkenny@paradigm.co.jp. **ISSN:** 0002-7847. **Subscription Rates:** Included in membership; 9,000¥ nonmembers; 15,000¥ nonmembers two years. **Remarks:** Advertising accepted; rates available upon request. **URL:** http://www.accj.or.jp/details.php?id=journal.
Circ: 4,500

782 Acta Anatomica Nipponica
Japanese Association of Anatomists
5-16-9 Honkomagome
Bunkyo-ku
Tokyo 113-0021, Japan
Ph: 81 358145811

Journal related to biology. **Founded:** 1928. **Freq:** Bimonthly. **ISSN:** 0022-7722. **Subscription Rates:** 15,000¥. **Remarks:** Advertising accepted; rates available upon request.
Circ: Paid 1,950

783 Acta Asiatica
Institute of Eastern Culture
The Toho Gakkai
1 Nishi Kanda 2-chome
Chiyoda-ku
Tokyo 101-0065, Japan
Ph: 81 332627221
Fax: 81 332627227

Journal on oriental studies. **Subtitle:** Bulletin of the Institute of Eastern Culture. **Founded:** 1961. **Freq:** Semiannual. **ISSN:** 0567-7254. **Subscription Rates:** 8,400¥.
Circ: Paid 1,000

784 Acta Criminologiae et Medicinae Legalis Japonica
Japanese Association of Criminology
c/o Dept. of Criminal Psychiatry
Medical and Dental University
2-3-10 Kanda-Surugadai
Chiyoda-ku
Tokyo 101-0062, Japan

Journal of criminology. **Founded:** 1929. **Freq:** Bimonthly. **ISSN:** 0302-0029. **Subscription Rates:** US$55. **Remarks:** Advertising accepted; rates available upon request.
Circ: Paid 800

785 Actinomycetologica
Society for Actinomycetes, Japan
c/o Kunimoto Hotta
Dept. of Bioactive Molecules, National
   Institute of Infectio
1-23-1, Toyama
Shinjuku-ku
Tokyo 162-8640, Japan
Publication E-mail: khotta@nih.go.jp

Journal of microbiology. **Founded:** 1962. **Freq:** Semiannual. **Key Personnel:** Sueharu Horinouchi, Editor, phone 81 352851111, fax 81 352851272. **ISSN:** 0914-5818. **Subscription Rates:** 7,000¥. **URL:** http://www.nih.go.jp/saj/journal.

786 Advances in Neurotrauma Research
Japanese Society for Neurotrauma Research
Nihon Daigaku Igakubu no Shinkei Geka
Oyaguchi Kamicho
Itabashi-ku
Tokyo, Japan

Journal of psychiatry and neurology. **Founded:** 1990. **Freq:** Annual. **ISSN:** 0916-698X. **Subscription Rates:** 3,500¥.

787 AMA - Agricultural Mechanization in Asia, Africa and Latin America
Farm Machinery Industrial Research Corp.
7 Kanda-Nishiki-cho 2-chome
Chiyoda-ku
Tokyo 101-0054, Japan   Ph: 81 332913674

Journal on agriculture. **Founded:** 1971. **Freq:** Quarterly. **Key Personnel:** Yoshisuke Kishida, Editor. **ISSN:** 0084-5841. **Subscription Rates:** 6,000¥. **Remarks:** Advertising accepted; rates available upon request.
Circ: Controlled 15,000

788 Analytical Sciences
Japan Society for Analytical Chemistry
Gotanda Sanhaitsu
26-2 Nishi-Gotanda 1-chome
Shinagawa-ku
Tokyo 141-0031, Japan   Ph: 81 334903351

Journal covering chemistry. **Founded:** 1985. **Freq:** Monthly. **Key Personnel:** T. Sawada, Editor. **ISSN:** 0910-6340. **Subscription Rates:** US$120. **URL:** http://wwwsoc.nii.ac.jp/jsac/analsci.html.
Circ: Paid 3,600

789 Animal Science Journal
Japanese Society of Animal Science
201 Nagatani Corporas
Ikenohata 2-9-4
Taito-ku
Tokyo 110-0008, Japan

Journal covering agriculture. **Founded:** 1985. **Freq:** Bimonthly. **Key Personnel:** Senkiti Sakai, Editor. **ISSN:** 1344-3941. **Subscription Rates:** 8,000¥. **Remarks:** Advertising accepted; rates available upon request. **URL:** http://wwwsoc.nii.ac.jp/jszs/contents/conte.html.
Circ: Paid 3,000

790 Annals of Nuclear Medicine
Japanese Society of Nuclear Medicine
Nihon Aisotopu Kyokai
28-45 Honkomagome 2-chome
Bunkyo-ku
Tokyo 113-0021, Japan

Medical science journal. **Founded:** 1987. **Freq:** Bimonthly. **ISSN:** 0914-7187. **Subscription Rates:** 1,500¥.

791 Annals of Thoracic and Cardiovascular Surgery
Axel Springer, Japan Publishing Inc.
2-1 Niban-cho
Chiyoda-ku
Tokyo 102-0084, Japan

Medical science journal. **Founded:** 1995. **Freq:** Quarterly. **ISSN:** 1341-1098. **Subscription Rates:** US$175.

792 Anritsu Technical Review
Anritsu Corporation
10-27 Minami-Azabu 5-chome
Minato-ku
Tokyo 106-0047, Japan

Journal of engineering. **Founded:** 1982. **ISSN:** 0914-7195.

793 Antarctic Record
National Institute of Polar Research
9-10, Kaga 1-chome
Itabashi-ku
Tokyo 173-8515, Japan   Ph: 81 339622214
Publication E-mail: www@nipr.ac.jp

Journal of geography. **Founded:** 1957. **Freq:** 3/year. **Key Personnel:** Kokichi Kamiyama, Editor. **ISSN:** 0085-7289. **URL:** http://www.nipr.ac.jp.
Circ: 1,000

794 Anthropological Science
Business Center for Academic Societies Japan
5-16-9 Honkomagome
Bunkyo-ku
Tokyo 113-0021, Japan   Ph: 81 358145811

Journal covering anthropology. **Founded:** 1993. **Freq:** Quarterly. **ISSN:** 0918-7960. **Subscription Rates:** US$150. **Remarks:** Advertising accepted; rates available upon request.
Circ: Paid 1,300

795 APO Productivity Journal
Asian Productivity Organization
2F Hirakawacho Daiichi Seimei Bldg.
1-2-10 Hirakawa-cho
Chiyoda-ku   Ph: 81 352263920
Tokyo 102-0093, Japan   Fax: 81 352263950
Publisher E-mail: apo@apo-tokyo.org

Journal covering business and economics. **Founded:** 1993. **Freq:** 2/year. **ISSN:** 0919-0589. **Subscription Rates:** US$10.
Circ: Paid 1,000

796 Apparel Production News
New Japan Sewing Machine News Ltd.
2nd Kosumo Bldg.
8-5 Sugamo 1-chome
Toshima-ku
Tokyo 170-0002, Japan   Ph: 81 339422574

Journal covering apparels. **Founded:** 1987. **Freq:** Monthly. **Key Personnel:** Makoto Nakajima, Editor. **ISSN:** 0914-7594. **Subscription Rates:** 9,600¥. **Remarks:** Advertising accepted; rates available upon request.
Circ: Paid 9,000

797 Applied Entomology and Zoology
Japanese Society of Applied Entomology and Zoology
c/o Japan Plant Protection Association
1-43-11 Komagome
Toshima-ku
Tokyo 170-0003, Japan   Ph: 81 339436021

Journal covering biology. **Founded:** 1966. **Freq:** Quarterly. **Key Personnel:** Masakazu Shiga, Editor. **ISSN:** 0003-6862. **Subscription Rates:** US$50. **Remarks:** Advertising accepted; rates available upon request.
Circ: Paid 1,900

798 Applied Human Science
Japan Society of Physiological Anthropology
c/o Business Center for Academic Societies
 Japan
5-16-9 Honkomagome
Bunkyo-ku
Tokyo 113-0021, Japan   Ph: 81 358145801

Journal covering biology. **Founded:** 1995. **Freq:** Bimonthly. **Key Personnel:** N. Nagai, Editor. **ISSN:** 1341-3473. **Subscription Rates:** 3,500¥.

799 Artificial Life and Robotics
Springer-Verlag Tokyo
3-13 Hongo 3-chome
Bunkyo-ku
Tokyo 113-0033, Japan   Ph: 81 338120617
Publication E-mail: orders@svt-ebs.co.jp

Journal of computers. **Founded:** 1997. **Freq:** Quarterly. **Key Personnel:** Masanori Sugisaka, Editor. **ISSN:** 1433-5298. **Subscription Rates:** 22,000¥. **URL:** http://link.springer.de/link/service/journals/10015/.

800 Asahi Evening News
Asahi Shimbun
5-3-2 Tsukiji
Chuou-ku   Ph: 81 355418785
Tokyo 104-8011, Japan   Fax: 81 355653286
Publisher E-mail: asacame@cg.pub.asahi-np.co.jp

General newspaper. **Founded:** 1954. **Freq:** Daily. **Key Personnel:** Yasunori Asai, Editor. **Subscription Rates:** 120¥ single issue. **Remarks:** Advertising accepted; rates available upon request. **URL:** http://www.asahi.com/english/english.hml.

Circ: Controlled 38,800

📖 801 Asia Electronics Industry
Dempa Publication Inc.
1-11-15 Higashi Gotanda
Tokyo 141, Japan

Journal of electrical engineering. **Founded:** 1996. **Freq:** Monthly. **Key Personnel:** Hideo Hirayama, Editor. **Remarks:** Advertising accepted; rates available upon request.

Circ: 51,000

📖 802 Asian Cultural Studies
International Christian University Institute of Asian Cultural Studies
3-10-2 Osawa
Mitaka-shi
Tokyo 181-0015, Japan

History journal. **Founded:** 1960. **Freq:** Irregular. **Key Personnel:** M. William Steele, Editor. **ISSN:** 0454-2150. **Subscription Rates:** 2,000¥.
Circ: Paid 1,000

📖 803 Asian Journal of Control
Chinese Automatic Control Society
c/o Prof. Hidenori Kimura
Dept. of Mathematics Eng. and Information
    Physics
University of Tokyo 7-3-1 Hongo
Bunkyo-ku
Tokyo 113-8656, Japan

Journal of computers. **Founded:** 1999. **Freq:** Quarterly. **Key Personnel:** Li-Chen Fu, Editor. **ISSN:** 1561-8625.

📖 804 Asian Oil and Gas
Intercontinental Marketing Corp.
IPO Box 5056
Tokyo 100-3191, Japan

Ph: 81 336617458
Fax: 81 336679646

Journal of petroleum and gas. **Freq:** 10/year.

📖 805 Asian-Pacific Book Development
Asia-Pacific Cultural Centre for Unesco
6 Fukuro-Machi
Shinjuku-ku
Tokyo 162-0828, Japan

Ph: 81 332694435

Journal of publishing and trade. **Founded:** 1989. **Freq:** Quarterly. **Key Personnel:** Muneharu Kusaba, Editor. **ISSN:** 0916-7838. **Subscription Rates:** US$20.

Circ: Paid 2,500

📖 806 Asian Research Trends
Centre for East Asian Cultural Studies for UNESCO
The Toyo Bunko
Honkomagome 2-28-21
Bunkyo-ku
Tokyo 113-0021, Japan

Ph: 81 339420124

History journal. **Founded:** 1991. **Freq:** Annual. **Key Personnel:** Yoneo Ishii, Editor. **ISSN:** 0917-1479. **Subscription Rates:** 2,200¥.

Circ: Paid 1,500

📖 807 Atoms in Japan
Japan Atomic Industrial Forum
Toshin Bldg.
1-1-13 Shinbashi
Minato-ku
Tokyo 105-8605, Japan

Ph: 81 335082411

Journal of nuclear energy. **Founded:** 1957. **Freq:** Monthly. **Key Personnel:** Kazuhisa Mori, Editor. **ISSN:** 0403-9319. **Subscription Rates:** 58,000¥.

📖 808 Axis
Axis Inc.
5-17-1 Roppongi
Minato-ku
Tokyo 106-0032, Japan
Publication E-mail: axismag@axisinc.co.jp

Ph: 81 335872781

Magazine covering interior decoration and design. **Subtitle:** World Design Journal. **Founded:** 1947. **Freq:** Bimonthly. **Key Personnel:** Yasuko Seki, Editor. **Subscription Rates:** 9,000¥.

📖 809 Bamboo Journal
Japan Society of Bamboo Development and Protection
Dento Sangyo Kaikan
9-2 Okazakiseishoji-cho
Sakyo-ku
Tokyo 606-8343, Japan

Journal covering biology. **Founded:** 1983. **Freq:** Annual. **ISSN:** 0289-2111.

📖 810 Benthos Research
Japanese Association of Benthology
Ocean Research Institute
University of Minami-Dai
Nakano-ku
Tokyo 164-0014, Japan

Ph: 81 353516469

Journal covering biology. **Founded:** 1970. **Freq:** Semiannual. **Key Personnel:** Seiji Goshima, Editor, phone 81 138405548, fax 81 138435015, goshima@pop.fish.hokudai.ac.jp. **ISSN:** 0289-4548. **Subscription Rates:** 4,000¥. **URL:** http://wwwsoc.nii.ac.jp/jab/index-e.html.

Circ: Paid 500

📖 811 Biomedical Research
Biomedical Research Press Inc
5 F Kyowa Bldg
2-1-3 Kyobashi
Chuo-ku
Tokyo 104-0031, Japan

Medical science journal. **Founded:** 1980. **Freq:** Bimonthly. **Key Personnel:** Tomio Kanno, Editor, t-kanno@yanaihara.co.jp. **ISSN:** 0388-6107. **Subscription Rates:** 23,000¥. **Remarks:** Advertising accepted; rates available upon request.

Circ: Paid 700

📖 812 Biomedical Research on Trace Elements
Japan Society for Biomedical Research on Trace Elements
Nihon Daigaku Igakubu Kagaku Kyoshitsu
30-1, Oyaguchi Kamicho
Itabashi-ku
Tokyo, Japan

Ph: 81 339728111

Journal covering biology. **Founded:** 1990. **Freq:** Semiannual. **Key Personnel:** Yasuyuki Arakawa, Editor. **ISSN:** 0916-717X. **Subscription Rates:** 75,000¥.

📖 813 Biophysics
Realize Inc
4-1-4 Hongo
Bunkyo-ku
Tokyo 113-0033, Japan

Ph: 81 338158511

Journal covering biophysics. **Founded:** 1961. **Freq:** Bimonthly. **Key Personnel:** Yutaka Kirino, Editor. **ISSN:** 0582-4052. **Subscription Rates:** 12,000¥. **Remarks:** Advertising accepted; rates available upon request.

Circ: Paid 3,500

📖 814 Bioscience, Biotechnology, and Biochemistry
Japan Society for Bioscience Biotechnology and Agrochemistry
2-4-16 Yayoi
Bunkyo-ku
Tokyo 113-0032, Japan

Ph: 81 338118789

Journal covering biology. **Founded:** 1992. **Freq:** Monthly. **Key Personnel:** Shuichi Kaminogawa, Editor. **ISSN:** 0916-8451. **Subscription Rates:** US$360. **Remarks:** Advertising accepted; rates available upon request.

Circ: Paid 3,600

◻ 815 Brain Tumor Pathology
Springer-Verlag Tokyo
3-13 Hongo 3-chome
Bunkyo-ku
Tokyo 113-0033, Japan   Ph: 81 338120617

Medical science journal. **Founded:** 1983. **Freq:** Semiannual. **Key Personnel:** Kintomo Takakura, Editor. **ISSN:** 1433-7398. **Subscription Rates:** 12,000¥. **URL:** http://link.springer.de/link/service/journals/10014/.

◻ 816 Breeding Science
Japanese Society of Breeding
c/o Faculty of Agriculture
University of Tokyo
Bunkyo-ku
Tokyo, Japan   Ph: 81 358415065

Journal covering agriculture. **Founded:** 1951. **Freq:** Quarterly. **Key Personnel:** Masahiro Nakagahra, Editor. **Subscription Rates:** 6,500¥. **Remarks:** Advertising accepted; rates available upon request.
                                           Circ: Paid 2,000

◻ 817 By the Way
Raifu-sha Co. Ltd.
2-1-8 Sarugaku-cho
Chiyoda-ku
Tokyo 101-0064, Japan   Ph: 81 332940579

Political science journal. **Subtitle:** Bridging the US-Japan Perception Gap. **Founded:** 1991. **Freq:** Bimonthly. **Key Personnel:** Yonnosake Tanaka, Editor. **ISSN:** 0917-7566. **Subscription Rates:** US$33. **Remarks:** Advertising accepted; rates available upon request.
                                           Circ: Paid 30,000

◻ 818 Calorimetry and Thermal Analysis
Japan Society of Calorimetry and Thermal Analysis
Miyazawa Bldg. 601
1-6-7 Iwamoto-cho
Chiyoda-ku
Tokyo 101-0032, Japan
Publication E-mail: netsu@mbd.niftys.com

Publishes the original papers, short notes, review articles, lectures, commentary and other various information for calorimetry and thermal analysis and its related fields. **Founded:** 1974. **Freq:** Quarterly. **ISSN:** 0386-2615. **URL:** http://wwwsoc.nii.ac.jp/jscta/e.

◻ 819 Catalysts & Catalysis
Catalysis Society of Japan
21-13-302
Higashi-Gotanda 5-chome
Shinagawa-ku
Tokyo 141-0022, Japan

Journal covering chemistry. **Founded:** 1959. **Freq:** 8/year. **Subscription Rates:** 2,000¥ single issue.

◻ 820 Clinical and Experimental Nephrology
Springer-Verlag Tokyo
3-13 Hongo 3-chome
Bunkyo-ku
Tokyo 113-0033, Japan   Ph: 81 338120617

Medical science journal. **Founded:** 1997. **Freq:** Quarterly. **Key Personnel:** Masashi Imai, Editor. **ISSN:** 1342-1751. **Subscription Rates:** 18,000¥. **URL:** http://link.springer.de/link/service/journals/10157/.

◻ 821 Commentarii Mathematici Universitatis Sancti Pauli
Kinokuniya Shoten - Kinokuniya Co. Ltd.
17-7 Shinjuku 3-chome
Shinjuku-ku
Tokyo 160-0022, Japan   Ph: 81 334390172

Mathematics journal. **Founded:** 1952. **Freq:** Semiannual. **ISSN:** 0010-258X. **Subscription Rates:** US$248.

◻ 822 Communications Research Laboratory Journal
Ministry of Posts and Telecommunications Communications Research Laboratory
2-1 Nukui-Kita-Machi 4-chome
Koganei-shi
Tokyo 184-0015, Japan   Ph: 81 423211211

Journal of communications. **Founded:** 1954. **Freq:** 3/year. **ISSN:** 0914-9260. **URL:** http://www.crl.go.jp.
                                           Circ: Free 1,000

◻ 823 The Communist
Kaihohsha
525-3 Waseda-Tsurumaki-cho
Shinjuku-ku
Tokyo 162-0041, Japan   Ph: 81 332071261

Political science journal. **Founded:** 1959. **Freq:** Bimonthly. **Key Personnel:** Yoshida Masao, Editor. **ISSN:** 1344-7904. **Subscription Rates:** 1,510¥ single issue. **Remarks:** Advertising accepted; rates available upon request.
                                           Circ: Paid 7,000

◻ 824 Computing Japan
LINC Media Inc.
Odakyu Minami-Aoyama Bldg. 8F
7-8-1 Minami Aoyama, Minato-ku   Ph: 81 334992099
Tokyo 107-0062, Japan   Fax: 81 334992199

Online journal of computers. **Founded:** 1999. **Freq:** Monthly. **Key Personnel:** Daniel Scuka, Editor. **Remarks:** Advertising accepted; rates available upon request. **URL:** http://www.japaninc.net/computingjapan/.
                                           Circ: (Not Reported)

◻ 825 Concrete Library International
Japan Society of Civil Engineers
Yotsuya 1-chome
Shinjuku-ku
Tokyo 160-0004, Japan

Journal covering civil engineering. **Founded:** 1983. **Freq:** Semiannual. **ISSN:** 0913-4913. **Subscription Rates:** 2,500¥. **URL:** http://www.jsce.or.jp/publication/e/c_l_i.html.

◻ 826 Crustacean Research
Carcinological Society of Japan
University of Fisheries
Dept .of Aquatic Bioscience
4-5-7 Ko-Unan
Minato-ku
Tokyo 108-0075, Japan   Ph: 81 354630535

Journal of zoology. **Founded:** 1963. **Freq:** Annual. **ISSN:** 0287-3478.

◻ 827 Cytologia
c/o Japan Mendel Society
Toshin Bldg.
Hongo 2-27-2
Bunkyo-ku
Tokyo 113-0033, Japan

Journal covering biology. **Founded:** 1929. **Freq:** Quarterly. **Key Personnel:** Tsuneyoshi Kuroiwa, Editor. **ISSN:** 0011-4545. **Subscription Rates:** 25,000¥. **Remarks:** Advertising accepted; rates available upon request.
                                           Circ: Paid 1,000

◻ 828 Dentistry in Japan
Japanese Dental Association
4-1-20 Kudan-Kita
Chiyoda-ku
Tokyo 102-0073, Japan   Ph: 81 332629214

Journal of dentistry. **Founded:** 1964. **Freq:** Annual. **Key Personnel:** Isao Ishikawa, Editor. **ISSN:** 0070-3737.
                                           Circ: Controlled 2,400

829 Dharma World
Kosei Publishing Co.
2-7-1 Suginami-ku
Tokyo 166-8535, Japan   Ph: 81 353852319
Publication E-mail: dharmaworld@mail.kosei-shuppan.co.jp

Magazine on Buddhism. **Freq:** Bimonthly. **Subscription Rates:** 3,700¥.
URL: http://www.kosei-shuppan.co.jp/english/text/mag/dindex.html.

830 Diamond Industria
Diamond Inc.
4-2 Kasumigaseki 1-chome
Chiyoda-ku
Tokyo 100-0013, Japan

Journal covering business and economics. **Founded:** 1971. **Freq:** Monthly.
Key Personnel: Natsuki Mori, Editor. **ISSN:** 0385-7360. **Subscription
Rates:** 9,960¥.
                                              Circ: Paid 47,000

831 Earth Planets and Space
Center for Academic Publications Japan
2-4-16 Yayoi
Bunkyo-ku
Tokyo 113-0032, Japan   Ph: 81 338175821

Earth sciences journal. **Founded:** 1997. **Freq:** Bimonthly. **Subscription
Rates:** US$143. **Remarks:** Advertising accepted; rates available upon
request.
                                              Circ: Paid 800

832 Earth Science
Association for the Geological Collaboration in Japan
8-7 Minami-Ikebukuro 1-chome
Toshima-ku
Tokyo 171-0022, Japan

Earth sciences journal. **Founded:** 1949. **Freq:** Bimonthly. **ISSN:** 0366-6611.

833 The East
The East Publications, Inc.
Mamiana Arc Bldg., 1F
2-1 Higashi-Azabu 3
Minato-ku   Ph: 81 332243751
Tokyo 106-0044, Japan   Fax: 81 332243754
Publication E-mail: east@japan.email.ne.jp

English language magazine covering Japanese culture for others. **Founded:**
1964. **Subscription Rates:** 4,800¥ Japan; US$38 other countries; 8,800¥ two
years Japan; US$70 two years other countries. **Remarks:** Advertising
accepted; rates available upon request. **URL:** http://www.theeast.co.jp.
                                              Circ: (Not Reported)

834 Economic Review
Iwanami Shoten Publishers
2-5-5 Hitotsubashi
Chiyoda-ku
Tokyo 101-0003, Japan

Journal covering economics. **Founded:** 1950. **Freq:** Quarterly. **Key Personnel:** R. Minami, Editor. **ISSN:** 0022-9733. **Subscription Rates:** 6,300¥.
Remarks: Advertising accepted; rates available upon request.
                                              Circ: Paid 1,500

835 Endocrine Surgery
Intermerc Co. Ltd.
39-15-104 Eifuku 1-chome
Suginami-ku
Tokyo 168-0064, Japan   Ph: 81 0353762820

Medical science journal. **Founded:** 1984. **Freq:** Quarterly. **ISSN:** 0914-9953.
Subscription Rates: 15,100¥.

836 Energy in Japan
Institute of Energy Economics Japan
Shuwa Kamiyacho Bldg
3-13 Toranomon 4-chome
Minato-ku
Tokyo 105-0001, Japan   Ph: 81 354014322

Journal covering energy. **Founded:** 1966. **Freq:** Bimonthly. **Key Personnel:**
Toshiaki Yuasa, Editor. **ISSN:** 0919-6080. **Subscription Rates:** US$200.
                                              Circ: Paid 800

837 Environmental Economics and Policy Studies
Springer-Verlag Tokyo
3-13 Hongo 3-chome
Bunkyo-ku
Tokyo 113-0033, Japan   Ph: 81 338120617
Publication E-mail: orders@svt-ebs.co.jp

Journal of environmental studies. **Founded:** 1998. **Freq:** Quarterly. **Key
Personnel:** E. Hosoda, Chief Managing Editor. **ISSN:** 1432-847X. **Subscription Rates:** 18,000¥. **URL:** http://link.springer.de/link/service/journals/
10018/.

838 Environmental Mutagen Research
Japanese Environmental Mutagen Society
c/o Mr. Ken-ichiro Tanabe
Koukuh Hoken Kyokai
1-44-2 Komagome
Toshima-ku
Tokyo 170-0003, Japan

Journal of genetics. **Founded:** 1978. **Freq:** 3/year. **Key Personnel:** Shizuyo
Sutoh, Editor. **ISSN:** 0910-0865. **URL:** http://wwwsoc.nii.ac.jp/jems/jems-
e.htmlSOCIETY.

839 Environmental Sciences
MYU, Scientific Publishing Division
2-32-3 Sendagi
Bunkyo-ku
Tokyo 113-0022, Japan   Ph: 81 338212930

Journal of environmental studies. **Founded:** 1991. **Freq:** Quarterly. **Key
Personnel:** Humio Tsunoda, Editor. **ISSN:** 0915-955X. **Subscription Rates:**
US$180.

840 Experimental Animals
Japanese Association for Laboratory Animal Science
Akamon Royal Heights
Rm. 1103
5-29-12 Hongo
Bunkyo-ku
Tokyo 113-0033, Japan   Ph: 81 338148276

Journal of experimental medicine. **Founded:** 1952. **Freq:** Quarterly. **Key
Personnel:** Yasuhiro Yoshikawa, Editor. **ISSN:** 1341-1357. **Subscription
Rates:** 3,000¥ individuals nonmembers. **Remarks:** Advertising accepted;
rates available upon request. **URL:** http://www.jalas.or.jp/.
                                              Circ: Paid 2,300

841 Extremophiles
Springer-Verlag Tokyo
3-13 Hongo 3-chome
Bunkyo-ku
Tokyo 113-0033, Japan   Ph: 81 338120617
Publication E-mail: orders@svt-ebs.co.jp

Journal covering biotechnology. **Subtitle:** Life Under Extreme Conditions.
Founded: 1997. **Freq:** Bimonthly. **Key Personnel:** K. Horikoshi, Managing
Editor. **ISSN:** 1431-0651. **Subscription Rates:** 34,000¥. **URL:** http://
link.springer.de/link/service/journals/00792/.

842 Financial Times Japan
Financial Times (Japan) Ltd.
Yamato Seimei Building 21F
1-1-7 Uchisaiwaicho
Chiyoda-ku
Tokyo 100-0011, Japan

General newspaper. **Founded:** 1990. **Freq:** Daily. **Remarks:** Advertising accepted; rates available upon request. **URL:** http://www.ftjapan.co.jp/html/home/index.html.

Circ: Paid 7,000

📖 843 Food Science and Technology Research
Business Center for Academic Societies
2nd Fl., Tsuna Bldg.
1-17-9 Hongo
Bunkyo-ku
Tokyo 113-0033, Japan   Ph: 81 338141363

Journal of food and food industry. **Founded:** 1995. **Freq:** Quarterly. **Key Personnel:** Tomohiko Mori, Editor. **ISSN:** 1344-6606. **Subscription Rates:** 16,000¥.

📖 844 Forma
Society for Science on Form Japan
Tokyo University of Agriculture
&Technology
Dept. of Mechanical Systems Engineering
24-16 Naka-cho 2-chome
Koganei-shi
Tokyo 184-0012, Japan   Ph: 81 423887224

Journal covering biology. **Founded:** 1985. **Freq:** Quarterly. **Key Personnel:** Ryuji Takaki, Editor-in-Chief, takaki@cc.tuat.ac.jp. **ISSN:** 0911-6036. **Subscription Rates:** US$150 nonmembers. **URL:** http://www.scipress.org/journals/forma/index.html.

Circ: Paid 400

📖 845 Gastric Cancer
Springer-Verlag Tokyo
3-13 Hongo 3-chome
Bunkyo-ku
Tokyo 113-0033, Japan   Ph: 81 338120617
Publication E-mail: orders@svt-ebs.co.jp

Publishes significant studies related to stomach neoplasms. **Founded:** 1999. **Freq:** Quarterly. **Key Personnel:** O. Kobori, Editor-in-Chief. **ISSN:** 1436-3291. **Subscription Rates:** 20,000¥. **URL:** http://link.springer-ny.com/link/service/journals/10120/.

📖 846 Geochemical Journal
Business Center for Academic Societies Japan
5-16-9 Honkomagome
Bunkyo-ku
Tokyo 113-0021, Japan   Ph: 81 358145811
Publication E-mail: gj@ess.sci.osaka-u.ac.jp

Earth sciences journal. **Founded:** 1966. **Freq:** Bimonthly. **Key Personnel:** J. Matsuda, Exec. Editor, phone 81 668505495, fax 81 668505541. **ISSN:** 0016-7002. **Subscription Rates:** 10,000¥. **Remarks:** Advertising accepted; rates available upon request. **URL:** http://www.terrapub.co.jp/journals/GJ/.

Circ: Paid 1,300

📖 847 Graphic Design in Japan
Intercontinental Marketing Corp.
IPO Box 5056   Ph: 81 336617458
Tokyo 100-3191, Japan   Fax: 81 336679646

Journal covering printing. **Freq:** Annual.

📖 848 Graphs and Combinatorics
Springer-Verlag Tokyo
3-13 Hongo 3-chome
Bunkyo-ku
Tokyo 113-0033, Japan   Ph: 81 338120617
Publication E-mail: orders@svt-ebs.co.jp

International journal devoted to research concerning all aspects of combinatorial mathematics. **Founded:** 1985. **Freq:** Quarterly. **Key Personnel:** J. Akiyama, Editor-in-Chief. **ISSN:** 0911-0119. **Subscription Rates:** 30,000¥. **URL:** http://link.springer-ny.com/link/service/journals/00373/.

📖 849 Guide to Japanese Taxes
Zaikei Shoho Sha. Co. Ltd.
1-2-14 Higashi-Shinbashi
Minato-ku
Tokyo 105-0021, Japan

Journal covering economics. **Founded:** 1965. **Freq:** Annual. **Key Personnel:** Yasuyuki Nagatomi, Editor. **ISSN:** 0072-8551. **Subscription Rates:** 7,000¥.
Circ: Paid 5,000

📖 850 Heart and Vessels
Springer-Verlag Tokyo
3-13 Hongo 3-chome
Bunkyo-ku
Tokyo 113-0033, Japan   Ph: 81 338120617
Publication E-mail: orders@svt-ebs.co.jp

Medical science journal. **Founded:** 1985. **Freq:** Semiannual. **Key Personnel:** Shigetake Sasayama, Editor-in-Chief. **ISSN:** 0910-8327. **Subscription Rates:** 10,000¥. **URL:** http://link.springer-ny.com/link/service/journals/00380/.
Ad Rates: BW: 70,000¥   **Circ:** Paid 1,000

📖 851 Heterocycles
Japan Institute of Heterocyclic Chemistry
1-7-17 Motoaka-Saka
Minato-ku
Tokyo 107-0051, Japan   Ph: 81 334045019

Journal covering chemistry. **Subtitle:** International Journal for Reviews and Communi. **Founded:** 1973. **Freq:** 15/year. **Key Personnel:** Keiichiro Fukumoto, Editor. **ISSN:** 0385-5414. **Subscription Rates:** US$3,798 all countries except Japan and Europe; €3,396 Europe. **URL:** http://www.elsevier.com/locate/heteroccles.
Circ: Paid 1,100

📖 852 Historia Scientiarum
History of Science Society of Japan
West Pine Bldg.
201, 2-15-19 Hirakawa-cho
Chiyoda-ku
Tokyo 102-0093, Japan

Science journal. **Subtitle:** International Journal of the History of Scien. **Founded:** 1962. **Freq:** 3/year. **Key Personnel:** Chikara Sasaki, Editor. **ISSN:** 0285-4821. **Subscription Rates:** 10,000¥.

📖 853 Hitachi Cable Review
Hitachi Cable Co. Ltd.
1-2 Marunochi 2-chome
Chiyoda-ku
Tokyo 100-0005, Japan

Journal of electrical engineering. **Founded:** 1982. **Freq:** Annual. **ISSN:** 0914-899X. **URL:** http://www.hitachi-cable.co.jp/en/review/20/index.htm.

📖 854 Hitotsubashi Journal of Arts and Sciences
Hitotsubashi University
Hitotsubashi Academy
2-1 Naka
Kunitachi-shi
Tokyo 186-0004, Japan

Journal covering arts and science. **Founded:** 1960. **Freq:** Annual. **Key Personnel:** T. Kubo, Editor. **ISSN:** 0073-2788. **Subscription Rates:** 2,500¥.
Circ: Paid 750

📖 855 Iberoamericana
Universidad Sofia Instituto Iberoamericano
7-1 Kioi-cho
Chiyoda-ku
Tokyo 102-0094, Japan   Ph: 81 332383530

Social science journal. **Founded:** 1979. **Freq:** Semiannual. **Key Personnel:** Kotaro Horisaka, Editor. **ISSN:** 0388-1237. **Subscription Rates:** 2,800¥.

856 Ichthyological Research
Springer-Verlag Tokyo
3-13 Hongo 3-chome
Bunkyo-ku
Tokyo 113-0033, Japan   Ph: 81 338120617
Publication E-mail: orders@svt-ebs.co.jp

Publishes research papers on original work, either descriptive or experimental, that advances the understanding of the diversity of fishes. **Founded:** 1950. **Freq:** Quarterly. **Key Personnel:** Hiroshi Kohno, Editor-in-Chief. **ISSN:** 1341-8998. **Subscription Rates:** 18,000¥. **Remarks:** Advertising accepted; rates available upon request. **URL:** http://link.springer-ny.com/link/service/journals/10228/.

                                                Circ: Paid 700

857 Idea
Seibundo Shinkosha Publishing Co. Ltd.
1-13-7 Yayoi-cho
Nakano-ku
Tokyo 164-0013, Japan

International graphic design magazine. **Subtitle:** International Advertising Art. **Founded:** 1953. **Freq:** Bimonthly. **Key Personnel:** Minoru Takita, Editor. **ISSN:** 0019-1299. **Subscription Rates:** 23,640¥. **Remarks:** Advertising accepted; rates available upon request.

                                                Circ: Paid 32,000

858 IEICE Journal
Institute of Electronics, Information and Communication Engineers
202 Kikai-Shikou-Kaikan Bldg.
3-5-8, Shibakouen
Minato-ku   Ph: 81 334336691
Tokyo 105, Japan   Fax: 81 334336659
Publisher E-mail: office@ieice.or.jp

Journal of electronics. **Founded:** 1917. **Freq:** Monthly. **Key Personnel:** Michiyuki Uenohara, Editor. **ISSN:** 0913-5693. **Subscription Rates:** 2,580¥. **Remarks:** Advertising accepted; rates available upon request.
                                                Circ: Paid 40,000

859 IHI Engineering Review
Ishikawajima-Harima Heavy Industries Co. Ltd.
2-16 Toyosu 3-chome
Koto-ku
Tokyo 135-0061, Japan

Journal of transportation. **Founded:** 1968. **Freq:** Quarterly. **Key Personnel:** Akira Tsutsui, Editor. **ISSN:** 0018-9820.

860 Illustration in Japan
Kodansha Ltd.
12-21 Otowa 2-chome
Bunkyo-ku
Tokyo 112-0013, Japan   Ph: 81 339466201

Journal covering arts. **Founded:** 1972. **Freq:** Annual.

861 Industries of Japan
Mainichi Newspapers
1-1-1 Hitotsubashi
Chiyoda-ku
Tokyo 100-0003, Japan   Ph: 81 332120321

Journal covering business and economics. **Founded:** 1958. **Freq:** Annual. **ISSN:** 0446-1266. **Subscription Rates:** 800¥.

862 Informatization White Paper
Japan Information Processing Development Center
Kikai Shinko Kaikan Bldg.
5-8 Shibakoen 3-chome
Minato-ku
Tokyo 105-0011, Japan   Ph: 81 334329381

Journal of computers. **Founded:** 1967. **Freq:** Annual. **Key Personnel:** Hiroshi Ikawa, Editor. **ISSN:** 0918-3752. **Subscription Rates:** 5,000¥. **Remarks:** Advertising accepted; rates available upon request.
                                                Circ: Paid 500

863 Intercommunication
NTT Publishing Co., Ltd.
4th Fl., Tokyo Opera City Tower
3-20-2 Nishishinjuku
Shinjuku-ku   Ph: 81 353530850
Tokyo 163-1404, Japan   Fax: 81 353530910
Publication E-mail: query@ntticc.or.jp

Magazine exploring the connection between the arts and scientific technology. **Subtitle:** A Journal of Exploring the Frontiers of Arts. **Freq:** Quarterly. **Subscription Rates:** 15,000¥. **URL:** http://www.ntticc.or.jp/pub/what_ic/index_e.html.

864 Internal Combustion Engine
Sankaido
5-18 Hongo 5-chome
Bunkyo-ku
Tokyo 113-0033, Japan

Journal of mechanical engineering. **Founded:** 1937. **Freq:** Monthly. **ISSN:** 0387-1142. **Subscription Rates:** 1,240¥ single issue.

865 Internal Medicine
Japanese Society of Internal Medicine
Hongo Daiichi Bldg. 8F
34-3, 3-chome
Hongo
Bunkyo-ku
Tokyo 113-8433, Japan   Ph: 81 338135991

Medical science journal. **Founded:** 1962. **Freq:** Monthly. **Key Personnel:** Hidehiko Saito, Editor. **ISSN:** 0918-2918. **Subscription Rates:** 20,000¥; US$270 other countries.
                                                Circ: Paid 6,500

866 International Journal of Clinical Oncology
Springer-Verlag Tokyo
3-13 Hongo 3-chome
Bunkyo-ku
Tokyo 113-0033, Japan   Ph: 81 338120617
Publication E-mail: orders@svt-ebs.co.jp

Publishes original research papers on all aspects of clinical human oncology. **Founded:** 1966. **Freq:** Bimonthly. **Key Personnel:** Yoshio Yamaoka, Editor-in-Chief. **ISSN:** 1341-9625. **Subscription Rates:** 22,000¥. **Remarks:** Advertising accepted; rates available upon request. **URL:** http://link.springer.de/link/service/journals/10147/.
                                                Circ: (Not Reported)

867 International Journal of Electrical Machining
Japan Society of Electrical-Machining Engineers (JSEME)
2-24-16 Naka-cho
Koganei-shi
Tokyo 184-0012, Japan

Journal of electrical engineering. **Freq:** Annual. **ISSN:** 1341-7908.

868 International Journal of Japan Society for Precision Engineering
Japan Society for Precision Engineering
Kudan-Seiwa Bldg. 5-9
Kudan-kita 1-chome
Chiyoda-ku
Tokyo 102-0073, Japan

Journal of engineering. **Founded:** 1963. **Freq:** Quarterly. **ISSN:** 0916-782X. **Subscription Rates:** US$100.

869 International Medical Journal
Japan International Cultural Exchange Foundation
2-15-5-207 Shoto
Shibuya-ku
Tokyo 150-0046, Japan   Ph: 81 334677422

Medical science journal. **Founded:** 1994. **Freq:** Quarterly. **Key Personnel:** Thomas Stapleton, Editor. **ISSN:** 1341-2051. **Subscription Rates:** 7,400¥; US$80 other countries. **Remarks:** Advertising accepted; rates available upon request. **Alt. Formats:** CD-ROM.
                                                Circ: (Not Reported)

📖 **870 International Medical News**
International Medical Society of Japan
4-12 Kami-Uma 1-chome
Setagaya-ku
Tokyo 154-0011, Japan

Medical science journal. **Founded:** 1952. **Freq:** Monthly. **ISSN:** 0535-1405.

📖 **871 International Travel Plan**
Far East Reporters Inc
Phoenix Bldg.
5F 1-4-3 Azabudai
Minato-ku
Tokyo 106-0041, Japan   Ph: 81 355709703

Journal of travel and tourism. **Founded:** 1997. **Freq:** Monthly. **Key Personnel:** Ed Mike Pokrovsky, Editor. **Subscription Rates:** 4,500¥. **Remarks:** Advertising accepted; rates available upon request.
Circ: Paid 50,000

📖 **872 Ionizing Radiation**
Japan Society of Applied Physics
1-12-3 Kudan-Kita
Chiyoda-ku
Tokyo 102-0073, Japan

Physics journal. **Founded:** 1974. **Freq:** 3/year. **ISSN:** 0285-3604. **Subscription Rates:** 4,000¥. **Remarks:** Advertising accepted; rates available upon request.
Circ: (Not Reported)

📖 **873 Japan Architect**
Japan Architect Co. Ltd.
31-2 Yushima 2-chome
Bunkyo-ku
Tokyo 113-0034, Japan   Ph: 81 338117101
Publication E-mail: ja-business@japan-architect.co.jp

Periodical containing information and detailed data of selected coverage of top-level Japanese architecture, projects, city planning and new trends. **Founded:** 1956. **Freq:** Quarterly. **Key Personnel:** Yasuhiro Teramatsu, Editor. **ISSN:** 0021-4302. **Subscription Rates:** 12,000¥. **Remarks:** Advertising accepted; rates available upon request. **URL:** http://www.japan-architect.co.jp.
Circ: Paid 18,000

📖 **874 Japan Automotive News**
JAN Corporation
5F Nikkan Jidosha Shimbun Bldg
2-1-25 Kaigan
Minato-ku
Tokyo 105-0022, Japan   Ph: 81 334380361

Newspaper covering automobiles. **Founded:** 1959. **Freq:** Monthly. **Key Personnel:** Makio Sakurazawa, Editor. **ISSN:** 0021-4329. **Subscription Rates:** 9,990¥. **Remarks:** Advertising accepted; rates available upon request. **URL:** http://www.japan-autonews.com/.
Circ: Paid 5,180

📖 **875 Japan Camera Trade News**
Genyosha Publications, Inc.
8-7 Shibuya 2-chome
Shibuya-ku
Tokyo 150, Japan   Ph: 81 334077521

Journal of photography. **Subtitle:** Monthly Information on Photographic Products,. **Founded:** 1950. **Freq:** Monthly. **Key Personnel:** K. Eda, Editor. **ISSN:** 0021-4345. **Subscription Rates:** US$130. **Remarks:** Advertising accepted; rates available upon request.
Circ: Paid 8,500

📖 **876 Japan Graphic Arts**
Japan Printing News Co. Ltd.
16-8 Shintomi 1-chome
Chuo-ku
Tokyo 104-0041, Japan   Ph: 81 335535681
Publication E-mail: info@nichiin.co.jp

Journal covering printing. **Founded:** 1959. **Freq:** Annual. **Key Personnel:** H. Kurihara, Editor. **ISSN:** 0072-548X. **Subscription Rates:** 5,000¥ single issue.
Ad Rates: BW: 150,000¥   **Circ:** Paid 5,000
                 4C: 450,000¥

📖 **877 Japan Harvest**
Japan Evangelical Missionary Association
2-1 Kanda-Surugadai
Chiyoda-ku
Tokyo 101-0062, Japan   Ph: 81 332951949
Publication E-mail: jema@jemanet.gol.com

Magazine catering to the evangelical community. **Founded:** 1951. **Freq:** Quarterly. **Key Personnel:** Gerald B.D. May, Editor. **ISSN:** 0021-440X. **Subscription Rates:** 2,500¥. **Remarks:** Advertising accepted; rates available upon request. **URL:** http://www.keikyo.com/jema/.
Circ: Paid 1,200

📖 **878 Japan Insurance News**
Insurance Research Institute Ltd.
17-3 Hon-Machi 1-chome
Shibuya-ku
Tokyo 151-0071, Japan   Ph: 81 333763331

Journal of insurance. **Founded:** 1974. **Freq:** Bimonthly. **Key Personnel:** Toshiaki Shirai, Editor. **ISSN:** 0910-4534. **Subscription Rates:** US$92. **Remarks:** Advertising accepted; rates available upon request.
Circ: Paid 2,000

📖 **879 Japan International Journal**
Business World Corp
2-8-6 Shirokanedai
Minato-ku
Tokyo 108-0071, Japan   Ph: 81 334420211

General interest magazine covering business, politics, culture and lifestyles. **Founded:** 1991. **Freq:** Monthly. **Key Personnel:** Hiro Miyata, Editor. **Subscription Rates:** 7,000¥. **Remarks:** Advertising accepted; rates available upon request.
Circ: (Not Reported)

📖 **880 Japan Journal of Industrial and Applied Mathematics**
Kinokuniya Shoten - Kinokuniya Co. Ltd.
Dept. of Information and System
  Engineering
Faculty of Science and Engineering, Chuo
  University
1-13-27 Kasuga   Ph: 81 338171690
Bunkyo-ku
Tokyo 112-8551, Japan   Fax: 81 338171681

Mathematics journal. **Founded:** 1984. **Freq:** 3/year. **Key Personnel:** Iri Masao, Editor-in-Chief, iri@ise.chuo-u.ac.jp. **ISSN:** 0916-7005. **Subscription Rates:** US$344. **URL:** http://wwwsoc.nii.ac.jp/jsiam/HTMLs/JJIAMintro.html.

📖 **881 Japan Law Journal**
Survey Japan
Ste. 603 Ichigaya-Mitsuke Heim
Ichigaya-Hachimancho 16
Shinjuku-ku   Ph: 81 332353421
Tokyo 162, Japan   Fax: 81 332353422

Journal of law. **Subtitle:** A Bimonthly on Legal Affairs in Japan and Abr. **Founded:** 1987. **Freq:** Bimonthly. **Key Personnel:** Kuni Sadamoto, Editor. **ISSN:** 1340-5349. **Subscription Rates:** 16,000¥.

---

882   Japan Marketing Data
Intercontinental Marketing Corp.
IPO Box 5056
Tokyo 100-3191, Japan
Ph: 81 336617458
Fax: 81 336679646

Journal covering economics. **Freq:** Annual. **Subscription Rates:** US$63.

883   Japan Mission Journal
Oriens Institute for Religious Research
2-28-5 Matsubara
Setagaya-ku
Tokyo 156-0043, Japan
Ph: 81 333227601

Periodical covering all aspects of evangelization and enculturation of Christianity in Japan. **Founded:** 1947. **Freq:** Quarterly. **Key Personnel:** M. Matata, Editor. **ISSN:** 1344-7297. **Subscription Rates:** 4,200¥. **Remarks:** Advertising accepted; rates available upon request. **URL:** http://www.oriens.or.jp/jmjback.htm.
Circ: Paid 1,000

884   Japan Quarterly
Asahi Shimbun
5-3-2 Tsukiji
Chuou-ku
Tokyo 104-8011, Japan
Ph: 81 355418785
Fax: 81 355653286
Publication E-mail: sekiguchi@dp.itochu.co.jp
Publisher E-mail: asacame@cg.pub.asahi-np.co.jp

Periodical featuring analysis of political and economic issues in Japan and on external developments which impact on Japan. **Founded:** 1954. **Freq:** Quarterly. **Key Personnel:** Yuji Oishi, Editor. **ISSN:** 0021-4590. **Subscription Rates:** US$58. **Available Online. URL:** http://www.c3.crc.co.jp/HomePage/reseach/JQ/index.html.
Ad Rates: BW: 400,000¥
4C: 800,000¥
Circ: Paid 11,000

885   Japan Times
The Japan Times Ltd.
4-5-4 Shibaura
Minato-ku
Tokyo 108-0023, Japan
Ph: 81 334535312
Publication E-mail: web@japantimes.co.jp

Newspaper covering world and domestic news, business and politics. **Founded:** 1897. **Freq:** Daily. **ISSN:** 0289-1956. **Subscription Rates:** 3,900¥ per month. **Remarks:** Advertising accepted; rates available upon request. **URL:** http://www.japantimes.co.jp/.
Circ: (Not Reported)

886   Japan Today
International Society for Educational Information
3-16-1 Minami Aoyama
Minato-ku
Tokyo 107-0062, Japan
Ph: 81 33479351
Fax: 81 334793352
Publication E-mail: kaya@isei.or.jp

Online general newspaper. **Freq:** Daily. **Key Personnel:** Chris Betros, Editor, editor@japantoday.com. **Subscription Rates:** 2,500¥ single issue. **URL:** http://www.japantoday.com/e/?content=home. **Alt. Formats:** CD-ROM.

887   Japanese Economy & Labor Series
Japan Institute of Labour
Shinjuku Monolith
PO Box 7040
Tokyo 163-0926, Japan
Ph: 81 359915165

Journal of labor and industrial relations. **Founded:** 1966. **Key Personnel:** Akira Takanashi, Editor.

888   Japanese Heart Journal
Nankodo Co Ltd.
Dept. of Cardiovascular Medicine
Graduate School of Medicine, University of Tokyo
Hongo 7-3-1
Bunkyo-ku
Tokyo 113-8655, Japan
Ph: 81 358006797
Fax: 81 338152087
Publication E-mail: jhj-adm@umin.ac.jp

Medical science journal. **Founded:** 1960. **Freq:** Bimonthly. **Key Personnel:** Ryozo Nagai, Editor-in-Chief. **ISSN:** 0021-4868. **Remarks:** Advertising accepted; rates available upon request. **URL:** http://square.umin.ac.jp/jhj/index.htm.
Circ: Paid 1,000

889   Japanese Journal of Applied Physics
Japan Society of Applied Physics
Daini Toyokaiji Bldg.
4-24-8 Shinbashi
Minato-ku
Tokyo 105-0004, Japan

Physics journal. **Founded:** 1962. **Freq:** Monthly. **Key Personnel:** Atsushi Koma, Editor. **ISSN:** 0021-4922.
Circ: 3,900

890   Japanese Journal of Bacteriology
Business Center for Academic Societies Japan
5-16-9 Honkomagome
Bunkyo-ku
Tokyo 113-0021, Japan
Ph: 81 358145811

Journal covering communicable diseases. **Founded:** 1944. **Freq:** Quarterly. **ISSN:** 0021-4930. **Subscription Rates:** 18,540¥. **Remarks:** Advertising accepted; rates available upon request.
Circ: Paid 3,700

891   Japanese Journal of Biofeedback Research
Society of Japanese Biofeedback Research
Jochi Daigaku Bungakubu Shinrigaku
Kenkyushitsu
7 Kioi-cho
Chiyoda-ku
Tokyo 102-0094, Japan

Journal of psychology. **Founded:** 1973. **Freq:** Annual. **ISSN:** 0386-1856. **Subscription Rates:** 1,000¥.

892   Japanese Journal of Biometeorology
IPEC Inc.
1-2-3 Sugamo
Toshima-ku
Tokyo 170-0002, Japan
Ph: 81 359784067

Journal of meteorology. **Founded:** 1966. **Freq:** Quarterly. **Key Personnel:** Yutaka Inaba, Editor. **ISSN:** 0389-1313. **Subscription Rates:** 5,000¥. **Remarks:** Advertising accepted; rates available upon request.
Circ: Paid 600

893   Japanese Journal of Biometrics
Biometric Society of Japan
c/o Statistical Information Institute for
Consulting and Ana
Daiwa Bldg. 2F
6-3-9 Minami-Aoyama
Minato-ku
Tokyo 107-0062, Japan
Ph: 81 354670481
Publication E-mail: biometrics@sinfonica.or.jp

Journal covering biology. **Founded:** 1980. **Freq:** Semiannual. **Key Personnel:** T. Sato, Editor-in-Chief. **ISSN:** 0918-4430. **Subscription Rates:** 10,000¥. **Remarks:** Advertising accepted; rates available upon request. **URL:** http://wwwsoc.nii.ac.jp/jbs/index_e.html.
Circ: (Not Reported)

894   Japanese Journal of Breast Cancer
Japanese Breast Cancer Society
c/o Cancer Institute Hospital
1-37-1, Kami-Ikebukuro
Toshima-ku
Tokyo 170-8455, Japan
Publication E-mail: t-mikami@kk-kyowa.ac.jp

Medical science journal. **Founded:** 1994. **Freq:** Quarterly. **Key Personnel:** Masakuni Noguchi, Editor-in-Chief. **ISSN:** 1340-6868. **URL:** http://www.jbcs.gr.jp/breast/top.html.

895 Japanese Journal of Chemotherapy
Japan Society of Chemotherapy
2-20-8 Kami-Osaki
Shinagawa-ku
Tokyo 141-0021, Japan   Ph: 81 334937129

Pharmacy journal. **Founded:** 1953. **Freq:** Monthly. **Key Personnel:** Kohya Shiba, Editor. **ISSN:** 1340-7007. **Subscription Rates:** 9,000¥. **Remarks:** Advertising accepted; rates available upon request.
                                         Circ: Paid 4,000

896 Japanese Journal of Health and Human Ecology
Kyorin Shoin
4-2-1 Yushima
Bunkyo-ku
Tokyo 113-0034, Japan   Ph: 81 38114887

Journal covering biology. **Founded:** 1935. **Freq:** Bimonthly. **Key Personnel:** M. Uematsu, Editor. **ISSN:** 0368-9395. **Subscription Rates:** 17,000¥. **Remarks:** Advertising accepted; rates available upon request.
                                         Circ: (Not Reported)

897 Japanese Journal of Hygiene
Japanese Society for Hygiene
c/o Dept. of Hygiene and Preventive
  Medicine
Faculty of Medicine
7-3-1 Hongo
Bunkyo-ku
Tokyo 113-0033, Japan

Journal of hygiene. **Founded:** 1946. **Freq:** Bimonthly. **Key Personnel:** K. Morimoto, Editor. **ISSN:** 0021-5082. **Subscription Rates:** 4,500¥. **Remarks:** Advertising accepted; rates available upon request.
                                         Circ: Paid 2,700

898 Japanese Journal of Infectious Diseases
National Institute of Infectious Diseases
23-1, Toyama 1-chome
Shinjuku-ku
Tokyo 162-8640, Japan   Ph: 81 352851111

Medical science journal. **Founded:** 1948. **Freq:** Bimonthly. **Key Personnel:** Yoshifumi Takeda, Editor. **ISSN:** 1344-6304.
                                         Circ: 1,100

899 Japanese Journal of Limnology
Japanese Society of Limnology
c/o Business Center for Academic Societies
  Japan
Honkomagome 5-16-9
Bunkyo-ku
Tokyo 113-8622, Japan   Ph: 81 358145810

Journal covering the scientific study of bodies of water. **Founded:** 1931. **Freq:** 3/year. **Key Personnel:** T. Nagata, Editor-in-Chief. **ISSN:** 0021-5104. **Subscription Rates:** 10,000¥.
                                         Circ: Paid 1,200

900 Japanese Journal of Lymphology
Japanese Society of Lymphology
Ika Daigaku Dai 1 Kaibogaku Kyoshitsu
1-1 Shinjuku 6-chome
Shinjuku-ku
Tokyo 160-0022, Japan

Medical science journal. **Founded:** 1978. **Freq:** Semiannual. **ISSN:** 0910-4186. **Subscription Rates:** 6,000¥.

901 Japanese Journal of Mathematics
Mathematical Society of Japan
C/o Kinokuniya Company Ltd
13-11, Higashi 3-chome
Shibuya-ku
Tokyo 150-8513, Japan

Mathematics journal. **Founded:** 1924. **Freq:** Semiannual. **Key Personnel:** Shigeo Kusuoka, Editor. **ISSN:** 0289-2316. **Subscription Rates:** US$239. **URL:** http://wwwsoc.nii.ac.jp/msj6/jjm/jjm-index.html.

902 Japanese Journal of Medical Mycology
Business Center for Academic Societies Japan
5-16-9 Honkomagome
Bunkyo-ku
Tokyo 113-0021, Japan   Ph: 81 358145811

Journal of microbiology. **Founded:** 1960. **Freq:** Quarterly. **ISSN:** 0916-4804. **Subscription Rates:** 10,300¥. **Remarks:** Advertising accepted; rates available upon request.
                                         Circ: Paid 1,000

903 Japanese Journal of Optics
Japan Society of Applied Physics
Daini Toyokaiji Bldg.
4-24-8 Shinbashi
Minato-ku
Tokyo 105-0004, Japan

Physics journal. **Founded:** 1972. **Freq:** Monthly. **ISSN:** 0389-6625. **Subscription Rates:** 800¥ single issue.

904 Japanese Journal of Ornithology
Ornithological Society of Japan
c/o Dept. of Zoology
National Science Museum
3-23-1 Hiyakunin-cho
Shinjuku-ku
Tokyo 169-0073, Japan   Ph: 81 333642311

Journal covering biology. **Founded:** 1915. **Freq:** Quarterly. **Key Personnel:** Hiroyuki Morioka, Editor. **ISSN:** 0913-400X. **Subscription Rates:** 6,000¥. **Remarks:** Advertising accepted; rates available upon request. **URL:** http://wwwsoc.nii.ac.jp/osj/english/home_e.html.
                                         Circ: Paid 900

905 Japanese Journal of Physical Fitness
Japanese Society of Physical Fitness and Sports Medicine
Business Center for Academic Societies
  Japan
5-16-9 Honkomagome
Bunkyo-ku
Tokyo 113-0021, Japan   Ph: 81 358145811

Journal covering physical fitness. **Founded:** 1950. **Freq:** Bimonthly. **Key Personnel:** Masahisa Usami, Editor. **ISSN:** 0039-906X. **Subscription Rates:** 12,000¥. **Remarks:** Advertising accepted; rates available upon request.
                                         Circ: Paid 4800

906 Japanese Journal of Physiology
Center for Academic Publications Japan
2-4-16 Yayoi
Bunkyo-ku
Tokyo 113-0032, Japan   Ph: 81 338175821
Publication E-mail: jjp-ed@capj.or.jp

Journal of physiology. **Founded:** 1951. **Freq:** Bimonthly. **Key Personnel:** Akinori Noma, Editor-in-Chief. **ISSN:** 0021-521X. **Subscription Rates:** US$160. **URL:** http://wwwsoc.nii.ac.jp/psj/jjp/jjphome.html.
                                         Circ: Paid 1,600

907 Japanese Journal of Sanitary Zoology
Japan Society of Sanitary Zoology
Business Center for Academic Societies
 Japan
5-16-9 Honkomagome
Bunkyo-ku
Tokyo 113-0021, Japan   Ph: 81 358145811

Journal of zoology. **Founded:** 1950. **Freq:** Quarterly. **ISSN:** 0424-7086. **Subscription Rates:** 10,300¥.
          Circ: Paid 1,000

908 Japanese Journal of Toxicology
Yakugyo Jiho Co. Ltd.
2-36 Kanda-Jinbo-cho
Chiyoda-ku
Tokyo 101-0051, Japan   Ph: 81 032657751

Journal of toxicology. **Founded:** 1988. **Freq:** Quarterly. **ISSN:** 0914-3777. **Subscription Rates:** 1,500¥ single issue.

909 Japanese Progress in Climatology
Japanese Climatological Seminar
Hosei Daigaku Bungakubu Chirigaku
 Kyoshitsu
17-1 Fujimi 2-chome
Chiyoda-ku
Tokyo 102-0071, Japan   Ph: 81 332649457

Journal of meteorology. **Founded:** 1964. **Freq:** Annual. **Key Personnel:** Norihito Satou, Editor. **ISSN:** 0075-3467. **Subscription Rates:** US$20.
          Circ: Controlled 1,050

910 Japan's Iron and Steel Industry
Kawata Publicity, Inc.
605, Otowa House
3-1-2, Otsuka
Bunkyo-ku   Ph: 81 339453878
Tokyo 112-0012, Japan   Fax: 81 339454870

Periodical covering the Japanese steel industry. **Founded:** 1951. **Freq:** Annual. **Key Personnel:** Sukeyuki Kawata, Editor. **ISSN:** 0075-3475. **Subscription Rates:** 4,000¥; US$40 other countries.
          Circ: Paid 3,000

911 JEOL News: Analytical Instrumentation
Japan Electron Optics Laboratory News
1-2 Musashino 3-chome
Akishima-shi
Tokyo 196-0021, Japan   Ph: 81 425422161

Journal of experimental medicine. **Founded:** 1963. **Freq:** Annual. **Key Personnel:** Shunichi Enomoto, Editor. **ISSN:** 0385-4418.
          Circ: 12,000

912 JEOL News: Electron Optics Instrumentation
JEOL Ltd.
1-2 Musashino 3-chome
Akishima-shi
Tokyo 196-0021, Japan   Ph: 81 425422161

Journal of experimental medicine. **Founded:** 1963. **Freq:** Semiannual. **Key Personnel:** Shunichi Enomoto, Editor. **ISSN:** 0385-4426.
          Circ: 18,000

913 Jikeikai Medical Journal
Jikei University School of Medicine
3-25-8 Nishi-Shinbashi
Minato-ku
Tokyo 105-0003, Japan

Medical science journal. **Founded:** 1954. **Freq:** Quarterly. **Key Personnel:** Tsuneya Ohno, Editor. **ISSN:** 0021-6968.
          Circ: 1,000

914 JJAP Series
Japan Society of Applied Physics
Daini Toyokaiji Bldg.
4-24-8 Shinbashi
Minato-ku
Tokyo 105-0004, Japan

Physics journal. **Founded:** 1988. **Freq:** Annual. **Key Personnel:** Atsushi Koma, Editor. **ISSN:** 0914-9090.

915 Journal of the Acoustical Society of Japan
Japan Audio-Visual Education Association
1-17-1 Toranomon
Minato-ku
Tokyo 105-0001, Japan

Journal covering education. **Founded:** 1963. **Freq:** Annual. **Key Personnel:** Morio Okabe, Editor. **ISSN:** 0065-0102. **Subscription Rates:** 1200¥. **URL:** http://ast.jstage.jst.go.jp/en/.
          Circ: Paid 2,000

916 Journal of Advanced Computational Intelligence
Fuji Technology Press Ltd.
Toranomon Sangyo Bldg.
1-2-29 Toranomon
Minato-ku
Tokyo 105-0001, Japan   Ph: 81 335080051

Journal of computers. **Freq:** Bimonthly. **Key Personnel:** Toshio Fukuda, Editor-in-Chief, phone 81 527894478, fax 81 527893909, fukuda@mein.nagoya-u.ac.jp. **ISSN:** 1343-0130. **Subscription Rates:** 66,000¥. **URL:** http://www.abo.fi/~rfuller/jaci.html.

917 Journal of Agricultural Meteorology
Society of Agricultural Meteorology of Japan
Dept. of Agricultural Engineering
Yayoi, Bunkyo-ku
Tokyo 113-0032, Japan

Journal of meteorology. **Founded:** 1943. **Freq:** Quarterly. **Key Personnel:** Taichi Maki, Editor. **ISSN:** 0021-8588. **Subscription Rates:** 2,060¥ single issue. **Remarks:** Advertising accepted; rates available upon request.
          Circ: Paid 1,100

918 Journal of American and Canadian Studies
Sophia University
7-1 Kioi-cho
Chiyoda-ku
Tokyo 102-8554, Japan   Ph: 81 332383908

Humanities journal. **Founded:** 1988. **Freq:** Annual. **Key Personnel:** Kazuyuki Matsuo, Editor. **ISSN:** 0914-8035. **Subscription Rates:** 1,000¥.
          Circ: Paid 2,000

919 Journal of Anesthesia
Springer-Verlag Tokyo
3-13 Hongo 3-chome
Bunkyo-ku
Tokyo 113-0033, Japan   Ph: 81 338120617
Publication E-mail: orders@svt-ebs.co.jp

Publishes original articles, review articles, special articles, clinical reports, short communications, letters to the editor and book and multimedia reviews. **Founded:** 1987. **Freq:** Quarterly. **Key Personnel:** Hidenori Toyooka, Editor-in-Chief. **ISSN:** 0913-8668. **Subscription Rates:** 20,000¥. **URL:** http://link.springer.de/link/service/journals/00540/.

920 Journal of Antibiotics
Japan Antibiotics Research Association
2-20-8 Kami-Osaki
Shinagawa-ku
Tokyo 141-0021, Japan   Ph: 81 334910181
Publication E-mail: journal@antibiotics.or.jp

Pharmacy journal. **Subtitle:** An International Journal Devoted to Research. **Founded:** 1947. **Freq:** Monthly. **Key Personnel:** M. Yagisawa, Managing Editor. **ISSN:** 0021-8820. **Subscription Rates:** US$300. **Remarks:** Advertising accepted; rates available upon request. **URL:** http://www.antibiotics.or.jp/

Circ: Paid 2,000

📖 **921 Journal of Architecture, Planning and Environmental Engineering**
Architectural Institute of Japan
26-20 Shiba 5-chome
Minato-ku
Tokyo 108-0014, Japan   Ph: 81 334562051

Journal covering architecture. **Founded:** 1936. **Freq:** Monthly. **ISSN:** 1340-4210. **Subscription Rates:** 33,600¥.

📖 **922 Journal of Artificial Organs**
Springer-Verlag Tokyo
3-13 Hongo 3-chome
Bunkyo-ku
Tokyo 113-0033, Japan   Ph: 81 338120617
Publication E-mail: orders@svt-ebs.co.jp

Medical science journal. **Founded:** 1998. **Freq:** Quarterly. **Key Personnel:** Hikaru Matsuda, Editor-in-Chief. **ISSN:** 1434-7229. **Subscription Rates:** 18,000¥. **URL:** http://link.springer-ny.com/link/service/journals/10047/.

📖 **923 Journal of Atherosclerosis and Thrombosis**
Japan Atherosclerosis Society
c/o MDS Co. Ltd
Gotanda First Bldg. 9F
2-8-1, Nishigotanda
Shinagawaku
Tokyo 141-0031, Japan   Ph: 81 354362970

Medical science journal. **Founded:** 1994. **Freq:** Quarterly. **Key Personnel:** Yoshiya Hata, Editor. **ISSN:** 1340-3478. **Subscription Rates:** 12,000¥. **URL:** http://jas.umin.ac.jp/en/index.html.

📖 **924 Journal of Biochemistry**
Japanese Biochemical Society
2nd Fl., Hongo-Tsuna Bldg
17-9 Hongo 6-chome
Bunkyo-ku
Tokyo 113-0033, Japan   Ph: 81 338151913
Publication E-mail: jbt@bcasj.or.jp

Publication devoted to publication of original papers in the fields of biochemistry, molecular biology, cell, and biotechnology. **Founded:** 1922. **Freq:** Monthly. **Key Personnel:** Tairo Oshima, Editor-in-Chief. **ISSN:** 0021-924X. **Subscription Rates:** US$250. **Remarks:** Advertising accepted; rates available upon request. **URL:** http://jb.bcasj.or.jp/.

Circ: Paid 2,650

📖 **925 Journal of Bone and Mineral Metabolism**
Springer-Verlag Tokyo
3-13 Hongo 3-chome
Bunkyo-ku
Tokyo 113-0033, Japan   Ph: 81 338120617
Publication E-mail: orders@svt-ebs.co.jp

Periodical aimed at providing an international forum for researchers and clinicians to present and discuss relevant issues in bone and mineral research. **Founded:** 1988. **Freq:** Bimonthly. **Key Personnel:** Fujio Suzuki, Editor-in-Chief. **ISSN:** 0914-8779. **Subscription Rates:** 22,000¥. **URL:** http://link.springer.de/link/service/journals/00774/.

Circ: Paid 2,500

📖 **926 Journal of the Ceramic Society of Japan**
Fuji Technology Press Ltd.
The Ceramic Society of Japan
22-17, Hyakunin-cho 2-chome
Shinjuku-ku
Tokyo 169-0073, Japan   Ph: 81 333625231

Journal of ceramics. **Founded:** 1987. **Freq:** Monthly. **Key Personnel:** Keiji

Hayashi, Editor. **ISSN:** 0914-5400. **Subscription Rates:** 200,000¥. **URL:** http://www.ceramic.or.jp/ihensyuj/journal.html.

Circ: Paid 6,000

📖 **927 Journal of Chemical Engineering of Japan**
Society of Chemical Engineers Japan
Kyoritsu Bldg.
4-6-19 Kohinata
Bunkyo-ku
Tokyo 112-0006, Japan   Ph: 81 339433529
Publication E-mail: journal@scej.org

Publishes original research in fields of chemical engineering ranging from fundamental principles to practical applications. **Founded:** 1968. **Freq:** Bimonthly. **Key Personnel:** Takeshi Fujie, Editor. **ISSN:** 0021-9592. **Subscription Rates:** US$85. **URL:** http://www.scej.org/.

📖 **928 Journal of Clinical and Experimental Medicine**
Ishiyaku Publishers, Inc
7-10 Honkomagome 1-chome
Bunkyo-ku
Tokyo 113-0021, Japan   Ph: 81 353957600

Medical science journal. **Founded:** 1946. **Freq:** Weekly. **Key Personnel:** Hiroshi Miura, Editor. **ISSN:** 0039-2359. **Subscription Rates:** 61,600¥. **Remarks:** Advertising accepted; rates available upon request. **URL:** http://www.ishiyaku.co.jp/ourco/aboutus.html.

Circ: Paid 8,800

📖 **929 Journal of Dermatology**
Japanese Dermatological Association
Taisei Bldg.
14-10 Hongo 3-chome
Bunkyo-ku
Tokyo 113-0033, Japan   Ph: 81 338115099

Journal of dermatology. **Founded:** 1974. **Freq:** Monthly. **Key Personnel:** Shinji Shimada, Editor-in-Chief. **ISSN:** 0385-2407. **Subscription Rates:** 10,000¥. **URL:** http://www.dermatol.or.jp/.

📖 **930 Journal of Development Assistance**
Overseas Economic Cooperation Fund
Takebashi Godo Bldg.
4-1 Ote-Machi 1-chome
Chiyoda-ku
Tokyo 100-0004, Japan

Discusses major development issues and the results of recent research. **Founded:** 1995. **Freq:** Semiannual. **ISSN:** 1341-3953.

📖 **931 Journal of Ethology**
Springer-Verlag Tokyo
3-13 Hongo 3-chome
Bunkyo-ku
Tokyo 113-0033, Japan   Ph: 81 338120617
Publication E-mail: orders@svt-ebs.co.jp

Periodical featuring reviews and original papers relating to all aspects of animal behavior, including traditional ethology. **Founded:** 1983. **Freq:** Semiannual. **Key Personnel:** Kazuki Tsuji, Editor-in-Chief. **ISSN:** 0289-0771. **Subscription Rates:** 16,000¥. **URL:** http://link.springer.de/link/service/journals/10164/.

📖 **932 Journal of Fertilization and Implantation**
Japan Society of Fertilization and Implantation
c/o Convex Inc.
Ichijoji Bldg
2-3-22 Azabudai
Minato-ku
Tokyo 106-0041, Japan   Ph: 81 335893460

Medical science journal. **Founded:** 1984. **Freq:** Annual. **Key Personnel:** Masahiko Hiroi, Editor. **ISSN:** 0914-6776. **Subscription Rates:** 6,000¥.

Circ: Paid 1,400

933 Journal of Food Hygienic Society of Japan
Food Hygienic Society of Japan
2-6-1 Jingu-Mae
Shibuya-ku
Tokyo 150-0001, Japan

Journal covering public health and safety. **Founded:** 1960. **Freq:** Bimonthly. **ISSN:** 0015-6426. **Remarks:** Advertising accepted; rates available upon request.

                                   Circ: (Not Reported)

934 Journal of Gastroenterology
Springer-Verlag Tokyo
3-13 Hongo 3-chome
Bunkyo-ku
Tokyo 113-0033, Japan   Ph: 81 338120617
Publication E-mail: helpdesk@link.springer.de

Medical science journal. **Founded:** 1966. **Freq:** Monthly. **Key Personnel:** Tsutomu Chiba, Editor-in-Chief. **ISSN:** 0944-1174. **Subscription Rates:** 40,000¥. **Remarks:** Advertising accepted; rates available upon request. **URL:** http://link.springer-ny.com/link/service/journals/00535/.

                                   Circ: Paid 4,500

935 The Journal of General and Applied Microbiology
Microbiology Research Foundation
Japan Academic Societies Center Bldg.
4-16 Yayoi 2-chome
Bunkyo-ku
Tokyo 113-0032, Japan   Ph: 81 338175821
Publication E-mail: naka-atsu@muj.biglobe.ne.jp

Publishes original papers pertaining to general and applied microbiology. **Founded:** 1955. **Freq:** Bimonthly. **Key Personnel:** Akira Yukota, Chief Managing Editor. **ISSN:** 0022-1260. **Subscription Rates:** 8,000¥. **URL:** http://www.iam.u-tokyo.ac.jp/JGAM/general.htm.

                                   Circ: Paid 680

936 Journal of Geological Society of Japan
Geological Society of Japan
10-4 Kaji-cho 1-chome
Chiyoda-ku
Tokyo 101-0044, Japan

Earth sciences journal. **Founded:** 1893. **Freq:** Monthly. **Key Personnel:** Yasumoto Suzuki, Editor. **ISSN:** 0016-7630. **Subscription Rates:** 12,000¥. **Remarks:** Advertising accepted; rates available upon request.
                                   Circ: Paid 5,500

937 Journal of Groundwater Hydrology
Japanese Association of Groundwater Hydrology
c/o Dept. of Earth Sciences Faculty of
  Science
3-8-6 Nihonbashi
Cyuo-ku
Tokyo 103-0027, Japan   Ph: 81 332739654

Journal of hydrology. **Founded:** 1959. **Freq:** Quarterly. **Key Personnel:** Norio Tase, Editor. **ISSN:** 0913-4182. **Subscription Rates:** 7,000¥. **Remarks:** Advertising accepted; rates available upon request.
                                 Circ: (Not Reported)

938 Journal of Health Science
Pharmaceutical Society of Japan
2-12-15 Shibuya 2-chome
Shibuya-ku
Tokyo 150-0002, Japan   Ph: 81 334063321

Journal of health science. **Founded:** 1953. **Freq:** Bimonthly. **Key Personnel:** Manabu Kunimoto, Editor-in-Chief. **ISSN:** 1344-9702. **Subscription Rates:** 9,600¥ institutions; 1,000¥ student members. **Remarks:** Advertising accepted; rates available upon request. **URL:** http://jhs.pharm.or.jp/home.htm.
                                 Circ: Controlled 1,700

939 Journal of Hepato-Biliary-Pancreatic Surgery
Springer-Verlag Tokyo
3-13 Hongo 3-chome
Bunkyo-ku
Tokyo 113-0033, Japan   Ph: 81 338120617
Publication E-mail: orders@svt-ebs.co.jp

Publishes original articles in the English language dealing with clinical investigations of and basic research on all aspects of the field of hepatic, biliary, and pancreatic surgery. **Founded:** 1993. **Freq:** Bimonthly. **Key Personnel:** Tadahiro Takada, Editor-in-Chief. **ISSN:** 0944-1166. **Subscription Rates:** 24,000¥. **URL:** http://link.springer-ny.com/link/service/journals/00534/.

940 Journal of Home Economics of Japan
Japan Society of Home Economics
No 502 Gakuendai - Haitsu
502-2-1-15 Otsuka
Bunkyo-ku
Tokyo 112-0012, Japan   Ph: 81 0339472627

Journal of home economics. **Founded:** 1950. **Freq:** Monthly. **ISSN:** 0913-5227. **Subscription Rates:** 12,000¥. **URL:** http://wwwsoc.nii.ac.jp/jshe/E-home.html.
                                 Circ: Paid 5,350

941 Journal of Human Ergology
Center for Academic Publications Japan
2-4-16 Yayoi
Bunkyo-ku
Tokyo 113-0032, Japan   Ph: 81 338175821

Medical science journal. **Founded:** 1972. **Freq:** Semiannual. **ISSN:** 0300-8134. **Subscription Rates:** US$74. **Remarks:** Advertising accepted; rates available upon request.
                                 Circ: Paid 500

942 Journal of Human Genetics
Springer-Verlag Tokyo
3-13 Hongo 3-chome
Bunkyo-ku
Tokyo 113-0033, Japan   Ph: 81 338120617
Publication E-mail: orders@svt-ebs.co.jp

Journal featuring articles on human genetics, including medical genetics and human genome analysis. **Founded:** 1956. **Freq:** Monthly. **Key Personnel:** Yusuke Nakamura, Editor, yusuke@ims.u-tokyo.ac.jp. **ISSN:** 1434-5161. **Subscription Rates:** 35,000¥. **Remarks:** Advertising accepted; rates available upon request. **URL:** http://link.springer.de/link/service/journals/10038/.
                                 Circ: Paid 1,200

943 Journal of Humanities and Natural Sciences
Tokyo Keizai University
34-7 Minami-cho 1-chome
Kokubunji-shi
Tokyo 185-0021, Japan

Humanities journal. **Founded:** 1962. **Freq:** 3/year. **ISSN:** 0495-8012.
                                 Circ: 2,200

944 Journal of Hydroscience and Hydraulic Engineering
Japan Society of Civil Engineers
Yotsuya 1-chome
Shinjuku-ku
Tokyo 160-0004, Japan

Journal of hydraulic engineering. **Founded:** 1983. **Freq:** Semiannual. **ISSN:** 0912-2508. **Subscription Rates:** 3,000¥ single issue.

945 Journal of Infection and Chemotherapy
Springer-Verlag Tokyo
3-13 Hongo 3-chome
Bunkyo-ku
Tokyo 113-0033, Japan   Ph: 81 338120617
Publication E-mail: orders@svt-ebs.co.jp

Pharmacy journal. **Founded:** 1995. **Freq:** Quarterly. **Key Personnel:** Kyoichi

Totsuka, Editor-in-Chief. **ISSN:** 1341-321X. **Subscription Rates:** 18,000¥. **URL:** http://link.springer-ny.com/link/service/journals/10156/.

Circ: Paid 1,500

946 Journal of Institute for the Comprehensive Study of Lotus Sutra
Rissho University Institute for the Comprehensive Study of Lotus Sutra
4-2-16 Osaki
Shinagawa-ku
Tokyo 141-0032, Japan   Ph: 81 354873253

Journal covering Buddhism. **Founded:** 1975. **Freq:** Annual. **Key Personnel:** Kokeu Sasaki, Editor. **ISSN:** 0287-1513.

947 Journal of Institute of Electrostatics
Institute of Electrostatics Japan
c/o Sharum 80 4F
1-3, Hongo 4-chome
Bunkyo-ku
Tokyo 113-0033, Japan   Ph: 81 338154171

Physics journal. **Founded:** 1977. **Freq:** Bimonthly. **ISSN:** 0386-2550.

948 Journal of International Studies
Sophia University Institute of International Relations
7-1 Kioi-cho
Chiyoda-ku
Tokyo 102-0094, Japan   Ph: 81 332383561

Political science journal. **Founded:** 1978. **Freq:** Semiannual. **Key Personnel:** David Wessels, Editor. **ISSN:** 0910-5476. **Subscription Rates:** 1,530¥ single issue.

Circ: Paid 500

949 Journal of Ion Exchange
Japan Association of Ion Exchange
Kogyo Daigaku Rigakubu Kagakka Abe
  Kenkyushitsu
12-1 Okayama 2-chome
Meguro-ku
Tokyo 152-0033, Japan

Journal covering chemistry. **Founded:** 1990. **Freq:** 3/year. **Key Personnel:** M. Igawa, Editor-in-Chief, phone 81 454815661, fax 81 454917915, igawam01@kanagawa-u.ac.jp. **ISSN:** 0915-860X. **URL:** http://www.jaie.gr.jp/JIE_E.html.

950 Journal of Japan Biomagnetism and Bioelectromagnetics Society
Nihon Seitai Jiki Gakkai
Daigaku Igakubu
Iyo Denshi Kenkyu Shisetsu
3-1 Hongo 7-chome
Bunkyo-ku
Tokyo 113-0033, Japan

Journal covering biophysics. **Founded:** 1988. **Freq:** Semiannual. **ISSN:** 0915-0374.

951 Journal of Japan Broncho-Esophagological Society
Japan Broncho-Esophagological Society
Hakuo Bldg.
2-3-10 Koraku
Bunkyo-ku
Tokyo 112-0004, Japan   Ph: 81 338183030

Medical science journal. **Founded:** 1950. **Freq:** Bimonthly. **Key Personnel:** Koshu Nagao, Editor. **ISSN:** 0029-0645. **Subscription Rates:** 12,000¥.
Ad Rates: BW: 60,000¥   **Circ:** Paid 3,700

952 Journal of Japan Institute of Navigation
Japan Institute of Navigation
c/o Tokyo University of Mercantile Marine
2-1-6 Ecchujima
Koto-ku
Tokyo 135-8533, Japan
Publication E-mail: navigation@nifty.com

Earth sciences journal. **Founded:** 1949. **Freq:** Semiannual. **Key Personnel:** H. Imazu, Editor. **ISSN:** 0388-7405. **Subscription Rates:** 3,000¥ single issue. **URL:** http://homepage2.nifty.com/navigation/english.html.

Circ: Paid 1,700

953 Journal of Japan Medical Society of Paraplegia
Nihon Parapurejia Igakkai
Keio Gijuku Daigaku Igakubu Seikei
Gekagaku Kyoshitsu
35 Shinano-Machi
Shinjuku-ku
Tokyo 160-0016, Japan

Medical science journal. **Founded:** 1988. **Freq:** Annual. **ISSN:** 0914-6822.

954 Journal of Japan Society of Aesthetic Surgery
Nippon Biyo Geka Gakkai
12-5 Shinbashi 1-chome
Minato-ku
Tokyo 105-0004, Japan   Ph: 81 335711270

Medical science journal. **Founded:** 1962. **Freq:** Quarterly. **Key Personnel:** Takashi Akamatsu, Editor. **ISSN:** 0387-9194. **Subscription Rates:** US$50. **Remarks:** Advertising accepted; rates available upon request.

Circ: Paid 750

955 Journal of Japan Society of Polymer Processing
Sigma Publishing Co., Ltd.
15-8-602 Sakuragaoka-cho
Shibuya-ku
Tokyo 150-0031, Japan   Ph: 81 334770336

Journal of plastics. **Founded:** 1989. **Freq:** Bimonthly. **Key Personnel:** Shinichi Izawa, Editor. **ISSN:** 0915-4027.

956 Journal of Japan Spine Research Society
Nihon Sekitsui Geka Gakkai
Keio Gijuku Daigaku Igakubu Seikei
Gekagaku Kyoshitsu
35 Shinano-Machi
Shinjuku-ku
Tokyo 160-0016, Japan

Medical science journal. **Founded:** 1990. **Freq:** Annual. **ISSN:** 0915-6496.

957 Journal of Japan Statistical Society
Japan Statistical Society
4-6-7 Minami-azabu
Minato-ku
Tokyo 106-8569, Japan   Ph: 81 0334425801

Journal of statistics. **Founded:** 1971. **Freq:** Semiannual. **Key Personnel:** Sadanori Konishi, Editor. **ISSN:** 0389-5602. **Subscription Rates:** 9,270¥; US$55 other countries. **Remarks:** Advertising accepted; rates available upon request. **URL:** http://www.jss.gr.jp.

Circ: Paid 1,500

958 Journal of Japan Welding Society
Japan Welding Society
1-11 Kanda-Sakuma-cho
Chiyoda-ku
Tokyo 101-0025, Japan   Ph: 81 332530488

Journal of metallurgy. **Founded:** 1926. **Freq:** Quarterly. **Key Personnel:** Masabumi Suzuki, Editor. **ISSN:** 0021-4787. **Subscription Rates:** 12,000¥. **Remarks:** Advertising accepted; rates available upon request.

Circ: (Not Reported)

959 Journal of Japanese Forestry Society
Japanese Forestry Society
c/o Japan Forest Technical Association
7 Roku-Ban-cho
Chiyoda-ku
Tokyo 102-0085, Japan   Ph: 81 332612766

Journal of forestry. **Founded:** 1918. **Freq:** Bimonthly. **Key Personnel:** Kazuo Suzuki, Editor. **ISSN:** 0021-485X. **Subscription Rates:** 8,000¥. **Remarks:** Advertising accepted; rates available upon request.
Circ: Paid 4,000

960 Journal of Japanese Society for Clinical Surgery
Nihon Rinsho Geka Igakkai
Eregansu Iidabashi 402
4-3 Iida-Bashi 3-chome
Chiyoda-ku
Tokyo 102-0072, Japan

Medical science journal. **Founded:** 1937. **Freq:** Monthly. **Key Personnel:** Junichi Ishii, Editor. **ISSN:** 0386-9776. **Subscription Rates:** 1,000¥ single issue.
Circ: Paid 16,000

961 Journal of Japanese Society of Computational Statistics
Japanese Society of Computational Statistics
c/o Statistical Information Institute for
   Consulting and Ana
Daiwa Bldg. 2F
6-3-9 Minami-Aoyama
Minato-ku
Tokyo 107-0062, Japan   Ph: 81 35676946
Publication E-mail: office@jscs.or.jp

Publishes scientific papers that address any aspect of the discipline of computational statistics. **Founded:** 1988. **Freq:** Annual. **Key Personnel:** Yoshimichi Ochi, Editor, phone 81 975547869, fax 81 975547886, ochi@csis.oita-u.ac.jp. **ISSN:** 0915-2350. **Subscription Rates:** 3,000¥. **URL:** http://www.jscs.or.jp/oubun/indexE.html.
Circ: Paid 400

962 Journal of Japanese Society of Dialysis Therapy
Japanese Society for Dialysis Therapy
Aramid Building 2F, 2-38-21 Hongo
Bunkyo-ku
Tokyo 113-0033, Japan
Publication E-mail: info@jsdt.or.jp

Publishes articles that are related to blood purification therapy. **Founded:** 1968. **Freq:** Monthly. **Subscription Rates:** 1,000¥ single issue. **URL:** http://www.jsdt.or.jp/index_e.html.

963 Journal of Japanese Society for Horticultural Science
Japanese Society for Horticultural Science
c/o Center for Academic Societies Japan
16-9 Honkomagome 5-chome
Bunkyo-ku
Tokyo 113-0021, Japan   Ph: 81 358145801

Journal of horticultural science. **Founded:** 1925. **Freq:** Quarterly. **Key Personnel:** Ken Ichi Arisumi, Editor. **ISSN:** 0013-7626. **Subscription Rates:** 7,000¥. **Remarks:** Advertising accepted; rates available upon request.
Circ: Paid 3,000

964 Journal of Japanese Trade and Industry
Maruzen Co. Ltd.
3-10 Nihombashi 2-chome
Chuo-ku
Tokyo 103-0027, Japan   Ph: 81 332727211

Journal covering economics. **Founded:** 1982. **Freq:** Bimonthly. **Key Personnel:** Yoshimichi Hori T. Iwasaki, Editor. **ISSN:** 0285-9556. **Subscription Rates:** 45¥. **Remarks:** Advertising accepted; rates available upon request.
Circ: Paid 35,000

965 Journal of Kagawa Nutrition College
Joshi Eiyo Daigaku
24-3 Komagome 3-chome
Toshima-ku
Tokyo 170-0003, Japan

Journal of nutrition. **Founded:** 1970. **Freq:** Annual. **Key Personnel:** Yoshiko Kagawa, Editor. **ISSN:** 0286-0511. **Remarks:** Advertising accepted; rates available upon request.
Circ: 900

966 Journal of Magnetics Society of Japan
Magnetics Society of Japan
Mitsui Sumitomo Kaijo
Surugadai Bldg. 6F
3-11 Kanda Surugadai
Chiyoda-ku
Tokyo 101-0062, Japan   Ph: 81 332721761

Physics journal. **Founded:** 1977. **Freq:** 5/year. **ISSN:** 0285-0192. **Subscription Rates:** 2,000¥ single issue. **URL:** http://wwwsoc.nii.ac.jp/msj2/english/index.html.

967 Journal of Marine Science and Technology
Springer-Verlag Tokyo
3-13 Hongo 3-chome
Bunkyo-ku
Tokyo 113-0033, Japan   Ph: 81 338120617
Publication E-mail: orders@svt-ebs.co.jp

Periodical aimed at providing a forum for the discussion of current issues in marine science and technology by publishing original, full-length, refereed contributions on research and/or developments in this field. **Founded:** 1996. **Freq:** Quarterly. **Key Personnel:** Hideaki Miyata, Editor-in-Chief. **ISSN:** 0948-4280. **Subscription Rates:** 16,000¥. **URL:** http://link.springer.de/link/service/journals/00773/.

968 Journal of Mathematical Sciences
University of Tokyo
Dept. of Mathematical Sciences
3-1, Hongo 7-chome
Bunkyo-ku
Tokyo, Japan   Ph: 81 0338161303

Mathematics journal. **Founded:** 1925. **Freq:** 3/year. **Key Personnel:** Yukio Matsumoto, Editor. **ISSN:** 1340-5705.
Circ: Paid 850

969 Journal of Medical and Dental Sciences
Tokyo Medical and Dental University
1-5-45 Yushima
Bunkyo-ku
Tokyo 113-0034, Japan

Medical science journal. **Founded:** 1954. **Freq:** Quarterly. **Key Personnel:** Sunao Nomoto, Editor. **ISSN:** 1342-8810.
Circ: 1,000

970 Journal of Meteorological Society of Japan
Meteorological Society of Japan
c/o Japan Meteorological Agency
1-3-4 Ote-Machi 1-chome
Chiyoda-ku
Tokyo 100-0004, Japan   Ph: 81 332128341
Publication E-mail: metsoc-j@aurora.ocn.ne.jp

Journal of meteorology. **Founded:** 1882. **Freq:** Bimonthly. **Key Personnel:** M. Murakami, Editor. **ISSN:** 0026-1165. **Subscription Rates:** 6,600¥. **URL:** http://wwwsoc.nii.ac.jp/msj/index-e.html.
Circ: Paid 2,000

971 Journal of Nippon Medical School
Nippon Medical School Medical Association
1-1-5 Sendagi
Bunkyo-ku
Tokyo 113-8602, Japan   Ph: 81 338222131

Medical science journal. **Founded:** 1927. **Freq:** Bimonthly. **Key Personnel:** Tsutomu Araki, Editor-in-Chief. **ISSN:** 1345-4676. **Subscription Rates:**

US$60. **Remarks:** Advertising accepted; rates available upon request. **URL:** http://www.nms.ac.jp/jnms.

Circ: Controlled 2,850

📖 **972 Journal of Nuclear Science and Technology**
Atomic Energy Society of Japan
Nihon Genshiryoku Gakkai
3-7, Shimbashi 2-chome
Minato-ku
Tokyo 105-0004, Japan
Publisher E-mail: atom@aesj.or.jp

Ph: 81 335081261
Fax: 81 335816128

Journal of nuclear physics. **Founded:** 1964. **Freq:** Monthly. **Key Personnel:** Chiken Kinoshita, Editor. **ISSN:** 0022-3131. **Subscription Rates:** 18,000¥. **Remarks:** Advertising accepted; rates available upon request. **URL:** http://www.ai-gakkai.or.jp/aesj/publication/jnst.html.

Circ: Paid 1,350

📖 **973 Journal of Nuclear Science and Technology**
Atomic Energy Society of Japan
Nihon Genshiryoku Gakkai
3-7, Shimbashi 2-chome
Minato-ku
Tokyo 105-0004, Japan
Publisher E-mail: atom@aesj.or.jp

Ph: 81 335081261
Fax: 81 335816128

Journal covering nuclear science and technology. **Freq:** Monthly. **ISSN:** 0022-3131. **Subscription Rates:** 18,000¥. **URL:** http://www.ai-gakkan.or.jp/aesj/publication/jnst.htm.

Circ: 1,500

📖 **974 Journal of Obstetrics and Gynaecology**
University of Tokyo Press Production Center
2-4-16 Yayoi
Bunkyo-ku
Tokyo 113-0032, Japan

Medical science journal. **Founded:** 1960. **Freq:** Bimonthly. **ISSN:** 1341-8076. **Subscription Rates:** 12,000¥. **Alt. Formats:** CD-ROM.

📖 **975 Journal of Occupational Health**
Japan Society for Occupational Health
IPEC Inc.
1-24-11 sugamo
Toshima-ku
Tokyo 170-0002, Japan
Publication E-mail: joh-editor@info.uoeh-u.ac.jp

Ph: 81 353959612

Publishes articles related to occupational and environmental health, including fundamental toxicological studies of industrial chemicals and other related studies. **Founded:** 1996. **Freq:** Quarterly. **Key Personnel:** Akio Koizumi, Editor. **ISSN:** 1341-9145. **Subscription Rates:** 10,000¥. **URL:** http://joh.med.uoeh-u.ac.jp/.

Circ: Paid 8,000

📖 **976 Journal of Operations Research Society of Japan**
Elsevier Science Inc. - Japan Regional Office
9-15 Higashi-Azabu 1-chome
Minato-ku
Tokyo 106-0044, Japan

Journal covering economics. **Founded:** 1957. **Freq:** Quarterly. **Key Personnel:** Takashi Kobayashi, Editor. **ISSN:** 0453-4514. **Subscription Rates:** 13,200¥.

Circ: Paid 3,000

📖 **977 Journal of Oral Science**
Nihon University School of Dentistry
1-8-13 Kanda-Surugadai
Chiyoda-ku
Tokyo 101-8310, Japan

Ph: 81 332198060

Journal of dentistry. **Founded:** 1958. **Freq:** Quarterly. **Key Personnel:**

Minoru Takagi, Editor. **ISSN:** 1343-4934. **Subscription Rates:** 5,000¥. **URL:** http://www.dent.nihon-u.ac.jp/publ/journal/e-jou00.html.

Circ: Controlled 1,200

📖 **978 Journal of Orthopaedic Science**
Springer-Verlag Tokyo
3-13 Hongo 3-chome
Bunkyo-ku
Tokyo 113-0033, Japan
Publication E-mail: orders@svt-ebs.co.jp

Ph: 81 338120617

Periodical featuring the latest research and topical debates in all fields of clinical and experimental orthopedics. **Founded:** 1996. **Freq:** Bimonthly. **Key Personnel:** Koichiro Hayashi, Editor-in-Chief. **ISSN:** 0949-2658. **Subscription Rates:** 20,000¥. **URL:** http://link.springer.de/link/service/journals/00776/.

Circ: Paid 2,800

📖 **979 Journal of Pacific Society**
Pacific Society
4-15-29-3f Mita
Minato-ku
Tokyo 108-0073, Japan

Journal covering anthropology. **Founded:** 1979. **Freq:** Quarterly. **Key Personnel:** Hiroshi Nakajima, Editor. **ISSN:** 0387-4745. **Subscription Rates:** 5,000¥. **Remarks:** Advertising accepted; rates available upon request.

Circ: Paid 1,500

📖 **980 Journal of Pharmaceutical Science and Technology**
Business Center for Academic Societies Japan
5-16-9 Honkomagome
Bunkyo-ku
Tokyo 113-0021, Japan

Ph: 81 358145811

Pharmacy journal. **Founded:** 1940. **Freq:** Quarterly. **ISSN:** 0372-7629. **Subscription Rates:** 5,356¥.

Circ: Paid 1,200

📖 **981 Journal of Physical Society of Japan**
Physical Society of Japan
Rm. 211, Kikai-Shinko Bldg.
3-5-8 Shiba-Koen
Minato-ku
Tokyo 105-0011, Japan
Publication E-mail: journal@jps.or.jp

Physics journal. **Founded:** 1946. **Freq:** Monthly. **Key Personnel:** M. Matsushita, Editor. **ISSN:** 0031-9015. **Subscription Rates:** 75,000¥. **URL:** http://wwwsoc.nii.ac.jp/jps/index.html.

Circ: Paid 2,600

📖 **982 Journal of Physical Therapy Science**
Society of Physical Therapy Science
1-2-3 Sugamo
Toshima-ku
Tokyo 170-0002, Japan

Ph: 81 359784067

Medical science journal. **Founded:** 1989. **Freq:** Semiannual. **Key Personnel:** Hitoshi Maruyama, Editor. **ISSN:** 0915-5287.

Circ: Paid 1,800

📖 **983 Journal of Plant Research**
Botanical Society of Japan
Toshin Bldg.
2-27-2 Hongo
Bunkyo-ku
Tokyo 113-0033, Japan
Publication E-mail: orders@svt-ebs.co.jp

Ph: 81 338145675

Journal covering botany. **Founded:** 1887. **Freq:** Bimonthly. **Key Personnel:** Hiroshi Tobe, Editor-in-Chief. **ISSN:** 0918-9440. **Subscription Rates:** 22,000¥. **Remarks:** Advertising accepted; rates available upon request. **URL:** http://link.springer.de/link/service/journals/10265/.

Circ: Paid 2,600

📖 **984 Journal of Reproduction and Development**
Japanese Society of Animal Reproduction
c/o IPEC Inc.
1-24-11 Sugamo
Toshima
Tokyo 170-0002, Japan   Ph: 81 359784067

Journal of veterinary science. **Founded:** 1955. **Freq:** Bimonthly. **Key Personnel:** Eimei Sato, Editor-in-Chief. **ISSN:** 0916-8818. **Subscription Rates:** 9,000¥. **Remarks:** Advertising accepted; rates available upon request. **URL:** http://jrd.jstage.jst.go.jp/en/.
                                                         Circ: (Not Reported)

📖 **985 Journal of Robotics and Mechatronics**
Fuji Technology Press Ltd.
Toranomon Sangyo Bldg.
1-2-29 Toranomon
Minato-ku
Tokyo 105-0001, Japan   Ph: 81 335080051

Journal of computers. **Founded:** 1989. **Freq:** Bimonthly. **Key Personnel:** Keiji Hayashi, Editor. **ISSN:** 0915-3942. **Subscription Rates:** 72,000¥.

📖 **986 Journal of Science Education in Japan**
Japan Society for Science Education
22 Shimo-Meguro 6-chome
Meguro-ku
Tokyo 153-0064, Japan

Journal of education. **Founded:** 1977. **Freq:** Quarterly. **Key Personnel:** Yuichi Iiri, Editor. **ISSN:** 0386-4553. **Subscription Rates:** 8,000¥.
                                                         Circ: Paid 1,200

📖 **987 Journal of Science Policy and Research Management**
Japan Society for Science Policy and Research Management
c/o Institute for Policy Sciences
Toshiba EMI Nagatacho Bldg., 5th Fl.
4-8 Nagata-cho 2-chome
Chiyoda-ku
Tokyo 100-0014, Japan   Ph: 81 355211741

Journal covering economics. **Founded:** 1986. **Freq:** Semiannual. **Key Personnel:** Ryo Hirasawa, Editor, hirasawa@nistep.go.jp. **ISSN:** 0914-7020. **Subscription Rates:** 8,000¥.
                                                         Circ: Paid 900

📖 **988 Journal of Seismological Society of Japan**
Seismological Society of Japan
Daigaku Jishin Kenkyujo
1-1 Yayoi 1-chome
Bunkyo-ku
Tokyo 113-0032, Japan

Journal of geophysics. **Founded:** 1948. **Freq:** Quarterly. **ISSN:** 0037-1114. **Subscription Rates:** US$20.

📖 **989 Journal of Smooth Muscle Research**
Japanese Society of Smooth Muscle Research
Dept. of Surgery
The Jikei University School of Medicine
3-25-8 Nishishinbashi
Minatoku
Tokyo 105-8461, Japan   Ph: 81 334331111

Medical science journal. **Founded:** 1965. **Freq:** Quarterly. **Key Personnel:** Hikaru Suzuki, Chief Editor, phone 81 667212332, fax 81 667301394. **ISSN:** 0916-8737. **Remarks:** Advertising accepted; rates available upon request. **URL:** http://wwwsoc.nii.ac.jp/jsmr/jsmr1/jsmr1.html.
                                                         Circ: 950

📖 **990 Journal of Social Science**
International Christian University Social Science Research Institute
3-10-2 Osawa
Mitaka-shi
Tokyo 181-8585, Japan   Ph: 81 422333224

Social science journal. **Founded:** 1960. **Freq:** Semiannual. **ISSN:** 0454-2134.
                                                         Circ: 650

📖 **991 Journal of Space Technology and Science**
Japanese Rocket Society
c/o Business Center for Academic Societies
  Japan
5-16-9 Honkomagome
Bunkyo-ku
Tokyo 113-0021, Japan   Ph: 81 358145811

Journal of aeronautics. **Freq:** Semiannual. **Key Personnel:** Yoshiaki Ohkami, Editor. **ISSN:** 0911-551X. **Subscription Rates:** US$50.

📖 **992 Journal of Structural and Construction Engineering**
Architectural Institute of Japan
26-20 Shiba 5-chome
Minato-ku
Tokyo 108-0014, Japan   Ph: 81 334562051

Journal covering architecture. **Founded:** 1936. **Freq:** Monthly. **ISSN:** 1340-4202. **Subscription Rates:** 33,600¥.

📖 **993 Journal of Structural Engineering B**
Architectural Institute of Japan
26-20 Shiba 5-chome
Minato-ku
Tokyo 108-0014, Japan   Ph: 81 334562051

Journal covering civil engineering. **Founded:** 1985. **Freq:** Annual. **ISSN:** 0910-8033. **Subscription Rates:** 3,000¥. **URL:** http://www.aij.or.jp/aijhome.htm.

📖 **994 Journal of Three Dimensional Images**
Forum for Advancement of Three Dimensional Image Technology and
  Arts
c/o Hiroaki Yamada
Dept. of Electronic Engineering
Shibaura Institue of Technolog
3-9-14 Shibaura, Minato-ku
Tokyo, Japan   Ph: 81 358145810

Journal of communications. **Founded:** 1987. **Freq:** Quarterly. **ISSN:** 1342-2189. **Subscription Rates:** 1,000¥ single issue.

📖 **995 Journal of Toho University Medical Society**
Toho University Medical Society
c/o Library
School of Medicine
5-21-16 Omori-Nishi
Ota-ku
Tokyo 143-0015, Japan   Ph: 81 337624151

Medical science journal. **Founded:** 1954. **Freq:** Bimonthly. **Key Personnel:** Yoshio Toshifumi, Editor. **ISSN:** 0040-8670. **Subscription Rates:** 6,000¥. **Remarks:** Advertising accepted; rates available upon request.
                                                         Circ: Paid 1,200

📖 **996 Journal of Tokyo University of Fisheries**
Tokyo University of Fisheries
4-5-7 Ko-Unan
Minato-ku
Tokyo 108-0075, Japan   Ph: 81 354630400

Journal of fisheries. **Founded:** 1950. **Freq:** Semiannual. **Key Personnel:** Shigeru Kimura, Editor. **ISSN:** 0040-9014.

📖 **997 Journal of Tokyo University of Mercantile Marine**
Tokyo University of Mercantile Marine
1-6 Ecchujima 2-chome
Koto-ku
Tokyo 135-0044, Japan

Journal of transportation. **Founded:** 1957. **Freq:** Annual. **ISSN:** 0493-4474.

📖 **998   Journal of Toxicological Sciences**
Japanese Society of Toxicological Sciences
Gakkai CTR Bldg
4th Fl.
2-4-16 Yayoi
Bunkyo-ku
Tokyo 113-0032, Japan   Ph: 81 0338123093

Pharmacy journal. **Founded:** 1976. **Freq:** Quarterly. **ISSN:** 0388-1350.
Subscription Rates: 7,000¥. **URL:** http://wwwsoc.nii.ac.jp/jsts/index-e.html.

📖 **999   Journal of Transportation Medicine**
Japanese Association of Transportation Medicine
c/o Business Center for Academic Societies
   Japan
5-16-9 Honkomagome
Bunkyo-ku
Tokyo 113-0021, Japan   Ph: 81 0358145811

Medical science journal. **Founded:** 1947. **Freq:** Bimonthly. **Key Personnel:**
Takashi Murayama, Editor. **ISSN:** 0022-5274. **Subscription Rates:** 7,000¥.
Remarks: Advertising accepted; rates available upon request.
                                              Circ: Controlled 600

📖 **1000   Journal of Veterinary Medical Science**
Maruzen Co. Ltd.
3-10 Nihombashi 2-chome
Chuo-ku
Tokyo 103-0027, Japan   Ph: 81 332727211

Journal of veterinary science. **Founded:** 1939. **Freq:** Bimonthly. **Key
Personnel:** Hideaki Karaki, Editor. **ISSN:** 0916-7250. **Subscription Rates:**
25,000¥. **Remarks:** Advertising accepted; rates available upon request.
                                              Circ: Paid 5,000

📖 **1001   Journal of Visualization**
Ohmsha Ltd.
3-1 Kanda-Nishiki-cho
Chiyoda-ku
Tokyo 101-0054, Japan   Ph: 81 332330641

Physics journal. **Founded:** 1998. **Freq:** Quarterly. **Key Personnel:** Y.
Nakayama, Editor, phone 81 339240611, fax 81 339240611, y-
naka@mug.biglobe.ne.jp. **ISSN:** 1343-8875. **Subscription Rates:** 35,000¥;
US$294 other countries. **URL:** http://www.vsj.or.jp/jov/.

📖 **1002   Journal of Water and Environmental Issues**
Japanese Association for Water Resources and Environment
16-12-803 Nishi-Shinjuku 6-chome
Shinjuku-ku
Tokyo 160-0023, Japan

Journal of water resources. **Founded:** 1987. **Freq:** Annual. **ISSN:** 0913-8277.
Subscription Rates: 1,500¥.

📖 **1003   Journal of Wood Science**
Springer-Verlag Tokyo
3-13 Hongo 3-chome
Bunkyo-ku
Tokyo 113-0033, Japan   Ph: 81 338120617
Publication E-mail: orders@svt-ebs.co.jp

Publishes original articles on basic and applied research dealing with the
science, technology, and engineering of wood, wood components, wood and
wood-based products, and wood constructions. **Freq:** Bimonthly. **Key
Personnel:** Takao Itoh, Editor-in-Chief. **ISSN:** 1435-0211. **Subscription
Rates:** 20,000¥. **URL:** http://link.springer.de/link/service/journals/10086/.

📖 **1004   Journal of World Affairs**
Takushohu University Institute of World Studies
4-14 Kohinata 3-chome
Bunkyo-ku
Tokyo 112-0006, Japan

Political science journal. **Freq:** Monthly. **Key Personnel:** Muneyoshi Date,
Editor. **ISSN:** 0453-0950. **Subscription Rates:** 3,600¥.

📖 **1005   JSME International Journal Series A**
Japan Society of Mechanical Engineers
Shinanomachi-Rengakan Bldg.
35 Shinano-Machi
Shinjuku-ku
Tokyo 160-0016, Japan   Ph: 81 353603505
Publication E-mail: journal@jsme.or.jp

Journal of mechanical engineering. **Founded:** 1958. **Freq:** Quarterly. **Key
Personnel:** Junji Tani, Editor-in-Chief. **ISSN:** 1340-8046. **Subscription
Rates:** US$125. **Remarks:** Advertising accepted; rates available upon
request. **URL:** http://www.jsme.or.jp/English/.
                                              Circ: Paid 1,300

📖 **1006   JSME International Journal Series B Fluids and Thermal
      Engineering**
Japan Society of Mechanical Engineers
Shinanomachi-Rengakan Bldg.
35 Shinano-Machi
Shinjuku-ku
Tokyo 160-0016, Japan   Ph: 81 353603505
Publication E-mail: journal@jsme.or.jp

Journal of mechanical engineering. **Founded:** 1958. **Freq:** Quarterly. **Key
Personnel:** Junji Tani, Editor-in-Chief. **ISSN:** 1340-8054. **Subscription
Rates:** US$125. **URL:** http://www.jsme.or.jp/English/.

📖 **1007   JSME International Journal Series C Dynamics, Control,
      Robotics, Design and Manufacturing**
Japan Society of Mechanical Engineers
Shinanomachi-Rengakan Bldg.
35 Shinano-Machi
Shinjuku-ku
Tokyo 160-0016, Japan   Ph: 81 353603505
Publication E-mail: journal@jsme.or.jp

Journal of mechanical engineering. **Founded:** 1958. **Freq:** Quarterly. **Key
Personnel:** Junji Tani, Editor-in-Chief. **ISSN:** 1340-8062. **Subscription
Rates:** US$125. **URL:** http://www.jsme.or.jp/English/.

📖 **1008   Keidanren Review**
Japan Federation of Economic Organizations
9-4 Ote-Machi 1-chome
Chiyoda-ku
Tokyo 100-0004, Japan   Ph: 81 332791411

Journal covering economics. **Founded:** 1964. **Freq:** Bimonthly. **ISSN:** 0022-
9695. **Remarks:** Advertising accepted; rates available upon request.
                                              Circ: Free 12,000

📖 **1009   Keio Business Review**
Keio University Society of Business and Commerce
c/o Faculty of Business and Commerce
Mita
Minato-ku
Tokyo 108-0073, Japan   Ph: 81 334534511

Journal covering economics. **Founded:** 1978. **Freq:** Annual. **Key Personnel:**
T. Shimizu, Editor. **ISSN:** 0453-4557.

📖 **1010 Keio Economic Studies**
Keio University
Keio Economic Society
2-15-45 Mita
Minato-ku
Tokyo 108-8345, Japan   Ph: 81 334534511

Journal covering economics. **Founded:** 1963. **Freq:** Semiannual. **Key Personnel:** Naoyuki Yoshino, Managing Editor. **ISSN:** 0022-9709. **Subscription Rates:** 3,000¥. **Remarks:** Advertising accepted; rates available upon request. **URL:** http://www.econ.keio.ac.jp/org/kes/en/.

       Circ: Paid 800

📖 **1011 Keio Journal of Medicine**
Keio University
School of Medicine
35 Shinanomachi
Shinjuku-ku
Tokyo 160-8582, Japan   Ph: 81 333531211

Publication devoted to the advancement and dissemination of the fundamental knowledge of medical science. **Founded:** 1952. **Freq:** Quarterly. **Key Personnel:** Naoki Aikawa, Editor-in-Chief. **ISSN:** 0022-9717. **Subscription Rates:** 5,000¥. **URL:** http://www.kjm.keio.ac.jp/.

       Circ: Paid 500

📖 **1012 Kyodo News**
2-2-5 Toranomon
Minato-ku
Tokyo 105-8474, Japan
Publication E-mail: kaigai.web@kyodonews.jp

General online newspaper. **Founded:** 1945. **Freq:** Daily. **URL:** http://home.kyodo.co.jp/.

📖 **1013 Lamellicornia**
Society of Lamellicornians
c/o Mr. Masaaki Ishida
23-5 Miyamae 3-chome
Suginami-ku
Tokyo 168-0081, Japan

Journal of entomology. **Founded:** 1985. **Freq:** Annual. **ISSN:** 0915-3020.

📖 **1014 Language Teacher**
Japan Association for Language Teaching
Urban Edge Bldg. 5F
1-37-9 Taito
Taito-ku
Tokyo 110-0016, Japan   Ph: 81 338371630
       Fax: 81 338371631
Publication E-mail: tlt_ed1@jalt.org
Publisher E-mail: jalt@gol.com

Educational magazine. **Founded:** 1984. **Freq:** Monthly. **Key Personnel:** Brad Visgatis, Co-Editor, pubchair@jalt.org. **ISSN:** 0289-7938. **Remarks:** Advertising accepted; rates available upon request. **URL:** http://www.jalt-publications.org/tlt/.

       Circ: (Not Reported)

📖 **1015 Library and Information Science**
Mita Society for Library and Information Science
c/o Keio University
2-15-45 Mita
Minato-ku
Tokyo 108-0073, Japan   Ph: 81 334533920

Publishes scholarly research papers and technical reports containing thoughts and findings not published previously in the fields of library and information science. **Founded:** 1963. **Freq:** Semiannual. **Key Personnel:** Shunsaku Tamura, Editor. **ISSN:** 0373-4447. **Subscription Rates:** US$20. **URL:** http://wwwsoc.nii.ac.jp/mslis/.

       Circ: Paid 1,500

📖 **1016 Low Temperature Medicine**
Japan Society for Low Temperature Medicine
Tateishi 5-11-16
Katushika
Tokyo 124-0012, Japan   Ph: 81 356983505

Medical science journal. **Founded:** 1976. **Freq:** Quarterly. **Key Personnel:** Tohru Tamaki, Editor. **ISSN:** 0285-4473. **Subscription Rates:** 2,000¥ single issue.

📖 **1017 Management Japan**
International Management Association of Japan, Inc.
Mori 9th Bldg., 1-2-2 Atago
Minato-ku
Tokyo 105-0002, Japan   Fax: 81 354085588
Publisher E-mail: imaj001@js2.so-net.ne.jp

International business publication. **Subtitle:** IMAJ Management Review. **Founded:** 1967. **Freq:** Annual. **Key Personnel:** Y. Nakaune, Editor. **ISSN:** 0025-1828. **Subscription Rates:** US$22. **Remarks:** Advertising accepted; rates available upon request. **Online:** Gale Group. **URL:** http://www.iijnet.or.jp/imaj/publi-e.htm.

       Circ: Paid 10,000

📖 **1018 Medical Electron Microscopy**
Springer-Verlag Tokyo
3-13 Hongo 3-chome
Bunkyo-ku
Tokyo 113-0033, Japan   Ph: 81 338120617
Publication E-mail: orders@svt-ebs.co.jp

Journal covering biology. **Founded:** 1993. **Freq:** Quarterly. **Key Personnel:** M. Mori, Editor. **ISSN:** 0918-4287. **Subscription Rates:** 20,000¥. **URL:** http://link.springer.de/link/service/journals/00795/.

📖 **1019 Medical Imaging Technology**
Digital Press Inc.
Texico Bldg.
9-7 Higashi-Ikebukuro
Toshima-ku
Tokyo 170-0013, Japan   Ph: 81 339716702

Medical science journal. **Founded:** 1983. **Freq:** Bimonthly. **Key Personnel:** Toru Matsumoto, Editor. **ISSN:** 0288-450X. **Subscription Rates:** 2,000¥ single issue. **Remarks:** Advertising accepted; rates available upon request.

       Circ: (Not Reported)

📖 **1020 Medical Journal of the Government Printing Bureau**
Ministry of Finance
Medical Association of the Printing Bureau
Okurasho Insatsukyoku Byoin
3-6 Nishigahara 2-chome
Kita-ku
Tokyo 114-0024, Japan

Medical science journal. **Founded:** 1955. **Freq:** Semiannual. **ISSN:** 0288-7908.

📖 **1021 MEJ**
Genyosha Publications, Inc.
8-7 Shibuya 2-chome
Shibuya-ku
Tokyo 150, Japan   Ph: 81 334077521

Medical science journal. **Subtitle:** Monthly Information on Medical, Surgical & De. **Founded:** 1957. **Freq:** Monthly. **Key Personnel:** Masami Eda, Editor. **ISSN:** 0025-8830. **Subscription Rates:** US$130. **Remarks:** Advertising accepted; rates available upon request.

       Circ: Paid 6,984

📖 **1022 Metropolis**
Crisscross KK
3F Maison Tomoe Bldg.
3-16-1 Minami-Aoyama
Minato-ku
Tokyo 107, Japan   Ph: 81 334236932
Publication E-mail: forum@japantoday.com

General interest magazine. **Subtitle:** Japan's No. 1 English Magazine. **Freq:**

Weekly. **Key Personnel:** Georgia Jacobs, Managing Editor, editor@metropolis.co.jp. **Remarks:** Advertising accepted; rates available upon request. **URL:** http://metropolis.japantoday.com/default.asp.

Circ: (Not Reported)

⬚ 1023 Microbiology and Immunology
Center for Academic Publications Japan
2-4-16 Yayoi
Bunkyo-ku
Tokyo 113-0032, Japan   Ph: 81 338175821

Journal of microbiology and immunology. **Founded:** 1957. **Freq:** Monthly. **ISSN:** 0385-5600. **Subscription Rates:** US$255. **Remarks:** Advertising accepted; rates available upon request.

Circ: Paid 1,500

⬚ 1024 Mitsubishi Electric Advance
Mitsubishi Electric Corporation
2-2-3 Marunochi
Chiyoda-ku
Tokyo 100-8310, Japan

Journal of electrical engineering. **Founded:** 1977. **Freq:** Quarterly. **Key Personnel:** Shin Suzuki, Editor. **ISSN:** 0386-5096. **Subscription Rates:** 6,000¥.

Circ: Paid 2,000

⬚ 1025 Monthly Journal of Entomology
Mushisha
Nakano Yubinkyo-ku
PO Box 10
Tokyo, Japan

Journal of entomology. **Founded:** 1971. **Freq:** Monthly. **ISSN:** 0388-418X. **Subscription Rates:** 980¥ single issue.

⬚ 1026 Monumenta Nipponica
Sophia University
7-1 Kioi-cho
Chiyoda-ku
Tokyo 102-8554, Japan   Ph: 81 332383543

Journal of oriental studies. **Subtitle:** Studies in Japanese Culture. **Founded:** 1938. **Freq:** Quarterly. **Key Personnel:** Kate Wildman Nakai, Editor, kw-nakai@sophia.ac.jp. **ISSN:** 0027-0741. **Subscription Rates:** 4,280¥; US$46 other countries. **Remarks:** Advertising accepted; rates available upon request. **URL:** http://monumenta.cc.sophia.ac.jp.

Circ: Paid 1,150

⬚ 1027 Motorcycle Japan
JAN Corporation
5F Nikkan Jidosha Shimbun Bldg
2-1-25 Kaigan
Minato-ku
Tokyo 105-0022, Japan   Ph: 81 334380361

Journal of transportation. **Founded:** 1983. **Freq:** Annual. **Key Personnel:** Makio Sakurazawa, Editor. **Subscription Rates:** 3,150¥.
Ad Rates: BW: 150,000¥   **Circ:** Paid 3,880
                 4C: 350,000¥

⬚ 1028 Movie -TV Marketing
Kikuko M. Ireton
PO Box 30
Tokyo 100-8691, Japan   Ph: 81 335872855
Publication E-mail: info@movietvmarketing.com

Journal of communications. **Founded:** 1953. **Freq:** Monthly. **Key Personnel:** Koji Watanabe, Managing Editor. **ISSN:** 0047-8288. **Subscription Rates:** 30,000¥. **Remarks:** Advertising accepted; rates available upon request. **URL:** http://www.movietvmarketing.com.

Circ: Paid 28,000

⬚ 1029 Natural Medicines
Japanese Society of Pharmacognosy
c/o The Japanese Society Office
5-16-9 Honkomagome
Bunkyo-ku
Tokyo 113-8622, Japan   Ph: 81 358145801

Pharmacy journal. **Founded:** 1947. **Freq:** Quarterly. **Key Personnel:** Hidezi Itokawa, Editor. **ISSN:** 1340-3443. **Subscription Rates:** 12,000¥. **Remarks:** Advertising accepted; rates available upon request.

Circ: Paid 700

⬚ 1030 Naval Architecture and Ocean Engineering
Society of Naval Architects of Japan
15-16 Toranomon 1-chome
Minato-ku
Tokyo 105-0001, Japan

Journal of oceanography. **Founded:** 1968. **Freq:** Annual. **ISSN:** 0387-5504. **Subscription Rates:** 4,000¥.

⬚ 1031 Neurologia Medico-Chirurgica
Japan Neurosurgical Society
c/o Akamon-mae Iwata Bldg.
5-27-8 Hongo
Bunkyo-ku
Tokyo 113-0033, Japan   Ph: 81 338126226
Publication E-mail: jns@ss.iij4u.or.jp

Medical science journal. **Founded:** 1959. **Freq:** Monthly. **Key Personnel:** Akira Yamaura, Editor-in-Chief. **ISSN:** 0470-8105. **Subscription Rates:** US$145. **Remarks:** Advertising accepted; rates available upon request. **URL:** http://www.ff.iij4u.or.jp/~neuromed.

Circ: (Not Reported)

⬚ 1032 New Diamond and Frontier Carbon Technology
MYU, Scientific Publishing Division
FCT Central Resarch Dept.
Pros-Nishi-Shinbashi Bldg. 3F
2-4-3, Nishi-Shinbashi
Minato-ku
Tokyo 105-0003, Japan
Publication E-mail: myukk@kt.rim.or.jp

Journal of mechanical engineering. **Founded:** 1991. **Freq:** Bimonthly. **Key Personnel:** Masanori Yoshikawa, Editor, phone 81 335923911, fax 81 335923933, LEP02155@nifty.ne.jp. **ISSN:** 1344-9931. **Subscription Rates:** US$250.

⬚ 1033 News from Nisshin Steel
Nisshin Steel Co. Ltd.
Shinkokusai Bldg.
4-1, Marunouchi 3-chome
Chiyoda-ku
Tokyo 100-8366, Japan   Ph: 81 332165511

Journal of metallurgy. **Freq:** Quarterly. **ISSN:** 0911-8764.

⬚ 1034 Nihongo Journal
ALC Press Inc.
2-54-12 Eifuku
Suginami-ku
Tokyo 168-8611, Japan   Ph: 81 120120800
Publication E-mail: nj@alc.co.jp

Journal of linguistics. **Subtitle:** A Magazine for People Studying Japanese and D. **Founded:** 1998. **Freq:** Monthly. **ISSN:** 0912-5361. **Subscription Rates:** US$148.

⬚ 1035 Nikkei Net Interactive
Nihon Keizai Shimbun Inc.
1-9-5 Otemachi
Chiyoda-ku
Tokyo 100-8066, Japan   Ph: 81 352552312
Publication E-mail: esupport@nikkei.co.jp

Online business newspaper. **Freq:** Daily. **Subscription Rates:** 1,000¥ per month. **Remarks:** Advertising accepted; rates available upon request. **URL:** http://www.nni.nikkei.co.jp/.

Circ: (Not Reported)

📖 **1036 The Nikkei Weekly**
Nihon Keizai Shimbun Inc.
1-9-5 Otemachi
Chiyoda-ku
Tokyo 100-8066, Japan   Ph: 81 352552312

Business newspaper. **Founded:** 1962. **Freq:** Weekly. **Key Personnel:** Nobuo Oneda, Editor. **ISSN:** 0918-5348. **Subscription Rates:** 21,600¥. **Remarks:** Advertising accepted; rates available upon request. **URL:** http://www.nni.nikkei.co.jp/FR/TNW/.

Circ: Paid 36,500

📖 **1037 Nippon Steel News**
Nippon Steel Corporation
6-3 Ote-Machi 2-chome
Chiyoda-ku
Tokyo 100-0004, Japan   Ph: 81 032424111

Journal of metallurgy. **Founded:** 1970. **Freq:** Monthly. **ISSN:** 0048-0452.

📖 **1038 Nipponia**
Heibonsha Ltd.
Izumi-Hakusan Bldg.
2-29-4 Hakusan
Bunkyo-ku
Tokyo 112-0001, Japan   Ph: 81 338180788
Publication E-mail: jinmaster@jcic.or.jp

Magazine on modern Japan. **Founded:** 1997. **Freq:** Quarterly. **Key Personnel:** Tsuchiya Komei, Editor. **ISSN:** 1343-1196. **URL:** http://jin.jcic.or.jp/nipponia/.

📖 **1039 NIRA Review**
National Institute for Research Advancement
34F Yebisu Garden Place Tower
4-20-3 Ebisu
Shibuya-ku
PO Box 5004
Tokyo 150-6034, Japan   Ph: 81 354481740

Social science journal. **Subtitle:** A Journal of Opinion on Public Policy Worldwi. **Founded:** 1994. **Freq:** Quarterly. **ISSN:** 1340-5268. **Subscription Rates:** 6,000¥. **Remarks:** Advertising accepted; rates available upon request.
Circ: (Not Reported)

📖 **1040 Oceanographical Magazine**
Japan Meteorological Agency
3-4 Ote-Machi 1-chome
Chiyoda-ku
Tokyo 100-0004, Japan

Journal on oceanography. **Founded:** 1949. **Freq:** Annual. **ISSN:** 0369-707X. **Subscription Rates:** 1,900¥.
Circ: Paid 788

📖 **1041 Office Equipment and Products**
Dempa Publication Inc.
1-11-15 Higashi Gotanda
Tokyo 141, Japan

Journal of electronics. **Founded:** 1972. **Freq:** Monthly. **Key Personnel:** Tetsuo Hirayama, Editor. **ISSN:** 0387-5245. **Subscription Rates:** US$130.

📖 **1042 Okajima's Folia Anatomica Japonica**
Okajima Foria Anatomica Yaponika Henshubu
c/o Keio University
School of Medicine Dept of Anatomy
35 Shinano-Machi
Shinjuku-ku
Tokyo 160-0016, Japan   Ph: 81 333531211

Journal covering biology. **Founded:** 1922. **Freq:** Bimonthly. **Key Personnel:** Sadakazu Aiso, Editor. **ISSN:** 0030-154X. **Subscription Rates:** 18,000¥.
Circ: Paid 400

📖 **1043 Optical Review**
Optical Society of Japan
Kudan-Kita Bldg. 5F
1-12-3 Kudan-kita
Chiyoda-ku
Tokyo 102-0073, Japan
Publication E-mail: optrev@ipap.jp

Publishes research and review papers in all branches of optics. **Founded:** 1994. **Freq:** Bimonthly. **Key Personnel:** Y. Tsutsumi, Production Editor, phone 81 334324308, fax 81 334320728. **ISSN:** 1340-6000. **URL:** http://annex.jsap.or.jp/OSJ/opticalreview/.

📖 **1044 Oral Radiology**
Japanese Society for Oral and Maxillofacial Radiology
c/o Hitotsubashi Printing Co. Ltd
Gakkai Business Center
12-15 Kami-Osaki
Shinagawaku
Tokyo 141-0021, Japan

Journal of dentistry. **Founded:** 1985. **Freq:** Semiannual. **Key Personnel:** Kanji Kishi, Editor. **ISSN:** 0911-6028. **Subscription Rates:** 5,000¥. **Remarks:** Advertising accepted; rates available upon request.
Circ: (Not Reported)

📖 **1045 Orthopaedic and Traumatic Surgery**
Kanehara Shuppan Ltd.
PO Box 1
Hongo Post Office
Tokyo, Japan

Journal of orthopedics. **Founded:** 1958. **Freq:** Monthly. **Key Personnel:** Yoshio Yamauchi, Editor. **ISSN:** 0387-4095. **Subscription Rates:** 1,900¥ single issue.
Circ: Paid 7,100

📖 **1046 Patents and Licensing**
IPL Communications Inc
Rm. 202
Sun Mansion
1-11 Azabudai 1-chome
Minato-ku
Tokyo 106-0041, Japan   Ph: 81 335894749

Journal of patents. **Founded:** 1971. **Freq:** Bimonthly. **Key Personnel:** Osahito Makiyama, Editor. **ISSN:** 0388-7081. **Subscription Rates:** 5,000¥. **Remarks:** Advertising accepted; rates available upon request.
Circ: (Not Reported)

📖 **1047 Pediatric Dental Journal**
Japanese Society of Pediatric Dentistry Oral Health Association
1-44-2 Komagome
Toshima-ku
Tokyo 170-0003, Japan

Journal of dentistry. **Founded:** 1991. **Freq:** Annual. **Key Personnel:** Mizuho Nishino, Editor. **ISSN:** 0917-2394. **Subscription Rates:** US$10.

📖 **1048 Pharma Japan**
Yakugyo Jiho Co. Ltd.
2-36 Kanda-Jinbo-cho
Chiyoda-ku
Tokyo 101-0051, Japan   Ph: 81 032657751

Pharmacy journal. **Subtitle:** Japan Drug Industry News. **Founded:** 1960. **Freq:** Weekly. **ISSN:** 0285-4937. **Subscription Rates:** 1,300¥. **Remarks:** Advertising accepted; rates available upon request. **URL:** http://www.pharma-japan.com/pha/1highlights/index2.html.
Circ: Paid 700

1049 Plankton Biology and Ecology
Plankton Society of Japan
c/o Tokyo University of Fisheries
4-5-7 Kounan
Minato-ku
Tokyo 108-8477, Japan   Ph: 81 354630539

Journal covering biology. **Freq:** Semiannual. **Key Personnel:** Shuhei Nishida, Editor. **ISSN:** 1343-0874. **Subscription Rates:** 12,000¥.
Circ: Paid 700

1050 Plasma Processing
Japan Society of Applied Physics
Research Group of Plasma Electronics
Waseda Daigaku Rikogakubu
4-1 Okubo 3-chome
Shinjuku-ku
Tokyo 160-0000, Japan

Physics journal. **Freq:** Annual.

1051 Polar Bioscience
National Institute of Polar Research
9-10, Kaga 1-chome
Itabashi-ku
Tokyo 173-8515, Japan   Ph: 81 339622214

Journal of geography. **Founded:** 1967. **Freq:** Annual. **Key Personnel:** Kokichi Kamiyama, Editor. **ISSN:** 1344-6231.
Circ: 1,000

1052 Polymer Journal
Society of Polymer Science Japan
Irifune 32 Fuji Bldg.
3-10-9 Irifune
Chuo-ku
Tokyo 104-0042, Japan   Ph: 81 355403772
Publication E-mail: hpj@spsj.or.jp

Journal covering scientific research and new information in all the fields of polymer science. **Founded:** 1970. **Freq:** Monthly. **Key Personnel:** Akihiro Abe, Editor. **ISSN:** 0032-3896. **Subscription Rates:** 47,000¥. **URL:** http://www.spsj.or.jp/c5/pj/pj.htm.
Circ: Paid 2,000

1053 Population Ecology
Springer-Verlag Tokyo
3-13 Hongo 3-chome
Bunkyo-ku
Tokyo 113-0033, Japan   Ph: 81 338120617

Publishes original research articles and reviews on various aspects of population ecology. **Founded:** 1962. **Freq:** 3/year. **Key Personnel:** Masakazu Shimada, Chief Editor, mshimada@balmer.c.u-tokyo.ac.jp. **ISSN:** 1438-3896. **Subscription Rates:** 25,000¥. **URL:** http://link.springer.de/link/service/journals/10144/.
Circ: Paid 25,000

1054 Production Research
University of Tokyo Institute of Industrial Science
22-1 Roppongi 7-chome
Minato-ku
Tokyo 106-0032, Japan   Ph: 81 334026231

Journal of technology. **Founded:** 1949. **Freq:** Monthly. **ISSN:** 0037-105X.
Circ: Free 1,980

1055 Publications of Astronomical Society of Japan
Astronomical Society of Japan
c/o National Astronomical Observatory
2-21-1 Osawa
Mitaka-shi
Tokyo 181-0015, Japan

Journal covering astronomy. **Founded:** 1949. **Freq:** Bimonthly. **Key Person-** nel: N. Arimoto, Editor. **ISSN:** 0004-6264. **Subscription Rates:** 22,000¥.
Remarks: Advertising accepted; rates available upon request.
Circ: (Not Reported)

1056 Quaternary Research
Business Center for Academic Societies Japan
5-16-9 Honkomagome
Bunkyo-ku
Tokyo 113-0021, Japan   Ph: 81 358145811
Publication E-mail: kojiok@ipc.hiroshima-u.ac.jp

Earth sciences journal. **Founded:** 1957. **Freq:** 5/year. **ISSN:** 0418-2642. **Subscription Rates:** US$83.
Circ: Paid 1,900

1057 Radio Japan News
Japan Broadcasting Corp
2-2-1 Jinnan
Shibuya-ku
Tokyo 150-8001, Japan   Ph: 81 334651111
Publication E-mail: worldtv@intl.nhk.or.jp

Journal of communications. **Founded:** 1956. **Freq:** Monthly. **ISSN:** 0033-7927. **URL:** http://www.nhk.or.jp/nhkworld.
Circ: Free 14,000

1058 Radioisotopes
Japan Radioisotope Association
28-45 Honkomagome 2-chome
Bunkyo-ku
Tokyo 113-0021, Japan   Ph: 81 339467110

Journal covering chemistry. **Founded:** 1952. **Freq:** Monthly. **Key Personnel:** Tatsuyi Hamada, Editor. **ISSN:** 0033-8303. **Subscription Rates:** 15,000¥. **Remarks:** Advertising accepted; rates available upon request. **URL:** http://www.jrias.or.jp/jrias/index.cfm/4,531,97,html.
Circ: Paid 5,000

1059 Renal Transplantation, Vascular Surgery
Japanese Society of Renal Transplantation and Vascular Surgery
Women's Medical College
Dept. of Urology
8-1 Kawada-cho
Shinjuku-ku
Tokyo 162-0054, Japan

Medical science journal. **Founded:** 1989. **Freq:** Semiannual. **Key Personnel:** Hiroshi Toma, Editor. **ISSN:** 0915-9118. **Subscription Rates:** 2,000¥.

1060 Resource Geology
Society of Resource Geology
Nogizaka Bldg.
9-6-41 Akasaka
Minato-ku
Tokyo 107-0052, Japan   Ph: 81 334755287
Publication E-mail: srg@kt.rim.or.jp

Journal of geology. **Founded:** 1951. **Freq:** Quarterly. **Key Personnel:** H. Shimazaki, Editor. **Subscription Rates:** 3,000¥ single issue. **Remarks:** Advertising accepted; rates available upon request.
Circ: Paid 1,400

1061 Reviews on Heteroatom Chemistry
MYU, Scientific Publishing Division
2-32-3 Sendagi
Bunkyo-ku
Tokyo 113-0022, Japan   Ph: 81 338212930

Journal covering chemistry. **Founded:** 1988. **Freq:** Semiannual. **Key Personnel:** Shigeru Oae, Editor. **ISSN:** 0915-6151. **Subscription Rates:** 28,000¥.

📖 **1062 Rigaku Journal**
Rigaku Corp
3-9-12 Matsubara-cho
Akishima-shi
Tokyo 196-0003, Japan   Ph: 81 425458139

Physics journal. **Founded:** 1984. **Freq:** Semiannual. **Key Personnel:** Tomohiko Watanabe, Editor. **ISSN:** 0913-543X.

📖 **1063 Rural and Environmental Engineering**
Japanese Society of Irrigation Drainage and Reclamation Engineering
Nogyo Doboku Kaikan
34-4 Shinbashi 5-chome
Minato-ku
Tokyo 105-0004, Japan   Ph: 81 334363418

Journal covering agriculture and environmental engineering. **Founded:** 1982. **Freq:** Semiannual. **Key Personnel:** Sschiko Yoshitake, Editor. **Subscription Rates:** 4,000¥.

📖 **1064 Sciences**
Japan International Marine Science and Technology Federation
3-5 Nihonbashikakigara-cho 1-chome
Chuo-ku
Tokyo 103-0014, Japan

Journal of oceanography. **Founded:** 1988. **Freq:** Quarterly. **ISSN:** 0914-6105.

📖 **1065 Seishin Studies**
University of the Sacred Heart
4-3-1 Hiro
Shibuya-ku
Tokyo 150-0012, Japan   Ph: 81 334075811

Humanities journal. **Founded:** 1952. **Freq:** Semiannual. **ISSN:** 0037-1084. **Subscription Rates:** 1,000¥.
                                         Circ: Paid 1,000

📖 **1066 Sensors and Materials**
MYU
2-32-3 Sendagi
Bunkyo-ku
Tokyo 113-0022, Japan   Ph: 81 338278549
Publication E-mail: myukk@kt.rim.or.jp

Publishes original work in the experimental and theoretical fields, aimed at understanding sensing technology, related materials, associated phenomena, and applied systems. **Founded:** 1989. **Freq:** 8/year. **Key Personnel:** Susumu Sugiyama, Editor. **ISSN:** 0914-4935. **Subscription Rates:** US$310. **URL:** http://www.kt.rim.or.jp/~myukk/S&M/index.html.

📖 **1067 Shakespeare Studies**
Shakespeare Society of Japan
501 Kenkyusha Bldg.
2-9, Kanda-Surugadai
Chiyoda-ku
Tokyo 101-0062, Japan

Journal of literature. **Founded:** 1962. **Freq:** Annual. **Key Personnel:** Yasunari Takahashi, Editor. **ISSN:** 0582-9402. **Subscription Rates:** 2,000¥. **URL:** http://wwwsoc.nii.ac.jp/sh/sh-english/outlines-e.html.
                                         Circ: Paid 1,200

📖 **1068 Shipping and Trade News**
Tokyo News Service Ltd.
Tsukiji Hamarikyu Bldg., 10th Fl.
3-3 Tsukiji 5-chome
Chuo-ku   Ph: 81 335428521
Tokyo 104-0045, Japan   Fax: 81 335425086
Publisher E-mail: editorial@tokyonews.co.jp

Newspaper covering the shipping industry. **Founded:** 1949. **Freq:** Daily. **Key Personnel:** Chiaki Sakurai, Editor. **Subscription Rates:** 42,900¥.
                                         Circ: Paid 15,000

📖 **1069 Shukan ST**
The Japan Times Ltd.
4-5-4 Shibaura
Minato-ku
Tokyo 108-0023, Japan   Ph: 81 334535312

Newspaper covering education. **Founded:** 1990. **Freq:** Weekly. **Key Personnel:** Mitsuru Tanaka, Editor. **ISSN:** 0915-7875. **Subscription Rates:** 11,400¥. **Remarks:** Advertising accepted; rates available upon request. **URL:** http://www.japantimes.co.jp/shukan-st/.
                                         Circ: Paid 150,000

📖 **1070 Soil Science and Plant Nutrition**
Business Center for Academic Societies Japan
5-16-9 Honkomagome
Bunkyo-ku
Tokyo 113-0021, Japan   Ph: 81 358145811

Journal covering agriculture. **Founded:** 1955. **Freq:** Quarterly. **ISSN:** 0038-0768. **Subscription Rates:** US$100.

📖 **1071 Soils & Foundations**
Japanese Geotechnical Society
4F, Sugayama Bldg
2-23 Kanda-Awaji-cho
Chiyoda-ku
Tokyo 101-0063, Japan   Ph: 81 332517661

Journal covering civil engineering. **Founded:** 1960. **Freq:** Quarterly. **ISSN:** 0038-0806. **Subscription Rates:** US$42. **Remarks:** Advertising accepted; rates available upon request.
                                         Circ: Paid 600

📖 **1072 Space in Japan**
Science and Technology Agency
2-1 Kasumigaseki 2-chome
Chiyoda-ku
Tokyo 100-0013, Japan   Ph: 81 335815271

Journal covering aeronautics. **Freq:** Biennial. **Subscription Rates:** 1,500¥.

📖 **1073 Species Diversity**
Japanese Society of Systematic Zoology
c/o Dept. of Zoology
National Science Museum
23-1 Hiyakunin-cho 3-chome
Shinjuku-ku
Tokyo 169-0073, Japan   Ph: 81 333642311

Journal of zoology. **Founded:** 1965. **Freq:** Semiannual. **Key Personnel:** Haruo Katakura, Editor. **ISSN:** 1342-1670. **Subscription Rates:** 10,000¥.
                                         Circ: Paid 500

📖 **1074 Structural Engineering — Earthquake Engineering**
Maruzen Co. Ltd.
3-10 Nihombashi 2-chome
Chuo-ku
Tokyo 103-0027, Japan   Ph: 81 332727211

Journal covering civil engineering. **Founded:** 1984. **Freq:** Semiannual. **ISSN:** 0289-8063. **Subscription Rates:** 2,500¥ single issue.

📖 **1075 Studies of Broadcasting**
Maruzen Planning Network Co
Atago-Mori Tower 16F
2-5-1, Atago
Minato-ku
Tokyo 105-6216, Japan   Ph: 81 354006800

Journal aimed at promoting the exchange of information on mass communications research. **Subtitle:** An International Annual of Broadcasting Scien. **Founded:** 1963. **Freq:** Annual. **ISSN:** 0585-7325. **URL:** http://www.nhk.or.jp/bunken/book-en/b46-e.html.
                                         Circ: 1,000

📖 **1076 Studies in English Literature**
English Literary Society of Japan
501 Kenkyusha Bldg.
9 Surugadai 2-chome
Kanda
Chiyoda-ku
Tokyo 101-0062, Japan   Ph: 81 332937528

Journal of literature. **Founded:** 1919. **Freq:** 3/year. **Key Personnel:** Hiroshi Ogawa, Editor. **ISSN:** 0039-3649. **Subscription Rates:** 7,000¥. **Remarks:** Advertising accepted; rates available upon request.
                                          Circ: Controlled 3,800

📖 **1077 Study of Medical Supplies**
Society of Japanese Pharmacopoeia
12-15 Shibuya 2-chome
Shibuya-ku
Tokyo 150-0002, Japan   Ph: 81 334005634

Medical science journal. **Founded:** 1970. **Freq:** Monthly. **Key Personnel:** Alcira Takanaka, Editor. **ISSN:** 0287-0894. **Subscription Rates:** US$600.

📖 **1078 Sumo World**
Clyde Newton
1-2-16 Inokashira
Mitaka-shi
Tokyo 181-0001, Japan   Ph: 81 334763774
Publication E-mail: patrick430@excite.com

Magazine on sumo. **Founded:** 1973. **Freq:** Bimonthly. **Key Personnel:** Clyde Newton, Editor. **Subscription Rates:** 3,900¥. **URL:** http://www.sumoworld.com/index.html.
                                          Circ: Paid 10,000

📖 **1079 Surgery Today**
Springer-Verlag Tokyo
3-13 Hongo 3-chome
Bunkyo-ku
Tokyo 113-0033, Japan   Ph: 81 338120617
Publication E-mail: orders@svt-ebs.co.jp

Medical science journal. **Founded:** 1899. **Freq:** Monthly. **Key Personnel:** Morito Monden, Editor. **ISSN:** 0941-1291. **Subscription Rates:** 50,000¥. **URL:** http://link.springer.de/link/service/journals/00595/aims.htm.
                                          Circ: Paid 1,500

📖 **1080 SUT Journal of Mathematics**
Science University of Tokyo
1-3, Kagurazaka
Shinjuku-ku
Tokyo 162-8601, Japan   Ph: 81 332604271
Publication E-mail: sutjmath@ma.kagu.sut.ac.jp

Mathematics journal. **Founded:** 1965. **Freq:** Semiannual. **Key Personnel:** Naoto Abe, Editor. **ISSN:** 0916-5746.

📖 **1081 Techno Japan**
Fuji Technology Press Ltd.
Toranomon Sangyo Bldg.
1-2-29 Toranomon
Minato-ku
Tokyo 105-0001, Japan   Ph: 81 335080051

Journal covering economics. **Subtitle:** A Monthly Survey of Japanese Technology and I. **Founded:** 1968. **Freq:** Monthly. **Key Personnel:** Keiji Hayashi, Editor. **ISSN:** 0911-5544. **Subscription Rates:** 24,000¥. **Remarks:** Advertising accepted; rates available upon request.
                                          Circ: Paid 18,756

📖 **1082 Telecom Tribune**
Ogiwara Bldg.
1-17-5 Uchikanda
Chiyoda-ku
Tokyo 101-0047, Japan   Ph: 81 332946191
Publication E-mail: info@telecom-tribune.com

Publication reporting on telecommunications and technology issues in and around Japan. **Founded:** 1985. **Freq:** Monthly. **Key Personnel:** Akira Kadokura, Editor-in-Chief. **ISSN:** 0912-9235. **URL:** http://www.techjapan.co.jp.

📖 **1083 TM**
Travel Management Inc
Dai-ichi Akiyama Bldg., 7F
2-3-22 Toranomon
Minato-ku
Tokyo 105-0001, Japan

Journal of travel and tourism. **Founded:** 1978. **Freq:** Semimonthly. **Key Personnel:** Toshio Takahashi, Editor. **Subscription Rates:** 8,400¥. **Remarks:** Advertising accepted; rates available upon request.
                                          Circ: Paid 12,251

📖 **1084 Tokyo Journal**
NeXXus Communications KK
BIG Office Plaza 1002-1006
62-8 Higashi-Ikebukuro
Toshima-ku
Tokyo 170-0013, Japan   Ph: 81 39800029
Publication E-mail: tj@nexxus.co.jp

General interest magazine. **Freq:** Quarterly. **Key Personnel:** Stephan Hauser, Editor-in-Chief. **ISSN:** 0289-811X. **Subscription Rates:** US$15.95. **Remarks:** Advertising accepted; rates available upon request. **URL:** http://www.tokyo.to/.
                                          Circ: (Not Reported)

📖 **1085 Tokyo Journal of Mathematics**
Kinokuniya Company Ltd.
38-1 Sakuragaoka 5-chome
Setagaya-ku
Tokyo 156-0054, Japan   Ph: 81 334390172

Mathematics journal. **Founded:** 1978. **Freq:** Semiannual. **ISSN:** 0387-3870. **Subscription Rates:** US$230.
                                          Circ: Paid 120

📖 **1086 Tokyo Scene**
P & K Inc.
3F Shikokuya Bldg.
Nishi-Gotanda 3-8-14
Shinagawa-ku
Tokyo 141-0031, Japan   Ph: 81 354376358

General interest magazine on Tokyo. **Freq:** Monthly. **Remarks:** Advertising accepted; rates available upon request. **URL:** http://www.tokyo-scene.com.
                                          Circ: (Not Reported)

📖 **1087 Tombo**
Society of Odonatology, Tokyo
c/o Mr. Shojiro Asahina
4-24 Takadanobaba 4-chome
Shinjuku-ku
Tokyo 160-0000, Japan

Journal of entomology. **Founded:** 1958. **Freq:** Annual. **ISSN:** 0495-8314.

📖 **1088 Tour Companion**
Tokyo News Service Ltd.
Tsukiji Hamarikyu Bldg., 10th Fl.
3-3 Tsukiji 5-chome
Chuo-ku   Ph: 81 335428521
Tokyo 104-0045, Japan   Fax: 81 335425086
Publisher E-mail: editorial@tokyonews.co.jp

Journal of travel and tourism. **Founded:** 1973. **Freq:** Biweekly. **Key Personnel:** Takashi Takeda, Editor. **Remarks:** Advertising accepted; rates available upon request.
                                          Circ: Free 80,000

1089 Toyota Technical Review
Toyota Motor Corporation International Public Affairs Division
1-4-18 Koraku
Bunkyo-ku
Tokyo 112-0004, Japan

Journal covering automobiles. **Founded:** 1991. **Freq:** Quarterly. **Key Personnel:** Hideo Hattori, Editor. **ISSN:** 0917-3706.

1090 Tsuda Review
Tsuda College
2-1-1 Tsuda-Machi
Kodaira-shi
Tokyo 187-0025, Japan   Ph: 81 423425111

Journal of literature. **Founded:** 1956. **Freq:** Annual. **ISSN:** 0496-3547.
Circ: 1,000

1091 Union of Japanese Scientists and Engineers Reports of Statistical Application Research
Union of Japanese Scientists and Engineers
5-10-11 Sendagaya
Shibuya-ku
Tokyo 151-0051, Japan

Mathematics journal. **Founded:** 1951. **Freq:** Quarterly. **Key Personnel:** T. Okuno, Editor. **ISSN:** 0034-4842. **Subscription Rates:** 8,700¥. **Remarks:** Advertising accepted; rates available upon request.
Circ: Paid 1,000

1092 Venus: Japanese Journal of Malacology
Malacological Society of Japan
c/o National Science Museum
3-23-1 Hiyakunin-cho
Shinjuku-ku
Tokyo 169-0073, Japan

Journal of zoology. **Founded:** 1928. **Freq:** Quarterly. **Key Personnel:** Akihiko Inaba, Editor. **ISSN:** 0042-3580. **Subscription Rates:** 7,500¥.
Circ: Paid 900

1093 Water Report
MYU, Scientific Publishing Division
2-32-3 Sendagi
Bunkyo-ku
Tokyo 113-0022, Japan   Ph: 81 338212930

Journal of environmental studies. **Founded:** 1991. **Freq:** Quarterly. **Key Personnel:** Junko Nakanishi, Editor. **ISSN:** 0917-0456. **Subscription Rates:** US$100.

1094 Zaiken
Waseda University Kagami Memorials Laboratory for Materials Science and Technology
2-8-26 Nishi-Waseda
Shinjuku-ku
Tokyo 162-0051, Japan   Ph: 81 332034782

Journal of metallurgy. **Founded:** 1993. **Freq:** Annual. **Key Personnel:** M. Nagumo, Editor. **ISSN:** 0919-8423. **Remarks:** Advertising accepted; rates available upon request.
Circ: Free 500

1095 Zoological Science
Zoological Society of Japan
Toshin Bldg. 2F
2-27-2 Hongo
Bunkyo-ku
Tokyo 113-0033, Japan   Ph: 81 338145461

Journal of zoology. **Founded:** 1984. **Freq:** Monthly. **Key Personnel:** Norio Suzuki, Editor-in-Chief. **ISSN:** 0289-0003. **Remarks:** Advertising accepted; rates available upon request.
Circ: Paid 3,400

TOYAMA

1096 Journal of Traditional Medicines
Chuo Insatsu Co
1-4-5 Shimo-Okui
Toyama 930-0817, Japan   Ph: 81 0764326572

Pharmacy journal. **Founded:** 1967. **Freq:** Quarterly. **Key Personnel:** Hiroshi Watanabe, Editor. **Subscription Rates:** 10,000¥. **Remarks:** Advertising accepted; rates available upon request.
Circ: Paid 1,300

1097 Mathematics Journal of Toyama University
Toyama University
Dept. of Mathematics
3190 Gofuku
Toyama 930-0887, Japan

Mathematics journal. **Founded:** 1990. **Freq:** Annual. **ISSN:** 0916-6009.

WAKAYAMA

1098 Publications of Seto Marine Biological Laboratory
Kyoto University
Graduate School of Science
Seto Marine Biological Laboratory
Shirahama-cho 459
Nishimuro-gun
Wakayama 649-22, Japan   Ph: 81 739423515

Journal covering biology. **Founded:** 1949. **Freq:** Semiannual. **Key Personnel:** Yoshihisa Shirayama, Editor. **ISSN:** 0037-2870. **URL:** http://www.kurcis.kobe-u.ac.jp/station/Seto/seto.html.
Circ: 460

YAMAGUCHI

1099 The Caving Journal
Speleological Society of Japan
Akiyoshidai Kagaku Hakubutsukan Akiyoshi
Mine-gun
Shuho-cho
Yamaguchi 754-0511, Japan
Publication E-mail: ssj@netlaputa.ne.jp

Periodical covering Japanese caves and caving. **Freq:** 3/year. **URL:** http://www.netlaputa.ne.jp/~ssj/en/e_publish.html.

1100 Journal of Speleological Society of Japan
Speleological Society of Japan
Akiyoshidai Kagaku Hakubutsukan Akiyoshi
Mine-gun
Shuho-cho
Yamaguchi 754-0511, Japan
Publication E-mail: ssj@netlaputa.ne.jp

Earth sciences journal. **Founded:** 1976. **Freq:** Annual. **Key Personnel:** T. Kuramoto, Editor. **ISSN:** 0386-233X. **Subscription Rates:** 3,000¥. **URL:** http://www.netlaputa.ne.jp/~ssj/en/e_publish.html.
Circ: Paid 250

1101 Journal of Tosoh Research
Tosoh Corporation
4560 Kaisei-cho
Shinnanyo-shi
Yamaguchi 746-0006, Japan   Ph: 81 834639911

Journal of chemical engineering. **Founded:** 1957. **Freq:** Annual. **Key Personnel:** Taiji Suzuki, Editor, t_suzuki@tosoh.co.jp. **ISSN:** 0914-3106.
Circ: Controlled 750

YAMANASHI

1102 International Journal of Biometeorology
International Society of Biometeorology
Societe Internationale de Biometeorologie
c/o Prof. M. Iriki
Yamanashi Institute of Environmental
  Sciences
Kamiyoshida, Fujiyoshida-shi   Ph: 81 555726211
Yamanashi 403, Japan   Fax: 81 555726204
Publisher E-mail: paul.beggs@mq.edu.au

International journal covering biometeorology. **Freq:** Quarterly. **Key Personnel:** Prof. M. Iriki, Editor-in-Chief, iriki@yies.pref.yamanashi.jp; Prof. H.D. Johnson, Field Editor, Animals; Dr. Richard de Dear, Field Editor, Artificial Systems; Prof. Alistair Woodward, Field Editor, Epidemiology; Dr. M. Shibata, Field Editor, Humans; Prof. Dr. D. Overdieck, Field Editor, Plants. **ISSN:** 0020-7128. **Subscription Rates:** US$511 North America; US$15.90 single issue North America; €429.49 other countries; €128.85 single issue other countries. **Remarks:** Advertising accepted; rates available upon request. **URL:** http://link.springer.de. **Alt. Formats:** Microform. **Additional Contact Info: Advertising:** Springer-Verlag, E. Luckermann, Heidelberger Platz 3, Berlin D-14197, 49 3082787739, fax: 49 3082787300.
                      Circ: (Not Reported)

YOKOHAMA

1103 Asian Journal of Oral and Maxillofacial Surgery
Asian Association of Oral and Maxillofacial Surgeons
Tsurumi Daigaku Shigakubu
Koku Gekagaku Kyoshitsu
1-3 Tsurumi 2-chome, Tsurumi-ku
Kanagawaken
Yokohama 230-0063, Japan

Medical science journal. **Founded:** 1989. **Freq:** Semiannual. **ISSN:** 0915-6992.

1104 Joint
Kanagawa Society of Joint Surgery
Showa Daigaku Igakubu
Fuzoku Fujigaoka Byoin Seikei Geka
1-30, Fujigaoka, Midori-ku
Kanagawaken
Yokohama, Japan

Medical science journal. **Founded:** 1986. **Freq:** Semiannual. **ISSN:** 0912-0904.

1105 Mitsubishi Heavy Industries Technical Review
Mitsubishi Heavy Industries, Ltd.
Technical Administration Dept.
3-1, Minatomirai 3-chome
Nishi-ku
Yokohama 220-8401, Japan   Ph: 81 452249050
Publication E-mail: mhitr@tech.hq.mhi.co.jp

Journal of technology. **Founded:** 1964. **Freq:** 3/year. **Key Personnel:** A. Numata, Editor. **ISSN:** 0026-6817. **Subscription Rates:** 4,500¥. **URL:** http://www.mhi.co.jp/tech/etechidx.htm.
                      Circ: 3,000

1106 Poetry Kanto
Kanto Poetry Center
Kanto Gakuin University
Kamariya Minami 3-22-1
Kanazawa-ku
Yokohama, Japan   Ph: 81 457812001

Journal of literature. **Founded:** 1984. **Freq:** Annual. **Key Personnel:** William I. Elliott, Editor.
               Circ: Controlled 700

1107 The Yoke
Yokohama Association for International Communications and Exchanges
Sangyo Boeki Center Bldg.
2 Yamashita-cho
Naka-ku
Yokohama 231-0023, Japan   Ph: 81 456717128
Publication E-mail: intlyoke@iris.or.jp

Magazine pertaining to social and cultural life of Yokahama. **Freq:** Bimonthly. **URL:** http://www.yoke.city.yokohama.jp/theyoke/index.html.

YOKOSUKA

1108 Connective Tissue
Japanese Society for Connective Tissue Research
Editorial Board of the Japanese Society for
  Connective Tissu
c/o Dept. of Biochemistry and Molecular
  Biology
Kanagawa Dental College
82 Inaoka-cho
Yokosuka 238-8580, Japan   Ph: 81 468228840
                        Fax: 81 468228839
Publication E-mail: connect@kdcnet.ac.jp

Medical science journal. **Founded:** 1969. **Freq:** Quarterly. **Key Personnel:** Ryu-Ichiro Hata, Editor. **ISSN:** 0916-572X. **URL:** http://jsctr.bcasj.or.jp/pub_info.htm.

KENYA

NAIROBI

1109 Newslink
Association of Christian Resource Organizations Serving Sudan
PO Box 21033   Ph: 254 256968518
Nairobi, Kenya   Fax: 254 2564141
Publisher E-mail: across@maf.org

Publication covering rural development. **Freq:** Annual. **Key Personnel:** Mike Wall, Contact, phone 254 2569685, across-mikewall@maf.or.ke. **Subscription Rates:** Free. **Remarks:** Advertising not accepted.
                      Circ: (Not Reported)

REPUBLIC OF KOREA

INCHON

1110 Pacific Focus
Inha University Center for Pacific Studies
Inchon, Republic of Korea

Political science journal. **Freq:** Semiannual. **Key Personnel:** Kwang Il Baek, Editor. **ISSN:** 1225-4657. **Subscription Rates:** US$20.

JEONJU

1111 The Korean Journal of Systematic Zoology
Korean Society of Systematic Zoology
Jeonbuk National University
Jeonju 560-756, Republic of Korea   Ph: 82 654702783

Periodical containing information on biology and zoology. **Founded:** 1985. **Freq:** Semiannual. **Subscription Rates:** US$20.

KUNSAN

1112 Fisheries Science Research
Kunsan National University College of Fisheries
Kunsan, Republic of Korea

Fisheries journal. **Founded:** 1985. **Freq:** Annual.

KYUNGGI-DO

1113 Asian-Australasian Journal of Animal Sciences
Asian-Australasian Association of Animal Production Societies
806 Kwachon
1-14 Pyullyang-dong, Kwachon-shi
Kyunggi-do 427-040, Republic of Korea   Ph: 82 25020757
Publication E-mail: inkhan@kornet.net

Publication providing information on agriculture and biology. **Founded:**
1988. **Freq:** Monthly. **Key Personnel:** In K. Han, Editor. **ISSN:** 1011-2367.
Subscription Rates: US$70 institutions (member countries); US$120 institutions nonmember countries.

Circ: 1,000

POHANG

1114 RIST Journal of R & D
Research Institute of Industrial Science & Technology
Central Laboratories
PO Box 35
Pohang 790-600, Republic of Korea   Ph: 82 562750900

Periodical covering science and technology areas. **Freq:** Quarterly.

SEOUL

1115 Archives of Pharmacal Research
Pharmaceutical Society of Korea
1489-3 Suhcho 3 dong Suhcho-gu
Seoul 137-073, Republic of Korea   Ph: 82 25843257

Publishes research reports in the pharmaceutical-biomedical sciences. **Founded:** 1978. **Freq:** Bimonthly. **Key Personnel:** Uhtack Oh, Editor-in-Chief.
ISSN: 0253-6269. **Subscription Rates:** US$120. **Remarks:** Advertising
accepted; rates available upon request.

Circ: Paid 1,500

1116 Asian Perspective
Institute for Eastern Studies
28-42 Samchung-dong, Chongro-ku
Seoul 110-230, Republic of Korea   Ph: 82 237000700
Publication E-mail: ifes@kyungnam.ac.kr

Political science journal. **Founded:** 1977. **Freq:** Quarterly. **Key Personnel:**
Melvin Gurtov, Editor. **ISSN:** 0258-9184. **Subscription Rates:** 44,000 W.
Remarks: Advertising accepted; rates available upon request.
Circ: Paid 2,300

1117 Bank of Korea Quarterly Economic Review
Bank of Korea Research Department
110 3 Ka Namdaemun Ro Chung-Ku
Seoul 100-794, Republic of Korea   Ph: 82 27594172

Business and economics journal. **Founded:** 1969. **Freq:** Quarterly. **Key
Personnel:** Seong Tae Lee, Editor.

1118 Bug
Business Network Co., Ltd.
Ste. 302, Bokjo Bldg., 29-15
Chung-pa 3ka, Yongsanku   Ph: 82 27111927
Seoul 140-133, Republic of Korea   Fax: 82 27065682
Publisher E-mail: business@andyou.com

Asian culture magazine.

1119 Development and Society
Institute of Social Development and Policy Research Center for Social
  Sciences
Seoul National University
Seoul 151-742, Republic of Korea   Ph: 82 28789337
Publication E-mail: isdpr@prome.snu.ac.kr

Periodical that analyzes social causes and consequences of development.
Founded: 1972. **Freq:** Semiannual. **Key Personnel:** Il Chul Kim, Editor.
Subscription Rates: 18,000 W. **URL:** http://sociology.snu.ac.kr/isdpr.

1120 Experimental and Molecular Medicine
Korean Society of Medical Biochemistry and Molecular Biology
821 KOFST
635-4, Yoksam-dong Kangnam-gu
Seoul 135-703, Republic of Korea   Ph: 82 2651621
Publication E-mail: dbmaster@bric.postech.ac.kr

Publication providing information on biology and medical science. **Founded:**
1964. **Freq:** Quarterly. **Key Personnel:** Soo Il Chung, Editor-in-Chief. **ISSN:**
0378-8512. **Subscription Rates:** 30,000 W. **Remarks:** Advertising accepted;
rates available upon request. **URL:** http://bric.postech.ac.kr/publications/
emm.

Circ: Paid 1,500

1121 Global Economic Review
Yonsei University Institute of East and West Studies
134 Shinchon Dong, Seodaemoon-ku
Seoul 120-749, Republic of Korea   Ph: 82 23939027

Publication providing information on political science. **Founded:** 1973. **Freq:**
Quarterly. **Key Personnel:** Kap Young Jeong, Editor. **Subscription Rates:**
US$40. **Remarks:** Advertising accepted; rates available upon request.
Circ: Paid 1,000

1122 Inquiry into the Future
Korean Society for Future Studies
Graduate School of Environmental Studies,
  Seoul National Uni
Rm. 13-211
Seoul, Republic of Korea

Asian history journal. **Founded:** 1970. **Freq:** Annual. **Key Personnel:** An Jae
Kim, Editor. **Subscription Rates:** US$5.
Circ: Paid 200

1123 Journal of Communications and Networks
Korean Institute of Communication Sciences
Hyundai Kirim Officetel No. 1504-6
1330-18 Seochodong, Seochoku
Seoul 137-070, Republic of Korea   Ph: 82 25395588
Publication E-mail: publish@jcn.or.kr

Publication providing information on computer networks. **Founded:** 1999.
Freq: Quarterly. **Key Personnel:** Byeong Gi Lee, Editor-in-Chief,
blee@snu.ac.kr. **ISSN:** 1229-2370. **Subscription Rates:** 30,000 W student
members; 35,000 W nonmembers. **URL:** http://jcn.or.kr.

1124 Journal of Economic Integration
Sejong University
Sejong Institution
Center for International Economics
Kunja-Dong, Kwangjin-Gu
Seoul 143-747, Republic of Korea   Ph: 82 234083338
Publication E-mail: cie@sejong.ac.kr

Periodical covering business and economics. **Founded:** 1986. **Freq:** Quarterly. **Key Personnel:** Myung-gun Choo, Editor. **Subscription Rates:** US$40
individuals; US$120 institutions. **Remarks:** Advertising accepted; rates
available upon request. **URL:** http://dasan.sejong.ac.kr/~cie.

Circ: Paid 250

1125 Journal of Electrical Engineering and Information Science
Korean Institute of Electrical Engineers
Seoul, Republic of Korea

Electrical engineering journal. **Founded:** 1990. **Freq:** Monthly. **ISSN:** 1226-
1262.

1126 Journal of Humanities
Yonsei University Press
Seodaemoon-ku, 134 Sinchon Dong
Seoul 120-749, Republic of Korea

Humanities journal. **Founded:** 1957. **Freq:** Semiannual. **Key Personnel:**
Gene Yoon, Editor-in-Chief. **Subscription Rates:** 5,000 W.

□ **1127 Journal of Korean Astronomical Society**
Seoul National University
San 56-1, Shilim-dong, Kwanak-gu
Seoul 151-742, Republic of Korea   Ph: 82 28849055

Astronomy journal. **Founded:** 1968. **Freq:** Semiannual. **Key Personnel:**
Minn Y K, Editor. **ISSN:** 0253-3065. **Subscription Rates:** 10,000 W.
Circ: Paid 500

□ **1128 The Journal of Microbiology**
Microbiological Society of Korea
The Korea Science & Technology Center
   (Rm. 803)
635-4, Yeogsam-dong
Seoul 135-703, Republic of Korea   Ph: 82 234533321

Microbiology journal. **Founded:** 1995. **Freq:** Quarterly. **Key Personnel:**
Myeong-Hee Yu, Editor-in-Chief. **ISSN:** 1225-8873. **Subscription Rates:**
US$70. **URL:** http://www.msk.or.kr.

□ **1129 Journal of Plant Biology**
Botanical Society of Korea
968-3 Pongchon-Dong Kwanak-Gu
402 Keumsong Bldg., Kangnam-ku
Seoul 151-051, Republic of Korea   Ph: 82 28840384

International journal devoted to biotechnology, biochemistry and macromo-
lecular structure, cellular and developmental biology, ecology, genetics and
genomics, molecular biology, morphology, physiology, and taxonomy of
plants. **Founded:** 1958. **Freq:** Quarterly. **Key Personnel:** Gynheung An,
Editor-in-Chief. **ISSN:** 1226-9239. **Subscription Rates:** 24,000 W. **Remarks:** Advertising accepted; rates available upon request. **Alt. Formats:**
CD-ROM.
Circ: Paid 750

□ **1130 Journal of Population, Health and Social Welfare**
Korea Institute for Health and Social Affairs
Eunpyung-Ku
Seoul 122-040, Republic of Korea   Ph: 82 23558003

Journal devoted to social service and welfare. **Founded:** 1981. **Freq:**
Semiannual. **Alt. Formats:** CD-ROM.
Circ: 500

□ **1131 Journal of Population and Health Studies**
Korea Institute for Population and Health
SAN 42-14 Bulgwang-Dong, Eunpyung-Ku
Seoul, Republic of Korea

Publication providing information on birth control. **Founded:** 1974. **Freq:**
Semiannual. **Key Personnel:** Joung Joo Lee, Editor. **ISSN:** 0259-9112.

□ **1132 KDB Report**
Korea Development Bank
10-2 Kwanch'ol-dong, Chongno-gu
PO Box 28
Seoul, Republic of Korea

Publication providing information on business and economics. **Founded:**
1977. **Freq:** Monthly. **Key Personnel:** Bong Won Lee, Editor.
Circ: 2,800

□ **1133 Korea Business World**
Korea Businessworld Ltd.
107-6 Banpo-dong, Seocho-ku
4-F Suhgun Bldg.
Seoul 137-040, Republic of Korea   Ph: 82 25321464

Business and economics journal. **Founded:** 1985. **Freq:** Monthly. **Remarks:**
Advertising accepted; rates available upon request.
Circ: 40,200

□ **1134 Korea Buyers Guide Electronics**
Korea Foreign Trade Association
Korea World Trade Center
159-1 Samsung-dong, Kangnam-gu
Seoul 135-729, Republic of Korea   Ph: 82 2551237

Business journal. **Freq:** Monthly. **Key Personnel:** Sung Hwan Park, Editor.
ISSN: 1227-5336. **Subscription Rates:** US$70.

□ **1135 Korea Development Bank: Its Functions and Activities**
Korea Development Bank
10-2 Kwanch'ol-dong, Chongno-gu
PO Box 28
Seoul, Republic of Korea

Periodical covering information of business and economics. **Freq:** Monthly.
Key Personnel: Min Beoung Yun, Editor. **ISSN:** 0075-6806.

□ **1136 Korea Economic Weekly**
Korea Economic Daily Co. Ltd.
4th Fl., WISE-Naeil Venture Center
154-11 Samsung-dong
Kangnam-gu
Seoul, Republic of Korea   Ph: 82 234302177
Publication E-mail: subscription@koreaeconomy.com

Business and economics newspaper. **Founded:** 1988. **Freq:** Weekly. **Key
Personnel:** Timothy M. Chung, Editor. **Subscription Rates:** 60,000 W.

□ **1137 Korea Focus on Current Topics**
Korea Foundation
Diplomatic Center Bldg.
1376-1, Seocho 2 dong
Seocho-gu   Ph: 82 234635600
Seoul 137-072, Republic of Korea   Fax: 82 234636086
Publisher E-mail: webmaster@kofo.or.kr

Political science journal. **Founded:** 1993. **Freq:** Bimonthly. **Key Personnel:**
Son Chu Whan, Editor. **Subscription Rates:** 3,500 W.

□ **1138 Korea Herald**
Korea Herald Newspaper
1-12, 3-ga, Hoehyon-dong
Jung-gu
PO Box 6479
Seoul 100-771, Republic of Korea
Publication E-mail: info@koreaherald.co.kr

General interest newspaper. **Founded:** 1953. **Freq:** Daily except Mondays.
Key Personnel: Lee Kyong-hee, Editor-in-Chief, klee@koreaherald.co.kr.
Subscription Rates: US$48.90 per month. **Remarks:** Advertising accepted;
rates available upon request. **URL:** http://www.koreaherald.co.kr.
Circ: 55,000

□ **1139 Korea Non-Life Insurance**
Korea Non-Life Insurance Association
80 Soosong-dong, 6th Fl., Chongno-ku
Seoul, Republic of Korea

Publication providing information on insurance. **Founded:** 1979. **Freq:**
Annual. **Key Personnel:** Il Sun Hong, Editor.
Circ: 2,000

□ **1140 The Korea Post**
2nd Fl, Daeok Bldg.
241-4 Oksu-dong
Songdong-gu
Seoul 133-100, Republic of Korea   Ph: 82 222981740
Publication E-mail: koreapost@koreapost.com

General interest magazine. **Freq:** Monthly. **Subscription Rates:** 70,000 W;
US$66 East Asia. **URL:** http://www.koreapost.com.
Ad Rates: BW: US$2,160   **Circ:** (Not Reported)
        4C: US$3,240

Ad Rates: GLR = general line rate; BW = one-time black & white page rate; 4C = one-time four color page rate; SAU = standard advertising unit rate;
CNU = Canadian newspaper advertising unit rate; PCI = per column inch rate.
Circulation: ★ = ABC; △ = BPA; ♦ = CAC; ● = CCAB; □ = VAC; ⊕ = PO Statement; ‡ = Publisher's Report; Boldface figures = sworn; Light figures = estimated.
Entry type: □ = Print; ♨ = Broadcast.

105

📖 **1141 Korea Trade**
Korea Trade Investment Promotion Corp
300-9, Yomgok-dong
Seocho-ku, Seocho
PO Box 101
Seoul, Republic of Korea   Ph: 82 234607114
Publication E-mail: kti@kotra.or.kr

Periodical aimed at informing the international investment community of emerging opportunities in Korea. **Founded:** 1983. **Freq:** Bimonthly. **Key Personnel:** Doo-Yun Hwang, Editor. **ISSN:** 0023-3943. **Subscription Rates:** US$20. **Remarks:** Advertising accepted; rates available upon request.
Circ: (Not Reported)

📖 **1142 Korea Trade and Investment**
Korea Trade Promotion Corp.
300-9, Yomgok-dong
Seocho-gu
Seoul, Republic of Korea   Ph: 82 34607114
Publication E-mail: kti@kotra.or.kr

Trade and investment magazine. **Founded:** 1983. **Freq:** Bimonthly. **Subscription Rates:** US$20. **URL:** http://www.kt-i.org.

📖 **1143 Korean Business Journal**
Seoul National University
San 56-1, Shilim-dong, Kwanak-gu
Seoul 151-742, Republic of Korea

Periodical covering business and economics. **Founded:** 1967. **Freq:** Quarterly. **Key Personnel:** Chung Nyun Kim, Editor. **Remarks:** Advertising accepted; rates available upon request.
Circ: 2,000

📖 **1144 Korean Economic and Financial Outlook**
Korea Institute of Finance
411 Ga Myong dong, Chung-gu
Seoul 100-012, Republic of Korea   Ph: 82 237056300

Publication that analyzes and forecasts macroeconomic performances and developments in the money and financial markets in Korea and abroad. **Founded:** 1996. **Freq:** Quarterly. **URL:** http://www.kif.re.kr/english/publication/perio1_start.html.

📖 **1145 Korean Financial Review**
Korea Institute of Finance
411 Ga Myong dong, Chung-gu
Seoul 100-012, Republic of Korea   Ph: 82 237056300

Publication providing analysis and forecasts of the domestic financial markets. **Founded:** 1993. **Freq:** Quarterly. **ISSN:** 1225-9462.

📖 **1146 Korean Journal of Chemical Engineering**
Korean Institute of Chemical Engineers
307, Regent River View Officetel, 547-8
Kui-dong, Kwangjin-ku
Seoul 143-709, Republic of Korea   Ph: 82 24583078

Publication providing information on chemical engineering. **Founded:** 1984. **Freq:** Quarterly. **ISSN:** 0256-1115.

📖 **1147 The Korean Journal of Defense Analysis**
Korea Institute for Defense Analyses
Office of Research Cooperation
Chung Ryang
PO Box 250
Seoul 130-650, Republic of Korea   Ph: 82 29611334

Military journal. **Founded:** 1989. **Freq:** Semiannual. **Key Personnel:** Changsu Kim, Editor. **ISSN:** 1016-3271.

📖 **1148 Korean Journal of International Studies**
Korean Institute of International Studies
PO Box 426
Seoul 110-604, Republic of Korea   Ph: 82 27527727

Political magazine. **Founded:** 1970. **Freq:** Quarterly. **Key Personnel:** Chong

Ki Choi, Editor. **ISSN:** 0377-0451. **Subscription Rates:** US$35. **Remarks:** Advertising accepted; rates available upon request.
Circ: Paid 1,200

📖 **1149 Korean Journal of Mycology**
Korean Society of Mycology
Dept. of Agrobiology
College of Agriculture
Dongguk University
Seoul 100-715, Republic of Korea

Biology and botany journal. **Founded:** 1972. **Freq:** Quarterly. **Key Personnel:** Kwon Sang Yoon, Editor. **Subscription Rates:** 30,000 W.
Circ: Paid 1,000

📖 **1150 The Korean Journal of Parasitology**
Korean Society for Parasitology
College of Medicine
Seoul National University
Seoul 110-799, Republic of Korea   Ph: 82 27408348
Publication E-mail: editor@parasitol.or.kr

Periodical containing original papers of research articles, case records, brief communications, and reviews or mini-reviews on parasites of humans or animals, and host-parasite relations. **Founded:** 1963. **Freq:** Quarterly. **Key Personnel:** Sung-Tae Hong, Editor. **ISSN:** 0023-4001. **Subscription Rates:** US$30. **URL:** http://www.parasitol.or.kr/kjp/.
Circ: Paid 1,000

📖 **1151 Korean Journal of Pharmacognosy**
Korean Society of Pharmacognosy
c/o Natural Products Research Institute
Jongro-ku, 28 Yeongun dong
Seoul 110-460, Republic of Korea   Ph: 82 27408925

Periodical containing information on pharmacy and pharmacology. **Founded:** 1970. **Freq:** Quarterly. **Key Personnel:** Jae Sue Choi, Editor. **ISSN:** 0253-3073. **Subscription Rates:** US$40. **Remarks:** Advertising accepted; rates available upon request.
Circ: Paid 800

📖 **1152 Korean Journal of Physiology and Pharmacology**
Eui-Hak Publishing and Printing Co.
448-13 Seokyo Dong Mapo-Gu
Seoul 121-210, Republic of Korea   Ph: 82 23260370
Publication E-mail: head@kosphar.org

Pharmacy and pharmacology journal. **Founded:** 1997. **Freq:** Bimonthly. **Key Personnel:** Soo Wan Chae, Editor. **ISSN:** 1226-4512. **Subscription Rates:** US$30.
Circ: Paid 1,000

📖 **1153 Korean Journal of Public Health**
Seoul National University
San 56-1, Shilim-dong, Kwanak-gu
Seoul 151-742, Republic of Korea   Ph: 82 27629101

Publication providing information on public health and safety. **Founded:** 1964. **Freq:** Semiannual. **Key Personnel:** Moonshik Zon, Editor.
Circ: 1,000

📖 **1154 Korean Journal of Zoology**
Zoological Society of Korea
Seoul National University
San 56-1, Shilli-dong, Kwanak-gu
Seoul 151-742, Republic of Korea   Ph: 82 28881803

Biology and zoology journal. **Founded:** 1959. **Freq:** Quarterly. **ISSN:** 0440-2510. **Subscription Rates:** 30,000 W.
Circ: Paid 500

📖 **1155 Korean Physical Society Journal**
Han'guk Mulli Hakhoe
Yuksam-Dong 635-4
Seoul 135-703, Republic of Korea   Ph: 82 25564737

Physics journal. **Founded:** 1968. **Freq:** Monthly. **ISSN:** 0374-4884.

1156 Korean Social Science Journal
Byung Young Ahn
PO Box 64
Seoul, Republic of Korea   Ph: 82 25629026

Periodical covering social sciences. **Founded:** 1973. **Freq:** Semiannual. **Key Personnel:** Hyun Chin Lim, Editor. **ISSN:** 1225-0368. **Subscription Rates:** US$13.

1157 Korean Society of Oceanography Journal
Hangug Haeyang Haghoe
Seoul National University
Seoul 151-742, Republic of Korea   Ph: 82 28725032

Publishes research papers and review articles on all aspects of oceanography. **Founded:** 1966. **Freq:** Quarterly. **ISSN:** 1225-1283. **Subscription Rates:** 30,000 W.
Circ: Paid 700

1158 KSME International Journal
Korean Society of Mechanical Engineers
KSTC New Bldg. 7th Fl.
635-4, Yeogsam dong Kangnam-ku
Seoul 135-705, Republic of Korea   Ph: 82 25013646
Publication E-mail: ksme@ksme.or.kr

Mechanical engineering journal. **Founded:** 1987. **Freq:** Monthly. **Key Personnel:** Dai Gil Lee, Editor. **ISSN:** 1226-4865. **Subscription Rates:** US$45. **URL:** http://www.ksme.or.kr/ksme/english/index-en.html.
Circ: Paid 700

1159 Maison
MCK Publishing
277-21 Nonhyundong
Kangnam-Ku
Seoul, Republic of Korea   Ph: 82 234852680

Magazine on architecture and construction. **Freq:** Monthly. **Subscription Rates:** US$54.98.

1160 Marie Claire
MCK Publishing
277-21 Nonhyundong
Kangnam-Ku
Seoul, Republic of Korea   Ph: 82 234852680

Magazine on apparel and fashion. **Freq:** Monthly. **Remarks:** Advertising accepted; rates available upon request.
Circ: (Not Reported)

1161 Mathematical Education
Korea Society of Mathematical Education
Seoul National University
Seoul, Republic of Korea

Mathematics journal. **Founded:** 1962. **Freq:** Semiannual. **Key Personnel:** Han Shick Park, Editor. **ISSN:** 1225-1380. **Subscription Rates:** 2,500 W. **Remarks:** Advertising accepted; rates available upon request.
Circ: Paid 500

1162 Metals and Materials
Korean Institute of Metals and Materials
POSCO Center 4th Fl.(East Wing)
892 Daechi 4-dong
Kangnam-ku
Seoul 135-777, Republic of Korea   Ph: 82 25571071

Publication providing information on metallurgy. **Founded:** 1995. **Freq:** Annual. **ISSN:** 1225-9438.

1163 Natural Product Sciences
Korean Society of Pharmacognosy
c/o Natural Products Research Institute
Jongro-ku, 28 Yeongun dong
Seoul 110-460, Republic of Korea   Ph: 82 27408925

Pharmacy and pharmacology journal. **Freq:** Quarterly. **Subscription Rates:** US$30.

1164 North Korea News
Naewoe Press
42-2 Chuja dong Chung-gu
PO Box 9708
Seoul 100-240, Republic of Korea

Periodical covering the political science field. **Freq:** Weekly. **Key Personnel:** One Hoe Kim, Editor. **ISSN:** 1012-4470.

1165 Ocean Research
Sang Joon Han
Ansan
PO Box 29
Seoul 426-600, Republic of Korea   Ph: 82 3454006000

Periodical covering information on earth science and oceanography. **Founded:** 1979. **Freq:** Semiannual. **Key Personnel:** Heung Jae Lie, Editor. **ISSN:** 1011-2723.
Circ: 1,500

1166 Performance Arts and Films
Hyundae Mihaksa Inc.
107 Hyehwa-dong
Chongro-ku
Seoul 110-530, Republic of Korea   Ph: 82 27663527

Magazine on costumes, film and music.

1167 The Plant Pathology Journal
Han Rim Won Publishing Co.
206-3 Ojang-Dong
Chung-gu   Ph: 82 222734201
Seoul 100-310, Republic of Korea   Fax: 82 222669083
Publication E-mail: yhokim@snu.ac.kr

Journal devoted to the publication of fundamental and applied investigations on all aspects of plant pathology and their traditional allies. **Founded:** 1985. **Freq:** Bimonthly. **Key Personnel:** Yin-Won Lee, Editor. **ISSN:** 0256-8608. **Subscription Rates:** US$100.

1168 Seoul Journal of Economics
Seoul National University Institute of Economic Research
Seoul 151-742, Republic of Korea   Ph: 82 28771629
Publication E-mail: sje@snu.ac.kr

Journal designed to carry both theoretical and empirical articles in all fields of economics. **Founded:** 1988. **Freq:** Quarterly. **Key Personnel:** Sibok Chang, Editorial Asst., sibok@hanmail.net. **ISSN:** 1225-0279. **Subscription Rates:** US$30. **Available Online.** **URL:** http://econ.snu.ac.kr/~ecores/english/sje.html.
Circ: Paid 300

1169 Seoul Journal of Korean Studies
Seoul National University Institute of Korean Studies
Seoul 151-742, Republic of Korea   Ph: 82 28885833
Publication E-mail: hanyon@plaza1.snu.ac.kr

Publication specializing in Korean Studies published within Korea in the English language. **Founded:** 1988. **Freq:** Annual. **Key Personnel:** Ryonggeun Lee, Editor. **ISSN:** 1225-0201. **Subscription Rates:** 8,000 W.

📖 **1170 Space**
Sea Young Chang
219 Wonseo dong, Chongro-gu
Seoul 110-280, Republic of Korea   Ph: 82 27472892

Journal devoted to architecture and construction. **Founded:** 1966. **Freq:** Monthly. **Key Personnel:** Heon Hun Kim, Editor. **Subscription Rates:** 60,000 W. **Remarks:** Advertising accepted; rates available upon request.
Circ: Paid ,5000

📖 **1171 This Month in Korea**
Korea International Relations Institute
37-2, 2-ka, Namsan-dong Chung-ku
Seoul, Republic of Korea   Ph: 82 7526310

Periodical covering political science. **Freq:** Monthly. **Key Personnel:** Suh Myung Suk, Editor.

📖 **1172 Vantage Point**
Naewoe Press
42-2 Chuja dong Chung-gu
PO Box 9708
Seoul 100-240, Republic of Korea

Business and politics journal. **Founded:** 1978. **Freq:** Monthly. **Key Personnel:** Li Ik Sang, Editor. **ISSN:** 0251-2971.
Circ: 3,000

📖 **1173 Wolgan Mot**
139 Sejongno
Chongno-gu
Seoul, Republic of Korea   Ph: 82 27217115

Magazine on apparel and fashion. **Key Personnel:** Kwon O-Kie, Editor.

📖 **1174 Women**
Korean National Council of Women
40-427 3ka Hangangro, Yongsan-ku
Seoul, Republic of Korea

Periodical covering women's interests. **Founded:** 1964. **Freq:** Monthly. **Key Personnel:** Yo Shik Lee, Editor.

📖 **1175 Women's Weekly**
14 Chunghak-dong Chongno-ku
Seoul, Republic of Korea

Pertains to women's interests. **Freq:** Weekly.

📖 **1176 World Friends**
International Friendship Society
PO Box 100
Seoul 100-601, Republic of Korea   Ph: 82 24612501

Hobbyist journal. **Founded:** 1966. **Freq:** Quarterly. **Key Personnel:** Yoo Suk Suh, Editor. **Subscription Rates:** US$12. **Remarks:** Advertising accepted; rates available upon request.
Circ: Paid 20,000

📖 **1177 Yonsei Business Review**
Yonsei University Industrial Management Research Centre
College of Business and Economics
134 Sinchon-Dong, Sudaemoon-ku
Seoul, Republic of Korea   Ph: 82 23920192

Business and economics journal. **Founded:** 1963. **Freq:** Semiannual. **Key Personnel:** Hwi Suck Choo, Editor. **ISSN:** 0036-4487. **Subscription Rates:** 8,000 W.
Circ: Paid 2,000

📖 **1178 Yonsei Medical Journal**
Yonsei University College of Medicine
PO Box 8044
Seoul 120-752, Republic of Korea   Ph: 82 23615061
Publication E-mail: ymj@yumc.yonsei.ac.kr

Periodical aimed at informing its readers of significant development in all areas related to medicine. **Founded:** 1960. **Freq:** Bimonthly. **Key Personnel:** Kwan Chul Tark, Editor-in-Chief, kctark@yumc.yonsei.ac.kr. **ISSN:** 0513-

5796. **Subscription Rates:** US$60. **URL:** http://www.eymj.org. **Alt. Formats:** Diskette; Magnetic tape.
Circ: Paid 1,400

📖 **1179 Yonsei Reports on Tropical Medicine**
Yonsei University Institute of Tropical Medicine
PO Box 8044
Seoul 120-752, Republic of Korea   Ph: 82 23615290

Medical journal. **Founded:** 1970. **Freq:** Annual. **ISSN:** 0375-5207.

SUWON

📖 **1180 FRI Journal of Forest Science**
Forest Research Institute Tree Breeding Department
Kyunggio-do
PO Box 24
Suwon 441-350, Republic of Korea

Forests and forestry journal. **Founded:** 1995. **Freq:** Annual. **ISSN:** 1225-9667.

📖 **1181 Korean Journal of Breeding**
Korean Breeding Society
School of Plant Sciences
Seoul National University
Suwon 441-744, Republic of Korea   Ph: 82 3312902307

Periodical covering information on agriculture and forestry. **Founded:** 1969. **Freq:** Quarterly. **Key Personnel:** Yeong-Ho Lee, Editor. **ISSN:** 0250-3360. **Subscription Rates:** 30,000 W. **Remarks:** Advertising accepted; rates available upon request. **Alt. Formats:** CD-ROM.
Circ: Paid 700

📖 **1182 Seoul National University Journal of Agricultural Sciences**
103 Seodoon-dong
Suwon, Republic of Korea

Agricultural journal. **Founded:** 1976. **Freq:** Semiannual. **ISSN:** 1013-4077.
Circ: 800

TAEJON

📖 **1183 ETRI Journal**
Electronics and Telecommunications Research Institute
161 Kajong dong Yusong-Gu
Taejon 305-350, Republic of Korea   Ph: 82 428605262
Publication E-mail: etrij@etri.re.kr

Academic journal in Korea in the field of electronics, information and telecommunications. **Founded:** 1993. **Freq:** Bimonthly. **Key Personnel:** Gil Rok Oh, Editor, groh@etri.re.kr. **ISSN:** 1225-6463. **URL:** http://e-trij.etri.re.kr.
Circ: 3,700

📖 **1184 Structural Engineering and Mechanics**
Korea Advanced Institute of Science and Technology
Dept. of Civil Engineering
373-1 Kusong-dong
Taejon 305-701, Republic of Korea   Ph: 82 428692441

Mechanical engineering journal. **Founded:** 1993. **Freq:** Bimonthly. **ISSN:** 1225-4568.

MALAYSIA

BATU CAVES

📖 **1185 Malayan Naturalist**
Malayan Nature Society
Jalan Bukit Idaman
68100 Batu Caves, Malaysia

Natural science journal. **Founded:** 1978. **Freq:** Quarterly. **ISSN:** 0127-0206.

1186 Malayan Nature Journal
Malayan Nature Society
Jalan Bukit Idaman
68100 Batu Caves, Malaysia

Natural science journal. **Founded:** 1949. **Freq:** Quarterly. **Key Personnel:** Geoffrey Davison, Editor. **ISSN:** 0025-1291. **Subscription Rates:** M$50 individuals; M$100 institutions.

         Circ: Paid 2,500

KAJANG

1187 Jurnal Sains Nuklear Malaysia
Malaysian Nuclear Society
Malaysian Institute for Nuclear Technology
  Research (MINT)
Bangi
Kajang, Malaysia
Publication E-mail: khairul@mint.gov.my

Nuclear science journal. **Founded:** 1983. **Freq:** Semiannual. **Key Personnel:** Ismail Bahari, Editor. **ISSN:** 0128-0155. **Subscription Rates:** M$100. **Remarks:** Advertising accepted; rates available upon request. **URL:** http://www.mint.gov.my/mns.

         Circ: Paid 1,000

KOTA KINABALU

1188 Borneo Review
Institute for Development Studies (SABAH)
Ste. 7 CF01, 7th Fl., Block C
Kompleks Karamunsing
88300 Kota Kinabalu, Malaysia   Ph: 60 88246166

Publishes research pertaining to economic, social, political and public administrative developments. **Founded:** 1990. **Freq:** Semiannual. **ISSN:** 0128-7397. **Subscription Rates:** M$32. **Remarks:** Advertising accepted; rates available upon request. **Available Online.**

         Circ: (Not Reported)

KUALA LUMPUR

1189 Asia-Pacific Military Balance
ADPR Consult (M) Sdn Bhd
19th Fl., SIME BANK Bldg.
No. 4, Jalan Sultan Sulaiman
50000 Kuala Lumpur, Malaysia   Ph: 60 322731355
Publication E-mail: enquiry@defencemagazine.com

Periodical covering geo-strategic developments of consequence to the Asia-Pacific region from an Asian perspective. **Freq:** Triennial. **ISSN:** 1511-3884. **URL:** http://www.adprconsult.com/.

1190 Asian Airlines & Aerospace
ADPR Consult (M) Sdn Bhd
19th Fl., SIME BANK Bldg.
No. 4, Jalan Sultan Sulaiman
50000 Kuala Lumpur, Malaysia   Ph: 60 322731355
Publication E-mail: enquiry@defencemagazine.com

Periodical containing special features, and profiles of the region's airline and aerospace industry. **Subtitle:** Asia's Leading Aviation Monthly. **Founded:** 1993. **Freq:** Monthly. **ISSN:** 1394-1798. **URL:** http://www.defencemagazine.com.
Ad Rates: BW: US$2,600   **Circ:** 18,000
         4C: US$3,500

1191 Asian Defence and Diplomacy
ADPR Consult (M) Sdn Bhd
19th Fl., SIME BANK Bldg.
No. 4, Jalan Sultan Sulaiman
50000 Kuala Lumpur, Malaysia   Ph: 60 322731355
Publication E-mail: enquiry@defencemagazine.com

Publication providing substantive reports and analysis on defence and security

issues. **Subtitle:** The Leading Magazine for Information on Regio. **Founded:** 1994. **Freq:** Monthly. **Key Personnel:** Gamal Fikry, Editorial Consultant. **ISSN:** 1394-178X. **URL:** http://www.defencemagazine.com.
Ad Rates: BW: US$3,000   **Circ:** 20,000
         4C: US$4,000

1192 Asian Defence Journal
Syed Hussain Publications Sdn Bhd
Haji Eusoff Damai Complex
61 A & B Jalan Dato
PO Box 10836
50726 Kuala Lumpur, Malaysia   Ph: 60 34420852

Periodical covering military, geopolitical affairs and all spheres of defense activities and industries from an Asia-Pacific perspective. **Founded:** 1971. **Freq:** Monthly. **ISSN:** 0126-6403. **Subscription Rates:** M$156.
         Circ: 20,000

1193 Auto International
Specialist Publications
15B Jalan Imbi
Kuala Lumpur, Malaysia

Automobile magazine. **Founded:** 1976. **Freq:** Monthly. **ISSN:** 0126-754X. **Remarks:** Advertising accepted; rates available upon request.
         Circ: Paid 20,000

1194 B & I Magazine
Eric Tan
32-2A Jalan Pandan 3/2
Pandan Jaya
55100 Kuala Lumpur, Malaysia   Ph: 60 392858223
Publication E-mail: et@b-i.com.my

Building and construction magazine. **Founded:** 1991. **Freq:** Bimonthly. **Key Personnel:** Joanne Gomez, Editor. **Subscription Rates:** M$1,500. **URL:** http://www.b-i.com.my.
Ad Rates: BW: M$1,900   **Circ:** (Not Reported)
         4C: M$3,000

1195 Banker's Journal Malaysia
Institut Bank-Bank Malaysia
Wisma IBI, No. 5 Jalan Semantan
Damansara Heights
50490 Kuala Lumpur, Malaysia   Ph: 60 320956833
Publication E-mail: publish@ibbm.org.my

Journal on banking and finance. **Subscription Rates:** M$50 members; M$60 nonmembers. **URL:** http://www.ibbm.org.my/bjm.

1196 Business Times
The New Straits Times Press (Malaysia) Berhad
Balai Berita 31
Jalan Riong
59100 Kuala Lumpur, Malaysia

Business newspaper. **Founded:** 1976. **Freq:** Daily. **Key Personnel:** Zainul Arifin, Editor, phone 60 320569800, zainul@nstp.com.my. **URL:** http://www.btimes.com.my.

1197 Dharma
Persatuan
Batu 6 Jalan Puchong
Jalan Kelang Lama Post Office
58200 Kuala Lumpur, Malaysia

Periodical that promotes the study of comparative theology and philosophy. **Subtitle:** A Quarterly Devoted to Universal Religion, Ri. **Founded:** 1949. **Freq:** Quarterly. **Key Personnel:** Mother A. Mangalam, Editor. **ISSN:** 0012-1746. **Subscription Rates:** M$6 single issue.
         Circ: Paid 3,000

1198 Discovering Mathematics
Malaysian Mathematical Society
Dept. of Mathematics
University of Malaya
50603 Kuala Lumpur, Malaysia

Mathematics journal. **Founded:** 1979. **Freq:** 3/year. **Key Personnel:** M.R. Wahidin, Editor. **ISSN:** 0126-9003. **Subscription Rates:** US$20.

1199 Engineering Science and Technology
University of Malaya
Lembah Pantai
59100 Kuala Lumpur, Malaysia   Ph: 60 37595504

Periodical covering the latest engineering discoveries and innovations. **Founded:** 1958. **Freq:** Annual. **Remarks:** Advertising accepted; rates available upon request.
                              Circ: (Not Reported)

1200 Esso in Malaysia
Esso Malaysia Berhad
PO Box 10601
Kuala Lumpur, Malaysia

Magazine covering petroleum and gas related aspects. **Founded:** 1979. **Freq:** Monthly. **Key Personnel:** Chan Soon Ching, Editor. **ISSN:** 0127-0710. **Subscription Rates:** Free.
                                Circ: Free 3,900

1201 Her World
Berita Publishing Sdn Bhd
16-20 Jalen 4/109E
Desa Business Park, Taman Desa
Off Jalan Kelang Lama   Ph: 60 0376208111
58100 Kuala Lumpur, Malaysia   Fax: 60 0376208026

Women's magazine. **Founded:** 1960. **Freq:** Monthly. **Key Personnel:** Datuk A. Kadir Jasin, Editor-in-Chief. **ISSN:** 0127-0079. **Subscription Rates:** M$68.75. **URL:** http://www.herworld.com.my.
Ad Rates: BW: M$2,970   **Circ:** Paid 35,000
           4C: M$4,620

1202 INFOFISH International
Infofish
1st Fl., Wisma PKNS
Jalan Raja Laut
PO Box 10899
50728 Kuala Lumpur, Malaysia   Ph: 60 326916804

Publication providing marketing information and technical advisory services for fishery products in the Asian and Pacific regions. **Founded:** 1981. **Freq:** Bimonthly. **ISSN:** 0127-2012. **Subscription Rates:** US$25 member countries; US$35 other developing countries. **URL:** http://www.infofish.org/.
Ad Rates: BW: US$1,330   **Circ:** Controlled 7,000
          4C: US$1,930

1203 Investors Digest Magazine
Kuala Lumpur Stock Exchange
Exchange Sq.
Bukit Kewangan
50200 Kuala Lumpur, Malaysia   Ph: 60 20267099
Publication E-mail: investorsdigest@beritapub.com.my

Addresses issues specific to the needs of those wishing to stay on top of investment opportunities. **Founded:** 1984. **Freq:** Monthly. **Key Personnel:** Datuk A. Kadir Jasin, Editor-in-Chief, akadirjasin@beritapub.com.my. **ISSN:** 0127-5461. **Subscription Rates:** M$86.40. **URL:** http://www.investorsdigest.com.my/index_html.
Ad Rates: BW: M$4,510   **Circ:** Paid 25,000
          4C: M$5,720

1204 Journal of the Malaysian Branch of the Royal Asiatic Society
Royal Asiatic Society Malaysian Branch
130M, Jalan Thamby Abdullah
Brickfields
50470 Kuala Lumpur, Malaysia   Ph: 60 322748345
Publication E-mail: mbras@tm.net.my

Scholarly publication. **Founded:** 1878. **Freq:** Semiannual. **Key Personnel:** Cheah Boon Kheng, Editor. **ISSN:** 0126-7353. **Subscription Rates:** M$30 individuals; M$50 institutions. **Remarks:** Advertising accepted; rates available upon request. **URL:** http://www.mbras.org.my/.
                               Circ: Paid 1,000

1205 Journal of Oil Palm Research
Malaysian Palm Oil Board
PO Box 10620
50720 Kuala Lumpur, Malaysia   Ph: 60 389259155
Publication E-mail: pub@mpob.gov.my

Oil palm research journal. **Founded:** 1989. **Freq:** Semiannual. **Key Personnel:** Yusof Basiron, Editor. **ISSN:** 1511-2780. **Subscription Rates:** M$30 single issue. **URL:** http://mpob.gov.my.

1206 Journal of Rubber Research
Malaysian Rubber Board
Public Relations, Publications and Library Unit
PO Box 10150
50908 Kuala Lumpur, Malaysia   Ph: 60 34567033

Publishes results and reviews on all aspects of rubber. **Founded:** 1928. **Freq:** Quarterly. **Key Personnel:** Datuk Alladin Bin Hashim, Editor. **ISSN:** 1511-1768. **Subscription Rates:** M$100. **Remarks:** Advertising accepted; rates available upon request.
                               Circ: Paid 1,000

1207 Journal of the Southeast Asian Archives
Southeast Asian Regional Branch International Council on Archives
National Archives of Malaysia
Jalan Duta
50568 Kuala Lumpur, Malaysia

Publishes mainly papers presented at seminars, conferences, workshops, colloquium, and etc organized by SARBICA (Southeast Asian Regional Branch of the International Council on Archives). **Founded:** 1968. **Freq:** Annual. **Key Personnel:** Shamsi Rih Sharifl, Editor. **Subscription Rates:** Included in membership; US$6 nonmembers. **Remarks:** Advertising accepted; rates available upon request. **URL:** http://arkib.gov.my/sarbica/publicat.htm.
                               Circ: (Not Reported)

1208 Journal of Tropical Agriculture & Food Science
Malaysian Agricultural Research & Development Institute
PO Box 12301
General Post Office
50774 Kuala Lumpur, Malaysia   Ph: 60 39437236

Publishes results of scientific studies in the fields of tropical agriculture and food science. **Founded:** 1973. **Freq:** Semiannual. **ISSN:** 1394-9829. **Subscription Rates:** M$40; US$40 other countries.
                               Circ: Paid 500

1209 Journal of Tropical Forest Products
Forest Research Institute Malaysia
Kepong
52109 Kuala Lumpur, Malaysia   Ph: 60 362797490
Publication E-mail: hoyf@frim.gov.my

Publishes original articles covering the entire field of science, processing and manufacture of wood and non-timber forest products. **Founded:** 1995. **Freq:** Semiannual. **ISSN:** 1394-2204. **Subscription Rates:** M$25 individuals; M$50 institutions.

1210 Journal of Tropical Forest Science
Forest Research Institute Malaysia
Kepong
52109 Kuala Lumpur, Malaysia   Ph: 60 362797490

Publishes original articles on current research related to tropical forestry and its associated sciences. **Founded:** 1988. **Freq:** Quarterly. **Key Personnel:** K.C. Khoo, Editor. **ISSN:** 0128-1283. **Subscription Rates:** M$45 individuals; M$90 institutions.
                               Circ: Paid 250

📖 **1211 Keretapi**
Malaya Railway Administration
PO Box 1
Kuala Lumpur, Malaysia

Transport journal. **Founded:** 1957. **Freq:** Quarterly. **ISSN:** 0047-3375. **Subscription Rates:** M$.60 single issue.
Circ: Paid 2,400

📖 **1212 Malaysiakini**
Mkini Dotcom Sdn. Bhd.
2-4 Jalan Bangsar Utama 9
59000 Kuala Lumpur, Malaysia   Ph: 60 322835567
Publication E-mail: subscribe@malaysiakini.com

Independent newspaper covering Malaysia. **Subtitle:** Only The News That Matters. **Key Personnel:** Steven Gan, Editor-in-Chief, steven@malaysiakini.com. **Subscription Rates:** M$100. **URL:** http://www.malaysiakini.com.
Ad Rates: BW: M$4,800   **Circ:** (Not Reported)

📖 **1213 The Malaysian Forester**
Forestry Department Headquarters
Jalan Sultan Salahuddin
50660 Kuala Lumpur, Malaysia   Ph: 60 326988244
Publication E-mail: hcthang@forestry.gov.my

Journal that deals with various aspects of tropical forestry and forest products. **Founded:** 1932. **Freq:** Quarterly. **Key Personnel:** Thai See Kiam, Chief Editor, skthai@forestry.gov.my. **ISSN:** 0302-2935. **Subscription Rates:** M$80. **URL:** http://www.forestry.gov.my/malforester.html.
Ad Rates: BW: M$550   **Circ:** (Not Reported)
4C: M$750

📖 **1214 Malaysian Journal of Economic Studies**
Persatuan
c/o Faculty of Economics & Administration
University of Malaya
50603 Kuala Lumpur, Malaysia   Ph: 60 379673600

Publishes original research related to the Malaysian economy. **Freq:** 2/year. **Key Personnel:** Tan Eu Chye, Editor. **ISSN:** 1511-4554. **URL:** http://www.pem.org.my/publications/journal-of-economic.htm.

📖 **1215 Malaysian Journal of Family Studies**
National Population and Family Development Board
PO Box 10416
50712 Kuala Lumpur, Malaysia

Publication providing various results of research in the area of family development in Malaysia. **Founded:** 1989. **Freq:** Annual. **Key Personnel:** Ang Eng Suan, Editor. **ISSN:** 0128-1232. **Subscription Rates:** US$10.
Circ: Paid 500

📖 **1216 Malaysian Journal of Library and Information Science**
University of Malaya
Faculty of Computer Science and Information Technology
50603 Kuala Lumpur, Malaysia   Ph: 60 379676316
Publication E-mail: kb@fsktm.um.edu.my

Publishes original articles based on professional policies, practices, principles and progress in the field of library and information science. **Founded:** 1996. **Freq:** Semiannual. **ISSN:** 1394-6234. **Subscription Rates:** US$30 individuals; US$30 institutions.

📖 **1217 The Malaysian Journal of Pathology**
Malaysian Society of Pathologists
University of Malaysia
Faculty of Medicine
Dept. of Pathology
59100 Kuala Lumpur, Malaysia   Ph: 60 37502064
Publication E-mail: msop@geocities.com

Publishes results of study and research in pathology, especially those relating to human disease occurring in Malaysia. **Founded:** 1978. **Freq:** Semiannual.

Key Personnel: Lai Meng Looi, Editor, lmlooi@medicine.med.um.edu.my. **ISSN:** 0126-8635. **Subscription Rates:** M$30; US$30 other countries. **Available Online.**

📖 **1218 Malaysian Journal of Science Series A: Life Sciences**
University of Malaya
Lembah Pantai
59100 Kuala Lumpur, Malaysia   Ph: 60 37595504

Periodical covering original research, communications, and reviews in the field of life sciences. **Founded:** 1971. **Freq:** 2/year. **Key Personnel:** Yong Hoi Sen, Editor. **ISSN:** 1394-1712.
Circ: 1,000

📖 **1219 Malaysian Journal of Science Series B: Physical & Earth Sciences**
University of Malaya
Lembah Pantai
59100 Kuala Lumpur, Malaysia   Ph: 60 37595504

Periodical covering original research, communications, and reviews in the fields of physical and earth sciences. **Founded:** 1972. **Freq:** 2/year. **Key Personnel:** Yong Hoi Sen, Editor. **ISSN:** 1394-3065.

📖 **1220 Malaysian Journal of Tropical Geography**
University of Malaya
Lembah Pantai
59100 Kuala Lumpur, Malaysia   Ph: 60 37595504

Periodical containing original papers on the human, physical and theoretical aspects of geography and the environment of tropical and sub-tropical areas. **Founded:** 1980. **Freq:** Semiannual. **Key Personnel:** Lee Boon Thong, Editor. **ISSN:** 0127-1474. **Subscription Rates:** M$40.
Circ: Paid 400

📖 **1221 Malaysian Panorama**
Ministry of Foreign Affairs
Jalan Wisma Putra
Kuala Lumpur, Malaysia

General interest periodical. **Founded:** 1971. **Freq:** Quarterly. **ISSN:** 0126-527X. **Subscription Rates:** Free single issue.
Circ: Paid 15,000

📖 **1222 Man and Society**
University of Malaya Press
University Library
Pantai Valley
50603 Kuala Lumpur, Malaysia   Ph: 60 37595524

Sociology journal. **Founded:** 1972. **Freq:** Annual. **Key Personnel:** Raziah Omar, Editor. **ISSN:** 0126-8678. **Subscription Rates:** US$15. **Remarks:** Advertising accepted; rates available upon request.
Circ: Paid 1,000

📖 **1223 Marie Claire**
M I Publishing
141A 1st Fl
Jalan Aminuddin Baki
Taman Tun Dr. Ismail
60000 Kuala Lumpur, Malaysia   Ph: 60 37194855

Periodical covering beauty and fashion trends. **Founded:** 1994. **Freq:** Monthly. **Key Personnel:** Jacqueline Pereira, Editor. **ISSN:** 0219-0206. **Subscription Rates:** M$63; M$63.
Ad Rates: BW: M$4,500   **Circ:** Paid 40,000
4C: M$4,800

📖 **1224 The Medical Journal of Malaysia**
Malaysian Medical Association
4th Fl., Mma House 124
Jalan Pahang
53000 Kuala Lumpur, Malaysia   Ph: 60 340411743
Publication E-mail: info@mma.org.my

Medical journal. **Founded:** 1890. **Freq:** Quarterly. **Print Method:** Offset. **URL:** http://www.mma.org.my/info/.
Ad Rates: BW: M$550   **Circ:** 8,000

📖 1225 The New Straits Times
The New Straits Times Press (Malaysia) Berhad
Balai Berita 31
Jalan Riong
59100 Kuala Lumpur, Malaysia
Publication E-mail: mishar@nstp.com.my

Business newspaper. **Subtitle:** Incorporating Business Times. **Founded:** 1845. **Freq:** Daily. **Subscription Rates:** M$30. **URL:** http://www.nst.com.my.
     Circ: 136,273

📖 1226 New Sunday Times
The New Straits Times Press (Malaysia) Berhad
Balai Berita 31
Jalan Riong
59100 Kuala Lumpur, Malaysia

English language newspaper for Malaysia. Includes tabloid magazine sections Sunday Style and Cars, Bikes, Trucks. **Founded:** 1931. **Freq:** Weekly. **URL:** http://adtimes.nstp.com.my/nsut.htm.
     Circ: 155,565

📖 1227 PC World Malaysia
Digital Access Sdn Bhd
P5-2 Podium Block
Plaza Dwitasik
No. 21 Jalan 5/106
Bandar Sri Permaisuri
56000 Kuala Lumpur, Malaysia

Computer magazine. **Founded:** 1999. **Freq:** Monthly. **Key Personnel:** Wilfred Lim, Editor, wilfred@daccess.com.my. **ISSN:** 1511-404X. **URL:** http://www.pcw.com.my/index.htm.

📖 1228 Show Daily
ADPR Consult (M) Sdn Bhd
19th Fl., SIME BANK Bldg.
No. 4, Jalan Sultan Sulaiman
50000 Kuala Lumpur, Malaysia   Ph: 60 322731355

Periodical featuring complete coverage of all press conferences, interviews with industry CEOs and top military brass, contract signing ceremonies, official VIP visits, live product demonstrations such as aerial displays and other newsworthy informat. **Freq:** Irregular. **Subscription Rates:** Free.

📖 1229 South Review
SNN Sdn Bhd
No 21-2, Jalan Setiawangsa 9
Taman Setiawangsa
54200 Kuala Lumpur, Malaysia   Ph: 60 342603944
Publication E-mail: snnmag@tm.net.my

Periodical aimed at providing a forum for voicing out the visions, concerns, and aspirations of the developing countries. **Founded:** 2000. **Freq:** Monthly. **Key Personnel:** A. Sri K. Nayagam, Managing Editor, phone 60 342603944, fax 60 342569676, snnmag@tm.net.my. **ISSN:** 1511-6956. **Subscription Rates:** M$58.80. **URL:** http://www.southreview.com.
Ad Rates: BW: US$790   **Circ:** (Not Reported)
     4C: US$1,200

📖 1230 Travel Agency
Phoenix Enterprise
KTM Godown No. 2A
Jalan Tun Sambanthan
50470 Kuala Lumpur, Malaysia

Periodical covering issues related to travel and tourism. **Founded:** 1978. **Freq:** Monthly. **Subscription Rates:** $A 20. **Remarks:** Advertising accepted; rates available upon request.
     Circ: (Not Reported)

📖 1231 Utusan Malaysia
Utusan Melayu (M) Bhd
46M, Jalan Lima
Off Jalan Chan Sow Lin
55200 Kuala Lumpur, Malaysia   Ph: 60 392877777
Publication E-mail: online@utusan.com.my

Newspaper catering to the multicultural, sophisticated public in Malaysia. **Key Personnel:** Dato' Mohd Khalid Mohd, Editor-in-Chief. **URL:** http://www.utusan.com.my.
Ad Rates: BW: M$36   **Circ:** Paid 235,483
     4C: M$3,000

📖 1232 Vision KL
Vision Kuala Lumpur
16, Jalan Liku Bangsar
59100 Kuala Lumpur, Malaysia

Lifestyle magazine for Kuala Lumpur. **Founded:** 1996. **Freq:** Monthly. **ISSN:** 1394-6382. **URL:** http://www.visionkl.com.

📖 1233 Watan
Kumpulan Akhbar Watan (KJ) Sdn Bhd
50-52 Lorong Rahim Kajai 14
Taman Tun Dr Ismail
60000 Kuala Lumpur, Malaysia

General interest periodical. **Founded:** 1977. **Freq:** Triweekly. **Key Personnel:** Encik Hishamuddin Haji Yaacub, Editor.
     Circ: Paid 80,000

PENANG

📖 1234 Environmental News Digest
Sahabat Alam Malaysia
19 Kelawai Rd.
Pulau
10250 Penang, Malaysia   Ph: 60 4376930

periodical that publishes papers devoted to the problems of environment science. **Founded:** 1983. **Freq:** 3/year. **Key Personnel:** David Heath, Editor. **ISSN:** 0127-7162. **Subscription Rates:** M$30.
     Circ: Paid 500

📖 1235 Penang Tourist Newspaper
Buildton Media Networks (M) Sdn Bhd
1-2-03 Jalan P. Ramlee
10460 Penang, Malaysia   Ph: 60 42826880
Publication E-mail: editor@pgtourist.com.my

Malaysian tourism newspaper. **URL:** http://pgtourist.com.my.

📖 1236 Suara SAM
Sahabat Alam Malaysia
19 Kelawai Rd.
Pulau
10250 Penang, Malaysia   Ph: 60 4376930

Periodical covering environmental issues. **Founded:** 1983. **Freq:** Bimonthly. **ISSN:** 0127-6409. **Subscription Rates:** M$16. **Remarks:** Advertising accepted; rates available upon request.
     Circ: Paid 2,500

📖 1237 Third World Economics
Third World Network
121-S, Jalan Utama
10450 Penang, Malaysia   Ph: 60 42266159
Publication E-mail: twn@igc.apc.org

Publication providing news and analyses that reflect the grassroots interests of people in the Third World. **Founded:** 1990. **Freq:** Biweekly. **Key Personnel:** Martin Khor Kok Peng, Editor. **ISSN:** 0128-4134. **Subscription Rates:** US$55 Third World countries; US$75 developed countries. **URL:** http://www.twnside.org.sg/twe.htm.

1238 Third World Resurgence
Third World Network
121-S, Jalan Utama
10450 Penang, Malaysia   Ph: 60 42266159

Periodical aimed at providing a Third World perspective on the issues confronting the Third World, including the environment, health and basic needs, international affairs, politics, economics, culture, and so on. **Founded:** 1990. **Freq:** Semiannual. **ISSN:** 0128-357X. **Subscription Rates:** US$45 institutions developed countries; US$30 individuals developed countries.

PETALING JAYA

1239 Art Corridor
Artext Publishing
Lot S1, 2nd Fl.
Centrepoint Bandar Utama
Lebuh Bandar Utama
47800 Petaling Jaya, Malaysia
Publication E-mail: artcorridor@koidholdings.com

Magazine specializing in fine arts. **Freq:** Quarterly. **Key Personnel:** Ming Chua, Editor. **URL:** http://www.artcorridor.net.

1240 Ethos
International Malaysia Forum
IMF Network Services
10, 2nd Fl., Jalan SS 21/62
Damansara Utama
47400 Petaling Jaya, Malaysia

Periodical that gives Malaysians living overseas a chance to voice their opinions. **URL:** http://www.ethos.com.my/.

1241 Ezyhealth Malaysia
Ezyhealth Asia Pacific Pte Ltd.
Optima Multimedia (M) Sdn. Bhd.
No. 58, Jalan SS22/21
Damansara Jaya, 1st Fl.   Ph: 60 377282399
47400 Petaling Jaya, Malaysia   Fax: 60 377252899
Publication E-mail: alisonlaw@ezyhealth.com

Health, beauty, and fitness magazine. **Founded:** 1999. **Freq:** Monthly. **Key Personnel:** Karen Koo, Advertising, karenkoo@ezyhealth.com. **Subscription Rates:** Free. **Remarks:** Advertising accepted; rates available upon request. **URL:** http://www.ezyhealth.com.
          Circ: Free 80,000

1242 Feminine
Life Publishers Bhd
2nd Fl., Nanyang Siang Pau Building
No. 1, Jalan SS 7/2
47301 Petaling Jaya, Malaysia

Women's magazine. **Founded:** 1978. **Freq:** Biweekly. **Key Personnel:** Yap Choy Hong, Editor. **Subscription Rates:** M$60.
Ad Rates: 4C: M$5,200   Circ: Paid 50,391

1243 Galaxie
Star Publications (M) Bhd
Menara Star, 15 Jalan 16/11
46350 Petaling Jaya, Malaysia   Ph: 60 379671388
Publication E-mail: cir.ccu@thestar.com.my

Entertainment magazine. **Founded:** 1974. **Freq:** Biweekly. **ISSN:** 1511-0133. **Subscription Rates:** M$40. **URL:** http://www.galaxie.com.my/home.asp.

1244 Golf Malaysia
Golf (Malaysia) Publications Sdn Bhd
No. 7-5, Block E2
Dataran Prima
Jalan PJU 1/42A
47301 Petaling Jaya, Malaysia   Ph: 60 378805060

Golf magazine. **Founded:** 1981. **Freq:** Monthly. **Key Personnel:** Shaun

Orange, Contributing Editor, shaunorange@golfmalaysia.com.my. **ISSN:** 0127-1997. **Subscription Rates:** M$120. **URL:** http://www.golfmalaysia.com.my/index.html.
          Circ: Paid 25,000

1245 Journal of the Institution of Engineers, Federation of Malaysia
Bangunan Ingenieur
Lot 60 & 62, Jalan 52/4
46720 Petaling Jaya, Malaysia   Ph: 60 37684001

Engineering journal. **Founded:** 1960. **Freq:** Semiannual. **ISSN:** 0538-0057. **Subscription Rates:** M$100 single issue.
Ad Rates: BW: M$700   Circ: (Not Reported)
                4C: M$1,300

1246 Jurutera
Institution of Engineers - Malaysia
Institusi Jurutera, Malaysia
Lots 60 & 62, Jalan 52/4
Peti Surat 223, Jalan Sultan   Ph: 60 37684001
46720 Petaling Jaya, Malaysia   Fax: 60 37577678
Publisher E-mail: sec@iem.po.my

Engineering journal. **Freq:** Monthly. **Key Personnel:** Haron Ismail, Editor. **Subscription Rates:** M$3 single issue. **Remarks:** Advertising accepted; rates available upon request.
          Circ: Paid 9,000

1247 The Malaysian Surveyor
Institution of Surveyors, Malaysia
3rd Fl., Bangunan Juruukur
64-66 Jalan 52-4   Ph: 60 379551773
46200 Petaling Jaya, Malaysia   Fax: 60 379550253
Publication E-mail: ism@po.jaring.my
Publisher E-mail: ism@po.jaring.my

Publication focusing on the development of the surveying profession, innovations in surveying technology and surveyors' contribution towards the property market and building industry. **Subtitle:** The Professional Journal of the Institution o. **Founded:** 1971. **Freq:** Quarterly. **Key Personnel:** Hj. Iskandar Hj. Ismail, Editor. **ISSN:** 0126-6268. **Subscription Rates:** M$40. **URL:** http://www.ism.org.my/library/journal/contents.htm.
Ad Rates: BW: US$650   Circ: Paid 3,000
                4C: US$900

1248 Rocket
Democratic Action Party of Malaysia
77 Jalan
20-9 Paramount Garden
Petaling Jaya, Malaysia
Publication E-mail: demoap@po.jaring.my

Focuses on the general news from the Democratic Action Party, component parties and NGOs in Malaysia. **Founded:** 1967. **Freq:** 3/week. **Key Personnel:** Tan Seng Giaw, Editorial Board Member, joonpin@pc.jaring.my. **ISSN:** 0048-8461. **URL:** http://www.jaring.my/daphome/edir/ehtm/econtrol.htm.

1249 The Star
Star Publications (M) Bhd
Menara Star, 15 Jalan 16/11
46350 Petaling Jaya, Malaysia   Ph: 60 379671388

General newspaper. **Subtitle:** The People's Paper. **Founded:** 1971. **Key Personnel:** Chua Yew Kay, Deputy Managing Editor. **URL:** http://thestar.com.my/info/thestar.asp.
          Circ: 279,647

Ad Rates: GLR = general line rate; BW = one-time black & white page rate; 4C = one-time four color page rate; SAU = standard advertising unit rate; CNU = Canadian newspaper advertising unit rate; PCI = per column inch rate.
Circulation: ★ = ABC; △ = BPA; ♦ = CAC; • = CCAB; ❑ = VAC; ⊕ = PO Statement; ‡ = Publisher's Report; Boldface figures = sworn; Light figures = estimated.
Entry type: ❑ = Print; ♠ = Broadcast.

113

📖 **1250 Union Herald**
National Union of Plantation Workers
Plantation Workers House
PO Box 73
46700 Petaling Jaya, Malaysia

Publication providing news about agriculture for plantation workers in Southeast Asia. **Founded:** 1961. **Freq:** Monthly. **ISSN:** 0049-528X. **Subscription Rates:** M$.50 single issue.
Circ: Paid 1,000

SABAH

📖 **1251 New Sabah Times**
PO Box 20119
Luyang, Kota Kinabalu
88758 Sabah, Malaysia   Ph: 60 88230055
Publication E-mail: inna@po.jaring.my

General newspaper. **Subtitle:** Sabah's First Established Paper. **Founded:** 1998. **URL:** http://www.newsabahtimes.com.my.
Ad Rates: BW: M$1,440   **Circ:** (Not Reported)

SERDANG

📖 **1252 Asia-Pacific Journal of Molecular Biology & Biotechnology**
Universiti Putra Malaysia
4th Fl., Administrative Bldg.
43400 Serdang, Malaysia   Ph: 60 389486101

Periodical covering topics relating to molecular biology & biotechnology. **Freq:** Semiannual. **ISSN:** 0128-7451.

📖 **1253 Pertanika Journal of Science and Technology**
Universiti Pertanian Malaysia Press
Serdang, Malaysia   Ph: 60 39433740

Science and technology journal. **Freq:** 2/year. **Key Personnel:** Abang Abdullah Abang Ali, Editor. **ISSN:** 0128-7680. **Subscription Rates:** US$60.
Circ: Paid 300

📖 **1254 Pertanika Journal of Social Science and Humanities**
Universiti Pertanian Malaysia Press
Serdang, Malaysia   Ph: 60 39433740

Social science journal. **Freq:** Semiannual. **Key Personnel:** Abdul Rahman Md Aroff, Editor. **ISSN:** 0128-7702. **Subscription Rates:** US$50 individuals; US$60 institutions.
Circ: Paid 200

📖 **1255 Pertanika Journal of Tropical Agricultural Science**
Universiti Pertanian Malaysia Press
Serdang, Malaysia   Ph: 60 39433740

Agricultural journal. **Founded:** 1978. **Freq:** 3/year. **Key Personnel:** Ruth Kiew, Editor. **ISSN:** 1511-3701. **Subscription Rates:** US$70. **Remarks:** Advertising accepted; rates available upon request.
Circ: (Not Reported)

SHAH ALAM

📖 **1256 SEAISI - Quarterly Journal**
South East Asia Iron & Steel Institute
PO Box 7094
Shah Alam, Malaysia   Ph: 60 355191102

Publication featuring technical papers presented during SEAISI's conferences and seminars and other related articles in iron and steel in South East Asia. **Founded:** 1972. **Freq:** Quarterly. **ISSN:** 0129-5721. **Subscription Rates:** US$100. **URL:** http://www.seaisi.org/index.htm.
Ad Rates: BW: US$500   **Circ:** Paid 2,000

UKM BANGI

📖 **1257 Journal of Education**
Jabatan Pendidikan
Universiti Kebangsaan Malaysia
43600 UKM Bangi, Malaysia

Periodical containing research, reports, commentaries and articles in the field of teaching and learning. **Founded:** 1970. **Freq:** Annual. **ISSN:** 0126-6020. **Subscription Rates:** US$15.

📖 **1258 Jurnal Ekonomi Malaysia**
Penerbit Universiti Kebangsaan Malaysia
43600 UKM Bangi, Malaysia

Business journal. **Founded:** 1980. **Freq:** Semiannual. **ISSN:** 0127-1962.
Circ: Paid 500

MALTA

VALLETTA

📖 **1259 Commercial Courier**
Chamber of Commerce - Malta
Exchange Bldgs.
Republic St.   Ph: 356 21 233873
Valletta, Malta   Fax: 356 21 245223
Publisher E-mail: admin@chamber.org.mt

Publication covering chambers of commerce. **Freq:** Monthly. **Key Personnel:** Kevin J. Borg, Contact, kjb@chamber.org.mt. **Subscription Rates:** 0.50 ML. **Remarks:** Advertising accepted; rates available upon request.
Circ: 1,300

NETHERLANDS

AMSTERDAM

📖 **1260 Journal of African Earth Sciences**
Elsevier Science
PO Box 211   Ph: 31 204853757
NL-1000 AE Amsterdam, Netherlands   Fax: 31 204853432
Publisher E-mail: nlinfo-f@elsevier.nl

Journal covering all aspects of geological investigations, especially the search for natural resources, on the African continent and surrounding Gondwana fragments. **Freq:** 8/year. **ISSN:** 0899-5362. **Subscription Rates:** 14,800¥ individuals Japan; €112 individuals Europe; US$125 individuals elsewhere; 228,600¥ institutions Japan; €1,722 institutions Europe; US$1,926 institutions elsewhere. **URL:** http://www.elsevier.com.

📖 **1261 Journal of Asian Earth Sciences**
Elsevier Science
PO Box 211   Ph: 31 204853757
NL-1000 AE Amsterdam, Netherlands   Fax: 31 204853432
Publisher E-mail: nlinfo-f@elsevier.nl

Journal covering all aspects of research related to the solid Earth Sciences of Asia worldwide. **Freq:** 8/year. **ISSN:** 1367-9120. **Subscription Rates:** 6,900¥ individuals Japan; €52 individuals Europe; US$58 individuals elsewhere; 113,600¥ institutions Japan; €856 institutions Europe; US$957 institutions elsewhere. **URL:** http://www.elsevier.com.

📖 **1262 Journal of South American Earth Sciences**
Elsevier Science
PO Box 211   Ph: 31 204853757
NL-1000 AE Amsterdam, Netherlands   Fax: 31 204853432
Publisher E-mail: nlinfo-f@elsevier.nl

Scientific journal covering earth sciences in the South American continent and surrounding oceans. **Freq:** 8/year. **ISSN:** 0895-9811. **Subscription Rates:** US$125 individuals except Europe & Japan; individuals Japan; €112 individuals European countries; US$798 institutions except Europe & Japan; institutions Japan; €713 institutions European countries.

📖 **1263 Nautique**
Multi Magazines BV
Prinsengracht 659-661
NL-1016 HV Amsterdam, Netherlands   Ph: 31 205353355
                                Fax: 31 205353344
Publication E-mail: nautique@multimag.nl

Consumer magazine covering yachting. **Subtitle:** The Dutch Yachting Magazine. **Founded:** Aug. 1995. **Freq:** Bimonthly. **Print Method:** Offset. **Trim Size:** 230 x 297 mm. **Key Personnel:** Sterre van Leer, Sub-Editor, s.vanleer@multimag.nl; Arthur van t Hoff, Editor-in-Chief; Fred van Ligten, Sales Mgr., f.vanligten@multimag.nl. **Subscription Rates:** €23.85 individuals; €5.15 single issue. **Remarks:** Accepts advertising. **URL:** http://www.nautique.nl.
Ad Rates: BW: €2,650   **Circ:** Combined 16,161
           4C: €3,600

DORDRECHT

📖 **1264 Feminist Legal Studies**
Kluwer Academic Publishers
Van Godewijckstraat 30
PO Box 17
NL-3300 AA Dordrecht, Netherlands   Ph: 31 786576000
                                Fax: 31 786576254
Publisher E-mail: kluwer@wkap.com

Law periodical. **Freq:** Semiannual. **ISSN:** 0966-3622. **Online:** Gale Group.

📖 **1265 International Journal for Philosophy of Religion**
Kluwer Academic Publishers
Van Godewijckstraat 30
PO Box 17
NL-3300 AA Dordrecht, Netherlands   Ph: 31 786576000
                                Fax: 31 786576254
Publisher E-mail: kluwer@wkap.com

Publication covering philosophy and religion. **Freq:** Bimonthly. **ISSN:** 0020-7047. **Online:** Gale Group.

📖 **1266 Liverpool Law Review**
Kluwer Academic Publishers
Van Godewijckstraat 30
PO Box 17
NL-3300 AA Dordrecht, Netherlands   Ph: 31 786576000
                                Fax: 31 786576254
Publisher E-mail: kluwer@wkap.com

Law periodical. **Freq:** Semiannual. **ISSN:** 0144-932X. **Online:** Gale Group.

📖 **1267 Res Publica**
Kluwer Academic Publishers
Van Godewijckstraat 30
PO Box 17
NL-3300 AA Dordrecht, Netherlands   Ph: 31 786576000
                                Fax: 31 786576254
Publisher E-mail: kluwer@wkap.com

Law periodical. **Freq:** Semiannual. **ISSN:** 1356-4765. **Online:** Gale Group.

MAASTRICHT

📖 **1268 Acta Neuropsychiatrica**
Blackwell Publishers Ltd
University Hospital of Maastricht
Dept. of Psychiatry
PO Box 5800
NL 6202 AZ Maastricht, Netherlands   Ph: 31 433877443
                                Fax: 31 433875444
Publication E-mail: crc.mh@skynet.be

Journal covering clinical, preclinical and molecular aspects of neuropsychiatric disorders. **Freq:** Bimonthly. **Key Personnel:** Michael Maes, Editor. **ISSN:** 0924-2708. **Subscription Rates:** US$224 institutions The Americas; print & premium online; 161 f institutions elsewhere; print & premium online; US$222 institutions The Americas; print & standard online; 146 f institutions elsewhere; print & standard online; US$200 institutions The Americas; premium online only; 131 f institutions elsewhere; premium online only; US$100 individuals The Americas; print & online; 66 f individuals elsewhere; print & online; US$90 individuals The Americas; online only; 59 f individuals

elsewhere; online only. **Available Online.** **URL:** http://www.blackwellpublishing.com.

RYSWYK

📖 **1269 Slagers Wereld**
Koninklijke Nederlandse Slagersorganisatie
Postbus 1234
NL-2280 CE Ryswyk, Netherlands   Ph: 31 703906365
                                Fax: 31 703904459
Publisher E-mail: slagershuis@wxs.nl

Dutch language publication covering the meat industry. **Freq:** Biweekly. **ISSN:** 0037-6698. **Remarks:** Advertising accepted; rates available upon request.
                                       Circ: 8,000

NEW ZEALAND

DUNEDIN NORTH

📖 **1270 New Zealand Journal of Archaeology**
New Zealand Archaeological Association, Inc.
PO Box 6337
Dunedin North, New Zealand   Ph: 64 34772372
                                Fax: 64 34775993
Publisher E-mail: dr.rock@clear.net.nz

Professional journal covering prehistoric and historic archaeology in New Zealand. **Freq:** Annual. **Key Personnel:** Janet Davidson, Editor. **ISSN:** 0110-540X. **Subscription Rates:** NZ$25 individuals; NZ$35 out of country. **URL:** http://www.nzarchaeology.org/nzja.html.

PALMERSTON NORTH

📖 **1271 New Zealand Veterinary Journal**
New Zealand Veterinary Association
Massey University
Private Bag 11-222
Palmerston North, New Zealand   Ph: 64 06 329 4045
                                Fax: 64 06 329 4047
Publication E-mail: nzvj@massey.ac.nz
Publisher E-mail: nzva@vets.org.nz

New Zealand journal covering veterinary medicine. **Freq:** Bimonthly. **Remarks:** Accepts advertising. **Alt. Formats:** CD-ROM.
                                    Circ: (Not Reported)

TIMARU

📖 **1272 Timaru Herald**
Timaru Herald Ltd.
PO Box 46
52 Bank St.
Timaru, New Zealand   Ph: 64 36844129
                                Fax: 64 36881042

General newspaper. **Founded:** Nov. 6, 1864. **Freq:** Mon.-Sat. **Print Method:** Web offset. **Key Personnel:** Barry Appleby, General Mgr.; Dave Wood, Editor, editor@timaruherald.co.nz; Kelvin Ayson, Business Mgr., kelvin.ayson@timaruherald.co.nz. **Subscription Rates:** NZ$216.45 individuals. **Remarks:** Accepts advertising. **URL:** http://www.stuff.co.nz. **Feature Editors:** Stephen Mitchell, *Features*.
                                    Circ: Combined 14,308

WELLINGTON

📖 **1273 In Business**
Business NZ
Level 6, Microsoft House
3 Hunter St.
PO Box 1925
Wellington, New Zealand   Ph: 64 4 4966555
                                Fax: 64 4 4966550
Publication E-mail: admin@businessnz.org.nz
Publisher E-mail: nzef@nzef.org.nz

Publication covering business and commerce. **Freq:** Bimonthly. **ISSN:** 0046-

Ad Rates: GLR = general line rate; BW = one-time black & white page rate; 4C = one-time four color page rate; SAU = standard advertising unit rate; CNU = Canadian newspaper advertising unit rate; PCI = per column inch rate.
Circulation: ★ = ABC; △ = BPA; ♦ = CAC; • = CCAB; ❑ = VAC; ⊕ = PO Statement; ‡ = Publisher's Report; Boldface figures = sworn; Light figures = estimated.
Entry type: 📖 = Print; 🎙 = Broadcast.

115

1903. **Subscription Rates:** Free for members only. **Remarks:** Advertising not accepted. **Formerly:** The Employer.

Circ: 15,000

1274 New Zealand Economic Papers
New Zealand Association of Economists
PO Box 568   Ph: 64 48017139
Wellington, New Zealand   Fax: 64 48017106
Publisher E-mail: economists@nzae.org.nz

Publication covering economics. **Founded:** 1967. **Freq:** 2/year. **Trim Size:** 230 x 150 cm. **Key Personnel:** Val Browning, Contact. **ISSN:** 0077-9954. **Subscription Rates:** NZ$90; NZ$100 New Zealand, airmail; NZ$120 Australia, airmail; NZ$130 other countries airmail. **Remarks:** Advertising not accepted.

Circ: (Not Reported)

POLAND

WARSAW

1275 Dos Yidishe Wort
Social and Cultural Association of Jews in Poland
Towarzystwo Spoleczno Kulturalne Zydow w Polsce
Grzybowski Sq. 12/16   Ph: 48 226200554
PL-00-104 Warsaw, Poland   Fax: 48 226522822
Publication E-mail: jwort@jewish.org.pl

Polish and Yiddish language publication covering Jewish religion, affairs, traditions, politics, history, and culture. **Founded:** 1992. **Freq:** Semimonthly. **Print Method:** Offset. **Trim Size:** A4. **Key Personnel:** Adam Rok, phone 48 226200548. **ISSN:** 0867-8421. **Subscription Rates:** US$30. **Remarks:** Advertising accepted; rates available upon request. **URL:** http://www.wort.prv.pl.

Circ: Paid 1,200

1276 Kwietnik
Agora S.A.
ul. Czerska 8/10   Ph: 48 226077650
PL-00-732 Warsaw, Poland   Fax: 48 226077651
Publication E-mail: kwietnik@agora.pl

Journal covering gardening and horticulture. **Founded:** Jan. 1995. **Freq:** Monthly. **Trim Size:** 204 x 275 mm. **Key Personnel:** Anna Slomczynska, Editor-in-Chief, phone 48 226077650, anna.slomczynska@agora.pl; Malgorzata Szymczykiewicz, Deputy Editor, phone 48 226077655, malgorzata.szymczykiewicz@agora.pl; Alicja Gawrys, Editor, phone 48 226077658; Magdalena Narkiewicz, Editor, phone 48 226077658; Anna Landowska, Secretary of the Board, phone 48 226077654, anna.landowska@agora.pl. **ISSN:** 1233-3808. **Remarks:** Accepts advertising.

Circ: (Not Reported)

1277 Postepy Astronautyki
Polish Astronautical Society
Polskie Towarzystwo Astronautyczne
Bartyckalba Str   Ph: 48 228403766
PL-00-716 Warsaw, Poland   Fax: 48 2284003131
Publisher E-mail: poczta@PTAstronaut.org.pl

English, Polish and Russian language publication covering aerospace. **Freq:** Biennial. **Subscription Rates:** 2.52 Zl.

Circ: 200

PORTUGAL

COIMBRA

1278 A Padaria Portuguesa
Bakery and Confectionery Products Association
Associacao do Conercio e da Industria de Panificacao, Pasterlaria e Similares
Apartado 1050   Ph: 351 239822845
P-3001 Coimbra 501, Portugal Fax: 351 239833099
Publication E-mail: aciprevista@netbi.pt

Portuguese language publication covering baking. **Founded:** Apr. 1997. **Freq:** Periodic. **Trim Size:** A4. **Key Personnel:** Jorge Ferreira Nunes,

Contact, jferreiranunes@clix.pt. **Remarks:** Advertising accepted; rates available upon request. **Available Online. Alt. Formats:** CD-ROM.

Circ: Non-paid ⊕**4,000**

RUSSIA

MOSCOW

1279 V Yedinom Stroyu
All-Russian Society of the Deaf
Vserossiiskoe Obshchestvo Glukhikh
ulitsa 1905-goda 10A
123022 Moscow, Russia   Ph: 7 952556704

Russian language publication covering the hearing impaired. **Founded:** 1933. **Freq:** Monthly. **Print Method:** Offset. **Trim Size:** 84 x 108. **Key Personnel:** V. Scripov, Editor-in-Chief. **Subscription Rates:** 12 Rb single issue. **Remarks:** Advertising accepted; rates available upon request. **Available Online. Formerly:** Tchizn Glyhih.

Circ: 3,000

SAUDI ARABIA

BAHRAIN

1280 Arab Gulf Journal of Scientific Research
Arab Gulf University
PO Box 26460
Manama
Bahrain, Saudi Arabia
Publication E-mail: riyad@agu.edu.bh.

Multidisciplinary science journal. **Founded:** 1983. **Freq:** 3/year. **Key Personnel:** Daham Alani, Editor. **ISSN:** 1015-4442. **Subscription Rates:** US$25 individuals; US$50 institutions. **URL:** http://www.agu.edu.bh/english/scientific/.

Circ: Paid 2,000

DHAHRAN

1281 Arabian Journal for Science and Engineering
King Fahd University of Petroleum and Minerals
PO Box 5033
Dhahran 31261, Saudi Arabia
Publication E-mail: ajse@kfupm.edu.sa

Journal of science and engineering. **Founded:** 1975. **Freq:** Bimonthly. **Key Personnel:** Harry A. Mavromatis, Editor. **ISSN:** 0377-9211. **Subscription Rates:** US$70. **Remarks:** Advertising accepted; rates available upon request.

Circ: Paid 800

JEDDAH

1282 Arab News
Saudi Research & Publishing Co.
SRP Bldg.
Madinah Rd.
PO Box 10452
Jeddah 21433, Saudi Arabia Ph: 966 26391888

General newspaper. **Subtitle:** Saudi Arabia's Frst English Daily. **Founded:** 1975. **Freq:** Daily. **Key Personnel:** Khaled Al-Maeena, Editor-in-Chief, almaeena@arabnews.com-. **ISSN:** 0254-833X. **URL:** http://www.arabnews.com/.

1283 Islamic World Medical Journal
Islamic Press Agency
PO Box 4288
Jeddah, Saudi Arabia

Journal of religion and theology. **Founded:** 1984. **Freq:** Bimonthly. **ISSN:** 0950-4567.

1284 King Abdul Aziz Medical Journal
King Abdul Aziz University College of Medicine and Allied Sciences
PO Box 1540
Jeddah 21441, Saudi Arabia

Medical journal. **Founded:** 1981. **Freq:** Quarterly. **ISSN:** 0254-413X. **Alt. Formats:** CD-ROM.

1285 Marine Science Journal of King Abdul Aziz University
King Abdul Aziz University Faculty of Marine Science
PO Box 1540
Jeddah 21441, Saudi Arabia   Ph: 966 26952386

Journal of marine science. **Founded:** 1981. **Freq:** Annual. **Key Personnel:** A.K. Behairy, Editor. **ISSN:** 1012-8840. **Subscription Rates:** US$5.

1286 Saudi Gazette
Okaz Organization for Press and Publication
PO Box 5576
Jeddah 21432, Saudi Arabia   Ph: 966 26722775
Publication E-mail: 105652.1670@compuserve.com

General newspaper. **Founded:** 1976. **Freq:** Daily. **Key Personnel:** Ahmed Al Yusuf, Editor-in-Chief. **ISSN:** 1319-0326. **Subscription Rates:** 600 SRl; 800 SRl other countries. **Remarks:** Advertising accepted; rates available upon request. **URL:** http://www.saudigazette.com.sa.
Circ: Paid 60,000

1287 Saudi Heart Journal
Saudi Heart Foundation
PO Box 6615
Jeddah 21452, Saudi Arabia   Ph: 966 26697043

Journal of cardiovascular diseases. **Founded:** 1989. **Freq:** 2/year. **Key Personnel:** Hassan Raffa, Editor. **ISSN:** 1018-077X. **Remarks:** Advertising accepted; rates available upon request. **Alt. Formats:** CD-ROM.
Circ: Free 5,000

RIYADH

1288 Administrative Sciences Journal of King Saud University
King Saud University University Libraries
PO Box 22480
Riyadh 11495, Saudi Arabia   Ph: 966 14676148

Journal of business and economics. **Founded:** 1989. **Freq:** Semiannual. **Key Personnel:** Khalid A Al Hamoudi, Editor. **ISSN:** 1018-3582. **Subscription Rates:** US$10.
Circ: Paid 3,000

1289 Agricultural Sciences Journal of King Saud University
King Saud University University Libraries
PO Box 22480
Riyadh 11495, Saudi Arabia   Ph: 966 14676148

Agricultural scientific journal. **Founded:** 1989. **Freq:** Semiannual. **Key Personnel:** Khalid A Al Hamoudi, Editor. **ISSN:** 1018-3590. **Subscription Rates:** US$10.
Circ: Paid 2,000

1290 Annals of Saudi Medicine
PO Box 3354
Riyadh 11211, Saudi Arabia   Ph: 966 14647272
Publication E-mail: renee@kfshrc.edu.sa

Multidisciplinary medical journal dealing with clinical, academic, and investigative medicine and research. **Founded:** 1981. **Freq:** Bimonthly. **Key Personnel:** Mohammed Akhtar, Editor, web_annals@kfshrc.edu.sa. **ISSN:** 0256-4947. **Subscription Rates:** 25 SRl. **Remarks:** Advertising accepted; rates available upon request. **URL:** http://www.kfshrc.edu.sa.
Circ: Controlled 17,000

1291 Arab Journal of Library and Information Science
Mars Publishing House
PO Box 10720
Riyadh 11443, Saudi Arabia

Journal of library and information science. **Founded:** 1980. **Freq:** Quarterly. **Key Personnel:** Abduaalh Al Majid, Editor. **Subscription Rates:** 120 SRl. **Remarks:** Advertising accepted; rates available upon request.
Circ: (Not Reported)

1292 Architecture and Planning Journal of King Saud University
King Saud University University Libraries
PO Box 22480
Riyadh 11495, Saudi Arabia   Ph: 966 14676148

Journal of architecture. **Founded:** 1989. **Freq:** Annual. **ISSN:** 1018-3604. **Subscription Rates:** US$5.

1293 Arts Journal of King Saud University
King Saud University University Libraries
PO Box 22480
Riyadh 11495, Saudi Arabia   Ph: 966 14676148

Journal of art and literature. **Founded:** 1993. **Freq:** Semiannual. **Key Personnel:** Khalid A Al Hamoudi, Editor. **ISSN:** 1018-3612. **Subscription Rates:** US$10.
Circ: Paid 3,000

1294 Computer and Information Sciences Journal of King Saud University
King Saud University University Libraries
PO Box 22480
Riyadh 11495, Saudi Arabia   Ph: 966 14676148

Computer science journal. **Founded:** 1993. **Freq:** Annual. **Key Personnel:** Khalid A Al Hamoudi, Editor. **ISSN:** 1319-1578. **Subscription Rates:** US$5.
Circ: Paid 2,000

1295 Educational Sciences and Islamic Studies Journal of King Saud University
King Saud University University Libraries
PO Box 22480
Riyadh 11495, Saudi Arabia   Ph: 966 14676148

Journal of Islamic religion and theology. **Founded:** 1989. **Freq:** Semiannual. **Key Personnel:** Khalid A Al Dobaian, Editor. **ISSN:** 1018-3620. **Subscription Rates:** US$10.
Circ: Paid 2,000

1296 Engineering Sciences Journal of King Saud University
King Saud University
PO Box 800
Riyadh 11421, Saudi Arabia   Ph: 966 14678687
Publication E-mail: ejournal@ksu.edu.sa

Journal of engineering. **Founded:** 1975. **Freq:** Semiannual. **Key Personnel:** Mohammed A. Alhaider, Editor, alhaider@ksu.edu.sa —. **ISSN:** 1018-3639. **Subscription Rates:** US$5. **URL:** http://www.eng.ksu.edu.sa/journal/history.html.
Circ: Paid 2,000

1297 Journal of Diplomatic Studies
Institute of Diplomatic Studies
PO Box 51988
Riyadh 11553, Saudi Arabia   Ph: 966 14018881

Political science journal. **Founded:** 1984. **Freq:** Annual. **Key Personnel:** Mohammed Omar Madani, Editor. **ISSN:** 1319-304X.

◫ **1298 Journal of Islamic University of Imam Muhammad Ibn Saud**
Islamic University of Imam Muhammad Ibn Saud
Deanery of Academic Research
PO Box 18011
Riyadh 11415, Saudi Arabia   Ph: 966 12582247

Journal of religion and theology. **Freq:** Quarterly. **Subscription Rates:** 100 SRl.

Circ: Paid 6,000

◫ **1299 Riyadh Daily**
PO Box 2943   Ph: 966 14417333
Riyadh 11476, Saudi Arabia   Fax: 966 14417107
Publication E-mail: secretary@riyadhdaily.com.sa

General newspaper. **Founded:** 1985. **Freq:** Daily. **Key Personnel:** Talaat Wafa, Editor, phone 96614871000. **ISSN:** 1319-027X. **Subscription Rates:** US$140. **Remarks:** Advertising accepted; rates available upon request. **URL:** http://www.riyadhdaily.com.sa.

Circ: (Not Reported)

◫ **1300 Saudi Arabia Business Week**
PO Box 2894
Riyadh, Saudi Arabia

Business and economics magazine. **Freq:** Weekly.

◫ **1301 The Saudi Journal of Disability and Rehabilitation (SJDR)**
Islamic World Council of Disability and Rehabilitation (ICDR)
PO Box 91409
Riyadh 11633, Saudi Arabia   Ph: 966 14780312
Publication E-mail: admin@dandrksa.com

Scientifically referred journal that publishes research in the field of disability and rehabilitation and disabled care with special attention on prosthetic/orthotics sciences and rehabilitation engineering. **Founded:** 1990. **Freq:** Quarterly. **Key Personnel:** Mohammed H.S. Al-Turaiki, Editor-in-Chief. **ISSN:** 1319-6499. **URL:** http://www.dandrksa.com/english/mag-e.htm.

◫ **1302 The Saudi Journal of Gastroenterology**
Saudi Gastroenterology Association
c/o Dallah Hospital
PO Box 87833
Riyadh 11652, Saudi Arabia   Ph: 966 14702777

Medical journal. **Founded:** 1995. **Freq:** 3/year. **Key Personnel:** Ibrahim A. Al, Editor. **ISSN:** 1319-3767. **URL:** http://www.ksu.edu.sa/societies/sga/journal.php.

◫ **1303 Saudi Journal of Kidney Diseases and Transplantation**
Saudi Center for Organ Transplantation
PO Box 27049
Riyadh 11417, Saudi Arabia   Ph: 966 14451100
Publication E-mail: scot@naseej.com.sa

Journal of urology and nephrology. **Founded:** 1990. **Freq:** Quarterly. **Key Personnel:** Hassan Abu Aisha, Editor-in-Charge. **ISSN:** 1319-2442. **Subscription Rates:** 150 SRl. **Remarks:** Advertising accepted; rates available upon request. **URL:** http://www.scot.org.sa/journal-abstracts-2.html.
Circ: Paid 3,500

◫ **1304 Saudi Medical Journal**
Riyadh Armed Forces Hospital
PO Box 7897
Riyadh 11159, Saudi Arabia   Ph: 966 14791000
Publication E-mail: info@smj.org.sa

Peer-reviewed medical publication. **Subtitle:** Integrating Medical Sciences and Health Care. **Founded:** 1979. **Freq:** Monthly. **Key Personnel:** Dr. Saleh Al Deeb, Editor, saldeeb@smj.org.sa; Dr. Basim Yaqub, Editor, byaqub@smj.org.sa. **ISSN:** 0379-5284. **Subscription Rates:** 375 SRl; US$100 other countries. **URL:** http://www.smj.org.sa.
Ad Rates: BW: 48,000   **Circ:** (Not Reported)
           SRl

◫ **1305 Science Journal of King Saud University**
King Saud University University Libraries
PO Box 22480
Riyadh 11495, Saudi Arabia   Ph: 966 14676148

Science journal. **Founded:** 1969. **Freq:** Semiannual. **Key Personnel:** Khalid A Al Hamoudi, Editor. **ISSN:** 1018-3647. **Subscription Rates:** US$10.
Circ: Paid 2,000

SINGAPORE

SINGAPORE

◫ **1306 Academy of Medicine, Singapore Annals**
Academy of Medicine, Singapore
142 Neil Rd.
Runme Shaw Building
Singapore 88871, Singapore   Ph: 65 62245166
Publication E-mail: annals@academyofmedicine.edu.sg

Periodical serving the various specialties that form the membership of the Academy of Medicine, Singapore. **Founded:** 1972. **Freq:** Bimonthly. **Key Personnel:** F.X. Sundram, Editor. **ISSN:** 0304-4602. **Subscription Rates:** S$90 individuals; S$180 other countries. **URL:** http://www.annals.edu.sg.

◫ **1307 Adasiaonline**
Resonance Solutions
99 Jervois Rd., Ste. 01-06
Singapore 249055, Singapore   Ph: 65 4790100
Publication E-mail: editor@adasiaonline.com

Periodical covering the advertising, marketing and media industry. **Key Personnel:** Allein G. Moore, Editor. **Subscription Rates:** S$70 Singapore and Malaysia; US$60 Asia Pacific. **URL:** http://www.adasiaonline.com/index.shtml/.
Ad Rates: BW: S$2,200   **Circ:** (Not Reported)
           4C: S$2,700

◫ **1308 The Arts**
The Esplanada Co Ltd.
1 Esplanade Dr.
Singapore 038981, Singapore   Ph: 65 68288222
Publication E-mail: editor@esplanade.com.sg

Singapore's pre-eminent magazine of art. **Freq:** Bimonthly. **Subscription Rates:** S$32; S$47 Singapore. **Remarks:** Advertising accepted; rates available upon request. **URL:** http://theartsmagazine.com.sg/.
Circ: (Not Reported)

◫ **1309 Asia-Pacific Aviation and Engineering Journal**
Singapore Institute of Aerospace Engineers Business Development Division
Airline House A 5F
25 Airline Rd.
Singapore 819829, Singapore   Ph: 65 5420688

Aeronautics and space flight periodical. **Founded:** 1976. **Freq:** Quarterly. **Key Personnel:** Poon Chia Wee, Editor. **ISSN:** 0129-9913. **Remarks:** Advertising accepted; rates available upon request.
Circ: Paid 10,000

◫ **1310 Asia-Pacific Information Technology Times**
RM Technology Media Pte Ltd.
1 North Bridge Rd., 24-06
High Street Center
Singapore 179094, Singapore   Ph: 65 3340393

Information technology magazine. **Freq:** Monthly.

◫ **1311 Asia-Pacific Journal of Education**
Oxford University Press Pte Ltd.
School of Education, NIE
469 Bukit Timah Rd.
Singapore 259756, Singapore

Journal of education. **Founded:** 1978. **Freq:** Semiannual. **Key Personnel:**

Gopinathan S, Managing Editor. **ISSN:** 0129-4776. **Subscription Rates:** S$25.60. **URL:** http://eduweb.nie.edu.sg/apje.

Circ: Paid 1,500

☐ **1312   Asia Pacific Journal of Finance**
John Wiley & Sons (Asia) Pte Ltd.
2 Clementi Loop 02-01
Singapore 129809, Singapore   Ph: 65 4632400
Publication E-mail: enquiry@wiley.com.sg

Periodical devoted to publishing original manuscripts that analyse financial and economic issues of concern to scholars, practitioners and policy makers in the Asia Pacific region. **Founded:** 1998. **Freq:** Semiannual. **Key Personnel:** Dorothy Chan, Editorial Asst., phone 65 8746324, fbacbrd@nus.edu.sg. **ISSN:** 0219-1466. **Subscription Rates:** US$70 ISU; US$45 individuals. **Remarks:** Advertising accepted; rates available upon request. **URL:** http://www.fba.nus.edu.sg/qm/journals/apjf.htm.

Circ: (Not Reported)

☐ **1313   Asia Pacific Journal of Management**
John Wiley & Sons (Asia) Pte Ltd.
The NUS Business School
Dept. of Business Policy, National
  University of Singapore
Biz 1 Bldg., 15 Law Link
Singapore 117592, Singapore
Publication E-mail: fbacbrd@nus.edu.sg

Publishes original manuscripts on subjects related to general and strategic management in the Asia Pacific region. **Founded:** 1983. **Freq:** Semiannual. **Key Personnel:** Kulwant Singh, Chief Editor, bizks@nus.edu.sg. **ISSN:** 0217-4561. **URL:** http://www.fba.nus.edu.sg/qm/journals/apjm.html.

Circ: Paid 400

☐ **1314   Asia-Pacific Journal of Operational Research**
National University of Singapore
Industrial and Systems Engineering Dept.
10 Kent Ridge Crescent
Singapore 119260, Singapore   Ph: 65 8742562
Publication E-mail: iseleecu@nus.edu.sg

Periodical aimed at providing a forum for practitioners, academics and researchers in operations research and related fields. **Founded:** 1984. **Freq:** Semiannual. **Key Personnel:** C. U. Lee, Managing Editor, iseleecu@nus.edu.sg. **ISSN:** 0217-5959. **Subscription Rates:** US$42. **URL:** http://sunsite.nus.edu.sg/ORSS/apjor.html.

Circ: Paid 1,100

☐ **1315   Asia-Pacific Journal of Ophthalmology**
Singapore National Eye Centre
11 Third Hospital Ave.
Singapore 168751, Singapore   Ph: 65 63224500

Medical science journal. **Founded:** 1987. **Freq:** Quarterly. **Key Personnel:** Arthur S. M. Lim, Editor. **ISSN:** 0129-1653. **Subscription Rates:** S$65. **Remarks:** Advertising accepted; rates available upon request.

Circ: Paid 500

☐ **1316   Asia-Pacific Journal of Pharmacology**
Singapore University Press (Pte) Ltd.
Yusof Ishak House, NUS
31 Lower Kent Ridge Rd.   Ph: 65 7761148
Singapore 119078, Singapore   Fax: 65 7740652
Publication E-mail: supbooks@nus.edu.sg
Publisher E-mail: supbooks@nus.edu.sg

Professional journal covering pharmacology. **Freq:** Quarterly. **Trim Size:** 19 x 26.5 cm. **ISSN:** 0217-9687. **Subscription Rates:** S$250 individuals.

☐ **1317   The Asia Water**
First Asia Publishing Pte Ltd.
6 New Industrial Rd., 02-02/04
Singapore 536199, Singapore   Ph: 65 8580040
Publication E-mail: asianwater@firstasia.com

Magazine covering issues related to water and wastewater. **Freq:** Monthly.
Circ: 7,803

☐ **1318   Asian Building & Construction**
Trend Publishing & Promotion Centre
529A Geylag Rd.
Singapore 389485, Singapore   Ph: 65 7423313
Publication E-mail: trendnet@singnet.com.sg

Journal aimed at promoting and supporting Asia's building and construction economies by disseminating quality information. **Freq:** Bimonthly. **Remarks:** Advertising accepted; rates available upon request. **URL:** http://www.abcnet.com.sg.

Circ: 18,000

☐ **1319   Asian Case Research Journal**
World Scientific Publishing Co. Pte Ltd.
NUS Business School
National University of Singapore
BIZ 1-02-29, Business Link
Singapore 117592, Singapore
Publication E-mail: wspc@wspc.com.sg

Journal that aims to provide case instructors such as academics, consultants, and company in-house trainers, a selection of high-quality cases on Asian companies and MNCs operating in the Asia-Pacific. **Founded:** 1997. **Freq:** Semiannual. **Key Personnel:** Lau Geok Theng, Chief Editor, bizlaugt@nus.edu.sg. **ISSN:** 0218-9275. **Subscription Rates:** S$122 institutions; S$92 individuals. **Remarks:** Advertising accepted; rates available upon request. **URL:** http://www.worldscinet.com/acrj/acrj.shtml.

Circ: (Not Reported)

☐ **1320   Asian Culture**
Singapore Society of Asian Studies
Kent Ridge
PO Box 1076
Singapore 911103, Singapore   Ph: 65 2713652

Sociology journal. **Founded:** 1983. **Freq:** Semiannual. **ISSN:** 0217-6742.

☐ **1321   Asian Diver**
Asian Diver Magazine
c/o EMAP Singapore Pte Ltd
250 Tanjong Pagar Rd.
Level 06-01, St. Andrews Centre
Singapore 088541, Singapore   Ph: 65 63241230
Publication E-mail: results@asiandiver.com

Magazine covering diving. **Founded:** 1992. **Freq:** Weekly. **Key Personnel:** Carol Lim, Editor, edit@asiandiver.com. **ISSN:** 0218-3064. **Remarks:** Advertising accepted; rates available upon request. **URL:** http://www.asiandiver.com/.

Circ: (Not Reported)

☐ **1322   Asian Furniture**
Toucan Publications Ltd.
322-C King George's Ave.
Singapore 0820, Singapore   Ph: 65 2997121

Magazine on furniture and furnishings.

☐ **1323   Asian Home Gourmet**
Geyling PO Box 0900
Singapore 9138, Singapore
Publication E-mail: info@asianhomegourmet.com

Culinary magazine. **Freq:** Quarterly. **Subscription Rates:** S$24. **URL:** http://www.asianhomegourmet.com/.

☐ **1324   Asian Journal of Marketing**
National University of Singapore
10 Kent Ridge Crescent
Singapore 119260, Singapore   Ph: 65 8743079
Publication E-mail: fbaweb@leonis.nus.sg

Periodical catering to a wide audience of academicians and practitioners in Asia and the rest of the world. **Founded:** 1992. **Freq:** Annual. **ISSN:** 0218-6101. **URL:** http://www.nus.edu.sg.

1325 Asian Journal of Political Science
Times Academic Press
Dept. of Political Science, Faculty of Arts
  and Social Scien
National University of Singapore
AS1 Level 4 11 Arts Link
Singapore 117570, Singapore

Publishes articles in the four sub-fields of political science, namely political theory, comparative politics, international relations and public administration. **Founded:** 1993. **Freq:** Semiannual. **Key Personnel:** Leo Suryadinata, Editor, fax 65 7796815. **ISSN:** 0218-5377. **Remarks:** Advertising accepted; rates available upon request.

Circ: Paid 250

1326 Asian Legal Business
121 Telok Ayer St., 12-01
Singapore 068590, Singapore   Ph: 65 64234631

Periodical covering the latest legal news, events and developments in Hong Kong, Singapore, China, Asia and the international business community. **Freq:** Monthly. **Key Personnel:** Stephen Mulrenan, Editor, stephen.mulrenan@kmimail.com. **Remarks:** Advertising accepted; rates available upon request. **URL:** http://www.asianlegalonline.com/.

Circ: (Not Reported)

1327 Asian Pacific Journal of Social Work
Times Academic Press
Dept. of Social Work and Psychology,
  Faculty of Arts and Soc
National Univeristy of Singapore
Block 6, Level 4, 11 Law Link
Singapore 117570, Singapore

Journal of social services and welfare. **Founded:** 1991. **Freq:** Semiannual. **ISSN:** 0218-5385. **Subscription Rates:** S$41.20.

1328 Asian and Pacific Labour
Trade Union House
3rd Fl., Shenton Way
Singapore 68810, Singapore

Human resources journal. **Founded:** 1963. **Freq:** Bimonthly. **Key Personnel:** V.S. Mathur, Editor. **Subscription Rates:** US$25. **Remarks:** Advertising accepted; rates available upon request.

Circ: Paid 25,000

1329 Asian Printer
Printer Magazines Pte Ltd.
37 Duxton Rd.
Singapore 089501, Singapore   Ph: 65 68423678

Magazine on graphics and typography. **Founded:** 1992. **Freq:** Bimonthly. **ISSN:** 0218-7876.

1330 Asian Sources Computer Products
Global Sources
c/o Media Data Systems Pte. Ltd
Raffles City
PO Box 0203
Singapore 911707, Singapore   Ph: 65 65472800

Publication featuring comprehensive coverage of new products, market and supply trends. **Founded:** 1983. **Freq:** Monthly. **Subscription Rates:** US$75. **Remarks:** Advertising accepted; rates available upon request. **URL:** http://www.globalsources.com/MAGAZINE/CP/CP.HTM.

Circ: (Not Reported)

1331 Asian Sources Gifts and Home Products
Global Sources
c/o Media Data Systems Pte. Ltd
Raffles City
PO Box 0203
Singapore 911707, Singapore   Ph: 65 65472800

Periodical featuring comprehensive coverage of new products, market and supply trends and features on the gifts and home products industries in Asia. **Founded:** 1982. **Freq:** Monthly. **Subscription Rates:** US$75. **Remarks:** Advertising accepted; rates available upon request. **URL:** http://www.allyoucanread.com/visits.asp?idSource=6633.

Circ: (Not Reported)

1332 Asian Sources Security Products
Global Sources
c/o Media Data Systems Pte. Ltd
Raffles City
PO Box 0203
Singapore 911707, Singapore   Ph: 65 65472800

Niche publication for volume buyers of security and safety products and accessories. **Founded:** 2002. **Freq:** Monthly. **Remarks:** Advertising accepted; rates available upon request. **URL:** http://www.globalsources.com/MAGAZINE/SECURITY/SECURITY.HTM.

Circ: (Not Reported)

1333 Asian Timber
First Asia Publishing Pte Ltd.
6 New Industrial Rd., 02-02/04
Singapore 536199, Singapore   Ph: 65 8580040

Publication covering wood. **Freq:** Monthly.

1334 Aunt Webby
Pacific Internet Limited
89B Science Park Dr.
02-05/06 The Rutherford
Singapore 118261, Singapore   Ph: 65 68720322
Publication E-mail: adsales@pacific.net.sg

Counselling magazine. **Freq:** Monthly. **Remarks:** Advertising accepted; rates available upon request. **URL:** http://www.pacific.net.sg/community/Magazines/Aunt%20Webby/.

Circ: (Not Reported)

1335 Banter
Banter Magazine
47 Jalan Puteh Jerneh
Singapore 278068, Singapore   Ph: 65 64761014
Publication E-mail: info@bantermag.com

Singapore's humour magazine. **Founded:** 2002. **Freq:** Bimonthly. **Subscription Rates:** S$30 Singapore; S$75 other countries. **URL:** http://www.bantermag.com/home.htm.
Ad Rates: BW: S$1,750   **Circ:** (Not Reported)
              4C: S$1,850

1336 BBnGG - Beautiful Brides & Gorgeous Grooms
WebImage International
51 Anson Rd.
07-53 Anson Centre
Singapore 079904, Singapore   Ph: 65 62247421
Publication E-mail: hype@bbngg.com

Online wedding resource. **Freq:** Monthly. **Remarks:** Advertising accepted; rates available upon request. **URL:** http://www.bbngg.com/.
Circ: (Not Reported)

1337 bc magazine
Carpe Diem Publications Ltd.
32 Maxwell Rd.
03-05/06 Whitehouse
Singapore 69115, Singapore   Ph: 65 63254070
Publication E-mail: sgeditorial@bcmagazine.net

Lifestyle magazine. **Freq:** Bimonthly. **Key Personnel:** Simon Durrant, Editor-in-Chief. **URL:** http://sg.bcmagazine.net/index.shtml.

 1338 **BigO**
Options Publications Pte Ltd.
PO Box 784
Marine Parade
Singapore 914410, Singapore   Ph: 65 63484007
Publication E-mail: singbigo@singnet.com.sg

Singapore's rock magazine. **Freq:** Weekly. **URL:** http://www.bigo.com.sg/.

 1339 **Building and Estate Management Society Proceedings**
Building and Estate Management Society
c/o Faculty of Architecture and Building
National University of Singapore
Kent Ridge
Singapore 511, Singapore   Ph: 65 7756666

Real estate journal. **Freq:** Semiannual.

 1340 **The Business Times**
Singapore Press Holdings Ltd.
SPH Podium Level 3
1000 Toa Payoh North
Singapore 318994, Singapore
Publication E-mail: btletter@sph.com.sg

Newspaper containing book reviews, film reviews, music reviews and theater reviews. **Founded:** 1976. **Freq:** Daily. **Key Personnel:** Patrick Daniel, Managing Editor, Patrick_Daniel@sph.com.sg. **Subscription Rates:** US$265.20. **Remarks:** Advertising accepted; rates available upon request. **URL:** http://business-times.asia1.com.sg/.

    Circ: Paid 32,118

 1341 **Catholic News**
The Catholic News
2 Highland Rd., 01-03
Singapore 549102, Singapore   Ph: 65 68583055
Publication E-mail: cathnews@catholic.org.sg

Periodical containing Catholic church news from Asia and around the world. **Freq:** 26/year. **Subscription Rates:** S$27. **URL:** http://www.veritas.org.sg/web_links/CN/.

 1342 **China Mail**
TWL Publishing (S) Pte Ltd.
37 Yu Li Industrial Bldg.
03-06 Geylang Lorong 23
Singapore 388371, Singapore   Ph: 65 67438606
Publication E-mail: cic@twlcic.com

Publication providing general information on China. **Founded:** 1988. **Freq:** Bimonthly. **ISSN:** 0218-1517. **Subscription Rates:** S$30. **URL:** http://www.twlcic.com/cm/icm3/Homepage.html.

 1343 **Cine News**
Singapore Cine Club
42 Branksome Rd.
Singapore 439580, Singapore

Journal of motion pictures. **Founded:** 1970. **Freq:** Monthly. **ISSN:** 0009-6954.

    Circ: Free 1,500

 1344 **CMPnet Asia**
CMP Business Media Pte Ltd.
390 Havelock Rd.
05-00 King's Centre   Ph: 65 67353366
Singapore 169662, Singapore   Fax: 65 67321191
Publication E-mail: feedback@cmpasia.com.sg
Publisher E-mail: info@cmpasia.com.sg

Business-to-business publication. **Freq:** Monthly. **Remarks:** Advertising accepted; rates available upon request. **URL:** http://www.cmpnetasia.com.
    Circ: (Not Reported)

 1345 **Coastal Engineering Journal**
World Scientific Publishing Co. Pte Ltd.
5 Toh Tuck Link
Singapore 596224, Singapore   Ph: 65 64665775
Publication E-mail: wspc@wspc.com.sg

Peer-reviewed periodical for the publication of research achievements and engineering practices in the fields of coastal, harbor and offshore engineering. **Founded:** 1958. **Freq:** Quarterly. **ISSN:** 0578-5634. **Subscription Rates:** S$593 institutions; S$215 individuals. **URL:** http://www.worldscinet.com/cej/cej.shtml.

 1346 **Commercial & Industrial Guide**
Integrated Databases India Ltd.
c/o Orchard
PO Box 389
Singapore, Singapore

Journal covering business, economics, trade and industrial directories. **Freq:** Annual.
Ad Rates: BW: **Circ:** 200,000
       US$17,600
       4C: US$21,725

 1347 **Communications of COLIPS**
Chinese and Oriental Languages Information Processing Society
Kent Ridge National University of
   Singapore
Singapore 119260, Singapore   Ph: 65 7722782
Publication E-mail: luatsemi@comp.nus.edu.sg

Periodical devoted to the publication of original theoretical and applied research in Chinese and oriental languages. **Founded:** 1991. **Freq:** Semiannual. **ISSN:** 0218-7019. **Subscription Rates:** S$25 members; S$120 nonmembers. **URL:** http://www.comp.nus.edu.sg/~colips/aboutus.html.
    Circ: Paid 400

 1348 **Communications in Contemporary Mathematics**
World Scientific Publishing Co. Pte Ltd.
5 Toh Tuck Link
Singapore 596224, Singapore   Ph: 65 64665775
Publication E-mail: wspc@wspc.com.sg

Publication communicating research in the fields of algebra, analysis, applied mathematics, dynamical systems, geometry, mathematical physics, number theory, partial differential equations, and topology. **Founded:** 1999. **Freq:** Bimonthly. **ISSN:** 0219-1997. **Subscription Rates:** S$590 institutions; S$236 individuals. **URL:** http://www.worldscinet.com/ccm/ccm.shtml.

 1349 **Computer Era**
Eastern Publishing Ltd.
8 Lorong Bakar Batu, 07-12
Singapore 348743-, Singapore   Ph: 65 62200552

Magazine on computers. **Freq:** Semiannual. **URL:** http://www.epl.com.sg/.

 1350 **Computerworld Singapore**
IDG Communications (S) Pte Ltd.
80 Marine Parade Rd.
17-01A Parkway Parade
Singapore 449269, Singapore   Ph: 65 63458383
Publication E-mail: jackieho@idg.com.sg; computerworld@idg.com.sg

Publication providing relevant news to Singapore's computer software professionals. **Freq:** Weekly. **Key Personnel:** Tan Ee Sze, Editor, eesze@idg.com.sg.

 1351 **Contemporary Southeast Asia**
Institute of Southeast Asian Studies
30 Heng Mui Keng Terrace
Pasir Panjang
Singapore 119614, Singapore   Ph: 65 67780955
Publication E-mail: pubsunit@iseas.edu.sg

Periodical covering the politics, international relations and security-related issues of Southeast Asia and the wider Asia-Pacific region. **Founded:** 1979. **Freq:** 3/year. **Key Personnel:** K.S. Nathan, Editor. **ISSN:** 0129-797X. **Subscription Rates:** S$46. **URL:** http://www.iseas.edu.sg/csea.html.

1352 CW Magazine
Peter Knipp Holdings Pte Ltd.
102F Pasir Panjang Rd.
05-06 Citilink Complex
Singapore 118530, Singapore   Ph: 65 2737707
Publication E-mail: grace@asiacuisine.com

Asia's leading food and bevarage portal. **Subtitle:** New Asia Cuisine & Wine Scene. **Freq:** Bimonthly. **Subscription Rates:** S$100 within Southeast Asia; S$140 outside Southeast Asia; S$180 two years within Southeast Asia. **Remarks:** Advertising accepted; rates available upon request. **URL:** http://www.asiacuisine.com.sg/.
Circ: (Not Reported)

1353 The Dental Mirror
National University of Singapore
National University Hospital
5 Lower Kent Ridge Rd.
Singapore 119074, Singapore   Ph: 65 67724987
Publication E-mail: denlaug@nus.edu.sg

Journal of dentistry. **Freq:** Semiannual. **URL:** http://www.nus.edu.sg/NUSinfo/DENT/faculty/mirror.htm.

1354 Digital Nanyang Chronicle
The Nanyang Chronicle
School of Communication and Information Bldg.
Nanyang Technological University
Singapore 639798, Singapore   Ph: 65 7906446
Publication E-mail: chronicle@ntu.edu.sg

Independent student newspaper. **Freq:** Monthly. **Key Personnel:** Gail Wan, Chief Editor. **URL:** http://www.ntu.edu.sg/chronicle.
Ad Rates: BW: US$665   **Circ:** (Not Reported)
                4C: US$1,165

1355 East
East Corp
20 Raffles Pl.
10-05/06 Ocean Towers
Singapore 048620, Singapore   Ph: 65 3243342
Publication E-mail: info@east.com

Lifestyle and fashion magazine. **Freq:** Monthly. **Remarks:** Advertising accepted; rates available upon request. **URL:** http://www.east.com/.
Circ: (Not Reported)

1356 8 Days
Media Corp Publishing Pte Ltd.
Caldecott Broadcast Centre
Andrew Rd.
Singapore 299939, Singapore   Ph: 65 63333888
Publication E-mail: Feedback@8daysonline.com

Movie, music and food magazine. **Freq:** Weekly. **Key Personnel:** Tan Lee Sun, Editor-in-Chief. **Remarks:** Advertising accepted; rates available upon request. **URL:** http://8days.mediacorppublishing.com/thisweekissue/index.htm.
Circ: (Not Reported)

1357 EndoSource Magazine
Endometriosis Association (Singapore)
c/o Mt. Alvernia Hospital
820 Thomson Rd.
Singapore 574623, Singapore   Ph: 65 63476640
Publication E-mail: lsl_endo@excite.com

Magazine of the Endometriosis Association (Singapore). **Freq:** Quarterly. **URL:** http://sg.geocities.com/easespore/endosource/endosource.html.

1358 Energy Asia
The Strategist Pte Ltd.
7500A Beach Rd.
23-304 The Plaza
Singapore 199591, Singapore   Ph: 65 62983839
Publication E-mail: editor@EnergyAsia.com

Publication providing information about oil, gas, power and petrochemical industries in the Asia Pacific region. **Founded:** 1979. **Freq:** Weekly. **Key Personnel:** Ng Weng Hoong, Editor, editor@EnergyAsia.com. **Subscription Rates:** US$150. **URL:** http://www.energyasia.com.
Circ: Paid 6,000

1359 Enquires
Singapore Indian Chamber of Commerce & Industry
101 Cecil St.
23-01/04 Tong Eng Bldg.   Ph: 65 62222855
Singapore 069533, Singapore   Fax: 65 62231707
Publisher E-mail: sicci@singnet.com.sg

Journal covering business and economics. **Freq:** Biweekly.

1360 Envision
Singapore Broadcasting Authority
140 Hill St.
MITA Bldg. 04-01
Singapore 179 369, Singapore   Ph: 65 68379973

Broadcasting technology magazine. **Freq:** Quarterly. **URL:** http://www.sba.gov.sg; http://www.sba.gov.sg/sba/a_envpublications.jsp.

1361 Ezyhealth Chinese
Ezyhealth Asia Pacific Pte Ltd.
12 Science Park Dr., 02-03/04
The Mendel Singapore Science Park
Singapore 118225, Singapore   Ph: 65 63959393
Publication E-mail: alisonlaw@ezyhealth.com

Health, beauty, and fitness magazine. **Founded:** 1999. **Freq:** Monthly. **Key Personnel:** Janice Yeo, Publisher. **Subscription Rates:** Free. **Remarks:** Advertising accepted; rates available upon request. **URL:** http://www.ezyhealth.com.
Circ: (Not Reported)

1362 Ezyhealth Singapore
Ezyhealth Asia Pacific Pte Ltd.
12 Science Park Dr., 02-03/04
The Mendel Singapore Science Park
Singapore 118225, Singapore   Ph: 65 63959393
Publication E-mail: alisonlaw@ezyhealth.com

Health, beauty, and fitness magazine. **Founded:** 1999. **Freq:** Monthly. **Key Personnel:** Josephine Cheong, Advertising, josephine-cheong@ezyhealth.com. **Subscription Rates:** Free. **Remarks:** Advertising accepted; rates available upon request. **URL:** http://www.ezyhealth.com.
Circ: Free 100,000

1363 FDM Asia
Eastern Publishing Ltd.
8 Lorong Bakar Batu, 07-12
Singapore 348743-, Singapore   Ph: 65 62200552

Magazine for professionals in the woodworking and furniture manufacturing industry. **Freq:** 8/year. **URL:** http://www.epl.com.sg/.

1364 Female Brides
MPH Magazines (S) Pte Ltd.
20 Martin Rd., 08-01
01 Seng Kee Bldg.
Singapore 239070, Singapore   Ph: 65 68794137
Publication E-mail: editor@femalebridesonline.com

Singapore's leading wedding and bridal magazine. **Freq:** Monthly. **Remarks:** Advertising accepted; rates available upon request. **URL:** http://www.femalebridesonline.com/main.php.
Circ: (Not Reported)

📖 **1365 Female Cookbook**
MPH Magazines (S) Pte Ltd.
20 Martin Rd., 08-01
01 Seng Kee Bldg.
Singapore 239070, Singapore   Ph: 65 68794137

Magazine on cooking. **Founded:** 1975. **Freq:** Annual.

📖 **1366 FHM Singapore**
Emap Singapore Pte Ltd.
250 Tanjong Pagar Rd., 07-01
St Andrew's Centre
Singapore 088541, Singapore   Ph: 65 62209339
Publication E-mail: r.schofield@emap.com.sg

Men's interest magazine. **Freq:** Monthly. **Key Personnel:** Dylan Tan, Editor, dylant@emap.com.sg. **Subscription Rates:** S$68. **Remarks:** Advertising accepted; rates available upon request. **URL:** http://www.fhm.com.sg/.
Circ: (Not Reported)

📖 **1367 Food & Entertainment**
Asian Trade Press (Pte) Ltd.
9 Raffles Pl.
27-01 Republic Plaza
Singapore 048619, Singapore   Ph: 65 62780771
Publication E-mail: enquiries_fneonline@asiantp.com

Periodical covering dining out in Singapore. **Freq:** Semiannual. **Subscription Rates:** S$10. **Remarks:** Advertising accepted; rates available upon request. **URL:** http://www.food-entertainment.com.sg/.
Circ: (Not Reported)

📖 **1368 Four Walls**
Panpac Media Group Ltd.
371 Beach Rd.
03-18 Keypoint
Singapore 199597, Singapore   Ph: 65 62920300
Publication E-mail: dawson.kan@panpacmedia.com

Publication focusing on residential interiors. **Freq:** Bimonthly. **Key Personnel:** John Low, Senior Editor, john.low@panpacmedia.com. **URL:** http://www.panpacmedia.com/singapore/print/4walls_pg.htm.
Ad Rates: 4C: S$2,500   **Circ:** (Not Reported)

📖 **1369 4x4 Magazine (Singapore)**
4X4 Magazine Co Ltd.
No. 33B Mosque St.
Singapore 059511, Singapore   Ph: 65 2224244

Magazine about four wheel drive vehicles. **Freq:** Monthly. **URL:** http://www.jeepnation.net/4x4mag/contact3.html.

📖 **1370 Fractals**
World Scientific Publishing Co. Pte Ltd.
5 Toh Tuck Link
Singapore 596224, Singapore   Ph: 65 64665775
Publication E-mail: wspc@wspc.com.sg

Publication focusing on complex geometry, patterns and scaling. **Founded:** 1993. **Freq:** Quarterly. **ISSN:** 0218-348X. **Subscription Rates:** S$1,040 institutions; S$378 individuals. **URL:** http://www.worldscinet.com/fractals/fractals.shtml.

📖 **1371 Garden Asia**
Garden Asia Pte Ltd.
240 Neo Tiew Crescent
Singapore 718878, Singapore   Ph: 65 67936500
Publication E-mail: info@gardenasia.com

Magazine on gardening. **URL:** http://www.gardenasia.com/.

📖 **1372 Golf**
Eastern Publishing Ltd.
8 Lorong Bakar Batu, 07-12
Singapore 348743-, Singapore   Ph: 65 62200552

Periodical covering local, regional and international golf events. **Freq:** Monthly. **URL:** http://www.epl.com.sg/.

📖 **1373 Groom n' Bride**
WO Pte Ltd.
123 Alexandra Village
Bukit Merah Lane 1, 03-82
Singapore 150123, Singapore   Ph: 65 62716388
Publication E-mail: mailling@wo.com.sg

Publication covering bridal fashion, beauty, hotels, men and women's fashion, entertainment, fitness and well-being, jewellery, interior styles, insurance and banking, photography, alternative wedding venues and travel. **Freq:** Quarterly. **Remarks:** Advertising accepted; rates available upon request. **URL:** http://www.gb.com.sg/.
Circ: (Not Reported)

📖 **1374 Hand Surgery**
World Scientific Publishing Co. Pte Ltd.
5 Toh Tuck Link
Singapore 596224, Singapore   Ph: 65 64665775
Publication E-mail: wspc@wspc.com.sg

Periodial covering injury and diseases of the hand and upper limb and related research. **Founded:** 1996. **Freq:** Semiannual. **ISSN:** 0218-8104. **Subscription Rates:** S$167 institutions; S$106 individuals. **URL:** http://www.worldscinet.com/hs/mkt/editorial.shtml.

📖 **1375 Happening**
Pacific Internet Limited
89B Science Park Dr.
02-05/06 The Rutherford
Singapore 118261, Singapore   Ph: 65 68720322
Publication E-mail: editor@happening.com.sg

Singapore's online arts and entertainment guide. **Freq:** Weekly. **Remarks:** Advertising accepted; rates available upon request. **URL:** http://www.happening.com.sg/livehtml/index.shtml.
Circ: (Not Reported)

📖 **1376 Hardware Mag**
Hardware Zone Pte Ltd.
Blk 20 Ayer Rajah Crescent, 09-04/05/10
Singapore 139964, Singapore   Ph: 65 68722725
Publication E-mail: sales@hwzcorp.com

Computer hardware magazine. **Freq:** Monthly. **Subscription Rates:** S$68 members; S$82.80 nonmembers. **Remarks:** Advertising accepted; rates available upon request. **URL:** http://www.hardwaremag.com/.
Circ: (Not Reported)

📖 **1377 HealthToday**
MediMedia Asia Pte Ltd.
No. 3, Lim Teck Kim Road 10-01
Singapore Technologies Building
Singapore 088934, Singapore   Ph: 65 62263556
Publication E-mail: enquiry@medimedia.com.sg

Consumer health magazine for the Asia Pacific region. **Freq:** 11/year. **Subscription Rates:** S$30. **Remarks:** Advertising accepted; rates available upon request. **URL:** http://www.healthtoday.net/.
Circ: (Not Reported)

📖 **1378 Her World**
Singapore Press Holdings Ltd.
Toa Payoh North
1000 Toa Payoh North
Singapore 318994, Singapore   Ph: 65 63196319
Publication E-mail: dtay@sph.com.sg

Ad Rates: GLR = general line rate; BW = one-time black & white page rate; 4C = one-time four color page rate; SAU = standard advertising unit rate; CNU = Canadian newspaper advertising unit rate; PCI = per column inch rate.
Circulation: ★ = ABC; △ = BPA; ♦ = CAC; • = CCAB; ❑ = VAC; ⊕ = PO Statement; ‡ = Publisher's Report; Boldface figures = sworn; Light figures = estimated.
Entry type: 📖 = Print; 🎙 = Broadcast.

123

Women's magazine on fashion, beauty and relationships. **Freq:** Monthly. **Key Personnel:** Caroline Ngui, Editor, nguislc@sph.com.sg. **Subscription Rates:** S$5. **Remarks:** Advertising accepted; rates available upon request. **URL:** http://herworld.asiaone.com.sg/.

Circ: (Not Reported)

□ 1379 Her World Brides
Singapore Press Holdings Ltd.
Toa Payoh North
1000 Toa Payoh North
Singapore 318994, Singapore   Ph: 65 63196319

Magazine for modern brides. **Founded:** 1998. **Freq:** Quarterly. **URL:** http://www.sph.com.sg/.
Ad Rates: BW: US$3,220   **Circ:** 11,000
              4C: US$4,290

□ 1380 Highway Magazine
Automobile Association of Singapore
336 River Valley Rd., 03-00
AA Centre
Singapore 238366, Singapore   Ph: 65 67372444
Publication E-mail: aasmail@aas.com.sg

Publication of the Automobile Association of Singapore. **Freq:** Monthly. **URL:** http://www.aas.com.sg.

□ 1381 Home Concepts
Panpac Media Group Ltd.
371 Beach Rd.
03-18 Keypoint
Singapore 199597, Singapore   Ph: 65 62920300
Publication E-mail: dawson.kan@panpacmedia.com

Architectural magazine. **Freq:** Bimonthly. **Key Personnel:** John Low, Senior Editor, john.low@panpacmedia.com. **URL:** http://www.panpacmedia.com/singapore/print/hc_pg.htm.
Ad Rates: BW: S$2,200   **Circ:** (Not Reported)
              4C: S$2,500

□ 1382 Home & Decor
Singapore Press Holdings Ltd.
Toa Payoh North
1000 Toa Payoh North
Singapore 318994, Singapore   Ph: 65 63196319

Decor magazine for Singapore. **Founded:** 1999. **Freq:** Monthly. **Subscription Rates:** S$5. **URL:** http://shop.asia1.com/stores/stoppress/hdecor.html.

□ 1383 Hydrocarbon Asia
AP Energy Business Publications Pte. Ltd.
63 Robinson Rd., 02-16
Singapore 068894, Singapore   Ph: 65 62223422
Publication E-mail: eraj@safan.com

Refining, gas processing and petrochemical business and technical magazine. **Freq:** 8/year. **Key Personnel:** George Croy, Editor, phone 65 63253055, george@safan.com. **Subscription Rates:** US$110. **URL:** http://hcasia.safan.com/.
Ad Rates: BW: US$2,970   **Circ:** (Not Reported)

□ 1384 I-S Magazine
Asia City Publishing Pte Ltd.
180 Cecil St.
13-01 Bangkok Bank Bldg.
Singapore 69546, Singapore   Ph: 65 63232512
Publication E-mail: ismag@asia-city.com.sg

Magazine about Asian city living. **Freq:** Weekly. **Key Personnel:** Andy Che, Deputy Editor, achen@asia-city.com.sg. **Remarks:** Advertising accepted; rates available upon request. **URL:** http://www.is-weekend.com/.

Circ: (Not Reported)

□ 1385 The IEA Journal of Ergonomics
International Ergonomics Association
School of Mechanical and Production
    Engineering
Nanyang Technological University
Nanyang Ave.
Singapore 639798, Singapore   Ph: 65 67911744

Journal covering business, economics and engineering. **Founded:** 1998. **Freq:** Quarterly. **Key Personnel:** Martin G. Helander, Editor. **URL:** http://www.iea.cc/.

□ 1386 Incentives & Meetings Asia
TTG Asia Media Pte Ltd.
Robinson Road Post Office
PO Box 657
Singapore 901307, Singapore

Publication providing information on meetings, incentive travel, conventions and exhibitions industry in the Asia-Pacific regional markets. **Founded:** 1994. **Freq:** Bimonthly. **Key Personnel:** Joyce Wong, Editor, joyce.wong@hk.hongkong.com. **URL:** http://www.ima.com.sg/.

□ 1387 Infinite Dimensional Analysis, Quantum Probability and
  Related Topics
World Scientific Publishing Co. Pte Ltd.
5 Toh Tuck Link
Singapore 596224, Singapore   Ph: 65 64665775
Publication E-mail: wspc@wspc.com.sg

Publication focusing on infinite dimensional analysis and quantum probability. **Founded:** 1998. **Freq:** Quarterly. **ISSN:** 0219-0257. **Subscription Rates:** S$481 institutions; S$175 individuals. **URL:** http://www.worldscinet.com/idaqp/idaqp.html.

□ 1388 Innovation
World Scientific Publishing Co. Pte Ltd.
5 Toh Tuck Link
Singapore 596224, Singapore   Ph: 65 64665775
Publication E-mail: glor@magma.ca

Publication devoted to the sharing of ideas and discussion of public sector innovation. **Subtitle:** The Magazine of Research and Technology. **Founded:** 2000. **Freq:** Quarterly. **Key Personnel:** Eleanor Glor, Editor-in-Chief, eglor@magma.ca. **ISSN:** 0219-4023. **Subscription Rates:** S$45. **URL:** http://www.innovation.cc.

□ 1389 Innovations in Materials Research
World Scientific Publishing Co. Pte Ltd.
5 Toh Tuck Link
Singapore 596224, Singapore   Ph: 65 64665775

Journal of engineering, mechanics and materials. **Subtitle:** International Journal Reporting Advances in S. **Founded:** 1996. **Freq:** Bimonthly. **Key Personnel:** Roy Rustum, Editor. **ISSN:** 0218-7566. **Subscription Rates:** S$120 institutions; S$390 institutions. **URL:** http://www.singnet.com.sg/~wspclib.

□ 1390 Intelligent Enterprise Asia
CMP Business Media Pte Ltd.
390 Havelock Rd.
05-00 King's Centre   Ph: 65 67353366
Singapore 169662, Singapore   Fax: 65 67321191
Publication E-mail: feedback@cmpasia.com.sg
Publisher E-mail: info@cmpasia.com.sg

Periodical for Asia's business leaders. **Founded:** 2000. **Freq:** Monthly. **Key Personnel:** Isabelle Chan, Editor, isabelle_chan@cmpasia.com.sg. **URL:** http://www.intelligentasia.com/.
Ad Rates: BW: US$4,235   **Circ:** 5,000
              4C: US$5,335

□ 1391 International Game Theory Review
World Scientific Publishing Co. Pte Ltd.
5 Toh Tuck Link
Singapore 596224, Singapore   Ph: 65 64665775
Publication E-mail: wspc@wspc.com.sg

Periodical offering up-to-date insights and perspectives through original research in game theory and its applications. **Founded:** 1999. **Freq:** Quarterly. **ISSN:** 0219-1989. **Subscription Rates:** S$406 institutions; S$153 individuals. **URL:** http://www.worldscinet.com/igtr/igtr.shtml.

1392 International Journal of Algebra and Computation
World Scientific Publishing Co. Pte Ltd.
5 Toh Tuck Link
Singapore 596224, Singapore   Ph: 65 64665775
Publication E-mail: wspc@wspc.com.sg

Publishes original papers in mathematics. **Founded:** 1991. **Freq:** Bimonthly. **ISSN:** 0218-1967. **Subscription Rates:** S$1,040 institutions; S$369 individuals. **URL:** http://www.worldscinet.com/ijac/ijac.shtml.

1393 International Journal of Artificial Intelligence Tools
World Scientific Publishing Co. Pte Ltd.
5 Toh Tuck Link
Singapore 596224, Singapore   Ph: 65 64665775
Publication E-mail: wspc@wspc.com.sg

Periodical aimed at providing a forum for scientists to share their knowledge on artificial intelligence tools. **Founded:** 1992. **Freq:** Quarterly. **ISSN:** 0218-2130. **Subscription Rates:** S$694 institutions; S$252 individuals. **URL:** http://www.worldscinet.com/ijait/ijait.shtml.

1394 International Journal of Bifurcation and Chaos in Applied Sciences and Engineering
World Scientific Publishing Co. Pte Ltd.
5 Toh Tuck Link
Singapore 596224, Singapore   Ph: 65 64665775
Publication E-mail: wspc@wspc.com.sg

Journal covering the field of chaos and nonlinear science. **Founded:** 1991. **Freq:** Monthly. **ISSN:** 0218-1274. **Subscription Rates:** S$4,023 institutions; S$1,460 individuals. **URL:** http://www.worldscinet.com/ijbc/ijbc.shtml.

1395 International Journal of Computational Geometry and Applications
World Scientific Publishing Co. Pte Ltd.
5 Toh Tuck Link
Singapore 596224, Singapore   Ph: 65 64665775
Publication E-mail: wspc@wspc.com.sg

Periodical devoted to the field of computational geometry. **Founded:** 1991. **Freq:** Bimonthly. **ISSN:** 0218-1959. **Subscription Rates:** S$756 institutions; S$275 individuals. **URL:** http://www.worldscinet.com/ijcga/ijcga.shtml.

1396 International Journal of Foundations of Computer Science
World Scientific Publishing Co. Pte Ltd.
5 Toh Tuck Link
Singapore 596224, Singapore   Ph: 65 64665775

Publishes articles that contribute new theoretical results in all areas of the foundations of computer science. **Founded:** 1990. **Freq:** Bimonthly. **ISSN:** 0129-0541. **Subscription Rates:** S$956 institutions; S$347 individuals. **URL:** http://www.cs.ucsb.edu/~ijfcs.

1397 International Journal of Genome Research
World Scientific Publishing Co. Pte Ltd.
5 Toh Tuck Link
Singapore 596224, Singapore   Ph: 65 64665775

Journal covering biology and genetics. **Founded:** 1992. **Freq:** Bimonthly. **ISSN:** 0218-1932. **Subscription Rates:** S$240.

1398 International Journal of High Speed Computing
World Scientific Publishing Co. Pte Ltd.
5 Toh Tuck Link
Singapore 596224, Singapore   Ph: 65 64665775
Publication E-mail: wspc@wspc.com.sg

Periodical directed at researchers, educators, and engineers in the field of parallel computations. **Founded:** 1989. **Freq:** Quarterly. **ISSN:** 0129-0533. **Subscription Rates:** S$853 institutions; S$310 individuals. **URL:** http://www.worldscinet.com/ijhsc/ijhsc.shtml.

1399 International Journal of High Speed Electronics and Systems
World Scientific Publishing Co. Pte Ltd.
5 Toh Tuck Link
Singapore 596224, Singapore   Ph: 65 64665775
Publication E-mail: wspc@wspc.com.sg

Journal that aims to promote engineering education by advancing interdisciplinary science between electronics and systems. **Founded:** 1990. **Freq:** Quarterly. **ISSN:** 0129-1564. **Subscription Rates:** S$894 institutions; S$356 individuals. **URL:** http://www.worldscinet.com/ijhses/ijhses.shtml.

1400 International Journal of Information Technology
World Scientific Publishing Co. Pte Ltd.
5 Toh Tuck Link
Singapore 596224, Singapore   Ph: 65 64665775
Publication E-mail: wspc@wspc.com.sg

Periodical aimed at providing a global forum for exchanging research findings and case studies that bridge the latest information technology and various decision-making techniques. **Founded:** 1995. **Freq:** Quarterly. **ISSN:** 0219-6220. **Subscription Rates:** S$425 institutions; S$170 individuals. **URL:** http://www.worldscinet.com/ijitdm/ijitdm.shtml.

1401 International Journal of Innovation Management
World Scientific Publishing Co. Pte Ltd.
5 Toh Tuck Link
Singapore 596224, Singapore   Ph: 65 64665775
Publication E-mail: wspc@wspc.com.sg

Publication dedicated to the advancement of academic research and management practice in the field of innovation management. **Founded:** 1997. **Freq:** Quarterly. **ISSN:** 1363-9196. **Subscription Rates:** S$582 institutions; S$233 individuals. **URL:** http://www.worldscinet.com/ijim/ijim.shtml.

1402 International Journal of Manufacturing System Design
World Scientific Publishing Co. Pte Ltd.
5 Toh Tuck Link
Singapore 596224, Singapore   Ph: 65 64665775

Journal of computers and automation. **Founded:** 1994. **Freq:** Quarterly. **ISSN:** 0218-3382. **Subscription Rates:** US$83.

1403 International Journal of Mathematical Logic
World Scientific Publishing Co. Pte Ltd.
5 Toh Tuck Link
Singapore 596224, Singapore   Ph: 65 64665775

Mathematics journal. **Founded:** 1998. **Freq:** Quarterly. **ISSN:** 0219-0613. **Subscription Rates:** S$127.

1404 International Journal of Mathematics
World Scientific Publishing Co. Pte Ltd.
5 Toh Tuck Link
Singapore 596224, Singapore   Ph: 65 64665775
Publication E-mail: wspc@wspc.com.sg

Publishes original papers in mathematics. **Founded:** 1990. **Freq:** 10/year. **ISSN:** 0129-167X. **Subscription Rates:** S$1,667 institutions; S$605 individuals. **URL:** http://www.worldscinet.com/ijm/ijm.shtml.

1405 International Journal of Modern Physics A
World Scientific Publishing Co. Pte Ltd.
5 Toh Tuck Link
Singapore 596224, Singapore   Ph: 65 64665775
Publication E-mail: wspc@wspc.com.sg

Periodical containing review articles and original papers covering the latest research developments in particles and fields, gravitation and cosmology. **Founded:** 1986. **Freq:** 32/year. **ISSN:** 0217-751X. **Subscription Rates:** S$6,477 institutions; S$2,351 individuals. **URL:** http://www.worldscinet.com/ijmpa/ijmpa.html.

Circ: Paid 500

1406 International Journal of Modern Physics B
World Scientific Publishing Co. Pte Ltd.
5 Toh Tuck Link
Singapore 596224, Singapore   Ph: 65 64665775
Publication E-mail: wspc@wspc.com.sg

Periodical covering the most important aspects as well as the latest developments in condensed matter, statistical, applied physics and high TC superconductivity. **Founded:** 1987. **Freq:** 32/year. **ISSN:** 0217-9792. **Subscription Rates:** S$4,885 institutions; S$1,773 individuals. **URL:** http://www.worldscinet.com/ijmpb/ijmpb.shtml.

Circ: Paid 300

1407 International Journal of Modern Physics C: Physics and Computers
World Scientific Publishing Co. Pte Ltd.
5 Toh Tuck Link
Singapore 596224, Singapore   Ph: 65 64665775
Publication E-mail: wspc@wspc.com.sg

Periodical covering computational physics, physical computation and related subjects. **Founded:** 1990. **Freq:** 10/year. **ISSN:** 0129-1831. **Subscription Rates:** S$1,418 institutions; S$522 individuals. **URL:** http://journals.wspc.com.sg/ijmpc/ijmpc.shtml.

1408 International Journal of Modern Physics D: Gravitation, Astrophysics and Cosmology
World Scientific Publishing Co. Pte Ltd.
5 Toh Tuck Link
Singapore 596224, Singapore   Ph: 65 64665775
Publication E-mail: wspc@wspc.com.sg

Journal covering astrophysics, gravitation and cosmology. **Founded:** 1992. **Freq:** 10/year. **ISSN:** 0218-2718. **Subscription Rates:** S$1,168 institutions; S$424 individuals. **URL:** http://ejournals.wspc.com.sg/ijmpd/ijmpd.html.

1409 International Journal of Modern Physics E: Report on Nuclear Physics
World Scientific Publishing Co. Pte Ltd.
5 Toh Tuck Link
Singapore 596224, Singapore   Ph: 65 64665775
Publication E-mail: wspc@wspc.com.sg

Periodical covering the topics on experimental, theoretical and computational nuclear science. **Founded:** 1992. **Freq:** Bimonthly. **ISSN:** 0218-3013. **Subscription Rates:** S$744 institutions; S$264 individuals. **URL:** http://ejournals.wspc.com.sg/ijmpe/ijmpe.html.

1410 International Journal of Neural Systems
World Scientific Publishing Co. Pte Ltd.
5 Toh Tuck Link
Singapore 596224, Singapore   Ph: 65 64665775
Publication E-mail: wspc@wspc.com.sg

Periodical containing peer-reviewed journal covering information processing in natural and artificial neural systems. **Founded:** 1989. **Freq:** Bimonthly. **ISSN:** 0129-0657. **Subscription Rates:** S$830 institutions; S$301 individuals. **URL:** http://www.worldscinet.com/ijns/ijns.shtml.

1411 International Journal of Pattern Recognition and Artificial Intelligence
World Scientific Publishing Co. Pte Ltd.
5 Toh Tuck Link
Singapore 596224, Singapore   Ph: 65 64665775
Publication E-mail: wspc@wspc.com.sg

Publishes both applications and theory-oriented articles on new developments in the fields of pattern recognition and artificial intelligence. **Founded:** 1987. **Freq:** 8/year. **ISSN:** 0218-0014. **Subscription Rates:** S$1,331 institutions; S$483 individuals. **URL:** http://www.worldscinet.com/ijprai/ijprai.shtml.

1412 International Journal of PIXE
World Scientific Publishing Co. Pte Ltd.
5 Toh Tuck Link
Singapore 596224, Singapore   Ph: 65 64665775
Publication E-mail: wspc@wspc.com.sg

Periodical covering the latest developments in the various aspects of particle-induced X-ray emission. **Founded:** 1990. **Freq:** Quarterly. **ISSN:** 0129-0835.

Subscription Rates: S$644 institutions; S$257 individuals. **URL:** http://www.worldscinet.com/ijpixe/ijpixe.shtml.

1413 International Journal of Reliability, Quality & Safety Engineering
World Scientific Publishing Co. Pte Ltd.
5 Toh Tuck Link
Singapore 596224, Singapore   Ph: 65 64665775
Publication E-mail: wspc@wspc.com.sg

Publication focusing on both the theoretical and practical aspects of reliability, quality, and safety in engineering. **Founded:** 1997. **Freq:** Quarterly. **ISSN:** 0218-5393. **Subscription Rates:** S$705 institutions; S$256 individuals. **URL:** http://www.worldscinet.com/ijrqse/mkt/archive.shtml.

1414 International Journal of Shaping Modeling
World Scientific Publishing Co. Pte Ltd.
5 Toh Tuck Link
Singapore 596224, Singapore   Ph: 65 64665775

Journal of computer graphics. **Founded:** 1994. **Freq:** Quarterly. **ISSN:** 0218-6543. **Subscription Rates:** S$83.

1415 International Journal of Software Engineering and Knowledge Engineering
World Scientific Publishing Co. Pte Ltd.
5 Toh Tuck Link
Singapore 596224, Singapore   Ph: 65 64665775

Periodical intended to serve as a forum for researchers, practitioners, and developers to exchange ideas and results for the advancement of software engineering and knowledge engineering. **Founded:** 1991. **Freq:** Quarterly. **ISSN:** 0218-1940. **Subscription Rates:** S$395 institutions; S$158 individuals.

1416 International Journal of Theoretical and Applied Finance
World Scientific Publishing Co. Pte Ltd.
5 Toh Tuck Link
Singapore 596224, Singapore   Ph: 65 64665775
Publication E-mail: wspc@wspc.com.sg

Publication focusing on theoretical modelling and application of financial instruments. **Founded:** 1998. **Freq:** Quarterly. **ISSN:** 0219-0249. **Subscription Rates:** S$658 institutions; S$263 individuals. **URL:** http://www.worldscinet.com/ijtaf/ijtaf.shtml.

1417 International Journal of Uncertainty, Fuzziness and Knowledge-Based Systems
World Scientific Publishing Co. Pte Ltd.
5 Toh Tuck Link
Singapore 596224, Singapore   Ph: 65 64665775
Publication E-mail: wspc@wspc.com.sg

Forum for research on various methodologies for the management of imprecise, vague, uncertain or incomplete information. **Founded:** 1993. **Freq:** Bimonthly. **ISSN:** 0218-4885. **Subscription Rates:** S$524 institutions; S$190 individuals. **URL:** http://www.worldscinet.com/ijufks/ijufks.shtml.

1418 Investor's Guide to Singapore
Singapore International Chamber of Commerce
John Hancock Tower
6 Raffles Quay, No.10-01   Ph: 65 2241255
Singapore 048580, Singapore   Fax: 65 2242785
Publication E-mail: SME First Stop@SICCI
Publisher E-mail: general@sicc.com.sg

Journal covering business, economics and investments. **Founded:** 1973. **Freq:** Annual. **ISSN:** 0129-5276. **Subscription Rates:** S$32. **URL:** http://www.sicc.com.sg.

Circ: Paid 4,500

1419 ISO Link
Temasek Polytechnic
21 Tampines Ave. 1
Singapore 529757, Singapore   Ph: 65 67882000
Publication E-mail: corporate_communications@tp.edu.sg

Publication for international students. **Freq:** Quarterly. **URL:** http://www.tp.edu.sg/admin/ss/ssd/isolink/cca.htm.

📖 **1420　IT Asia**
Newscom Pte Ltd.
105 Boon Keng Rd., 04-17
Singapore 339776, Singapore　　　　　　　　Ph: 65 2919861

Journal of data communication and data transmission systems. **Founded:** 1987. **Freq:** Monthly. **Key Personnel:** Austin Morais, Editor. **ISSN:** 1012-8328.
Ad Rates:　BW: S$6,545　　　　　　　　**Circ:** Paid 22,266
　　　　　　　4C: S$7,415

📖 **1421　JCA Forecast**
James Cowan Associates (S.E. Asia) Pte Ltd.
9th Fl., Phillip Grand Bldg.
Singapore 48695, Singapore

Journal covering business, economics and investments. **Founded:** 1971. **Freq:** Weekly. **Key Personnel:** Sabastian Anthony Samy, Editor. **Subscription Rates:** S$350.

　　　　　　　　　　　　　　　　　　Circ: Paid 9,000

📖 **1422　Journal of Biological Systems**
World Scientific Publishing Co. Pte Ltd.
5 Toh Tuck Link
Singapore 596224, Singapore　　　　　　　Ph: 65 64665775
Publication E-mail: wspc@wspc.com.sg

Journal that aims to promote interdisciplinary approaches in biology and in medicine. **Founded:** 1993. **Freq:** Quarterly. **ISSN:** 0218-3390. **Subscription Rates:**　S$626　institutions;　S$227　individuals.　**URL:**　http://www.worldscinet.com/jbs/jbs.shtml.

📖 **1423　Journal of Circuits, Systems and Computers**
World Scientific Publishing Co. Pte Ltd.
5 Toh Tuck Link
Singapore 596224, Singapore　　　　　　　Ph: 65 64665775
Publication E-mail: wspc@wspc.com.sg

Publication covering topics ranging from mathematical foundations to practical engineering design. **Founded:** 1991. **Freq:** Bimonthly. **ISSN:** 0218-1266. **Subscription Rates:** S$743 institutions; S$273 individuals. **URL:** http://www.worldscinet.com/jcsc/jcsc.shtml.

📖 **1424　Journal of Computational Acoustics**
World Scientific Publishing Co. Pte Ltd.
5 Toh Tuck Link
Singapore 596224, Singapore　　　　　　　Ph: 65 64665775
Publication E-mail: wspc@wspc.com.sg

Journal that aims to provide an international forum for the dissemination of the state-of-the-art information in the field of computational acoustics. **Freq:** Quarterly. **ISSN:** 0218-396X. **Subscription Rates:** S$661 institutions; S$24 individuals. **URL:** http://www.worldscinet.com/jca/jca.shtml.

📖 **1425　Journal of Earthquake Engineering**
World Scientific Publishing Co. Pte Ltd.
5 Toh Tuck Link
Singapore 596224, Singapore　　　　　　　Ph: 65 64665775
Publication E-mail: wspc@wspc.com.sg

Periodical containing peer-reviewed papers on research and development in analytical, experimental and field studies of earthquakes. **Founded:** 1997. **Freq:** Quarterly. **ISSN:** 1363-2469. **Subscription Rates:** S$492 institutions; S$197 individuals. **URL:** http://www.worldscinet.com/jee/jee.shtml.

📖 **1426　Journal of Electronics Manufacturing**
World Scientific Publishing Co. Pte Ltd.
5 Toh Tuck Link
Singapore 596224, Singapore　　　　　　　Ph: 65 64665775
Publication E-mail: wspc@wspc.com.sg

Publishes quality technical papers associated with the manufacture and assembly of circuit boards, semiconductors and other components. **Founded:** 1991. **Freq:** Quarterly. **ISSN:** 0960-3131. **Subscription Rates:** S$613

institutions;　S$220　individuals.　**URL:**　http://www.worldscinet.com/jem/jem.shtml.

📖 **1427　Journal of Enterprising Culture**
World Scientific Publishing Co. Pte Ltd.
5 Toh Tuck Link
Singapore 596224, Singapore　　　　　　　Ph: 65 64665775
Publication E-mail: wspc@wspc.com.sg

Journal that publishes conceptual, research, and/or case based works that can be of practical value to business persons, educators, students and advocates. **Freq:** Quarterly. **ISSN:** 0218-4958. **Subscription Rates:** S$294 institutions. **URL:** http://www.worldscinet.com/jec/jec.shtml.

📖 **1428　Journal of Environmental Assessment Policy and Management**
World Scientific Publishing Co. Pte Ltd.
5 Toh Tuck Link
Singapore 596224, Singapore　　　　　　　Ph: 65 64665775
Publication E-mail: wspc@wspc.com.sg

Interdisciplinary, peer-reviewed international journal covering policy and decision-making relating to environmental assessment (EA) in the broadest sense. **Founded:** 1999. **Freq:** Quarterly. **ISSN:** 1464-3332. **Subscription Rates:**　S$513　institutions;　S$163　individuals.　**URL:**　http://www.worldscinet.com/jeapm/jeapm.shtml.

📖 **1429　Journal of Knot Theory and Its Ramifications**
World Scientific Publishing Co. Pte Ltd.
5 Toh Tuck Link
Singapore 596224, Singapore　　　　　　　Ph: 65 64665775
Publication E-mail: wspc@wspc.com.sg

Periodical intended as a forum for new developments in knot theory. **Founded:** 1992. **Freq:** 8/year. **ISSN:** 0218-2165. **Subscription Rates:** S$1,183 institutions; S$429 individuals. **URL:** http://www.worldscinet.com/jktr/jktr.shtml.

📖 **1430　Journal of Musculoskeletal Research**
World Scientific Publishing Co. Pte Ltd.
5 Toh Tuck Link
Singapore 596224, Singapore　　　　　　　Ph: 65 64665775
Publication E-mail: wspc@wspc.com.sg

International, interdisciplinary journal aimed at publishing up-to-date contributions on clinical and basic research on the musculoskeletal system. **Founded:** 1997. **Freq:** Quarterly. **ISSN:** 0218-9577. **Subscription Rates:** S$288 institutions; S$141 individuals. **URL:** http://www.worldscinet.com/jmr/jmr.shtml.

📖 **1431　Journal of Nonlinear Optical Physics and Materials**
World Scientific Publishing Co. Pte Ltd.
5 Toh Tuck Link
Singapore 596224, Singapore　　　　　　　Ph: 65 64665775
Publication E-mail: wspc@wspc.com.sg

Periodical devoted to the rapidly advancing research and development in the field of nonlinear interactions of light with matter. **Founded:** 1992. **Freq:** Quarterly. **ISSN:** 0218-8635. **Subscription Rates:** S$1,087 institutions; S$387 individuals. **URL:** http://www.worldscinet.com/jnopm/jnopm.shtml.

📖 **1432　Juice**
Catcha.com Pte Ltd.
1 Scotts Rd.
20-13 Shaw Centre
Singapore 228208, Singapore　　　　　　　Ph: 65 7336166
Publication E-mail: editor@getforme.com

Lifestyle magazine. **Freq:** Monthly. **Key Personnel:** Tricia Lee, Managing Editor. **Remarks:** Advertising accepted; rates available upon request. **URL:** http://www.juiceonline.com.
　　　　　　　　　　　　　　　　　　Circ: Free 30,000

📖 **1433   Law Gazette**
The Law Society of Singapore
39 South Bridge Rd.
Singapore 58673, Singapore   Ph: 65 65382500

Law journal. **Subtitle:** An Official Publication of the Law Society of. **Freq:** Monthly. **Key Personnel:** Elizabeth Sheares, Editor. **Subscription Rates:** S$185.40. **URL:** http://www.lawgazette.com.sg.
                                    Circ: Paid 4,300

📖 **1434   LawLink**
The Alumni Relations Committee, NUS Law School
13 Law Link
Kent Ridge
Singapore 117590, Singapore
Publication E-mail: lawweb@nus.edu.sg

Alumni magazine of the National University of Singapore Law School. **Freq:** Semiannual. **ISSN:** 0219-6441. **URL:** http://law.nus.edu.sg/alumni/lawlink.htm.

📖 **1435   Lien**
Alliance Francaise
1 Sarkies Rd.
Singapore 258130, Singapore   Ph: 65 7378422

Online Franco-Singaporean arts magazine. **Freq:** Bimonthly. **Remarks:** Advertising accepted; rates available upon request. **URL:** http://www.alliancefrancaise.org.sg.
                                    Circ: (Not Reported)

📖 **1436   Lime**
Media Corp Publishing Pte Ltd.
Caldecott Broadcast Centre
Andrew Rd.
Singapore 299939, Singapore   Ph: 65 63333888
Publication E-mail: subhelp@mediacorppub.com.sg

Entertainment magazine. **Freq:** Monthly. **URL:** http://lime.mediacorppublishing.com/2002_11/index.htm.

📖 **1437   LookBook**
Panpac Media Group Ltd.
371 Beach Rd.
03-18 Keypoint
Singapore 199597, Singapore   Ph: 65 62920300
Publication E-mail: aun.koh@panpacmedia.com

Fashion and lifestyle magazine. **Freq:** Monthly. **Key Personnel:** Chong Wan Tay, Editor, chongwan.tay@panpacmedia.com. **Remarks:** Advertising accepted; rates available upon request. **URL:** http://www.panpacmedia.com/singapore/print/lookbook_pg.htm.
                                    Circ: (Not Reported)

📖 **1438   Male by Birth, Man by Choice**
MBMC International
59 Devonshire Lodge
09-01 Devonshire Rd.
Singapore 239856, Singapore   Ph: 65 67377290
Publication E-mail: advertise@newurbanmale.com

Men's lifestyle webzine. **Remarks:** Advertising accepted; rates available upon request. **URL:** http://www.newurbanmale.com/.
                                    Circ: (Not Reported)

📖 **1439   Mallal's Monthly Digest**
Butterworths Asia
Shenton House
3 Shenton Way 14-03
Singapore 68805, Singapore   Ph: 65 2203684

Law journal. **Founded:** 1987. **Freq:** Monthly. **ISSN:** 0961-5563. **Subscription Rates:** S$299.
                                    Circ: Paid 500

📖 **1440   Marketwatch**
Fraser Roach & Co Pte Ltd.
Maxwell Rd.
PO Box 789
Singapore 9015, Singapore

Journal covering banking and finance. **Founded:** 1926. **Freq:** Monthly. **ISSN:** 0016-0083.
                                    Circ: Paid 2,250

📖 **1441   Mathematical Models and Methods in Applied Sciences**
World Scientific Publishing Co. Pte Ltd.
5 Toh Tuck Link
Singapore 596224, Singapore   Ph: 65 64665775
Publication E-mail: wspc@wspc.com.sg

Periodical aimed at providing a medium of exchange for scientists engaged in applied sciences. **Founded:** 1991. **Freq:** Monthly. **ISSN:** 0218-2025. **Subscription Rates:** S$1,376 institutions; S$499 individuals. **URL:** http://www.worldscinet.com/m3as/m3as.shtml.

📖 **1442   Messenger**
Southeast Asia Union Mission of Seventh-Day Adventists
251 Upper Serangoon Rd.
Singapore 34768, Singapore

Journal covering the religion and theology of Protestants. **Founded:** 1968. **Freq:** Bimonthly. **Key Personnel:** Loralyn Horning, Editor. **ISSN:** 0026-0371. **Subscription Rates:** S$3.50.
                                    Circ: Controlled 2,000

📖 **1443   Mineral Resources Engineering**
World Scientific Publishing Co. Pte Ltd.
5 Toh Tuck Link
Singapore 596224, Singapore   Ph: 65 64665775
Publication E-mail: wspc@wspc.com.sg

Publishes papers on advances in research, development and practical applications in all aspects of mining science and mining engineering technology. **Freq:** Quarterly. **ISSN:** 0950-6098. **Subscription Rates:** S$625 institutions; S$225 individuals. **URL:** http://www.worldscinet.com/mre/mre.shtml.

📖 **1444   Mirror of Opinion**
Ministry of Information and the Arts Media Division
PSA Bldg., 36th Fl.
460 Alexandra Rd.
Singapore 119963, Singapore

General interest newspaper. **Founded:** 1965. **Freq:** Daily. **ISSN:** 0544-4055. **Subscription Rates:** S$130.
                                    Circ: Paid 400

📖 **1445   Modern Physics Letters A**
World Scientific Publishing Co. Pte Ltd.
5 Toh Tuck Link
Singapore 596224, Singapore   Ph: 65 64665775
Publication E-mail: wspc@wspc.com.sg

Periodical containing research papers covering current research developments in gravitation, cosmology, nuclear physics, and particles and fields. **Founded:** 1986. **Freq:** 40/year. **ISSN:** 0217-7323. **Subscription Rates:** S$4,248 institutions; S$1,542 individuals. **URL:** http://www.worldscinet.com/mpla/mpla.html.
                                    Circ: Paid 550

📖 **1446   Modern Physics Letters B**
World Scientific Publishing Co. Pte Ltd.
5 Toh Tuck Link
Singapore 596224, Singapore   Ph: 65 64665775
Publication E-mail: wspc@wspc.com.sg

Periodical featuring important and useful research findings in condensed matter physics, statistical physics, applied physics and high-Tc superconductivity. **Founded:** 1987. **Freq:** 30/year. **ISSN:** 0217-9849. **Subscription Rates:** S$3,337 institutions; S$1,211 individuals. **URL:** http://www.worldscinet.com/mplb/mplb.html.
                                    Circ: Paid 350

📖 **1447 Motherhood**
Eastern Publishing Ltd.
8 Lorong Bakar Batu, 07-12
Singapore 348743-, Singapore   Ph: 65 62200552
Publication E-mail: VivienNg@epl.com.sg

Magazine for an online parenting audience. **Freq:** Monthly. **Key Personnel:** Eileen Chan, Editor-in-Chief, EileenChan@epl.com.sg. **Subscription Rates:** S$4.50. **Remarks:** Advertising accepted; rates available upon request. **URL:** http://www.motherhood.com.sg/.

                                        Circ: (Not Reported)

📖 **1448 Motherhood Handbook**
Eastern Publishing Ltd.
8 Lorong Bakar Batu, 07-12
Singapore 348743-, Singapore   Ph: 65 62200552

Publication providing information on concise and succinct information on pregnancy, birth and early baby care. **Freq:** Annual. **URL:** http://www.epl.com.sg/.

📖 **1449 Motoring**
Eastern Publishing Ltd.
8 Lorong Bakar Batu, 07-12
Singapore 348743-, Singapore   Ph: 65 62200552

Automotive publication. **URL:** http://www.epl.com.sg/.

📖 **1450 Motoring Annual**
Eastern Publishing Ltd.
8 Lorong Bakar Batu, 07-12
Singapore 348743-, Singapore   Ph: 65 62200552

Automotive publication. **Freq:** Annual. **URL:** http://www.epl.com.sg/.

📖 **1451 Nature Aquarium World**
Vectrapoint Publishing (Singapore) Pte Ltd.
Towner Road
PO Box 1898
Singapore 913299, Singapore   Ph: 65 7670177
Publication E-mail: aquajournal@vectrapoint.com

Nature magazine. **URL:** http://www.vectrapoint.com/.

📖 **1452 Nature Watch**
Nature Society (Singapore)
510 Geylang Rd., 02-05
The Sunflower
Singapore 389466, Singapore   Ph: 65 67412036
Publication E-mail: contact@nss.org.sg

Periodical featuring articles of interest to nature lovers. **Freq:** Quarterly. **URL:** http://habitatnews.nus.edu.sg/pub/naturewatch/.

📖 **1453 Newman**
Panpac Media Group Ltd.
371 Beach Rd.
03-18 Keypoint
Singapore 199597, Singapore   Ph: 65 62920300

Singapore's magazine for men. **Freq:** Monthly. **Subscription Rates:** S$48. **URL:** http://www.newman.com.sg/.

📖 **1454 9to5Asia.com**
Worklife Asia Pte Ltd.
Robinson Road Post Office
PO Box 292
Singapore 900542, Singapore   Ph: 65 63388078
Publication E-mail: sales@9to5asia.com

E-zine about work and life. **Founded:** 1998. **Freq:** Monthly. **URL:** http://coldfusion.9to5asia.com/.

📖 **1455 NUS Economic Journal**
National University of Singapore
c/o Dept. of Economics
10 Kent Ridge Crescent
Singapore 511, Singapore   Ph: 65 7779117

Journal covering business and economics. **Founded:** 1962. **Freq:** Annual. **Key Personnel:** Cadence Wong Yim Hwa, Editor. **ISSN:** 0218-3269. **Subscription Rates:** S$10. **Remarks:** Advertising accepted; rates available upon request. **URL:** http://nussu.nus.edu.sg/nussu/Nclubsoc.

                                        Circ: Paid 10,000

📖 **1456 The Padang**
Singapore Cricket Club
Connaught Dr.
Singapore 179681, Singapore   Ph: 65 63389271
Publication E-mail: scc@scc.org.sg

Cricketing magazine. **Freq:** Bimonthly. **URL:** http://www.scc.org.sg/.

📖 **1457 Paper Asia**
First Asia Publishing Pte Ltd.
6 New Industrial Rd., 02-02/04
Singapore 536199, Singapore   Ph: 65 8580040

Magazine on pulp and papers industry. **Freq:** Monthly.
                                        Circ: 5,621

📖 **1458 Parallel Processing Letters**
World Scientific Publishing Co. Pte Ltd.
5 Toh Tuck Link
Singapore 596224, Singapore   Ph: 65 64665775
Publication E-mail: wspc@wspc.com.sg

Periodical that aims to rapidly disseminate results on a worldwide basis in the field of parallel processing in the form of short papers. **Founded:** 1991. **Freq:** Quarterly. **ISSN:** 0129-6264. **Subscription Rates:** S$664 institutions; S$241 individuals. **URL:** http://www.worldscinet.com/ppl/ppl.shtml.

📖 **1459 PC World Singapore**
Block 1008
Toa Payoh North 07-11
Singapore 318996, Singapore
Publication E-mail: gene@comres.com.sg

Publication focusing on computers and information technology. **Freq:** Monthly. **Key Personnel:** Gene Vallejo-Yeo, Editor, gene@comres.com.sg. **Subscription Rates:** S$70. **URL:** http://www.pcworld.com.sg/.

📖 **1460 Petromin**
AP Energy Business Publications Pte. Ltd.
63 Robinson Rd., 02-16
Singapore 068894, Singapore   Ph: 65 62223422
Publication E-mail: petromin@safan.com

Publication providing companies with maximum business exposure in print and online. **Founded:** 1983. **Freq:** Monthly. **Key Personnel:** Khin Bo, Technical Editor, phone 65 63253055, khinbo@safan.com. **ISSN:** 0129-1122. **URL:** http://www.petromin.safan.com/.

📖 **1461 Planews**
Singapore Institute of Planners
c/o 23 Duxton Hill
Singapore 89906, Singapore   Ph: 65 62250322
Publication E-mail: Info@sip.org.sg

Journal of housing and urban planning. **Founded:** 1972. **Freq:** Semiannual. **Key Personnel:** Ole Johan Dale, Editor. **ISSN:** 0129-3184. **Subscription Rates:** S$5. **Remarks:** Advertising accepted; rates available upon request. **URL:** http://www.sip.org.sg/Planews/planews.htm.

                                        Circ: Paid 1,000

Ad Rates: GLR = general line rate; BW = one-time black & white page rate; 4C = one-time four color page rate; SAU = standard advertising unit rate; CNU = Canadian newspaper advertising unit rate; PCI = per column inch rate.
Circulation: ★ = ABC; △ = BPA; ♦ = CAC; ● = CCAB; ❑ = VAC; ⊕ = PO Statement; ‡ = Publisher's Report; Boldface figures = sworn; Light figures = estimated.
Entry type: 📖 = Print; 🕮 = Broadcast.

129

⏏ 1462   Plastichem
Singapore Polytechnic Polymer Society
Dover Rd.
Singapore, Singapore

Journal of chemical engineering and physical chemistry. **Founded:** 1969. **Freq:** Annual. **Key Personnel:** Tang Sook Mui, Editor. **ISSN:** 0129-2889. **Remarks:** Advertising accepted; rates available upon request.
Circ: 1,000

⏏ 1463   Plastics & Rubber Singapore Journal
Plastics and Rubber Institute of Singapore
Tanglin Post Office Box 354
Singapore 912412, Singapore
Publication E-mail: chmcsoh@nus.edu.sg

Technical publication on the science and technology that drives the plastics and rubber industries. **Remarks:** Advertising accepted; rates available upon request. **URL:** http://www.pris.org.sg/Journal.htm.
Circ: (Not Reported)

⏏ 1464   Politeia
National University of Singapore
Kent Ridge
Singapore 511, Singapore

Political science journal. **Founded:** 1971. **Freq:** Annual. **ISSN:** 0217-7587. **Subscription Rates:** S$2.50. **Remarks:** Advertising accepted; rates available upon request.
Circ: Paid 2,000

⏏ 1465   Port O'Call
Panpac Media Group Ltd.
371 Beach Rd.
03-18 Keypoint
Singapore 199597, Singapore   Ph: 65 62920300
Publication E-mail: janet.teo@panpacmedia.com

Magazine reaching out to U.S., UK, Australian and New Zealand naval armed services personnel who make port calls at Singapore. **Freq:** Semiannual. **Key Personnel:** Ho Sum Kwong, Editor-in-Chief, sk@panpacmedia.com. **URL:** http://www.panpacmedia.com/singapore/print/portocall_pg.htm.
Ad Rates: 4C: S$3,000   **Circ:** (Not Reported)

⏏ 1466   Pregnancy & Babycare
Panpac Media Group Ltd.
371 Beach Rd.
03-18 Keypoint
Singapore 199597, Singapore   Ph: 65 62920300
Publication E-mail: dawson.kan@panpacmedia.com

Parenting magazine. **Key Personnel:** Erniza Johari, Editor, erniza.johari@panpacmedia.com. **Remarks:** Advertising accepted; rates available upon request. **URL:** http://www.panpacmedia.com/singapore/print.
Circ: (Not Reported)

⏏ 1467   Premier Golf Annual
Eastern Publishing Ltd.
8 Lorong Bakar Batu, 07-12
Singapore 348743-, Singapore   Ph: 65 62200552

Magazine featuring information on where to buy golf clubs, putters, drivers, golf shoes and golf balls. **Freq:** Annual. **URL:** http://www.epl.com.sg/.

⏏ 1468   Regional Outlook: Southeast Asia
Institute of Southeast Asian Studies
30 Heng Mui Keng Terrace
Pasir Panjang
Singapore 119614, Singapore   Ph: 65 67780955
Publication E-mail: admin@iseas.edu.sg

Periodical that aims to provide a succinct analysis of current political and economic trends in the ten countries of Southeast Asia. **Founded:** 1992. **Freq:** Annual. **Key Personnel:** Triena Ong, Editor. **ISSN:** 0218-3056. **Subscription Rates:** US$19.9. **URL:** http://www.iseas.edu.sg/journals.html.

⏏ 1469   Research and Practice in Human Resource Management
Singapore Human Resources Institute
60A Collyer Quay
5th Level, Change Alley Aerial Plaza
   Tower
Singapore 049322, Singapore   Ph: 65 4380012
Publication E-mail: shri98@signt.com.sg

Publishes articles in fields of interest to scholars and practitioners of personnel management and human resource management. **Founded:** 1993. **Freq:** Annual. **Key Personnel:** Donald J Campbell, Editor. **ISSN:** 0218-5180. **Subscription Rates:** S$18.54 Singapore; US$35 other countries. **URL:** http://www.fba.nus.edu.sg/rphrm/Astart.htm.

⏏ 1470   Review of Pacific Basin Financial Markets and Policies
World Scientific Publishing Co. Pte Ltd.
5 Toh Tuck Link
Singapore 596224, Singapore   Ph: 65 64665775
Publication E-mail: wspc@wspc.com.sg

Publication focusing on global interdisciplinary research in finance, economics and accounting. **Founded:** 1998. **Freq:** Quarterly. **ISSN:** 0219-0915. **Subscription Rates:** S$331 institutions; S$132 individuals. **URL:** http://www.worldscinet.com/rpbfmp/rpbfmp.shtml.

⏏ 1471   Reviews in Mathematical Physics
World Scientific Publishing Co. Pte Ltd.
5 Toh Tuck Link
Singapore 596224, Singapore   Ph: 65 64665775
Publication E-mail: wspc@wspc.com.sg

Publishes papers of relevance to mathematical physicists, mathematicians and theoretical physicists interested in interdisciplinary topic. **Founded:** 1989. **Freq:** 10/year. **ISSN:** 0129-055X. **Subscription Rates:** S$1,514 institutions; S$548 individuals. **URL:** http://www.worldscinet.com/rmp/rmp.shtml.
Circ: Paid 150

⏏ 1472   RSYC
Republic of Singapore Yacht Club
52 West Coast Ferry Rd.
Singapore 126887, Singapore   Ph: 65 67689288
Publication E-mail: info@rsyc.org.sg

Official magazine of the Republic of Singapore Yacht Club. **Freq:** Bimonthly. **Remarks:** Advertising accepted; rates available upon request. **URL:** http://www.rsyc.org.sg/magazine/.
Circ: Free 2,200

⏏ 1473   SEAMEO Regional Language Centre Guidelines
SEAMEO Regional Language Centre
30 Orange Grove Rd.   Ph: 65 8857888
Singapore 258352, Singapore   Fax: 65 7342753
Publication E-mail: admn@relc.org.sg
Publisher E-mail: admin@relc.org.sg

Publication focusing on language teaching and learning disciplines. **Founded:** 1979. **Freq:** Semiannual. **ISSN:** 0129-7767. **Subscription Rates:** US$181. **URL:** http://www.seameo.org/centers/relc.htm.
Circ: Paid 1,000

⏏ 1474   SG News
Singapore Ministry of Information, Communications and the Arts
140 Hill St., No. 02-02
MITA Bldg.   Ph: 65 22707988
Singapore 179369, Singapore   Fax: 65 68379480
Publication E-mail: mita_news@mita.gov.sg
Publisher E-mail: mita_pa@gov.sg

General newspaper for Singapore. **Founded:** 1999. **Freq:** Daily. **URL:** http://www.sgnews.info/.

⏏ 1475   Sgezine
Singapore International Foundation
9 Penang Rd.
12-01 Park Mall
Singapore 238459, Singapore   Ph: 65 68378700
Publication E-mail: sifnet@sif.org.sg

General interest magazine for Singaporeans. **Freq:** Quarterly. **Key Personnel:**

Lea Wee, Editor, leawee@pacific.net.sg. **Remarks:** Advertising accepted; rates available upon request. **URL:** http://www.sgezine.com.sg/.
Circ: (Not Reported)

📖 **1476 Shipping Times**
Singapore Press Holdings Ltd.
82 Genting Ln., News Centre
Singapore 349567, Singapore   Ph: 65 7435318
Publication E-mail: btship@cyberway.com.sg

Shipping industry newspaper. **Founded:** 1976. **Freq:** Daily. **Key Personnel:** George Joseph, Editor, phone 65 63195772. **Subscription Rates:** S$265.20. **Remarks:** Advertising accepted; rates available upon request. **URL:** http://business-times.asia1.com.sg/shippingtimes/.
Circ: 35,000

📖 **1477 Showcase**
Hagley & Hoyle Pte Ltd.
70 Shenton Way
03-03 Marina House
Singapore 0207, Singapore   Ph: 65 2240688

Journal covering business and economics. **Founded:** 1975. **Freq:** Annual. **ISSN:** 0129-5179.

📖 **1478 Signature**
Signature Publishing Pte Ltd.
2-201 Merlin Pl.
Beach Rd.
Singapore, Singapore

Journal of travel and tourism. **Freq:** Monthly. **Key Personnel:** Filipina Elizabeth Reyes, Editor. **Remarks:** Advertising accepted; rates available upon request. **URL:** http://www.sigpubs.com.
Circ: 32,000

📖 **1479 Silver Kris**
MPH Magazines (S) Pte Ltd.
20 Martin Rd., 08-01
01 Seng Kee Bldg.
Singapore 239070, Singapore   Ph: 65 68794137

Magazine of Singapore Airlines. **Freq:** Monthly. **Key Personnel:** Steve Thompson, Group Editor.

📖 **1480 Singapore Accountant**
Longman Singapore Publishers (Pte) Ltd.
25 First Lok Yang Rd.
Singapore 629734, Singapore   Ph: 65 2682666

Journal covering business and economics. **Founded:** 1984. **Freq:** Bimonthly. **Key Personnel:** June Oei, Editor. **ISSN:** 0217-4456. **Subscription Rates:** S$86.
Circ: Paid 8,000

📖 **1481 Singapore Architect**
Singapore Institute of Architects
79 Neil Rd.   Ph: 65 62262668
Singapore 088907, Singapore   Fax: 65 62262663
Publication E-mail: info@sia.org.sg
Publisher E-mail: info@sia.org.sg

Official magazine of the Singapore Institute of Architects. **Freq:** Quarterly. **Remarks:** Advertising accepted; rates available upon request. **URL:** http://www.sia.org.sg/magazine/magz-info/.
Circ: (Not Reported)

📖 **1482 Singapore Economic Review**
World Scientific Publishing Co. Pte Ltd.
5 Toh Tuck Link
Singapore 596224, Singapore   Ph: 65 64665775
Publication E-mail: admn@relc.org.sg

Periodical devoted to the publication of high-quality theoretical and empirical papers on all aspects of economics. **Founded:** 1956. **Freq:** Semiannual. **Key**

Personnel: Koh Ai Tee, Editor. **ISSN:** 0217-5908. **Subscription Rates:** S$108. **Remarks:** Advertising accepted; rates available upon request. **URL:** http://www.worldscinet.com/ser/ser.shtml.
Circ: Paid 800

📖 **1483 The Singapore Family Physician**
College of Family Physicians Singapore
16 College Rd., No. 01-02
Singapore 169854, Singapore   Ph: 65 62230606

Medical journal. **Freq:** Quarterly. **Key Personnel:** Matthew N.G. Joo Ming, Editor.

📖 **1484 Singapore Journal of Legal Studies**
National University of Singapore
Faculty of Law
National University of Singapore
13 Law Link   Ph: 65 8743102
Singapore 117590, Singapore   Fax: 65 7790979
Publication E-mail: lawsjls@nus.edu.sg

Publication focusing on legal developments in Singapore. **Founded:** 1959. **Freq:** Semiannual. **Key Personnel:** Michael Hor Yew Meng, Chief Editor, lawhorym@nus.edu.sg. **ISSN:** 0218-2173. **Subscription Rates:** S$66.95 Singapore. **Remarks:** Advertising accepted; rates available upon request. **URL:** http://law.nus.edu.sg/sjls.
Circ: Paid 1,850

📖 **1485 Singapore Journal of Obstetrics & Gynaecology**
Obstetrical and Gynaecological Society of Singapore
Unit 8K38, Level 8, Women's Tower
KK Women's & Children's Hospital
100 Bukit Timah Rd.
Singapore 229899, Singapore   Ph: 65 2951383
Publication E-mail: ogss@pacific.net.sg

Journal of obstetrics and gynaecology. **Founded:** 1956. **Freq:** 3/year. **Key Personnel:** Loganath A, Editor. **ISSN:** 0129-3273. **Subscription Rates:** US$25. **URL:** http://www.ogss.net.
Circ: Paid 1,000

📖 **1486 Singapore Journal of Primary Industries**
Ministry of National Development
National Development Bldg.
5 Maxwell Rd., 03-00
Singapore 69110, Singapore

Publication of original research findings and review of progress in fisheries, horticulture, animal husbandry and veterinary science and allied subjects. **Founded:** 1973. **Freq:** Annual. **ISSN:** 0129-6485. **Subscription Rates:** S$15.
Circ: Paid 500

📖 **1487 Singapore Journal of Tropical Geography**
Blackwell Publishers Ltd
Dept. of Geography
National University of Singapore
1 Arts Link
Singapore 117570, Singapore

Geography journal. **Freq:** Monthly. **Key Personnel:** James D. Sidaway, Guest Editor, geojds@nus.edu.sg. **URL:** http://www.fas.nus.edu.sg/geog/pub1.htm.

📖 **1488 Singapore Law Review**
National University of Singapore
10 Kent Ridge Crescent
Singapore 119260, Singapore   Ph: 65 7723603
Publication E-mail: bm_slr@yahoo.com.sg

Periodical aimed at promoting legal thinking, legal writing and discussions amongst the students of the Law Faculty. **Founded:** 1969. **Freq:** Semiannual. **Key Personnel:** Benedict Teo, Chief Editor. **ISSN:** 0080-9691. **Subscription Rates:** S$20 Singapore; S$27 other countries. **Remarks:** Advertising

Ad Rates: GLR = general line rate; BW = one-time black & white page rate; 4C = one-time four color page rate; SAU = standard advertising unit rate; CNU = Canadian newspaper advertising unit rate; PCI = per column inch rate.
Circulation: ★ = ABC; △ = BPA; ♦ = CAC; • = CCAB; ❑ = VAC; ⊕ = PO Statement; ‡ = Publisher's Report; Boldface figures = sworn; Light figures = estimated.
Entry type: 📖 = Print; 🎤 = Broadcast.

131

accepted; rates available upon request. **URL:** http://law.nus.edu.sg/lawclub/slr.

Circ: Paid 1,350

📖 **1489 Singapore Management Review**
Singapore Institute of Management
Research and Publications Dept.
461 Clementi Rd.
Singapore 599491, Singapore
Publication E-mail: research@sim.edu.sg

Publication focusing on the latest business issues in Singapore and around the Asian region. **Founded:** 1979. **Freq:** Semiannual. **Key Personnel:** Hing-Man Leung, Editor. **ISSN:** 0129-5977. **Subscription Rates:** S$48. **Remarks:** Advertising accepted; rates available upon request. **URL:** http://www2.sim.edu.sg.

Circ: (Not Reported)

📖 **1490 Singapore National Academy of Science Journal**
National University of Singapore
Lower Kent Ridge Rd.
Singapore 511, Singapore

Journal covering biology and botany. **Founded:** 1977. **Freq:** Annual. **Key Personnel:** A.N. Rao, Editor. **ISSN:** 0129-3729. **Subscription Rates:** S$32.

Circ: Paid 1,500

📖 **1491 Singapore Paediatric Journal**
Singapore Paediatric Society
Lower Kent Ridge Rd.
National University Hospital
Singapore 119074, Singapore

Journal of pediatrics. **Founded:** 1958. **Freq:** Quarterly. **Key Personnel:** H.B. Wong, Editor. **ISSN:** 0218-9941. **Subscription Rates:** US$50. **Remarks:** Advertising accepted; rates available upon request.

Circ: Paid 1,000

📖 **1492 Singapore Source Book for Architects & Designers**
Times Media Pte Ltd.
1 New Industrial Rd.
Times Centre
Singapore 536196, Singapore   Ph: 65 2848844

Journal covering building, construction and interior design. **Founded:** 1989. **Freq:** Annual. **ISSN:** 0218-3153. **Subscription Rates:** S$60. **Remarks:** Advertising accepted; rates available upon request. **URL:** http://www.timesbiz.com.sg.

Circ: (Not Reported)

📖 **1493 Singapore Visitor**
Panpac Media Group Ltd.
371 Beach Rd.
03-18 Keypoint
Singapore 199597, Singapore   Ph: 65 62920300
Publication E-mail: janet.teo@panpacmedia.com

Magazine for English speaking tourists in Singapore. **Freq:** Monthly. **Key Personnel:** Ho Sum Kwong, Editor-in-Chief, sk@panpacmedia.com. **URL:** http://www.panpacmedia.com/singapore/print/tsv_pg.htm.
Ad Rates: 4C: S$3,200   **Circ:** (Not Reported)

📖 **1494 Smart Investor**
Panpac Media Group Ltd.
371 Beach Rd.
03-18 Keypoint
Singapore 199597, Singapore   Ph: 65 62920300
Publication E-mail: liew.leekuen@panpacmedia.com

Magazine that explores opportunities and options available to the serious retail investor. **Freq:** Monthly. **Key Personnel:** Timmy Tan, Editor, timmy.tan@panpacmedia.com. **Subscription Rates:** S$55 Singapore; S$97 Asian countries. **URL:** http://www.smartinvestor.com.sg/.
Ad Rates: BW: S$3,000   **Circ:** (Not Reported)
             4C: S$3,800

📖 **1495 The SMS Magazine**
Debenhams Management Services Pte Ltd.
No. 3, Woodlands Industrial Park E1, 03-04
Northland Industrial Bldg.
Singapore 757726, Singapore   Ph: 65 3684511
Publication E-mail: sales@thesmsmagazine.com

Lifestyle magazine. **Freq:** Quarterly. **ISSN:** 0219-5801. **Subscription Rates:** S$28 two years. **URL:** http://www.thesmsmagazine.com/.
Ad Rates: 4C: US$3,772   **Circ:** (Not Reported)

📖 **1496 Sojourn**
Institute of Southeast Asian Studies
30 Heng Mui Keng Terrace
Pasir Panjang
Singapore 119614, Singapore   Ph: 65 67780955

Sociology journal. **Founded:** 1986. **Freq:** Semiannual. **Key Personnel:** Triena Ong, Editor. **ISSN:** 0217-9520. **Subscription Rates:** S$40 ISU. **URL:** http://www.iseas.edu.sg/pub.html.

📖 **1497 South Seas Society Journal**
South Seas Society
PO Box 709
Singapore 901409, Singapore   Ph: 65 4661940

Journal covering Asian history. **Founded:** 1940. **Freq:** Semiannual. **Key Personnel:** Gwee Yee Hean, Editor. **ISSN:** 0081-2889. **Subscription Rates:** US$20.

Circ: Paid 1,000

📖 **1498 Southeast Asian Affairs**
Institute of Southeast Asian Studies
30 Heng Mui Keng Terrace
Pasir Panjang
Singapore 119614, Singapore   Ph: 65 67780955
Publication E-mail: admin@iseas.edu.sg

Annual review of significant trends and developments in Southeast Asia. **Founded:** 1974. **Freq:** Annual. **Key Personnel:** Daljit Singh, Editor. **ISSN:** 0377-5437. **Subscription Rates:** US$23.9. **URL:** http://www.iseas.edu.sg.

📖 **1499 Southeast Asian Journal of Social Sciences**
Times Academic Press
1 New Industrial Rd.
Times Centre
Singapore 536196, Singapore   Ph: 65 3807463

Social science journal. **Founded:** 1968. **Freq:** Semiannual. **Key Personnel:** Chan Knok Sun, Editor. **ISSN:** 0303-8246. **URL:** http://www.timesone.com.sg/.

📖 **1500 Space**
Panpac Media Group Ltd.
371 Beach Rd.
03-18 Keypoint
Singapore 199597, Singapore   Ph: 65 62920300
Publication E-mail: dawson.kan@panpacmedia.com

Magazine on architecture and interior design. **Freq:** Bimonthly. **Key Personnel:** John Low, Senior Editor, john.low@panpacmedia.com. **URL:** http://www.panpacmedia.com/singapore/print/space_pg.htm.
Ad Rates: 4C: S$2,700   **Circ:** (Not Reported)

📖 **1501 Sports**
Singapore Sports Council
National Stadium Kallang
Singapore 1439, Singapore

Journal of sports and games. **Founded:** 1972. **Freq:** 10/year. **Key Personnel:** Ong Poh Choo, Editor. **ISSN:** 0217-3123. **Subscription Rates:** S$9. **Remarks:** Advertising accepted; rates available upon request. **URL:** http://www.ssc.gov.sg.

Circ: Paid 17,000

📖 **1502 Square Rooms**
SNP Corporation
1 Kim Seng Promenade
18-01 Great World City East Tower
Singapore 237994, Singapore · Ph: 65 68269600

The new living magazine for homeowners. **Freq:** Bimonthly. **Subscription Rates:** S$4.85. **Remarks:** Advertising accepted; rates available upon request. **URL:** http://www.myepb.com/script/SquareRooms.asp.
Circ: (Not Reported)

📖 **1503 The Straits Times**
Singapore Press Holdings Ltd.
82 Genting Ln., News Centre
Singapore 349567, Singapore · Ph: 65 7435318
Publication E-mail: circs@starhub.net.sg

Newspaper with a special focus on Singapore and the Asian region. **Founded:** 1845. **Freq:** Daily. **Key Personnel:** Yeong Ah Seng, Editor, yeong@sph.com.sg. **Remarks:** Advertising accepted; rates available upon request. **URL:** http://straitstimes.asia1.com.sg/.
Circ: Paid 400,000

📖 **1504 Surface Review and Letters**
World Scientific Publishing Co. Pte Ltd.
5 Toh Tuck Link
Singapore 596224, Singapore · Ph: 65 64665775
Publication E-mail: wspc@wspc.com.sg

Periodical devoted to the elucidation of properties and processes that occur at the boundaries of materials. **Founded:** 1994. **Freq:** Bimonthly. **Key Personnel:** Tong S Y, Editor. **ISSN:** 0218-625X. **Subscription Rates:** S$1,262 institutions; S$458 individuals. **URL:** http://www.worldscinet.com/srl/srl.shtml.

📖 **1505 Teach**
Teach Magazine
59a Club S.
Singapore 069434, Singapore · Ph: 65 62254100
Publication E-mail: teach@teachmagazine.com.sg

Magazine for Singapore's education community. **Freq:** 11/year. **Subscription Rates:** S$77. **Remarks:** Advertising accepted; rates available upon request. **URL:** http://www.teachmagazine.com.sg/.
Circ: (Not Reported)

📖 **1506 Teenage**
Teenage.com Pte Ltd.
57 Loyang Dr.
Singapore 508968, Singapore · Ph: 65 5469852
Publication E-mail: admin@teenage.com.sg

Magazine covering topics of interest to teenagers. **Founded:** 1988. **Freq:** Monthly. **URL:** http://www.teenage.com.sg/.

📖 **1507 teens**
Teens Pte Ltd.
8 Lorong Bakar Batu, 04-09
Singapore 348743, Singapore · Ph: 65 7448708
Publication E-mail: info@teensmag.com.sg

Magazine covering fashion, beauty and entertainment. **Remarks:** Advertising accepted; rates available upon request. **URL:** http://www.teensmag.com.sg/.
Circ: (Not Reported)

📖 **1508 Teens Annual**
Eastern Publishing Ltd.
8 Lorong Bakar Batu, 07-12
Singapore 348743-, Singapore · Ph: 65 62200552

Teen magazine focusing on fashion, health, and beauty. **Freq:** Annual. **URL:** http://www.epl.com.sg/.

📖 **1509 Tenders Estimating Data Service**
Construction Industry Development Board
Annexe A MND Complex
9 Maxwell Rd. 03-00
Singapore 69112, Singapore · Ph: 65 2256711

Journal covering building and construction. **Founded:** 1988. **Freq:** Semiannual. **Subscription Rates:** US$103.
Circ: Paid 200

📖 **1510 Today's Parents**
Panpac Media Group Ltd.
371 Beach Rd.
03-18 Keypoint
Singapore 199597, Singapore · Ph: 65 62920300
Publication E-mail: dawson.kan@panpacmedia.com

Magazine on parenting. **Freq:** Monthly. **Key Personnel:** Erniza Johari, Editor, erniza.johari@panpacmedia.com. **URL:** http://www.panpacmedia.com/singapore/print/tp_pg.htm.
Ad Rates: BW: S$2,200
4C: S$2,700
Circ: (Not Reported)

📖 **1511 Travel Asia**
Venture Asia Publishing
10 Craig Rd.
Singapore 089670, Singapore · Ph: 65 62231866

Travel magazine. **Freq:** Weekly. **ISSN:** 0218-9321. **URL:** http://www.travel-asia.com/.

📖 **1512 Travel Trade Gazette Asia**
TTG Asia Media Pte Ltd.
9 Battery Rd.
17-02/12, Straits Trading Bldg.
Singapore 049910, Singapore · Ph: 65 63957555
Publication E-mail: ttgnewsdesk@ttgasia.com

Publication focusing on travel and tourism. **Remarks:** Advertising accepted; rates available upon request. **URL:** http://www.ttg.com.sg/.
Circ: (Not Reported)

📖 **1513 TSEA: Targeting Singapore Electronics Audience**
RLFC
Singapore Science Park
89 Science Park Dr.
04-32 The Rutherford
Singapore 118261, Singapore · Ph: 65 8721915

Journal of electronics. **Freq:** Quarterly. **Key Personnel:** Lee Frost, Editor. **ISSN:** 0218-9461.
Ad Rates: BW: US$2065
4C: US$2950
Circ: 25,000

📖 **1514 Twenty Four Seven**
Panpac Media Group Ltd.
371 Beach Rd.
03-18 Keypoint
Singapore 199597, Singapore · Ph: 65 62920300
Publication E-mail: circulation@panpacmedia.com

Lifestyle magazine. **Freq:** Monthly. **Key Personnel:** Annette Tan, Editor, annette.tan@panpacmedia.com. **Subscription Rates:** S$5. **Remarks:** Advertising accepted; rates available upon request. **URL:** http://www.panpacmedia.com/singapore/print/index.html.
Circ: (Not Reported)

📖 **1515 Unibeam**
Building and Estate Management Society
c/o Faculty of Architecture and Building
National University of Singapore
Kent Ridge
Singapore 511, Singapore · Ph: 65 7756666

Real estate journal. **Freq:** Annual. **ISSN:** 0129-3680.

1516 University of Singapore History Society Journal
National University of Singapore
Kent Ridge
Singapore 511, Singapore   Ph: 65 7723839

Journal covering Asian history. **Founded:** 1963. **Freq:** Annual. **Key Personnel:** Boey Swee Siang, Editor. **Subscription Rates:** S$3. **Remarks:** Advertising accepted; rates available upon request.
Circ: Paid 500

1517 Wedding & Travel
Fullhouse Communications Private Limited
246 MacPherson Rd., 06-01
Betime Bldg.
Singapore 348578, Singapore   Ph: 65 68427266

Wedding magazine. **Freq:** Semiannual. **URL:** http://www.wedding-travel.com.sg/.

1518 Wine & Dine
Panpac Media Group Ltd.
371 Beach Rd.
03-18 Keypoint
Singapore 199597, Singapore   Ph: 65 62920300
Publication E-mail: cecilia.goh@panpacmedia.com

Magazine covering food, wine, travel and good living. **Freq:** Monthly. **Key Personnel:** Tan Su-Lyn, Managing Editor, tan.sulyn@panpacmedia.com. **Subscription Rates:** S$54. **URL:** http://www.wineanddine.com.sg/.
Ad Rates: BW: S$3,500   **Circ:** (Not Reported)
                 4C: S$4,500

1519 Woman's World
Eastern Publishing Ltd.
8 Lorong Bakar Batu, 07-12
Singapore 348743-, Singapore   Ph: 65 62200552

Woman's lifestyle magazine. **Freq:** Monthly. **URL:** http://www.epl.com.sg/.

1520 World Literature Written in English
National Institute of Education
Bukit Timah Rd.
Singapore 1025, Singapore   Ph: 65 4605622

Journal of literature. **Freq:** Semiannual. **Key Personnel:** Kirpal Singh, Editor. **ISSN:** 0093-1705. **Subscription Rates:** S$30.90.

1521 Young Buddhist
Singapore Buddhist Youth Organisations Joint Celebrations Committee
83 Silat Rd.
Singapore, Singapore

Journal covering Buddhist religion and theology. **Freq:** Annual.

1522 Young Generation
SNP Corporation
1 Kim Seng Promenade
18-01 Great World City East Tower
Singapore 237994, Singapore   Ph: 65 68269600

Magazine for children aged between 7 and 13 years. **Freq:** Monthly. **Subscription Rates:** US$2.43. **Remarks:** Advertising accepted; rates available upon request. **URL:** http://www.myepb.com/script/yg.asp.
Circ: (Not Reported)

1523 Young Parents
Singapore Press Holdings Ltd.
Toa Payoh North
1000 Toa Payoh North
Singapore 318994, Singapore   Ph: 65 63196319

Magazine for parents. **Founded:** 1986. **Freq:** Monthly. **Subscription Rates:** S$5. **URL:** http://shop.asiaone.com/stores/stoppress/yp.html.

SLOVAKIA

BRATISLAVA

1524 Computing and Informatics
Slovak Academy of Sciences
Institute of Informatics
Dubravska cesta 9   Ph: 42 1259412204
842 37 Bratislava, Slovakia   Fax: 42 1254771004
Publication E-mail: cai.ui@savba.sk
Publisher E-mail: upsycai@savba.sk

Professional journal covering computer science. **Founded:** 1982. **Freq:** Bimonthly. **Key Personnel:** Dr. Ladislav Hluchy, Editor-in-Chief. **ISSN:** 0232-0274. **Subscription Rates:** US$140 individuals. **Remarks:** Advertising not accepted. **Former name:** Computers and Artificial Intelligence.
Circ: (Not Reported)

SLOVENIA

LJUBLJANA

1525 Obzornik za Matematiko in Fiziko
DMFA-ZALOZNISTVO
Jadranska 19
P.P. 2964   Ph: 386 12512005
SI-1001 Ljubljana, Slovenia   Fax: 386 12517281
Publication E-mail: dmfa.zaloznistvo@fmf.uni-lj.si
Publisher E-mail: dmfa.zaloznistvo@fmf.uni-li.si

Slovenian language publication covering math and physics. **Founded:** 1951. **Freq:** Bimonthly. **Trim Size:** 17 x 24 cm. **Key Personnel:** Roman Drnovsek, Contact, phone 386 1 4766 632, roman.drnovsek@fmf.uni-lj.si. **ISSN:** 0473-7466. **Subscription Rates:** 8,000 Din institutions; 4,000 Din members; 2,000 Din students; €30 other countries. **Remarks:** Advertising accepted; rates available upon request. **URL:** http://www.fmf.uni-lj.si/~zaloznistvo/omf.htm.
Circ: 1,450

REPUBLIC OF SOUTH AFRICA

PARKLANDS

1526 Essentials
Box 1346
Parklands 2121, Republic of South Africa   Ph: 27 011 293 6000

Consumer magazine covering inspirational and other issues for women. **Founded:** Nov. 1994. **Freq:** Monthly. **Key Personnel:** Frith Harris, Editor, frithh@caxton.co.za; Belinda dos Santos, Managing Editor.

WALKERVILLE

1527 Pit & Quarry
Institute of Quarrying - Southern Africa
PO Box 940   Ph: 27 119491608
Walkerville 1876, Republic of South Africa   Fax: 27 119491534
Publication E-mail: mining@brookpattrick.co.za
Publisher E-mail: iqsa@global.co.za

Publications covering quarrying and surface mining. **Founded:** July 2001. **Key Personnel:** Dale Kelly, Editor, phone 2711 6224666, fax 2711 6167146, dale@brookpattrick.co.za. **Remarks:** Accepts advertising.
Circ: Paid 4,000

WITS

1528 South African Journal on Human Rights
JUTA Law
Centre for Applied Legal Studies
University of Witwatersrand, Johannesburg   Ph: 27 117178600
Wits 2050, Republic of South Africa   Fax: 27 114032341
Publication E-mail: sajhr@law.wits.ac.za

Professional journal covering public law in South Africa. **Founded:** 1985. **Freq:** Quarterly. **Key Personnel:** Glenda Fick, Editor, fickgc@law.wits.ac.za; Iain Currie, Editor, currieib@law.wits.ac.za; Jonathan Klaaren, Editor, klaarenje@law.wits.ac.za; Cathi Albertyn, Editor, albertync@law.wits.ac.za;

Theunis Roux, Editor, rouxt@law.wits.ac.za; Marius Pieterse, Editor, pieter-sem@law.wits.ac.za. **ISSN:** 0258-7203. **Subscription Rates:** R 360 individuals South Africa; R 315 individuals (directly through JUTA); R 309.50 students; R 315.79 individuals Southern Africa; £45 individuals Europe; US$75 individuals Australia, North & South America; R 435.79 other countries (includes p&p). **Remarks:** Advertising not accepted. **URL:** http://www.law.wits.ac.za/sajhr/sajhr.html; http://www.jutastat.com.

Circ: (Not Reported)

SPAIN

LA CORUNA

◫ **1529 Oficio & Arte**
Organizacion de los Artesanos de Espana
Montes 13 entreplanta Dcha. Local 3   Ph: 34 981288104
E-15009 La Coruna, Spain   Fax: 34 981282796
Publication E-mail: correo@oficioyarte.org
Publisher E-mail: correo@oficioyarte.org

Trade periodical covering arts and crafts in Spain and elsewhere. **Founded:** 1992. **Freq:** Bimonthly. **Trim Size:** A4. **Key Personnel:** Manuel Gonzalez Arias, Director; Isabel Prada, Composition. **ISSN:** 1135-1152. **Subscription Rates:** €16.80 individuals; €2.80 single issue. **Remarks:** Accepts advertising. **URL:** http://www.oficioyarte.org.
Ad Rates: BW: €408.69   **Circ:** Paid ⊕**4,000**
              4C: €823.39

MADRID

◫ **1530 Heavyrock**
C/Lopez de Hoyos 133 - Posterior   Ph: 34 915193689
E-28002 Madrid, Spain   Fax: 34 914163774
Publication E-mail: mariskal@mariskalrock.com
Publisher E-mail: mariskal@mariskalrock.com

Consumer magazine covering heavy metal rock music. **Freq:** Monthly. **URL:** http://www.mariskalrock.com.

Circ: Combined 241,000

◫ **1531 Scherzo**
Scherzo Editorial S.A.
C/Cartagena, 10-1 C   Ph: 34 913567622
E-28028 Madrid, Spain   Fax: 34 917261864
Publication E-mail: revista@scherzo.es

Consumer magazine covering classical music. **Founded:** Dec. 1985. **Freq:** 10/year. **Trim Size:** 170 x 250 mm. **Cols./Page:** 3. **Col. Width:** 5.2 millimeters. **Col. Depth:** 250 millimeters. **Key Personnel:** Tomas Martin de Vidales, Editor; Enrique Martinez, Contact; Arantza Quintanilla, Publicity, arantza@scherzo.es. **ISSN:** 0213-4802. **Subscription Rates:** €54 Spain; €84 Europe, airmail; €96 U.S. and Canada; €102 Central and South America. **Remarks:** Accepts advertising. **URL:** http://www.scherzo.es.
Ad Rates: BW: €1,140   **Circ:** Combined 17,500
              4C: €1,500

SAN SEBASTIAN DE LOS REYES

◫ **1532 Cognitiva**
Fundacion Infancia y Aprendizaje
C/Naranjo de Bulnes 69   Ph: 34 916589100
E-28707 San Sebastian de los Reyes, Spain   Fax: 34 916589100
Publication E-mail: coginitiv@ull.es
Publisher E-mail: fundacionia@fia.es

Journal covering cognitive processes, including perception, attention, memory, language comprehension, reasoning, problem solving and mental representation for researchers and scholars in the field in Spanish and English. **Founded:** 1989. **Freq:** Semiannual. **Key Personnel:** Manuel Carreiras, Editor. **ISSN:** 0214-3550. **Remarks:** Accepts advertising scientific and cultural contents only.

Circ: (Not Reported)

◫ **1533 Cultura y Educacion**
Fundacion Infancia y Aprendizaje
C/Naranjo de Bulnes 69   Ph: 34 916589100
E-28707 San Sebastian de los Reyes, Spain   Fax: 34 916589100
Publication E-mail: cultured@usal.es
Publisher E-mail: fundacionia@fia.es

Journal covering historical-cultural theory in education for researchers and scholars in education, anthropology, psychology, sociology, communication, teachers, counselors, and social workers. In Spanish and English. **Founded:** 1989. **Freq:** Quarterly. **Print Method:** Offset. **Trim Size:** 150 x 240 cm. **Col. Width:** 125 millimeters. **Col. Depth:** 200 millimeters. **Key Personnel:** Amelia Alvarez, Editor; Pilar Lacasa, Editor. **ISSN:** 1135-6405. **Remarks:** Accepts advertising scientific and cultural content only.
Ad Rates: BW: 300.51   **Circ:** Combined 600
              Ptas

◫ **1534 Estudios de Psicologia**
Fundacion Infancia y Aprendizaje
C/Naranjo de Bulnes 69   Ph: 34 916589100
E-28707 San Sebastian de los Reyes, Spain   Fax: 34 916589100
Publication E-mail: revista.estudios.psicologia@uam.es
Publisher E-mail: fundacionia@fia.es

Journal covering psychology and related disciplines for researchers, professionals, and scholars in the field in Spanish and English. **Founded:** 1980. **Freq:** Triennial. **Key Personnel:** Alberto Rosa, Editor. **ISSN:** 0210-9395. **Remarks:** Accepts advertising scientific and cultural content only.

Circ: (Not Reported)

◫ **1535 Infancia Y Aprendizaje/Journal for the Study of
    Education and Development**
Fundacion Infancia y Aprendizaje
C/Naranjo de Bulnes 69   Ph: 34 916589100
E-28707 San Sebastian de los Reyes, Spain   Fax: 34 916589100
Publication E-mail: infanciap@usal.es
Publisher E-mail: fundacionia@fia.es

Journal covering developmental and educational psychology for psychologists, counselors, and educators in Spanish and English. **Founded:** 1978. **Freq:** Quarterly. **Key Personnel:** Pablo del Rio, Editor; Emilio Sanchez, Editor. **ISSN:** 0210-3702. **Remarks:** Accepts advertising science and cultural contents only.

Circ: (Not Reported)

◫ **1536 Revista de Psicologia Social**
Fundacion Infancia y Aprendizaje
C/Naranjo de Bulnes 69   Ph: 34 916589100
E-28707 San Sebastian de los Reyes, Spain   Fax: 34 916589100
Publication E-mail: avarias@psi.uned.es
Publisher E-mail: fundacionia@fia.es

Journal covering the study of behavior from a social perspective for researchers, scholars, social psychologists, and social workers in Spanish, Italian, Portuguese, French and English. **Founded:** 1986. **Freq:** Triennial. **Print Method:** Offset. **Trim Size:** 150 x 260 cm. **Col. Width:** 125 millimeters. **Col. Depth:** 200 millimeters. **Key Personnel:** Amalio Blanco, Editor; Jose Miguel Fernandez-Dols, Editor; Francisco Morales, Editor. **ISSN:** 0213-1748. **Remarks:** Accepts advertising science and cultural content only.

Circ: Paid 350
Non-paid 70

SWEDEN

NORRA RADA

◫ **1537 Fritid & Gronyte Leverantorerna**
Arvidson Promotion
Prastbol   Ph: 46 056360502
SE-683 93 Norra Rada, Sweden   Fax: 46 056360512
Publication E-mail: editor@arvidsonpromotion.com
Publisher E-mail: arvidson@algonet.se

Trade magazine for the groundskeeping and garden industry. **Founded:** Sept. 1995. **Freq:** 5/year. **Print Method:** Offset. **Cols./Page:** 3. **Key Personnel:** Birgitta Niemi, Contact, phone 46 08 7714650, adnews@telia.com. **Subscription Rates:** 290 SKr individuals; 64 SKr single issue. **Remarks:** Accepts advertising. **URL:** http://www.gronyte.com. **Formerly:** Gronyteleveran Torerna.

Ad Rates:	BW: 8,900 SKr	Circ: Combined ‡11,300
	4C: 13,900	
	SKr	

STOCKHOLM

1538 TF-bladet
Swedish Dental Patients' Organization
Bergsunds Strand 9
SE-117 38 Stockholm, Sweden

Journal of the Swedish Dental Patients' Organization for members. **Founded:** 1986. **Freq:** Quarterly. **Print Method:** Offset. **Trim Size:** 210 x 297 mm. **Cols./Page:** 3. **ISSN:** 0349-263X. **Subscription Rates:** 175 SKr individuals. **Remarks:** Accepts advertising.

Circ: Paid 12,000

SWITZERLAND

EINSIEDELN

1539 Schweizer Jager
Verlag Schweizer Jager
Postfach 261
CH-8840 Einsiedeln, Switzerland

Ph: 41 554184343
Fax: 41 554184344

Trade magazine covering hunting. **Founded:** 1916. **Freq:** Monthly. **Print Method:** Offset. **Key Personnel:** Werner Grond, Editorial, phone 41 417552906, fax 41 417552819, redaktion@schweizerjaeger.ch. **ISSN:** 0036-8016. **Remarks:** Accepts advertising.

Circ: (Not Reported)

GENEVA

1540 The Ecumenical Review
World Council of Churches
PO Box 2100
CH-1211 Geneva 2, Switzerland

Ph: 41 227916111
Fax: 41 227981346

Publisher E-mail: infowcc@wcc-coe.org

Publication covering philosophy and religion. **Founded:** 1948. **Freq:** Quarterly. **Print Method:** Offset. **Trim Size:** 16 x 24. **Key Personnel:** Thedore Gill, Contact, phone 41 227916150, tag@wcc-coe.org. **ISSN:** 0013-0796. **Remarks:** Accepts advertising. **Online:** Gale Group; ATLA. **Alt. Formats:** Microform, Bell & Howell Information and Learning.

Ad Rates: BW: 395 SFr   Circ: Paid ‡3,000

1541 Interavia Business & Technology
Aerospace Media Publishing
Le Voie des Truz 20
PO Box 1192
CH-1211 Geneva 5, Switzerland

Ph: 41 227882788
Fax: 41 227882726

Publisher E-mail: info@interavia.ch

Publication for the aerospace and defense industries. **Freq:** Monthly. **USPS:** 660-669. **Subscription Rates:** US$175; US$16 single issue. **Remarks:** Accepts advertising. **Online:** Gale Group.

Ad Rates: BW: US$4,700   Circ: △20,000
         4C: US$8,000

1542 Un Special
Room 356
Palais des Nations
CH-1211 Geneva, Switzerland

Ph: 41 229172501
Fax: 41 229170505

Publication E-mail: unspecial@unece.org

Staff magazine. **Founded:** 1947. **Freq:** Monthly. **Key Personnel:** J.M. Jakobowicz, Editor-in-Chief. **Subscription Rates:** Free. **Remarks:** Accepts advertising.

Circ: (Not Reported)

LAUSANNE

1543 Revue Militaire Suisse
Association de la Revue Militaire Suisse
Av. Florimont 3
CH-1006 Lausanne, Switzerland

Ph: 41 2131189707
Fax: 41 3213119709

Publisher E-mail: JCRC@vtxnet.ch

Swiss military publication. **Founded:** 1856. **Freq:** Monthly. **Cols./Page:** 3. **Key Personnel:** Herve de Weck, Editor, phone 41 324665232, fax 41 324662974, herve.deweck@bluewin.ch. **ISSN:** 0035-368X. **Remarks:** Accepts advertising.

Circ: (Not Reported)

NEUCHATEL

1544 Tsantsa
Swiss Ethnological Society
Schweizerische Ethnologische Gesellschaft
c/o Institut d'ethnologie de l'Universite de
    Neuchatel
Rue Saint-Nicholas 4
CH-2000 Neuchatel, Switzerland

Ph: 41 327181710
Fax: 41 327181711

Publisher E-mail: secretariat.sse@unine.ch

Publication covering anthropology and ethnology. **Freq:** Annual. **ISSN:** 1420-7834. **URL:** http://www.seg-sse.ch.

TAIWAN

CHUNGLI

1545 Technical Journal of Telecommunication Laboratories
Ministry of Communications Telecommunication Laboratories
PO Box 71
Chungli, Taiwan

Periodical containing articles related to electrical engineering. **Founded:** 1971. **Freq:** Quarterly. **ISSN:** 1015-0730. **Subscription Rates:** US$35; US$40 other countries.

Circ: Paid 800

CHUTUNG HSINCHU

1546 Chinese Journal of Materials Science
Chinese Society for Materials Science
195-5 Chung-Hsing Rd.
Chutung Hsinchu 31015, Taiwan

Ph: 886 35916836

Periodical containing abstracts and articles covering mechanical engineering and materials. **Founded:** 1969. **Freq:** Quarterly. **Key Personnel:** Sing Tien Wu, Editor. **ISSN:** 0379-6906. **Subscription Rates:** US$22.

Circ: Paid 1,500

HSINCHU

1547 Journal of Chinese Institute of Chemical Engineers
Chinese Institute of Chemical Engineers
c/o Dept. of Chemical Engineering, National
    Tsing Hua Univer
Hsinchu 300, Taiwan

Publication E-mail: wtwu@faculty.nthu.edu.tw

Periodical containing articles related to chemical engineering. **Founded:** 1970. **Freq:** Bimonthly. **Key Personnel:** Wen Teng Wu, Editor. **ISSN:** 0368-1653. **Subscription Rates:** NTs 900; US$30 other countries. **Remarks:** Advertising accepted; rates available upon request.

Circ: Paid 500

1548 The Taiwanese Journal of Mathematics
The Mathematical Society of the Republic of China
National Chiao Tung University, Dept. of
    Mathematics
Hsinchu 300, Taiwan

Ph: 886 223630231

Publication E-mail: mathsoc@math.nctu.edu.tw

Publishes original research papers and survey articles in all areas of mathematics. **Founded:** 1997. **Freq:** Quarterly. **Key Personnel:** Sze-Bi Hsu,

Editor-in-Chief. **Subscription Rates:** US$60. **URL:** http://www.math.nthu.edu.tw/~tjm/myweb/FrameGenInfo.htm.

KAOHSIUNG

☐ **1549 Export Processing Zone Concentrates**
Export Processing Zone Administration
Kaohsiung, Taiwan

Periodical covering export processing and international business aspects. **Founded:** 1955. **Freq:** Annual. **Key Personnel:** Wu Sze Yung, Editor. **Subscription Rates:** Free.

Circ: Paid 3,200

☐ **1550 Kaohsiung Journal of Medical Sciences**
Kaohsiung Medical College
No. 100 Shih-Chuan 1st Rd.
Kaohsiung 80708, Taiwan   Ph: 886 73121101
Publication E-mail: m835003@!kmu.edu.tw

Periodical containing scientific papers in all fields of medicine, review articles, original articles, and case reports. **Founded:** 1985. **Freq:** Monthly. **Key Personnel:** Hong Wen Liu, Editor. **ISSN:** 1607-551X. **Subscription Rates:** US$60. **URL:** http://kjms.kmu.edu.tw/index.html.

Circ: Paid 1,500

NAN-TOU HSIEN

☐ **1551 Journal of the Experimental Forest of National Taiwan University**
Experimental Forest of National Taiwan University
No. 12, Chien-Shan Rd., Section 1, Chu-Shan
Nan-Tou Hsien 55704, Taiwan   Ph: 886 49642181

Periodical covering forests and forestry related aspects. **Founded:** 1952. **Freq:** Quarterly. **Key Personnel:** Ju-Yuan Liu, Editor. **ISSN:** 0255-6014.

TAIPEI

☐ **1552 Acta Geologica Taiwanica**
National Taiwan University
Dept. of Geology
No. 1, Sec. 4
Taipei 10764, Taiwan   Ph: 886 223630231
Publication E-mail: loch@ccms.ntu.edu.tw

Periodical covering earth sciences and geology aspects. **Founded:** 1947. **Freq:** Annual. **Key Personnel:** Tsung Kwei Liu, Editor, li-utk@ccms.ntu.edu.tw. **ISSN:** 0065-1265.

Circ: Paid 600

☐ **1553 Acta Neurologica Taiwanica**
Taiwan Neurological Society
Section 3 No. 8
Taipei 100, Taiwan
Publication E-mail: gant@mail.hato.com.tw

Periodical covering psychology and neurology aspects. **Founded:** 1997. **Freq:** Quarterly. **ISSN:** 1028-768X.

☐ **1554 Acta Oceanographica Taiwanica**
National Taiwan University
College of Science
Institute of Oceanography
PO Box 23-13
Taipei 106, Taiwan   Ph: 886 23625983
Publication E-mail: ctliu@ccms.ntu.edu.tw

Periodical containing original articles, notes, and letters on oceanographic research. **Founded:** 1971. **Freq:** Annual. **Key Personnel:** Wung Yang Shieh, Editor. **ISSN:** 0379-7481. **Subscription Rates:** US$30.

Circ: Paid 800

☐ **1555 Acta Paediatrica Sinica Taiwanica**
Taiwan Pediatric Association
10F/1, No. 69, Sec. 1, Hang Chow S. Rd   Ph: 886 223516446
Taipei 10022, Taiwan   Fax: 886 223516448
Publication E-mail: pediatr@www.pediatr.org.tw
Publisher E-mail: pediatr@pediatr.org.tw

Periodical covering pediatrics related articles. **Founded:** 1960. **Freq:** Bimonthly. **Key Personnel:** Ching Yuan Lin, Editor. **ISSN:** 0001-6578. **Subscription Rates:** NTs 3,000; US$100 other countries. **URL:** http://www.pediatr.org.tw/contents/english.htm.

Circ: Paid 3,000

☐ **1556 Acta Zoologica Taiwanica**
National Taiwan University
College of Science
PO Box 23-13
Taipei 10764, Taiwan   Ph: 886 223630231
Publication E-mail: ctyen@ccms.ntu.edu.tw

Periodical containing original research on any aspects of zoological science from worldwide. **Founded:** 1988. **Freq:** Semiannual. **Key Personnel:** Tai Sheng Chiu, Editor. **ISSN:** 1019-5858. **URL:** http://www.zo.ntu.edu.tw/azt/index_e.htm.

Circ: Controlled 500

☐ **1557 African Studies**
National Chengchi University
Program of African Studies
Social Sciences Materials Center
187 Chin Hua St.
Taipei, Taiwan   Ph: 886 229393091
Publication E-mail: mts@nccu.edu.tw

Periodical containing aspects related to the history of Africa. **Founded:** 1973. **Freq:** Annual. **ISSN:** 0378-0597. **URL:** http://www.nccu.edu.tw/english.

☐ **1558 Asian Air Transport**
Tzeng Brothers Information Group
PO Box 43-345
7G-09 World Trade Ctr.
Taipei 105, Taiwan   Ph: 886 27251904

Aviation magazine. **Founded:** 1988. **Freq:** Monthly. **Key Personnel:** Robert Tzeng, Editor. **ISSN:** 1021-3740. **Subscription Rates:** US$80. **Remarks:** Advertising accepted; rates available upon request.

Circ: Paid 11,750

☐ **1559 Asian Pacific Culture Quarterly**
Asian-Pacific Cultural Center
6F, 66 Aikuo East Rd.
Taipei 107, Taiwan   Ph: 886 223222139
Publication E-mail: apccapcc@ms23.hinet.net

General articles on Asian-Pacific culture and creative writings. **Founded:** 1973. **Freq:** Quarterly. **Key Personnel:** Eric T.S. Wu, Editor. **ISSN:** 0378-8911. **Subscription Rates:** NTs 960; US$36 other countries.

Circ: Paid 3,000

☐ **1560 Business and Industry: Taiwan**
Business & industry Taiwan
No. 31, Ln. 697, Tunhwa S. Rd
Taipei, Taiwan

Business and industry magazine. **Founded:** 1974. **Freq:** Weekly. **Key Personnel:** Kenneth M. Jalleh, Editor. **ISSN:** 1015-003X. **Subscription Rates:** NTs 700; US$34 other countries.

☐ **1561 Centerpoint**
Asian Vegetable Research and Development Center
Shanhua, PO Box 42
Taipei 741, Taiwan   Ph: 886 65837801
Publication E-mail: avrdcbox@netra.avrdc.org.tw

Periodical containing the latest news about the association and the vegetable research field. **Founded:** 1981. **Freq:** 3/year. **Key Personnel:** Ming-Tong Kow, Editor. **ISSN:** 0258-3070. **Remarks:** Advertising accepted; rates available upon request. **URL:** http://www.avrdc.org.tw.

Circ: (Not Reported)

1562 The China News
Simone Wei
40 Tung Hsing Rd., 10th Fl.
Taipei, Taiwan   Ph: 886 227686002

General interest periodical. **Founded:** 1949. **Freq:** Daily. **Key Personnel:** Anthony Lawrance, Editor. **Subscription Rates:** NTs 650.
Ad Rates: BW: NTs   **Circ:** Paid 100,000
                 80,000
                 4C: NTs
                 120,000

1563 The China Post
5F 8 Fu Shun St.
Taipei 104, Taiwan   Ph: 886 225969971
Publication E-mail: cpost@mail.chinapost.com.tw

General interest newspaper covering domestic and international news, investment, commerce, trade, health, science and technology, life and family. **Founded:** 1952. **Freq:** Daily. **Key Personnel:** Jack C. Huang, Editor. **Subscription Rates:** US$45.30. **Remarks:** Advertising accepted; rates available upon request. **URL:** http://www.chinapost.com.tw/thechinapost/.
Circ: Paid 180,000

1564 Chinese Journal of Administration
National Chengchi University
Center for Public and Business Administration Education
187 Chin Hua St.
Taipei, Taiwan   Ph: 886 23940690

Periodical aimed at providing a forum for exchanging ideas and information among administrators, scholars, and others interested in public and business administration and related fields. **Founded:** 1963. **Freq:** Semiannual. **Key Personnel:** Kuo-Liang Wang, Editor. **ISSN:** 0009-4579. **Subscription Rates:** NTs 400; US$20 other countries. **Remarks:** Advertising accepted; rates available upon request.
Circ: Paid 1,500

1565 Chinese Journal of Physics
The Physical Society of the Republic of China
PO Box 23-30
Taipei 106, Taiwan   Ph: 886 223634923
Publication E-mail: cjp@PSROC.phys.ntu.edu.tw

Publishes reviews, regular articles, and refereed conference papers in various branches of physics. **Founded:** 1963. **Freq:** Quarterly. **Key Personnel:** Tzihong Chiueh, Editor-in-Chief, chiuehth@phys.ntu.edu.tw. **ISSN:** 0577-9073. **Subscription Rates:** US$200. **URL:** http://psroc.phys.ntu.edu.tw/cjp/.

1566 Chinese Journal of Physiology
Chinese Physiological Society
Dept. of Physiology, National Yan-Ming
   Medical College
Shih-pai
Taipei 11221, Taiwan

Periodical containing original papers concerned with all fields of physiology, pharmacology, anatomy, and biochemistry. **Founded:** 1927. **Freq:** Quarterly. **Key Personnel:** Paulus S. Wang, Editor. **ISSN:** 0304-4920. **Subscription Rates:** NTs 1,600.
Circ: Paid 1,000

1567 Chinese Journal of Psychology
Chinese Psychological Association
c/o Dept. of Psychology, National Taiwan
   University
Taipei 10764, Taiwan

Periodical containing articles related to psychology. **Founded:** 1973. **Freq:** Semiannual. **Key Personnel:** Chia Hung Hsu, Editor, chhsu@ccms.ntu.edu.tw. **ISSN:** 1013-9656. **Subscription Rates:** US$40.
Circ: Paid 500

1568 Chinese Medical Journal
Excerpta Medica Asia Ltd.
Chinese Medical Association
201 Sec. 2 Shih-Pai Rd.
Taipei, Taiwan   Ph: 886 228757358
Publication E-mail: effie@excerptahk.com

Periodical covering basic, experimental and clinical medical sciences, includes original articles and case reports and review articles. **Founded:** 1915. **Freq:** Monthly. **Key Personnel:** Mau Song Chang, Editor. **ISSN:** 0578-1337. **Subscription Rates:** NTs 1,250; NTs 1,100 students. **URL:** http://www.vghtpe.gov.tw/~cmj/.

1569 Commodity Price Statistics Monthly in Taiwan Area
Executive Yuan Directorate-General of Budget, Accounting & Statistics
2 Kwangchow St.
Taipei, Taiwan   Ph: 886 223711521

Publication providing statistics on recent changing conditions of commodity prices in the Taiwan area of the Republic of China. Includes export and import price indices. **Founded:** 1971. **Freq:** Monthly. **ISSN:** 0257-5728. **Subscription Rates:** NTs 100. **URL:** http://www.dgbasey.gov.tw/english/dgbas-e0.htm.
Circ: Paid 1,300

1570 Digital Times
DigiTimes Publication Inc.
9F, 135, Section 2, Chien Kuo N. Rd.
Taipei 104, Taiwan   Ph: 886 225177700
Publication E-mail: editor@mail.digitimes.com.tw

Newspaper focusing on the IT industry. **Founded:** 1998. **Freq:** Daily. **ISSN:** 1607-4114. **Remarks:** Advertising accepted; rates available upon request. **Available Online. URL:** http://www.digitimes.com/.
Circ: (Not Reported)

1571 Dynasty
China Airlines Ltd.
131 Nanking East Rd., Sec. 3
Taipei, Taiwan   Ph: 886 225062345
Publication E-mail: ju-rung_chen@email.china-airlines.com

Airlines and aviation magazine. **Founded:** 1969. **Freq:** Bimonthly. **Key Personnel:** Wu I. Shou, Editor. **Subscription Rates:** Free. **URL:** http://chunying.free.fr/dynasty/dynasty.htm.
Circ: Paid 60,000

1572 Environmental Policy Monthly
Environmental Protection Administration
41, Section 1, Chung-Hwa Rd.
Taipei, Taiwan   Ph: 886 223117722
Publication E-mail: mail@sun.epa.gov.tw

Environmental policy journal. **Freq:** Monthly. **Key Personnel:** Y.F. Liang, Editor. **URL:** http://www.epa.gov.tw/english/Epm/.

1573 Evensongs
Tamkang University
English Dept.
Tamsui Campus, Room T1101
151 Ying-chuan Rd., Taipei County
Taipei 251, Taiwan   Ph: 886 226215656

Periodical covering literary and political issues in Taiwan. **Founded:** 1970. **Freq:** Quarterly. **Key Personnel:** Lily H.M. Chang, Editor. **ISSN:** 0378-6153. **Remarks:** Advertising accepted; rates available upon request.
Circ: Paid 3,000

1574 Financial Statistics Monthly
Central Bank of China
2 Roosevelt Rd., Sec. 1
Taipei 107, Taiwan   Ph: 886 223936161
Publication E-mail: adminrol@mail.cbc.gov.tw

Periodical containing financial statistical updates on Taiwan. **Founded:** 1951. **Freq:** Monthly. **Subscription Rates:** US$40. **URL:** http://www.cbc.gov.tw/EngHome/publications.htm.
Circ: Paid 2,250

📖 **1575   Flow of Funds**
Central Bank of China
2 Roosevelt Rd., Sec. 1
Taipei 107, Taiwan   Ph: 886 223936161

Periodical covering banking and finance related aspects. **Founded:** 1968. **Freq:** Annual. **ISSN:** 1017-9658. **Subscription Rates:** US$5. **URL:** http://www.cbc.gov.tw/EngHome/publications.htm.
Circ: Paid 1,200

📖 **1576   Food Science and Agricultural Chemistry**
Chinese Agricultural Chemical Society
c/o Dept of Agricultural Chemistry,
   National Taiwan Universi
No. 1, Sec. 4, Roosevelt Rd.
Taipei 10617, Taiwan

Publishes original research papers and review articles dealing with all aspects of food science and agricultural chemistry, including soil science, biochemistry, biotechnology, and nutrition. **Founded:** 1999. **Freq:** Quarterly. **Key Personnel:** Jong-Ching Su, Editor. **ISSN:** 1560-4152. **Subscription Rates:** US$80. **URL:** http://www.agrichem.org.tw/Publish/FSAC.htm.

📖 **1577   Formosan Journal of Surgery**
Surgical Association, Taiwan
c/o National Taiwan University Hospital,
   Dept. of Surgery
No. 7, Chung-Shan Rd.
Taipei 100, Taiwan   Ph: 886 223970800
Publication E-mail: journal@surgery.org.tw

Publishes scholarly research in all clinical and experimental areas of surgery and related fields. **Founded:** 1970. **Freq:** Bimonthly. **Key Personnel:** Chun-Jean Lee, Editor. **ISSN:** 1682-606X.

📖 **1578   Formosan Science**
Formosan Association for Advancement of Science
341 Hwa Cheng Rd, Hsinchuang Chen
Taipei, Taiwan

Comprehensive works journal. **Founded:** 1947. **Freq:** Quarterly. **ISSN:** 0015-7791.
Circ: Paid 500

📖 **1579   Fu Jen Studies**
Fu Jen University
College of Foreign Languages & Literatures
510 Chung Cheng Rd.
Hsinchuang
Taipei 24205, Taiwan   Ph: 886 29031111
Publication E-mail: engl1006@mails.fju.edu.tw

Periodical covering Chinese and western literature and linguistics. **Subtitle:** Literature & Linguistics. **Founded:** 1973. **Freq:** Annual. **Key Personnel:** Raphael Schulte, Editor. **ISSN:** 1015-0021. **Subscription Rates:** US$15. **Remarks:** Advertising accepted; rates available upon request.
Circ: Paid 300

📖 **1580   Graphical Survey of the Economy**
Central Bank of China
Economic Research Dept.
2 Roosevelt Rd., Sec. 1
Taipei 107, Taiwan

Periodical that publishes articles related to the economic situations. **Founded:** 1972. **Freq:** Annual. **ISSN:** 1017-9631. **Subscription Rates:** US$5.
Circ: Paid 2,000

📖 **1581   IBS Asian Electronics News**
Asia-I B S Publications
3-1 Fl., No. 75, Nanking E. Rd., Sec. 4
Taipei, Taiwan

Periodical containing information regarding electrical engineering. **Founded:**
1979. **Freq:** Monthly. **Key Personnel:** Charles Adarne, Editor. **ISSN:** 0888-4943. **Subscription Rates:** US$100.
Circ: Paid 15,000

📖 **1582   IBS Electronic Component & Equipment Exhibition**
Asia-I B S Publications
3-1 Fl., No. 75, Nanking E. Rd., Sec. 4
Taipei, Taiwan

Periodical covering electronics and electrical engineering aspects. **Founded:** 1981. **Freq:** Monthly. **Key Personnel:** Charles Adarne, Editor. **Subscription Rates:** US$50.
Circ: Paid 8,000

📖 **1583   Industry of Free China**
Publishing Committee of Industry of Free China/Council for Economic
   Planning and Development
9th Fl., No 87, Nanking E. Rd., Sec 2
Taipei 10408, Taiwan   Ph: 886 25225404

Publishes extensive economic statistics and articles about current economic performance. **Founded:** 1954. **Freq:** Monthly. **Key Personnel:** W.P. Chang, Editor. **ISSN:** 0019-946X. **Subscription Rates:** NTs 800; US$75 other countries.
Circ: Paid 2,500

📖 **1584   Industry Weekly**
Trade Winds Inc.
No. 7, Ln. 75, Yung Kang St.
Taipei 106, Taiwan   Ph: 886 223967791
Publication E-mail: tradwind@ms2.hinet.net

Periodical covering Taiwan's export industries and products, especially hardware, autoparts, machinery and industrial supplies. **Founded:** 1975. **Freq:** Weekly. **Key Personnel:** Donald Shapiro, Editor. **ISSN:** 1024-9028. **Subscription Rates:** US$90; US$110 other countries. **Remarks:** Advertising accepted; rates available upon request. **URL:** http://www.tradewinds.net.
Circ: Paid 12,000

📖 **1585   International Journal of Peace Studies**
Grassroots Publishing Co.
PO Box 26 447
Taipei 106, Taiwan   Ph: 886 227060962
Publication E-mail: ohio3106@ms8.hinet.net

Periodical containing articles on conceptual ideas on aspects of world peace; examines the role of the UN in terms of security and development, disarmament, and non-offensive defense. **Founded:** 1996. **Freq:** Semiannual. **Key Personnel:** Cheng-Feng Shih, Editor. **ISSN:** 1085-7494. **Subscription Rates:** US$20. **Remarks:** Advertising accepted; rates available upon request. **URL:** http://www.copri.dk/copri/ipra/ijps.htm.
Circ: (Not Reported)

📖 **1586   Journal of Agricultural Research of China**
Taiwan Agricultural Research Institute
189 Chung-cheng Rd., Wufeng
Taipei, Taiwan

Agricultural research journal. **Founded:** 1950. **Freq:** Quarterly. **ISSN:** 0376-477X. **Subscription Rates:** Free single issue.

📖 **1587   Journal of Chinese Agricultural Chemical Society**
Chinese Agricultural Chemical Society
PO Box 23-77
Taipei 10764, Taiwan   Ph: 886 23633783

Reports on research in analytical and biological chemistry, food and nutrition, microbiology, fermentation, and plant nutrition. **Founded:** 1963. **Freq:** Bimonthly. **Key Personnel:** Dar Yuan Lee, Editor. **ISSN:** 0578-1736. **Subscription Rates:** NTs 250.
Circ: Paid 850

📖 **1588 Journal of Chinese Chemical Society**
PO Box 1-9
Nankang   Ph: 886 227898512
Taipei 115, Taiwan   Fax: 886 226533995
Publication E-mail: jccs@chem.sinica.edu.tw

Periodical containing both experimental and theoretical research on funda-
mental aspects of chemistry. **Founded:** 1932. **Freq:** Bimonthly. **Key
Personnel:** Sheng Hsien Lin, Editor. **ISSN:** 0009-4536. **Subscription Rates:**
NTs 650.

Circ: Paid 2,000

📖 **1589 Journal of Chinese Institute of Engineers**
Chinese Institute of Engineers
4-F, No. 1, Sec 2
Taipei, Taiwan   Ph: 886 23925128
Publication E-mail: joy6220@mail.ntust.edu.tw

Periodical containing research and short commentary on issues and phenome-
na in many areas of engineering. **Founded:** 1978. **Freq:** Bimonthly. **Key
Personnel:** Ching Tien Liou, Editor. **ISSN:** 0253-3839. **Subscription Rates:**
NTs 1,800.

Circ: Paid 1800

📖 **1590 Journal of the Formosan Medical Association**
Formosan Medical Association
No. 1, Chang-Te St.
Taipei 10016, Taiwan   Ph: 886 223810367
Publication E-mail: ting@ms33.url.com.tw

General medical journal for Taiwan. **Freq:** Monthly. **Key Personnel:** Kwen-
Tay Luh, Editor-in-Chief, jeethan@excerptahk.com. **ISSN:** 0929-6646. **Subscription Rates:** US$60. **URL:** http://fma.mc.ntu.edu.tw/jfma/.

📖 **1591 Journal of Geographical Science**
National Taiwan University
Dept. of Geography
Taipei, Taiwan   Ph: 886 23629908

Geographic journal. **Founded:** 1962. **Freq:** Annual. **Key Personnel:** Chin
Hong Sun, Editor. **ISSN:** 0494-5387. **Subscription Rates:** Free single issue.
Circ: Paid 500

📖 **1592 Journal of Geological Society of China**
Geological Society of China
PO Box 23-59
Taipei 10764, Taiwan
Publication E-mail: geolsoc@w2.ohya.com.tw

Journal covering geological aspects pertinent to China. **Founded:** 1958. **Freq:**
Quarterly. **Key Personnel:** Yuan Wang, Editor. **ISSN:** 1018-7057. **Subscription Rates:** US$30.

📖 **1593 Journal of Microbiology, Immunology and Infection**
Chinese Society of Microbiology
National Taiwan University, College of
  Medicine
1, Jenai Rd., Sec. 1
Taipei, Taiwan   Ph: 886 228757532

Periodical covering microbiology, immunology and various infections.
Founded: 1968. **Freq:** Quarterly. **Key Personnel:** Yu Tien Liu, Editor.
Subscription Rates: US$90. **Alt. Formats:** CD-ROM.

Circ: Paid 4,000

📖 **1594 Journal of Nursing Research**
Nurses' Association of the Republic of China
4F, 281, Section 4, Hsin-Yi Rd.
Taipei 106, Taiwan   Ph: 886 227552291
Publication E-mail: tnaj@twna.org.tw

Nursing research journal. **Founded:** 2001. **Freq:** Bimonthly. **Key Personnel:**
Teresa J.C. Yin, Chief Editor. **ISSN:** 1682-3141.

📖 **1595 Journal of Social Science**
National Taiwan University
College of Law
21 Hsu Chow Rd.
Taipei, Taiwan   Ph: 886 223918758
Publication E-mail: Law@ms.cc.ntu.edu.tw

Social science journal. **Founded:** 1950. **Freq:** Irregular. **ISSN:** 0077-5835.

📖 **1596 Journal of Social Sciences and Philosophy**
Academia Sinica Sun Yat-Sen Institute for Social Sciences and
  Philosophy
Academia Sinica, Nankang
Taipei 11529, Taiwan   Ph: 886 227898100
Publication E-mail: issppub@gate.sinica.edu.tw

Publishes contributions in the fields of philosophy, political science, history,
economics social studies and law. **Founded:** 1988. **Freq:** Semiannual. **Key
Personnel:** Yun Peng Chu, Editor. **ISSN:** 1018-189X. **Subscription Rates:**
Free single issue.
Circ: Paid 1,000

📖 **1597 Journal of Sociology**
National Taiwan University
Dept. of Sociology
1 Roosevelt Rd., Sec. 4
Taipei 106, Taiwan   Ph: 886 023630231
Publication E-mail: social@ms.cc.ntu.edu.tw

Sociology journal. **Founded:** 1963. **Freq:** Annual. **Key Personnel:** Cheng
Han Chang, Editor. **ISSN:** 0077-5851. **Subscription Rates:** US$5.
Circ: Paid 500

📖 **1598 Journal of Taiwan Museum**
Taiwan Provincial Museum
2 Siangyang Rd.
Taipei 100, Taiwan   Ph: 886 23979396
Publication E-mail: ckku@eden.tpm.gov.tw

Periodical containing museum and art related information. **Founded:** 1948.
Freq: Semiannual. **Key Personnel:** Li Zer Ning, Editor. **ISSN:** 0256-257X.
Subscription Rates: Free single issue.
Circ: Paid 1,000

📖 **1599 Journal of the Taiwan Society of Anesthesiologists**
Taiwan Society of Anesthesiologists
201, Shih-Pai Rd., Sec. 2
Taipei 11217, Taiwan
Publication E-mail: saroc@tpts5.seed.net.tw

Anesthesiology magazine. **Founded:** 1960. **Freq:** Quarterly. **Key Personnel:**
Tak-Yu Lee, Editor-in-Chief. **ISSN:** 0254-1319. **Subscription Rates:** NTs
250 single issue. **URL:** http://www.anesth.org/.

📖 **1600 Let's Talk in English**
Overseas Radio & Television, Inc.
10 Ln. 62, Tachih St.
Taipei 104, Taiwan   Ph: 886 225338082
Publication E-mail: Letters@ortv.com.tw

English-language magazine recommended for junior high students. **Founded:**
1981. **Freq:** Monthly. **ISSN:** 1015-5899. **URL:** http://www.letstalk.com.tw/lt/
lt12/index.html.

📖 **1601 Postal Service Today**
Postal Authorities of the Republic of China (Taiwan)
55, Chin Shan South Rd., Section 2
Taipei, Taiwan   Ph: 886 223569670

Postal service magazine. **Founded:** 1958. **Freq:** Monthly. **Key Personnel:**
W.Y. Fang, Editor. **ISSN:** 0529-2786. **Subscription Rates:** NTs 400; US$24
other countries.
Circ: Paid 20,000

1602　Sinorama Magazine
Government Information Office, Taiwan
5F, No.54, Chunghsiao
East Rd., Sec.1
Taipei 100, Taiwan　　　　　　　　Ph: 886 0223922256

Publication about Taiwan. **Founded:** 1978. **Freq:** Monthly. **ISSN:** 0256-9043. **Subscription Rates:** US$40; US$45 other countries.

1603　Soochow Journal of Economics and Business
Soochow University
Wai Shuang Hsi, Shih Lin
Taipei 111, Taiwan　　　　　　　　Ph: 886 228819471

Economics and business journal. **Founded:** 1977. **Freq:** Annual. **ISSN:** 0259-3769. **Subscription Rates:** US$20.

　　　　　　　　　　　　　　　　　　Circ: Paid 500

1604　Soochow Journal of Foreign Languages and Literatures
Soochow University
Wai Shuang Hsi, Shih Lin
Taipei 111, Taiwan　　　　　　　　Ph: 886 228819471

Foreign language and literature journal. **Founded:** 1985. **Freq:** Annual. **ISSN:** 0259-3777. **Subscription Rates:** US$20.

1605　Soochow Journal of History
Soochow University
Wai Shuang Hsi, Shih Lin
Taipei 111, Taiwan　　　　　　　　Ph: 886 228819471
Publication E-mail: thi@www.scu.edu.tw

History journal. **Founded:** 1995. **Freq:** Annual. **ISSN:** 1025-0689. **Subscription Rates:** US$15.

1606　Soochow Journal of Political Science
Soochow University
Wai Shuang Hsi, Shih Lin
Taipei 111, Taiwan　　　　　　　　Ph: 886 228819471

Political science journal. **Founded:** 1977. **Freq:** Semiannual. **ISSN:** 1019-8636. **Subscription Rates:** US$20 single issue.

1607　Soochow Journal of Social Work
Soochow University
Wai Shuang Hsi, Shih Lin
Taipei 111, Taiwan　　　　　　　　Ph: 886 228819471
Publication E-mail: tsw@www.scu.edu.tw

Periodical covering social work. **Founded:** 1995. **Freq:** Annual. **ISSN:** 1026-4493. **Subscription Rates:** US$21.

1608　Stationery and Office Supplies
Taiwan Trade Pages Corp
PO Box 72-50
Taipei, Taiwan　　　　　　　　Ph: 886 023050759

Periodical covering information regarding office and art supplies and stationery. **Freq:** Semiannual. **Subscription Rates:** US$30.

1609　Statistica Sinica
Academia Sinica
Institute of Statistical Science
128, Sec. 2 Yen-chiu-Yuan Rd.
Taipei 115, Taiwan　　　　　　　　Ph: 886 227835611
Publication E-mail: ss@stat.sinica.edu.tw

Publishes original work in all areas of statistics and probability, including theory, methods and applications. **Founded:** 1991. **Freq:** Quarterly. **Key Personnel:** Y.C. Yao, Editor. **ISSN:** 1017-0405. **Subscription Rates:** NTs 2,250. **Available Online.**

1610　Studio Classroom
Overseas Radio & Television, Inc.
10 Ln. 62, Tachih St.
Taipei 104, Taiwan　　　　　　　　Ph: 886 225338082
Publication E-mail: letters@ortv.com

English-language teaching magazine. **Founded:** 1978. **Freq:** Monthly. **ISSN:** 1015-5902. **URL:** http://www.studioclassroom.com.tw/sc/. **Alt. Formats:** CD-ROM.

1611　The Taiwan Economic News
China Economic News Service (CENS)
561 Chunghsiao E. Rd., Sec. 4　　　　Ph: 886 227681234
Taipei, Taiwan　　　　　　　　　　Fax: 886 227629143
Publisher E-mail: news@cens.com

Economic newspaper. **Remarks:** Advertising accepted; rates available upon request. **URL:** http://news.cens.com/.

　　　　　　　　　　　　　　　　　　Circ: (Not Reported)

1612　Taiwan International Trade
Importers & Exporters Association of Taipei
Information & Publications Dept.
5F, 350, Sung Chiang Rd.
Taipei 104, Taiwan　　　　　　　　Ph: 886 0225813521

International trade magazine. **Freq:** Quarterly. **URL:** http://test.ieatpe.org.tw/tit/titweb14_index.htm.

1613　Taiwan News
Luis Ko
7F, 88 Hsin Yi Rd., Sec. 2
Taipei 106, Taiwan
Publication E-mail: edop@etaiwannews.com

English language newspaper for Taiwan. **Founded:** 1949. **Freq:** Daily. **Key Personnel:** Sen-hong Yang, Editor. **ISSN:** 1607-2626. **Remarks:** Advertising accepted; rates available upon request. **URL:** http://www.etaiwannews.com/.
　　　　　　　　　　　　　　　　　　Circ: (Not Reported)

1614　Taiwan Outlook
The Taiwan Studies Institute
134 Hsichang St.
Taipei, Taiwan
Publication E-mail: info@taiwanstudies.org

General interest magazine. **Freq:** Bimonthly. **ISSN:** 1682-797X. **URL:** http://www.taiwanstudies.org/tsi_publications/taiwan_outlook.

1615　Travel In Taiwan
Vision International Publishing Co.
Rm. 5, 10/F, 2 Fuhsing N. Rd.
Taipei, Taiwan　　　　　　　　Ph: 886 027115403

Travel magazine. **Freq:** Monthly. **URL:** http://www.sinica.edu.tw/tit/.

1616　Zoological Studies
Institute of Zoology
Academia Sinica
Taipei 115, Taiwan　　　　　　　　Ph: 886 227899529
Publication E-mail: zoolstud@gate.sinica.edu.tw

Journal on zoological studies. **Founded:** 1994. **Freq:** Quarterly. **Key Personnel:** Kwang Wang Shao, Editor. **ISSN:** 1021-5506. **URL:** http://www.sinica.edu.tw/zool/zoolstud/content.htm.

TAMSUI

1617　International Journal of Information and Management Sciences
Tamkang University
Dept. of Management Sciences & Decision Making
Tamsui 25137, Taiwan　　　　　　　Ph: 886 0286313221

Publishes original contributions on information systems, general systems,

Ad Rates:　GLR = general line rate; BW = one-time black & white page rate; 4C = one-time four color page rate; SAU = standard advertising unit rate;
CNU = Canadian newspaper advertising unit rate; PCI = per column inch rate.
Circulation: ★ = ABC; △ = BPA; ♦ = CAC; ● = CCAB; ❑ = VAC; ⊕ = PO Statement; ‡ = Publisher's Report; Boldface figures = sworn; Light figures = estimated.
Entry type: ▱ = Print; ☊ = Broadcast.

141

stochastic systems, transportation systems, industrial management, industrial engineering, management sciences, regional science, decision science, operations research, and app. **Founded:** 1990. **Freq:** Quarterly. **Key Personnel:** Kuo-Ren Lou, Editor. **ISSN:** 1017-1819. **Subscription Rates:** NTs 1,000; US$60 other countries.

Circ: Paid 400

📖 **1618 Journal of Educational Media and Library Sciences**
Tamkang University
Graduate Institute of Educational Media and Library Sciences
151, Ying-chuan Rd.
Tamsui 25137, Taiwan   Ph: 886 226215656

Journal devoted to studies regarding the fields of library science, information science, audio-visual and educational technology. **Founded:** 1970. **Freq:** Quarterly. **Key Personnel:** Shih Hsion Huang, Editor, Shhuang@mail.tku.edu.tw. **ISSN:** 1013-090X. **Subscription Rates:** NTs 400. **Available Online.**

Circ: Paid 1,200

📖 **1619 Tamkang Journal of Futures Studies**
Tamkang University
College of Education
Center for Futures Studies
Tamsui 251, Taiwan   Ph: 886 226215656
Publication E-mail: future@mail.tku.edu.tw

Publication focusing on integrating sociology, technology, environment, economy, politics and other sciences, as well as on future trends forecasting. **Key Personnel:** Hong-Zen Wang, Managing Editor. **URL:** http://www.ed.tku.edu.tw/develop/JFS.

📖 **1620 Tamkang Journal of International Affairs**
Tamkang University
College of International Studies
Rm. 917, Ching Sheng Bldg.
Tamsui 251, Taiwan   Ph: 886 226215656
Publication E-mail: 066368@mail.tku.edu.tw

Publication providing an open forum for discussions on a wide range of topics related to a scholarly understanding of international relations in the contemporary world, as well as a historical approach in culture, economy and politics of particular a. **Founded:** 1997. **Freq:** Quarterly. **Key Personnel:** Edward I-hsin Chen, Co-Editor. **ISSN:** 1027-4979.

📖 **1621 Tamkang Journal of Mathematics**
Tamkang University
Dept. of Mathematics
Tamsui 25137, Taiwan
Publication E-mail: bsm01@mail.tku.edu.tw

Publishes in English research papers of broad interest in all fields of pure and applied mathematics. **Founded:** 1970. **Freq:** Quarterly. **Key Personnel:** Bit-Shun Tam, Managing Editor. **ISSN:** 0376-4079. **Subscription Rates:** US$50.

📖 **1622 Tamkang Journal of Tamkang Review**
Tamkang University
Rm. 1101, Ching Sheng Bldg.
Tamsui 251, Taiwan   Ph: 886 226215656
Publication E-mail: jwu@mail.tku.edu.tw

Publishes studies of Chinese Literature from a critical point of view that places the subject within the context of world literature and studies dealing with theoretical aspects of East-West comparative literature. **Founded:** 1970. **Freq:** Semiannual. **Key Personnel:** Yao-Fu Lin, Editor. **ISSN:** 0049-2949.

TAOYUAN

📖 **1623 Journal of Explosives and Propellants**
Society of Explosives and Propellants, R.O.C.
Chung Cheng Institute of Technology,
  National Defense Univer
Ta-His
Taoyuan 335, Taiwan   Ph: 886 33891716

Publication providing information on explosives and propellants. **Founded:** 1985. **Freq:** Semiannual. **Key Personnel:** M.D. Ger, Asst. Editor, mdger@ccit.edu.tw. **ISSN:** 1013-767X. **Subscription Rates:** Free single issue.

THAILAND

BANGKOK

📖 **1624 Agricultural Engineering Journal**
Asian Association for Agricultural Engineering
c/o Div. of Agricultural & Food
  Engineering, Asian Institute
Klane Luong
PO Box 4
Bangkok 12120, Thailand   Ph: 66 25245479
Publication E-mail: aaae@ait.ac.th

Periodical covering soil and water engineering, farm machinery, farm structures, post-harvest technology, and food processing and emerging technologies. **Founded:** 1992. **Freq:** Quarterly. **Key Personnel:** V.M. Salokhe, Editor, salokhe@ait.ac.th. **ISSN:** 0858-2114. **Subscription Rates:** US$25 individuals; US$85 institutions. **URL:** http://www.ait.ac.th.

Circ: 300

📖 **1625 Asian Pacific Journal of Allergy and Immunology**
Allergy and Immunology Society Thailand
Dept. of Immunology, Faculty of Medicine
  Siriraj Hospital
Mahidol University
2 Prannok Rd.
Bangkoknoi
Bangkok 10700, Thailand   Ph: 66 24180569
Publication E-mail: sisso@mahidol.ac.th

Immunology journal. **Founded:** 1983. **Freq:** Semiannual. **ISSN:** 0125-877X.

📖 **1626 BAMBI Magazine**
Bangkok Babies & Mothers International
PO Box 1078
Suanphlub
Bangkok 10121, Thailand

Magazine providing support and information for pregnant women and parents of babies and young children living in Thailand. **Founded:** 1982. **Key Personnel:** Janine Taylor, Contact, janinetaylor1@yahoo.com. **URL:** http://www.bambi-bangkok.org.

📖 **1627 Bangkok Post Student Weekly**
The Post Publishing Public Co., Ltd.
Bangkok Post Bldg.
136 Na Ranong Rd.
Klong Toey   Ph: 66 22403700
Bangkok 10110, Thailand   Fax: 66 26713174
Publication E-mail: student-weekly@bangkokpost.net

News magazine for teenagers. **Founded:** 1969. **Freq:** Weekly. **Key Personnel:** Anussorn Thavisin, Editor. **Subscription Rates:** 38,000 Bht. **URL:** http://www.student-weekly.com.

Circ: 110,000

📖 **1628 Buffalo Journal**
Chulalongkorn University
Research Centre for Bioscience in Animal Production
Faculty of Veterinary Science
Chulalongkorn
Bangkok 10330, Thailand   Ph: 66 22518936
Publication E-mail: kmaneewa@netserv.chula.ac.th

Publishes research paper, reviews and comments on buffalo anatomy, breeding, diseases, genetics, management, nutrition, physiology, reproduction, and socio-economic problem. **Subtitle:** An International Journal of Buffalo Science. **Founded:** 1985. **Freq:** 3/year. **Key Personnel:** M. Kamonpatana Kamonpatana, Editor. **ISSN:** 0857-1554. **Subscription Rates:** US$85.

📖 **1629 Business Day**
Business Day Co., Ltd.
22nd Fl., Olympia Tower
444 Ratchadapisak Rd.   Ph: 66 25123579
Bangkok 10320, Thailand   Fax: 66 251235656
Publication E-mail: bday@bday.net
Publisher E-mail: info@bday.net

International business newspaper. **Subtitle:** Thailand's First International Business Daily. **URL:** http://www.bday.net.

1630 Business in Thailand Magazine
Business (Thailand) Co., Ltd.
972, Soi Saeng Cham
Rama IX Rd.   Ph: 66 22471519
Bangkok 10310, Thailand   Fax: 66 224832579
Publication E-mail: editor@business-in-thailand.com

English language magazine keeping both local and foreign decision makers constantly in touch with the fast changing business climate and economic conditions in Thailand. **Freq:** Monthly. **Subscription Rates:** 1,200 Bht. **URL:** http://www.businessinthailandmag.com/msindex.html.
Ad Rates: BW: 38,000   **Circ:** (Not Reported)
                       Bht
                       4C: 45,000 Bht

1631 Business Times
Thai Bldg., 1400 Rama IV Rd.
Bangkok 10110, Thailand

Business magazine. **Founded:** 1979. **Freq:** Weekly. **ISSN:** 0125-2313. **Available Online.**

1632 Confluence
United Nations Economic and Social Commission for Asia and the Pacific
United Nations Bldg.
Rajadamnern Ave.
Bangkok 10200, Thailand   Ph: 66 22881598
Publication E-mail: library-escap@un.org

Periodical covering the range of technological, managerial and conceptual information related to water resource developments. **Founded:** 1982. **Freq:** Semiannual. **ISSN:** 0257-3520.
                                                                              Circ: 600

1633 Decor International Magazine
Media Access Co. Ltd.
Lardprao Soi 8, Lardyao
99-3-4 Legacy Bldg.
Bangkok 10900, Thailand   Ph: 66 29387040

Periodical covering interior design and home decoration trends. **Founded:** 1991. **Freq:** Monthly. **Key Personnel:** Pravut Kanchanawat, Editor. **ISSN:** 0858-4028. **Subscription Rates:** 950 Bht.
                                                                              Circ: 5,000

1634 Electronic Journal of School of Advanced Technologies
School of Advanced Technologies
Telecommunications Program
Asian Institute of Technology
PO Box 4
Klong Luang
Bangkok 12120, Thailand   Ph: 66 25245739

Periodical covering basic and applied research in computer science and information management. **Key Personnel:** Nandana Rajatheva, Editor, rajath@ait.ac.th. **ISSN:** 1513-1432. **URL:** http://www.sat.ait.ac.th/ej-sat/.

1635 The English Teacher Online
IELE, Assumption University (ABAC)
Ramkhamhaeng soi 24
Bangkok 10240, Thailand   Ph: 66 23004543
Publication E-mail: artasp@au.edu

Publication designed primarily as a pragmatic resource for professionals involved in primary, secondary or higher education. **Subtitle:** An International Journal. **Key Personnel:** Melinda Tan, Managing Editor, Melinda.Tan@iele.au.edu. **URL:** http://www.elt.au.edu.

1636 Geotechnical Engineering
Southeast Asian Geotechnical Society
c/o Asian Institute of Technology
PO Box 4
Bangkok 12120, Thailand   Ph: 66 25162126

Geotechnical engineering journal. **Founded:** 1970. **Freq:** Semiannual. **Key Personnel:** D.T. Bergado, Editor. **ISSN:** 0046-5828. **Subscription Rates:** US$20 individuals; US$30 institutions. **Alt. Formats:** Microfiche; Microfilm.
                                                                              Circ: 1,120

1637 Good Morning Chiangmai News Magazine
Good Morning Chiangmai News Magazine Co., Ltd.
20/1 Ratchamanka Rd.
A.Muang
Bangkok 50200, Thailand
Publication E-mail: gmorning@loxinfo.co.th

News magazine covering Chiangmai and the North of Thailand. Includes features, pen pals and more. **Freq:** Monthly. **URL:** http://chiangmai-on-line.com/gmcm.

1638 Hobby Electronics
Se-Education Public Company Ltd.
800/43-45 Soi Trakulsuk
Asok-Dindaeng
Bangkok 10400, Thailand   Ph: 66 2248280
Publication E-mail: marketing@se-ed.com

Publication providing information for fledgling electronics enthusiasts and interested readers. **Subtitle:** for inventors and experimenters. **Founded:** 1997. **Freq:** Monthly. **Key Personnel:** Prasert Rojsutheewat, Editor. **ISSN:** 0858-9976. **Subscription Rates:** 400 Bht. **Remarks:** Advertising accepted; rates available upon request.
                                                                              Circ: (Not Reported)

1639 Investor
Thailand's Board of investment
Pansak Bldg., 4th Fl.
138-1 Petchburi Rd.
Bangkok 10400, Thailand

Publication providing business, economics and investment related information. **Founded:** 1968. **Freq:** Monthly. **Key Personnel:** Tos Patumsen, Editor. **ISSN:** 0125-0248. **Subscription Rates:** 95 Bht.

1640 Journal of Euro-Asian Management
Asian Institute of Technology School of Management
PO Box 4
Klong Luang
Bangkok 12120, Thailand   Ph: 66 25160110
Publication E-mail: somwebmaster@ait.ac.th

Periodical containing information pertaining to Asian and European business and management. **Founded:** 1995. **Freq:** Semiannual. **Key Personnel:** Jyoti P. Gupta, Editor. **ISSN:** 0859-449X. **Subscription Rates:** US$40.
                                                                              Circ: 500

1641 Journal of Ferrocement
Asian Institute of Technology
PO Box 2754
Bangkok 10501, Thailand   Ph: 66 25245864
Publication E-mail: geoferro@ait.ac.th

Periodical covering concrete, cement, low-cost composite materials and related topics. **Founded:** 1971. **Freq:** Quarterly. **Key Personnel:** Lilia Robles Austriaco, Editor. **ISSN:** 0125-1759. **Subscription Rates:** US$35; US$85 institutions. **Alt. Formats:** Microfilm.
                                                                              Circ: 400

 1642 **Journal of the Medical Association of Thailand**
Medical Association of Thailand
67/9 Soi Soonvichai
New Pechburi Rd.
Bangkok, Thailand   Ph: 66 23144333
Publication E-mail: math@loxinfo.co.th

Medical sciences journal. **Founded:** 1929. **Freq:** Monthly. **ISSN:** 0125-2208.
Subscription Rates: US$40.
Circ: 3,500

 1643 **Journal of National Research Council of Thailand**
National Research Council of Thailand
196 Phahonyothin Rd.
Chatuchak
Bangkok 10900, Thailand   Ph: 66 29407051
Publication E-mail: tfrd@fc.nrct.go.th

Publishes research in many areas of the natural and social sciences. **Founded:**
1960. **Freq:** Quarterly. **Key Personnel:** Chirapandh Arthachinta, Editor.
ISSN: 0028-0011. **Subscription Rates:** 100 Bht.

 1644 **Journal of Research Methodology**
Chulalongkorn University Press
Phyathai Rd.
Pathumwan
Bangkok 10330, Thailand   Ph: 66 22153626
Publication E-mail: psomwung@chul.ac.th

Periodical covering research methodology, statistics, measurement and
evaluation and research results in education and social sciences. **Founded:**
1989. **Freq:** Semiannual. **Key Personnel:** Somwung Pitiyanuwat, Editor.
ISSN: 0857-2933. **Subscription Rates:** 90 Bht.
Circ: 1,000

 1645 **Journal of the Science Society of Thailand**
Thailand's National Science and Technology Development Agency
(NSTDA)
Public Information Dept.
Ratchathewi
Bangkok 10400, Thailand

Periodical covering natural science, mathematics, computer science and
engineering. **Founded:** 1975. **Freq:** Quarterly. **ISSN:** 0303-8122.

 1646 **Journal of Southeast Asian Education**
SEAMEO Secretariat
4th Fl., Darakarn Bldg. 920
Sukhumvir Rd.
Bangkok 10110, Thailand   Ph: 66 23910144
Publication E-mail: narerat@pearson-indochina.com

Publication focusing on education. **Founded:** 2000. **Freq:** Semiannual. **ISSN:**
1513-4601. **Subscription Rates:** 395 Bht single issue. **URL:** http://
www.seameo.org/journal.

 1647 **Journal of Thai Chamber of Commerce**
Bamrung Nukoulkit Press
83 Bamrung Muang Rd.
Bangkok, Thailand

Business and economics journal. **Freq:** Monthly. **Key Personnel:** L. Chara,
Editor.

 1648 **Kasetsart Journal**
Kasetsart University Research and Development Institute
Bangkok 10900, Thailand
Publication E-mail: kurdi@nontri.ku.ac.th

Life science journal. **Founded:** 1961. **Freq:** Semiannual. **Key Personnel:** S.
Panichsakpatana, Editor. **ISSN:** 0075-5192.

 1649 **Kinnaree Magazine**
Thai Airways International Public Company Limited
Ground Fl., Bldg. 9
89 Vibhavadi Rangsit Rd.
Bangkok 10900, Thailand   Ph: 66 25453321
Publication E-mail: info@kinnaree.com

In-flight magazine. **Freq:** Monthly. **Key Personnel:** Manisa E. Piyasing, Web
Editor. **URL:** http://www.kinnaree.com.

 1650 **Living in Thailand**
Media Transasia (Thailand) Ltd.
14/F, Ocean Tower II, 75/10 Soi Wattana
Sukhumvit Soi 21, Asoke Rd., Klongtoey
Prakanong
Bangkok 10110, Thailand   Ph: 66 22042370

General interest periodical. **Founded:** 1972. **Freq:** Monthly. **Key Personnel:**
J.S. Uberoi, Editor. **ISSN:** 0125-1953. **Subscription Rates:** 100 Bht.
Available Online.
Circ: 26,450

 1651 **LookEast**
Advertising & Media Consultants Co. Ltd.
12th Fl., Silom Condominium
52/38 Soi Saladaeng 2, Silom Rd.
Bangkok 10500, Thailand   Ph: 66 22336839
Publication E-mail: ravisehgal1@hotmail.com

Travel and tourism related magazine. **Key Personnel:** Asha Narula Sehgal,
Editor. **ISSN:** 0857-1139.

 1652 **Metro Magazine**
The Post Publishing Public Co., Ltd.
Bangkok Post Bldg.
136 Na Ranong Rd.
Klong Toey   Ph: 66 22403700
Bangkok 10110, Thailand   Fax: 66 26713174
Publication E-mail: subscription@bangkokpost.co.th

Magazine presenting featured articles, film reviews, restaurant guides and
more. **Freq:** Monthly. **Subscription Rates:** 1,000 Bht; 2,400 Bht other
countries. **URL:** http://www.bkkmetro.com/indexx.php.

 1653 **Microcomputer**
Se-Education Public Company Ltd.
800/43-45 Soi Trakulsuk
Asok-Dindaeng
Bangkok 10400, Thailand   Ph: 66 2248280
Publication E-mail: marketing@se-ed.com

Computer magazine. **Subtitle:** For General PC User. **Founded:** 1983. **Freq:**
Monthly. **Key Personnel:** Mongkol Kaewchan, Editor. **ISSN:** 0857-0140.
Subscription Rates: 720 Bht. **Remarks:** Advertising accepted; rates avail-
able upon request.
Circ: (Not Reported)

 1654 **Microcomputer User Magazine**
Se-Education Public Company Ltd.
800/43-45 Soi Trakulsuk
Asok-Dindaeng
Bangkok 10400, Thailand   Ph: 66 2248280
Publication E-mail: math@loxinfo.co.th

Publication providing information for PC buyers and general users. **Subtitle:**
For PC Buyers and General Public. **Founded:** 1993. **Freq:** Monthly. **Key
Personnel:** Wirath Winijwatanawong, Editor. **ISSN:** 0857-0140. **Subscrip-
tion Rates:** 600 Bht. **Remarks:** Advertising accepted; rates available upon
request.
Circ: (Not Reported)

 1655 **MuangBoran Journal**
Muang Boran Publishing House
397 Phrasumain Rd.
Bangkok 10200, Thailand   Ph: 66 22816110

Educational journal. **Founded:** 1974. **Freq:** Quarterly. **Subscription Rates:**
440 Bht; US$26 other countries.

 1656 **National Junior Magazine**
Nation Multimedia Group
44 Moo 10, Bang Na-Trat KM 4.5
Bang Na District   Ph: 66 23255555
Bangkok 10260, Thailand   Fax: 66 23172071
Publication E-mail: enj@nationjunior.com

Leading English-language magazine in Thailand. **Key Personnel:** Chusri Ngamprasert, Editor, jujang@nationgroup.com. **Remarks:** Advertising accepted; rates available upon request. **URL:** http://www.nationjunior.com.
Circ: (Not Reported)

📖 **1657 Pink Ink**
MBE Surawong 227
173/3 Surawong Rd.
Bangkok 10500, Thailand   Ph: 66 26613150
Publication E-mail: pinkink@khsnet.com

Thailand's gay and lesbian magazine. **Freq:** Bimonthly. **Key Personnel:** Nick Wilde, Editor. **URL:** http://www.khsnet.net/pinkink.

📖 **1658 Population Headliners**
United Nations Economic and Social Commission for Asia and the Pacific
United Nations Bldg.
Rajadamnern Ave.
Bangkok 10200, Thailand   Ph: 66 22881598
Publication E-mail: library-escap@un.org

Population studies journal. **Founded:** 1971. **Freq:** Bimonthly. **ISSN:** 0252-3639. **Subscription Rates:** Free.
Circ: 5,500

📖 **1659 The Rubber International**
TRI Global Co Ltd.
238/9 (Behind the Grand Hotel)
Ratchada-Pisek Rd.
Hui-Kwang
Bangkok 10320, Thailand   Ph: 66 22740770
Publication E-mail: trigb@ksc.th.com

Rubber business magazine. **Freq:** Monthly. **Remarks:** Advertising accepted; rates available upon request. **URL:** http://www.rubbmag.com.
Circ: (Not Reported)

📖 **1660 Science Asia**
Science Society of Thailand
c/o Department of Biochemistry
Faculty of Science, Mahidol University
73/1 Rama VI Rd., Rajdhevee   Ph: 66 22460063
Bangkok 10400, Thailand   Fax: 66 22480375

Science journal. **Freq:** Quarterly. **Key Personnel:** M.R. Jisnuson Svasti, Editor, scjsv@mahidol.ac.th. **Subscription Rates:** 600 Bht individuals; 1,200 Bht institutions. **URL:** http://scienceasia.tiac.or.th.

📖 **1661 SET Journal**
Stock Exchange of Thailand
62 Rachadapisek Rd.
Klongtoey
Bangkok 10110, Thailand   Ph: 66 22292000
Publication E-mail: webmaster@setinter1.set.or.th

Stock exchange and economics journal. **Founded:** 1997. **Freq:** Monthly. **ISSN:** 0859-709X.

📖 **1662 Siriraj Hospital Gazette**
Mahidol University
Faculty of Medicine Siriraj Hospital
Bldg. 3 Rm. 312, Bangkoknoi
Bangkok 10700, Thailand
Publication E-mail: simai@mahidol.ac.th

Publication focusing on medical science and health. **Founded:** 1949. **Freq:** Monthly. **ISSN:** 0125-152X.

📖 **1663 Stock Market in Thailand**
Stock Exchange of Thailand
62 Rachadapisek Rd.
Klongtoey
Bangkok 10110, Thailand   Ph: 66 22292000

Trade publication. **Founded:** 1983. **Freq:** Annual. **Subscription Rates:** 70 Bht.

📖 **1664 Telcom Journal**
Telcom Journal Co Ltd.
327/17-19 Soi Sri-Amporn (Phaholyothin 32)
Senanikom Rd., Ladyao
Chatuchak
Bangkok 10900, Thailand   Ph: 66 25614993
Publication E-mail: info@tj.co.th

Newspaper covering the telecom business. **Freq:** Weekly. **Key Personnel:** Yupayao Inthirat, Exec. Editor. **Subscription Rates:** 1,000 Bht. **URL:** http://www.tj.co.th.
Ad Rates: BW: 120,000   **Circ:** 120,000
              Bht
              4C: 150,000
              Bht

📖 **1665 Thai-American Business**
The American Chamber of Commerce in Thailand
18th Floor Kian Gwan Bldg. 2
140/1 Wireless Rd.
Lumphini
Pathumwan
Bangkok 10330, Thailand   Ph: 66 222519266
Publication E-mail: info@amchamthailand.com

Business and economics journal. **Founded:** 1967. **Freq:** Bimonthly. **ISSN:** 0125-0191. **Subscription Rates:** 400 Bht. **Remarks:** Advertising accepted; rates available upon request.
Circ: Paid 3,000

📖 **1666 Thai Economic Review**
Chulalongkorn University
Phyathai Rd.
Bangkok 10500, Thailand

Journal covering issues related to economics. **Founded:** 1972. **Freq:** 3/year. **Key Personnel:** Supachai Manuspaibool, Editor. **ISSN:** 0125-3905. **Remarks:** Advertising accepted; rates available upon request.
Circ: (Not Reported)

📖 **1667 Thai Journal of Agricultural Science**
Agricultural Science Society of Thailand
Kasetsart University
PO Box 1070
Bangkok 10903, Thailand   Ph: 66 25790308

Agricultural journal. **Founded:** 1967. **Freq:** Quarterly. **Key Personnel:** Suranant Subhadrabandhu, Editor. **ISSN:** 0049-3589. **Subscription Rates:** 600 Bht nonmembers; US$60 nonmembers other countries. **Remarks:** Advertising accepted; rates available upon request.
Circ: (Not Reported)

📖 **1668 Thai Journal of Anesthesiology**
Royal College of Anesthesiologists of Thailand
Dept. of Anesthesiology
Faculty of Medicine
Chulalongkorn University
Rama 4 Rd., Pathumwan
Bangkok, Thailand

Medical journal.

📖 1669 Thai Journal of Development Administration
National Institute of Development Administration
Research Center
118 Seri Thai Rd.
Bangkok 10240, Thailand   Ph: 66 23777400
Publication E-mail: nisnida@nida.nida.ac.th

Periodical covering issues related to production of goods and services.
Founded: 1960. **Freq:** Quarterly. **Key Personnel:** Juree Vichit Vadakan,
Editor. **ISSN:** 0125-3689. **Subscription Rates:** US$30. **Remarks:** Advertis-
ing accepted; rates available upon request.
                                                              Circ: Paid 1,500

📖 1670 Thai Junior Red Cross Magazine
Chatra Press
77 Rama V
Bangkok, Thailand

Community service magazine. **Founded:** 1923. **Freq:** Bimonthly. **Key
Personnel:** Prem Burachatra, Editor. **ISSN:** 0040-5361. **Subscription Rates:**
10 Bht.
                                                              Circ: 4,131

📖 1671 Thailand Airline Timetable
Advertising & Media Consultants Co. Ltd.
12th Fl., Silom Condominium
52/38 Soi Saladaeng 2, Silom Rd.
Bangkok 10500, Thailand   Ph: 66 22336839

Air transport journal. **Founded:** 1976. **Freq:** Monthly. **Key Personnel:** Asha
Narula Sehgal, Editor. **ISSN:** 0125-1090.
                                                              Circ: Paid 40,000

📖 1672 Thailand Travel Magazine
The Post Publishing Public Co., Ltd.
Bangkok Post Bldg.
136 Na Ranong Rd.
Klong Toey   Ph: 66 22403700
Bangkok 10110, Thailand   Fax: 66 26713174

Tourism industry magazine. **Founded:** 1994. **Freq:** Monthly. **ISSN:** 0858-
8392. **URL:** http://ksc.goldsite.com/Publication/Travel.

📖 1673 Thailand Update
Office of the Board of Investment
555 Vibhavadi-Rangsit Rd.
Chatuchak
Bangkok 10900, Thailand   Ph: 66 25378111
Publication E-mail: head@boi.go.th

Business and economics journal. **Freq:** Monthly. **URL:** http://www.boi.go.th/
english/thailandupdate.
                                                              Circ: 10,000

📖 1674 TISNET Trade and Investment Bulletin
United Nations Economic and Social Commission for Asia and the
   Pacific
Trade Information Service, International Trade and Industry Division
United Nations Bldg.
Rajadamnern Ave.   Ph: 66 22881601
Bangkok 10200, Thailand   Fax: 66 22881019
Publisher E-mail: trade_inf@unescap.org

Publication covering economic development. **Founded:** 1982. **Freq:** Monthly. **Trim Size:** 21 x 30 cm. **Subscription Rates:** US$50. **Remarks:**
Advertising not accepted.
                                                              Circ: (Not Reported)

📖 1675 Tobacco Asia
Lockwood Trade Journal Co., Inc.
Ste. 711, SNC Tower, 33 Soi 4
Sukhumvit Rd., Klong Toey
Bangkok 10110, Thailand   Ph: 66 26569394
Publication E-mail: smokeasia@aol.com

Tobacco business magazine. **Founded:** 1997. **Freq:** Quarterly. **Key Person-**

nel: Glenn A. John, Editor, glenn@tobaccoasia.com. **Subscription Rates:**
US$30. **URL:** http://www.tobaccoasia.com.
Ad Rates: BW: US$2,100   **Circ:** 5,000
              4C: US$2,900

📖 1676 Top Fashion Magazine
40/11 Soi Indramara 8 Suthisarn
   Samsaennai Phrayathai
Bangkok 10400, Thailand
Publication E-mail: webmaster@topfashion.in.th

Fashion periodical featuring a catalog of men's and women's clothing, Thai
traditional dress, and underwear from local merchants and exporters.
Founded: 1991. **Freq:** Monthly. **ISSN:** 0858-2769. **URL:** http://
www.topfashion.in.th/Default.HTM.

📖 1677 Travel Trade Report
Ross Publishing Ltd.
18th Fl., Ste. 1801 Wave Pl.
55 Wireless Rd.
Patumwan
Bangkok 10330, Thailand   Ph: 66 2254742
Publication E-mail: editor@ttreport.com

Periodical containing information related to Thailand and Mekong Region's
tourism industry. **Founded:** 1978. **Freq:** Weekly. **Key Personnel:** Don Ross,
Editor. **URL:** http://www.ttreport.com.

📖 1678 Traveller Magazine
Quest Media Co. Ltd.
Thaniya Plaza Bldg., 12th Fl.
52 Silom Rd., Suryawongse
Bangrak
Bangkok 10500, Thailand   Ph: 66 22312772
Publication E-mail: pgoodfellow@dreamasia.com

Travel journalism. **Freq:** Bimonthly. **Key Personnel:** Jonathan Hopfner,
Editor, jhopfner@dreamasia.com.

📖 1679 Update Magazine
Se-Education Public Company Ltd.
800/43-45 Soi Trakulsuk
Asok-Dindaeng
Bangkok 10400, Thailand   Ph: 66 2248280
Publication E-mail: marketing@se-ed.com

Periodical covering the latest developments in the world of science and
technology. **Subtitle:** Up to Date Reading Material for Modern People.
Founded: 1978. **Freq:** Monthly. **Key Personnel:** Jumpol Hayakirin, Editor.
ISSN: 0858-6934. **Subscription Rates:** 720 Bht.

CHIANG MAI

📖 1680 Bangkok Magazine
Infothai CM Co. Ltd.
299/50 Mooban Natongville I
Tasala, Muang
Chiang Mai, Thailand
Publication E-mail: sales@infothai.com

Magazine providing useful information about Bangkok, its people, and the
many things to do and places to go in the City of Angels. **URL:** http://
www.infothai.com/bangkokmag.

📖 1681 Chiangmai Mail
Chiangmai Mail Publishing Co. Ltd.
142 Im-boon Housing Estate
Soi 1, Muangsamut Rd.
Tambon Changmoi
Muang District
Chiang Mai 50300, Thailand
Publication E-mail: cnxmail@loxinfo.co.th

General newspaper. **Subtitle:** Serving the North of Thailand. **Freq:** Weekly.
URL: http://www.chiangmai-mail.com.

📖 **1682 Welcome to Chiangmai & Chiangrai Magazine**
PO Box 100
Chiang Mai 50000, Thailand
Publication E-mail: Marji@chiangmai-chiangrai.com

Periodical covering advice to tourists, Buddhism, business, bars, food, guest houses, and more. **Freq:** Monthly. **Key Personnel:** Khun Margaret, Contact. **Subscription Rates:** 160 Bht; US$40. **URL:** http://welcome-to.chiangmai-chiangrai.com.

NAKHON PATHOM

📖 **1683 Journal of Population and Social Studies**
Thai Association of Population and Social Researchers
Institute for Population and Social Research
Mahidol University
Salaya Campus
Nakhon Pathom 73170, Thailand

Journal covering matters related to social sciences. **Key Personnel:** Boonlert Leoprapai, Editor.

📖 **1684 SABRAO Journal of Breeding and Genetics**
Society for the Advancement of Breeding Researches in Asia and
  Oceania
Faculty of Agriculture, Kasetsart University
Kamphaeng Saen Campus
Nakhon Pathom 73140, Thailand   Ph: 66 234351399
Publication E-mail: fscisil@nontri.ku.ac.th

Publication devoted to the basic and practical aspects of breeding research in economic organisms. **Founded:** 1969. **Freq:** Semiannual. **Key Personnel:** Peerasak Srinives, Asst. Editor, agrpss@ku.ac.th. **ISSN:** 1029-7073. **Subscription Rates:** US$30. **Remarks:** Advertising accepted; rates available upon request. **Available Online.**
                                        Circ: (Not Reported)

NONTHABURI

📖 **1685 On Air Magazine**
Sahasarn Media
199/444 Kaerai Tower, 1st Fl.
Kaerai Junction, Tiwanon Rd.
Ampher Muang
Nonthaburi 11000, Thailand   Ph: 66 29501628
Publication E-mail: manager@onairmag.com

International music magazine. **Freq:** Monthly. **URL:** http://www.onair.atfreeweb.com.

PHATTAYA

📖 **1686 NewsToday.co.th**
Quick News Co. Ltd.
Bangkok Post Bldg.
Phattaya 20260, Thailand
Publication E-mail: quicknews@newstoday.co.th.

Newspaper delivered in Bangkok and Pattaya. **Subtitle:** Your Favourite Newspaper Daily Delivered. **Freq:** Daily. **URL:** http://www.newstoday.co.th.

PHUKET

📖 **1687 The Phuket Gazette**
The Phuket Gazette Co., Ltd.
367/2 Yaowarat Rd.
Amphur Muang   Ph: 66 076236555
Phuket 83000, Thailand   Fax: 66 076213971
Publication E-mail: info@phuketgazette.net

Online English community newspaper for Phuket. **Freq:** Weekly. **Key Personnel:** Alasdair- Forbes, Managing Editor. **Subscription Rates:** 2,800 Bht; 8,000 Bht other countries. **URL:** http://www.phuketgazette.net.

TURKEY

ISTANBUL

📖 **1688 Archives of the Turkish Society of Cardiology**
Turkish Society of Cardiology
Turk Kardiyoloji Dernegi
Darilaceze cad Flinye sok. Eksioglu Is
  Merkezi, 9/1
Okneydan   Ph: 90 2122211730
TR-80270 Istanbul, Turkey   Fax: 90 2122211754
Publisher E-mail: tkd@ixir.com

Scientific publication covering cardiology. **Founded:** 1966. **Freq:** Monthly. **Trim Size:** A4. **ISSN:** 1016-5169. **Subscription Rates:** US$70. **URL:** http://www.tkd.org.tr. **Alt. Formats:** Magnetic tape.
Ad Rates: 4C: US$300   **Circ:** 1,200

UNITED ARAB EMIRATES

ABU DHABI

📖 **1689 Abu Dhabi Economy**
Abu Dhabi Chamber of Commerce & Industry
Publication & Press Relations Dept.
PO Box 662
Abu Dhabi, United Arab Emirates   Ph: 971 22214000
Publication E-mail: services@adcci-uae.com

Periodical featuring Abu Dhabi's latest situation in non-oil trade, stock market and world energy markets. **Freq:** Monthly. **URL:** http://www.adcci.gov.ae.

📖 **1690 Bee Sagheer**
Food and Environment Control Centre (FECC)
Salam St.
Abu Dhabi, United Arab Emirates
Publication E-mail: Webmaster@beesagheer.com

Online environment magazine for UAE children in English and Arabic. **Subtitle:** Children Environment Magazine. **URL:** http://www.beesagheer.com/english.

DUBAI

📖 **1691 Ad-Vocate**
Motivate Publishing
PO Box 2331   Ph: 971 42824060
Dubai, United Arab Emirates   Fax: 971 42824436
Publication E-mail: motivate@emirates.net.ae
Publisher E-mail: executive@motivate.co.ae

Reports latest developments within the advertising association and the industry as a whole. **Freq:** Quarterly. **Remarks:** Advertising accepted; rates available upon request. **URL:** http://www.motivatepublishing.com/files/bus-pub.html.
                                        Circ: (Not Reported)

📖 **1692 Afsaar Magazine**
Afsaar Group
PO Box 45594
Dubai, United Arab Emirates   Ph: 971 26811102
Publication E-mail: Asfaar@emirates.net.ae

International tourism related magazine. **Subtitle:** The First Tourism & Travel Magazine in UAE. **Subscription Rates:** 120 Dh individuals. **URL:** http://www.asfaar.net/home_eng.htm.
Ad Rates: BW: 6,000 Dh   **Circ:** (Not Reported)
             4C: 8,000 Dh

📖 **1693 Al Shindagah**
Al Habtoor Group LLC
PO Box 25444
Dubai, United Arab Emirates   Ph: 971 43431111
Publication E-mail: shindaga@alhabtoorgroup.com

Periodical covering general news section. **Key Personnel:** Nadia Jones, Editor. **URL:** http://www.alshindagah.com/index.html.

📖 **1694 Arabian Business**
The Information & Technology Publishing Co. Ltd.
PO Box 500024
Dubai, United Arab Emirates   Ph: 971 42829996
Publication E-mail: abc@itp.net

English-language business magazine for the Middle East. **Key Personnel:** David Ingham, Editor, david.ingham@itp.net. **Subscription Rates:** 125 Dh; 365 Dh other countries. **Remarks:** Advertising accepted; rates available upon request. **URL:** http://www.itp.net/corporate/current/97478350998941.htm.
     Circ: (Not Reported)

📖 **1695 Arabian Computer News**
The Information & Technology Publishing Co. Ltd.
PO Box 500024
Dubai, United Arab Emirates   Ph: 971 42829996
Publication E-mail: acn@itp.net

Technology and business magazine for the Middle East. **Key Personnel:** Greg Wilson, Editor, greg.wilson@itp.net. **Subscription Rates:** Free; 365 Dh other countries. **Remarks:** Advertising accepted; rates available upon request. **URL:** http://www.itp.net/corporate/current/9747883908353.htm.
     Circ: (Not Reported)

📖 **1696 Arabian Woman**
GoDubai.com
Atrium Centre, Office 409
PO Box 43577
Dubai, United Arab Emirates
Publication E-mail: arbwoman@emirates.net.ae

Periodical covering information related to Arabian women. **Subtitle:** Woman's Magazine in English. **Key Personnel:** Samreen Fowad, Editor. **URL:** http://www.godubai.com/arabianwoman.

📖 **1697 Channel Middle East**
The Information & Technology Publishing Co. Ltd.
PO Box 500024
Dubai, United Arab Emirates   Ph: 971 42829996
Publication E-mail: crn@itp.net

Information technology channel magazine for the Middle East. **Freq:** Monthly. **Key Personnel:** Mark Sutton, Editor, mark.sutton@itp.net. **Subscription Rates:** Free; 365 Dh other countries. **Remarks:** Advertising accepted; rates available upon request. **URL:** http://www.itp.net/corporate/media/crn.htm.
     Circ: (Not Reported)

📖 **1698 Charged Middle East**
The Information & Technology Publishing Co. Ltd.
PO Box 500024
Dubai, United Arab Emirates   Ph: 971 42829996
Publication E-mail: neil.petch@itp.net

Magazine covering tatest technology from MP3 to DVD players. **Subtitle:** Where Life Meets Technology. **Key Personnel:** Rob Corder, Editorial Dir., rob.corder@itp.net. **Subscription Rates:** 80 Dh; 365 Dh other countries. **Remarks:** Advertising accepted; rates available upon request. **URL:** http://www.itp.net/corporate/current/97842461565587.htm.
     Circ: (Not Reported)

📖 **1699 City Times**
Galadari Printing and Publishing LLC
PO Box 3082
Dubai, United Arab Emirates   Ph: 971 43382400
Publication E-mail: kteditor@emirates.net.ae

General newspaper. **Freq:** Daily. **Remarks:** Advertising accepted; rates available upon request. **URL:** http://www.khaleejtimes.co.ae/ctimeshome.htm.
     Circ: (Not Reported)

📖 **1700 Communications Africa**
The Information & Technology Publishing Co. Ltd.
PO Box 500024
Dubai, United Arab Emirates   Ph: 971 42829996

Communications magazine for Africa. **Freq:** Quarterly. **Subscription Rates:** Free; 365 Dh other countries.

📖 **1701 Communications Egypt**
The Information & Technology Publishing Co. Ltd.
PO Box 500024
Dubai, United Arab Emirates   Ph: 971 42829996
Publication E-mail: cmea@itp.net

Communications magazine. **Freq:** Quarterly. **Key Personnel:** Mats Palmgren, Editor, mats.palmgren@itp.net. **Subscription Rates:** Free; 365 Dh other countries. **Remarks:** Advertising accepted; rates available upon request. **URL:** http://www.itp.net/corporate/current/9754195066451.htm.
     Circ: (Not Reported)

📖 **1702 Communications Maghreb**
The Information & Technology Publishing Co. Ltd.
PO Box 500024
Dubai, United Arab Emirates   Ph: 971 42829996

Maghreb communications magazine. **Freq:** Quarterly. **Subscription Rates:** Free; 365 Dh other countries.

📖 **1703 Communications Middle East & Africa**
The Information & Technology Publishing Co. Ltd.
PO Box 500024
Dubai, United Arab Emirates   Ph: 971 42829996
Publication E-mail: cmea@itp.net

Communications magazine for the Middle East. **Key Personnel:** Daniel Anderson-Ford, Editor, daniel.anderson@itp.net. **Subscription Rates:** Free; 365 Dh other countries. **Remarks:** Advertising accepted; rates available upon request. **URL:** http://www.itp.net/corporate/current/97478918465888.htm.
     Circ: (Not Reported)

📖 **1704 Digital Studio**
The Information & Technology Publishing Co. Ltd.
PO Box 500024
Dubai, United Arab Emirates   Ph: 971 42829996
Publication E-mail: ds@itp.net

Magazine for broadcast professionals. **Key Personnel:** David Cass, Editor, david.cass@itp.net. **Subscription Rates:** Free; 365 Dh other countries. **Remarks:** Advertising accepted; rates available upon request. **URL:** http://www.itp.net/corporate/current/97479109555779.htm.
     Circ: (Not Reported)

📖 **1705 Dubai International**
Motivate Publishing
PO Box 2331   Ph: 971 42824060
Dubai, United Arab Emirates   Fax: 971 42824436
Publication E-mail: motivate@emirates.net.ae
Publisher E-mail: executive@motivate.co.ae

Periodical highlighting major developments at the airport and events in the city's entertainment and sporting calendar. **URL:** http://www.motivatepublishing.com/files/dxtinter.html.
Ad Rates: 4C: 10,750 Dh   **Circ:** (Not Reported)

📖 **1706 Emirates Inflight**
Motivate Publishing
PO Box 2331   Ph: 971 42824060
Dubai, United Arab Emirates   Fax: 971 42824436
Publication E-mail: motivate@emirates.net.ae
Publisher E-mail: executive@motivate.co.ae

Magazine containing features of wide-ranging and topical interest, commissioned from international writers and photographers. **URL:** http://www.motivatepublishing.com/files/einflight.html.
Ad Rates: 4C: 18,000 Dh   **Circ:** (Not Reported)

1707 Emirates Medical Journal
The Emirates Medical Association (EMA)
PO Box 6600
Sh. Rashid Bldg.
Flat No. 305, Zabil St.
Dubai, United Arab Emirates   Ph: 971 43377377
Publication E-mail: emaad@emirates.net.ae

Publishes information related to developing medicine and science. **Subtitle:** Official Publication of the Emirates Medial A. **Founded:** 1980. **Freq:** 3/year. **Key Personnel:** Ali Shakar, Gen. Secretary. **ISSN:** 0250-6882. **URL:** http://www.emiratesma.org/medical.html.

1708 Emirates Woman
Motivate Publishing
PO Box 2331
Dubai, United Arab Emirates   Ph: 971 42824060
                                     Fax: 971 42824436
Publication E-mail: motivate@emirates.net.ae
Publisher E-mail: executive@motivate.co.ae

Periodical covering information related to Emirates women. **Founded:** 1981. **URL:** http://www.motivatepublishing.com/files/ewoman.html.
Ad Rates: 4C: 9,000 Dh   **Circ:** Paid 21,745

1709 Gulf Industry Magazine
Al Hilal Publishing & Marketing Group
Office M03, Al Moosa Group Building
   Umm
Hurair Rd.
PO Box 6387
Dubai, United Arab Emirates   Ph: 971 43371366
Publication E-mail: editor@gulfindustryworldwide.com

Trade journal for the building and construction industries of Saudi Arabia and the Arabian Gulf. **Freq:** Bimonthly. **URL:** http://www.gulfindustryworldwide.com/cover.asp.
Ad Rates: BW: US$2,680   **Circ:** (Not Reported)
                 4C: US$4,285

1710 Gulf Marketing Review
Pegasus Publishing Ltd.
PO Box 7269
Dubai, United Arab Emirates
Publication E-mail: graybiz@emirates.net.ae

Publishes information regarding marketing and advertising. **Founded:** 1993. **Freq:** Monthly. **URL:** http://www.gmr-online.com/access/gmr-online.
Ad Rates: 4C: US$4,400   **Circ:** (Not Reported)

1711 Gulf News
Al Nisr Publishing LLC
PO Box 6519
Dubai, United Arab Emirates   Ph: 971 43447100
Publication E-mail: edit@gulf-news.co.ae

English language newspaper of the United Arab Emirates covering the Gulf region. **Founded:** 1978. **Freq:** Daily. **Key Personnel:** Abdul Hamid Ahmad, Editor-in-Chief, ahamid@gulfnews.com. **URL:** http://www.gulf-news.com.
Ad Rates: BW: US$17.50   **Circ:** 91,000

1712 The Gulf Today
Dar Alkhaleej Publishing and Press
PO Box 7955
Dubai, United Arab Emirates   Ph: 971 42625304

General newspaper. **Freq:** Daily. **URL:** http://www.thegulftoday.com.

1713 Khaleej Times
Galadari Printing and Publishing LLC
PO Box 3082
Dubai, United Arab Emirates   Ph: 971 43382400
Publication E-mail: kteditor@emirates.net.ae

General newspaper. **Freq:** Daily. **ISSN:** 1563-5856. **Subscription Rates:** 560 Dh. **URL:** http://www.khaleejtimes.co.ae.
Ad Rates: BW: 60 Dh   **Circ:** 72,000

1714 Living in the Gulf
Motivate Publishing
PO Box 2331   Ph: 971 42824060
Dubai, United Arab Emirates   Fax: 971 42824436
Publication E-mail: motivate@emirates.net.ae
Publisher E-mail: executive@motivate.co.ae

Magazine for Spinneys' customers. **URL:** http://www.motivatepublishing.com/files/living.html.
Ad Rates: 4C: 11,500 Dh   **Circ:** (Not Reported)

1715 MEED - The Middle East Business Weekly
MEED Communications
MEED Regional Office, Office 109, West
   Bldg.
Dubai Airport Free Zone
PO Box 25960
Dubai, United Arab Emirates   Ph: 971 42995300
Publication E-mail: ronjana@meed-dubai.com

Periodical covering business and economic news in the Middle East. **Subtitle:** Middle East Economic Digest. **Founded:** 1957. **Freq:** Weekly. **Key Personnel:** Richard Baker, Contact, richard@meed-dubai.com. **URL:** http://www.meed.com/nav?page=meed.
                                       Circ: 60,000

1716 Mobile Executive
The Information & Technology Publishing Co. Ltd.
PO Box 500024
Dubai, United Arab Emirates   Ph: 971 42829996
Publication E-mail: mex@itp.net

Periodical featuring technology solutions for people on the move. **Freq:** Bimonthly. **Key Personnel:** Justin Etheridge, Editor, justin.etheridge@itp.net. **Remarks:** Advertising accepted; rates available upon request. **URL:** http://www.itp.net/corporate/current/97479188512267.htm.
                                       Circ: (Not Reported)

1717 Money Works Magazine
Rasalmal Financial Publishing FZ-LLC
PO Box 10656
Dubai, United Arab Emirates   Ph: 971 43912160
Publication E-mail: info@getyourmoneyworking.com

Personal finance magazine. **Subtitle:** The UAE's First Money Magazine. **Founded:** 1998. **Key Personnel:** Wendy Jackson, Deputy Editor. **URL:** http://www.iirgulf.com/e-bank/sponsors.htm.
                                       Circ: 10,000

1718 Network Middle East
The Information & Technology Publishing Co. Ltd.
PO Box 500024
Dubai, United Arab Emirates   Ph: 971 42829996
Publication E-mail: nme@itp.net

Magazine for network professionals. **Key Personnel:** Zoe Moleshead, Editor, Zoe.Moleshead@itp.net. **Subscription Rates:** Free; 365 Dh other countries. **Remarks:** Advertising accepted; rates available upon request. **URL:** http://www.itp.net/corporate/media/nme.htm.
                                       Circ: (Not Reported)

1719 PC Magazine Middle & Near East
Dabbagh Information Technology
PO Box 60934
Dubai, United Arab Emirates   Ph: 971 42240500

Information technology and business publication. **Subtitle:** The Middle East's First Guide to Technology. **Key Personnel:** Gia Marie Lacuna, Managing Editor, jennifer@ditnet.co.ae. **URL:** http://www.pcmag-mideast.com.
Ad Rates: BW: US$3,500   **Circ:** 4,870

◫ **1720 Photography Middle East**
The Information & Technology Publishing Co. Ltd.
PO Box 500024
Dubai, United Arab Emirates   Ph: 971 42829996
Publication E-mail: photography@itp.net

Magazine covering photography. **Key Personnel:** Kieran Potts, Editor, kieran.potts@itp.net. **Subscription Rates:** 80 Dh; 275 Dh other countries. **Remarks:** Advertising accepted; rates available upon request. **URL:** http://www.itp.net/corporate/media/photography.htm.
     Circ: (Not Reported)

◫ **1721 RaceWeek**
Gray Business Communications
PO Box 7260
Dubai, United Arab Emirates   Ph: 971 43499007
Publication E-mail: info@raceweek.co.uk

Reports information about horse sports and related industries in the Gulf. **Founded:** 1994. **Freq:** Biweekly. **Key Personnel:** Kirstie Hepburn, Editor, editorial@raceweek.co.uk. **URL:** http://www.raceweek.co.uk/access/raceweekcouk/raceweek.html.
Ad Rates: BW: US$2850   **Circ:** Controlled 3,840

◫ **1722 Time Out Dubai**
The Information & Technology Publishing Co. Ltd.
PO Box 500024
Dubai, United Arab Emirates   Ph: 971 42829996
Publication E-mail: sallyann.casciani@itp.net

General interest magazine. **Freq:** Monthly. **Key Personnel:** Steve Lee, Contact, steve.lee@itp.net. **Remarks:** Advertising accepted; rates available upon request. **URL:** http://www.timeoutdubai.com.
     Circ: (Not Reported)

◫ **1723 UPDATE Magazine**
Dubai Port and Jebel Ali Free Zone Authorities
PO Box 17000
Dubai, United Arab Emirates   Ph: 971 48815000
Publication E-mail: mktg@dpa.co.ae

Periodical containing information regarding Dubai port authorities. **Freq:** Monthly. **URL:** http://sids.com/update.

◫ **1724 The Weekend Magazine**
Galadari Printing and Publishing LLC
PO Box 3082
Dubai, United Arab Emirates   Ph: 971 43382400

Entertainment magazine. **Freq:** Weekly (Fri.). **Key Personnel:** Patrick Michael, Editor, ktwkd@emirates.net.ae.

◫ **1725 What's On**
Motivate Publishing
PO Box 2331
Dubai, United Arab Emirates   Ph: 971 42824060
     Fax: 971 42824436
Publication E-mail: motivate@emirates.net.ae
Publisher E-mail: executive@motivate.co.ae

Leisure magazine for the Gulf. **URL:** http://www.motivatepublishing.com/files/whatson.html.
Ad Rates: 4C: 10,000 Dh   **Circ:** (Not Reported)

◫ **1726 Windows Middle East**
The Information & Technology Publishing Co. Ltd.
PO Box 500024
Dubai, United Arab Emirates   Ph: 971 42829996
Publication E-mail: windows@itp.net

English-language IT magazine for the Middle East. **Key Personnel:** Graham Stacey, Editor, graham.stacey@itp.net. **Subscription Rates:** 135 Dh; 365 Dh other countries. **Remarks:** Advertising accepted; rates available upon request. **URL:** http://www.itp.net/corporate/current/97479350451128.htm.
     Circ: (Not Reported)

◫ **1727 Windows Southern Africa**
The Information & Technology Publishing Co. Ltd.
PO Box 500024
Dubai, United Arab Emirates   Ph: 971 42829996

Publication targeting small, medium and micro-enterprises (SMMEs). Features a mix of news, features, reviews, workshops and a wealth of other information relevant to the SMME market. **Subscription Rates:** 70 Dh; 365 Dh other countries. **Remarks:** Advertising accepted; rates available upon request.
     Circ: (Not Reported)

◫ **1728 Young Times**
Galadari Printing and Publishing LLC
PO Box 3082
Dubai, United Arab Emirates   Ph: 971 43382400
Publication E-mail: feedback@youngtimes.com

Magazine covering youth interests. **Freq:** Weekly (Tues.). **URL:** http://www.youngtimes.co.ae/index.html.

SHARJAH

◫ **1729 TeenzSpot.com**
Hussain Najmuddin Tinwala
PO Box 243
Sharjah, United Arab Emirates
Publication E-mail: theteam@teenzspot.com

Online magazine for teens. **Subtitle:** The Leading Teen Magazine. **URL:** http://www.teenzspot.com.

UNITED KINGDOM

ABERYSTWYTH

◫ **1730 Reformation**
Ashgate Publishing Ltd.
c/o Professor Andrew Hadfield
Department of English
University of Wales, Aberystwyth
Hugh Owne Bldg.
Aberystwyth SY23 3DY, United Kingdom
Publisher E-mail: info@gowerpub.com

Scholarly journal covering the Reformation era. **Freq:** Annual. **Key Personnel:** Prof. Andrew Hadfield, Editor; Nicky Staszkiewicz, Subscriptions, phone 44 1252 351804, fax 44 1252 351839, nstaszkiewicz@ashgatepub.co.uk. **ISSN:** 1357-4175. **URL:** http://www.ashgate.com/subject_area/history/reformation.htm.

◫ **1731 Y Ddolen**
CILIP Cymru/Wales
DILS
Llanbadarn Fawr   Ph: 44 1970622174
Aberystwyth SY23 3AS, United Kingdom   Fax: 44 1970622190

Professional journal covering libraries and librarianship in Wales. **Subtitle:** Supplement to Update. **Freq:** 3/year. **Trim Size:** A4. **Key Personnel:** H. Evans, Exec. Officer, hle@aber.ac.uk. **ISSN:** 0261-3557. **Subscription Rates:** Free to qualified subscribers. **Remarks:** Accepts advertising. **URL:** http://www.dil.aber.ac.uk/holi/pdf/ddolen.pdf.
     Circ: Non-paid ‡1,500

ABINGDON

◫ **1732 Distance Education**
Carfax Publishing Ltd.
PO Box 25   Ph: 44 2078422344
Abingdon OX14 3UE, United Kingdom   Fax: 44 2088422134
Publication E-mail: distance-education@unimelb.edu.au

Journal covering research and other topics in distance education. **Subtitle:** An International Journal. **Key Personnel:** Dr. Som Naidu, Editor, s.naidu@unimelb.edu.au. **ISSN:** 0158-7919. **Subscription Rates:** US$164 institutions; US$53 individuals.

ALDERSHOT

1733 Alexandria
Ashgate Publishing Ltd.
Gower House
Croft Rd.   Ph: 44 1252331551
Aldershot GU11 3HR, United Kingdom   Fax: 44 1252344405
Publisher E-mail: info@gowerpub.com

Professional journal covering library and information issues worldwide. **Freq:** Triennial. **Key Personnel:** Maurice Line, Editor; Nicky Staszkiewicz, Subscriptions, phone 44 1252 351804, fax 44 1252 351839, nstaszkiewicz@ashgatepub.co.uk. **ISSN:** 0955-7490. **URL:** http://www.ashgate.com.

1734 Crusades
Ashgate Publishing Ltd.
Gower House
Croft Rd.   Ph: 44 1252331551
Aldershot GU11 3HR, United Kingdom   Fax: 44 1252344405
Publisher E-mail: info@gowerpub.com

Scholarly journal covering the crusades from the First Crusade (1095-1102) to the fall of Malta (1798). **Key Personnel:** Prof. B. Z. Kedar, Editor; Prof. J. S. C. Riley-Smith, Editor; Dr. Helen Nicholson, Assoc. Editor; Nicky Staszkiewicz, Subscriptions, phone 44 1252 351804, fax 44 1252 351839, nstaszkiewicz@ashgatepub.co.uk. **ISSN:** 1476-5276. **URL:** http://www.ashgate.com/subject_area/history/history_page.htm.

1735 The Design Journal
Ashgate Publishing Ltd.
Gower House
Croft Rd.   Ph: 44 1252331551
Aldershot GU11 3HR, United Kingdom   Fax: 44 1252344405
Publisher E-mail: info@gowerpub.com

Journal covering all aspects of design practice, theory, management and education for all design professionals worldwide. **Freq:** Triennial. **Key Personnel:** Prof. Rachel Cooper, Editorial Chair; Jack Ingram, Exec. Editor; Nicky Staszkiewicz, Subscriptions, phone 44 1252 351804, fax 44 1252 351839, nstaszkiewicz@ashgatepub.co.uk. **ISSN:** 1460-6965. **URL:** http://www.ashgate.com.

1736 The European Yearbook of Business History
Ashgate Publishing Ltd.
Gower House
Croft Rd.   Ph: 44 1252331551
Aldershot GU11 3HR, United Kingdom   Fax: 44 1252344405
Publisher E-mail: info@gowerpub.com

Scholarly journal covering business history in Europe. **Freq:** Annual. **Key Personnel:** Wilfred Feldenkirchen, Editor; Terry Gourvish, Editor; Nicky Staszkiewicz, Subscriptions, phone 44 1252 351804, fax 44 1252 351839, nstaszkiewicz@ashgatepub.co.uk. **ISSN:** 1462-186X. **URL:** http://www.ashgate.com.

1737 Human Factors and Aerospace Safety
Ashgate Publishing Ltd.
Gower House
Croft Rd.   Ph: 44 1252331551
Aldershot GU11 3HR, United Kingdom   Fax: 44 1252344405
Publisher E-mail: info@gowerpub.com

Journal covering the study of the human element in the aerospace system and its role either avoiding or contributing to accidents and incidents, and promoting safe operations worldwide. **Freq:** Quarterly. **Key Personnel:** Don Harris, Editor-in-Chief; Helen C. Muir, Editor-in-Chief; Charles Billings, Assoc. Editor; R. Curtis Graeber, Assoc. Editor; Peter Jorna, Assoc. Editor; Rob Lee, Assoc. Editor; John Ernsting, Assoc. Editor; Nicky Staszkiewicz, Subscriptions, phone 44 1252 351804, fax 44 1252 351839, nstaszkiewicz@ashgatepub.co.uk. **ISSN:** 1468-9456. **Subscription Rates:** US$175 institutions; US$74.95 individuals. **URL:** http://www.ashgate.com.

1738 Journals in Art and Architectural History
Ashgate Publishing Ltd.
Gower House
Croft Rd.   Ph: 44 1252331551
Aldershot GU11 3HR, United Kingdom   Fax: 44 1252344405
Publisher E-mail: info@gowerpub.com

Scholarly journal covering art, architecture, design, film, photography and the performing arts in the U.K. **Founded:** 2000. **Freq:** Semiannual. **Key Personnel:** Ysanne Holt, Editor; Paul Barlow, Reviews Editor; Nicky Staszkiewicz, Subscriptions, phone 44 1252 351804, fax 44 1252 351839, nstaszkiewicz@ashgatepub.co.uk. **ISSN:** 1471-4787. **Subscription Rates:** £30 institutions; £15 individuals. **URL:** http://www.ashgate.com/.

1739 The Shakespearean International Yearbook
Ashgate Publishing Ltd.
Gower House
Croft Rd.   Ph: 44 1252331551
Aldershot GU11 3HR, United Kingdom   Fax: 44 1252344405
Publisher E-mail: info@gowerpub.com

Scholarly journal covering Shakespearean studies. **Freq:** Annual. **Key Personnel:** W. R. Elton, Editor; Nicky Staszkiewicz, Subscriptions, phone 44 1252 351804, fax 44 1252 351839, nstaszkiewicz@ashgatepub.co.uk. **ISSN:** 1465-6098. **URL:** http://www.ashgate.com.

BATH

1740 Tools and Trades
Tool and Trades History Society
Barrow Mead Cottage
Rush Hill   Ph: 44 225837031
Bath BA2 2QP, United Kingdom   Fax: 44 225835470
Publisher E-mail: taths@reestools.co.uk

Publication covering tools and trades. **Founded:** 1984. **Freq:** Every 18 months. **Trim Size:** 200 x 250 cm. **Subscription Rates:** Included in membership; £15 nonmembers plus p&p. **Remarks:** Advertising not accepted.

                                                 Circ: (Not Reported)

BRADFORD

1741 Journal of Documentation
Emerald
60/62 Toller Ln.   Ph: 44 1274777700
Bradford BD8 9BY, United Kingdom   Fax: 44 1274785200
Publisher E-mail: editorial@emeraldinsight.com

Journal covering information management. **Founded:** 1944. **Freq:** Quarterly. **ISSN:** 0022-0418. **Remarks:** Advertising not accepted. **URL:** http://www.emeraldinsight.com.

                                                 Circ: (Not Reported)

1742 Records Management Journal
Emerald
60/62 Toller Ln.   Ph: 44 1274777700
Bradford BD8 9BY, United Kingdom   Fax: 44 1274785200
Publisher E-mail: editorial@emeraldinsight.com

Scholarly journal covering records management worldwide. **Founded:** 1989. **Freq:** Triennial. **Cols./Page:** 1. **Key Personnel:** Catherine Hare, Editor, catherine.hare@northumbria.ac.uk; Dr. Julie McLeod, Editor, julie.mcleod@northumbria.ac.uk. **ISSN:** 0956-5698. **Subscription Rates:** £69 individuals. **Remarks:** Accepts advertising. **URL:** http://www.emeraldinsight.com.

                                                 Circ: (Not Reported)

Ad Rates: GLR = general line rate; BW = one-time black & white page rate; 4C = one-time four color page rate; SAU = standard advertising unit rate; CNU = Canadian newspaper advertising unit rate; PCI = per column inch rate.
Circulation: ★ = ABC; △ = BPA; ♦ = CAC; • = CCAB; ❑ = VAC; ⊕ = PO Statement; ‡ = Publisher's Report; Boldface figures = sworn; Light figures = estimated.
Entry type: ❑ = Print; ♣ = Broadcast.

151

BRIGHTON

□ 1743 Journal of Ethnic and Migration Studies (JEMS)
Carfax Publishing
Sussex Centre for Migration Research
School of European Studies
University of Sussex
Falmer   Ph: 44 1273877778
Brighton BN1 9SH, United Kingdom   Fax: 44 1273623246
Publication E-mail: jems@sussex.ac.uk
Publisher E-mail: enquiries@tandf.co.uk

Journal covering the migration and ethnic studies. **Founded:** 1971. **Freq:** Quarterly. **Key Personnel:** Russell King, Editor; Richard R.D. Bedford, Assoc. Editor; Adrian Favell, Assoc. Editor; Jenny Money, Editorial Mgr. **ISSN:** 1369-183X. **Subscription Rates:** £49 individuals; £251 institutions. **Online:** Gale Group. **URL:** http://www.cemes.org/jems.htm. **Former name:** New Community.

□ 1744 The Law Teacher
Brighton Business School
University of Brighton
Lewes Road   Ph: 44 1273 642174
Brighton BN2 4AT, United Kingdom   Fax: 44 1273 642980

Publication covering legal education. **Freq:** 3/year. **ISSN:** 0303-9400. **Subscription Rates:** £35; £18 single issue. **Remarks:** Advertising accepted; rates available upon request.
                               Circ: (Not Reported)

BRISTOL

□ 1745 Journal of Physics A: Mathematical and General
Institute of Physics Publishing Ltd.
Dirac House
Temple Back   Ph: 44 1179297481
Bristol BS1 6BE, United Kingdom   Fax: 44 1179294318
Publication E-mail: jphysa@iop.org
Publisher E-mail: physics@iop.org

Journal covering physics and mathematics. **Founded:** Jan. 1968. **Freq:** Weekly. **Print Method:** Litho. **Trim Size:** 171 x 248 mm. **Key Personnel:** Neil Scriven, Contact, phone 44 1179301079, neil.scriven@iop.org. **Subscription Rates:** US$5,690. **Remarks:** Advertising accepted; rates available upon request. **URL:** http://www.iop.org/Journals/jphysa.
                               Circ: (Not Reported)

CAMBRIDGE

□ 1746 Scottish Journal of Theology
Cambridge University Press
The Edinburgh Bldg.
Shaftesbury Rd.   Ph: 44 1223312393
Cambridge CB2 2RU, United Kingdom   Fax: 44 1223315052
Publisher E-mail: journals@cambridge.org

Scholarly journal covering historical and systematic theology and bible study. **Freq:** Quarterly. **Key Personnel:** Iain R. Torrance, Editor; Bryan D. Spinks, Editor. **ISSN:** 0036-9306. **Subscription Rates:** £97 institutions electronic; £108 institutions print and electronic. **Remarks:** Advertising accepted; rates available upon request. **Available Online.**
                               Circ: (Not Reported)

COVENTRY

□ 1747 The British Journal of Religious Education
Christian Education Publications
c/o Prof. Robert Jackson
Institute of Education
University of Warwick   Ph: 44 2476523190
Coventry CV4 7AL, United Kingdom   Fax: 44 2476524110
Publication E-mail: r.jackson@warwick.ac.uk
Publisher E-mail: cem@cem.org.uk

Scholarly journal covering religious education. **Founded:** 1975. **Freq:** Triennial. **Key Personnel:** Mary Hayward, Contact, phone 44 1904707130, m.hayward@leeds.ac.uk. **ISSN:** 0141-6200. **Subscription Rates:** £37 individuals. **Remarks:** Advertising not accepted.
                               Circ: Paid 2,000

□ 1748 The Organic Way
Henry Doubleday Research Association
Ryton-on-Dunsmore   Ph: 44 2476303517
Coventry CV8 3LG, United Kingdom   Fax: 44 2476639229
Publisher E-mail: enquiry@hdra.org.co.uk

Members only journal covering organic farming, gardening, and food. **Freq:** Quarterly. **Print Method:** Web offset. **Trim Size:** 292 x 191 mm. **Key Personnel:** Judy Steele, Contact, phone 44 2476308231, jsteele@hdra.org.uk. **Remarks:** Accepts advertising. **Available Online.** **Alt. Formats:** Audio tape. **Formerly:** Growing Organically.
Ad Rates: BW: £570   **Circ:** 30,400
               4C: £825

DERBY

□ 1749 Mathematics Teaching
Association of Teachers of Mathematics
7 Shaftesbury St.   Ph: 44 1332346599
Derby DE23 8YB, United Kingdom   Fax: 44 1332204357
Publisher E-mail: admin@atm.org.uk

Publication covering mathematics. **Founded:** 1955. **Freq:** Quarterly. **Print Method:** Offset litho. **Trim Size:** 286 x 210. **Key Personnel:** Helen Williams, Editor, helenwilliams@atm.org; Geoff Dunn, Editor, geoffdunn@atm.org; Robin Stewart, Editor, robinstewart@atm.org. **ISSN:** 0025-5785. **Subscription Rates:** £49 individuals membership; £67 institutions membership; £19.50 students membership; £37 newly qualified teachers, membership.
Ad Rates: BW: £290   **Circ:** (Not Reported)
               4C: £475

□ 1750 RE Today
Christian Education Publications
RE Today Services
Royal Buildings
Victoria St.
Derby DE1 1GW, United Kingdom
Publication E-mail: director@christianeducation.org.uk
Publisher E-mail: cem@cem.org.uk

Professional magazine for teachers of religious education in the UK. **Founded:** 1984. **Freq:** Triennial. **ISSN:** 0266-7738. **Subscription Rates:** £27 individuals. **Remarks:** Accepts advertising.
Ad Rates: BW: £624   **Circ:** Paid 7,000
               4C: £686.40

DEREHAM

□ 1751 Journal of the Cheirological Society
Cheirological Society
29 London Rd.   Ph: 44 1362693962
Dereham NR19 1AS, United Kingdom   Fax: 44 1362693962

Journal covering palm reading. **Founded:** 1889. **Freq:** Quarterly. **Print Method:** Litho. **Trim Size:** A4. **Key Personnel:** Elizabeth Hertzog, Contact, liz@hertzog.idps.co.uk. **Subscription Rates:** Included in membership. **Remarks:** Advertising not accepted.
                               Circ: (Not Reported)

DESBOROUGH

□ 1752 The Powys Review
Beeches House
Harborough Rd.   Ph: 44 1536 763916
Desborough NN14 2QX, United Kingdom   Fax: 44 1536 763916

Literary journal covering the works of John C. Powys, T. F. Powys and Llewelyn Powys, and English literature from the 1890s to the 1960s. **Founded:** 1977. **Freq:** Annual. **Trim Size:** 9 x 25 cm. **Cols./Page:** 2. **Col. Width:** 7 centimeters. **Col. Depth:** 21.5 centimeters. **Key Personnel:** Belinda Humfrey, Editor, belinda.humfrey@talk21.com. **ISSN:** 0309-1619. **Subscription Rates:** £8 individuals. **Remarks:** Accepts advertising.
                               Circ: Controlled 620

EDINBURGH

1753 Forestry and Timber News
Forestry and Timber Association
5 Dublin St. Lane South
Edinburgh EH1 3PX, United Kingdom Ph: 44 1315387111
            Fax: 44 1315387222
Publication E-mail: ftn@forestryandtimber.org
Publisher E-mail: info@forestryandtimber.org

Publication covering forestry and Association news. **Founded:** Mar. 2002. **Freq:** Quarterly. **ISSN:** 1476-8615. **Subscription Rates:** £18 individuals. **Remarks:** Advertising accepted; rates available upon request. **Formed by the merger of:** Timber Grower; APF News.

            Circ: ⊕3,500

EPSOM

1754 Dental Practice
A. E. Morgan Publications Ltd.
Stanley House
9 West St.   Ph: 44 1372741411
Epsom KT18 7RL, United Kingdom Fax: 44 1372744493
Publisher E-mail: t.morgan@easynet.co.uk

Trade magazine for dentists. **Subtitle:** The Journal for the Dental Team. **Founded:** 1962. **Freq:** Monthly. **Print Method:** Web offset. **Trim Size:** 285 x 405 mm. **Key Personnel:** Stephen Tidman, Contact. **Subscription Rates:** £40 surface mail; £44 letter rate; £60 airmail rate, others; £90 letter rate, others. **Remarks:** Accepts advertising.

Ad Rates: GLR: £11.30   **Circ:** Controlled 18,500
     BW: £1,300
     4C: £1,530
     PCI: £11.30

HEMEL HEMPSTEAD

1755 New Specialist Angler
Specialist Anglers Alliance
41 Crofts Path
Hemel Hempstead HP3 8HB, United Ph: 44 1442398022
 Kingdom   Fax: 44 1442398044
Publication E-mail: editor@saauk.org
Publisher E-mail: secretary@saauk.org

Publication covering fishing. **Freq:** Periodic. **Subscription Rates:** Included in membership. **Remarks:** Advertising accepted; rates available upon request. **Formerly:** Specialist Angler.

          Circ: (Not Reported)

HITCHIN

1756 Milk Industry
Dairy Industry Association Ltd.
59 Coleridge Close
Hitchin SG4 0QX, United Kingdom Ph: 44 1462457813
           Fax: 44 1462457815
Publication E-mail: milkindustry@aol.com
Publisher E-mail: info@dia-ltd.org.uk

Publication covering the worldwide milk industry. **Freq:** Monthly. **Print Method:** Litho. **Trim Size:** A4. **Key Personnel:** Geoff Platt, Editor. **Subscription Rates:** £75; £5 single issue. **Remarks:** Accepts advertising. **Formerly:** Milk Industry International.

Ad Rates: BW: £800   **Circ:** Combined 3,000
     4C: £1,350

KEMPSTON

1757 Investment Now
70 Singer Way   Ph: 44 1234843905
Kempston MK42 7PU, United Kingdom Fax: 44 1234843901
Publication E-mail: inedit@aol.com

Journal covering economic development issues in the U.K. and worldwide. **Remarks:** Accepts advertising.

Ad Rates: BW: £2,055   **Circ:** Combined 70,000
     4C: £2,550

KENILWORTH

1758 Multi-Skills
The Academy of Multi-Skills
Warwick Corner
42 Warwick Rd.   Ph: 44 1926855498
Kenilworth CV8 1HE, United Kingdom Fax: 44 1926513100

Professional journal of the Academy of the Multi-Skills. **ISSN:** 1359-9755. **Subscription Rates:** Free to qualified subscribers; £7 nonmembers.

KIDLINGTON

1759 Complementary Therapies in Medicine
Elsevier Science Ltd.
The Boulevard
Langford Ln.   Ph: 44 1865843000
Kidlington OX5 1GB, United Kingdom Fax: 44 1865843010

Health publication. **Freq:** Quarterly. **Key Personnel:** Rebecca Scott, Publishing Editor, phone 44 1865843824, fax 44 1865843997, R.Scott@elsevier.co.uk. **ISSN:** 0965-2299. **Subscription Rates:** £64 individuals; £164 institutions; £52 trainees; £52 members The British Holistic Medical Association. **Online:** Gale Group.

1760 Journal of Adolescence
Elsevier Science Ltd.
The Boulevard
Langford Ln.   Ph: 44 1865843000
Kidlington OX5 1GB, United Kingdom Fax: 44 1865843010

Publication covering adolescent psychology and mental health. **Founded:** 1978. **Freq:** Quarterly. **ISSN:** 0140-1971. **Subscription Rates:** £275 institutions. **Online:** Science Direct. **URL:** http://www.sciencedirect.com.

LEEDS

1761 Faster Higher Stronger
Sports Coach UK
114 Cardigan Rd.
Headingley
Leeds LS6 3BJ, United Kingdom Ph: 44 1132744802
           Fax: 44 1132755019
Publication E-mail: fhs@sportscoachuk.org
Publisher E-mail: coaching@sportscoachuk.org

Publication covering coaching. **Freq:** Quarterly. **ISSN:** 1464-4495. **Subscription Rates:** £15. **Remarks:** Advertising accepted; rates available upon request.

           Circ: 10,000

LEICESTER

1762 The Journal of Infection
British Infection Society
Dept. of Infection and Tropical Medicine
Leicester Royal Infirmary
Leicester LE1 SWW, United Kingdom Ph: 44 116 257 3952
          Fax: 44 116 258 5067
Publisher E-mail: martin.wiselka@uhl-tr.nhs.uk

Professional journal covering epidemiology and infection. **Freq:** Bimonthly. **Remarks:** Advertising accepted; rates available upon request.

          Circ: (Not Reported)

LONDON

📖 **1763 e-Health Business**
Informa Pharmaceuticals
Mortimer House
37-41 Mortimer St.   Ph: 44 2074535467
London W1T 3JH, United Kingdom   Fax: 44 2074532384
Publication E-mail: enquiries@informapharma.com
Publisher E-mail: enquiries@informapharma.com

Trade publication covering the consumer health care industry worldwide. **Subtitle:** News, Analysis and Marketing Insight for Global e-Health Developments. **Founded:** 2001. **Freq:** Monthly. **Trim Size:** 210 x 297 mm. **Cols./Page:** 3. **Key Personnel:** Sarah Walkley, Editor, phone 44 207453 5467, fax 44 207453 2384, sarah.walkley@informa.com. **Subscription Rates:** £325 individuals; £585 two years. **Remarks:** Accepts advertising.
Circ: (Not Reported)

📖 **1764 Elements**
The Environment Council
212 High Holborn   Ph: 44 2078362626
London WC1V 7BF, United Kingdom Fax: 44 2072421180
Publication E-mail: publications@envcouncil.org.uk
Publisher E-mail: info@envcouncil.org.uk

Publication covering environmental decision making. **Subtitle:** For Environmental Decisions. **Founded:** Oct. 2000. **Freq:** Bimonthly. **ISSN:** 1472-815X. **Remarks:** Accepts advertising.
Circ: Combined 2,200

📖 **1765 European Voice**
The Economist Group
15 Regent St.   Ph: 44 2075638900
London SW1Y 4LR, United Kingdom Fax: 44 2075638913

Newspaper covering European issues. **Freq:** Weekly. **URL:** http://www.european-voice.com.

📖 **1766 Family Law Journal**
Legalese Ltd.
28-33 Cato St.   Ph: 44 2073969313
London W1H 5HS, United Kingdom   Fax: 44 2073969302

Professional magazine covering family law, including adoption, children, child support, death, legal aid, mediation, pensions, public law, and practice and procedure. **Freq:** Monthly. **Key Personnel:** Laura Morrison, Editor; Claire Bostock, Advertising; Marie Kraus, Subscriptions. **Subscription Rates:** £120 individuals. **Remarks:** Accepts advertising. **URL:** http://www.legalease.co.uk/law_jour_fl.htm.
Circ: (Not Reported)

📖 **1767 Flying Angel News**
The Mission to Seafarers
St. Michael Paternoster Royal
College Hill   Ph: 44 2072485202
London EC4R 2RL, United Kingdom Fax: 44 2072484761
Publication E-mail: pr@missiontoseafarers.org
Publisher E-mail: general@missiontoseafarers.org

Newspaper covering seafarers. **Founded:** 1958. **Freq:** Quarterly. **Key Personnel:** Gillian Ennis, Editor, gillian@missiontoseafarers.org. **Subscription Rates:** £2. **Remarks:** Advertising not accepted.
Circ: 18,800

📖 **1768 Health Policy and Planning**
Oxford University Press
Department of Public Health and Policy
London School of Hygiene and Tropical
  Medicine
Keppel St.
London WC1E 7HT, United Kingdom
Publisher E-mail: enquiries@oup.co.uk

Professional journal covering health care issues. **Freq:** Quarterly. **Key Personnel:** Kara Hanson, Editor; Ruairi Brugha, Editor. **ISSN:** 0268-1080. **Subscription Rates:** £75 individuals; £175 institutions; £155 institutions online only; £88 institutions developing countries; £50 institutions developing countries; online only; £36 students. **URL:** http://www3.oup.co.uk/jnls/list/heapol/scope.

📖 **1769 Journal of Common Market Studies**
Blackwell Publishers Ltd
c/o University Association for Contemporary
  European Studies
King's College
Strand
London WC2R 2LS, United Kingdom

International business publication covering integration issues related to the politics and economics of the European Union. Annual subscription includes The European Union: Annual Review. **Founded:** 1962. **Freq:** 5/year. **Key Personnel:** Iain Begg, Editor, phone 44 2078158279, fax 44 2078158277, iain.begg@sbu.acu.uk; John Peterson, Editor, phone 44 1413303895, fax 44 1413305071, jcms@gla.ac.uk. **ISSN:** 0021-9886. **Subscription Rates:** £321 institutions Europe; £161 institutions Eastern Europe; £557 institutions The Americas; £387 institutions elsewhere; £91 individuals Europe/Eastern Europe; £158 individuals The Americas; £110 individuals elsewhere. **Remarks:** Accepts advertising. **Online:** Gale Group.
Ad Rates: BW: £275   **Circ:** (Not Reported)

📖 **1770 Journal of Pathology**
John Wiley & Sons Ltd.
2 Carlton House Terrace   Ph: 44 209304315
London SW1Y 5AF, United Kingdom   Fax: 44 209761267
Publisher E-mail: cs-journals@wiley.co.uk

Professional journal covering pathology. **Founded:** 1892. **Freq:** Monthly. **Key Personnel:** Jeremy Theobald, Managing Editor, managing_editor@jpathol.org. **ISSN:** 0022-3417. **Remarks:** Accepts advertising. **Available Online.**
Circ: (Not Reported)

📖 **1771 Lex**
Legalese Ltd.
28-33 Cato St.   Ph: 44 2073969313
London W1H 5HS, United Kingdom   Fax: 44 2073969302

Magazine covering the legal profession for students in the UK's leading law faculties. **Freq:** Triennial. **Key Personnel:** Mathew Lyons, Editor, mathew.lyons@legalease.co.uk; Laura Marsh, Reporter, laura.marsh@legalease.co.uk; Felicity Williams, Reporter, felicity.williams@legalease.co.uk; Johnathan Briggs, Production Mgr., jonathan.briggs@legalease.co.uk; Aine Kelly, Sr. Sub-Editor, aine.kelly@legalease.co.uk; Nick Hayes, Advertising, nick.hayes@legalease.co.uk. **Subscription Rates:** £22.50 individuals. **Remarks:** Accepts advertising. **URL:** http://www.lexonthenet.com.
Circ: (Not Reported)

📖 **1772 London Bulletin**
Association of London Government
59 1/2 Southwark St.   Ph: 44 2079349761
London SE1 0AL, United Kingdom   Fax: 44 2079349769
Publisher E-mail: reception@alg.gov.uk

Corporate magazine covering municipal government. **Subtitle:** The Magazine for London Local Government. **Founded:** June 2000. **Freq:** Bimonthly. **Key Personnel:** Lucy Shubbs, Contact, lucy.shubbs.alg.gov.uk; Julian Blake, Contact, julian.blake@alg.gov.uk. **Subscription Rates:** £30. **Remarks:** Advertising accepted; rates available upon request.
Circ: Combined 6,000

📖 **1773 London Housing**
Association of London Government
59 1/2 Southwark St.   Ph: 44 2079349761
London SE1 0AL, United Kingdom   Fax: 44 2079349769
Publisher E-mail: reception@alg.gov.uk

Trade magazine covering municipal government. **Subtitle:** News & Analysis of London's Social Housing. **Founded:** 1989. **Freq:** Bimonthly. **Key Personnel:** Lucy Shubbs, Contact, lucy.shubbs@alg.gov.uk; Julian Blake, Contact, julian.blake@alg.gov.uk. **Subscription Rates:** £24. **Remarks:** Advertising accepted; rates available upon request.
Circ: Combined 4,000

📖 **1774 Mezzo**
International Planned Parenthood Federation (IPPF)
Regent's College
Inner Circle
Regent's Park   Ph: 44 2074877900
London NW1 4NS, United Kingdom   Fax: 44 2074877950
Publisher E-mail: info@ippf.org

Magazine in English, Spanish and French covering health, sexual, and general interest issues for a youth audience worldwide. **Key Personnel:** Jessica Nott, Asst. Technical Officer, phone 02074877866, fax 02074877865, jnott@ippf.org; Kathryn Faulkner, Asst. Technical Officer, phone 02074877911, fax 02074877865, kfaulkner@ippf.org. **Subscription Rates:** Free. **Remarks:** Advertising not accepted.

                                          Circ: Non-paid 6,000

📖 **1775 Pulse**
CMP Information Ltd.
City Reach
5 Greenwich View Pl.
Millharbour   Ph: 44 2078616423
London E14 9NN, United Kingdom   Fax: 44 2078616256
Publication E-mail: pulse@cmpinformation.com

Medical newspaper for general practitioners in the UK. **Founded:** 1959. **Freq:** Weekly. **Trim Size:** 287 x 400 mm. **Col. Width:** 42 millimeters. **Col. Depth:** 377 millimeters. **Key Personnel:** Elisabeth Ravi, Publishing Dir., phone 44 02078616183, fax 44 02078616256, eravi@cmpinformation.com; Richard Purdy, Advertising, phone 44 02078616425, fax 44 02078616255. **Remarks:** Accepts advertising.

                                          Circ: Combined 42,175

📖 **1776 Survival**
Oxford University Press
IISS
Arundel House
13-25 Arundel St.
Temple Place
London WC2R 3DX, United Kingdom
Publisher E-mail: enquiries@oup.co.uk

Journal covering strategic and international studies, including military and security issues worldwide. **Freq:** Quarterly. **Key Personnel:** Dr. Dana Allin, Editor. **ISSN:** 0039-6338. **Subscription Rates:** £100 institutions; £90 institutions online only; £45 individuals; £27 students; senior citizens. **Available Online. URL:** http://www3.oup.co.uk/jnls/list/surviv/scope.

📖 **1777 Trusts & Estates Tax Journal**
Legalese Ltd.
28-33 Cato St.   Ph: 44 2073969313
London W1H 5HS, United Kingdom   Fax: 44 2073969302

Journal covering tax issues arising out of trusts, estates, wills and inheritance tax planning for practitioners. **Founded:** 1999. **Freq:** 10/year. **Key Personnel:** Sarah Horsfield, Editor; Claire Bostock, Advertising; Marie Kraus, Subscriptions. **Subscription Rates:** £144 individuals. **Remarks:** Accepts advertising. **URL:** http://www.legalease.co.uk/law_journ/jour_tj.htm.

                                          Circ: (Not Reported)

📖 **1778 Viewpoint**
Royal Mencap Society
123 Golden Ln.   Ph: 44 1714540454
London EC1Y 0RT, United Kingdom   Fax: 44 1716083254
Publisher E-mail: info@mencap.org.uk

Publication covering the mentally disabled. **Freq:** Monthly.

MANCHESTER

📖 **1779 Plane Talk**
Manchester Airport plc
Rm. 1023
First Fl., Olympic House
Manchester Airport   Ph: 44 1614892024
Manchester M90 1QX, United Kingdom   Fax: 44 1614892775
Publication E-mail: plane.talk@manairport.co.uk

Newspaper covering issues for airport employees and others. **Founded:** Nov. 1987. **Freq:** Monthly. **Print Method:** Web offset. **Trim Size:** 297 x 420 mm. **Cols./Page:** 6. **Col. Width:** 41 millimeters. **Col. Depth:** 400 millimeters. **Key Personnel:** Janice Bonner, Editor, phone 0161 489 3662, fax 0161 489 2775, j.bonner@manairport.co.uk; Linda Toy, Advertising Coord., phone 0161 489 2844, fax 0161 489 2775, asplane.talk@manairport.co.uk. **Subscription Rates:** £10 individuals. **Remarks:** Accepts advertising.
Ad Rates: GLR: £2   **Circ:** Controlled 12,000
                 BW: £700
                 4C: £820
                 PCI: £6

MIDDLESEX

📖 **1780 Veterinary Dermatology**
Blackwell Science Ltd.
2 Kempton Ct.
Kemton Ave.
Sunbury
Middlesex TW16 5PA, United Kingdom
Publisher E-mail: martine.cairou.keen@blacksci.co.uk

Journal covering all aspects of the skin of mammals, birds, reptiles, amphibians and fish. **Freq:** Bimonthly. **Key Personnel:** Ian Mason, Editor-in-Chief; Peter Hill, Editor; Karen Moriello, Editor. **ISSN:** 0959-4493. **Subscription Rates:** US$782 institutions The Americas, print & premium online; £468 institutions Europe, print & premium online; £515 institutions elsewhere, print & premium online; US$711 institutions The Americas, print & standard online; £425 institutions Europe, print & standard online; £468 institutions elsewhere, print & standard online; US$640 institutions The Americas, premium online only; £383 institutions Europe, premium online only; £421 institutions elsewhere, premium online only. **Remarks:** Accepts advertising. **Available Online. URL:** http://www.blackwellpublishing.com.
Ad Rates: BW: £477   **Circ:** (Not Reported)
                 4C: £1,197

MIDLOTHIAN

📖 **1781 Veterinary Anaesthesia and Analgesia**
Blackwell Science Ltd.
c/o Eddie Clutton
University of Edinburgh
Veterinary Field Station, Easter Bush
Roslin
Midlothian EH25 9RG, United Kingdom   Ph: 44 1316506220
Publisher E-mail: martine.cairou.keen@blacksci.co.uk

Journal covering all branches of anaesthesia and the pain relief in animals. **Freq:** Quarterly. **Key Personnel:** Eddie Clutton, Editor, eclutton@vet.ed.ac.uk; Peter J. Pascoe, Editor, phone 1 530 752 3151, fax 1 530 752 6042, pjpascoe@ucdavis.edu; Leslie Hall, Review Editor, phone 44 1223 262676, lwh2@cus.cam.ac.uk. **ISSN:** 1467-2987. **Subscription Rates:** US$341 institutions The Americas, print & premium online; £204 institutions Europe, print & premium online; £224 institutions elsewhere, print & premium online; US$310 institutions The Americas, print & standard online; £185 institutions Europe, print & standard online; £204 institutions elsewhere, print & standard online; US$279 institutions The Americas, premium online only; £167 institutions Europe, premium online only; £184 institutions elsewhere, premium online only. **Remarks:** Accepts advertising. **Available Online. URL:** http://www.blackwellpublishing.com.
Ad Rates: BW: £477   **Circ:** (Not Reported)
                 4C: £1,197

Ad Rates: GLR = general line rate; BW = one-time black & white page rate; 4C = one-time four color page rate; SAU = standard advertising unit rate; CNU = Canadian newspaper advertising unit rate; PCI = per column inch rate.
Circulation: ★ = ABC; △ = BPA; ♦ = CAC; ● = CCAB; ❑ = VAC; ⊕ = PO Statement; ‡ = Publisher's Report; Boldface figures = sworn; Light figures = estimated.
Entry type: 📖 = Print; 🎤 = Broadcast.

OLD WOKING

📖 **1782 The Stocktaker**
Institute of Licensed Trade Stock Auditors
Stockwell House
Kingfield Rd.   Ph: 44 1483770102
Old Woking GU22 9AB, United Kingdom   Fax: 44 1483770102
Publication E-mail: secretary@iltsa.co.uk
Publisher E-mail: iltsuk@aol.com

Publication covering finance. **Founded:** 1982. **Freq:** 12/year. **Key Personnel:** Trevor Perrott, Contact, trevor@iltsa.co.uk. **ISSN:** 1471-0471. **Subscription Rates:** £24. **Remarks:** Advertising accepted; rates available upon request.

Circ: 650

OXFORD

📖 **1783 Abacus**
Blackwell Publishers Ltd
108 Cowley Rd.   Ph: 44 1865791100
Oxford OX4 1JF, United Kingdom   Fax: 44 1865791347

Journal covering academic and professional aspects of accounting, finance and business. **Subtitle:** A Journal of Accounting, Finance and Business Studies. **Freq:** Triennial. **Key Personnel:** G. W. Dean, Editor, phone 61 29351 3107, fax 61 29351 6638, graeme@econ.usyd.edu.au. **ISSN:** 0001-3072. **Subscription Rates:** $A 303 institutions Australia & New Zealand, print & premium online; US$310 institutions The Americas, print & premium online; £193 institutions Europe, print & premium online; £216 institutions elsewhere, print & premium online; $A 275 institutions Australia & New Zealand, print & standard online; US$282 institutions The Americas, print & standard online; £175 institutions Europe, print & standard online; £196 institutions elsewhere, print & standard online; $A 248 institutions Australia & New Zealand, premium online only; US$254 institutions The Americas, premium online only. **Remarks:** Accepts advertising. **Available Online.** **URL:** http://www.blackwellpublishing.com.
Ad Rates: BW: £260   **Circ:** (Not Reported)

📖 **1784 Anatomical Science**
Blackwell Publishers Ltd
108 Cowley Rd.   Ph: 44 1865791100
Oxford OX4 1JF, United Kingdom   Fax: 44 1865791347

Official English journal of the Japanese Association of Anatomists covering the morphological sciences in animals and humans. **Freq:** Quarterly. **Key Personnel:** Tanemichi Chiba, Editor. **ISSN:** 0022-7722. **Subscription Rates:** 38,500¥ institutions Japan; print & premium online; US$259 institutions elsewhere; print & premium online; 35,000¥ institutions Japan; print & standard online; US$235 institutions elsewhere; print & standard online; 31,500¥ institutions Japan; premium online only; US$212 institutions elsewhere; premium online only. **Available Online.** **URL:** http://www.blackwellpublishing.

📖 **1785 Animal Science Journal**
Blackwell Publishers Ltd
108 Cowley Rd.   Ph: 44 1865791100
Oxford OX4 1JF, United Kingdom   Fax: 44 1865791347

Official journal of the Japanese Society of Animal Science covering all fields of animal and poultry science. **Freq:** Bimonthly. **Key Personnel:** Toshio Tanaka, Editor. **ISSN:** 1344-3941. **Remarks:** Accepts advertising. **Available Online.** **URL:** http://www.blackwellpublishing.com.
Circ: (Not Reported)

📖 **1786 APLAR Journal of Rheumatology**
Blackwell Publishers Ltd
108 Cowley Rd.   Ph: 44 1865791100
Oxford OX4 1JF, United Kingdom   Fax: 44 1865791347

Official journal of the Asia Pacific League of Associations for Rheumatology covering rheumatic diseases. **Freq:** Triennial. **Key Personnel:** Pao Hsii Feng, Editor. **ISSN:** 0219-0494. **Subscription Rates:** US$198 institutions print & premium online; US$180 institutions print & standard online; US$162 institutions premium online only; US$90 individuals. **Remarks:** Accepts advertising. **Available Online.** **URL:** http://www.blackwellpublishing.com.
Circ: (Not Reported)

📖 **1787 Australian Economic Review**
Blackwell Publishers Ltd
108 Cowley Rd.   Ph: 44 1865791100
Oxford OX4 1JF, United Kingdom   Fax: 44 1865791347

Publication covering economics. **Freq:** Quarterly. **ISSN:** 0004-9018. **Online:** Gale Group.

📖 **1788 The European Union**
Blackwell Publishers Ltd
108 Cowley Rd.   Ph: 44 1865791100
Oxford OX4 1JF, United Kingdom   Fax: 44 1865791347

Journal covering political, economic, and legal developments in the European Union and its Member States. Included in the annual subscription to the *Journal of Common Market Studies.*. **Freq:** Annual. **Trim Size:** 152 x 229 mm. **Key Personnel:** Geoffrey Edwards, Editor; Georg Wiessala, Editor. **Subscription Rates:** £15.99 single issue. **URL:** http://www.blackwellpublishing.com.

📖 **1789 The Japanese Economic Review**
Blackwell Publishers Ltd
108 Cowley Rd.   Ph: 44 1865791100
Oxford OX4 1JF, United Kingdom   Fax: 44 1865791347

Professional journal of the Japanese Economic Association. **Freq:** Quarterly. **Key Personnel:** Nobuhiro Kiyotaki, Editor; Makoto Yano, Editor; Shinichi Fukuda, Editor; Masanori Hasimoto, Editor; Akira Okada, Editor; Taku Yamamoto, Editor. **ISSN:** 1352-4739. **Subscription Rates:** US$62 individuals North & South America; £43 elsewhere; US$144 institutions North & South America; £100 elsewhere. **URL:** http://www.blackwellpublishers.co.uk/journals/jere. **Former name:** The Economic Studies Quarterly.

📖 **1790 Landscape Research**
Landscape Research Group
Oxford Brookes University
Gipsy Lane
Meadington   Ph: 44 1865 483950
Oxford OX3 0BP, United Kingdom   Fax: 44 1865 483937

Landscaping publication. **Freq:** 4/year. **Key Personnel:** P. Graham, Contact, pgraham@brookes.ac.uk. **Remarks:** Advertising accepted; rates available upon request. **URL:** http://www.landscaperesearch.org.uk.
Circ: (Not Reported)

📖 **1791 Psychology of Women Quarterly**
Blackwell Publishers Ltd
108 Cowley Rd.   Ph: 44 1865791100
Oxford OX4 1JF, United Kingdom   Fax: 44 1865791347

Publication covering psychology and mental health. **Freq:** Quarterly. **ISSN:** 0361-6843. **Online:** Gale Group.

READING

📖 **1792 Journal of Medical Microbiology**
Society for General Microbiology
Marlborough House
Basingstoke Rd.
Spencers Wood   Ph: 44 1189881800
Reading RG7 1AG, United Kingdom   Fax: 44 1189885656
Publication E-mail: jmm@sgm.ac.uk
Publisher E-mail: admin@sgm.ac.uk

Journal covering medical microbiology. **Freq:** Monthly. **Key Personnel:** Aidan Parte, Contact. **ISSN:** 0022-2615. **Remarks:** Advertising accepted; rates available upon request. **URL:** http://jmm.sgmjournals.org.
Circ: Paid 700

ST. ALBANS

📖 **1793 Journal of Chemical Research**
Science Reviews
PO Box 314   Ph: 44 1727 847322
St. Albans AL1 4ZG, United Kingdom   Fax: 44 1727 847323
Publication E-mail: jcr@scilet.com

Professional journal covering chemical research. **Freq:** Monthly.

SWANSEA

📖 **1794 The Journal of International Commercial Law**
Ashgate Publishing Ltd.
c/o Iwan Davies
Head of Department of Law
University of Wales
Singleton Park
Swansea SA2 8PP, United Kingdom
Publisher E-mail: info@gowerpub.com

Academic legal journal covering commerical law worldwide. **Founded:** 2002. **Freq:** Triennial. **Key Personnel:** Iwan Davies, Editor, i.r.davies@swansea.ac.uk; Rhidian Thomas, Asst. Editor; Nicky Staszkiewicz, Subscriptions, phone 44 1252 351804, fax 44 1252 351839, nstaszkiewicz@ashgatepub.co.uk. **ISSN:** 1476-7546. **URL:** http://www.ashgate.com/subject_area/law/law_journals.htm.

TELFORD

📖 **1795 The Sound Magazine**
Chatterbox Recording Club
Welland Stafford St.
St. Georges
Telford TF2 9DT, United Kingdom   Ph: 44 1952616410

Magazine on audio tape for club members. **Freq:** Quarterly. **URL:** http://www.btinternet.com/~phil.jones8/chatterbox2.htm. **Alt. Formats:** Audio tape.

TUNBRIDGE WELLS

📖 **1796 Transportation Professional**
Barrett, Byrd Associates
BBA Linden House
Linden Close
Tunbridge Wells TN4 8HH, United   Ph: 44 207387525
    Kingdom   Fax: 44 2073873808
Publication E-mail: info@transportation-mag.com
Publisher E-mail: info@iht.org

Trade publication covering transportation. **Freq:** 10/year. **Key Personnel:** Ty Byrd, phone 44 1892 524656. **Remarks:** Advertising accepted; rates available upon request. **Formerly:** Highways & Transportation (June 1902).
     Circ: (Not Reported)

WEYBRIDGE

📖 **1797 Glass's Guide to Used Vehicle Prices**
Glass's Information Services Ltd.
1 Princes Rd.   Ph: 44 1932823823
Weybridge KT13 9TU, United Kingdom   Fax: 44 1932846564
Publisher E-mail: customer@glass.co.uk

Trade magazine covering used vehicle values. **Founded:** 1933. **Freq:** Monthly. **Key Personnel:** David Wilde, Production Mgr., phone 44 01932823839, fax 44 01932849299, david.wilde@glass.co.uk; Lisa King, Marketing Mgr., phone 44 01932823814, fax 44 01932849299, lisa.king@glass.co.uk. **Subscription Rates:** £32 individuals. **Remarks:** Accepts advertising. **Alt. Formats:** CD-ROM.
     Circ: (Not Reported)

WINDSOR

📖 **1798 Songlines**
1 Leworth Pl.
Mellor Walk
Bachelors Acre   Ph: 44 1753865342
Windsor SL4 1EB, United Kingdom   Fax: 44 1753621547
Publication E-mail: info@songlines.co.uk

Consumer magazine covering world music. **Subtitle:** The World Music Magazine. **Freq:** Bimonthly. **Key Personnel:** Simon Broughton, Editor, editor@songlines.co.uk; Paul Geoghegan, Publisher/Adv. Mgr., paul@songlines.co.uk; Jo Frost, Asst. Editor, jo@songlines.co.uk; Nikki Hoffman, Subscription Mgr., subs@songlines.co.uk. **Subscription Rates:** £19

individuals; £25 out of country surface mail; £31 out of country airmail. **Remarks:** Accepts advertising. **URL:** http://www.songlines.co.uk.
     Circ: (Not Reported)

BRITISH VIRGIN ISLANDS

TORTOLA

📖 **1799 The Island Sun**
Sun Enterprises (BVI) Ltd.
PO Box 21
Road Town   Ph: (284)494-2476
Tortola, British Virgin Islands   Fax: (284)494-3510
Publication E-mail: issun@candwbvi.net

Community newspaper. **Founded:** 1962. **Freq:** Weekly (Sat.). **Print Method:** Litho offset. **Cols./Page:** 5. **Key Personnel:** Vernon Pickering, Editor; Peggy Carney, Advertising Mgr. **Subscription Rates:** US$55 British Virgin Islands; US$85 Caribbean, U.S., and Canada; US$65 U.S. Virgin Islands; US$95 UK; US$110 Europe, Asia, Africa, and Australia. **Remarks:** Accepts advertising. **URL:** http://www.islandsun.com.
Ad Rates: BW: US$300   **Circ:** Paid 3,300
          4C: US$795
          PCI: US$8

The Master Index is a comprehensive listing of all entries, both print and broadcast, included in this *Directory*. Citations in this index are interfiled alphabetically throughout regardless of media type. Publications are cited according to title and important keywords within titles; broadcast citations are by station call letters or cable company names. Indexed here also are: notices of recent cessations; former call letters or titles; foreign language and other alternate publication titles; other types of citations. Indexing is word-by-word rather than letter-by-letter, so that "New York" files before "News". Listings in the Master Index include geographic locations and entry numbers. An asterisk (*) after a number indicates that the title is mentioned within the text of the cited entry.

A

A & U (Tokyo, JPN) **780**
Abacus (Oxford, GBR) **1783**
Abdominal Imaging (New York, NY, USA) **153**
Abraham Lincoln Association; Journal of the (Springfield, IL, USA) **76**
Abu Dhabi Economy (Abu Dhabi, UAE) **1689**
Academic Journal of Agriculture **337***
Academy of Medicine, Singapore Annals (Singapore, SGP) **1306**
Acarological Society of Japan; Journal of (Chiba, JPN) **584**
ACCJ Journal (Tokyo, JPN) **781**
Accountant; Singapore (Singapore, SGP) **1480**
Acoustical Society of Japan; Journal of the (Tokyo, JPN) **915**
Acoustics Australia (Castlemaine, VI, AUS) **311**
Acoustics; Journal of Computational (Singapore, SGP) **1424**
Acta Agronomica Sinica (Beijing, CHN) **337**
Acta Anatomica Nipponica (Tokyo, JPN) **782**
Acta Arachnologica (Osaka, JPN) **722**
Acta Asiatica (Tokyo, JPN) **783**
Acta Criminologiae et Medicinae Legalis Japonica (Tokyo, JPN) **784**
Acta Dipterologica (Fukuoka, JPN) **591**
Acta Geographica Sinica (Beijing, CHN) **338**
Acta Geologica Taiwanica (Taipei, TWN) **1552**
Acta Histochemica et Cytochemica (Kyoto, JPN) **665**
Acta Medica et Biologica (Niigata, JPN) **712**
Acta Medica Kinki University (Osaka, JPN) **723**
Acta Medica Nagasakiensia (Nagasaki, JPN) **705**
Acta Medica Okayama (Okayama, JPN) **715**
Acta Neurologica Taiwanica (Taipei, TWN) **1553**
Acta Neuropsychiatrica (Maastricht, NLD) **1268**
Acta Oceanographica Taiwanica (Taipei, TWN) **1554**
Acta Paediatrica Sinica Taiwanica (Taipei, TWN) **1555**
Acta Phytotaxonomica et Geobotanica (Kyoto, JPN) **666**
Acta Zoologica Taiwanica (Taipei, TWN) **1556**
Actinomycetologica (Tokyo, JPN) **785**
Action Asia (Hong Kong, CHN) **364**
Ad-Vocate (Dubai, UAE) **1691**
Adasiaonline (Singapore, SGP) **1307**
Administrative Sciences Journal of King Saud University (Riyadh, SAU) **1288**
Adolescence; Journal of (Kidlington, GBR) **1760**
Adult Education and Development (Bonn, GER) **493**
Advances in Neurotrauma Research (Tokyo, JPN) **786**
The Advertizer **218***
Advertizer-Herald (Bamberg, SC, USA) **218**
Aero Information; China (Beijing, CHN) **343**
Aeronautical Materials; Journal of (Beijing, CHN) **357**
Aerospace; Asian Airlines & (Kuala Lumpur, MYS) **1190**
Aerospace Power; Journal of (Beijing, CHN) **358**
Aerospace Safety; Human Factors and (Aldershot, GBR) **1737**
Aesthetic Surgery; Journal of Japan Society of (Tokyo, JPN) **954**
Africa; China and (Beijing, CHN) **344**
Africa; Communications (Dubai, UAE) **1700**
Africa; Communications Middle East & (Dubai, UAE) **1703**
Africa and Latin America; AMA - Agricultural Mechanization in Asia, (Tokyo, JPN) **787**
African Earth Sciences; Journal of (Amsterdam, NLD) **1260**

African Journal on Human Rights; South (Wits, SAF) **1528**
African Studies (Taipei, TWN) **1557**
Afro-Asian Journal of Rural Development (New Delhi, DH, IND) **544**
Afsaar Magazine (Dubai, UAE) **1692**
Agricultural Chemical Society; Journal of Chinese (Taipei, TWN) **1587**
Agricultural Chemistry; Food Science and (Taipei, TWN) **1576**
Agricultural Engineering Journal (Bangkok, THA) **1624**
Agricultural Journal of Kyushu University (Fukuoka, JPN) **592**
Agricultural Mechanization in Asia, Africa and Latin America; AMA - (Tokyo, JPN) **787**
Agricultural Meteorology; Journal of (Tokyo, JPN) **917**
Agricultural Research of China; Journal of (Taipei, TWN) **1586**
Agricultural Research; Tohoku Journal of (Miyagi, JPN) **699**
Agricultural Science; Pertanika Journal of Tropical (Serdang, MYS) **1255**
Agricultural Science; Thai Journal of (Bangkok, THA) **1667**
Agricultural Sciences Journal of King Saud University (Riyadh, SAU) **1289**
Agricultural Sciences; Seoul National University Journal of (Suwon, KOR) **1182**
Agriculture & Food Science; Journal of Tropical (Kuala Lumpur, MYS) **1208**
Agro Food (Milan, ITA) **558**
Aikido Journal (Kanagawa, JPN) **647**
Aikuiskasvatus (Helsinki, FIN) **470**
Air Transport; Asian (Taipei, TWN) **1558**
Airline Timetable; Thailand (Bangkok, THA) **1671**
Airlines & Aerospace; Asian (Kuala Lumpur, MYS) **1190**
Airone (Milan, ITA) **559**
Akita Journal of Medicine (Akita, JPN) **578**
AKK-Motorsport (A-lehdet, FIN) **450**
Akron Sun; West (Cleveland, OH, USA) **194**
Al Shindagah (Dubai, UAE) **1693**
Alexandria (Aldershot, GBR) **1733**
Algebra and Computation; International Journal of (Singapore, SGP) **1392**
Algorithmica (New York, NY, USA) **154**
Alpin (Nuremberg, GER) **504**
Alpinismus **504***
AMA - Agricultural Mechanization in Asia, Africa and Latin America (Tokyo, JPN) **787**
Amakusa Marine Biological Laboratory; Publications of (Kumamoto, JPN) **664**
American Brewer **245***
American Brewer (Alexandria, VA, USA) **245**
American and Canadian Studies; Journal of (Tokyo, JPN) **918**
American Cueist Magazine (McKinney, TX, USA) **239**
The American Journal of Criminal Law (Austin, TX, USA) **224**
American Literary Realism (Albuquerque, NM, USA) **148**
American Literature; Kyushu (Fukuoka, JPN) **599**
American Orthoptic Journal (Madison, WI, USA) **267**
American Philosophical Quarterly (University Park, PA, USA) **211**
American Police Beat (Cambridge, MA, USA) **100**
American Studies; Doshisha (Kyoto, JPN) **669**
American Studies; Indian Journal of (Hyderabad, AP, IND) **523**
American Studies; Nanzan Review of (Aichi, JPN) **574**

Ammattiautoilija **473***
Anaesthesia and Analgesia; Veterinary (Midlothian, GBR) **1781**
Analgesia; Veterinary Anaesthesia and (Midlothian, GBR) **1781**
Analytical Instrumentation; JEOL News: (Tokyo, JPN) **911**
Analytical Sciences (Tokyo, JPN) **788**
Anatomia, Histologia, Embryologia (Wilrijk, BEL) **332**
Anatomical Science (Oxford, GBR) **1784**
L'Anello Che Non Tiene (Madison, WI, USA) **268**
Anesthesia; Journal of (Tokyo, JPN) **919**
Anesthesiologists; Journal of the Taiwan Society of (Taipei, TWN) **1599**
Anesthesiology; Thai Journal of (Bangkok, THA) **1668**
Angler; New Specialist (Hemel Hempstead, GBR) **1755**
Animal Psychology; Japanese Journal of (Ibaraki, JPN) **629**
Animal Science Journal (Tokyo, JPN) **789**
Animal Science Journal (Oxford, GBR) **1785**
Animal Sciences; Asian-Australasian Journal of (Kyunggi-do, KOR) **1113**
Animals; Experimental (Tokyo, JPN) **840**
Annals of Nuclear Medicine (Tokyo, JPN) **790**
Annals of Saudi Medicine (Riyadh, SAU) **1290**
Annals of Thoracic and Cardiovascular Surgery (Tokyo, JPN) **791**
Anritsu Technical Review (Tokyo, JPN) **792**
Antarctic Record (Tokyo, JPN) **793**
Anthropological Science (Tokyo, JPN) **794**
Anthropological Survey of India; The Journal of the (Calcutta, WB, IND) **514**
Anthropology; Arctic (Madison, WI, USA) **269**
Antibiotics; Journal of (Tokyo, JPN) **920**
Aomori Prefectural Central Hospital; Medical Journal of (Aomori, JPN) **582**
Aomori Society of Obstetricians and Gynecologists; Journal of (Aomori, JPN) **581**
APF News **1753***
APLAR Journal of Rheumatology (Oxford, GBR) **1786**
APO Productivity Journal (Tokyo, JPN) **795**
Appalachian Journal (Boone, NC, USA) **185**
Apparel; Hong Kong (Hong Kong, CHN) **383**
Apparel Journal; Asia Textile & (Hong Kong, CHN) **371**
Apparel Production News (Tokyo, JPN) **796**
Applied Entomology and Zoology (Tokyo, JPN) **797**
Applied Human Science (Tokyo, JPN) **798**
Applied Linguistics; Hong Kong Journal of (Hong Kong, CHN) **398**
Applied Mathematics; Japan Journal of Industrial and (Tokyo, JPN) **880**
Applied Mathematics and Optimization (New York, NY, USA) **155**
Applied Physics; Japanese Journal of (Tokyo, JPN) **889**
Apu (A-lehdet, FIN) **451**
Aquarium World; Nature (Singapore, SGP) **1451**
Arab Gulf Journal of Scientific Research (Bahrain, SAU) **1280**
Arab Journal of Library and Information Science (Riyadh, SAU) **1291**
Arab News (Jeddah, SAU) **1282**
Arabian Business (Dubai, UAE) **1694**
Arabian Computer News (Dubai, UAE) **1695**
Arabian Journal for Science and Engineering (Dhahran, SAU) **1281**
Arabian Woman (Dubai, UAE) **1696**
Archaeology; New Zealand Journal of (Dunedin North, NZL) **1270**

B

Education; Asia-Pacific Journal of (Singapore, SGP) 1311

Education and Development; Infancia Y Aprendizaje/ Journal for the Study of (San Sebastian de los Reyes, SPA) 1535

Education; Distance (Abingdon, GBR) 1732

Education; Hiroshima Journal of Mathematics (Hiroshima, JPN) 609

Education in Japan; Journal of Science (Tokyo, JPN) 986

Education; Journal of (UKM Bangi, MYS) 1257

Education; Journal of Southeast Asian (Bangkok, THA) 1646

Education; Psychology and (Orangeburg, SC, USA) 220

Education & Recreation; Journal of Physical (Hong Kong, CHN) 428

Education Series 3; Journal of Hyogo University of Teacher (Hyogo, JPN) 623

Educational Media and Library Sciences; Journal of (Tamsui, TWN) 1618

Educational Sciences and Islamic Studies Journal of King Saud University (Riyadh, SAU) 1295

Educational Technology; Australian Journal of (Como, WA, AUS) 312

Eeva (A-lehdet, FIN) 454

EGA Needle Arts Magazine (Dillwyn, VA, USA) 252

Egypt; Communications (Dubai, UAE) 1701

8 Days (Singapore, SGP) 1356

El Mundo (Wenatchee, WA, USA) 263

Electric Advance; Mitsubishi (Tokyo, JPN) 1024

Electrical Engineering and Information Science; Journal of (Seoul, KOR) 1125

Electrical Engineering; Research Reports on Information Science and (Fukuoka, JPN) 601

Electrical Machining; International Journal of (Tokyo, JPN) 867

Electron Optics Instrumentation; JEOL News: (Tokyo, JPN) 912

Electronic Component & Equipment Exhibition; IBS (Taipei, TWN) 1582

Electronic Components & Parts; Hong Kong (Hong Kong, CHN) 387

Electronic Journal of School of Advanced Technologies (Bangkok, THA) 1634

Electronics Asia; Nikkei (Hong Kong, CHN) 431

Electronics Audience; TSEA: Targeting Singapore (Singapore, SGP) 1513

Electronics; Hobby (Bangkok, THA) 1638

Electronics; Hong Kong (Hong Kong, CHN) 388

Electronics Industry; Asia (Tokyo, JPN) 801

Electronics; Korea Buyers Guide (Seoul, KOR) 1134

Electronics Manufacturing; Journal of (Singapore, SGP) 1426

Electronics News; IBS Asian (Taipei, TWN) 1581

Electronics and Systems; International Journal of High Speed (Singapore, SGP) 1399

Electrostatics; Journal of Institute of (Tokyo, JPN) 947

Elements (London, GBR) 1764

ellipse (Fredericton, NB, CAN) 286

Embryologia; Anatomia, Histologia, (Wilrijk, BEL) 332

Emirates Inflight (Dubai, UAE) 1706

Emirates Medical Journal (Dubai, UAE) 1707

Emirates Woman (Dubai, UAE) 1708

The Employer 1273*

Endemain 448*

Endocrine Surgery (Tokyo, JPN) 835

Endocrinology; Clinical Pediatric (Sapporo, JPN) 753

EndoSource Magazine (Singapore, SGP) 1357

Energy Asia (Singapore, SGP) 1358

Energy in Japan (Tokyo, JPN) 836

Engine; Internal Combustion (Tokyo, JPN) 864

Engineer; Midwest (Chicago, IL, USA) 57

Engineering; Arabian Journal for Science and (Dhahran, SAU) 1281

Engineering B; Journal of Structural (Tokyo, JPN) 993

Engineering — Earthquake Engineering; Structural (Tokyo, JPN) 1074

Engineering; Geotechnical (Bangkok, THA) 1636

Engineering and Information Science; Journal of Electrical (Seoul, KOR) 1125

Engineering; International Journal of Bifurcation and Chaos in Applied Sciences and (Singapore, SGP) 1394

Engineering; International Journal of Japan Society for Precision (Tokyo, JPN) 868

Engineering; International Journal of Reliability, Quality & Safety (Singapore, SGP) 1413

Engineering of Japan; Journal of Chemical (Tokyo, JPN) 927

Engineering Journal; Agricultural (Bangkok, THA) 1624

Engineering; Journal of Architecture, Planning and Environmental (Tokyo, JPN) 921

Engineering Journal; Asia-Pacific Aviation and (Singapore, SGP) 1309

Engineering; Journal of Earthquake (Singapore, SGP) 1425

Engineering; Journal of Hydroscience and Hydraulic (Tokyo, JPN) 944

Engineering; Journal of Structural and Construction (Tokyo, JPN) 992

Engineering; Journal of Textile (Osaka, JPN) 735

Engineering; JSME International Journal Series B Fluids and Thermal (Tokyo, JPN) 1006

Engineering and Knowledge Engineering; International Journal of Software (Singapore, SGP) 1415

Engineering; Korean Journal of Chemical (Seoul, KOR) 1146

Engineering and Mechanics; Structural (Taejon, KOR) 1184

Engineering; Mineral Resources (Singapore, SGP) 1443

Engineering; Naval Architecture and Ocean (Tokyo, JPN) 1030

Engineering and Related Fields; Kyoto University Research Activities in Civil (Kyoto, JPN) 683

Engineering; Research Reports on Information Science and Electrical (Fukuoka, JPN) 601

Engineering Review of Doshisha University; Science and (Kyoto, JPN) 689

Engineering Review; IHI (Tokyo, JPN) 859

Engineering; Review of Laser (Osaka, JPN) 744

Engineering Science and Technology (Kuala Lumpur, MYS) 1199

Engineering Sciences Journal of King Saud University (Riyadh, SAU) 1296

Engineers; Federation of Malaysia; Journal of the Institution of (Petaling Jaya, MYS) 1245

Engineers; Journal of Chinese Institute of (Taipei, TWN) 1589

Engineers; Journal of Chinese Institute of Chemical (Hsinchu, TWN) 1547

Engineers Reports of Statistical Application Research; Union of Japanese Scientists and (Tokyo, JPN) 1091

English; Let's Talk in (Taipei, TWN) 1600

English Literature; Studies in (Tokyo, JPN) 1076

The English Teacher Online (Bangkok, THA) 1635

English; World Literature Written in (Singapore, SGP) 1520

Enquires (Singapore, SGP) 1359

Enterprise; Hong Kong (Hong Kong, CHN) 389

Entomological Science (Mito, JPN) 695

Entomological Society; Journal of Kyoto (Kyoto, JPN) 679

Entomologist; New (Minamiminowa, JPN) 694

Entomology; Monthly Journal of (Tokyo, JPN) 1025

Entomology and Zoology; Applied (Tokyo, JPN) 797

Entomology and Zoology; Japanese Journal of Environment, (Osaka, JPN) 726

Environment and Conservation; Ecology, (Karad, MH, IND) 528

Environment, Entomology and Zoology; Japanese Journal of (Osaka, JPN) 726

Environment News; China (Beijing, CHN) 350

Environmental Assessment Policy and Management; Journal of (Singapore, SGP) 1428

Environmental Chemistry; Journal of (Ibaraki, JPN) 634

Environmental Economics and Policy Studies (Tokyo, JPN) 837

Environmental Engineering; Journal of Architecture, Planning and (Tokyo, JPN) 921

Environmental Engineering; Rural and (Tokyo, JPN) 1063

Environmental Health; Journal of University of Occupational and (Fukuoka, JPN) 597

Environmental Issues; Journal of Water and (Tokyo, JPN) 1002

Environmental Medicine (Aichi, JPN) 571

Environmental Mutagen Research (Tokyo, JPN) 838

Environmental News Digest (Penang, MYS) 1234

Environmental Policy Monthly (Taipei, TWN) 1572

Environmental Sciences (Tokyo, JPN) 839

Environmental Sciences; Asian Journal of Microbiology, Biotechnology and (Aligarh, UP, IND) 510

Envision (Singapore, SGP) 1360

Epoche (Villanova, PA, USA) 212

Equipment Solutions (Chicago, IL, USA) 54

Ergology; Journal of Human (Tokyo, JPN) 941

Ergonomics; The IEA Journal of (Singapore, SGP) 1385

Esophagological Society; Journal of Japan Broncho- (Tokyo, JPN) 951

Essentials (Parklands, SAF) 1526

Esso in Malaysia (Kuala Lumpur, MYS) 1200

Estates Tax Journal; Trusts & (London, GBR) 1777

Estudios de Psicologia (San Sebastian de los Reyes, SPA) 1534

Ethnic and Migration Studies (JEMS); Journal of (Brighton, GBR) 1743

Ethnobotany (New Delhi, DH, IND) 548

Ethnomusicology (Champaign, IL, USA) 47

Ethology; Journal of (Tokyo, JPN) 931

Ethos (Petaling Jaya, MYS) 1240

ETRI Journal (Taejon, KOR) 1183

Euro-Asian Management; Journal of (Bangkok, THA) 1640

Europe; Lifelong Learning in (Helsinki, FIN) 475

European Edition; Business Travel Planner - (Secaucus, NJ, USA) 141

European Journal of Hospital Pharmacy (Oosterzele-Bal, BEL) 330

The European Union (Oxford, GBR) 1788

European Voice (London, GBR) 1765

The European Yearbook of Business History (Aldershot, GBR) 1736

Evensongs (Taipei, TWN) 1573

L'Exclusif 301*

Experimental Animals (Tokyo, JPN) 840

Experimental Medicine; Japanese Journal of Clinical and (Fukuoka, JPN) 596

Experimental Medicine; Journal of Clinical and (Tokyo, JPN) 928

Experimental Medicine; Tohoku Journal of (Miyagi, JPN) 700

Experimental and Molecular Medicine (Seoul, KOR) 1120

Experimental Nephrology; Clinical and (Tokyo, JPN) 820

Explosives and Propellants; Journal of (Taoyuan, TWN) 1623

Export Processing Zone Concentrates (Kaohsiung, TWN) 1549

Extremophiles (Tokyo, JPN) 841

Ezyhealth Chinese (Singapore, SGP) 1361

Ezyhealth Malaysia (Petaling Jaya, MYS) 1241

Ezyhealth Singapore (Singapore, SGP) 1362

F

Fabrics & Accessories; Hong Kong (Hong Kong, CHN) 390

Faculty of Science and Technology of Kinki University; Journal of the (Osaka, JPN) 728

Famiglia Cristiana (Milan, ITA) 562

Family Law Journal (London, GBR) 1766

Family Studies; Malaysian Journal of (Kuala Lumpur, MYS) 1215

Far Eastern Affairs (Minneapolis, MN, USA) 120

Farming; Successful (Des Moines, IA, USA) 81

Fashion Flash; Hong Kong (Hong Kong, CHN) 391

Fashion Magazine; Top (Bangkok, THA) 1676

Faster Higher Stronger (Leeds, GBR) 1761

FATE Magazine (Lakeville, MN, USA) 118

FDM Asia (Singapore, SGP) 1363

Female Brides (Singapore, SGP) 1364

Female Cookbook (Singapore, SGP) 1365

Feminine (Petaling Jaya, MYS) 1242

Feminist Legal Studies (Dordrecht, NLD) 1264

Femme Fatales (Oak Park, IL, USA) 74

Fence (New York, NY, USA) 163

Ferris State Torch (Big Rapids, MI, USA) 106

Ferrocement; Journal of (Bangkok, THA) 1641

Fertilization and Implantation; Journal of (Tokyo, JPN) 932

FHM Singapore (Singapore, SGP) 1366

Films; Performance Arts and (Seoul, KOR) 1166

Finance; Asia Pacific Journal of (Singapore, SGP) 1312

Finance; International Journal of Theoretical and Applied (Singapore, SGP) 1416

Financial Law Briefing; Asian (Hong Kong, CHN) 373

Financial Markets and Policies; Review of Pacific Basin (Singapore, SGP) 1470

Financial Outlook; Korean Economic and (Seoul, KOR) 1144

Financial Statistics Monthly (Taipei, TWN) 1574

Financial Times Japan (Tokyo, JPN) 842

Finish 540*

Fish Pathology (Hiroshima, JPN) 608

Fisher; The Canadian Fly (Belleville, ON, CAN) 287

Fisheries; Journal of Tokyo University of (Tokyo, JPN) 996

Fisheries Prefectural University Mie; Journal of the Faculty of (Mie, JPN) 693

Fisheries Science Research (Kunsan, KOR) 1112

Fitness; Japanese Journal of Physical (Tokyo, JPN) 905

Flash Opel Scene International (Herten, GER) 498

Flora of Hokkaido; Illustrated (Hokkaido, JPN) 616

Flora Magazine (Chicago, IL, USA) 55

The Florida Bar Journal (Tallahassee, FL, USA) 41

Flortecnica Data e Fiori (Vernasca, ITA) 568

Flow of Funds (Taipei, TWN) 1575

Fly Fisher; The Canadian (Belleville, ON, CAN) 287

Flying Angel News (London, GBR) 1767

Folia Ugentia (Genval, BEL) 328

F1 Racing (A-lehdet, FIN) 455

Food; Agro (Milan, ITA) 558

Master Index Gale Directory of Publications & Broadcast Media/137th Ed. Supp.

Master Index

International Journal of Computer Processing of Oriental Languages (Hong Kong, CHN) **423**

International Journal of Electrical Machining (Tokyo, JPN) **867**

International Journal of Foundations of Computer Science (Singapore, SGP) **1396**

International Journal of Genome Research (Singapore, SGP) **1397**

International Journal of Hematology (Kyoto, JPN) **671**

International Journal of High Speed Computing (Singapore, SGP) **1398**

International Journal of High Speed Electronics and Systems (Singapore, SGP) **1399**

International Journal of Image and Graphics (Hong Kong, CHN) **424**

International Journal of Information and Management Sciences (Tamsui, TWN) **1617**

International Journal of Information Technology (Singapore, SGP) **1400**

International Journal of Innovation Management (Singapore, SGP) **1401**

International Journal of Japan Society for Precision Engineering (Tokyo, JPN) **868**

International Journal of Kobe University Law Review (Hyogo, JPN) **620**

International Journal of Manufacturing System Design (Singapore, SGP) **1402**

International Journal of Mathematical Logic (Singapore, SGP) **1403**

International Journal of Mathematics (Singapore, SGP) **1404**

International Journal of Modern Physics A (Singapore, SGP) **1405**

International Journal of Modern Physics B (Singapore, SGP) **1406**

International Journal of Modern Physics C: Physics and Computers (Singapore, SGP) **1407**

International Journal of Modern Physics D: Gravitation, Astrophysics and Cosmology (Singapore, SGP) **1408**

International Journal of Modern Physics E: Report on Nuclear Physics (Singapore, SGP) **1409**

International Journal of Neural Systems (Singapore, SGP) **1410**

International Journal of Pattern Recognition and Artificial Intelligence (Singapore, SGP) **1411**

International Journal of Peace Studies (Taipei, TWN) **1585**

International Journal for Philosophy of Religion (Dordrecht, NLD) **1265**

International Journal of PIXE (Singapore, SGP) **1412**

International Journal of Reliability, Quality & Safety Engineering (Singapore, SGP) **1413**

International Journal of Shaping Modeling (Singapore, SGP) **1414**

International Journal of Software Engineering and Knowledge Engineering (Singapore, SGP) **1415**

International Journal of Theoretical and Applied Finance (Singapore, SGP) **1416**

International Journal of Uncertainty, Fuzziness and Knowledge-Based Systems (Singapore, SGP) **1417**

International Medical Journal (Tokyo, JPN) **869**

International Medical News (Tokyo, JPN) **870**

International Medical Sciences Academy; Journal of the (New Delhi, DH, IND) **552**

International Organization (Cambridge, MA, USA) **101**

International Peat Journal (Jyvaskyla, FIN) **479**

International Railway Journal (New York, NY, USA) **165**

International Sociology; Journal of Institute of (Hyogo, JPN) **624**

International Studies; Journal of (Tokyo, JPN) **948**

International Studies; Journal of College of (Aichi, JPN) **572**

International Studies; Korean Journal of (Seoul, KOR) **1148**

International Travel Plan (Tokyo, JPN) **871**

Inver Grove Heights Sun Current; South St. Paul/ (South St. Paul, MN, USA) **124**

Investment; Korea Trade and (Seoul, KOR) **1142**

Investment Now (Kempston, GBR) **1757**

Investor (Bangkok, THA) **1639**

Investor; Smart (Singapore, SGP) **1494**

Investors Digest Magazine (Kuala Lumpur, MYS) **1203**

Investor's Guide to Singapore (Singapore, SGP) **1418**

Ion Exchange; Journal of (Tokyo, JPN) **949**

Ionizing Radiation (Tokyo, JPN) **872**

Iron and Steel Industry; Japan's (Tokyo, JPN) **910**

Ishikawa Prefectural Central Hospital; Medical Journal of (Ishikawa, JPN) **644**

Islamic Studies Journal of King Saud University; Educational Sciences and (Riyadh, SAU) **1295**

Islamic University of Imam Muhammad Ibn Saud; Journal of (Riyadh, SAU) **1298**

Islamic World Medical Journal (Jeddah, SAU) **1283**

Island Studies in Okinawa (Okinawa, JPN) **720**

The Island Sun (Tortola, BVI) **1799**

ISO Link (Singapore, SGP) **1419**

(ISR); Information Systems Research (Linthicum Heights, MD, USA) **93**

IT Asia (Singapore, SGP) **1420**

Iwate Prefectural Miyako Hospital; Medical Journal of (Iwate, JPN) **645**

J

Jacket (Balmain, NW, AUS) **308**

Japan Architect (Tokyo, JPN) **873**

Japan; Atoms in (Tokyo, JPN) **807**

Japan Automotive News (Tokyo, JPN) **874**

Japan Biomagnetism and Bioelectromagnetics Society; Journal of (Tokyo, JPN) **950**

Japan Broncho-Esophagological Society; Journal of (Tokyo, JPN) **951**

Japan Camera Trade News (Tokyo, JPN) **875**

Japan; Computing (Tokyo, JPN) **824**

Japan; Dentistry in (Tokyo, JPN) **828**

Japan; Energy in (Tokyo, JPN) **836**

Japan; Financial Times (Tokyo, JPN) **842**

Japan Glaucoma Society; Journal of (Miyazaki, JPN) **703**

Japan Graphic Arts (Tokyo, JPN) **876**

Japan; Graphic Design in (Tokyo, JPN) **847**

Japan Harvest (Tokyo, JPN) **877**

Japan; Illustration in (Tokyo, JPN) **860**

Japan; Industries of (Tokyo, JPN) **861**

Japan Institute of Navigation; Journal of (Tokyo, JPN) **952**

Japan Insurance News (Tokyo, JPN) **878**

Japan International Journal (Tokyo, JPN) **879**

Japan; Journal of Acarological Society of (Chiba, JPN) **584**

Japan; Journal of Chemical Engineering of (Tokyo, JPN) **927**

Japan; Journal of Food Hygienic Society of (Tokyo, JPN) **933**

Japan; Journal of Geodetic Society of (Ibaraki, JPN) **635**

Japan; Journal of Geological Society of (Tokyo, JPN) **936**

Japan; Journal of Home Economics of (Tokyo, JPN) **940**

Japan Journal of Industrial and Applied Mathematics (Tokyo, JPN) **880**

Japan; Journal of Magnetics Society of (Tokyo, JPN) **966**

Japan; Journal of Meteorological Society of (Tokyo, JPN) **970**

Japan; Journal of Operations Research Society of (Tokyo, JPN) **976**

Japan; Journal of Physical Society of (Tokyo, JPN) **981**

Japan; Journal of Science Education in (Tokyo, JPN) **986**

Japan; Journal of Sedimentological Society of (Matsumoto, JPN) **692**

Japan; Journal of Seismological Society of (Tokyo, JPN) **988**

Japan; Journal of Sericultural Science of (Ibaraki, JPN) **636**

Japan; Journal of Speleological Society of (Yamaguchi, JPN) **1100**

Japan Law Journal (Tokyo, JPN) **881**

Japan Marketing Data (Tokyo, JPN) **882**

Japan Medical Society of Paraplegia; Journal of (Tokyo, JPN) **953**

Japan Mission Journal (Tokyo, JPN) **883**

Japan; Motorcycle (Tokyo, JPN) **1027**

Japan; Neuro-Ophthalmology (Kanagawa, JPN) **654**

Japan News; Radio (Tokyo, JPN) **1057**

Japan; Pharma (Tokyo, JPN) **1048**

Japan; Physiology and Ecology (Kyoto, JPN) **685**

Japan; Publications of Astronomical Society of (Tokyo, JPN) **1055**

Japan Quarterly (Tokyo, JPN) **884**

Japan Salivary Gland Society; Journal of (Kanagawa, JPN) **651**

Japan Society of Aesthetic Surgery; Journal of (Tokyo, JPN) **954**

Japan Society of Polymer Processing; Journal of (Tokyo, JPN) **955**

Japan Society for Precision Engineering; International Journal of (Tokyo, JPN) **868**

Japan; Solvent Extraction Research and Development, (Sendai, JPN) **767**

Japan; Space in (Tokyo, JPN) **1072**

Japan Spine Research Society; Journal of (Tokyo, JPN) **956**

Japan Statistical Society; Journal of (Tokyo, JPN) **957**

Japan Times (Tokyo, JPN) **885**

Japan Today (Tokyo, JPN) **886**

Japan Update (Okinawa City, JPN) **721**

Japan Welding Society; Journal of (Tokyo, JPN) **958**

Japanese Association for Chest Surgery; Journal of (Kyoto, JPN) **678**

Japanese Circulation Journal (Kyoto, JPN) **672**

The Japanese Economic Review (Oxford, GBR) **1789**

Japanese Economy & Labor Series (Tokyo, JPN) **887**

Japanese Forestry Society; Journal of (Tokyo, JPN) **959**

Japanese Heart Journal (Tokyo, JPN) **888**

Japanese Journal of Animal Psychology (Ibaraki, JPN) **629**

Japanese Journal of Applied Physics (Tokyo, JPN) **889**

Japanese Journal of Bacteriology (Tokyo, JPN) **890**

Japanese Journal of Behavior Therapy (Ibaraki, JPN) **630**

Japanese Journal of Biofeedback Research (Tokyo, JPN) **891**

Japanese Journal of Biometeorology (Tokyo, JPN) **892**

Japanese Journal of Biometrics (Tokyo, JPN) **893**

Japanese Journal of Breast Cancer (Tokyo, JPN) **894**

Japanese Journal of Chemotherapy (Tokyo, JPN) **895**

Japanese Journal of Clinical and Experimental Medicine (Fukuoka, JPN) **596**

Japanese Journal of Crop Science (Sendai, JPN) **763**

Japanese Journal of Environment, Entomology and Zoology (Osaka, JPN) **726**

Japanese Journal of Health and Human Ecology (Tokyo, JPN) **896**

Japanese Journal of Herpetology (Kyoto, JPN) **673**

Japanese Journal of Hygiene (Tokyo, JPN) **897**

Japanese Journal of Infectious Diseases (Tokyo, JPN) **898**

Japanese Journal of Limnology (Tokyo, JPN) **899**

Japanese Journal of Lymphology (Tokyo, JPN) **900**

Japanese Journal of Malacology; Venus: (Tokyo, JPN) **1092**

Japanese Journal of Mathematics (Tokyo, JPN) **901**

Japanese. Journal of Medical Imaging and Information Sciences (Kyoto, JPN) **674**

Japanese Journal of Medical Mycology (Tokyo, JPN) **902**

Japanese Journal of Nematology (Ibaraki, JPN) **631**

Japanese Journal of Obstetrical, Gynecological and Neonatal Hematology (Shizuoka, JPN) **771**

Japanese Journal of Optics (Tokyo, JPN) **903**

Japanese Journal of Ornithology (Tokyo, JPN) **904**

The Japanese Journal of Pharmacology (Kyoto, JPN) **675**

Japanese Journal of Physical Fitness (Tokyo, JPN) **905**

Japanese Journal of Physiology (Tokyo, JPN) **906**

Japanese Journal of Protozoology (Gifu, JPN) **605**

Japanese Journal of Rheumatism and Joint Surgery (Shiga, JPN) **768**

Japanese Journal of Sanitary Zoology (Tokyo, JPN) **907**

Japanese Journal of Toxicology (Tokyo, JPN) **908**

Japanese Journal of Tropical Medicine and Hygiene (Nagasaki, JPN) **706**

Japanese Journal of Veterinary Research (Sapporo, JPN) **758**

Japanese Paediatric Orthopaedic Association; Journal of (Sendai, JPN) **764**

Japanese Poultry Science (Ibaraki, JPN) **632**

Japanese Progress in Climatology (Tokyo, JPN) **909**

Japanese Religions (Kyoto, JPN) **676**

Japanese Scientists and Engineers Reports of Statistical Application Research; Union of (Tokyo, JPN) **1091**

Japanese Society of Autologous Blood Transfusion; Journal of (Okayama, JPN) **717**

Japanese Society for Clinical Surgery; Journal of (Tokyo, JPN) **960**

Japanese Society of Computational Statistics; Journal of (Tokyo, JPN) **961**

Japanese Society of Dialysis Therapy; Journal of (Tokyo, JPN) **962**

Japanese Society for Horticultural Science; Journal of (Tokyo, JPN) **963**

Japanese Taxes; Guide to (Tokyo, JPN) **849**

Japanese Trade and Industry; Journal of (Tokyo, JPN) **964**

Japan's Iron and Steel Industry (Tokyo, JPN) **910**

JCA Forecast (Singapore, SGP) **1421**

(JEMS); Journal of Ethnic and Migration Studies (Brighton, GBR) **1743**

JEOL News: Analytical Instrumentation (Tokyo, JPN) **911**

JEOL News: Electron Optics Instrumentation (Tokyo, JPN) **912**

Jesus (Milan, ITA) **563**

Jewellery Collection; Hong Kong (Hong Kong, CHN) **396**

Jewelry Express Magazine; Hong Kong (Hong Kong, CHN) **397**

Jikeikai Medical Journal (Tokyo, JPN) **913**

JJAP Series (Tokyo, JPN) **914**

Joint (Yokohama, JPN) **1104**

Joint Surgery; Japanese Journal of Rheumatism and (Shiga, JPN) **768**

The Journal 241*
Journal of the Abraham Lincoln Association (Springfield, IL, USA) 76
Journal of Acarological Society of Japan (Chiba, JPN) 584
Journal of the Acoustical Society of Japan (Tokyo, JPN) 915
Journal of Adolescence (Kidlington, GBR) 1760
Journal of Advanced Computational Intelligence (Tokyo, JPN) 916
Journal of Advanced Transportation (Calgary, AB, CAN) 274
Journal of Aeronautical Materials (Beijing, CHN) 357
Journal of Aerospace Power (Beijing, CHN) 358
Journal of African Earth Sciences (Amsterdam, NLD) 1260
Journal of Agricultural Meteorology (Tokyo, JPN) 917
Journal of Agricultural Research 337*
Journal of Agricultural Research of China (Taipei, TWN) 1586
Journal of Allergy and Immunology; Asian Pacific (Bangkok, THA) 1625
Journal of American and Canadian Studies (Tokyo, JPN) 918
Journal of Anesthesia (Tokyo, JPN) 919
The Journal of the Anthropological Survey of India (Calcutta, WB, IND) 514
Journal of Antibiotics (Tokyo, JPN) 920
Journal of Aomori Society of Obstetricians and Gynecologists (Aomori, JPN) 581
Journal of Applied Medicine (Kyoto, JPN) 677
Journal of Architecture, Planning and Environmental Engineering (Tokyo, JPN) 921
Journal of Argentine Dermatology (Buenos Aires, ARG) 306
Journal of Artificial Organs (Tokyo, JPN) 922
Journal of Asian Earth Sciences (Amsterdam, NLD) 1261
Journal of the Asiatic Society (Calcutta, WB, IND) 515
Journal of Atherosclerosis and Thrombosis (Tokyo, JPN) 923
Journal of Australian Studies (St. Lucia, QL, AUS) 320
Journal of Biochemistry (Tokyo, JPN) 924
Journal of Biological Systems (Singapore, SGP) 1422
Journal of Bioscience and Bioengineering (Osaka, JPN) 727
Journal of Bone and Mineral Metabolism (Tokyo, JPN) 925
Journal of Brain Science (Okayama, JPN) 716
Journal of the Ceramic Society of Japan (Tokyo, JPN) 926
Journal of the Cheirological Society (Dereham, GBR) 1751
Journal of Chemical Engineering of Japan (Tokyo, JPN) 927
Journal of Chemical Research (St. Albans, GBR) 1793
Journal of Chemical Software (Fukui, JPN) 590
Journal of the China University of Geosciences (Beijing, CHN) 359
Journal of Chinese Agricultural Chemical Society (Taipei, TWN) 1587
Journal of Chinese Chemical Society (Taipei, TWN) 1588
Journal of Chinese Institute of Chemical Engineers (Hsinchu, TWN) 1547
Journal of Chinese Institute of Engineers (Taipei, TWN) 1589
Journal of Circuits, Systems and Computers (Singapore, SGP) 1423
Journal of Clinical Biochemical and Nutrition (Ibaraki, JPN) 633
Journal of Clinical and Experimental Medicine (Tokyo, JPN) 928
Journal of College of International Studies (Aichi, JPN) 572
Journal of Common Market Studies (London, GBR) 1769
Journal of Communications and Networks (Seoul, KOR) 1123
Journal of Computational Acoustics (Singapore, SGP) 1424
Journal of Counseling and Development (Alexandria, VA, USA) 246
Journal of Dermatology (Tokyo, JPN) 929
Journal of Development Assistance (Tokyo, JPN) 930
Journal of Diplomatic Studies (Riyadh, SAU) 1297
Journal of Documentation (Bradford, GBR) 1741
Journal of Earthquake Engineering (Singapore, SGP) 1425
Journal of Economic Integration (Seoul, KOR) 1124
Journal of Education (UKM Bangi, MYS) 1257
Journal of Educational Media and Library Sciences (Tamsui, TWN) 1618
Journal of Electrical Engineering and Information Science (Seoul, KOR) 1125

Journal of Electronics Manufacturing (Singapore, SGP) 1426
Journal of Enterprising Culture (Singapore, SGP) 1427
Journal of Environmental Assessment Policy and Management (Singapore, SGP) 1428
Journal of Environmental Chemistry (Ibaraki, JPN) 634
Journal of Ethnic and Migration Studies (JEMS) (Brighton, GBR) 1743
Journal of Ethology (Tokyo, JPN) 931
Journal of Euro-Asian Management (Bangkok, THA) 1640
Journal of the Experimental Forest of National Taiwan University (Nan-Tou Hsien, TWN) 1551
Journal of Explosives and Propellants (Taoyuan, TWN) 1623
Journal of Faculty of Applied Biological Science of Hiroshima University (Higashi-Hiroshima City, JPN) 607
Journal of the Faculty of Fisheries Prefectural University Mie (Mie, JPN) 693
Journal of Faculty of Marine Science and Technology of Tokai University (Shizuoka, JPN) 772
Journal of Faculty of Nutriiton of Kobe Gakuin University (Hyogo, JPN) 621
Journal of the Faculty of Science and Technology of Kinki University (Osaka, JPN) 728
Journal of Ferrocement (Bangkok, THA) 1641
Journal of Fertilization and Implantation (Tokyo, JPN) 932
Journal of Food Hygienic Society of Japan (Tokyo, JPN) 933
Journal of the Formosan Medical Association (Taipei, TWN) 1590
Journal of Fujita Technical Research Institute (Kanagawa, JPN) 650
Journal of Gastroenterology (Tokyo, JPN) 934
Journal of Gem Industry (Jaipur, RJ, IND) 526
The Journal of General and Applied Microbiology (Tokyo, JPN) 935
Journal of Geodetic Society of Japan (Ibaraki, JPN) 635
Journal of Geographical Science (Taipei, TWN) 1591
Journal of Geographical Sciences (Beijing, CHN) 360
Journal of Geological Society of China (Taipei, TWN) 1592
Journal of Geological Society of Japan (Tokyo, JPN) 936
Journal of Geosciences (Osaka, JPN) 729
Journal of Germfree Life and Gnotobiology (Kobe, JPN) 659
Journal of Groundwater Hydrology (Tokyo, JPN) 937
Journal of Health Science (Tokyo, JPN) 938
Journal of Hepato-Biliary-Pancreatic Surgery (Tokyo, JPN) 939
Journal of Himeji Red Cross Hospital (Hyogo, JPN) 622
Journal of Hiroshima City Medical Association (Hiroshima, JPN) 611
Journal of Hiroshima University Dental Society (Hiroshima, JPN) 612
Journal of the History of Philosophy (Baltimore, MD, USA) 87
Journal of Home Economics of Japan (Tokyo, JPN) 940
Journal of the Hong Kong College of Cardiology (Hong Kong, CHN) 425
The Journal of the Hong Kong Geriatrics Society (Hong Kong, CHN) 426
Journal of Human Ergology (Tokyo, JPN) 941
Journal of Human Genetics (Tokyo, JPN) 942
Journal of Human Resources (Madison, WI, USA) 270
Journal of Humanities (Seoul, KOR) 1126
Journal of Humanities and Natural Sciences (Tokyo, JPN) 943
Journal of Hydroscience and Hydraulic Engineering (Tokyo, JPN) 944
Journal of Hyogo University of Teacher Education Series 3 (Hyogo, JPN) 623
Journal of Industrial Pollution Control (Karad, MH, IND) 529
The Journal of Infection (Leicester, GBR) 1762
Journal of Infection and Chemotherapy (Tokyo, JPN) 945
The Journal of the Institute 543*
Journal of Institute for the Comprehensive Study of Lotus Sutra (Tokyo, JPN) 946
Journal of Institute of Electrostatics (Tokyo, JPN) 947
Journal of Institute of International Sociology (Hyogo, JPN) 624
Journal of the Institution of Engineers, Federation of Malaysia (Petaling Jaya, MYS) 1245
Journal of Intensive Care Medicine (Creteil, FRA) 488
The Journal of International Commercial Law (Swansea, GBR) 1794
Journal of the International Medical Sciences Academy (New Delhi, DH, IND) 552
Journal of International Studies (Tokyo, JPN) 948
Journal of Ion Exchange (Tokyo, JPN) 949

Journal of Islamic University of Imam Muhammad Ibn Saud (Riyadh, SAU) 1298
Journal of Japan Biomagnetism and Bioelectromagnetics Society (Tokyo, JPN) 950
Journal of Japan Broncho-Esophagological Society (Tokyo, JPN) 951
Journal of Japan Glaucoma Society (Miyazaki, JPN) 703
Journal of Japan Institute of Navigation (Tokyo, JPN) 952
Journal of Japan Medical Society of Paraplegia (Tokyo, JPN) 953
Journal of Japan Salivary Gland Society (Kanagawa, JPN) 651
Journal of Japan Society of Aesthetic Surgery (Tokyo, JPN) 954
Journal of Japan Society of Polymer Processing (Tokyo, JPN) 955
Journal of Japan Spine Research Society (Tokyo, JPN) 956
Journal of Japan Statistical Society (Tokyo, JPN) 957
Journal of Japan Welding Society (Tokyo, JPN) 958
Journal of Japanese Association for Chest Surgery (Kyoto, JPN) 678
Journal of Japanese Forestry Society (Tokyo, JPN) 959
Journal of Japanese Paediatric Orthopaedic Association (Sendai, JPN) 764
Journal of Japanese Society of Autologous Blood Transfusion (Okayama, JPN) 717
Journal of Japanese Society for Clinical Surgery (Tokyo, JPN) 960
Journal of Japanese Society of Computational Statistics (Tokyo, JPN) 961
Journal of Japanese Society of Dialysis Therapy (Tokyo, JPN) 962
Journal of Japanese Society for Horticultural Science (Tokyo, JPN) 963
Journal of Japanese Trade and Industry (Tokyo, JPN) 964
Journal of Juzen Medical Society (Ishikawa, JPN) 643
Journal of Kagawa Nutrition College (Tokyo, JPN) 965
Journal of Kansai Medical University Journal (Osaka, JPN) 730
Journal of Kansai Society of Naval Architects (Osaka, JPN) 731
Journal of Knot Theory and Its Ramifications (Singapore, SGP) 1429
Journal of Korean Astronomical Society (Seoul, KOR) 1127
Journal of Kyoto Entomological Society (Kyoto, JPN) 679
Journal of Kyoto Prefectural University of Medicine (Kyoto, JPN) 680
Journal of Magnetics Society of Japan (Tokyo, JPN) 966
Journal of the Malaysian Branch of the Royal Asiatic Society (Kuala Lumpur, MYS) 1204
Journal of Marine Science Museum of Tokai University (Shizuoka, JPN) 773
Journal of Marine Science and Technology (Tokyo, JPN) 967
Journal of Mathematical Sciences (Tokyo, JPN) 968
Journal of Mathematics (Tokushima, JPN) 777
Journal of the Medical Association of Thailand (Bangkok, THA) 1642
Journal of Medical and Dental Sciences (Tokyo, JPN) 969
Journal of Medical Investigation (Tokushima, JPN) 778
Journal of Medical Microbiology (Reading, GBR) 1792
Journal of Medicinal and Aromatic Plant Science (Lucknow, UP, IND) 533
Journal of Membrane Biology (New York, NY, USA) 166
Journal of Meteorological Society of Japan (Tokyo, JPN) 970
The Journal of Microbiology (Seoul, KOR) 1128
Journal of Microbiology, Immunology and Infection (Taipei, TWN) 1593
Journal of Microwave Surgery (Osaka, JPN) 732
Journal of Mineralogy, Petrology and Economic Geology (Sendai, JPN) 765
Journal of Modern Literature in Chinese (Hong Kong, CHN) 427
Journal of Molecular Evolution (New York, NY, USA) 167
Journal of Musculoskeletal Research (Singapore, SGP) 1430
Journal of Musicological Research (Philadelphia, PA, USA) 205
Journal of National Defense Medical College (Saitama, JPN) 751
Journal of National Research Council of Thailand (Bangkok, THA) 1643
Journal of Nippon Medical School (Tokyo, JPN) 971
Journal of Nonlinear Optical Physics and Materials (Singapore, SGP) 1431

K

Naval Architects; Journal of Kansai Society of (Osaka, JPN) **731**

Naval Architecture and Ocean Engineering (Tokyo, JPN) **1030**

Navigation; Journal of Japan Institute of (Tokyo, JPN) **952**

Navy News; Royal Australian (Canberra, AC, AUS) **310**

Needle Arts Magazine; EGA (Dillwyn, VA, USA) **252**

Nematology; Japanese Journal of (Ibaraki, JPN) **631**

Neonatal Hematology; Japanese Journal of Obstetrical, Gynecological and (Shizuoka, JPN) **771**

Nephrology; Clinical and Experimental (Tokyo, JPN) **820**

Network Middle East (Dubai, UAE) **1718**

Neural Systems; International Journal of (Singapore, SGP) **1410**

Neuro-Ophthalmology Japan (Kanagawa, JPN) **654**

Neurologia Medico-Chirurgica (Tokyo, JPN) **1031**

New Cicada (Fukushima, JPN) **603**

New Community **1743***

New Diamond and Frontier Carbon Technology (Tokyo, JPN) **1032**

New England Wine Gazette (Bernardsville, NJ, USA) **133**

New Entomologist (Minamiminowa, JPN) **694**

New Era Magazine (Huntington Beach, CA, USA) **11**

The New Food & Drug Packaging **75***

New Hope/Golden Valley Sun-Post (New Hope, MN, USA) **121**

New Jersey Reporter (Trenton, NJ, USA) **146**

New Sabah Times (Sabah, MYS) **1251**

New Specialist Angler (Hemel Hempstead, GBR) **1755**

The New Straits Times (Kuala Lumpur, MYS) **1225**

New Sunday Times (Kuala Lumpur, MYS) **1226**

New Zealand Economic Papers (Wellington, NZL) **1274**

New Zealand Journal of Archaeology (Dunedin North, NZL) **1270**

New Zealand Veterinary Journal (Palmerston North, NZL) **1271**

Newbury Street and Back Bay Guide (Boston, MA, USA) **99**

Newman (Singapore, SGP) **1453**

News from Nisshin Steel (Tokyo, JPN) **1033**

Newslink (Nairobi, KEN) **1109**

NewsToday.co.th (Phattaya, THA) **1686**

Nihongo Journal (Tokyo, JPN) **1034**

Nihonkai Mathematical Journal (Niigata, JPN) **714**

Nikkei Electronics Asia (Hong Kong, CHN) **431**

Nikkei Net Interactive (Tokyo, JPN) **1035**

The Nikkei Weekly (Tokyo, JPN) **1036**

9to5Asia.com (Singapore, SGP) **1454**

Nippon Medical School; Journal of (Tokyo, JPN) **971**

Nippon Steel News (Tokyo, JPN) **1037**

Nippon Tungsten Review (Fukuoka, JPN) **600**

Nipponia (Tokyo, JPN) **1038**

NIRA Review (Tokyo, JPN) **1039**

Nisshin Steel; News from (Tokyo, JPN) **1033**

Nonlinear Science; Journal of (New York, NY, USA) **168**

North American Edition; Business Travel Planner - (Secaucus, NJ, USA) **142**

The North American Technocrat (Ferndale, WA, USA) **253**

North Korea News (Seoul, KOR) **1164**

North Trade Journal (Bamberg, SC, USA) **219**

Northern Light (Conway, NH, USA) **128**

The Northern Miner (Toronto, ON, CAN) **295**

Northern Occupational Health; Journal of (Sapporo, JPN) **759**

The Northwest Technocrat **253***

Northwestern University Law Review (Champaign, IL, USA) **48**

Nuclear Medicine; Annals of (Tokyo, JPN) **790**

Nuclear Science and Technology; Journal of (Tokyo, JPN) **973**

Nuclear Science and Technology; Journal of (Tokyo, JPN) **972**

Nuklear Malaysia; Jurnal Sains (Kajang, MYS) **1187**

Nuorten Tasavalta (Helsinki, FIN) **476**

Nursing Education; Journal of (Thorofare, NJ, USA) **144**

Nursing Home; Today's **73***

Nursing Journal; The Hong Kong (Hong Kong, CHN) **410**

Nursing and Mental Health Services; Journal of Psychosocial (Thorofare, NJ, USA) **145**

Nursing Research; Journal of (Taipei, TWN) **1594**

NUS Economic Journal (Singapore, SGP) **1455**

Nutriiton of Kobe Gakuin University; Journal of Faculty of (Hyogo, JPN) **621**

Nutrition, Allergy, Diet - Taplalkozas, anyagcsere, dieta (Budapest, HUN) **507**

Nutrition College; Journal of Kagawa (Tokyo, JPN) **965**

Nutrition & Dietetics (Deakin, AC, AUS) **313**

Nutrition; Journal of Clinical Biochemical and (Ibaraki, JPN) **633**

Nutrition; Soil Science and Plant (Tokyo, JPN) **1070**

N.W. Navigator (Silverdale, WA, USA) **262**

O

OAG Business Travel Planner **143***

OAG Business Travel Planner **142***

OAG Business Travel Planner **141***

OAG Business Travel Planner, North American Edition **142***

OAG Travel Planner Hotel & Motel Redbook (North American Edition) **142***

Observer-Tribune (Chester, NJ, USA) **135**

Obstetrical, Gynecological and Neonatal Hematology; Japanese Journal of (Shizuoka, JPN) **771**

Obstetricians and Gynecologists; Journal of Aomori Society of (Aomori, JPN) **581**

Obstetrics and Gynaecology; Journal of (Tokyo, JPN) **974**

Obstetrics & Gynaecology; Singapore Journal of (Singapore, SGP) **1485**

Obzornik za Matematiko in Fiziko (Ljubljana, SVA) **1525**

Occupational and Environmental Health; Journal of University of (Fukuoka, JPN) **597**

Occupational Health; Journal of (Tokyo, JPN) **975**

Occupational Health; Journal of Northern (Sapporo, JPN) **759**

Ocean Engineering; Naval Architecture and (Tokyo, JPN) **1030**

Ocean Research (Seoul, KOR) **1165**

Oceanographical Magazine (Tokyo, JPN) **1040**

Oceanography Journal; Korean Society of (Seoul, KOR) **1157**

Office Equipment and Products (Tokyo, JPN) **1041**

Office Supplies; Stationery and (Taipei, TWN) **1608**

Official Journal of the European Patent Office (Munich, GER) **502**

Oficio & Arte (La Coruna, SPA) **1529**

Oil and Gas; Asian (Tokyo, JPN) **804**

Oil Palm Research; Journal of (Kuala Lumpur, MYS) **1205**

Okajima's Folia Anatomica Japonica (Tokyo, JPN) **1042**

Okayama University; Mathematical Journal of (Okayama, JPN) **719**

Okinawa; Island Studies in (Okinawa, JPN) **720**

On Air Magazine (Nonthaburi, THA) **1685**

ON-CALL **309***

Oncology (Melville, NY, USA) **152**

Oncology; International Journal of Clinical (Tokyo, JPN) **866**

101 Fun Things to Do (Marble Falls, TX, USA) **236**

Open City (New York, NY, USA) **175**

Openings (Jinan, SD, CHN) **440**

Operational Research; Asia-Pacific Journal of (Singapore, SGP) **1314**

Operations Research Society of Japan; Journal of (Tokyo, JPN) **976**

Ophthalmology; Asia-Pacific Journal of (Singapore, SGP) **1315**

Optical; Hong Kong (Hong Kong, CHN) **411**

Optical Physics and Materials; Journal of Nonlinear (Singapore, SGP) **1431**

Optical Review (Tokyo, JPN) **1043**

Optics Instrumentation; JEOL News: Electron (Tokyo, JPN) **912**

Optics; Japanese Journal of (Tokyo, JPN) **903**

Optics; Journal of (Calcutta, WB, IND) **516**

OR/MS Today (Linthicum Heights, MD, USA) **96**

Oral and Maxillofacial Surgery; Asian Journal of (Yokohama, JPN) **1103**

Oral Radiology (Tokyo, JPN) **1044**

Oral Science; Journal of (Tokyo, JPN) **977**

The Organic Way (Coventry, GBR) **1748**

Organs; Journal of Artificial (Tokyo, JPN) **922**

Orient Aviation (Hong Kong, CHN) **432**

Oriental Languages; International Journal of Computer Processing of (Hong Kong, CHN) **423**

Orientations (Hong Kong, CHN) **433**

Ornithology; Japanese Journal of (Tokyo, JPN) **904**

Ornithology; Journal of Yamashina Institute for (Chiba, JPN) **587**

Orthomolecular Medicine; Journal of (Toronto, ON, CAN) **293**

Orthopaedic Association; Journal of Japanese Paediatric (Sendai, JPN) **764**

Orthopaedic Ceramic Implants (Osaka, JPN) **738**

Orthopaedic Science; Journal of (Tokyo, JPN) **978**

Orthopaedic Surgery; The Hong Kong Journal of (Hong Kong, CHN) **400**

Orthopaedic and Traumatic Surgery (Tokyo, JPN) **1045**

Orthoptic Journal; American (Madison, WI, USA) **267**

Osaka Dental University; Journal of (Osaka, JPN) **733**

Osaka Journal of Mathematics (Osaka, JPN) **739**

The Outdoor Edge (Vancouver, BC, CAN) **280**

The Owl of Minerva (Chicago, IL, USA) **58**

P

Pacific/Asia Edition; Business Travel Planner - (Secaucus, NJ, USA) **143**

Pacific Basin Financial Markets and Policies; Review of (Singapore, SGP) **1470**

Pacific Focus (Inchon, KOR) **1110**

Pacific Labour; Asian and (Singapore, SGP) **1328**

Pacific Society; Journal of (Tokyo, JPN) **979**

Pacific Study; South (Kagoshima, JPN) **646**

Packaging; Food & Drug (St. Charles, IL, USA) **75**

Packaging; Hong Kong (Hong Kong, CHN) **412**

The Padang (Singapore, SGP) **1456**

A Padaria Portuguesa (Coimbra, PRT) **1278**

Paediatric Journal; Singapore (Singapore, SGP) **1491**

Paediatric Orthopaedic Association; Journal of Japanese (Sendai, JPN) **764**

Paediatrics; Hong Kong Journal of (Hong Kong, CHN) **401**

Pain Digest (New York, NY, USA) **176**

Pain and Palliative Care Pharmacotherapy; Journal of (Salt Lake City, UT, USA) **243**

Paintindia (Mumbai, MH, IND) **540**

Pancreatic Surgery; Journal of Hepato-Biliary- (Tokyo, JPN) **939**

Paper Asia (Singapore, SGP) **1457**

(Paper & Pulp); Papir a Celuloza (Prague, CZE) **443**

Papers in Meteorology and Geophysics (Ibaraki, JPN) **638**

Papir a Celuloza (Paper & Pulp) (Prague, CZE) **443**

Parallel Processing Letters (Singapore, SGP) **1458**

Paraplegia; Journal of Japan Medical Society of (Tokyo, JPN) **953**

Parasitology; The Korean Journal of (Seoul, KOR) **1150**

Parents; Today's (Singapore, SGP) **1510**

Parents; Young (Singapore, SGP) **1523**

Pasta Magazine (Riverside, CA, USA) **15**

Patents and Licensing (Tokyo, JPN) **1046**

Patents and Trademarks; The Gazette of (Budapest, HUN) **506**

Pathology; Brain Tumor (Tokyo, JPN) **815**

Pathology; Fish (Hiroshima, JPN) **608**

Pathology; Journal of (London, GBR) **1770**

Pathology; The Malaysian Journal of (Kuala Lumpur, MYS) **1217**

PC Magazine Middle & Near East (Dubai, UAE) **1719**

PC World Hong Kong (Hong Kong, CHN) **434**

PC World Malaysia (Kuala Lumpur, MYS) **1227**

PC World Singapore (Singapore, SGP) **1459**

Peace and Freedom (Redcliffe North, QL, AUS) **316**

Peace Studies; International Journal of (Taipei, TWN) **1585**

Pearland Journal (Pearland, TX, USA) **241**

Peat Journal; International (Jyvaskyla, FIN) **479**

Peatlands International (Jyvaskyla, FIN) **480**

Pediatric Cardiology (New York, NY, USA) **177**

Pediatric Dental Journal (Tokyo, JPN) **1047**

Pedologist (Ibaraki, JPN) **639**

Penang Tourist Newspaper (Penang, MYS) **1235**

Pennsylvania History (State College, PA, USA) **210**

People's Daily (Beijing, CHN) **362**

Peptide Information (Osaka, JPN) **740**

Performance Arts and Films (Seoul, KOR) **1166**

Perspectives on Work (Champaign, IL, USA) **49**

Pertanika Journal of Science and Technology (Serdang, MYS) **1253**

Pertanika Journal of Social Science and Humanities (Serdang, MYS) **1254**

Pertanika Journal of Tropical Agricultural Science (Serdang, MYS) **1255**

Pesticide Science; Journal of (Osaka, JPN) **734**

Petrology and Economic Geology; Journal of Mineralogy, (Sendai, JPN) **765**

Petromin (Singapore, SGP) **1460**

Pharma Japan (Tokyo, JPN) **1048**

Pharmacal Research; Archives of (Seoul, KOR) **1115**

Pharmaceutical Journal; Canadian (Ottawa, ON, CAN) **290**

Pharmaceutical Science and Technology; Journal of (Tokyo, JPN) **980**

Pharmaceuticals and Specialties; Compendium of (Ottawa, ON, CAN) **291**

Pharmacognosy; Korean Journal of (Seoul, KOR) **1151**

Pharmacology; Asia-Pacific Journal of (Singapore, SGP) **1316**

Pharmacology; The Japanese Journal of (Kyoto, JPN) **675**

Pharmacology; Korean Journal of Physiology and (Seoul, KOR) **1152**
Pharmacometrics (Sendai, JPN) **766**
Pharmacotherapy; Journal of Pain and Palliative Care (Salt Lake City, UT, USA) **243**
Pharmacy; European Journal of Hospital (Oosterzele-Bal, BEL) **330**
Philosophical Quarterly; American (University Park, PA, USA) **211**
Philosophy; International Journal of Applied (Ft. Pierce, FL, USA) **38**
Philosophy; Journal of the History of (Baltimore, MD, USA) **87**
Philosophy; Journal of Social Sciences and (Taipei, TWN) **1596**
Philosophy Now (Charlottesville, VA, USA) **250**
Philosophy, Psychiatry & Psychology (Baltimore, MD, USA) **90**
Philosophy Quarterly; History of (Vancouver, BC, CAN) **279**
Philosophy of Religion; International Journal for (Dordrecht, NLD) **1265**
Philosophy; Research Notes and Memoranda of Applied Geometry for Prevenient Natural (Chiba, JPN) **589**
Philosophy & Theology (Milwaukee, WI, USA) **273**
Photography Middle East (Dubai, UAE) **1720**
The Phuket Gazette (Phuket, THA) **1687**
Physical & Earth Sciences; Malaysian Journal of Science Series B: (Kuala Lumpur, MYS) **1219**
Physical Education & Recreation; Journal of (Hong Kong, CHN) **428**
Physical Fitness; Japanese Journal of (Tokyo, JPN) **905**
Physical Medicine and Rehabilitation; Archives of (Chicago, IL, USA) **51**
Physical Society of Japan; Journal of (Tokyo, JPN) **981**
Physical Society Journal; Korean (Seoul, KOR) **1155**
Physical Therapy Science; Journal of (Tokyo, JPN) **982**
Physician; The Singapore Family (Singapore, SGP) **1483**
Physico-Chemical Biology (Kanagawa, JPN) **655**
Physics A; International Journal of Modern (Singapore, SGP) **1405**
Physics A: Mathematical and General; Journal of (Bristol, GBR) **1745**
Physics B; International Journal of Modern (Singapore, SGP) **1406**
Physics C: Physics and Computers; International Journal of Modern (Singapore, SGP) **1407**
Physics; Chinese Journal of (Taipei, TWN) **1565**
Physics D: Gravitation, Astrophysics and Cosmology; International Journal of Modern (Singapore, SGP) **1408**
Physics E: Report on Nuclear Physics; International Journal of Modern (Singapore, SGP) **1409**
Physics For You (New Delhi, DH, IND) **553**
Physics; Indian Journal of Theoretical (Calcutta, WB, IND) **513**
Physics; Japanese Journal of Applied (Tokyo, JPN) **889**
Physics Letters A; Modern (Singapore, SGP) **1445**
Physics Letters B; Modern (Singapore, SGP) **1446**
Physics and Materials; Journal of Nonlinear Optical (Singapore, SGP) **1431**
Physics; Progress of Theoretical (Kyoto, JPN) **686**
Physics; Reviews in Mathematical (Singapore, SGP) **1471**
Physics - Supplement; Progress of Theoretical (Kyoto, JPN) **687**
Physiology; Chinese Journal of (Taipei, TWN) **1566**
Physiology and Ecology Japan (Kyoto, JPN) **685**
Physiology; Japanese Journal of (Tokyo, JPN) **906**
Physiology and Pharmacology; Korean Journal of (Seoul, KOR) **1152**
Physiotherapy Journal; Hong Kong (Hong Kong, CHN) **413**
Phytogeography and Taxonomy; Journal of (Kanazawa, JPN) **658**
Phytotaxonomy (New Delhi, DH, IND) **554**
The Picayune (Marble Falls, TX, USA) **237**
PILC Journal of Dravidic Studies (Pondicherry, PN, IND) **556**
Pink Ink (Bangkok, THA) **1657**
Pipeline News (Houston, TX, USA) **232**
Pit & Quarry (Walkerville, SAF) **1527**
Plainfield Sun (Naperville, IL, USA) **70**
Plane Talk (Manchester, GBR) **1779**
Planews (Singapore, SGP) **1461**
Plankton Biology and Ecology (Tokyo, JPN) **1049**
Planning and Environmental Engineering; Journal of Architecture, (Tokyo, JPN) **921**
Plant Biology; Journal of (Seoul, KOR) **1129**
Plant Growth Regulation; Journal of (New York, NY, USA) **169**
Plant Nutrition; Soil Science and (Tokyo, JPN) **1070**

The Plant Pathology Journal (Seoul, KOR) **1167**
Plant Production Science (Tanashi, JPN) **774**
Plant Research; Journal of (Tokyo, JPN) **983**
Plant Science; Journal of Medicinal and Aromatic (Lucknow, UP, IND) **533**
Plasma and Fusion Research; Journal of (Aichi, JPN) **573**
Plasma and Fusion Research; Journal of (Nagoya, JPN) **708**
Plasma Processing (Tokyo, JPN) **1050**
Plastichem (Singapore, SGP) **1462**
Plastics Auxiliaries **26***
Plastics Auxiliaries & Machinery (Denver, CO, USA) **26**
Plastics & Rubber Singapore Journal (Singapore, SGP) **1463**
Poetry Kanto (Yokohama, JPN) **1106**
Polar Bioscience (Tokyo, JPN) **1051**
Police Beat; American (Cambridge, MA, USA) **100**
Politeia (Singapore, SGP) **1464**
Political Science; Asian Journal of (Singapore, SGP) **1325**
Political Science; Soochow Journal of (Taipei, TWN) **1606**
Politics & Policy Quarterly; State (Champaign, IL, USA) **50**
Pollution Control; Journal of Industrial (Karad, MH, IND) **529**
Pollution Research (Karad, MH, IND) **530**
Polymer Journal (Tokyo, JPN) **1052**
Polymer Processing; Journal of Japan Society of (Tokyo, JPN) **955**
Population Ecology (Tokyo, JPN) **1053**
Population Headliners (Bangkok, THA) **1658**
Population, Health and Social Welfare; Journal of (Seoul, KOR) **1130**
Population and Health Studies; Journal of (Seoul, KOR) **1131**
Population and Social Studies; Journal of (Nakhon Pathom, THA) **1683**
Port O'Call (Singapore, SGP) **1465**
Port Orchard Advantage **255***
The Port Orchard Independent (Port Orchard, WA, USA) **255**
Portal (Baltimore, MD, USA) **91**
The Post (Willingboro, NJ, USA) **147**
Postal Service Today (Taipei, TWN) **1601**
Postepy Astronautyki (Warsaw, POL) **1277**
Poultry Science; Japanese (Ibaraki, JPN) **632**
Power & Gas Marketing (Houston, TX, USA) **233**
The Powys Review (Desborough, GBR) **1752**
Practitioner; The Hong Kong (Hong Kong, CHN) **414**
Pregnancy & Babycare (Singapore, SGP) **1466**
Premier Golf Annual (Singapore, SGP) **1467**
Prices; Glass's Guide to Used Vehicle (Weybridge, GBR) **1797**
Primary Care; Hokkaido Journal of (Sapporo, JPN) **756**
Primates (Aichi, JPN) **575**
PrintAction (Toronto, ON, CAN) **296**
Printer; Asian (Singapore, SGP) **1329**
Printing Bureau; Medical Journal of the Government (Tokyo, JPN) **1020**
Printing; Hong Kong (Hong Kong, CHN) **415**
Production Research (Tokyo, JPN) **1054**
Productivity News; Hong Kong (Hong Kong, CHN) **416**
Profile (Hong Kong, CHN) **435**
Progress of Theoretical Physics (Kyoto, JPN) **686**
Progress of Theoretical Physics - Supplement (Kyoto, JPN) **687**
The Prosecutor (Alexandria, VA, USA) **247**
Protozoology; Japanese Journal of (Gifu, JPN) **605**
Psychiatry; The Hong Kong Journal of (Hong Kong, CHN) **402**
Psychiatry & Psychology; Philosophy, (Baltimore, MD, USA) **90**
Psychologia (Kyoto, JPN) **688**
Psychologica Folia; Tohoku (Miyagi, JPN) **702**
Psychologie; Report (Bonn, GER) **495**
Psychology—A Journal of Human Behavior **220***
Psychology; Chinese Journal of (Taipei, TWN) **1567**
Psychology and Education (Orangeburg, SC, USA) **220**
Psychology; Japanese Journal of Animal (Ibaraki, JPN) **629**
Psychology; Philosophy, Psychiatry & (Baltimore, MD, USA) **90**
Psychology of Women Quarterly (Oxford, GBR) **1791**
Psychomusicology (Tallahassee, FL, USA) **42**
ptah (Helsinki, FIN) **477**
Public Affairs Quarterly (Pittsburgh, PA, USA) **209**
Public Health; Korean Journal of (Seoul, KOR) **1153**
Publications of Amakusa Marine Biological Laboratory (Kumamoto, JPN) **664**
Publications of Astronomical Society of Japan (Tokyo, JPN) **1055**
Publications of Seto Marine Biological Laboratory (Wakayama, JPN) **1098**

Pulse (London, GBR) **1775**

Q

Quantitative Structure-Activity Relationships (Bonn, GER) **494**
Quaternary Research (Tokyo, JPN) **1056**
Queensland Law Journal; University of (St. Lucia, QL, AUS) **321**
Questions (Charlottesville, VA, USA) **251**
Questions and Answers in General Topology (Osaka, JPN) **741**

R

RaceWeek (Dubai, UAE) **1721**
Racing; F1 (A-lehdet, FIN) **455**
Racing Journal; The Hong Kong (Hong Kong, CHN) **417**
Radiation; Ionizing (Tokyo, JPN) **872**
Radiation Research; Journal of (Chiba, JPN) **585**
Radical History Review (New York, NY, USA) **178**
Radio Japan News (Tokyo, JPN) **1057**
Radioisotopes (Tokyo, JPN) **1058**
Radiology; Cardiovascular and Interventional (New York, NY, USA) **157**
Radiology; Oral (Tokyo, JPN) **1044**
Railway Age (New York, NY, USA) **179**
Railway Journal; International (New York, NY, USA) **165**
Rare Earths (Osaka, JPN) **742**
RE Today (Derby, GBR) **1750**
Real Estate Letter; The Institutional (Walnut Creek, CA, USA) **22**
Realty **139***
Records Management Journal (Bradford, GBR) **1742**
Recreation Digest; Special (Iowa City, IA, USA) **82**
Recreation; Journal of Physical Education & (Hong Kong, CHN) **428**
Red Cross Hospital; Journal of Himeji (Hyogo, JPN) **622**
Red Cross Magazine; Thai Junior (Bangkok, THA) **1670**
Reformation (Aberystwyth, GBR) **1730**
Refractories; China's (Henan, CHN) **363**
Regional Development Dialogue (Aichi, JPN) **576**
Regional Development Studies (Aichi, JPN) **577**
Regional Outlook: Southeast Asia (Singapore, SGP) **1468**
Rehabilitation; Archives of Physical Medicine and (Chicago, IL, USA) **51**
Rehabilitation (SJDR); The Saudi Journal of Disability and (Riyadh, SAU) **1301**
Rehabilitation Technology (Houston, TX, USA) **234**
REITStreet Magazine (Walnut Creek, CA, USA) **23**
Religion; International Journal for Philosophy of (Dordrecht, NLD) **1265**
Religions; Japanese (Kyoto, JPN) **676**
Religious Education; The British Journal of (Coventry, GBR) **1747**
Remix (Emeryville, CA, USA) **7**
Renaissance and Reformation/Renaissance et Reforme (Toronto, ON, CAN) **297**
Renaissance et Reforme; Renaissance and Reformation/ (Toronto, ON, CAN) **297**
Renal Transplantation, Vascular Surgery (Tokyo, JPN) **1059**
Report Psychologie (Bonn, GER) **495**
The Reporter (Lansdale, PA, USA) **203**
Reproduction and Development; Journal of (Tokyo, JPN) **984**
Res Publica (Dordrecht, NLD) **1267**
Research Methodology; Journal of (Bangkok, THA) **1644**
Research Notes and Memoranda of Applied Geometry for Prevenient Natural Philosophy (Chiba, JPN) **589**
Research and Practice in Forensic Medicine (Miyagi, JPN) **697**
Research and Practice in Human Resource Management (Singapore, SGP) **1469**
Research Reports on Information Science and Electrical Engineering (Fukuoka, JPN) **601**
Resource Geology (Tokyo, JPN) **1060**
Resource News **275***
Review of Development and Change (Chennai, TN, IND) **519**
Review of Economics and Business (Osaka, JPN) **743**
Review of Industrial Property Protection and Copyright (Budapest, HUN) **508**
Review of Laser Engineering (Osaka, JPN) **744**

Review of Modern Literature in Chinese (Hong Kong, CHN) **436**

Review of Pacific Basin Financial Markets and Policies (Singapore, SGP) **1470**

Reviews on Heteroatom Chemistry (Tokyo, JPN) **1061**

Reviews in Mathematical Physics (Singapore, SGP) **1471**

Revista de Psicologia Social (San Sebastian de los Reyes, SPA) **1536**

Revue Militaire Suisse (Lausanne, SWI) **1543**

Rheedea (Calicut, KE, IND) **518**

Rheumatism and Joint Surgery; Japanese Journal of (Shiga, JPN) **768**

Rheumatology; APLAR Journal of (Oxford, GBR) **1786**

Richfield Sun Current (Richfield, MN, USA) **123**

Rigaku Journal (Tokyo, JPN) **1062**

RINSE (Toronto, ON, CAN) **298**

RIST Journal of R & D (Pohang, KOR) **1114**

River Cities Tribune (Marble Falls, TX, USA) **238**

Riyadh Daily (Riyadh, SAU) **1299**

Robotics; Artificial Life and (Tokyo, JPN) **799**

Robotics, Design and Manufacturing; JSME International Journal Series C Dynamics, Control, (Tokyo, JPN) **1007**

Robotics and Mechatronics; Journal of (Tokyo, JPN) **985**

Rocket (Petaling Jaya, MYS) **1248**

Rocky Mountain Golf Magazine (Steamboat Springs, CO, USA) **27**

Roctober (Chicago, IL, USA) **59**

Roxbury Register (Roxbury Township, NJ, USA) **140**

Royal Asiatic Society; Journal of the Malaysian Branch of the (Kuala Lumpur, MYS) **1204**

Royal Australian Navy News (Canberra, AC, AUS) **310**

RSYC (Singapore, SGP) **1472**

RTI—Redes, Telecom and Instalacoes (Sao Paulo, SP, BRZ) **336**

The Rubber International (Bangkok, THA) **1659**

Rubber Research; Journal of (Kuala Lumpur, MYS) **1206**

Rubber Singapore Journal; Plastics & (Singapore, SGP) **1463**

Rural Development; Afro-Asian Journal of (New Delhi, DH, IND) **544**

Rural and Environmental Engineering (Tokyo, JPN) **1063**

S

SABRAO Journal of Breeding and Genetics (Nakhon Pathom, THA) **1684**

Safety; Human Factors and Aerospace (Aldershot, GBR) **1737**

SAGGI-Child Development and Disabilities (Ponte Lambro, ITA) **565**

Sago Communication (Ibaraki, JPN) **640**

Sahko-Electricity In Finland **478***

SAHKO & TELE (Helsinki, FIN) **478**

St. Charles Sun (Naperville, IL, USA) **71**

St. Polten Konkret (St. Polten, AUT) **324**

Saitama Mathematical Journal (Saitama, JPN) **752**

Salivary Gland Society; Journal of Japan (Kanagawa, JPN) **651**

Sanitary Zoology; Japanese Journal of (Tokyo, JPN) **907**

Sapporo Medical Journal (Sapporo, JPN) **761**

Satellite 1-416 (Toronto, ON, CAN) **299**

Saudi Arabia Business Week (Riyadh, SAU) **1300**

Saudi Gazette (Jeddah, SAU) **1286**

Saudi Heart Journal (Jeddah, SAU) **1287**

The Saudi Journal of Disability and Rehabilitation (SJDR) (Riyadh, SAU) **1301**

The Saudi Journal of Gastroenterology (Riyadh, SAU) **1302**

Saudi Journal of Kidney Diseases and Transplantation (Riyadh, SAU) **1303**

Saudi Medical Journal (Riyadh, SAU) **1304**

Saudi Medicine; Annals of (Riyadh, SAU) **1290**

Savage Sun Current; Burnsville/ (Burnsville, MN, USA) **111**

SBA: Controle e Automacao (Campina Grande, PB, BRZ) **333**

Scherzo (Madrid, SPA) **1531**

School of Advanced Technologies; Electronic Journal of (Bangkok, THA) **1634**

Schweinzucht und Schweinemast (Munich, GER) **503**

Schweizer Jager (Einsiedeln, SWI) **1539**

Science Asia (Bangkok, THA) **1660**

Science Education in Japan; Journal of (Tokyo, JPN) **986**

Science and Engineering; Arabian Journal for (Dhahran, SAU) **1281**

Science and Engineering Review of Doshisha University (Kyoto, JPN) **689**

Science; Formosan (Taipei, TWN) **1578**

Science and Industry (Osaka, JPN) **745**

Science Journal of King Saud University (Riyadh, SAU) **1305**

Science; Journal of Nonlinear (New York, NY, USA) **168**

Science Journal; Singapore National Academy of (Singapore, SGP) **1490**

Science Policy and Research Management; Journal of (Tokyo, JPN) **987**

Science Research; Fisheries (Kunsan, KOR) **1112**

Science Series A: Life Sciences; Malaysian Journal of (Kuala Lumpur, MYS) **1218**

Science Series B: Physical & Earth Sciences; Malaysian Journal of (Kuala Lumpur, MYS) **1219**

Science Society of Thailand; Journal of the (Bangkok, THA) **1645**

Science and Technology; Engineering (Kuala Lumpur, MYS) **1199**

Science and Technology of Kinki University; Journal of the Faculty of (Osaka, JPN) **728**

Science and Technology; Pertanika Journal of (Serdang, MYS) **1253**

Sciences (Tokyo, JPN) **1064**

Sciences; Hitotsubashi Journal of Arts and (Tokyo, JPN) **854**

Scientific Research; Arab Gulf Journal of (Bahrain, SAU) **1280**

Scientists and Engineers Reports of Statistical Application Research; Union of Japanese (Tokyo, JPN) **1091**

Scottish Journal of Theology (Cambridge, GBR) **1746**

Screen (Mumbai, MH, IND) **541**

Sea and Sky (Kobe, JPN) **660**

SEAISI - Quarterly Journal (Shah Alam, MYS) **1256**

SEAMEO Regional Language Centre Guidelines (Singapore, SGP) **1473**

Seattle University Spectator (Seattle, WA, USA) **258**

Seattle's Child (Snohomish County Edition) (Seattle, WA, USA) **259**

Security Products; Asian Sources (Singapore, SGP) **1332**

Sedimentological Society of Japan; Journal of (Matsumoto, JPN) **692**

Seishin Studies (Tokyo, JPN) **1065**

Seismological Society of Japan; Journal of (Tokyo, JPN) **988**

Semigroup Forum (New York, NY, USA) **180**

Sensors and Materials (Tokyo, JPN) **1066**

Seoul Journal of Economics (Seoul, KOR) **1168**

Seoul Journal of Korean Studies (Seoul, KOR) **1169**

Seoul National University Journal of Agricultural Sciences (Suwon, KOR) **1182**

Sericultural Science of Japan; Journal of (Ibaraki, JPN) **636**

SET Journal (Bangkok, THA) **1661**

Seto Marine Biological Laboratory; Publications of (Wakayama, JPN) **1098**

Setsunan University Review of Humanities and Social Sciences (Osaka, JPN) **746**

Sewing Savvy (Berne, IN, USA) **79**

SG; News (Singapore, SGP) **1474**

Sgezine (Singapore, SGP) **1475**

Shakespeare Studies (Tokyo, JPN) **1067**

The Shakespearean International Yearbook (Aldershot, GBR) **1739**

Shanghai Today (Shanghai, CHN) **441**

Shareholder Value (Peterborough, NH, USA) **130**

Shimane Journal of Medical Science (Shimane, JPN) **769**

The Shinano Mainichi Shimbun (Nagano City, JPN) **704**

Shipping Times (Singapore, SGP) **1476**

Shipping and Trade News (Tokyo, JPN) **1068**

Shopping News South (Bristol, RI, USA) **214**

Show Daily (Kuala Lumpur, MYS) **1228**

Showcase (Singapore, SGP) **1477**

Shukan ST (Tokyo, JPN) **1069**

The Shuttle Sheet (Greensboro, NC, USA) **189**

Signature (Singapore, SGP) **1478**

Silk & Satin (Dorval, QC, CAN) **302**

Silver Kris (Singapore, SGP) **1479**

Singapore Accountant (Singapore, SGP) **1480**

Singapore Annals; Academy of Medicine, (Singapore, SGP) **1306**

Singapore Architect (Singapore, SGP) **1481**

Singapore; Computerworld (Singapore, SGP) **1350**

Singapore Economic Review (Singapore, SGP) **1482**

Singapore Electronics Audience; TSEA: Targeting (Singapore, SGP) **1513**

Singapore; Ezyhealth (Singapore, SGP) **1362**

The Singapore Family Physician (Singapore, SGP) **1483**

Singapore; FHM (Singapore, SGP) **1366**

(Singapore); 4x4 Magazine (Singapore, SGP) **1369**

Singapore; Investor's Guide to (Singapore, SGP) **1418**

Singapore Journal of Legal Studies (Singapore, SGP) **1484**

Singapore Journal of Obstetrics & Gynaecology (Singapore, SGP) **1485**

Singapore Journal; Plastics & Rubber (Singapore, SGP) **1463**

Singapore Journal of Primary Industries (Singapore, SGP) **1486**

Singapore Journal of Tropical Geography (Singapore, SGP) **1487**

Singapore Law Review (Singapore, SGP) **1488**

Singapore Management Review (Singapore, SGP) **1489**

Singapore National Academy of Science Journal (Singapore, SGP) **1490**

Singapore Paediatric Journal (Singapore, SGP) **1491**

Singapore; PC World (Singapore, SGP) **1459**

Singapore Source Book for Architects & Designers (Singapore, SGP) **1492**

Singapore Visitor (Singapore, SGP) **1493**

Sinorama Magazine (Taipei, TWN) **1602**

Siriraj Hospital Gazette (Bangkok, THA) **1662**

60504 Sun; The Fox Valley Villages/ (Naperville, IL, USA) **63**

(SJDR); The Saudi Journal of Disability and Rehabilitation (Riyadh, SAU) **1301**

Skyscraper (New York, NY, USA) **181**

Slagers Wereld (Ryswyk, NLD) **1269**

Smart Investor (Singapore, SGP) **1494**

Smooth Muscle Research; Journal of (Tokyo, JPN) **989**

The SMS Magazine (Singapore, SGP) **1495**

(Snohomish County Edition); Seattle's Child (Seattle, WA, USA) **259**

Social Science and Humanities; Pertanika Journal of (Serdang, MYS) **1254**

Social Science; Journal of (Tokyo, JPN) **990**

Social Science; Journal of (Taipei, TWN) **1595**

Social Science Journal; Korean (Seoul, KOR) **1156**

Social Science Research of University of Tokushima (Tokushima, JPN) **779**

Social Sciences and Philosophy; Journal of (Taipei, TWN) **1596**

Social Sciences; Setsunan University Review of Humanities and (Osaka, JPN) **746**

Social Sciences; Southeast Asian Journal of (Singapore, SGP) **1499**

Social Studies; Journal of Population and (Nakhon Pathom, THA) **1683**

Social Welfare; Journal of Population, Health and (Seoul, KOR) **1130**

Social Work; Asian Pacific Journal of (Singapore, SGP) **1327**

Social Work; The Hong Kong Journal of (Hong Kong, CHN) **403**

Social Work; Soochow Journal of (Taipei, TWN) **1607**

Sociology; Journal of (Taipei, TWN) **1597**

Sociology; Journal of Institute of International (Hyogo, JPN) **624**

Software Engineering and Knowledge Engineering; International Journal of (Singapore, SGP) **1415**

Software; Journal of Chemical (Fukui, JPN) **590**

Soil Microorganisms (Matsudo City, JPN) **691**

Soil Science and Plant Nutrition (Tokyo, JPN) **1070**

Soils & Foundations (Tokyo, JPN) **1071**

Sojourn (Singapore, SGP) **1496**

Solvent Extraction Research and Development, Japan (Sendai, JPN) **767**

Sonderhefte (Hannover, GER) **496**

Songlines (Windsor, GBR) **1798**

Soochow Journal of Economics and Business (Taipei, TWN) **1603**

Soochow Journal of Foreign Languages and Literatures (Taipei, TWN) **1604**

Soochow Journal of History (Taipei, TWN) **1605**

Soochow Journal of Political Science (Taipei, TWN) **1606**

Soochow Journal of Social Work (Taipei, TWN) **1607**

Sophia (Melbourne, VI, AUS) **315**

The Sound Magazine (Telford, GBR) **1795**

Soundi (A-lehdet, FIN) **466**

South African Journal on Human Rights (Wits, SAF) **1528**

South American Earth Sciences; Journal of (Amsterdam, NLD) **1262**

South County Independent (Wakefield, RI, USA) **217**

South Pacific Study (Kagoshima, JPN) **646**

South Review (Kuala Lumpur, MYS) **1229**

South St. Paul/Inver Grove Heights Sun Current (South St. Paul, MN, USA) **124**

South Seas Society Journal (Singapore, SGP) **1497**

Southeast Asia; Contemporary (Singapore, SGP) **1351**

Southeast Asia; Regional Outlook: (Singapore, SGP) **1468**

Southeast Asian Affairs (Singapore, SGP) **1498**

Southeast Asian Archives; Journal of the (Kuala Lumpur, MYS) **1207**

Southeast Asian Journal of Social Sciences (Singapore, SGP) **1499**

Southern Africa; Windows (Dubai, UAE) **1727**

Southern California Brides (Riverside, CA, USA) **16**
Southern California Golf (Riverside, CA, USA) **17**
Soviet Metal Technology (New York, NY, USA) **182**
Space (Seoul, KOR) **1170**
Space (Singapore, SGP) **1500**
Space; Biological Sciences in (Kanagawa, JPN) **648**
Space; Earth Planets and (Tokyo, JPN) **831**
Space in Japan (Tokyo, JPN) **1072**
Space Technology and Science; Journal of (Tokyo, JPN) **991**
Special Recreation Digest (Iowa City, IA, USA) **82**
Specialist Angler **1755***
Species Diversity (Tokyo, JPN) **1073**
Spectroscopy; Infrared and Raman (Saitama, JPN) **750**
Speleological Society of Japan; Journal of (Yamaguchi, JPN) **1100**
Spices and Aromatic Crops; Journal of (Marikunnu, KE, IND) **534**
Spinal Surgery (Osaka, JPN) **747**
Spine Research Society; Journal of Japan (Tokyo, JPN) **956**
Sports (Singapore, SGP) **1501**
Sports; China (Beijing, CHN) **353**
Sports Medicine and Sports Science; The Hong Kong Journal of (Hong Kong, CHN) **404**
Sports Science; The Hong Kong Journal of Sports Medicine and (Hong Kong, CHN) **404**
Square Rooms (Singapore, SGP) **1502**
The Standard (Hong Kong, CHN) **437**
The Star (Petaling Jaya, MYS) **1249**
State News; Delaware (Dover, DE, USA) **32**
State Politics & Policy Quarterly (Champaign, IL, USA) **50**
Stationery; Hong Kong Gifts, Premiums & (Hong Kong, CHN) **393**
Stationery and Office Supplies (Taipei, TWN) **1608**
Stations-Service Acutalites (Clichy, FRA) **486**
Statistica Sinica (Taipei, TWN) **1609**
Statistical Abstract of Maharashtra State (Mumbai, MH, IND) **542**
Statistics Monthly in Taiwan Area; Commodity Price (Taipei, TWN) **1569**
Steel Industry; Japan's Iron and (Tokyo, JPN) **910**
Steel News; Nippon (Tokyo, JPN) **1037**
Steel; News from Nisshin (Tokyo, JPN) **1033**
Stock Market in Thailand (Bangkok, THA) **1663**
The Stocktaker (Old Woking, GBR) **1782**
The Straits Times (Singapore, SGP) **1503**
Structural Engineering — Earthquake Engineering (Tokyo, JPN) **1074**
Structural Engineering and Mechanics (Taejon, KOR) **1184**
Student Weekly; Bangkok Post (Bangkok, THA) **1627**
Studia Leibnitiana Supplementa (Hannover, GER) **497**
Studies of Broadcasting (Tokyo, JPN) **1075**
Studies in English Literature (Tokyo, JPN) **1076**
Studio Classroom (Taipei, TWN) **1610**
Study of Elementary Particles (Kyoto, JPN) **690**
Study of Medical Supplies (Tokyo, JPN) **1077**
Suara SAM (Penang, MYS) **1236**
Successful Farming (Des Moines, IA, USA) **81**
Sumo World (Tokyo, JPN) **1078**
The Sun (Cleveland, OH, USA) **193**
Sun Marketplace (Hanover, PA, USA) **202**
Sun Prarie Sailor **115***
Surface Review and Letters (Singapore, SGP) **1504**
Surgery; Annals of Thoracic and Cardiovascular (Tokyo, JPN) **791**
Surgery; Asian Journal of Oral and Maxillofacial (Yokohama, JPN) **1103**
Surgery; Endocrine (Tokyo, JPN) **835**
Surgery; Formosan Journal of (Taipei, TWN) **1577**
Surgery; The Hong Kong Journal of Orthopaedic (Hong Kong, CHN) **400**
Surgery; Japanese Journal of Rheumatism and Joint (Shiga, JPN) **768**
Surgery; Journal of Japan Society of Aesthetic (Tokyo, JPN) **954**
Surgery; Journal of Japanese Association for Chest (Kyoto, JPN) **678**
Surgery; Journal of Japanese Society for Clinical (Tokyo, JPN) **960**
Surgery; Journal of Microwave (Osaka, JPN) **732**
Surgery; Orthopaedic and Traumatic (Tokyo, JPN) **1045**
Surgery; Renal Transplantation, Vascular (Tokyo, JPN) **1059**
Surgery; Spinal (Osaka, JPN) **747**
Surgery Today (Tokyo, JPN) **1079**
Surgery; World Journal of (New York, NY, USA) **183**
Surveyor; The Malaysian (Petaling Jaya, MYS) **1247**
Survival (London, GBR) **1776**
SUT Journal of Mathematics (Tokyo, JPN) **1080**
Svaz prumyslu papiru a celulozy/SPPaC **443***
Symploke (Victoria, TX, USA) **242**

T

Taiwan Area; Commodity Price Statistics Monthly in (Taipei, TWN) **1569**
Taiwan; Business and Industry: (Taipei, TWN) **1560**
The Taiwan Economic News (Taipei, TWN) **1611**
Taiwan International Trade (Taipei, TWN) **1612**
Taiwan Museum; Journal of (Taipei, TWN) **1598**
Taiwan News (Taipei, TWN) **1613**
Taiwan Outlook (Taipei, TWN) **1614**
Taiwan Society of Anesthesiologists; Journal of the (Taipei, TWN) **1599**
Taiwan; Travel In (Taipei, TWN) **1615**
The Taiwanese Journal of Mathematics (Hsinchu, TWN) **1548**
Tamkang Journal of Futures Studies (Tamsui, TWN) **1619**
Tamkang Journal of International Affairs (Tamsui, TWN) **1620**
Tamkang Journal of Mathematics (Tamsui, TWN) **1621**
Tamkang Journal of Tamkang Review (Tamsui, TWN) **1622**
Taplalkozas, anyagcsere, dieta; Nutrition, Allergy, Diet - (Budapest, HUN) **507**
Targeting Singapore Electronics Audience; TSEA: (Singapore, SGP) **1513**
Tax Journal; Trusts & Estates (London, GBR) **1777**
Taxation (New Delhi, DH, IND) **555**
Taxes; Guide to Japanese (Tokyo, JPN) **849**
Taxonomy; Journal of Phytogeography and (Kanazawa, JPN) **658**
Tchizn Glyhih **1279***
Teach (Singapore, SGP) **1505**
Teacher Education Series 3; Journal of Hyogo University of (Hyogo, JPN) **623**
Teacher; Language (Tokyo, JPN) **1014**
Teacher Online; The English (Bangkok, THA) **1635**
Technical Journal of Telecommunication Laboratories (Chungli, TWN) **1545**
Techno Japan (Tokyo, JPN) **1081**
Technocrat; The North American (Ferndale, WA, USA) **253**
Technology; Engineering Science and (Kuala Lumpur, MYS) **1199**
Technology; Journal of Nuclear Science and (Tokyo, JPN) **972**
Technology Research; Food Science and (Tokyo, JPN) **843**
Teenage (Singapore, SGP) **1506**
teens (Singapore, SGP) **1507**
Teens Annual (Singapore, SGP) **1508**
TeenzSpot.com (Sharjah, UAE) **1729**
Telcom Journal (Bangkok, THA) **1664**
Telecom Asia (Hong Kong, CHN) **438**
Telecom Tribune (Tokyo, JPN) **1082**
Telecommunication Laboratories; Technical Journal of (Chungli, TWN) **1545**
Tenders Estimating Data Service (Singapore, SGP) **1509**
Tensor (Kanagawa, JPN) **656**
Texas Forum on Civil Liberties and Civil Rights (Austin, TX, USA) **225**
Texas Intellectual Property Law Journal (Austin, TX, USA) **226**
Texas International Law Journal (Austin, TX, USA) **227**
Texas Journal of Women and the Law (Austin, TX, USA) **228**
Texas Law Review (Austin, TX, USA) **229**
Textile & Apparel Journal; Asia (Hong Kong, CHN) **371**
Textile Engineering; Journal of (Osaka, JPN) **735**
Tezukayama College Food Sciences; Journal of (Nara, JPN) **711**
TF-bladet (Stockholm, SWE) **1538**
Thai-American Business (Bangkok, THA) **1665**
Thai Chamber of Commerce; Journal of (Bangkok, THA) **1647**
Thai Economic Review (Bangkok, THA) **1666**
Thai Journal of Agricultural Science (Bangkok, THA) **1667**
Thai Journal of Anesthesiology (Bangkok, THA) **1668**
Thai Journal of Development Administration (Bangkok, THA) **1669**
Thai Junior Red Cross Magazine (Bangkok, THA) **1670**
Thailand Airline Timetable (Bangkok, THA) **1671**
Thailand; Journal of National Research Council of (Bangkok, THA) **1643**
Thailand; Journal of the Science Society of (Bangkok, THA) **1645**
Thailand; Living in (Bangkok, THA) **1650**
Thailand Magazine; Business in (Bangkok, THA) **1630**
Thailand; Stock Market in (Bangkok, THA) **1663**
Thailand Travel Magazine (Bangkok, THA) **1672**
Thailand Update (Bangkok, THA) **1673**

theIndian (Westland, MI, USA) **109**
Theology; Philosophy & (Milwaukee, WI, USA) **273**
Theology; Scottish Journal of (Cambridge, GBR) **1746**
Theoretical Physics; Progress of (Kyoto, JPN) **686**
Theoretical Physics - Supplement; Progress of (Kyoto, JPN) **687**
Theory & Event (Baltimore, MD, USA) **92**
Theosophist (Chennai, TN, IND) **520**
Therapy; Japanese Journal of Behavior (Ibaraki, JPN) **630**
Third World Economics (Penang, MYS) **1237**
Third World Resurgence (Penang, MYS) **1238**
This Month in Korea (Seoul, KOR) **1171**
Thoracic and Cardiovascular Surgery; Annals of (Tokyo, JPN) **791**
Three Dimensional Images; Journal of (Tokyo, JPN) **994**
Thrombosis; Journal of Atherosclerosis and (Tokyo, JPN) **923**
Tibet Journal (Dharamsala, HP, IND) **521**
Timaru Herald (Timaru, NZL) **1272**
Timber Grower **1753***
Timber News; Forestry and (Edinburgh, GBR) **1753**
Time Asia (Hong Kong, CHN) **439**
Time Out Dubai (Dubai, UAE) **1722**
Tishomingo Journal; Belmont- (Belmont, MS, USA) **125**
TISNET Trade and Investment Bulletin (Bangkok, THA) **1674**
TM (Tokyo, JPN) **1083**
Tobacco Asia (Bangkok, THA) **1675**
Today's Facility Manager (Red Bank, NJ, USA) **139**
Today's Nursing Home **73***
Today's OEA (Portland, OR, USA) **199**
Today's Parents (Singapore, SGP) **1510**
Tohoku Geophysical Journal (Miyagi, JPN) **698**
Tohoku Journal of Agricultural Research (Miyagi, JPN) **699**
Tohoku Journal of Experimental Medicine (Miyagi, JPN) **700**
Tohoku Mathematical Journal (Miyagi, JPN) **701**
Tohoku Psychologica Folia (Miyagi, JPN) **702**
Tokai University; Journal of Faculty of Marine Science and Technology of (Shizuoka, JPN) **772**
Tokai University; Journal of Marine Science Museum of (Shizuoka, JPN) **773**
Tokushima; Social Science Research of University of (Tokushima, JPN) **779**
Tokyo Dental College Society; Journal of (Chiba, JPN) **586**
Tokyo Journal (Tokyo, JPN) **1084**
Tokyo Journal of Mathematics (Tokyo, JPN) **1085**
Tokyo Scene (Tokyo, JPN) **1086**
Tokyo University of Fisheries; Journal of (Tokyo, JPN) **996**
Tokyo University of Mercantile Marine; Journal of (Tokyo, JPN) **997**
Tombo (Tokyo, JPN) **1087**
Tool and Tillage (Frederiksberg, DEN) **446**
Tools and Trades (Bath, GBR) **1740**
Top Fashion Magazine (Bangkok, THA) **1676**
Topology; Questions and Answers in General (Osaka, JPN) **741**
Tosoh Research; Journal of (Yamaguchi, JPN) **1101**
Tour Companion (Tokyo, JPN) **1088**
Tourist (Oakville, ON, CAN) **289**
Tourist Newspaper; Penang (Penang, MYS) **1235**
Toxicology; Japanese Journal of (Tokyo, JPN) **908**
Toyama University; Mathematics Journal of (Toyama, JPN) **1097**
Toyota Technical Review (Tokyo, JPN) **1089**
Toys; Hong Kong (Hong Kong, CHN) **418**
Tractor; Implement & (Cedar Falls, IA, USA) **80**
Trade; China's Foreign (Beijing, CHN) **355**
Trade and Investment; Korea (Seoul, KOR) **1142**
Trade Services; Hong Kong (Hong Kong, CHN) **419**
Trademarks; The Gazette of Patents and (Budapest, HUN) **506**
Traditional Medicines; Journal of (Toyama, JPN) **1096**
Transfusion; Journal of Japanese Society of Autologous Blood (Okayama, JPN) **717**
Transplantation; Saudi Journal of Kidney Diseases and (Riyadh, SAU) **1303**
Transport Service (Clichy, FRA) **487**
Transportation; Journal of Advanced (Calgary, AB, CAN) **274**
Transportation & Logistics; Canadian (Toronto, ON, CAN) **292**
Transportation Medicine; Journal of (Tokyo, JPN) **999**
Transportation Professional (Tunbridge Wells, GBR) **1796**
Transporter; Milk & Liquid Food (Appleton, WI, USA) **266**
Traumatic Surgery; Orthopaedic and (Tokyo, JPN) **1045**
Travel Agency (Kuala Lumpur, MYS) **1230**
Travel Asia (Singapore, SGP) **1511**

Numbers cited in bold after listings are entry numbers rather than page numbers.